The Zohar

by
Rav Shimon bar Yochai
From The Book of Avraham

with
The Sulam Commentary

by
Rav Yehuda Ashlag

The First Ever Unabridged
English Translation with Commentary

Published by
The Kabbalah Centre International Inc.
Dean Rav S. P. Berg Shlita

Edited and Compiled by
Rabbi Michael Berg

בברכה לבריאות, שמחה,
אריכות ימים וממון רב
לעומרי בן יגאל ושולמית

אשתו
קרן בת דוד וצפורה

ולביתם
נווה בת עומרי וקרן

ברכה לבריאות, שמחה ואריכות ימים
לרחל בת מרים
ולמיכאל הבר

APPLYING THE POWER OF THE ZOHAR

The Zohar is a book of great mystical power and wisdom. It is Universally recognized as the definitive work on the Kabbalah – and it is also so Much more.

The Zohar is a wellspring of spiritual energy, a fountainhead of metaphysical power that not only reveals and explains, but literally brings blessing, protection, and well-being into the lives of all those who read or peruse its sacred texts. All that is required is worthy desire, the certainty of a trusting heart, and an open and receptive mind. Unlike other books, including the great spiritual texts of other traditions, The Zohar is written in a kind of code, through which metaphors, parables, and cryptic language at first conceal but ultimately reveal the forces of creation.

As electrical current is concealed in wire and cable before disclosing itself as an illuminated light bulb, the spiritual Light of the Creator is wrapped in allegory and symbolism throughout the Aramaic text of the Zohar. And while many books contain information and knowledge, the Zohar both expresses and embodies spiritual Light. The very letters on its pages have the power to bring spiritual wisdom and positive energy into every area of our lives.

As we visually scan the Aramaic texts and study the accompanying insights that appear in English, spiritual power is summoned from above – and worlds tremble as Light is sent forth in response.

It's primary purpose is not only to help us acquire wisdom, but to draw Light from the Upper Worlds and to bring sanctification into our lives. Indeed, the book itself is the most powerful of all tools for cleansing the soul and connecting to the Light of the Creator. As you open these pages, therefore, do not make understanding in the conventional sense your primary goal.

Although you may not have a knowledge of Aramaic, look first at the Aramaic text before reading the English. Do not be discouraged by difficulties with comprehension. Instead, open your heart to the spiritual transformation the Zohar is offering you.

Ultimately, the Zohar is an instrument for refining the individual soul – for removing darkness from the earth – and for bringing well being and blessing to our fellow man.

Its purpose is not only to make us intellectually wise, but to make us spiritually pure.

Torah

Also known as the Five Books of Moses, the Torah is considered to be the physical body of learning, whereas the Zohar is the internal soul. The literal stories of the Torah conceal countless hidden secrets. The Zohar is the Light that illuminates all of the Torah's sublime mysteries.

Beresheet	Genesis
Shemot	Exodus
Vayikra	Leviticus
Bemidbar	Numbers
Devarim	Deuteronomy

Prophets

Amos	Amos
Chagai	Haggai
Chavakuk	Habakkuk
Hoshea	Hosea
Malachi	Malachi
Melachim	Kings
Michah	Micah
Nachum	Nahum
Ovadyah	Obadiah
Shmuel	Samuel
Shoftim	Judges
Tzefanyah	Zephaniah
Yechezkel	Ezekiel
Yehoshua	Joshua
Yeshayah	Isaiah
Yirmeyah	Jeremiah
Yoel	Joel
Yonah	Jonah
Zecharyah	Zechariah

Writings

Daniel	Daniel
Divrei Hayamim	Chronicles
Eicha	Lamentations
Ester	Esther
Ezra	Ezra
Nechemiah	Nehemiah
Iyov	Job
Kohelet	Ecclesiastes
Mishlei	Proverbs
Rut	Ruth

Sir Hashirim	Songs of Songs
Tehilim	Psalms

The Ten Sfirot – Emanations

To conceal the blinding *Light* of the Upper World, and thus create a tiny point into which our universe would be born, ten *curtains* were fabricated. These ten *curtains* are called Ten Sfirot. Each successive Sfirah further reduces the emanation of *Light*, gradually dimming its brilliance to a level almost devoid of *Light* – our physical world known as *Malchut*. The only remnant of Light remaining in this darkened universe is a *pilot light* which sustains our existence. This Light is the life force of a human being and the force that gives birth to stars, sustains suns and sets everything from swirling galaxies to busy ant hills in motion. Moreover, the Ten Sfirot act like a prism, refracting the Light into many *colors* giving rise to the diversity of life and matter in our world.

The Ten Sfirot are as follows:

Keter	Crown
Chochmah	Wisdom
Binah	Understanding
Da'at	Knowledge
Zeir Anpin	Small Face,
	(includes the next six Sfirot):
Chesed	Mercy (Chassadim - plural)
Gvurah	Judgment (Gvurot - Plural)
Tiferet	Splendor
Netzach	Victory (Eternity)
Hod	Glory
Yesod	Foundation
Malchut	Kingdom

The Partzufim - Spiritual forms

One complete structure of the Ten Sfirot creates a *Partzuf* or Spiritual Form. Together, these forces are the building blocks of all reality. As water and sand combine to create cement, the Ten Sfirot

combine to produce a Spiritual Form [*Partzuf*]. Each of the Spiritual Forms below are therefore composed of one set of Ten Sfirot.

These Spiritual Forms are called:

Atik	Ancient
Atik Yomin	Ancient of Days
Atika Kadisha	Holy Ancient
Atik of Atikin	Anceint of Ancients
Aba	Father
Arich Anpin	Long Face
Ima	Mother
Nukva	Female
Tevunah	Intelligence
Yisrael Saba	Israel Grandfather
Zachar	Male

These names are not meant to be understood literally. Each represents a unique spiritual force and building block, producing a substructure and foundation for all the worlds make up reality.

The Five Worlds

All of the above Spiritual Forms [*Partzufim*] create one spiritual world. There are Five Worlds in total that compose all reality, therefore, five sets of the above Spiritual Forms are required.

Our physical world corresponds to the world of: Asiyah – Action

Adam Kadmon	Primordial Man
Atzilut	Emanation
Briyah	Creation
Yetzirah	Formation
Asiyah	Action

The Five Levels of the soul

Nefesh	First, Lowest level of Soul
Ruach	Second level of Soul
Neshamah	Third level of Soul
Chayah	Fourth level of Soul
Yechidah	Highest, fifth level of Soul

Names of God

As a single ray of white sunlight contains the seven colors of the spectrum, the one Light of the Creator embodies many diverse spiritual forces. These different forces are called *Names of God*. Each Name denotes a specific attribute and spiritual power. The Hebrew letters that compose these Names are the interface by which these varied Forces act upon our physical world. The most common Name of God is the Tetragrammaton (the four letters, *Yud Hei Vav Hei* יהוה.) Because of the enormous power that the Tetragrammaton transmits, we do not utter it aloud. When speaking of the Tetragrammaton, we use the term *Hashem* which means, *The Name*.

Adonai, El, Elohim, Hashem, Shadai, Eheyeh, Tzevaot, Yud Hei Vav Hei

People

Er	The son of Noach
Rabbi Elazar	The son of Rabbi Shimon bar Yochai
Rabbi Shimon bar Yochai	Author of the Zohar
Shem, Cham, Yefet	Noach's children
Shet	Seth
Ya'akov	Jacob
Yishai	Jesse (King David's father)
Yitzchak	Isaac
Yosef	Joseph
Yitro	Jethro
Yehuda	Judah

Angels

Angels are distinct energy components, part of a vast communication network running through the upper worlds. Each unique Angel is responsible for transmitting various forces of influence into our physical universe.

Adriel, Ahinael, Dumah (name of Angel in charge of the dead), Gabriel, Kadshiel, Kedumiel, Metatron, Michael, Rachmiel,

Raphael, Tahariel, Uriel

Nations

Nations actually represent the inner attributes and character traits of our individual self. The nation of Amalek refers to the doubt and uncertainty that dwells within us when we face hardship and obstacles. Moab represents the dual nature of man. Nefilim refers to the sparks of Light that we have defiled through our impure actions, and to the negative forces that lurk within the human soul as a result of our own wrongful deeds.

Amalek, Moab, Nefilim

General

Aba	Father
	Refers to the male principle and positive force in our universe. Correlates to the proton in an atom.
Arvit	The Evening prayer
Chayot	Animals
Chupah	Canopy (wedding ceremony)
Et	The
Avadon	Hell
Gehenom	Hell
Sheol	Hell
	The place a soul goes for purification upon leaving this world.
Ima	Mother
	The female principle and minus force in our universe. Correlates to the electron in an atom.
Kiddush	Blessing over the wine
Klipah	Shell (negativity)
Klipot	Shells (Plural)
Kriat Sh'ma	The Reading of the Sh'ma
Mashiach	Messiah
Minchah	The Afternoon prayer
Mishnah	Study
Mochin	Brain, Spiritual levels of Light
Moed	A designated time or holiday
Negev	The south of Israel
Nukva	Female

Partzuf	Face
Shacharit	The Morning prayer
Shamayim	Heavens (sky)
Shechinah	The Divine presence, The female aspect of the Creator
Tefilin	Phylacteries
The Dinur river	The river of fire
Tzadik	Righteous person
Zion	Another name for Jerusalem
Yisrael	The land of Israel The nation of Israel or an individual Israelite
Zohar	Splendor

The Hebrew vowels

Chirik אִ, Cholam אֹ אוֹ, Kamatz אָ, Patach אַ, Segol אֶ, Sh'va אְ, Shuruk אוּ אֻ, Tzere אֵ.

The Twelve Tribes

Asher, Dan, Ephraim, Gad, Issachar, Judah, Levi, Menasheh, Naphtali, Reuben, Shimon, Zebulun

Jewish Holidays

Rosh Hashanah	The Jewish New Year
Yom Kippur	Day of Atonement
Sukkot	Holiday of the Booths
Shmini Atzeret	The day of Convocation
Simchat Torah	Holiday on which we dance with the Torah
Pesach	Passover
Shavout	Holiday of the Weeks

כרך כ

פרשת פנחס חלק א׳

Vol. XX

Pinchas A

A Prayer from The Ari

To be recited before the study of the Zohar

Ruler of the universe, and Master of all masters, The Father of mercy and forgiveness, we thank You, our God and the God of our fathers, by bowing down and kneeling, that You brought us closer to Your Torah and Your holy work, and You enable us to take part in the secrets of Your holy Torah. How worthy are we that You grant us with such big favor, that is the reason we plead before You, that You will forgive and acquit all our sins, and that they should not bring separation between You and us.

And may it be your will before You, our God and the God of our fathers, that You will awaken and prepare our hearts to love and revere You, and may You listen to our utterances, and open our closed heart to the hidden studies of Your Torah, and may our study be pleasant before Your Place of Honor, as the aroma of sweet incense, and may You emanate to us Light from the source of our soul to all of our being. And, may the sparks of your holy servants, through which you revealed Your wisdom to the world, shine.

May their merit and the merit of their fathers, and the merit of their Torah, and holiness, support us so we shall not stumble through our study. And by their merit enlighten our eyes in our learning as it stated by King David, The Sweet Singer of Israel: "Open my eyes, so that I will see wonders from Your Torah" (Tehilim 119:18). Because from His mouth God gives wisdom and understanding.

"May the utterances of my mouth and the thoughts of my heart find favor before You, God, my Strength and my Redeemer" (Tehilim 19:15).

PINCHAS

❧

Name of Articles

1. "Hear, my son, the instruction of your father"

A Synopsis
Rabbi Elazar deconstructs the title verse to teach us that people must follow the Torah that was given to them by God along with His rebukes and punishments. When someone who has studied the Torah dies, it precedes him and opens all the gates for him to the World to Come. Rabbi Elazar says that God takes most joy in those who get up at night to study the Torah.

The Relevance of this Passage
The concepts of punishment and reward have no basis in spirituality. If one inadvertently, or even purposely, touches a burning coal and incurs injury, one does not profess to have been punished by the fiery ember. Conversely, if one uses this coal to heat one's home, feed one's family, or bathe oneself in warmed waters, one does not construe this as a reward. It is one's knowledge – or lack of it – that determines its influence in one's life.

Spiritual Light functions under the same principle. Rabbi Elazar is telling us that if we connect to the spiritual current of the Creator through Torah and Kabbalah, we attain spiritual growth and manage these magnificent spiritual forces in a positive, productive fashion. If we connect to spiritual Light through the ego, we inevitably short-circuit and incur injury, be it emotional, physical, or spiritual.

Here we conjoin our souls to the Light in a balanced, safe way. The ego, along with its appetite for self-indulgence, is subjugated. The resulting illumination opens up all the gates that lead to the World to Come – for us, and for all our fellow human beings.

The righteous who have engaged in Torah study in the still of night, all through history, now bestow their blessings upon the reader so that the Holy One's joy reigns over all Creation.

١. וַיְדַבֵּר יְיָ׳ אֶל מֹשֶׁה לֵאמֹר, פִּנְחָס בֶּן אֶלְעָזָר וְגוֹ׳, רִבִּי אֶלְעָזָר פָּתַח וְאָמַר, שְׁמַע בְּנִי מוּסַר אָבִיךְ וְאַל תִּטּוֹשׁ תּוֹרַת אִמֶּךְ. שְׁמַע בְּנִי מוּסַר אָבִיךְ, דָּא קוּדְשָׁא בְּרִיךְ הוּא. וְאַל תִּטּוֹשׁ תּוֹרַת אִמֶּךְ, דָּא כְּנֶסֶת יִשְׂרָאֵל. מַאי מוּסַר אָבִיךְ, מוּסָר, דָּא אוֹרַיְיתָא, דְּאִית בָּהּ כַּמָּה תּוֹכָחִין, כַּמָּה עוֹנָשִׁין. כד״א, מוּסַר יְיָ׳ בְּנִי אַל תִּמְאָס וְאַל תָּקוֹץ בְּתוֹכַחְתּוֹ.

1. "And Hashem spoke to Moses, saying, Pinchas, the son of Elazar..." (Bemidbar 25:10-11). Rabbi Elazar began, "Hear, my son, the instruction of your father, and do not forsake the Torah of your mother" (Mishlei 1:8). "Hear, my son, the instruction of your father..." refers to the Holy One, blessed be He. "and do not forsake the Torah of your mother," refers to the Congregation of Yisrael. What is the instruction of your father? Instruction is the Torah which contains a number of rebukes and punishments, as it is said: "My son, do not despise the chastening of Hashem, nor be weary of His correction" (Mishlei 3:11).

2. וּבְגִין דְּכָל מַאן דְּאִשְׁתְּדַּל בְּאוֹרַיְיתָא בְּהַאי עָלְמָא, זָכֵי דְּיִפְתְּחוּן לֵיהּ כַּמָּה תַּרְעִין לְהַהוּא עָלְמָא, כַּמָּה נְהוֹרִין. בְּשַׁעֲתָא דְּיִנְפּוֹק מֵהַאי עָלְמָא, הִיא אַקְדִּימַת קַמֵּיהּ, וְאַזְלָא לְכָל נְטוּרֵי תַּרְעִין, מַכְרֶזֶת וְאוֹמֶרֶת, פִּתְחוּ שְׁעָרִים וְיָבֹא גּוֹי צַדִּיק. אַתְקִינוּ כֻּרְסְיָין לִפְלָנַיָּא עַבְדָּא דְּמַלְכָּא. דְּלֵית חֵדוּ לְקוּדְשָׁא בְּרִיךְ הוּא אֶלָּא מַאן דְּאִשְׁתְּדַּל בְּאוֹרַיְיתָא, כָּ"שׁ בַּ"נ דְּמִתְעַר בְּלֵילְיָא לְאִשְׁתַּדְּלָא בְּאוֹרַיְיתָא, דְּהָא כָּל צַדִּיקַיָּיא דִּבְגִנְתָּא דְּעֵדֶן, צַיְיתִין לְקַלֵּיהּ, וְקוּדְשָׁא בְּרִיךְ הוּא מִשְׁתַּכַּח בֵּינַיְיהוּ, כְּמָה דְּאוּקְמוּהָ הַיּוֹשֶׁבֶת בַּגַּנִּים חֲבֵרִים מַקְשִׁיבִים לְקוֹלֵךְ הַשְׁמִיעִינִי.

2. And since everyone who engages in Torah in this world is worthy that a number of gates, a number of lights to the World to Come, be opened for him, therefore when he departs from this world THE TORAH precedes him, going to all the gate keepers proclaiming, "Open the gates, that the righteous nation...may enter in" (Yeshayah 26:2). Prepare a seat for so-and-so, the King's servant! The Holy One, blessed be He, has no joy other than with one who engages in Torah. How much more so with a man who rises up at night to engage in Torah, for all the righteous in the Garden of Eden are attentive to his voice and the Holy One, blessed be He, is among them, as they put it: "You that dwell in the gardens, the companions hearken for your voice: Cause me to hear it" (Shir Hashirim 8:13).

2. "The companions hearken for your voice"

A Synopsis

Rabbi Shimon tells us that everyone who studies the Torah at night is strengthened by the Shechinah, and this is even more true of those who guard the covenant. He says that Yisrael would have been destroyed had Pinchas not killed Cozbi and Zimri, but his act appeased God's anger. Lastly we hear that if a person reincarnates the second time without improving his soul he has betrayed God's truth.

The Relevance of this Passage

The *Shechinah* protects us and fortifies the immune system, personally and globally. Its presence removes airborne diseases from our planet and purges from our bodies the negative forces that cause ailments. For this reason, the Righteous souls of antiquity and present day devote time and energy to Torah study after the stroke of midnight. Their cumulative efforts are now ignited so that Earth and all its inhabitants may possess the divine presence called *Shechinah*. Diseases are decimated by the healing Light that shines here, while the collective immune system of humanity is bolstered, forever protecting us from the scourge of illness.

The energy arising through Pinchas's action abolishes all sentences of death and disease decreed against us. This energy cleanses away the negative residue created by sexual misdeeds and corruption. Although we may not merit such mercy, our appreciation of the Zohar's power and of Rabbi Shimon's might assures complete nullification.

Finally, our efforts to share all that we now receive with friends and foes, secures for us spiritual change and growth. Thus, we have not, and shall not ever, betray "the truth of the King."

3. ר"ש אָמַר הַאי קְרָא רָזָא דְחָכְמְתָא אִית בֵּיה. הַיּוֹשֶׁבֶת בַּגַּנִּים, דָּא כְּנֶסֶת יִשְׂרָאֵל, דְּאִיהִי בְּגָלוּתָא עִם יִשְׂרָאֵל, וְאַזְלָא עִמְּהוֹן בְּעָקַתַּיְיהוּ. חֲבֵרִים מַקְשִׁיבִים לְקוֹלֵךְ, מַשִׁרְיָין עִלָּאִין. כֻּלְּהוּ צַיְיתִין לְקוֹלֵךְ, לְקוֹל תּוּשְׁבַּחְתֵּךְ בְּגָלוּתָא. הַשְׁמִיעִינִי, כד"א הַרְאִינִי אֶת מַרְאַיִךְ הַשְׁמִיעִנִי אֶת קוֹלֵךְ. הַשְׁמִיעִינִי, קָלָא דְּאִינּוּן חַבְרַיָּיא דְּמִשְׁתַּדְּלֵי בְּאוֹרַיְיתָא דְּהָא לֵית תּוּשְׁבַּחְתָּא קַמָּאי, כְּאִינּוּן דְּמִשְׁתַּדְּלֵי בְּאוֹרַיְיתָא.

-7-

3. Rabbi Shimon said: This verse has in it the secret of wisdom. "You that dwell in the gardens" (Shir Hashirim 8:13) refers to the Congregation of Yisrael, THAT IS MALCHUT, which is with Yisrael in exile and accompanies them in their troubles. "the companions hearken for your voice..." (Ibid.) refers to the camps of the higher heavenly ANGELS, all of whom listen to your voice, the voice of your praises in exile. "Cause me to hear it" (Ibid.) is as it is said: "let me see your countenance, let me hear your voice" (Shir Hashirim 2:14). "let me hear your voice" refers to the voice of those companions who engage in Torah, for I have no praise such as those who engage in Torah.

4. אָמַר ר״ש, כִּבְיָכוֹל, כָּל אִינוּן דְּזַכָּאן לְאִשְׁתַּדְּלָא בְּאוֹרַיְיתָא, וּמִכַּד פָּלִיג לֵילְיָא, וְאַתְיָין בִּמְטרוֹנִיתָא כַּד נָהִיר יְמָמָא, לְקַבְּלָא אַנְפֵּי מַלְכָּא, אִתְקִיף וְאַחֲסִין בִּשְׁכִינְתָּא. וְלֹא עוֹד, אֶלָּא דְּשַׁרְיָא בֵּיהּ חוּט שֶׁל חֶסֶד, כְּמָה דְּאוֹקִימְנָא.

4. Rabbi Shimon said: It is as if all those who are privileged to engage in Torah at midnight and ad the day begins to dawn come with the Queen to welcome the King, grow stronger and take possession of the Shechinah. Moreover, a thread of grace hangs over such a one, as the sages have explained.

5. ת״ח, כָּל מַאן דְּזָכֵי לְאִתְתַּקָּף בִּשְׁכִינְתָּא, יִסְתְּמַר גַּרְמוֹהִי מֵאִנּוּן מִלִּין דַּאֲחִידָן לְקַבְלָה. כְּגוֹן מַאן. אִינוּן דְּלָא מְשַׁקְּרֵי בְּאָת קַדִּישָׁא, כְּגוֹן בַּת אֵל נֵכָר. וְכָל מַאן דְּנָטִיר גַּרְמֵיהּ, כִּבְיָכוֹל כְּנֶסֶת יִשְׂרָאֵל אֲחִידָא בֵּיהּ, וְנַטְרָא לֵיהּ, וְהִיא אַקְדִּימַת לֵיהּ שְׁלָם. וְכ״ש אִי זָכֵי וְקָנֵי לְהַאי.

5. Come and see: Everyone who is privileged to be strengthened in the Shechinah gains protection for himself from those matters that are considered to be opposed TO THE SHECHINAH. Who is protected? Those who do not falsify by the sign of the Holy Covenant LIKE MATING WITH the daughter of a foreign El. And he who is careful, as it were, the Congregation of Yisrael is linked to him, in turn, and protects him and welcomes him. And this is even more so if he has been privileged to attain it, THE SIGN OF THE HOLY COVENANT.

6. וְאָמַר ר"ש, אִתְחֲזִיִין יִשְׂרָאֵל לְאִשְׁתֵּצָאָה בְּהַהוּא שַׁעֲתָא, בַּר דְּאַקְדִּים פִּנְחָס לְהַאי עוֹבָדָא, וְשָׁכִיךְ רוּגְזָא. הה"ד, פִּנְחָס בֶּן אֶלְעָזָר בֶּן אַהֲרֹן הַכֹּהֵן הֵשִׁיב וְגוֹ'. ד"א, פִּנְחָס בֶּן אֶלְעָזָר וְגוֹ'. אר"ש, בֶּן בֶּן תְּרֵי זִמְנֵי, לְאַשְׁלְמָא עוֹבָדָא קָא אָתֵי.

6. Rabbi Shimon said: Yisrael at that time would have deserved to have been extirpated from the world had not Pinchas first done the deed OF KILLING ZIMRI AND COZBI, and thus the anger abated. This is what is said: "Pinchas, the son of Elazar, the son of Aaron the priest, has turned my wrath away" (Bemidbar 25:11). Another explanation: "Pinchas, the son of Elazar, the son of...": Rabbi Shimon said, The word son occurs twice to complete the act.

7. אָמַר רִבִּי שִׁמְעוֹן, הַאי ב"נ דְּנָטִיל גִּלְגּוּלָא דְּנִשְׁמָתָא, וְלָא זָכֵי דְּיִתְתָּקַּן בֵּיהּ, כְּאִילוּ מְשַׁקֵּר בְּקוּשְׁטָא דְּמַלְכָּא. וַאֲנָא קָרֵינָא עֲלֵיהּ הַאי קְרָא אוֹ מָצָא אֲבֵידָה וְכִחֵשׁ בָּהּ וְנִשְׁבַּע עַל שָׁקֶר. וְכִחֵשׁ בָּהּ, טַב לֵיהּ דְּלָא אִבְרֵי.

7. Rabbi Shimon said: When the soul of a person reincarnates, MEANING A SECOND TIME AROUND, without gaining merits to be changed for the better, it is as though he betrays the truth of the King and I apply to him the verse, "...or has found that which was lost, and have lied concerning it, and have sworn falsely..." (Vayikra 5:22). "And have lied concerning it," MEANING TO THE SOUL, it would have been better for him had he not been created, FOR IT WOULD HAVE BEEN BETTER HAD HE NOT REINCARNATED INTO THIS WORLD.

3. Completely righteous and incompletely righteous

A Synopsis
In this section we learn that a completely righteous person is allowed to challenge an evil person, but an incompletely righteous person is not. The latter is defined as someone who did evil deeds himself in his first incarnation but now in this incarnation has done only good deeds. These good deeds are required to repair his earlier bad deeds. Rabbi Shimon says that even one who is not destined for greatness can achieve it through dedication to the Holy Name, as did Pinchas.

The Relevance of this Passage
The effects of our sins, committed this life and past, are henceforth remedied. The darkness generated by our iniquities vanishes as lambent flames of Light are dispersed into the present and distant past. This illumination, which traverses time itself, cleanses us, completes us, and makes us whole and righteous in the eyes of the Creator.

Moreover, we are protected from the deeds of the wicked. And although spiritual greatness may not have been in our destiny, we attain it now in the act of embracing this holy book and remaining steadfast in our commitment to the Light. We imbue our fellow man with holiness, correcting the transgressions of all humanity, and thus commencing our Final Redemption with untold benevolence. All of this is achieved upon the merit of the true Righteous, including Pinchas, Nadab, and Abihu, who desire nothing less for us.

8. תָּנֵינָן צַדִּיק גָּמוּר, אֵינוֹ נִדְחֶה. וְצַדִּיק שָׁאֵינוֹ גָּמוּר, נִדְחֶה. מַאן הוּא צַדִּיק גָּמוּר, וּמַאן הוּא צַדִּיק שָׁאֵינוֹ גָּמוּר, וְכִי מַאן דְּלָא שָׁלִים בְּמִלּוֹי, צַדִּיק אִקְרֵי. אֶלָּא, צַדִּיק גָּמוּר, יָדִיעַ, דְּהָא לָא נָטִיל גִּלְגּוּלִין עַקִימִין, וּבְאַחֲסַנְתֵּיה בָּנֵי בִּנְיָין, וְאַתְקִין שׁוּרִין, וְחָצַב בֵּירִין, וְנָטַע אִילָנִין.

8. We have learned: A totally righteous person is not put off BY AN EVIL PERSON AND MAY CHALLENGE HIM, but one who is not totally righteous is held back AND IS FORBIDDEN TO CHALLENGE AN EVIL PERSON. HE ASKS, Who is totally righteous? And who is incompletely righteous? And could it be that one who is not perfect in his deeds is nevertheless called 'righteous',

THAT IS, THAT YOU REFER TO HIM AS AN INCOMPLETE RIGHTEOUS? FOR
SOMEONE WHO IS LACKING IN HIS DEEDS, ACCORDING TO HOW THEY
SHOULD BE, OUGHT TO BE CALLED 'EVIL'. HE ANSWERS, it is known that
a totally righteous person is one who has not undergone crooked
incarnations THAT IS, HE IS NOT INCARNATED and within his OWN
inheritance he constructs edifices, puts up walls, digs wells and plants trees.
THAT IS TO SAY, ALL THE GOOD DEEDS THAT HE DID PERTAIN TO HIM,
FOR HE HAS NO NEED OF IMPROVING OTHERS.

9. צַדִּיק שֶׁאֵינוֹ גָמוּר, דְּבָנֵי בִּנְיָין בְּאַחֲסַנְתָּא אָחֳרָא, חָפַר בָּהּ בֵּירִין,
וְאַעֲדָר, הָא אַתְקִין אַבְנֵי יְסוֹדָא כְּמִלְּקַדְמִין, וְאַעֲמַל בָּהּ, וְלָא יָדַע אִי
אִשְׁתְּאַר דִּילֵיהּ. מִסִּטְרָא דִּילֵיהּ, טַב וְצַדִּיק אִקְרֵי. וּמִסִּטְרָא דְּהַהוּא
אַחֲסַנְתָּא, לָאו הָכִי.

9. An incompletely righteous person IS one who constructs edifices on
someone else's inheritance, THAT IS TO SAY, WHOSE SOUL IS ON ITS
SECOND INCARNATION BECAUSE HE WAS WICKED THE FIRST TIME, WITH
THE RESULT THAT ALL HIS GOOD DEEDS ARE NEEDED TO REPAIR THE
SOUL FROM THE FIRST TIME THAT IT CAME INTO THE WORLD, AND SO
HIS EDIFICES ARE BUILT WITHIN SOMEONE ELSE'S INHERITANCE. He
digs wells within it and cultivates it, restores the foundation stones to the
way they were, and labors there, but does not know whether it will remain
his. For in terms of himself, THAT IS, ACCORDING TO HIS DEEDS IN THIS
INCARNATION, he is good, and is considered righteous person. But in terms
of the legacy, THAT IS, IN TERMS OF HIS DEEDS ON THE FIRST TIME HE
CAME INTO THE WORLD, he is not so. THAT IS TO SAY, HE HAS NOT YET
REMEDIED THE EFFECTS OF THE SINS COMMITTED THE FIRST TIME.

10. לב"נ דְּבָנֵי בִּנְיָין שְׁפִירָן, יָאָן לְמֶחֱזֵי, אִסְתַּכַּל בִּיסוֹדָא, וְחָמֵי לֵיהּ
שְׁקִיעַ עֲקִימָא מִכָּל סְטְרִין. הָא בִּנְיָינָא לָא שְׁלִים, עַד דְּסָתַר לֵיהּ,
וְאַתְקִין לֵיהּ כְּמִלְּקַדְמִין. מִסִּטְרָא דְּהַהוּא בִּנְיָינָא דִּילֵיהּ, אִשְׁתְּכַח טַב
וְשַׁפִּיר. מִסִּטְרָא דִּיסוֹדָא, בִּישׁ וְעָקִים. וּבְגִין כָּךְ, לָא אִקְרֵי עוֹבָדָא
שְׁלִים, לָא אִקְרֵי בִּנְיָינָא שְׁלִים. בְּג"כ צַדִּיק שֶׁאֵינוֹ גָמוּר אִקְרֵי, וְנִדְחָה.
וע"ד כְּבַלַּע רָשָׁע צַדִּיק מִמֶּנּוּ.

10. HE IS LIKENED TO a man who constructs beautiful and attractive buildings. Look at the foundation and see how it is sunken and twisted in all directions. The building will not be perfect until he has demolished it and rebuilt it as it was, NAMELY, AS IT SHOULD BE. Thus in terms of the superstructure of the building that he constructed, everything was good and fine but in terms of the edifice's foundation it is bad and twisted, and for this reason is not referred to as a perfect deed, and not considered a perfect building. AND SO IT IS WITH THE INCARNATED MAN. ALTHOUGH IN TERMS OF HIS DEEDS HE IS RIGHTEOUS, NEVERTHELESS, SINCE HE HAS NOT YET REMEDIED THE EFFECTS OF THE SINS HE COMMITTED THE FIRST TIME THAT HE CAME INTO THE WORLD, he is called 'an incompletely righteous person' because of it and he is held back BY A WICKED MAN. And about this SCRIPTURE SAYS, "when the wicked devours the man that is more righteous than he" (Chavakuk 1:13).

11. ת"ח, מַאן דִּמְקַנֵּא לִשְׁמָא קַדִּישָׁא דְּקוּדְשָׁא בְּרִיךְ הוּא, דַּאֲפִילוּ לָא יִזְכֵּי לַגְדוּלָה, וְלָא אִתְחֲזֵי לָה, רָוַח לָה וְנָטִיל לָה. פִּנְחָס לָא אִתְחֲזֵי לֵיהּ בְּהַהוּא זִמְנָא, וּבְגִין דְּקַנֵּא לִשְׁמָא דְּמָארֵיהּ, רָוַח לְכֹלָּא, וְסָלִיק לְכֹלָּא, וְאִתְתְּקַן בֵּיהּ כֹּלָּא וְזָכָה לְאִשְׁתַּמְּשָׁא בִּכְהוּנָה עִלָּאָה. מֵהַהִיא שַׁעֲתָא, פִּנְחָס בֶּן אֶלְעָזָר בֶּן אַהֲרֹן הַכֹּהֵן, דְּאַשְׁלִים לִתְרֵין דַּרְגִּין, בְּגִין דְּקַנֵּא לִשְׁמָא דְּמָארֵיהּ, דְּאִתְתְּקַן מַה דְּאִתְעֲקַם.

11. Come and see: One who is zealous for the Holy Name of the Holy One, blessed be He, even if he is not designated for greatness and is not worthy of it, he earns it and gains it. Pinchas was not worthy OF THE PRIESTHOOD at that time, but because he was zealous for the name of his Master, he earned everything and rose to the highest position, and everything was put right within him, and he was privileged to serve in the supreme priesthood. From then on he was referred to as Pinchas the son of Elazar, the son of Aaron the priest, WITH THE WORD 'SON' OCCURRING TWICE since he completed two levels, THAT IS, HE MADE GOOD FOR HIMSELF AND ALSO FOR THE SOULS OF NADAV AND ABIHU WHICH HAD INCARNATED IN HIM, WHO ARE THE SONS OF AARON AND IT IS THEREFORE WRITTEN "THE SON OF ELAZAR, THE SON OF AARON." And this was because he was zealous for the name of his Master and put the wrong right, FOR HE CORRECTED HIMSELF AND ALSO THE ASPECT OF THE SOULS OF NADAV AND ABIHU THAT WERE INCARNATED IN HIM.

4. "Preserve my soul; for I am pious"

A Synopsis
Rabbi Shimon tells Rabbi Yehuda that "Preserve my soul" means "preserve the Hei," for the soul holds onto the Hei. If the soul is deserving when it leaves this world it is welcomed to the World to Come, but if it is not deserving, the angels of destruction push it outside. When David prayed for the preservation of his soul, he called himself pious because he was receiving the flow of Chassadim, and Rabbi Yitzchak says that Chassadim is bestowed by the Righteous, Yesod.

The Relevance of this Passage
The letter *Hei* appears twice in the Holy Name of God, the Tetragrammaton יהוה. The first *Hei* corresponds to the Sfirah of *Binah*. *Binah* is vastly important. It is a boundless bank of Light from which we draw the beneficence of the Creator. The Light of *Binah* also denotes the *World to Come* – namely, paradise in the here and now, when we are fortunate enough to connect to it.

The second *Hei* corresponds to our mundane, material world of *Malchut*. Through his spiritual might, King David likewise embodies the perfection of *Malchut*. Our soul is preserved and made worthy of the *World to Come* – the Light of *Binah*. As *Binah's* Light is now cast upon the world, the tables are suddenly turned: *Binah's* rays are directed against the angels of destruction, and they are pushed outside, cast out forever from this world and the next. We are now free to inherit a land of peace, prosperity, and paradise.

12. רִבִּי יְהוּדָה פָּתַח וְאָמַר, שָׁמְרָה נַפְשִׁי כִּי חָסִיד אָנִי הוֹשַׁע עַבְדְּךָ וְגוֹ'. סוֹפֵיהּ דִּקְרָא אִית לְאִסְתַּכְּלָא, וּלְבָתַר קְרָא כֹּלָּא, סוֹפֵיהּ דִּקְרָא כְּתִיב, הַבּוֹטֵחַ אֵלֶיךָ, הַבּוֹטֵחַ בָּךְ מִבְּעֵי לֵיהּ, מַאי הַבּוֹטֵחַ אֵלֶיךָ. אֶלָּא כִּבְיָכוֹל דָּוִד מִבְטַח לֵיהּ, דְּלָא יַעֲבַר לֵיהּ פַּלְגוּת לֵילְיָא בְּשִׁנְתָּא, כְּמָה דִּכְתִיב חֲצוֹת לַיְלָה אָקוּם לְהוֹדוֹת לָךְ. קַמָּתִי מִבְּעֵי לֵיהּ. אֶלָּא, אָקוּם, וְאֶתְקַשַּׁר בָּךְ לְעָלְמִין.

12. Rabbi Yehuda began: "Preserve my soul; for I am pious: Save Your servant..." (Tehilim 86:2). One has to look at the end of the verse, and then at the whole verse. At the end of the verse it says, "who trusts in You." HE

ASKS, Should it not have said, "who trusts You"? HE ANSWERS: apparently David promised not to be asleep when midnight passed, as it is written: "At midnight I will rise to give thanks to You" (Tehilim 119:62). He should have said, "I arose," but THE MEANING IS, I will arise and be bound to You for ever.

13. שָׁמְרָה נַפְשִׁי, שָׁמוֹר מִבָּעֵי לֵיהּ. וְהָא תָּנֵינָן דְּלֵית אָת בְּאוֹרַיְיתָא דְּלָא אִית בָּהּ רָזִין עִלָּאִין וְיַקִּירִין. שָׁמְרָה. לְקוּדְשָׁא בְּרִיךְ הוּא קָאָמַר, שָׁמְרָה לְהַהוּא חוּלָקָא, דְּאִתְאֲחָד בֵּיהּ נָפֶשׁ. דְּכַד נַפְשָׁא נָפְקָאת מֵהַאי עָלְמָא, אַתְיָא לְמֵירַת עָלְמָא דְּאָתֵי. אִי זָכֵי, כַּמָּה חֵילִין עִלָּאִין נָפְקִין לְקַבְּלָא לָהּ, וּלְנַטְרָא לָהּ, וּלְאַעֲלָא לָהּ בְּמָדוֹרָא דְּדוּכְתָּהָא, וְהַאי ה' נָטִיל לָהּ, לְאִתְאַחֲדָא עִמָּהּ בְּרֵישׁ יַרְחֵי וְשַׁבַּתֵּי.

13. HE ASKS "Preserve (Heb. *shomrah*) my soul." He should have used the form '*shemor*', but we have learned that there is no letter in the Torah that does not have heavenly and precious secrets. HE ANSWERS '*shomrah*', for he was saying to the Holy One, blessed be He, '*shomrah*', NAMELY SHEMOR (PRESERVE) THE HEI, for it is that same part onto which the soul holds. When the soul leaves this world it enters to inherit the domain of the World to Come. If it so merits, a number of heavenly hosts come out to greet it, guard it, and bring it into its residence in its place. That letter Hei, NAMELY MALCHUT, preserves it, so as to unite with it on new moons and Shabbatot.

14. וְאִי לָא זָכֵי, כַּמָּה גַּרְדִּינֵי טְהִירִין אִזְדַּמְּנָן לְקַבְּלָהּ, וְדַחוּ לָהּ לְבַר. וַוי לְהַהִיא נַפְשָׁא, דְּמִתְגַּלְגְּלָא בְּרֵיקַנְיָא, כְּאַבְנָא בְּקוּסְפִיתָא. הה"ד, וְאֵת נֶפֶשׁ אוֹיְבֶיךָ יְקַלְעֶנָּה בְּתוֹךְ כַּף הַקָּלַע. וְדָוִד בָּעֵי בְּעוּתֵיהּ קַמֵּי קוּדְשָׁא בְּרִיךְ הוּא וְאָמַר, שָׁמְרָה נַפְשִׁי, דְּלָא יִדְחוּן לָהּ לְבַר. וְכַד מָטֵי לְקַבְּלָהּ, יִפְתְּחוּן לָהּ פִּתְחִין, וּתְקַבֵּל לָהּ קַמָּךְ. כִּי חָסִיד אָנִי, וְכִי חָסִיד אִקְרֵי. א"ר יְהוּדָה, אִין. דִּכְתִיב, חַסְדֵי דָוִד הַנֶּאֱמָנִים. בְּגִין כָּךְ שָׁמְרָה נַפְשִׁי, דְּלָא תִשְׁבּוֹק לָהּ לְמֵהַךְ לְבַר.

14. But if it does not so merit, a number of angels of destruction are directed against it, and push it outside. Woe to that soul that wanders in vain as a

stone in the hollow of the sling. This is what was said: "and the souls of your enemies, them shall he sling out, as out of the hollow of a sling" (I Shmuel 25:29). And David made his request before the Holy One, blessed be He, and said, "Preserve my soul" that it be not rejected, and when they come out against it, may the portals be opened for it, and may You accept it before You. "for I am pious...": HE ASKS, was David really called 'pious'? WAS HE NOT A KING, AND WAS NOT KINGSHIP (MALCHUT) HIS CHARACTERISTIC? Rabbi Yehuda said, Yes, HE WAS CALLED 'PIOUS', for it is written, "the sure loving promises (Heb. *chassadim*) of David" (Yeshayah 55:3). THAT IS, SINCE HE WAS RECEIVING CHASSADIM THAT ARE SURE, HE IS 'PIOUS' (HEB. *CHASID*) and this is the reason for "Preserve my soul," namely, do not abandon it to wander on the outside.

‏15. ר' יִצְחָק אָמַר, כָּל ב״נ דְּאִית לֵיהּ חוּלָקָא בְּצַדִּיק, יָרִית לְהַאי אֶרֶץ, כְּמָה דִכְתִּיב, וְעַמֵּךְ כֻּלָּם צַדִּיקִים וְגוֹ'. וְהַאי צַדִּיק חָסִיד אִקְרֵי. אָמַר דָּוִד בָּתַר דִּבְהַאי אֲתָר אֲחִידְנָא, חָסִיד אֲנִי, ובג״כ שָׁמְרָה נַפְשִׁי, לְאִתְקַשְּׁרָא בָּךְ.

15. Rabbi Yitzchak said: Everyone who has a portion in the Righteous, NAMELY WHO GUARDS HIS COVENANT, inherits this land, THAT IS MALCHUT, as it is said: "Your people also shall be all righteous: they shall inherit the land for ever" (Yeshayah 60:21). And this Righteous, WHICH IS YESOD, is called 'pious' SINCE HE BESTOWS CHASSADIM. THAT IS WHY David said, Since I am linked and holding onto that place, UNTO THE RIGHTEOUS, THEREFORE, "I am pious"; and because of this, "Preserve my soul" that it be bound up with You.

5. The Hei added to the name of Joseph and the Yud to Pinchas

A Synopsis

Rabbi Chiya begins by saying that the angel taught Joseph the seventy languages that the Pharaoh knew but also taught him the Holy Language that the Pharaoh did not. Rabbi Shimon says that even though Joseph pretended not to understand the language of Potiphar's wife she eventually caught on to him and knew that he did understand; then the Holy Spirit known as 'testimony' gave him a warning. It is this testimony that is the Hei that was added to Joseph's name and the Yud that was added to the name of Pinchas.

The Relevance of this Passage

Joseph's greatness was found when he resisted the seductive words and sexual advances of Potiphar's wife, one of the most enchanting women in the world. The inner strength and virtue deeply rooted in Joseph is implanted within us so that we forever triumph over the seductions of our material world.

Pharoah symbolizes man's self-destructive ego. The narrative that expounds upon Joseph's mastery over Pharoah in the Holy Tongue instills in us self-mastery and might, so that we may, at last, triumph over our Evil Inclination. This great Light extends to all human beings. Humanity now achieves its final victory over the angel Satan and his entire legion.

The addition of the Hebrew letters *Hei* and *Yod* into the names of Joseph and Pinchas, respectively, indicates the alteration of human nature, the divine aspect of the Creator being imbued into the very being of these people. Here, we too receive an injection of divinity through these two "genetic-like" Hebrew letters. Our essence is forever changed.

16. רִבִּי חִיָּיא פָּתַח, עֵדוּת בִּיהוֹסֵף שָׂמוֹ וְגוֹ'. הָא אוּקְמוּהָ, דְּאוֹלִיף שִׁבְעִין פִּתְקִין, וְלָשׁוֹן הַקֹּדֶשׁ יַתִּיר. הה"ד, שְׂפַת לֹא יָדַעְתִּי אֶשְׁמָע. אֲבָל מַאי עֵדוּת. ת"ח, בְּשַׁעֲתָא דְּאַתְּתֵּיהּ דְּפוֹטִיפַר הֲוַת אֲחִידָא בֵּיהּ לְהַהִיא מִלָּה, הֲוָה יוֹסֵף עָבֵיד גַּרְמֵיהּ כְּמַאן דְּלָא יָדַע לִישָׁנָא דִּילָהּ, וְכֵן בְּכָל יוֹמָא עַד הַהִיא שַׁעֲתָא בַּתְרַיְיתָא, דִּכְתִיב וַתִּתְפְּשֵׂהוּ בְּבִגְדוֹ. מַאי וַתִּתְפְּשֵׂהוּ. אֶלָּא בְּגִין דְּעָבֵיד גַּרְמֵיהּ כְּמַאן דְּלָא יָדַע לִישָׁנָא. וְרוּחַ הַקֹּדֶשׁ צָוַוח לָקֳבְלֵיהּ, לְשַׁמָּרֶךָ מֵאִשָּׁה זָרָה מִנָּכְרִיָּה אֲמָרֶיהָ הֶחֱלִיקָה.

מַאי קמ״ל. אֶלָּא כָּל מַאן דְּנָטִיר גַּרְמֵיהּ מֵהַאי, אִתְקְשַׁר בָּהּ בִּשְׁכִינְתָּא,
וְאָחִיד בְּהַהוּא עֵדוּת. וּמַאי הוּא. ה׳ דְּאִתּוֹסַף בֵּיהּ. דִּכְתִיב, עֵדוּת
בִּיהוֹסֵף שָׂמוֹ. אוּף הָכָא י׳ אִתּוֹסַף בְּפִנְחָס, עַל דְּקַנֵּי בְּהַאי.

16. Rabbi Chiya began: "This he ordained in Jehoseph for testimony, when he went out over the land of Egypt, I heard the language of him whom I had not known" (Tehilim 81:6). We have learned THAT THE ANGEL taught Joseph seventy languages, AS WERE KNOWN BY PHARAOH, but also in the Holy Tongue HE WAS greater THAN PHARAOH, FOR PHARAOH DID NOT KNOW THE HOLY TONGUE. This is meant by "I heard the language of him whom I had not known" FOR HE TAUGHT HIM LANGUAGES THAT HE HAD NOT KNOWN PREVIOUSLY. But, IF THIS IS SO, what is "testimony"? AND HE ANSWERS, Come and see: When Potiphar's wife took hold of him for the reason, Joseph made himself as one who did not know her language, and so it was each day until the last time, as it is written: "And she caught him by his garment" (Beresheet 39:12). What is the meaning of "she caught him"? Until that time he had pretended that he did not know her language, BUT THEN SHE SAW THROUGH HIM, THAT HE DID KNOW HER LANGUAGE, MEANING THAT HE UNDERSTOOD HER INTENTION. THIS IS THE MEANING OF "SHE CAUGHT HIM": THAT SHE CAUGHT THE TRICKERY IN HIM. "HIS GARMENT (HEB. *BEGED*)," IS DERIVED FROM TRICKERY (HEB. *BEGIDAH*). And the Holy Spirit, THAT IS, MALCHUT, cried out to him, "that they may keep you from the strange woman, from the alien woman who makes smooth her words" (Mishlei 7:5). HE ASKS, what is this trying to teach us here? AND ANSWERS, THIS IS TEACHING US that everyone who keeps himself from such a thing AS JOSEPH DID is bound up with the Shechinah and holds on to this testimony WHICH IS MALCHUT. And which is it? This is the Hei that was added to him, as it is written: "This he ordained in Jehoseph for testimony." Also in our section, a Yud was added to the name of Pinchas because he was zealous over the same matter, THE AFFAIR OF ZIMRI, FOR THE YUD HINTS AT MALCHUT.

6. Keeper of the covenant

A Synopsis

Rabbi Yesa wonders why when the children of Yisrael were exiled to Babylon and wept, they were remembering Zion and not Jerusalem. Rabbi Shimon's answer is that the whole purpose of the Righteous, Yesod, is to bestow blessings, and if the Shechinah is in exile it has no one to bestow blessings upon and therefore the Righteous has perished. Rabbi Yesa says that whoever respects God is honored in his life and in his death, as were Joseph and Pinchas. From Rabbi Shimon we learn why Pinchas was granted the priesthood, even though he had killed and all those who kill are normally barred from the priesthood.

The Relevance of this Passage

The righteous souls throughout history experience untold anguish over our exile, for they know the Thought of Creation is bestowing boundless blessings upon our souls. These blessings occur when the *Shechinah* rests upon us and we connect to *Yesod,* the gateway through which divinity pours into our world.

Here we employ the almightiness of the Righteous to summon forth and redeem the *Shechinah* from her exile (our exile) so that we may receive the abundance of Light from *Yesod* that was intended for us since the dawn of creation. The sorrow of saintly men herewith ceases, for even the simple meditation of the average reader will now ease the burden of the Righteous, who have carried us on their backs for millennia. Such is the power of the Zohar.

As Jacob fled the seductive solicitations of Potiphar's wife, we escape the tug and pull of the material world, of Satan, and of our egocentric impulses, which are all, in truth, one and the same. By virtue of Joseph's righteousness, we merit honor and peace in this world and into the *World to Come.* We become rulers over Egypt. We command all negative forces throughout the land, and are inspired to fervently embrace the Creator. Our inspiration, rising on the wings of Pinchas's zealous love of the Holy One, corrects our past sins and earns us long life, priestly holiness, and a portion of the World to Come.

Most importantly, the Angel of Death's lethal grip over mankind is unalterably broken. The pain, torment, and suffering associated with death dies by the hand of Pinchas. The court of supernal judgment is adjourned – *permanently!*

17. רִבִּי יֵיסָא פָּתַח, עַל נַהֲרוֹת בָּבֶל שָׁם יָשַׁבְנוּ גַּם בָּכִינוּ בְּזָכְרֵנוּ אֶת

צִיּוֹן. אֶת יְרוּשָׁלַם מִבָּעֵי לֵיהּ, כְּמָה דִּכְתִיב אִם אֶשְׁכָּחֵךְ יְרוּשָׁלַם תִּשְׁכַּח

יְמִינִי, מַאי בְּזָכְרֵנוּ אֶת צִיּוֹן. לְב״ן דהו״ל הֵיכָלָא יַקִּירָא, יָאָה וְשַׁפִּירָא,

אָתוּ לִסְטִין וְאוֹקִידוּ לֵיהּ. צַעֲרָא דְּמַאן הוּא, לָאו דְּמָארֵיהּ דְּהֵיכָלָא.

אוּף הָכָא שְׁכִינְתָּא בְּגָלוּתָא שַׁרְיָא, צַעֲרָא דְּמַאן הוּא, לָאו דְּצַדִּיק.

וְאַזְלָא הָא כְּמָה דְּאוּקִמוּהָ, דִּכְתִיב הַצַּדִּיק אָבָד, אָבָד מַמָּשׁ. אוּף הָכָא

בְּזָכְרֵנוּ אֶת צִיּוֹן, בְּזָכְרֵנוּ הַהוּא צַעֲרָא דִּילֵיהּ עַל זוּוּגָהָא, צַעֲרָא דִּילֵיהּ

הוּא.

17. Rabbi Yesa began: "By the rivers of Babylon, there we sat down, we also wept, when we remembered Zion" (Tehilim 137:1). HE ASKS, should it not have said Jerusalem since it is written, "If I forget you, Jerusalem, let my right hand forget its cunning" (Ibid. 5). Why then, "when we remembered Zion"? AND HE ANSWERS: IT IS LIKE a man who had a precious and beautiful palace, and robbers came and burned it down. Whose is the anguish IF not that of the palace owner? Here also, whose anguish is it that the Shechinah is in exile, if not that of the Righteous, NAMELY YESOD? And this fits in with what they taught, as it is written: "The righteous perishes" (Yeshayah 57:1) literally, perished. FOR THE WHOLE PURPOSE OF YESOD IS TO BESTOW. BUT IF THE SHECHINAH IS IN EXILE HE HAS NO ONE TO BESTOW UPON, AND THEREFORE IT IS AS IF IT DOES NOT EXIST, BUT HAD PERISHED. Here also, "when we remembered Zion," MEANS when we remembered the anguish OF ZION, WHICH IS YESOD, because of its LACK OF mating, for the anguish is indeed his.

18. אָמַר רִבִּי יֵיסָא, מַאן דְּאוֹקִיר שְׁמָא דְּמָארֵיהּ בְּהַאי, וְנָטִיר הַאי,

זָכָה דְּיוֹקִיר לֵיהּ מָארֵיהּ עַל כֹּלָּא. מְנָלָן. מִיּוֹסֵף. דִּכְתִיב וַיַּרְכֵּב אוֹתוֹ

בְּמִרְכֶּבֶת הַמִּשְׁנֶה אֲשֶׁר לוֹ, וּכְתִיב וְנָתֹן אוֹתוֹ עַל כָּל אֶרֶץ מִצְרָיִם וְלֹא

עוֹד, אֶלָּא כַּד עָבְרוּ יִשְׂרָאֵל יַת יַמָּא, אֲרוֹנָא דְּיוֹסֵף עָאל בְּגוֹ

בְּקַדְמֵיתָא, וְלָא הֲווֹ מַיָּא קַיְימִין עַל קִיּוּמַיְיהוּ קַמֵּיהּ, הֲדָא הוּא דִכְתִיב,

הַיָּם רָאָה וַיָּנֹס. מַאי רָאָה וַיָּנֹס. אֶלָּא רָאָה הַהוּא דִּכְתִיב בֵּיהּ וַיָּנָס וַיֵּצֵא

הַחוּצָה.

18. Rabbi Yesa said: Whoever respects the name of his Master in this

-19-

matter, and keeps THE COVENANT, is privileged to have his Master respect him over all. How do we know this? Because regarding Joseph, it is written, "And he made him to ride in the second chariot which he had... and made him ruler over all the land of Egypt" (Beresheet 41:43). Furthermore, when Yisrael crossed the sea, Joseph's coffin entered the water first and the waters in front of it were unable to stay as they were. Therefore it is written, "The sea saw it, and fled" (Tehilim 114:3). What is the meaning of "and fled"? The sea saw him about whom this is written, "and fled, and went outside" (Beresheet 39:12).

19. ת״ח, זָכֵי לִיקָרָא בְּחַיּוֹי וְזָכֵי לִיקָרָא בְּמִיתָתֵיה. בְּחַיָּיו אֲמַאי. בְּגִין הַהוּא זְמַן דְּלָא בָּעָא לְאִתְדַּבְּקָא בָּה, דִּכְתִּיב וַיְמָאֵן וַיֹּאמֶר אֶל אֵשֶׁת אֲדֹנָיו. וּכְתִיב וְלֹא שָׁמַע אֵלֶיהָ לִשְׁכַּב אֶצְלָה לִהְיוֹת עִמָּהּ. בְּגִין כָּךְ זָכָה בְּהַאי עָלְמָא. כֵּיוָן דִּכְתִּיב וַתִּתְפְּשֵׂהוּ בְּבִגְדוֹ, וּכְתִיב וַיָּנָס וַיֵּצֵא הַחוּצָה, זָכֵי לְבָתַר דְּעָאל לְגוֹ פָּרוֹכְתָּא עִלָּאָה, וְהָכִי אִתְחֲזֵי לֵיה, דִּידֵיה נָטַל בְּהַאי עָלְמָא, וְדִידֵיה נָטַל בְּעָלְמָא אַחֲרָא.

19. Come and see: He was honored in his life and honored in his death. Why in his life? Because during that time he did not want to cleave TO POTIPHAR'S WIFE, as it is written: "But he refused, and said to his master's wife..." (Ibid. 8), and, "that he hearkened not to her, to lie by her, or to be with her" (Ibid. 10). For this reason he was honored in this world. Since it is written, "And she caught him by his garment...and he fled, and went outside," BECAUSE OF THAT he earned entry after HIS DEMISE into the heavenly curtain THAT IS IN THE SANCTUARY OF THE HOLY OF HOLIES. And so it was befitting to him, RESULTING that he received his due in this world and in the other world.

20. פִּנְחָס זָכֵי בְּהַאי עָלְמָא, וְזָכָה בְּעָלְמָא דְּאָתֵי, וְזָכָה לְקַיְּימָא יַתִּיר מִכָּל אִינּוּן דְּנַפְקוּ מִמִּצְרַיִם, וְזָכָה לְכַהֲנָא עִלָּאָה, הוּא וְכָל בְּנוֹי אֲבַתְרֵיה. וְאִי תֵּימָא דְּלָא זָכָה לְכַהֲנָא עַד לָא עֲבַד עוֹבָדָא דָּא. לָא. דְּהָא אִינּוּן דְּאָמְרֵי דְּזָכָה קוֹדֶם. לָאו הָכִי אֶלָּא בְּמַאי אוֹקִימְנָא תַּחַת אֲשֶׁר קִנֵּא לֵאלֹהָיו, דְּמַשְׁמַע דְּבְגִין עוֹבָדָא דָּא רָוַוח כְּהוּנְתָא, מַה דְּלָא הֲוָה קוֹדֶם.

20. Pinchas was privileged in this world and in the World to Come, and meritted to live and exist longer than all those who came out of Egypt. He also merited to serve as High Priest, both he and all his descendants after him. You may argue that he earned priesthood only after this act. However, this is incorrect, there are those who say that he had earned the priesthood previously. If so, how should we understand the words, "because he was zealous for his Elohim" (Bemidbar 25:13), which meaning is that he earned the priesthood because of this deed and had not gained it previously?

‫21. ת״ח, כָּל כֹּהֵן דְּקָטִיל נֶפֶשׁ, פָּסִיל לֵיהּ כְּהוּנָתֵיהּ לְעָלְמִין. דְּהָא‬
‫וַדַּאי פָּסִיל הַהוּא דַּרְגָּא דִּילֵיהּ לְגַבֵּיהּ. וּפִנְחָס מִן דִּינָא פָּסִיל לְכַהֲנָא‬
‫הֲוָה, וּבְגִין דְּקַנֵּא לֵיהּ לְקוּדְשָׁא בְּרִיךְ הוּא, אִצְטְרִיךְ לְיַחֲסָא לֵיהּ כְּהוּנַת‬
‫עָלְמִין, לֵיהּ, וְלִבְנוֹי אֲבַתְרֵיהּ, לְדָרֵי דָּרִין. א״ר יִצְחָק, ת״ח, רָשִׁים הוּא‬
‫פִּנְחָס לְעֵילָא, וְרָשִׁים הוּא לְתַתָּא, עַד לָא יִפּוּק לְעָלְמָא דְּהָא עִם אִינּוּן‬
‫דְּנַפְקוּ מִמִּצְרַיִם אִתְמְנֵי.‬

21. HE RESPONDS: come and see, any priest who kills a person is considered forever unfit for the priesthood because he has marred his own level, BECAUSE PRIESTHOOD IS THE LEVEL OF CHESED AND KILLING A PERSON IS ITS OPPOSITION. SINCE Pinchas HAD KILLED ZIMRI AND COZBI, he was legally barred from remaining a priest. But because he was zealous for the Holy One, blessed be He, He had to reinstate him, and also his seed after him for all time, into the priesthood. THIS IS THE MEANING OF THE WORDS, "BECAUSE HE WAS ZEALOUS FOR HIS ELOHIM." Rabbi Yitzchak said, Come and see: Pinchas is recorded above and below. ABOVE MEANS before he came into the world BELOW, is as he was among those who came out of Egypt.

‫22. רִבִּי אֶלְעָזָר וְר׳ יוֹסֵי וְר׳ חִיָּיא, הֲווֹ אָזְלֵי בְּמַדְבְּרָא, א״ר יוֹסֵי, הָא‬
‫דִּכְתִיב בְּפִנְחָס הִנְנִי נוֹתֵן לוֹ אֶת בְּרִיתִי שָׁלוֹם. שָׁלוֹם מִמַּלְאַךְ הַמָּוֶת,‬
‫דְּלָא שַׁלִּיט בֵּיהּ לְעָלְמִין, וְלָא אִתְדָּן בְּדִינוֹי. וְאִי תֵּימָא דְּלָא מִית.‬
‫וַדַּאי לָא מִית כִּשְׁאַר בְּנֵי עָלְמָא, וְאוֹרִיךְ יוֹמִין עַל כָּל בְּנֵי דָּרָא, בְּגִין‬
‫דְּבְהַאי בְּרִית עִלָּאָה אָחִיד, וְכַד אִסְתְּלַק מֵעָלְמָא, בְּתִיאוּבְתָּא עִלָּאָה‬
‫וּבִדְבִיקוּתֵיהּ שַׁפִּירָא אִסְתַּלַּק מִשְּׁאַר בְּנֵי עָלְמָא.‬

22. Rabbi Elazar, Rabbi Yosi, and Rabbi Chiya were walking in the wilderness. Rabbi Yosi said, This that is written concerning Pinchas, "Behold I give him My covenant of peace" (Ibid. 12), refers to peace from the Angel of Death, the Angel who will never have control over him or have power to judge him. If you were to suggest that he did not die, you would be mistaken. HE DID DIE but certainly not in the same way as others do and he lived longer than all the other members of his generation because he held on to that heavenly covenant. And when he did leave this world he departed from other people with a supreme longing and with wonderful devoutness.

7. The attire of that world

A Synopsis
Rabbi Elazar deduces from some verses in Zecharyah that it is a person's bad deeds that make a filthy garment for his spirit, and that everyone will be joyful if they can don a more suitable garment in the World to Come. Next the rabbis sit in the shade of a rock while they pause from their travels, and Rabbi Elazar says, 'Shade is without doubt the joy of the soul'.

The Relevance of this Passage
Throughout our life and our past lives, there have been countless times when we succumbed to our immoral impulses. When this occurred, we created a blemish, a blockage that soiled our soul. These blockages must be cleansed for the following reasons: Each negative deed committed is akin to placing a filthy piece of cloth over a lamp. A room, lit by a lamp, grows progressively darker each time another layer of cloth is draped over the lamp. It is this added darkness that incites chaos, turmoil, pain, and suffering in life. When these dirty cloths are removed, the Light is free to shine with maximum intensity.

According to the Zohar, Joshua and Pinchas wore garments that sparkled with cleanliness. Pinchas, we're told, "changed clothes" in one hour. Thus, one hour of contrite meditation upon this particular passage purifies our souls from all its iniquities. The passage allows us to "change clothes" like Pinchas did. And in the moment we share this purifying Light with our neighbors and the souls languishing in the underworld, the Gates of Entry into Hell are slammed shut for good. We liberate these newly cleansed souls from their burning abode as Hell undergoes a final meltdown. The entire world is attired in gleaming garments befitting the purity of this holy Book of Splendor.

23. רְבִּי אֶלְעָזָר פָּתַח וְאָמַר, וַיַּרְאֵנִי אֶת יְהוֹשֻׁעַ הַכֹּהֵן הַגָּדוֹל עוֹמֵד לִפְנֵי מַלְאַךְ יְיָ' וְגוֹ'. ת"ח, וַוי לְאִינוּן בְּנֵי נָשָׁא, דְּלָא מִסְתַּכְּלָאן בִּיקָרָא דְּמָארֵיהוֹן, וְכָל יוֹמָא וְיוֹמָא כְּרוֹזָא קָארֵי עֲלַיְיהוּ, וְלָא מַשְׁגִּיחִין. אָתָא ב"נ לְאִסְתַּכְּלָא בְּפִקוּדֵי אוֹרַיְיתָא, כַּמָה סַנֵּיגוֹרִין קַיְימִין לְאַדְכְּרָא עֲלֵיה לְטָב. אָתָא ב"נ וְאַעֲבַר עַל פְּקוּדֵי אוֹרַיְיתָא, אִינוּן עוֹבָדִין קַטֵיגוֹרִין עֲלֵיה לְבִישׁ, קַמֵּי קוּדְשָׁא בְּרִיךְ הוּא. יְהוֹשֻׁעַ כֹּהֵן גָּדוֹל הֲוָה,

וְאוֹקְמוּהָ, מַה כְּתִיב בֵּיהּ. וְהַשָּׂטָן עוֹמֵד עַל יְמִינוֹ לְשִׂטְנוֹ. וּמַה בְּהַאי כָּךְ, בִּשְׁאַר בְּנֵי עָלְמָא דְּלָא מִסְתַּכְּלֵי בִּיקָרָא דְּמָארֵיהוֹן, עַל אַחַת כַּמָּה וְכַמָּה.

23. Rabbi Elazar began: "And he showed me Joshua the High Priest, standing before the angel of Hashem..." (Zecharyah 3:1). Come and see: woe to those people who do not look out for their Master's glory and do not pay attention to the fact that He daily issues a proclamation about them. When a person observes the commandments of the Torah, many defenders rise to recall his good points, but if a person transgresses the commandments his deeds accuse him before the Holy One, blessed be He. We have been told that Joshua was a High Priest. And what is written about him? "...and the adversary standing at his right hand to thwart him" (Ibid.). If this is how it was for him, then how much more so for other people who do not care for the glory of their Master.

24. חָמֵי מַה כְּתִיב, וִיהוֹשֻׁעַ הָיָה לָבוּשׁ בְּגָדִים צוֹאִים, וְאוֹקְמוּהָ. אֲבָל בְּגָדִים צוֹאִים, וַדַּאי אִינּוּן לְבוּשִׁין דְּאִתְלַבְּשָׁא בֵּיהּ רוּחָא בְּהַהוּא עָלְמָא. זַכָּאָה חוּלָקֵיהּ דְּמַאן דִּלְבוּשׁוֹי מִתְתַּקְנִין וּשְׁלֵמִין בְּהַהוּא עָלְמָא. וְהָא אִתְּמַר, כָּל מַאן דְּבַעְיָין לְאַעֲלָא לַגֵּיהִנָּם, אִינּוּן לְבוּשִׁין דִּמְלַבְּשִׁין לֵיהּ, הֵיךְ אִינּוּן. מַה כְּתִיב הָכָא, וִיהוֹשֻׁעַ הָיָה לָבוּשׁ בְּגָדִים צוֹאִים וְעוֹמֵד לִפְנֵי הַמַּלְאָךְ. מַאן מַלְאָךְ. דָּא מַלְאָךְ דִּמְמָנָא עַל גֵּיהִנָּם, וּמְמָנָא עַל מַאן דְּחָמֵי בְּאִינּוּן לְבוּשִׁין. עַד דְּאָתִיב קָלָא וְאָמַר, הָסִירוּ הַבְּגָדִים הַצּוֹאִים מֵעָלָיו.

24. Look what is written: "Now Joshua was clothed in filthy garments..." (Ibid. 3). This has been explained. Yet the filthy garments were surely the garments in which the spirit is attired in that world. Happy is the portion of he whose garments are fixed and complete in that world! We have already learned what raiment they clothe one whom they want to send to Gehenom, what these raiments are that they dress him in. AND HE ANSWERS: here it is written, "Now Joshua was clothed in filthy garments, and he stood before the angel." Which angel? The Angel in charge of Gehenom and who is also in charge of everyone whom he sees in such clothes. Then a voice said, "Take off the filthy garments from him" (Ibid. 4).

25. מֵהָכָא אִית לְאִסְתַּכְּלָא, דְּעוֹבָדִין בִּישִׁין דב"נ, עַבְדִין לֵיהּ אִינּוּן לְבוּשִׁים צוֹאִים. וַיֹּאמֶר אֵלָיו רְאֵה הֶעֱבַרְתִּי מֵעָלֶיךָ עֲוֹנֶךָ וְהַלְבֵּשׁ אוֹתְךָ מַחֲלָצוֹת. אַלְבִּישֵׁינֵיהּ לְבוּשִׁין אַחֲרָנִין מְתַתְּקְנָן, דִּבְהוּ אִסְתָּכַּל ב"נ בְּזִיו יְקָרָא דְּמָארֵיהּ.

25. It follows from this that it is a person's bad deeds that make the filthy garments for him. "And he said to him, 'Behold I have caused your iniquity to pass from you; and I clothe you in festive garments'" (Ibid.). For they clothed him in other more suitable garments, in which a person may observe the splendor of his Master's glory.

26. ת"ח, כְּגַוְונָא דָּא פִּנְחָס, דְּלָא אִסְתַּלָּק מֵעָלְמָא, עַד דְּאִתְתָּקָנוּ קַמֵּיהּ לְבוּשִׁין אַחֲרָנִין, דְּרוּחָא אִתְהֲנֵי בְּהוּ, לְעָלְמָא דְּאָתֵי. בְּשַׁעֲתָא חֲדָא אִתְפְּשַׁט מֵאִלֵּין. וְאִתְלְבַּשׁ בְּאִלֵּין, לְקַיְּימָא דִּכְתִיב הִנְנִי נוֹתֵן לוֹ אֶת בְּרִיתִי שָׁלוֹם. עַד דַּהֲווֹ אַזְלֵי, שִׁמְשָׁא הֲוָה תַּקִּיפָא, וְיָתְבוּ תְּחוֹת צְלָא דְּחַד טִנָרָא דְּמַדְבְּרָא. אָמַר ר' אֶלְעָזָר, וַדַּאי צְלָּא חֶדְוָתָא דְּנַפְשָׁא הוּא.

26. Come and see the similarity: Pinchas, who did not leave this world until he had changed into other fitted garments which the spirit would enjoy in the World to Come, had at the same time taken off one set and put on the other, to fulfil that which is written: "Behold, I give to him My covenant of peace" (Bemidbar 25:12). While they were on their way and the sunlight was strong, they sat down in the shade of a rock in the wilderness. Rabbi Elazar said, Shade is without doubt joy to the soul.

8. From Rosh Hashanah to the last day of Sukkot

A Synopsis

Rabbi Elazar explains to Rabbi Chiya the significance of the days mentioned in the title of this section. We hear that it has to do with the order in which God lifts up his right arm and extends it to embrace Malchut and unite with her. It includes the purification and fasting that the children of Yisrael do at this time.

The Relevance of this Passage

This passage expounds upon the deep secrets underlying the days between Rosh Hashanah and Sukkot. The words of Rabbi Chiya and Rabbi Elazar ignite the unification and cleansing powers of these cosmic instruments.

These spiritual influences uproot all immoral qualities from our nature in a merciful, softhearted fashion. They cleanse all the iniquities of humanity, our sins, and our misdeeds, purifying and preparing us for union with the Light of Creator. Judgments are overturned. Sentences are repealed. The Right, Left, and Central Columns are balanced and perfected. All the worlds are refined and corrected.

And because the Zohar is above time and place, outside the laws of physics; because this mystical tome deals with the mysteries of the soul and the secrets of secrets, the effect and results are all-embracing – universal, macrocosmic, and in the Now. Our actions here are the ultimate atonement, bringing forth our Final Redemption and unification with the Light, thanks to the righteousness and power of the rabbis cited throughout this ancient holy book.

27. אָמַר רַבִּי חִיָּיא לְרַבִּי אֶלְעָזָר, אִלֵּין יוֹמִין, מֵרֹאשׁ הַשָּׁנָה עַד יוֹמָא בַּתְרָאָה דְּחַג, בָּעֵינָא לְמֵיקֶם עָלַיְיהוּ. א"ר אֶלְעָזָר, הָא אִתְּמַר וְחַבְרַיָּיא אִתְּעָרוּ בְּהוּ. א"ר חִיָּיא, וַדַּאי הָכִי הוּא, אֲבָל אֲנָא שְׁמַעֲנָא לְבוּצִינָא קַדִּישָׁא עִלָּאָה מִלָּה בְּהוּ. אָמַר לֵיהּ, אֵימָא הַהוּא מִלָּה. א"ל עַד לָא קָאִימְנָא בֵּיהּ. א"ר אֶלְעָזָר, אַף עַל גַּב דְּחַבְרַיָּיא אוֹקְמוּ מִלָּה, וְשַׁפִּיר הוּא, אֲבָל סִדּוּרָא דְּהָנֵי יוֹמֵי, רָזָא דְּחָכְמְתָא הוּא, בֵּין מְחַצְדֵי חַקְלָא.

27. Rabbi Chiya said to Rabbi Elazar, I should like to discuss these days from Rosh Hashanah until the last day of Sukkot. Rabbi Elazar said, But we

have already studied them, and the friends have made their comments about them. Rabbi Chiya said, Of course, but I heard something about them from the great and Holy Luminary, RABBI SHIMON. He said to him, Tell us. To which Rabbi Chiya replied, I still do not grasp it AND IT IS NOT AS CLEAR AS IT SHOULD BE. Rabbi Elazar said, Although the friends have already discussed this matter, and it is beautiful, the order of these days is the secret of wisdom, among the reapers in the field, NAMELY, AMONG THOSE SCHOLARS WHO HAVE ALREADY COMPLETED ALL THE CLARIFICATIONS OF MALCHUT, WHICH IS TERMED 'A FIELD'.

28. ת״ח, הָא אִתְּמַר סְדוּרָא דְיִחוּדָא כֹּלָא בְּחַד הֵיךְ הֲוֵי. וְהָא אִתְּמַר. פָּתַח וְאָמַר, חָשַׂף יְיָ' אֶת זְרוֹעַ קָדְשׁוֹ, דָּא דְרוֹעָא חֲדָא, דְּבֵיהּ תַּלְיָא יְשׁוּעָה, דְּבֵיהּ תַּלְיָא נוּקְמָא, דְּבֵיהּ תַּלְיָא פוּרְקָנָא. וְלָמָה, לְמֵיקַם לָהּ לכנ״י מֵעַפְרָא, וּלְקַבְּלָא לָהּ לְגַבֵּיהּ, לְאִזְדַּוְּוגָא כַּחֲדָא. וְכַד הַאי אִתְּעַר לְקַבְלָהּ, כַּמָה דְחִילוּ שַׁרְיָא בְּעָלְמָא, עַד דְּיָנַח הַהוּא דְרוֹעָא תְּחוֹת רֵישָׁהָא לְאִתְחַבְּרָא. כְּמָה דְאַתְּ אָמַר, שְׂמֹאלוֹ תַּחַת לְרֹאשִׁי וְגוֹ', וּכְדֵין נַיְיחָא דִינָא, וּמְכַפֵּר חוֹבִין.

28. Come and see: The order of unifying all into one, how does that go? We have learned, He began, "Hashem has made bare His holy arm" (Yeshayah 52:10). This is one arm, WHICH IS THE LEFT COLUMN on which are dependent salvation, vengeance, and redemption. But why DID HASHEM MAKE BARE THIS HOLY ARM OF HIS? It was to raise up the Congregation of Yisrael, NAMELY, MALCHUT, from the dust and to welcome her with Him so as to unite as one. When that ARM is raised up toward her, there is much fear present in the world, until He rests that arm under her head to unite with her, as it is said: "His left hand is under my head..." (Shir Hashirim 2:6). And then judgment rests and He atones for sins.

29. לְבָתַר אָתֵי יְמִינָא לְחַבְּקָא, כְּדֵין חֶדְוָותָא שַׁרְיָיא בְּעָלְמָא, וְכָל אַנְפִּין נְהִירִין. לְבָתַר אִזְדַּוְּוגַת בְּגוּפָא, וּכְדֵין כֹּלָּא אִקְרֵי אֶחָד, בְּלָא פֵּרוּדָא, כְּדֵין הוּא שְׁלִימוּ דְּכֹלָּא, וְחֶדְוָותָא דְּכֹלָּא, וְאָחִידוּ וַדַּאי, מַה דְּלָא אִשְׁתְּכַח הָכִי בִּשְׁאַר זִמְנֵי.

29. Later the Right COLUMN comes to embrace her. Then rejoicing engulfs the world, and all countenances shine. Subsequently, she, MALCHUT, unites with the body, NAMELY, THE CENTRAL COLUMN, and then everything is considered one without schism, FOR THE CENTRAL COLUMN INCORPORATES THE RIGHT AND THE LEFT. Then everything is perfect and everything is joyous and they, ZEIR ANPIN AND MALCHUT, certainly unite, which is not the case at other times.

30. כְּגַוְונָא דְּהַאי, סִדּוּרָא דְּהָנֵי יוֹמִין, מֵרֹאשׁ הַשָּׁנָה עַד יוֹמָא בַּתְרָאָה דְּחַג. בְּרֹאשׁ הַשָּׁנָה, אִתְּעַר דְּרוֹעָא דִשְׂמָאלָא, לְקַבְּלָא לָהּ לְמַטְרוֹנִיתָא, וּכְדֵין כָּל עָלְמָא בִּדְחִילוּ בְּדִינָא, וּבָעֵי הַהוּא זִמְנָא בִּתְיוּבְתָּא שְׁלִים, לְאִשְׁתַּכְּחָא עָלְמָא קַמֵּי קוּדְשָׁא בְּרִיךְ הוּא. לְבָתַר אַתְיַאת מַטְרוֹנִיתָא, וּבַעְיָין בְּנֵי הֵיכָלָא בְּתִשְׁעָה לְיַרְחָא, לְמֶעְבַּד חֶדְוָותָא, וּלְמִטְבַּל בְּנַהֲרָא, לְדַכְּאָה גַרְמַיְיהוּ בְּזִוּוּגָא דְּמַטְרוֹנִיתָא, בְּיוֹמָא אַחֳרָא, הוּא זִוּוּגָא דִּילָהּ לְשַׂוְואָה שְׂמָאלָא תְּחוֹת רֵישָׁהָא, כְּמָה דְאַתְּ אָמַר שְׂמֹאלוֹ תַּחַת לְרֹאשִׁי.

30. Likewise is the order of those days, from Rosh Hashanah until the last day of Sukkot, is like this. On Rosh Hashanah, the left arm is awakened, NAMELY, THE LEFT COLUMN OF ZEIR ANPIN, to welcome the Queen. The whole world is then in fear of Judgment, and the whole world has to be in complete repentance before the Holy One, blessed be He. Later, on the ninth of the month, the Queen comes and the palace retinue, NAMELY, THE CHILDREN OF YISRAEL, make merry and immerse themselves in the river to purify themselves SO AS TO BE WORTHY OF the union of the Queen WITH ZEIR ANPIN, on the other day, NAMELY, THE TENTH OF THE MONTH, YOM KIPPUR (DAY OF ATONEMENT). For her union is accomplished by ZEIR ANPIN placing his left hand under her head, in accordance with the text, "His left hand is under my head."

31. וּכְדֵין יִשְׂרָאֵל בְּתַעֲנִיתָא עַל חוֹבַיְיהוּ, וּמְכַפְּרָא לְהוּ. דְּהָא אִימָּא עִלָּאָה אַנְהִירַת אַנְפָּהָא לְמַטְרוֹנִיתָא בְּזִוּוּגָהָא, וּמִתְכַּפְּרִין כָּל בְּנֵי הֵיכָלָא. כֵּיוָן דִּשְׂמָאלָא מְקַבְּלָה לָהּ בְּהַאי יוֹמָא, דְּרֵישָׁא דְּמַטְרוֹנִיתָא שַׁרְיָיא עַל שְׂמָאלָא.

31. Then, on the tenth day Yisrael fast for their sins and are forgiven. For Supernal Ima, NAMELY, BINAH, looks kindly on Malchut in the union, FOR ON YOM KIPPUR MALCHUT RISES AND COATS BINAH, and makes atonement for all of the retinue of the palace, NAMELY, YISRAEL, since the left OF ZEIR ANPIN welcomes her on this day, for the head of Malchut rests on the left.

32. בְּיוֹמָא קַדְמָאָה דְּחַג, יִתְּעַר יְמִינָא לְקַבְּלָהּ, בְּגִין לְחַבְּקָהּ וּכְדֵין כָּל חֶדְווֹא וְכָל אַנְפִּין נְהִירִין, וְחֶדְוָותָא דְּמַיִם צְלִילָן, לְנַסְּכָא עַל מַדְבְּחָא. וּבַעְיָין בְּנֵי נָשָׁא לְמֶחֱדֵי בְּכָל זִינִין דְּחֶדְוָה, דְּהָא יְמִינָא גָּרִים. בְּכָל אֲתָר דְּשָׁארִי יְמִינָא, חֶדְוָותָא אִצְטְרִיךְ בְּכֹלָּא, כְּדֵין חֶדְוָותָא הִיא לְאִשְׁתַּעְשְׁעָא.

32. On the first day of Sukkot, the Right COLUMN OF ZEIR ANPIN begins to move towards MALCHUT to embrace her. THIS IS THE HIDDEN MEANING OF THE VERSE, "AND HIS RIGHT HAND EMBRACES ME" (SHIR HASHIRIM 2:6). Then everyone rejoices and all countenances shine. There is joy in pouring pure water on the altar. People should be happy by rejoicing in many different ways. This is brought about by the right, for wherever the right side, NAMELY, CHASSADIM, rests, there has to be joy everywhere. Then there is joy with which to be happy.

33. לְבָתַר בְּיוֹמָא תְּמִינָאָה, חֶדְוָותָא דְּאוֹרַיְיתָא הוּא, דְּהָא כְּדֵין זוּוּגָא דְּגוּפָא, הוּא זוּוּגָא דְּכֹלָּא, לְמֶהֱוֵי כֹּלָּא חַד, וְדָא הוּא שְׁלִימוּ דְּכֹלָּא, וְדָא יוֹמָא דְּיִשְׂרָאֵל אִיהוּ וַדַּאי, וְעַדְבָא דִּידְהוּ בִּלְחוֹדַיְיהוּ, דְּלֵית בֵּיהּ חוּלָקָא לְאַחֲרָא. זַכָּאִין אִינּוּן יִשְׂרָאֵל בְּעָלְמָא דֵּין, וּבְעָלְמָא דְּאָתֵי, עֲלַיְיהוּ כְּתִיב כִּי עַם קָדוֹשׁ אַתָּה לַיְיָ' אֱלֹהֶיךָ וְגוֹ'.

33. Later, on the day of Shmini Atzeret, is Simchat Torah, as then the mating of the body NAMELY, THE CENTRAL COLUMN CALLED 'BODY' is taking place. This is the union of all parts, FOR IT INCLUDES THE MATING OF THE LEFT SIDE, OF ROSH HASHANAH AND YOM KIPPUR AS WELL AS THE UNION OF THE RIGHT SIDE OF THE HOLIDAY OF SUKKOT SINCE THE CENTRAL COLUMN INCORPORATES THE RIGHT AND THE LEFT. Thus all is

one and this is overall perfection. And this day is definitely Yisrael's. Its portion belongs to them alone, for no other people has a part in it. THAT IS TO SAY, IT IS NOT LIKE THE FESTIVAL OF SUKKOT WHEN SEVENTY BULLS ARE SACRIFICED FOR THE SEVENTY NATIONS, BECAUSE THE NATIONS HAVE NO PART IN SHMINI ATZERET. Happy are Yisrael in this world and in the World to Come. About them it is written, "Because you are a holy people for Hashem your Elohim" (Devarim 14:2).

9. The rainbow

A Synopsis

Rabbi Yehuda says the rainbow appears to remind people of God's promise never again to destroy the world, and we also hear that the rainbow appears whenever there is no righteous person to protect the world. When Rabbi Elazar talks about the green, red and white colors in the rainbow that correspond to the three patriarchs, Rabbi Aba disagrees with his assignment of each color. He ends by talking about the letter Yud in Pinchas' name, and mentions that Nadab and Abihu were reincarnated in Pinchas.

The Relevance of this Passage

This one passage alone is so potent that one heartfelt reading has the power to forever establish serenity in our souls and lasting peace in the world.

Sin is a constant trademark of man. And although transgressors physically outnumber the few righteous men of this world, the good deeds of these saintly souls outweigh all the sins of the wicked combined. Such is the power of Light over darkness. The righteous, we're told, protect us with their presence. And the rainbow, which appeared after the Flood as a sign of God's promise never to destroy this world, protects us when there are no righteous men among us.

The reason for this tale is crystal-clear – the Zohar is drawing upon the righteous *and* the rainbow to lay gently a blanket of protection over the entire world. And because this truth is emerging through the Zohar for the first time in history, the effect is unprecedented: Judgments looming over the horizon are cast off to sea forevermore as we evoke the name of Pinchas. The Earth's waters, once used to destroy mankind, are restored to their pre-Flood molecular structure. This divine substance transmutes into waters of healing that regenerate the soul and the cells of body.

The Zohar speaks of the colors green and white, which are healing colors. They shine here brightly; and they rectify us, heal us, and make us well again.

The color red – attributed to the war planet Mars, and to our Left Column trait of receiving – sparkles! Its illumination brings personal and global conflict to a peaceful end. Moreover, the seed of all conflict and strife – the brothers Isaac and Ishmael, and Jacob and Esau, combine and blend into one color, just as the colors of the rainbow unite into the color of white. This exquisite unity engenders love between the brothers, and among their

posterity – the Jews, the Moslems, the Christians, and the entire family of man. Intolerance is thereby banished from the hearts of humans. Racial and religious barriers dissolve into nothingness.

The letter *Yud* is inserted into the spelling of our own spiritual name, into our essence, so that we experience an existence of perfection. Metaphysically, we will never again perish from this world.

The true hidden colors of the Three Columns burst forth in this breathtaking moment of meditation, marking the end of our personal and global exile. Our Lower World of *Malchut* joins together with the Upper World of *Zeir Anpin*; and in the process, the garments of black worn by *Malchut* are replaced "with the garments of the shining colors of the secrets of the Torah." Namely, darkness is removed, eternally, from civilization.

34. פִּנְחָס בֶּן אֶלְעָזָר בֶּן אַהֲרֹן הַכֹּהֵן הֵשִׁיב אֶת חֲמָתִי מֵעַל בְּנֵי יִשְׂרָאֵל וְגוֹ'. ר' יְהוּדָה פָּתַח, זְכָר נָא מִי הוּא נָקִי אָבָד וְאֵיפֹה יְשָׁרִים נִכְחָדוּ, תַּמָּן תָּנֵינָן, מַאן דְּחָמֵי קֶשֶׁת בִּגְוָונוֹי, אִצְטְרִיךְ לְבָרְכָא בָּרוּךְ זוֹכֵר הַבְּרִית. בְּגִין דְּדָא אִיהוּ בְּרִית קַיָּימָא קַדִּישָׁא, דְּשַׁוֵּי קוּדְשָׁא בְּרִיךְ הוּא בְּאַרְעָא דְּלָא יֵיתֵי עָלָה מֵי טוֹפָנָא. בְּגִין דְּכַד סַגִּיאוּ חַיָּיבִין בְּעָלְמָא, בָּעֵי קוּדְשָׁא בְּרִיךְ הוּא לְאוֹבָדָא לוֹן, וּכְדֵין דָּכִיר לוֹן הַאי אוֹמָאָה דְּאוֹמֵי לְאַרְעָא, דִּכְתִיב תְּרֵי זִמְנֵי לֹא לֹא. לֹא אוֹסִיף לְקַלֵּל, וְלֹא אוֹסִיף עוֹד לְהַכּוֹת, דָּא אִיהוּ אוֹמָאָה. כְּמָה דִּכְתִיב אֲשֶׁר נִשְׁבַּעְתִּי מֵעֲבוֹר מֵי נֹחַ.

34. "Pinchas, the son of Elazar, the son of Aaron the priest, has turned My wrath away from the children of Yisrael..." (Bemidbar 25:11). Rabbi Yehuda began: "Recall, now, who that was innocent ever perished? or where were the upright cut off?" (Iyov 4:7). We learned there that whoever sees the rainbow in all its colors has to say the blessing: 'Blessed is He who remembers the covenant', since this is the sign of a holy covenant that the Holy One, blessed be He, placed on earth that the waters of the flood will not cover it again. This is because, when the numbers of wicked people increase in the world, the Holy One, blessed be He, wants to destroy them, but then He recalls for them that oath that He swore to the land, as it is twice written 'not': "I will not again curse...neither will I again smite any more..." (Beresheet 8:21). And TWICE 'NOT' constitutes an oath, as it is said: "as I

have sworn that the waters of Noah should no more go over the earth"
(Yeshayah 54:9).

35(1). רִבִּי יוֹסֵי אָמַר, קֶשֶׁת אָתָא לְאַגָּנָא עַל עָלְמָא. לְמַלְכָּא, דְּכָל
זִמְנִין דִּבְרֵיהּ חָב לְקַבְּלֵיהּ, אָתָא מַלְכָּא לְאַלְקָאָה לֵיהּ, אִתְגַּלְיָא עֲלֵיהּ
מַטְרוֹנִיתָא בִּלְבוּשֵׁי יְקָר דְּמַלְכוּ, מַלְכָּא חָמֵי לָהּ סָלִיק רוּגְזָא דִּבְרֵיהּ,
וְחַדֵּי בָּהּ, דִּכְתִּיב, וּרְאִיתִיהָ לִזְכּוֹר בְּרִית עוֹלָם. וע״ד, לָא אִתְחֲזֵי קֶשֶׁת
בְּעָלְמָא, אֶלָּא בִּלְבוּשֵׁי יְקָר דְּמַלְכוּ. וּבְשַׁעֲתָא דְּאִית צַדִּיק בְּעָלְמָא,
אִיהוּ בְּרִית, לְמֵיקָם בְּרִית, וְאַגִּין עַל עָלְמָא. לָא הֲוֵי צַדִּיק, הָא קֶשֶׁת,
לְאִתְחַזָּאָה דְּהָא עָלְמָא אִיהוּ קַיְּימָא לְאוֹבָדָא, אֶלָּא בְּגִין קֶשֶׁת דָּא.

35a. Rabbi Yosi said: A rainbow comes to protect the world. It is like a
queen wearing royal apparel who appears before the king every time he is
about to hit his son because he has sinned against him. The king sees her
and his anger with his son leaves him and he rejoices with her, as it is
written: "and I will look upon it, that I may remember the everlasting
covenant" (Beresheet 9:16). And this is why a rainbow appears in the world,
only in the royal apparel of Malchut. THESE GARMENTS OF MALCHUT
ARE: WHITE, RED AND GREEN, AND THEY SUGGEST THE THREE
COLUMNS AS WILL BE EXPLAINED. When there is a righteous person in the
world, he upholds the covenant and thus protects the world. But if there is
no righteous person, then there is a rainbow to indicate that the world is
about to perish but SURVIVES because of it.

35(2). ר' אֶלְעָזָר אָמַר, לְעוֹלָם לָא אִתְלַבַּשׁ קֶשֶׁת דָּא, אֶלָּא בִּלְבוּשָׁא
דַּאֲבָהָן קַדְמָאֵי. יָרוֹק וְסוּמָק וְחִיוָּור. יְרוֹקָא, דָּא לְבוּשָׁא דְּאַבְרָהָם,
אִצְטַבַּע לְבוּשָׁא דָּא, כַּד נָפַק מִנֵּיהּ יִשְׁמָעֵאל. סוּמָקָא, דָּא גָּוֶון יִצְחָק.
דְּאַתְיָא סוּמָקָא וְאִצְטַבַּע, כַּד נָפִיק מִנֵּיהּ עֵשָׂו. וְאִתְמְשַׁךְ הַהוּא סוּמָקָא
לְתַתָּא, עַד כֹּכְבָא דְּמַאְדִּים, דְּאִתְאַחִיד בֵּיהּ עֵשָׂו. חִוָּורָא, דָּא אִיהוּ
לְבוּשָׁא טָבָא דְּיַעֲקֹב, דְּהָא לָא אִשְׁתַּנּוּ אַנְפּוֹהִי לְעָלְמִין.

35b. Rabbi Elazar said: This rainbow, NAMELY MALCHUT, has never worn
anything except the apparel of the patriarchs, NAMELY, CHESED, GVURAH
AND TIFERET OF ZEIR ANPIN, NAMELY green, red and white. The raiment

of Abraham is green, and it was so colored when Ishmael issued from him. 'Red' is Isaac, who acquired this color when Esau issued from him. This red stretches down to the planet Mars – *Ma'adim* (from red - Heb. *adom*), which Esau is holding onto. White is the fine garment of Jacob, whose good countenance never changed, FOR HIS BED WAS PERFECT AND THERE WAS NO BLEMISH IN HIM.

35(3). ר' אַבָּא אָמַר יָאוּת הוּא, אֲבָל הָכִי אָמַר בּוּצִינָא קַדִּישָׁא, חִוְּור, דָּא אַבְרָהָם. דְּאִתְלַבַּן בְּחִוְּורָא דְּנוּרָא. סוּמָקָא, דָּא יִצְחָק וַדַּאי. יָרוֹק, דָּא הוּא יַעֲקֹב, דְּקַיְּימָא בֵּין תְּרֵין גְּוונִין, וּכְתִיב בֵּיה בְּיַעֲקֹב, לֹא עַתָּה יֵבוֹשׁ יַעֲקֹב וְלֹא עַתָּה פָּנָיו יֶחֱוָרוּ דְּהָא כָּל עַרְסֵיה שְׁלִים הֲוָה. וְהָכִי הוּא לֹא עַתָּה יֵבוֹשׁ יַעֲקֹב, לְאִתְחֲזָאָה בְּגַוֵון סוּמָק, כְּיִצְחָק דְּנָפַק מִנֵּיה עֵשָׂו. וְלֹא עַתָּה פָּנָיו יֶחֱוָרוּ, כְּאַבְרָהָם לְאִתְחֲזָאָה בְּגַוֵון חִוְּור, דְּנָפַק מִנֵּיה יִשְׁמָעֵאל. אֶלָּא נָטַל גְּוונִין, לְאִתְעַטְּרָא בְּהוּ, עַל אֲבָהָן דִּילֵיה, וּבְאִלֵּין לְבוּשִׁין מִתְלַבְּשַׁת קֶשֶׁת, בְּשַׁעֲתָא דְּאִתְחֲזֵי קַמֵּי מַלְכָּא.

35c. Rabbi Aba said: That is good, but the Holy Luminary, NAMELY RABBI SHIMON, said, 'White' is Abraham, who was purified ('whitened') in the white-hot heat of the fire BY NIMROD, WHO CAST HIM INTO *UR* (FIRE) OF THE CHALDEES. 'Red' is obviously Isaac, and 'green' is Jacob, who is between the other two colors, FOR GREEN INCLUDES WHITE AND RED. THIS GREEN STANDS FOR THE GREEN COLOR OF THE SUN. And about Jacob it is written, "Jacob shall not now be ashamed, neither shall his face now wax pale" (Yeshayah 29:22) because his whole bed was perfect. AND THE INTERPRETATION OF this is: "Jacob shall not now be ashamed" because he shall not be seen in red like Isaac, who fathered Esau. "neither shall his face now grow pale." This means that he shall not be seen in white like Abraham, who fathered Ishmael. Instead he took the colors WHITE AND RED and enveloped them to adorn himself in his ancestors. HE INCORPORATED WITHIN HIMSELF THE TWO PATRIARCHS ABRAHAM AND ISAAC, WHO ARE WHITE AND RED, AND THIS IS WHY HIS COLOR IS GREEN, WHICH INCLUDES WHITE AND RED. And the rainbow, NAMELY, MALCHUT, puts on these garments OF WHITE, RED, AND GREEN when it appears before the King, ZEIR ANPIN.

35(4). תָּא חֲזֵי, רָזָא דִּבְרִית קַדִּישָׁא, הִיא אָת יוֹ"ד, דְּמִתְעַטְּרָא

בְּרְשִׁימוּ עִלָּאָה, וְדָא אִיהוּ דְּאִתְרְשִׁים בִּבְרִית תָּדִיר לְעָלְמִין, וּבְגִין דְּקַנֵּי פִּנְחָס עַל בְּרִית, אִתְרְשִׁים בִּשְׁמֵיהּ הָכָא אָת דָּא, פִּנְחָס יו״ד זְעֵירָא, אִיהוּ יו״ד דְּאִיהוּ בְּרִית וַדַּאי, דְּנָפִיק מִגּוֹ יו״ד עִלָּאָה קַדִּישָׁא. וע״ד, אִיהוּ קָאִים בְּקִיּוּמָא שְׁלִים קַמֵּי מַלְכָּא קַדִּישָׁא, דְּלָא אִתְאֲבִיד מִגּוֹ עָלְמָא. וְהָכִי הוּא נָקִי מֵהַהוּא חוֹבָא דִּפְעוֹר, וְלָא אִתְאֲבִיד תָּדִיר מִגּוֹ קַדִּישָׁא דְּעָלְמָא. וְאֵיפֹה יְשָׁרִים נִכְחָדוּ, אִלֵּין נָדָב וַאֲבִיהוּא, דְּלָא אִשְׁתְּצִיאוּ מִן הַהוּא עָלְמָא בְּגִינֵיהּ.

35d. Come and see: The secret of the holy covenant is the letter Yud that adorns itself with a supreme heavenly impression, NAMELY THE CORONA OF YESOD OF ZEIR ANPIN and this is recorded forever in the everlasting covenant. And because Pinchas was zealous for the Covenant, that letter Yud was inserted into the spelling of his name. The Yud in the spelling of 'Pinchas' is a small one, WHICH IS THE SECRET OF MALCHUT, THE SECRET OF THE CORONA OF YESOD, FOR 'PINCHAS' HERE IS SPELLED WITH YUD, which is definitely the Covenant, which emanated from the upper holy Yud BECAUSE MALCHUT EMANATES FROM YUD OF YUD HEI VAV HEI IN THE SECRET OF THE FATHER ESTABLISHING HIS DAUGHTER. And this is why PINCHAS has a perfect existence before the Holy King and shall never perish from the world. And because of this he was without guilt at Peor. For he never lost himself from the world's holiness. "or where were the upright cut off?" this refers to Nadab and Abihu, who did not totally perish from the world BECAUSE THEIR SOULS INCARNATED IN PINCHAS, WHO CORRECTED THEM.

A Synopsis

Moses tells the Rabbis that Elijah is Pinchas so they must come up with some new interpretations. Rabbi Yehuda's opinion is that the rainbow does not shine with its proper colors, but the colors hint at the merits of the priests and Levites and Yisrael in all their beauty. Next we hear that Malchut in exile can only be dressed in black, and that the rainbow is really the angel Metatron, the eldest servant of God. God's promise to look at the rainbow and remember His covenant refers to the shining secrets of the Torah, for light signifies all the mysteries of the Torah. Lastly we hear that every one of the names of God testifies about God who is above everything, and that all of Yisrael, as they are all the sons of Adam, must serve God.

רעיא מהימנא

36. אָמַר לֵיהּ רַעְיָא מְהֵימָנָא, שַׁפִּיר קָאמַרְתְּ, אֲבָל בְּגִין דְּאֵלִיָּהוּ
דְּאִיהוּ פִּנְחָס, קַנִּי עַל בְּרִית, צָרִיךְ לְחַדְתָּא מִלִּין סַגִּיאִין בֵּיהּ, דְּהַאי
פַּרְשְׁתָא כְּתִיבָא בְּאוֹרַיְיתָא עַל שְׁמֵיהּ, דַּעֲלֵיהּ אִתְּמַר קַנֹּא קַנֵּאתִי, תְּרֵי
קִנְאוֹת, חַד בְּשַׁדַּ"י דִּלְעֵילָּא, וְתִנְיָינָא בְּשַׁדַּ"י דִּלְתַתָּא, וּבְגִין דָּא עָבֵיד
תְּרֵין שְׁבוּעוֹת בְּתַרְוַוייהוּ, וּתְרֵין זִמְנִין לֹא לֹא.

Ra'aya Meheimna (the Faithful Shepherd)

36. The Faithful Shepherd said to him: What you said is good, but since Elijah is Pinchas, who was zealous for the Covenant, one must establish new and important interpretations about him. This is because this portion in the Torah is named Pinchas after him, NAMELY ELIJAH, WHO WAS PINCHAS, of whom it is said, "I have been very (lit. 'zealously') zealous" (I Melachim 19:10). This refers to two forms of zealousness, one for the heavenly name of Shadai, YESOD of ZEIR ANPIN, and the other for the lower name of Shadai, METATRON CALLED 'SHADAI'. And this is why he made two oaths for the two of them and it is twice WRITTEN, 'Not, not.'

37. אֲבָל רִבִּי יְהוּדָה אָמַר, מַאן דְּחָמֵי קֶשֶׁת בִּגְוָונוֹי נְהִירִין, צָרִיךְ
לְבָרְכָא בָּרוּךְ זוֹכֵר הַבְּרִית. וּבְגָלוּתָא דְּלָאו אִיהוּ נָהִיר בִּגְוָונוֹי כַּדְקָא
יֵאוֹת, וְלֹא עוֹד אֶלָּא דִּלְזִמְנִין נָהִיר זְעֵיר, וְזִמְנִין לָא נָהִיר כְּלָל, זִמְנִין
אִתְחֲזֵי בִּשְׁלִימוּ, וְזִמְנִין לָאו. דְּקֶשֶׁת קָא רָמִיז גְּוָונוֹי, לְזַכְווָן דְּכֹהֲנִים
לְוִיִם וְיִשְׂרְאֵלִים, כַּד אִינּוּן שַׁפִּירִין, דְּנָהִיר קֶשֶׁת בִּגְוָונוֹי דְּאִינּוּן תְּלַת.

37. But Rabbi Yehuda said: Whoever sees a rainbow in shining colors must recite the blessing, 'Blessed be He who remembers the covenant.' In exile the rainbow does not shine in its colors properly BECAUSE IN EXILE MALCHUT DOES NOT RECEIVE PROPERLY, AS FITTING THE UNIFICATION OF THE THREE COLUMNS, STAND FOR THE RAINBOW'S THREE COLORS. Furthermore, sometimes it hardly shines and at other times it doesn't shine at all. Sometimes it is seen complete, and sometimes not. The rainbow's colors hint at the merits of the priests Levites, and Yisrael when they are in

their beauty, since the rainbow is radiant in its three colors, THE SECRET OF
THE THREE COLUMNS.

38. קוּם אַנְתְּ רִבִּי יוֹסֵי הַגְּלִילִי, וְאֵימָא, דְּהָא מִלִּין שַׁפִּירִין קָאֲמַרַת
בַּחֲבוּרָה קַדְמָאָה, דְּקֶשֶׁת לָא אַתְיָא אֶלָּא לְאַגָּנָא עַל עָלְמָא. לְמַלְכָּא,
דִּבְכָל זִמְנָא דִּבְרֵיהּ חָב, וּמַלְכָּא חֲזֵי לְמַטְרוֹנִיתָא, סָלִיק רוּגְזָא דִּבְרֵיהּ,
דִּכְתִּיב וּרְאִיתִיהָ לִזְכּוֹר בְּרִית עוֹלָם. וְעַ"ד לָא אִתְחֲזֵי קֶשֶׁת, אֶלָּא
לְאַגָּנָא עַל עָלְמָא. וְלָא אִתְגַּלְיָא, אֶלָּא בִּלְבוּשׁ יְקָר דְּמַלְכוּ, וּבְשַׁעֲתָא
דְּאִית צַדִּיק בְּאַרְעָא, אִיהוּ בְּרִית. לְמֵיקַם בְּרִית.

38. Rise up now, Rabbi Yosi of Galilee, and speak, for you said beautiful
things in the previous discussion, that the rainbow only comes to protect the
world. IT IS LIKE the king who, whenever his son sins, and he sees the
queen, it takes away his anger with his son, as it is written: "and I will look
upon it, that I may remember the everlasting covenant" (Beresheet 9:16).
Therefore the rainbow only appears in order to protect the world FOR IT IS
THE SECRET OF MALCHUT, AS EXPLAINED ABOVE. It appears only in
precious royal apparel, THE SECRET OF THE THREE COLORS. But when
there is a righteous person in the world, he is the covenant, upholding of the
covenant. THIS MEANS HE ESTABLISHES THE UNION BETWEEN ZEIR
ANPIN AND MALCHUT, THEREFORE THERE IS NO NEED TO AROUSE
MALCHUT BY MEANS OF THE RAINBOW.

39. וְכִי בְּגָלוּתָא, קוּדְשָׁא בְּרִיךְ הוּא אִתְרְחַק מִמַּטְרוֹנִיתָא, וְאֵיךְ
מַטְרוֹנִיתָא אִתְלַבְּשַׁת לְבוּשֵׁי מַלְכוּתָא בְּגָלוּתָא לָא. אֲבָל בְּגָלוּתָא,
לְבוּשָׁה דְּקַדְרוּת, וְאִיהוּ אַמְרַת אַל תִּרְאוּנִי שֶׁאֲנִי שְׁחַרְחֹרֶת. אֶלָּא וַדַּאי
הַהוּא קֶשֶׁת דְּאִתְגַּלְיָיא בְּגָלוּתָא, לָאו אִיהוּ אֶלָּא מְטַטְרוֹ"ן, דְּאִתְקְרֵי
שַׁדַּ"י וְאִיהוּ עַבְדוֹ זָקֵן בֵּיתוֹ, דְּשַׁלִּיט בְּכָל דִּילֵיהּ, וּבְנוֹי, אִתְקְרִיאוּ
עֲבָדִים דְּקוּדְשָׁא בְּרִיךְ הוּא. וּבְנֵי מַטְרוֹנִיתָא בָּנִים, וּבְגִין דָּא, אִם
כְּבָנִים אִם כַּעֲבָדִים.

39. HE ASKS, but how can the Queen put on royal apparel, THE SECRET OF
THE THREE COLUMNS, in exile? For in exile the Holy One, blessed be He,

draws away from the Queen. AND HE ANSWERS, No, IN EXILE SHE DOES
NOT WEAR ROYAL APPAREL, but is dressed in gloomy darkness, NAMELY IN
BLACKNESS, and says: "Do not gaze upon me, because I am black" (Shir
Hashirim 1:6). On the contrary, the rainbow that is viewed as appearing in
exile is none other than THE ANGEL Metatron, who is called 'Shadai', and
he is "the eldest servant" OF ZEIR ANPIN "of his house, that ruled over all
that he had" (Beresheet 24:2), while his sons, NAMELY THOSE WHO
ATTAINED RUACH FROM THE ASPECT OF METATRON are called 'the
servants of the Holy One, blessed be He'. The queen's sons, NAMELY
THOSE WHO ATTAINED NEFESH FROM MALCHUT OF ATZILUT, ARE
CALLED 'sons'. This is the reason WHY WE PRAY 'whether as sons or as
servants'.

40. וּבְזִמְנָא דְּאִתְחָרַב בֵּי מַקְדְּשָׁא, אוּקְמוּהָ דַּעֲבָדִים חָפוּ רֹאשָׁם,
וְנִתְדַּלְדְּלוּ אַנְשֵׁי מַעֲשֶׂה. וַדַּאי אַנְשֵׁי מַעֲשֶׂה אִתְקְרִיאוּ, עַל שֵׁם
מַטְרוֹנִיתָא, דְּאִתְּמַר עָלָהּ רַבּוֹת בָּנוֹת עָשׂוּ חָיִל וְאַתְּ עָלִית עַל כֻּלָּנָה.
אֲבָל אִי אִית לֵיהּ צַדִּיק, דְּזַכְווֹי וְעוֹבָדוֹי לְאַנְהָרָא, בְּהוֹן מַטְרוֹנִיתָא,
וּלְמִפְשַׁט מִנָּהּ לְבוּשֵׁי קַדְרוּתָא דִּפְשָׁטִין וּלְקַשְּׁטָא לָהּ בִּלְבוּשִׁין דִּגְוָונִין
נְהִירִין דְּרָזִין דְּאוֹרַיְיתָא, מַה כְּתִיב בֵּיהּ, וּרְאִיתִיהָ לִזְכּוֹר בְּרִית עוֹלָם.
וּרְאִיתִיהָ, בְּרָזִין נְהִירִין דְּאוֹרַיְיתָא, דְּאוֹר רָ"ז אִתְקְרֵי, הַה"ד, כִּי נֵר
מִצְוָה תּוֹרָה אוֹר. וּבְאִלֵּין רָזִין אִתְּמַר וּרְאִיתִיהָ.

40. When the Temple was destroyed, so we are told, servants covered their
heads in shame and men of action were weakened. This term 'men of
action' is definitely derived from the name of 'Malchut,' about whom it is
said: "Many daughters have done valiantly, but you have excelled them all"
(Mishlei 31:29). THAT IS, EXCELLED REGARDING ACTION, FOR MALCHUT
IS CALLED "ACTION." However, if there is a righteous person whose merits
and actions are such as to enlighten Malchut and to strip her of the black of
literal MEANING WITHOUT THE ESOTERIC MEANING, and adorn her with
the garments of the shining colors of secrets of the Torah, what is written
about him? "and I will look upon it, that I may remember the everlasting
covenant." "and I will look upon it" – this refers to the shining secrets of the
Torah, for light is called 'a secret', NAMELY THE NUMERICAL VALUE OF OR
(ENG. 'LIGHT') IS THE SAME AS THAT OF RAZ (ENG. 'SECRET'). THUS,
LIGHT SIGNIFIES ALL THE MYSTERIES OF THE TORAH, as it is said: "For

the commandment is a lamp; and the Torah is light" (Mishlei 6:23). And about these secrets it was said: "and I will look upon it."

41. וּבְהַהוּא זִמְנָא סָלִיק מִנֵּיהּ רוּגְזָא דִּבְרֵיהּ, וַחֲמַת הַמֶּלֶךְ שָׁכָכָה, וְיֵימָא לָהּ מַלְכָּא בִּצְלוֹתָא דַעֲמִידָה קַמֵּיהּ, מַה שְׁאֵלָתֵךְ וְיִנָּתֵן לָךְ וּמַה בַּקָּשָׁתֵךְ. בְּהַהוּא זִמְנָא, שְׁאֵלָתָא עַל פּוּרְקָנָא דִּילָהּ, וּבְנָהָא עִמֵּיהּ, הה"ד תִּנָּתֶן לִי נַפְשִׁי בִּשְׁאֵלָתִי וְעַמִּי בְּבַקָּשָׁתִי. אֲבָל קֶשֶׁת דְּאִתְחֲזְיָא בְּעָלְמָא בְּגָלוּתָא, דְּעַבְדָּא אִיהוּ, זִמְנִין דְּנָפִיק בִּשְׁלִימוּ, כַּד בְּנוֹי מַכְשִׁירִין עוֹבָדוֹי, וּלְזִמְנִין לָא אִשְׁתְּכַח בִּשְׁלִימוּ, כַּד בְּנוֹי לָא מַכְשִׁירִין עוֹבָדוֹי.

41. When HE LOOKS AT THE RAINBOW, NAMELY MALCHUT, his anger at his son leaves him, "Then the king's wrath was pacified" (Ester 7:10). And the King says to her, when she is in the Amidah prayer before Him, "What is your petition? and it shall be granted you: and what is your request..." (Ester 5:6). Then she asks for her redemption and that of her children, as it is said: "let my life be given me at my petition, and my people at my request" (Ester 7:3). But a rainbow that appears in the world at a time of exile is of the servant, NAMELY METATRON. THAT IS TO SAY, THE LIGHT OF THE HEAVENLY UNION IS CLOTHED IN METATRON, AND HE IS BEARER OF THE THREE COLORS OF THE RAINBOW, WHICH ARE THE THREE COLUMNS. And sometimes it appears complete, when His children act correctly, while at other times it is incomplete, when His children do not act correctly.

42. אִלֵּין דִּמְכַשְׁרִין עוֹבָדֵיהוֹן קַמֵּי מַלְכָּא, וּמְקַנִּין עַל שְׁמֵיהּ, וּמְקַדְּשִׁין לֵיהּ בָּרַבִּים. הָכִי מְקַדְּשִׁין לֵיהּ לְעֵילָּא, בֵּין מְמָנָן דִּשְׁאַר עַמִּין, וְאִשְׁתְּמוֹדְעִין לֵיהּ כָּל מְמָנָא בִּכְנוּיֵּיהּ. אֲבָל יִשְׂרָאֵל אִשְׁתְּמוֹדְעִין לְעֵילָּא כֹּלָּא בְּשֵׁם יְדֹוָ"ד, דְּאִיהוּ חַיֵּי כָל כִּנּוּיִין.

42. (THE BEGINNING IS MISSING) and those who make their acts worthy before the King and are zealous for His name, sanctifying it in public, as they sanctify it in heaven amongst the angels who are appointed over the other nations — each chieftain being known by the name of the nation.

Yisrael, however, are known above by the name Yud Hei Vav Hei, which is the life to all titles.

43. וְכָל שֵׁם וְכִנּוּי סָהִיד עֲלֵיהּ, אַ״ל סָהִיד עֲלֵיהּ, דְּאִית לֵיהּ יְכוֹלֶת עַל כָּל אֵל, הַה״ד אֲנִי אֶדְרוֹשׁ אֶל אֵל. אֵל, מָארֵי דְּאֵל. אֱלֹהִים סָהִיד עֲלֵיהּ, דְּאִיהוּ אֱלֹהֵי הָאֱלֹהִים. אֲדֹנָ״י סָהִיד עֲלֵיהּ, דְּאִיהוּ אֲדוֹנֵי הָאֲדוֹנִים. אוֹף הָכִי כָּל שֵׁם. דְּכָל מַלְאָךְ אִית לְכָל חַד שֵׁם יְדִיעַ, לְאִשְׁתְּמוֹדְעָא לְכָל כַּת בְּהַהוּא שֵׁם דְּמַלְכָּא דִּילֵיהּ. אֲבָל יִשְׂרָאֵל, אִשְׁתְּמוֹדְעָן לֵיהּ בִּיהוּ״ה.

43. And every name and appellation testifies about Him, ABOUT THE HOLY ONE, BLESSED BE HE. The name El testifies that He can overcome every other El, as it is said: "But as for me, I would seek to El" (Iyov 5:8). El is the master of every El. Elohim testifies that He is the Elohim of the Elohim. Adonai testifies that He is the Master (Heb. *adon*) over masters. And so it is with each name. And each angel has a proper name so each group OF ANGELS is known by the name of its king. Yisrael, however, is known to Him by the Yud Hei Vav Hei.

44. וְרָזָא דְּמִלָּה, ב״נ חַד יָכִיל לְמֶהֱוֵי לֵיהּ כַּמָּה סוּסְוָון, אוֹף הָכִי כָּל יִשְׂרָאֵל אִינּוּן בְּנוֹי דְּאָדָם, וְכָל בְּרָא צָרִיךְ לְמֶהֱוֵי לֵיהּ לַאֲבוּי כַּסּוּס וְכַחֲמוֹר לְמַשּׂוּי, וּלְמֶהֱוֵי כָּפִיף תְּחוֹתוֹי, וְהַאי אִיהוּ רָזָא אָדָם וּבְהֵמָה תּוֹשִׁיעַ יְיָ׳. דְּאִיהוּ בָּרָא דְּאָדָם, וְעָבֵיד גַּרְמֵיהּ כִּבְהֵמָה תְּחוֹתוֹי.

44. And the secret of the matter is that just as one man (Heb. *adam*) can have a number of horses, so it is that all of Yisrael are the sons of Adam; THE SECRET OF THE NUMERICAL VALUE OF YUD HEI VAV HEI, FULLY SPELLED WITH ALEPHS, WHICH AMOUNTS TO THE NUMERICAL VALUE OF 'ADAM'. FOR THE SOULS OF YISRAEL ARE THE PROGENY OF ZEIR ANPIN AND MALCHUT. And every son must be like a horse and beast of burden for his father, and be subject to him. This secret is expressed thus: "Hashem, You preserve man and beast" (Tehilim 36:7). FOR YISRAEL are the children of Adam, WHICH IS YUD HEI VAV HEI OF THE NUMERICAL VALUE OF 45. And they make themselves as a beast under him.

10. Levirate marriage and reincarnation

A Synopsis

We learn why levirate marriage is permitted even though it is normally forbidden for a man to marry his brother's wife. We are told that the flow of the letter Vav causes the letter Yud to turn, and from here the explanation uses the concept of flow to show how the soul of man returns to God. If it returns in perfection it runs back into the great sea, but if not, it reincarnates. And if a man has no children his soul is not perfect. When a man has committed evil during three incarnations he will not be given a fourth chance, but is sent to Gehenom for judgment. A parallel is drawn between the three colors of the rainbow, the three incarnations, and the three Sfirot associated with them. Someone who becomes righteous through the experience of many incarnations will not then come back to this world again. For the soul of the man who died childless, his widow becomes a home and his brother who fathers children by her becomes a redeemer. We learn that Moses has reincarnated in a number of generations to save the souls of Yisrael, and that God ascribed the merit of all these people to Moses. Moses had been destined to receive the Torah in the generation of the Flood, but this did not happen due to the sins of the people. Rabbi Shimon stands up and concludes this section by giving an example of a poor rabbi who is being punished now for his sins in an earlier incarnation.

The Relevance of this Passage

The Zohar converses upon the Sfirot of *Binah* and *Zeir Anpin* and the letters *Yud, Hei* and *Vav* along with their respective numerical values. The significance of this is positive on many fronts: Sexual iniquities, associated with incest, are purified by the Zohar's sacred verses. Our own souls are rectified, freeing us from another incarnation and from the decrees of judgments which are executed in Hell. Those who have left this world childless are redeemed by our heartfelt reading of this passage. Repentance is stirred in our hearts so that our souls merge with the Creator, as a river merges with the sea, in the *World to Come.*

Our visual embrace of these verses sets the supernal sun into motion as it rises majestically on the horizon. Its Light moves upon the face of the Earth. For us, the rays are warming and blissful; but for the wicked, these flames are the fires of Hell itself. The wicked are the genuinely evil who walk among us, lifetime upon lifetime, soulless beings who seek, not repentance or spiritual change, but

only the propagation of greater evil. As the Light scintillates everywhere, its rays catch the wicked, blotting them out of existence in one fell swoop.

45. וּבְגִין דָּא אִיהוּ פְּקוּדָא דְקוּדְשָׁא בְּרִיךְ הוּא בְּאוֹרַיְתָא, לְמֶהֱוֵי אָח מִיַּבֵּם לְאִתְּתֵיהּ דְּאָח, לְמֶעְבַּד בְּרָא לַאֲחוּי, בְּגִין דְּלָא יִתְאֲבִיד מֵהַהוּא עָלְמָא. וְהַאי אִיהוּ כְּגוֹן רָזָא דְּכִלְאַיִם בְּצִיצִית. דְּאָמְרוּ, מַה שֶּׁאָסַרְתִּי לָךְ כָּאן, הִתַּרְתִּי לָךְ כָּאן. אָסַרְתִּי לָךְ כִּלְאַיִם דְּעָלְמָא, הִתַּרְתִּי לָךְ כִּלְאַיִם דְּצִיצִית. אָסַרְתִּי לָךְ אֵשֶׁת אָח, הִתַּרְתִּי לָךְ יְבָמָה. כְּגוֹן מַרְכִּיבִים תַּפּוּחִים אוֹ דְּקָלִים מִן בְּמִינוֹ. וְאָסוּר לְאַרְכָּבָא מִין בְּשֶׁאֵינוֹ מִינוֹ. וְאִתְּמַר בֵּיהּ כִּי הָאָדָם עֵץ הַשָּׂדֶה. וּבְיַבָּמָה מַרְכִּיבִין מִין בְּשֶׁאֵינוֹ מִינוֹ, בְּגִין דְּלָא לְתַאֲבִיד נֶפֶשׁ הַמֵּת. וְלֹא יִמָּחֶה שְׁמוֹ מִיִּשְׂרָאֵל.

45. And for this reason it is a commandment of the Holy One, blessed be He, that a man should marry his deceased brother's widow, to have a son for his brother that he be not lost to that world. And this is like the secret of the mixed kinds in the fringes (Heb. *Tzitzit*). For it has been said: What I have forbidden to you in one place, I have permitted in another. I have forbidden mixed kinds in general, but permitted mixed kinds in the fringes. I have forbidden you to marry your brother's wife, but have permitted his widow marriage. Similarly, one may graft apples or dates, each on its own species, but it is forbidden to graft one species onto another. And on this it is said: "For man is a tree of the field" (Devarim 20:19), FOR MAN IS ALSO FORBIDDEN TO MATE WITH ONE WHO IS NOT OF HIS SPECIES, WHICH IS INCEST, but, for levirate marriage, one may graft two different species so that the soul of the deceased shall not be lost, "that his name be not wiped out in Yisrael" (Devarim 25:6).

46. וְהַאי אִיהוּ רָזָא דְּגִלְגּוּל. גִּלְגּוּל לֵית לֵיהּ תְּנוּעָה בְּלָא אֲמַת הַמַּיִם, אוֹף הָכִי, אֲמַת הַמַּיִם רָזָא דְּאָת ו', בֵּיהּ אִתְעֲבֵיד גַּלְגַּל גִּלְגּוּל. וְרָזָא דְּמִלָּה, מַה גַּלְגַּל אֵין לוֹ תְּנוּעָה בְּלָא אֲמַת הַמַּיִם, אוֹף הָכִי, גַּלְגַּל אִיהוּ י', וְלֵית לֵיהּ תְּנוּעָה בְּלָא אֲמַת הַמַּיִם דְּאִיהוּ ו'. יְבָמָה ה'. לְהַאי אִיהוּ בִּינָ"ה בֵּ"ן יָ"ה. בְּאוֹת י' בָּרָא עָלְמָא דְּאָתֵי, עוֹלָם אָרוֹךְ, דְּאִיהוּ ו'.

46. And this is the secret of reincarnation (lit. 'rolling'). The wheel does not move without the flow of water through the conduit TO TURN IT. So also, the conduit is the secret of the letter Vav, by which the wheel is turned. And the secret of the matter is that just as the wheel will have no motion without the aqueduct, so also the wheel which is the letter Yud will have no motion without the aqueduct which is the letter Vav. A deceased brother's widow is Hei, and we thus have THE LETTERS OF Binah, *Ben* (lit. 'the son of') Yah. FOR THE SON, WHO IS ZEIR ANPIN, ISSUES FROM THE UNION OF YUD HEI, THAT ARE CHOCHMAH AND BINAH, AND HENCE HE IS IMPLIED IN HIS MOTHER'S NAME, BEN YAH, NAMELY THE LETTERS OF BINAH. With the letter Yud, THAT IS CHOCHMAH, He created the World to Come, which is an extended world, namely the letter Vav, WHICH IS ZEIR ANPIN.

47. בְּגִין דָּא, מַאן דְּלֵית לֵיהּ בֵּן, לָאו אִיהוּ מִבְּנֵי עָלְמָא דְּאָתֵי, דְּיַמָּא לְקָבְלֵיהּ, וּמְנֵיהּ נָפִיק, מִבֵּינַיְיהוּ וי', וּמְנֵיהּ מִתְפַּלְּגִין כַּמָּה נַחֲלֵי, דְּאִינּוּן מְסַבְּבִין עָלְמָא, עַד דְּהַחְזְרוּ לְיַמָּא דְּנַפְקוּ מִתַּמָּן, וּבְגִין דָּא אָמַר קְרָא, כָּל הַנְּחָלִים הוֹלְכִים אֶל הַיָּם וְהַיָּם אֵינֶנּוּ מָלֵא אֶל מְקוֹם שֶׁהַנְּחָלִים וְגוֹ'. עַד דְּאָהַדְרוּ כְּגַוְונָא דְּנַפְקוּ.

47. For this reason, anyone who has no son, WHO CORRESPONDS TO ZEIR ANPIN, WHICH IS THE SECRET OF VAV, WHICH IS THE WORLD TO COME, will not be among the inhebitants of the World to Come. For the sea, WHICH is BINAH, THE SECRET OF THE WORLD TO COME, corresponds to it, TO THE VAV, for the Vav emerges from between THE YUD-HEI, WHERE THE YUD IS THE SECRET OF CHOCHMAH AND THE HEI OF BINAH, WHICH IS CALLED 'SEA'. THEREFORE THE VAV IS LIKEWISE CALLED 'THE WORLD TO COME' LIKE IT. And from the sea, WHICH IS BINAH, a number of rivers separate, THESE BEING THE SFIROT OF THE VAV, WHICH IS ZEIR ANPIN, and they circumscribe the world, WHICH IS MALCHUT, until they return to the sea, WHICH IS BINAH, from which THE RIVERS, WHICH ARE ZEIR ANPIN, issued. This is why scripture said: "All the rivers run into the sea; yet the sea is not full; to the place where the rivers flow, thither they return" (Kohelet 1:7). That is to say, until they return to it as they came out; NAMELY IN THE SAME CONDITION AS THE RIVERS FLOW OUT OF BINAH, SO DO THEY RETURN TO BINAH.

48. אוֹף הָכִי, וְהָרוּחַ תָּשׁוּב אֶל הָאֱלֹהִים אֲשֶׁר נְתָנָהּ. כְּגַוְונָא דְּיָהִיב

לָהּ שְׁלֵימָתָא. אִם תָּשׁוּב בְּתִיוּבְתָּא, דְּאִיהוּ בִּינָ"ה בֶּ"ן יָ"ה, עִלָּאָה. אָת ה' סְלִיקַת בְּאָת י' לְחַמְשִׁין, עֶשֶׂר זִמְנִין חָמֵשׁ. הָא אִיהוּ יָ"ם, יָ"ה. בֶּ"ן, נַחַל דְּנָפַק מִן יַמָּא, וְאִתְפְּלִיג לְכַמָּה נַחֲלִין, כְּגַוְונָא דְּאִילָנָא דְּאִתְפְּשַׁט לְכַמָּה עַנְפִּין.

48. So also, REGARDING THE SOUL OF MAN, IT IS WRITTEN, "and the spirit returns to the Elohim who gave it" (Kohelet 12:7), NAMELY IT RETURNS TO HIM IN PERFECTION, as He gave it in perfect condition. If it returns in repentance, which is the supernal Binah, THAT IS CALLED 'REPENTANCE', WHICH IS THE LETTERS OF Ben-Yah, the letter Hei IN THIS WORD is multiplied by the letter Yud IN IT, which means ten (= Yud) times five (= Hei) equals fifty. This, ACCORDING TO THE NUMERICAL VALUE, is the sea (Heb. *Yam* = 50). THIS IS THE SECRET OF THE LETTERS Yud-Hei IN BINAH, HEI TIMES YUD. THE LETTERS OF 'BEN' OF BINAH ARE the river flowing from it, ZEIR ANPIN, and it divides into several rivers, NAMELY SIX ENDS, like a tree spreading into a number of branches. AND WHEN A MAN REPENTS, HE CLINGS TO THE RIVER, WHICH IS ZEIR ANPIN AND RETURNS WITH ITS RIVERS TO BINAH, WHICH IS CALLED 'REPENTANCE', AND IS ALSO CALLED 'SEA'. AND THIS IS THE SECRET OF THE VERSE, "ALL THE RIVERS RUN INTO THE SEA," AS MENTIONED ABOVE.

49. וְאִי לָא חָזַר נִשְׁמָתָא שְׁלֵימָתָא, כְּגַוְונָא דְּאִשְׁתְּלָמַת. אִתְּמַר בָּהּ, שָׁם הֵם שָׁבִים לָלָכֶת, אִיהִי וְכָל נִשְׁמָתִין אַחֲרָנִין. אוֹף הָכִי לָאו אִיהוּ שְׁלִים בְּבֵן, אִי לֵית לֵיהּ בַּת, דְּאִיהוּ עָלְמָא דֵּין, לְמֶהֱוֵי שְׁלִים בְּהַאי עָלְמָא דְּאִתְבְּרֵי בְּה', הה"ד אֵלֶּה תוֹלְדוֹת הַשָּׁמַיִם וְהָאָרֶץ בְּהִבָּרְאָם.

49. And if the soul does not return perfect as it was WHEN IT WAS GIVEN, the verse says about it, "thither they return" (Kohelet 1:7), it and all the other souls WHICH ARE LIKE IT, NAMELY IMPERFECT. IN OTHER WORDS, THEY RETURN TO THIS WORLD IN AN INCARNATION. And so also if he is incomplete, in not having a son, or if he has no daughter, who is ALLUDED TO in this world, BEING MALCHUT, so that he can be perfected by her in this world, MALCHUT, which was created with Hei, as it is written: "These are the generations of the heaven and the earth when they were created (Heb. *behibaram*)" (Beresheet 2:4), MEANING *BEHEI BERA'AM* (HE

CREATED THEM WITH HEI). SO A MAN HAS TO INCARNATE A SECOND
TIME BECAUSE HIS SOUL IS NOT PERFECT, AND TO HIM IS THE VERSE
APPLIED "THITHER THEY RETURN."

50. יְהֹ"ו, הֵן כָּל אֵלֶה יִפְעַל אֵל פַּעֲמַיִם שָׁלֹשׁ עִם גָּבֶר. וְרַשִׁיעַיָּיא
דְּאִתְּמַר בְּהוֹן, וּבְכֵן רָאִיתִי רְשָׁעִים קְבוּרִים וָבָאוּ, גַּרְמוּ אֵלֶּה אֱלֹהֶיךָ
יִשְׂרָאֵל, דְּאִתְּמַר עֲלַיְיהוּ, עַל שְׁלֹשָׁה פִּשְׁעֵי יִשְׂרָאֵל. בָּתַר דְּקִלְקְלוּ
גַּרְמַיְיהוּ תְּלַת זִמְנִין, וְלָא זָכֵי בֵּיה"ו, דְּאִתְּמַר בֵּיהּ מְקוֹם שֶׁיִּפּוֹל הָעֵץ
שָׁם יְהוּ. עַל אַרְבָּעָה לֹא אֲשִׁיבֶנּוּ, דְּהַיְינוּ ה'. וְאִתְדָנוּ בַּגֵּיהִנָּם,
בְּמַשְׁחִית אַף וְחֵימָה.

50. Yud-Hei-Vav OF YUD HEI VAV HEI FORM THE SECRET OF CHESED,
GVURAH AND TIFERET. THIS IS THE SECRET OF THE VERSE: "Lo, El does
all these things twice or three times with a man" (Iyov 33:29). THAT IS TO
SAY THAT THE SOULS INCARNATE ACCORDING TO THE PRINCIPLE OF THE
LETTERS YUD-HEI-VAV, ABOUT WHICH SCRIPTURE SAYS: "LO, EL DOES
ALL THESE THINGS..." Regarding the wicked, it is said: "And so I saw the
wicked buried, and come" (Kohelet 8:10). THAT IS, DESPITE BEING
INCARNATED THEY REMAINED WICKED, causing "These (Heb. *eleh*) are
your Elohim, O Yisrael" (Shemot 32:4). THEY DO HARM TO "*ELEH*,"
NAMELY THE SECRET OF THE YUD-HEI-VAV, and about them it is said:
"For three transgressions of Yisrael, I will turn away his punishment, but for
the fourth I will not turn away his punishment" (Amos 2:6). THIS MEANS
THAT, after they have corrupted themselves three times IN THEIR
INCARNATIONS, and they have not merited TO BE CORRECTED by Yud-Hei-
Vav, about which it is said: "in the place where the tree falls, there (Heb.
yehu, *Yud Hei Vav*) shall it lie" (Kohelet 11:3). THAT IS TO SAY, THE
REPAIR OF THE TREE, WHICH IS MAN, IS AFFECTED BY YUD-HEI-VAV.
THEN "but for the fourth I will not turn away his punishment." THIS
REFERS TO THE LAST HEI, THE FOURTH LETTER OF THE YUD HEI VAV
HEI, AND MEANS, HE WILL NOT SEND THE SOUL BACK FOR A FOURTH
REINCARNATION, CORRESPONDING TO IT, BUT it will be judged in
Gehenom by destruction, anger, and wrath.

51. וּלְבוּשִׁין דִּתְלַת אַתְוָון אִלֵּין, אִשְׁתְּמוֹדְעִין בַּקֶּשֶׁת, דְּאִינּוּן חִיוָּור
סוּמָק וְיָרוֹק. מַאן דְּיֵיתֵי בְּזִמְנָא חֲדָא, אִיהוּ חִיוָּור. בְּתִנְיָינָא, סוּמָק.

בִּתְלִיתָאָה, יָרוֹק. וּבְגִין דְּבַיַעֲקֹב אִתְכְּלִילוּ אַתְוָון, וְאִשְׁתְּרָשׁ אִילָנָא
וְאִתְנְטַע וְאִתְרַבָּא, וְאִתְעֲבֵיד אִיבָּא טָבָא, לֹא עַתָּה יֵבוֹשׁ יַעֲקֹב וְלֹא
עַתָּה פָּנָיו יֶחֱוָרוּ, לְמֶהֱוֵי מֶרְכַּבְתֵּיה בְּיֵצֶר הָרָע, דְּאִיהוּ נָחָשׁ, וְכָל מִינֵי
חֵיוָה בִּישָׁא. ובג"ד, וַיָּשַׂר אֶל מַלְאָךְ וַיּוּכָל. וּבְגִין דְּאִתְקְרֵי אָדָם אִילָנָא,
אִיהוּ רָזָא דָּא, לְאִילָנָא דְּאִתְנְטַע בַּאֲתַר דְּלָא עָבֵיד אִיבָּא. מֶה עֲבַד.
עָקַר לֵיה וּנְטָעֵיה בַּאֲתַר אַחֲרָא. וּבְגִין דָּא אוּקְמוּהָ מ"מ דְּלָא הֲוֵי
מוּחְזָק לְמֶהֱוֵי עָקַר, עַד דְּאָזִיל לְאֶרֶץ יִשְׂרָאֵל, וְאִתְנְטַע תַּמָּן בְּאִתְּתָא.

51. And the garments of these three letters, YUD-HEI-VAV, are recognizable in the rainbow, namely white, red, and green. A person in his first time OF REINCARNATION is white, CORRESPONDING TO THE LETTER YUD OF THE YUD HEI VAV HEI, WHICH IS CHESED; in the second he is red, CORRESPONDING TO THE HEI OF THE YUD HEI VAV HEI, WHICH IS GVURAH; and in the third he is green, CORRESPONDING TO THE VAV OF THE YUD HEI VAV HEI, WHICH IS TIFERET, CALLED 'JACOB', THE CENTRAL COLUMN INCORPORATING THE OTHER TWO, CHESED AND GVURAH. And since the letters YUD AND HEI, WHICH ARE CHESED AND GVURAH, are included in Jacob, and the tree takes root, grows, and gives good fruits, THEREFORE IT IS SAID: "Jacob shall not now be ashamed, neither shall his face now wax pale" (Yeshayah 29:22), so that his Chariot should not journey with the Evil Inclination, which is the serpent, nor with any other type of evil beasts. And for this reason, IT IS WRITTEN ABOUT HIM: "and he strove with an angel, and prevailed" (Hoshea 12:5). And because man is called 'a tree', he is, in this secret, SIMILAR TO a tree planted in a place where it does not bear fruit. What can one do about it? One removes it and replants it elsewhere. This is why the scholars of the Mishnah taught that A MAN is not considered barren until he be replanted in the land of Yisrael and tries to make a woman conceive there.

52. אוֹף הָכִי צַדִּיק, דְּאִיהוּ מְטַלְטֵל מֵאֲתַר לַאֲתַר, מִבַּיִת לְבַיִת, כְּאִילּוּ
יֵיתֵי בְּגִלְגּוּלָא זִמְנִין סַגִּיאִין. וְהַיְינוּ וְעוֹשֶׂה חֶסֶד לַאֲלָפִים לְאוֹהֲבָיו, עַד
דְּיִזְכֶּה לְעָלְמָא. דְּאָתֵי שְׁלִים. אֲבָל לְחַיָּיבַיָא, לָא אַיְיתֵי לֵיה יַתִּיר
מִתְּלַת זִמְנִין. וְאִי חָזַר בְּתִיוּבְתָּא, אִתְּמַר בֵּיה גָּלוּת מְכַפֶּרֶת עָוֹן. וּבְגִין
דָּא אוּקְמוּהָ מ"מ, צַדִּיקִים שׁוּב אֵינָן חוֹזְרִים לַעֲפָרָם.

52. So also, a righteous man who wanders from place to place, from house to house, is like a person who goes through many incarnations. That is what is meant by "but showing mercy to thousands of generations of those that love Me" (Shemot 20:6), until he achieves perfection in the World to Come. But, a wicked person is not allowed more than three INCARNATIONS. If he repents, however, HIS WANDERING IS CONSIDERED A REINCARNATION AND HE ACHIEVES THE PERFECTION OF A RIGHTEOUS MAN. For we have learned that 'Exile atones for transgression'. This is why the sages of the Mishnah taught: 'The righteous do not return to their dust' again, NAMELY DO NOT INCARNATE.

53. אֶלָּא קָא רָמִיז, וְעָפָר אַחֵר יִקַּח וְטָח אֶת הַבָּיִת. וְאָדָם עַל עָפָר יָשׁוּב. וְיָשׁוֹב הֶעָפָר עַל הָאָרֶץ כְּשֶׁהָיָה. בְּגִין דְּהוּא מְנוּגַע, וְלֵית בֵּיהּ אֶלָּא אִשָּׁה רָעָה, יֵצֶר הָרָע, דְּאִתְּמַר בָּהּ אִשָּׁה רָעָה צָרַעַת לְבַעְלָהּ. מַאי תַּקְנְתֵיהּ. יְגָרְשֶׁנָּה וְיִתְרַפֵּא. דְּאִיהִי גַרְמַת וַיְגָרֶשׁ אֶת הָאָדָם הָאָדָם, דָּא נִשְׁמָתָא. אֶ"ת, בַּת זוּגוֹ דְּאָדָם. כְּצִפּוֹר נוֹדֶדֶת מִן קִנָּהּ כֵּן אִישׁ נוֹדֵד מִמְּקוֹמוֹ.

53. But CONCERNING THE WICKED, scripture says: "and he shall take other mortar, and shall plaster the house" (Vayikra 14:42), NAMELY THAT HE SHALL TAKE ANOTHER BODY COMING FROM THE DUST, IN A REINCARNATION, AND AMEND HIS SOUL. "and man shall return to dust" (Iyov 34:15) MEANS THAT HE WILL RETURN IN REINCARNATION. AND ALSO, "the dust returns to the earth as it was" (Kohelet 12:7) INTIMATES THAT HE WILL RETURN IN A REINCARNATION. This is because the wicked person is afflicted and has but a bad woman – that is, the Evil Inclination, about which we have learned that 'a bad woman is like leprosy to her husband' FOR SHE IS THE BODY OF THE WICKED. What remedy does the wicked person have? Let him divorce her and be healed. THAT IS, HE SHOULD GET RID OF HIS PRESENT BODY, TAKE ANOTHER BODY, AND SO BE HEALED. For she, THE WICKED WOMAN, THAT IS, THE BODY, was the cause of: "So He drove out the man" (Beresheet 3:24). "the man" refers to the soul; the particle "et (Eng. 'the')" REFERS TO THE BODY, which is the spouse of man, WHO IS THE SOUL, AS IT SAYS: "As a bird who wanders from her nest, so is man who wanders from his place" (Mishlei 27:8). IN OTHER WORDS, BECAUSE THE MAN CAUSED THE BIRD, WHICH IS THE SOUL, TO WANDER FROM ITS NEST, FOR IT WAS DRIVEN OUT FROM ITS

HEAVENLY PLACE BECAUSE OF HIS SINS, SO ALSO DOES A MAN WANDER FROM HIS PLACE IN ORDER THAT HE SHOULD RETURN IN A REINCARNATION.

54. וּבְגִין דָּא, גַּם צִפּוֹר מָצְאָה בַיִת, הַיְינוּ יְבָמָה. וּדְרוֹר קֵן לָהּ, הַיְינוּ גּוֹאֵל, אֲשֶׁר שָׁתָה אֶפְרוֹחֶיהָ, בֵּן וּבַת. זַכָּאָה אִיהוּ מַאן דְּעָבֵד קִינָא, וְגָאַל אֶת מִמְכַּר אָחִיו. דְּאִיהוּ מָכוּר בַּעֲבוּר דְּלָאו דִּילֵיהּ.

54. And that is why: "Even the sparrow has found a home" (Tehilim 84:4), meaning the deceased brother's wife. THIS MEANS THAT THE SPARROW, THE DEAD CHILDLESS MAN'S SOUL, HAS FOUND A HOME, AS IT WAS INCARNATED IN THE BODY OF THE WIDOW, WHO BECAME A HOME TO IT. "and the swallow a nest for herself" (Ibid.) refers to the redeemer WHO MARRIES THE DECEASED BROTHER'S WIDOW AND FINDS HIMSELF A NEST IN HER. "where she may lay her young" (Ibid.) refers to a son and a daughter THEY BEGET. Happy is he who makes a nest, THAT IS, WHO MARRIES THE WIDOW OF HIS CHILDLESS DECEASED BROTHER. "and shall redeem that which his brother sold" (Vayikra 25:25), FOR THE WIDOW OF HIS DECEASED BROTHER is considered as though sold to him, for she is not his, BUT HIS BROTHER'S, AND SHE IS THEREFORE CALLED "THAT WHICH HIS BROTHER SOLD."

55. וּבְגִין דָּא אָמַר מֹשֶׁה, וַיִּתְעַבֵּר יְיָ' בִּי לְמַעַנְכֶם. הָכָא הוּא סוֹד הָעִבּוּר. רַעְיָא מְהֵימָנָא, שֶׁזִּיב שִׁתִּין רִבּוֹא, כַּמָּה זִמְנִין דְּאָתֵי בְּגִלְגּוּלָא, וּבְגִין דָּא זְכוּת כֻּלְּהוּ תַּלְיָיא קוּדְשָׁא בְּרִיךְ הוּא בֵּיהּ. וּבְגִין דָּא אוֹקְמוּהָ רַבָּנָן, אִשָּׁה אַחַת יָלְדָה בְּמִצְרַיִם שִׁשִּׁים רִבּוֹא בְּכֶרֶס אֶחָד. וְאע"ג דְּאוֹקְמוּהָ רַבָּנָן בְּמִלִּין אַחֲרָנִין, שִׁבְעִים פָּנִים לַתּוֹרָה.

55. And this was why Moses said: "And Hashem was angry (Heb. vayit'aber) with me for your sakes" (Devarim 3:26). And this is the secret of the conception (Heb. Ibur), FOR MALCHUT CONCEIVED BY THE SOUL OF MOSES. The Faithful Shepherd saved sixty thousand SOULS in Yisrael a number of times, for he incarnated IN A NUMBER OF GENERATIONS AND SAVED THEM. For this reason, the Holy One, blessed be He, ascribed TO MOSES the merit of all of them, and this is why the sages taught: 'One

woman in Egypt brought forth in one womb six hundred thousand at one birth'. THIS IS MOSES WHO WAS CONSIDERED AS EQUAL TO SIX HUNDRED THOUSAND SOULS OF YISRAEL. And although the sages expounded this verse with regard to other matters, THERE IS NO DIFFICULTY BECAUSE 'there are seventy aspects to the Torah'.

56. דְּהָכִי אֹרַח דְּמָארֵי רָזִין, אַמְרִין מַרְגְּלִית לְתַלְמִידֵיהוֹן, וְלָא אִשְׁתְּמוֹדְעוּן בֵּיהּ בְּרְמִיזָא, אַהֲדָר לוֹן הַהוּא מִלָּה בְּמִלֵּי שְׂחוֹק, כְּגַוְונָא דְּהַהוּא דְּאָמַר, דְּבֵיצָה אַחַת, אַפִּילַת שִׁתִּין כְּרָכִין. וְאָתָא בֵּיצָה וְנָפְלַת מִן עוֹפָא דַּהֲוָה פָּרַח בַּאֲוֵירָא, וּמְחָאַת אִלֵּין שִׁתִּין כְּרָכִין, וּמָארֵי דְּלֵיצָנוּתָא אָמְרוּ, דְּלָא אָמַר הוּא אֶלָּא דב״ן כָּתַב שִׁשִּׁים כְּרָכִין, וְאָתָא בֵּיצָה דְּנָפְקַת מִן עוֹפָא וּמְחָקַת שִׁתִּין כְּרָכִין דִּכְתִיבָה. וְחַס וְשָׁלוֹם דְּמָארֵי אוֹרַיְיתָא אַמְרִין מִלִּין דִּשְׂחוֹק, וּדְבָרִים בְּטֵלִים בְּאוֹרַיְיתָא.

56. This is the way in which the mystics offer a pearl to their pupils, and if THE PUPILS do not understand the hint, it is explained to them as a jest. For example, a man says that a single egg overthrew sixty villages, because the egg was dropped by a bird that was flying in the air and struck the villages. The jesters said that this is not what he said, but that a man wrote ON A PIECE OF PAPER 'sixty villages' and the egg dropped by the bird erased THE WORDS 'sixty villages'. And heaven forbid that the sages of the Torah should say jocular and useless things of the Torah!

57. אֶלָּא הָא אוֹקְמוּהָ, אֶפְרוֹחִים, אִלֵּין מָארֵי מִשְׁנָה. אוֹ בֵּיצִים, אִלֵּין מָארֵי מִקְרָא. וּכְגַוְונָא דְּנָפַל מֵהַהוּא נְפוֹל, דְּאִיהוּ בַּר נָפְלֵי, נְפִילַת בֵּיצָה דְּאִיהוּ אֶתְרוֹג שִׁיעוּרָא בְּכַבֵּיצָה. וּבְגִינָהּ אִתְּמַר בְּיוֹם הַהוּא אָקִים אֶת סֻכַּת דָּוִד הַנּוֹפֶלֶת. וְנָפְלוּ עִמָּהּ שִׁשִּׁים הֵמָּה מְלָכוֹת, דְּאִינּוּן כְּרִיכִין בָּהּ, כְּגוֹן כֵּיצַד כּוֹרְכִין אֶת שְׁמַע. וְאִינּוּן לָקֳבֵל שִׁשִּׁים מַסֶּכְתּוֹת. וַעֲלָמוֹת אֵין מִסְפָּר, אִלֵּין בְּתוּלוֹת אַחֲרֵיהָ רֵעוֹתֶיהָ, דְּאִינּוּן הֲלָכוֹת, דְּלֵית לוֹן חוּשְׁבַּן.

57. But they taught: "Young ones" (Devarim 22:6) are the sages of the Mishnah, "eggs" (Ibid.) are the Scripture scholars, THAT IS TO SAY: THE

YOUNG ONES' ARE ZEIR ANPIN, ONTO WHICH THESE SAGES OF THE MISHNAH HOLD, WHEREAS THE EGGS ARE MALCHUT, ONTO WHICH THE SCRIPTURE SCHOLARS HOLD. And it is like falling (Heb. *nafal*) from that young bird (Heb. *nipol*), ZEIR ANPIN CALLED 'fallen', BECAUSE THE FALL ORIGINATES IN HIM, JUST AS AN EGG DROPS FROM A BIRD. For FROM HIM falls the egg, which is like an Etrog, as it is the same size as an egg, WHICH IS TO SAY THAT BOTH AN EGG AND AN ETROG ARE MALCHUT. THAT IS WHY AN ETROG IS EGG-SIZE, and it is said about it: "On that day I will raise up the tabernacle of David that is fallen" (Amos 9:11), FOR IT HAS FALLEN INTO EXILE AND HAS TO BE RAISED UP AGAIN. And with it fell INTO EXILE "sixty queens" (Shir Hashirim 6:8) – CHESED, GVURAH, TIFERET, NETZACH, HOD AND YESOD, EACH ONE OF WHICH INCLUDES TEN, AND THEY ARE CALLED VILLAGES (HEB. *KRACHM*) since they are bound (Heb. *kruchim*) to it. It has the same sense as in 'how are the portions of the Sh'ma bound together', NAMELY JOINED TOGETHER WITHOUT INTERRUPTION. AND HERE ALSO ITS MEANING IS THAT ITS SIX ENDS ARE TIED TOGETHER IN IT, and they correspond to the sixty tractates, FOR THE ORAL LAW, WHICH IS MALCHUT, IS DIVIDED INTO SIXTY TRACTATES, WHICH CORRESPOND TO THE SIXTY QUEENS REFERRED TO ABOVE. "and young women without number" (Ibid.) – these are: "the virgins, her companions that follow her" (Tehilim 45:15), NAMELY THE PALACES THAT ARE IN BRIYAH, which are Halachot (legal rulings) that are innumerable, BEING IN BRIYAH.

נח. וְהַהוּא נִיפוֹל אִיהוּ בֶּן יָ"ה אִיהוּ בְּתוֹךְ נ' תַּרְעִין דְּבִינָ"ה, דְּהַיְינוּ יָ"ה חָמֵשׁ זִמְנִין עֲשַׂר ו' אִיהוּ נִיפוֹל, דְּנָפַל בָּתַר הַהִיא דְּאִתְּמַר, אֵיךְ נָפַלְתָּ מִשָּׁמַיִם הֵילֵל בֶּן שָׁחַר וְאִקְרֵי נִיפוֹל, וְלָא נָפַל, וְלָא נוֹפֵל. בְּגִין דְּבֵיה נִיפוֹל יִ"וּ וְנָחִית בְּהוֹן לְגַבֵּי ה' ה', דְּאִתְּמַר בְּהוֹן וַתֵּלַכְנָה שְׁתֵּיהֶן. הה"ד שַׁלַּח תְּשַׁלַּח חַד מִבַּיִת רִאשׁוֹן וְתִנְיָינָא מִבַּיִת שֵׁנִי, לְאַקְמָא לוֹן. הה"ד, יִ"שְׂמְחוּ הַ"שָּׁמַיִם וְ"תָגֵל הָ"אָרֶץ.

58. And that young bird is the son of Yud-Hei, NAMELY ZEIR ANPIN, which is within the fifty gates of Binah, namely Yud-Hei, where ten is multiplied by five AMOUNTING TO FIFTY. The Vav, WHICH IS ZEIR ANPIN, is CALLED a young bird (lit. 'fallen one') because it fell after that ABOUT WHOM it is said: "How are you fallen from Heaven, O bright star, son of the morning!"

(Yeshayah 14:12). THIS IS MALCHUT, WHICH IS SO CALLED BECAUSE OF ITS TWO STATES; IN ONE STATE IT IS BLACK AND IN THE OTHER IT IS BRIGHTLY LIGHTED, AND ZEIR ANPIN FOLLOWED HER WHEN SHE WAS IN EXILE, IN ORDER TO RAISE HER UP. AND THAT IS WHY he is called "fallen" and it is not written that he fell or falls. THAT IS TO SAY, IT IS NOT HE THAT FALLS BUT MALCHUT WHO FALLS FROM HIM, FROM HEAVEN TO EARTH. AND HE HAS IN HIM Yud and Vav; NAMELY ZEIR ANPIN INCLUDES THE YUD AND VAV OF THE YUD HEI VAV HEI, THAT ARE CHOCHMAH AND ZEIR ANPIN and he descends through them IN ORDER TO RAISE UP the two letters Hei OF THE YUD HEI VAV HEI, NAMELY BINAH AND MALCHUT, about whom it is said: "So the two of them went..." (Rut 1:19). This is the meaning of: "but you shall surely let...go" (Devarim 22:7) (lit. 'Letting go you shall let go'). The first LETTING GO refers to the first Temple, WHICH WAS DESTROYED, AND CORRESPONDS TO THE FIRST HEI. The second LETTING GO REFERS TO the second Temple, WHICH WAS ALSO DESTROYED, AND CORRESPONDS TO THE HEI THAT IS THAT LAST LETTER OF THE YUD HEI VAV HEI. THE YUD AND THE VAV OF THE YUD HEI VAV HEI DESCENDED in order to raise up THE TWO LETTERS HEI, as is written: "Let the heavens rejoice, and let the earth be glad" (Tehilim 96:11). THE INITIAL LETTERS OF THE FOUR HEBREW WORDS FORMING THIS VERSE ARE YUD, HEI, VAV AND HEI, AND SO THE YUD AND THE VAV ARE JOINED WITH THE TWO LETTERS HEI.

59. ת"ח, הַאי שִׁמְשָׁא אִתְגַּלְיָא בִּימָמָא, וְאִתְכַּסְיָא בְּלֵילְיָא. וְנָהִיר בְּשִׁתִּין רִבּוֹא כֹּכְבַיָּא. אוֹף הָכִי רַעְיָא מְהֵימְנָא, בָּתַר דְּאִתְכְּנִישׁ מֵעָלְמָא, נָהִיר בְּשִׁתִּין רִבּוֹא נִשְׁמָתִין דְּיִשְׂרָאֵל, אִי דָּרָא כַּדְקָא יָאוּת. וְהַאי אִיהוּ רָזָא דְּגִלְגּוּלָא, דְּאָמַר עֲלֵיהּ קֹהֶלֶת, דּוֹר הֹלֵךְ וְדוֹר בָּא. וְאוֹקְמוּהָ דְּלֵית דּוֹר פָּחוּת מִשִּׁשִּׁים רִבּוֹא. וְהָאָרֶץ לְעוֹלָם עוֹמָדֶת, דָּא כ"י. הַהִיא דְּאִתְּמַר בָּהּ, וְהָאָרֶץ הֲדֹם רַגְלָי, וְהָיָה זַרְעֲךָ כַּעֲפַר הָאָרֶץ.

59. Come and see: The sun is seen by day and hidden by night when it shines through six hundred thousand stars. The Faithful Shepherd is similar. After his departure from the world, HE RETURNS IN AN INCARNATION AND shines on the six hundred thousand souls of Yisrael, but only if the generation is worthy. This is the secret of reincarnation, concerning which Kohelet said: "One generation passes away, and another generation comes"

(Kohelet 1:4). We have learned that a generation is no less than six hundred thousand. "but the earth abides forever" (Ibid.) – this is the Congregation of Yisrael, WHICH IS MALCHUT, concerning which it is written: "and the earth is My footstool" (Yeshayah 66:1), "and your seed shall be as the dust of the earth" (Beresheet 28:14).

60. וְעוֹד רָזָא אַחֲרָא אוֹקְמוּהָ רַבָּנָן, הַדּוֹר שֶׁהוֹלֵךְ הוּא הַדּוֹר שֶׁבָּא, הָלַךְ חִגֵּר בָּא חִגֵּר, הֹלֵךְ סוּמָא בָּא סוּמָא. וְעוֹד אוֹקְמוּהָ רַבָּנָן, דְּעָתִיד הֲוָה מֹשֶׁה לְקַבְּלָא אוֹרַיְיתָא בְּדָרָא דְּטוֹפָנָא, אֶלָּא בְּגִין דַּהֲווֹ רְשִׁיעַיָּיא, הה"ד בְּשַׁגַּ"ם הוּא בָּשָׂר. בְּשַׁגַּ"ם זֶה מֹשֶׁ"ה. וַאֲמַאי קָרֵי לֵיה בְּשַׁגָּם. אֶלָּא קֹהֶלֶת חָסֵר ב' מִן בְּשַׁגַּ"ם לְכַסָּאָה מִלָּה. אָמַר אָמַרְתִּי שֶׁגַּם זֶה הָבֶל.

60. And the sages have taught us yet another secret. "ONE GENERATION PASSES AWAY, AND ANOTHER GENERATION COMES" MEANS THAT the generation that passes away is the same generation that comes. A cripple goes and a cripple comes; a blind man goes and a blind man comes. And the sages further taught that Moses was destined to receive the Torah in the generation of the Flood, but DID NOT RECEIVE IT THEN because of the wicked people, as it is written: "for that he also (Heb. *beshagam*) is flesh" (Beresheet 6:3). THE NUMERICAL VALUE OF THE WORD "*beshagam*" is the same as that of Moses. Why is he called "*beshagam*"? IN ORDER TO KEEP THE MATTER SECRET. And Kohelet EVEN removed the Bet from "*beshagam*" to conceal it even more, when he said: "I said that this also (Heb. *shegam*) is vanity" (Kohelet 8:14). "*SHEGAM*" HERE REFERS TO MOSES, AND KOHELET REMOVED THE BET IN ORDER TO CONCEAL THE MATTER.

61. וְאוֹקְמוּהָ עַל יִתְרוֹ, לָמָּה נִקְרָא שְׁמוֹ קֵינִי, שֶׁנִּפְרָד מִקַּיִן. קָם בּוּצִינָא קַדִּישָׁא וְאָמַר, עַל דָּא כְּתִיב, קָנִיתִי אִישׁ אֶת יְדֹוָ"ד. דְּחָזָאת לֵיה בְּרוּחַ הַקֹּדֶשׁ, דַּעֲתִידִין בְּנוֹי לְמֵיתַב בְּלִשְׁכַּת הַגָּזִית.

61. It has been taught about Jethro: Why is his name called 'Kenite'? Because he "had severed himself from Cain" (Shoftim 4:11). The Holy Luminary, RABBI SHIMON, arose and said: Therefore it is written ABOUT

CAIN, "I have acquired (Heb. *kaniti*) a manchild from Hashem" (Beresheet 4:1), for she saw JETHRO through the Holy Spirit and that his sons would in the future sit in the Chamber of Granit Stones, WHERE THE SANHEDRIN USED TO MEET.

62. וְאוּף הָכִי ר' פְּדָת, דַּהֲוָה דְּחִיקָא לֵיהּ שַׁעֲתָא, דְּלָא הֲוָה לֵיהּ אֶלָּא קַב חֲרוּבִין מֵע"ש לְע"ש, כְּמוֹ לר' חֲנִינָא. אֲמַאי הַאי, בָּתַר דַּהֲוַת בַּת קוֹל נָפְקַת וְאוֹמֶרֶת, כָּל הָעוֹלָם כֻּלּוֹ אֵינוּ נִיזוֹן אֶלָּא בִּשְׁבִיל חֲנִינָא בְּנִי.

62. And so it was with Rabbi Pedat, who was in distress and who had no more than a measure of carobs from one Shabbat Eve to the next, like Rabbi Chanina. HE ASKS why is this, since a heavenly voice had proclaimed: The whole world is fed only because of Chanina, my son?

63. אֶלָּא אִיהוּ גָּרִים קוֹדֶם, דְּחָרַב ק"ב מִן י', דְּאִיהוּ יַבּ"ק. אוּף הָכִי לָא הוּ"ל אֶלָּא קַב חֲרוּבִין. דְּאָת י' אִיהוּ יְחוּד, וּמִנֵּיהּ אַתְיָא נְבִיעוּ לְאָת ב', דְּאִיהִי בְּרָכָה, וְאִיהִי קֹדֶשׁ, וּמִנֵּיהּ אִתְקַדָּשׁ ק', דְּאִיהִי קְדוּשָׁיָה. וְר' פְּדָת גָּרִים לְמֶהֱוֵי חֲרוּבִין דִּילֵיהּ ק"ב, דְּאִינוּן קְ"דוּשָׁה בְּ"רָכָה, אוּף הָכִי לָא הוּ"ל אֶלָּא קַב חֲרוּבִין, אוּף הָכִי בֶּן אִיוֹב בֶּן יִבָמָה הֲוָה, וּבְגִין דָּא אִתְעֲנָשׁ, עַל מַה דְּאִירַע לוֹ כְּבָר.

63. AND HE ANSWERS THAT he caused this IN HIS FIRST REINCARNATION, when he destroyed (Heb. *charav*) the measure (Heb. *kav*, Kof Bet) from Yud, which makes Yud, Kof and Bet, hence he was left with only a measure of carobs (Heb. *charuv*). HE EXPLAINS HIS WORDS: YUD, BET AND KOF ARE THE INITIAL LETTERS OF THE WORDS *YICHUD* (ENG. 'UNIFICATION'), *BERACHAH* (ENG. 'BLESSING') AND *KEDUSHAH* (ENG. 'HOLINESS'). The letter Yud stands for unification, WHICH IS THE SECRET OF THE NAME *EHEYEH*, BINAH, from which the emanation comes to the letter Bet, standing for blessing, WHICH IS THE SECRET OF THE YUD HEI VAV HEI, WHICH IS ZEIR ANPIN, which is holy, from which Kof is sanctified, which is its sanctification NAMELY THE NAME ADONAI, WHICH IS MALCHUT. And Rabbi Pedat caused, IN HIS FIRST REINCARNATION, his measure (Kof Bet) to be destroyed, which are holiness and blessing, WITHOUT THE UNITY

SHINING UPON THEM. Thus he had only a measure of carobs. So, too, was it with Job, who was the son of a levirate widow, and he was punished because of what had already happened to him IN THE FIRST REINCARNATION.

11. Before the Giving of the Torah they depended on constellations

A Synopsis

We are told that before the Torah was given, even children, life and sustenance were dependent on constellations, but afterward God removed Yisrael from the influence of the stars and constellations. If a person does not keep the commandments, however, the stars and constellations will still hold sway over him. Finally we hear again that people grow old and die, and then return again as children.

The Relevance of this Passage

On the wings of Abraham and by the thrust of the letter *Hei* engraved into the parchment of Torah, we are now propelled above the plane of planetary influence. We become shepherds of the stars, pilots of the planets, reacquiring control over our fate. Our future is hereby transformed to one of an immediate and complete redemption, in a process that embodies the mercy and tenderness of this great Book of Splendor. Illnesses, conferred to us by the stars, flare out of existence, like falling stars in the distant heavens.

The Zohar's words "For PEOPLE die when old and return to this world as children" have the effect of arresting the aging process. The letters kindle Light that regenerates our cells and our souls, infusing us with rejuvenescence so that we become youthful again, like children – for this is the ultimate destiny of human beings.

64. וְאִינּוּן דְּלָא יַדְעֵי רָזָא דָּא, אַמְרֵי בְּנֵי חַיֵּי וּמְזוֹנֵי לָאו בִּזְכוּתָא תַּלְיָא מִלְתָא, אֶלָּא בְּמַזָּלָא תַּלְיָא מִלְתָא. וְהָא חֲזֵינָא לְאַבְרָהָם דְּחָזָא בְּמַזָּלֵיהּ, דְּלָא הֲוָה עָתִיד לְמֶהֱוֵי לֵיהּ בְּרָא, וְקוּדְשָׁא בְּרִיךְ הוּא אַפִּיק לֵיהּ לְבָרָא, כְּדִכְתִּיב וַיּוֹצֵא אוֹתוֹ הַחוּצָה וַיֹּאמֶר הַבֶּט וְגוֹ'. וְאַקְמוּהַ, דְּא"ל צֵא מֵאִצְטַגְנִינוּת שֶׁלָּךְ, וְהֶעֱלָהוּ לְמַעְלָה מֵהַכֹּכָבִים, וְאָמַר לוֹ הַבֶּט נָא הַשָּׁמַיְמָה וּסְפוֹר הַכֹּכָבִים. עַד הָכָא מִלִּין דְּרַבָּנָן, וְצָרִיךְ לְפָרְשָׁא לוֹן בְּדֶרֶךְ נִסְתָּר.

64. And those who do not know this secret say: 'Children, life and sustenance is not a matter of one's merit, rather it depends on constellations (Heb. *mazal*)'. Take the case of Abram, who saw that he was not destined to have a son, and the Holy One, blessed be He, took him outside, as it is said:

"And He brought him outside, and said, Look..." (Beresheet 15:5). And it has been taught that He said to him: 'Leave your astrology', NAMELY DO NOT CONSULT THE STARS AND CONSTELLATIONS. And He took him up above the stars and said to him: "Look now towards heaven, and count the stars" (Ibid.). So much for the words of the sages, but they have to be interpreted mystically!

65. ת"ח, כָּל בִּרְיָין דְּעָלְמָא, קוֹדֶם דְּאִתְיְיהִיבַת אוֹרַיְיתָא לְיִשְׂרָאֵל, הֲווֹ תַּלְיָין בְּמַזָּלָא, וַאֲפִילוּ בְּנֵי חַיֵּי וּמְזוֹנֵי. אֲבָל בָּתַר דְּאִתְיְיהִיבַת אוֹרַיְיתָא לְיִשְׂרָאֵל, אַפִּיק לוֹן מֵחִיּוּבָא דְּכֹכְבַיָּא וּמַזָּלֵי. וְדָא אוֹלִיפְנָא מֵאַבְרָהָם. בְּגִין דַּהֲווֹ עֲתִידִין בְּנוֹי לְקַבְּלָא ה' מֵאַבְרָהָם, דְּאִיהִי חֲמִשָּׁה חוּמְשֵׁי תּוֹרָה. דְּאִתְּמַר בָּהּ אֵלֶּה תוֹלְדוֹת הַשָּׁמַיִם וְהָאָרֶץ בְּהִבָּרְאָם, בְּה' בְּרָאָם. אָמַר לְאַבְרָהָם, בְּגִין הַאי ה' דְּאִתּוֹסַף בִּשְׁמָךְ, הַשָּׁמַיִם תַּחְתָּךְ, וְכָל כֹּכְבַיָּא וּמַזָּלֵי דִּנְהִירִין בָּהּ. וְלֹא עוֹד, אֶלָּא דְּאִתְּמַר בָּהּ הֵ"א לָכֶם זֶרַע, וּזְרַעְתֶּם בְּהֵ"א. כִּי בְּיִצְחָק יִקָּרֵא לְךָ זָרַע.

65. Come and see: All creatures in the world, before the Torah was given to Yisrael, were dependent on Mazal, even children, life and sustenance. But after the Torah was given to Yisrael, He removed Yisrael from the influences of the stars and constellations. This we have learned from Abraham, since his children were destined to receive Hei from Abraham, that is, the five books of the Torah, NAMELY MALCHUT, as it is said: "These are the generations of heaven and earth when they were created (Heb. *behibar'am*)" (Beresheet 2:4). *behibar'am*: *beHei bera'am* (meaning 'He created them with a Hei'). He said to Abraham 'Because of that Hei that was added to your name, the heavens below you and all the stars and constellations that shine in Hei will be subservient to your will' BECAUSE HE RAISED HIM ABOVE THEM. Moreover, it is said: "lo (Heb. *he*), here is grain for you, and you shall sow the land" (Beresheet 47:23) with Hei. That is, "for in Isaac shall your seed be called" (Beresheet 21:12), WHO IS THE SECRET OF THE LEFT COLUMN, FROM WHICH MALCHUT, THE SECRET OF HEI, IS DRAWN, AND SOWING IS THUS IN MALCHUT.

66. וּבְג"ד, כָּל הַמִּשְׁתַּדֵּל בְּאוֹרַיְיתָא, בָּטִיל מִנֵּיהּ חִיּוּבָא דְּכֹכְבַיָּא וּמַזָּלֵי. אִי אוֹלִיף לָהּ כְּדֵי לְקַיְּימָא פְּקוּדְהָא. וְאִם לָאו, כְּאִלּוּ לָא

אִשְׁתְּדַּל בָּהּ, וְלָא בָּטִיל מִנֵּיהּ חִיּוּבָא דְּכֹּכְבַיָּא וּמַזָּלֵי. כָּל שֶׁכֵּן עַמֵּי הָאָרֶץ דְּאִינּוּן אִתְמַתְלָן לִבְעִירָן. דְּאוֹקְמוּהָ עָלַיְיהוּ אָרוּר שׁוֹכֵב עִם כָּל בְּהֵמָה, דְּלָא אִתְבַּטָּלוּן מִנְּהוֹן חִיּוּבָא דְּכֹּכְבַיָּא וּמַזָּלֵי.

66. For this reason, everyone who engages in the Torah is released from the influence of stars and constellations. By learning Torah HERE IS MEANT with the intention of keeping its commandments. If it is not HIS INTENTION TO KEEP ITS COMMANDMENTS, then he is as one who does not engage in Torah, and the stars and constellations hold sway over him. This is even more true with respect to the common people, who are likened to animals, about which it has been taught: "Cursed be he who lies with any manner of beast" (Devarim 27:21). The hold of the stars and constellations over them is certainly not annulled.

67. אֱנוֹשׁ כֶּחָצִיר יָמָיו כְּצִיץ הַשָּׂדֶה כֵּן יָצִיץ, וְאִתְּמַר בֵּיהּ, נַעַר הָיִיתִי גַּם זָקַנְתִּי. לְבָתַר יָשׁוּב לִימֵי עֲלוּמָיו. דְּאִילָנָא דְּאִתְקְצִיצוּ עַנְפִין עַתִּיקִין דִּילֵיהּ, וְצָמְחוּ כְּמִלְּקַדְמִין בְּשָׁרְשׁוֹי, אַהַדְרוּ בְּעָלְמָא כְּמִלְּקַדְמִין. מִיתוּ סָבִין, וְאִתְהַדְרוּ לְהַאי עָלְמָא עוּלֵימִין. וְהַיְינוּ רָזָא דִּמְחַדֵּשׁ קוּדְשָׁא בְּרִיךְ הוּא בְּכָל יוֹם תָּמִיד מַעֲשֵׂה בְרֵאשִׁית. דְּמֵתִין אֶלֶף בְּכָל יוֹמָא וּמִתְחַדְּשִׁין אֶלֶף בְּכָל יוֹמָא.

67. "As for man, his days are as grass: as a flower of the field so he flourishes" (Tehilim 103:15). And ABOUT MAN it is said: "I was young and am now old" (Tehilim 37:25). And later IT IS SAID: "He returns to the days of his youth" (Iyov 33:25). IT IS LIKE a tree from which the old branches were cut off, but they grew again from its roots, as at the beginning. For PEOPLE die when old and return to this world as children. And this is the secret of the Holy One, blessed be He, 'renewing the creation every day continually'. For a thousand die each day and a thousand are renewed each day, REINCARNATING INTO THE WORLD.

12. "Wine makes glad the heart of man...the cypress trees are her house"

A Synopsis

The "wine" is said to be the Torah, but we are told that the secrets of the Torah should be disclosed only to those who fear God. The red and white colors of the wine are said here to be Judgment and Mercy. It is significant that certain commandments and blessings are performed with wine. "The heart of man" means two hearts, that of Binah and that of Malchut, and we read the numerology of the words, letters and vowels associated with this lesson. Next Rabbi Elazar asks his father how Nadab and Abihu could have reincarnated into Pinchas when he was already alive at the time of their deaths. Rabbi Shimon replies that both Nadab and Abihu died childless so they were not fit for the priesthood. When Pinchas saw the tribe of Shimon coming after him his soul fled out of him in terror; then the unamended souls of Nadab and Abihu joined with his soul and all returned to his body. After this he deserved the priesthood. Rabbi Shimon explains God's command to hang the chiefs up against the sun to demonstrate that everyone must make amends in his soul on the same level at which he sinned. Rabbi Shimon talks for a long time about the sustenance that is provided for the righteous.

The Relevance of this Passage

This passage is a well of wisdom that runs unfathomably deep, capable of producing innumerable volumes of medical journals if all of its secrets were unraveled and translated to written word.

As the Zohar speaks of the importance of wine – *red and white* – and the gladness of heart that wine provides, one cannot help but notice the similarity to the blood coursing through our veins, and to our heart, which pumps blood throughout the body.

Blood is made up of *red and white* blood cells. The white cells are constantly watchful for disease, fighting germs and infections that enter the body. Red blood cells deliver oxygen to the body and remove waste. Kabbalistically, any form of disease is considered judgment. The elimination of disease, according to Kabbalah, is mercy. The white blood cells are Mercy, eliminating disease and Judgment from the red blood cells.

A rose, the Zohar tells us, also conveys judgment and mercy – indicated by white - and red - colored roses, and by their thorns

and sweet scent. Their thorns represent judgment, and their fragrance represents mercy.

Fundamentally important to the reader are the healing forces that radiate from these ancient mysteries:

Our blood is purified, removing harmful germs and infections by virtue of our meditative reading. Blood clots and other blood-related ailments are healed.

Physically, wine is a rich dietary source of flavinoid phenolics, which are effective antioxidants. Antioxidants combat atherosclerosis, or clogging of the arteries.

The alcohol in wine alters blood lipid levels by lowering total cholesterol and raising high-density lipoprotein (HDL) levels, which retard and even reverse the formation of cholesterol plaque in the arteries.

These effects are merely minute physical manifestations of wine's spiritual power.

Thus, as our eyes now drink from the cup of wine, its blessings are aroused. Light "WHICH IS DRAWN FROM BINAH" purges the fury and vengeance that burns in our heart. Anger hardens our heart and clogs our arteries. Now that it is soothed and gladdened, our arteries are unblocked and cleared, and cholesterol is lowered.

Our hearts become filled with loving-kindness and mercy, strengthening this vital organ while cleansing our blood of viral and bacterial toxins, wastes, and microbial poisons.

Our sins are the source of all illness. And we learn from the Zohar that "at whatever level a man sins before the Holy One, blessed be He, he must make amends in his soul at that same level." The Light now drawn from *Pinchas* remedies our sins, past and present, measure for measure, engendering healing and the final restoration.

We invoke the essence of the angel *Metatron,* who embodies the restoration of youth and immortality, which, according to the Zohar, occurs through the "ILLUMINATION OF CHOCHMAH, WHICH IS DRAWN FROM BINAH." Thus, the verses that speak the mysteries of *Metatron* reverse the aging process and the decline of physiological function. Cells are reverted back to their embryonic state – a stem cell – where they are now purified and free to repopulate and regenerate the human body, eternally.

Medical science today acknowledges what the Zohar revealed long

ago – stem cells perform what have been called "acts of biological resurrection." The immortal telomerase enzyme causes cells to divide indefinitely, instead of dying. The spiritual essence of telomerase flourishes in our normal healthy cells, while vanishing from tumor cells.

"The Cypress trees are her house," we're told, indicates the middle point between *Chesed* and *Gvurah* which are Mercy and Judgment, respectively. Abraham's daughter sits among the Cypress trees. She is pious, having performed deeds of loving-kindness. Accordingly, through this passage we are infused with loving-kindness and Light from *Chochmah* and *Binah,* creating balance between judgment and mercy, our white and red blood cells, and our heart and our soul. This mitigates judgment and halts disease.

68. וְיַיִן יְשַׂמַּח לְבַב אֱנוֹשׁ, דָּא יֵינָא דְאוֹרַיְיתָא. דְּהָכִי סָלִיק יַיִן, כְּחוּשְׁבַּן סוֹ״ד. וּמַה יַי״ן צָרִיךְ לְמֶהֱוֵי סָתִים וְחָתִים, דְּלָא יִתְנְסַךְ לע״ז. אוֹף הָכִי צָרִיךְ לְמֶהֱוֵי סָתִים וְחָתִים סוֹד דְּאוֹרַיְיתָא, וְכָל רָזִין דִּילָהּ, וְלָא אִשְׁתַּכְּיָין אֶלָּא לִירֵאָיו. וְלָאו לְמַגָּנָא עַבְדִּין כַּמָּה פִּקוּדִין בְּיַיִן, וּמְבָרְכִין בֵּיהּ לְקוּדְשָׁא בְּרִיךְ הוּא, וְיַיִן אִית לֵיהּ תְּרֵי גַּוְונִין, חִיוָּר וְסוּמָק, דִּינָא וְרַחֲמֵי, וְהַיְינוּ ב׳ תּוֹסֶפֶת בְּיַיִן. כְּגַוְונָא דְּשׁוֹשַׁנָּה חִיוָּרָא וְסוּמָקָא. חִיוָּר מִסִּטְרָא דִּימִינָא, סוּמָק מִסִּטְרָא דִּשְׂמָאלָא.

68. "Wine makes glad the heart of man" (Tehilim 104:15). This is the wine of the Torah, for the numerical value of the word *yayin* (Eng. 'wine') is the same as the letters of *sod* (Eng. 'secret'). Just as wine has to be kept sealed so that it should not be used in a libation for idol worship, so also must the secret of the Torah be closed up and sealed, and none of its secrets be disclosed other than to those who fear Him. And it is not for nothing that several commandments are performed with wine, and blessings to the Holy One, blessed be He, are said. Wine comes in two colors: white and red, which are Judgment and Mercy. And this is why we have the added Bet (= 2) in *be'yayin* ('with wine'). THIS BET HINTS AT JUDGMENT AND MERCY. It is like the rose which has in it both white and red – white from the right side WHICH IS CHESED, and red from the left side WHICH IS GVURAH.

69. וּמַאי לְבַב אֱנוֹשׁ, לֵב הֲו״ל לְמֵימַר. אֶלָּא אִית לֵב מָסוּר לַלֵּב.

וְאִינּוּן ל"ב אֱלֹהִים דְּעוֹבָדָא דִּבְרֵאשִׁית, ב' מִן בְּרֵאשִׁית, ל' מִן לְעֵינֵי
כָּל יִשְׂרָאֵל, אִיהוּ ל"ב תִּנְיָינָא. דָּא ל"ב ל"ב שְׁנַיִם ס"ד, חָסֵר תְּמַנְיָא
לְע"ב, דְּאִיהוּ וַיְכֻלּוּ. אִינּוּן שִׁבְעָה יְמֵי בְּרֵאשִׁית. תְּמִינָאָה מַאי הִיא. ז'
יְמֵי בְּרֵאשִׁית, עִם זֶה סֵפֶר תּוֹלְדוֹת אָדָם. זֶה ע"ב, בְּחוּשְׁבָן בַּיַּיִן.

69. HE ASKS, what is "the heart (Heb. *levav*) of man"? It should have used "*lev* (Eng. 'heart')." HE ANSWERS, there is a heart (Heb. *lev*) gives to the heart (Heb. *lev*). They are THE FIRST Lamed Bet (= 32) times Elohim in the works of Creation, AND THIS *LEV* IS THE SECRET OF BINAH. THE SECOND *LEV* (LAMED-BET) IS the Bet of Beresheet ("In the beginning"), and the Lamed of "in the eyes of (Heb. *le'einei*) all Yisrael" (Devarim 34:12). AND THESE TWO LETTERS, THE BET AT THE BEGINNING OF THE TORAH AND THE LAMED WITH WHICH IT ENDS, ALSO FORM THE WORD *LEV*, NAMELY THE HEART OF MALCHUT. THIS IS WHY IT IS WRITTEN *LEVAV*. FOR THE WINE, WHICH IS THE ILLUMINATION OF CHOCHMAH, IS REVEALED IN AND GLADDENS THE HEART (HEB. *LEV*) OF BINAH AND THE HEART (HEB. *LEV*) OF MALCHUT, FROM WHERE MAN RECEIVES IT. THE NUMERICAL VALUE OF twice *lev* is 64, which is eight less than 72; and 72 IS THE NUMERICAL VALUE OF *vaychulu* ("And...were finished") (Beresheet 2:1). BUT IS THE NAME OF AYIN BET (72), ALLUDED TO IN *VAYCHULU*, THE SECRET OF THE NAME OF THE ILLUMINATION OF CHOCHMAH, THAT IT SHOULD BE ALLUDED TO IN THOSE *LEV LEV*? HE ANSWERS, these are the seven days of Creation THEMSELVES, IN WHICH *LEV* OR 32 ELOHIM SHINE. THEY ARE JOINED TO THE NUMBER 64. BUT 64 AND 7 IS ONLY 71, AND WE ARE STILL ONE SHORT. HE ASKS, what of the eighth, TO COMPLETE IT TO 72? HE ANSWERS, IT IS the seven days of Creation together with "This is the book of the generations of Adam" (Beresheet 5:1), WHICH IS ALSO CONSIDERED TO BE A DAY OF CREATION. It is 72, like the numerical value of the letters of *beyayin* ('with wine'), WHICH IS THE SECRET OF THE ILLUMINATION OF CHOCHMAH, AS DISCUSSED ABOVE.

70. מַאי לְהַצְהִיל פָּנִים מִשָּׁמֶן. אִינּוּן י"ב פָּנִים, ד' דְּאַרְיֵה, ד' דְּשׁוֹר,
ד' דְּנֶשֶׁר, דְּאִינּוּן מִיכָאֵל אַרְיֵה, אַרְבַּע אַנְפִּין דִּילֵיהּ יְהֹו"ה. אַרְבַּע
אַנְפִּין דְּשׁוֹר, וְאִיהוּ גַּבְרִיאֵל, וְאִינּוּן יהֹו"ה. ד' אַנְפִּין דְּנֶשֶׁר, וְאִיהוּ
נוּרִיאֵל, וְאִינּוּן יהֹו"ה. וְאִינּוּן מְמָנָן, תְּחוֹת חֶסֶ"ד פַּחַ"ד אֱמֶ"ת, דַּרְגִּין

דְּתְלַת אֲבָהָן. וְאוֹקְמוּהָ רַבָּנָן, הָאָבוֹת הֵן הֵן הַמֶּרְכָּבָה. וְסַלְּקִין נְהוֹרִין
לְחֶשְׁבָּן יַבּ"ק. וְאִינּוּן מֶלֶךְ מַלַךְ יִמְלוֹךְ, יְהֹוָ"ה אֶהְיֶ"ה אֲדֹנָ"י. סַךְ הַכֹּל
יַבּ"ק.

70. HE ASKS, What is the meaning of "oil to brighten his face" (Tehilim
104:15)? AND ANSWERS, these are the twelve faces: four of the lion, four of
the ox, and four of the eagle. There is Michael the lion, WHO IS THE
SECRET OF CHESED. His four faces are THE FOUR LETTERS Yud Hei Vav
Hei, WHERE THE YUD AND THE VAV HAVE THE VOWEL SEGOL ("E"). The
four faces of the ox, which is Gabriel, NAMELY GVURAH, are FOUR
LETTERS Yud Hei Vav Hei, WHICH YUD AND VAV HAVE THE VOWAL
PATACH ("A"). The four faces of the eagle, which is Nuriel, are THE FOUR
LETTERS Yud Hei Vav Hei, WHEN THE YUD HAS THE VOWAL CHIRIK
("I"), AND THE VAV HAS SH'VA (SEMI-VOWEL). They are appointed under
THE THREE SFIROT OF ZEIR ANPIN – Chesed, Fear and Truth, WHICH ARE
CHESED, GVURAH AND TIFERET. These are the grades of the three
patriarchs, ABRAHAM, ISAAC AND JACOB. The sages have taught: 'the
patriarchs are the Chariot'. The lights OF THE TWELVE COUNTENANCES
add up to Yud Bet Kof, which are 'reigns', 'reigned' and 'will reign'. They
are the secret of Yud Hei Vav He, Eheyeh and Adonai, for the total
NUMERICAL VALUE OF THESE THREE NAMES is Yud Bet Kof, WHICH IS
112.

71. רִבִּי שִׁמְעוֹן הֲוָה יָתִיב וְלָעֵי בְּפָרְשָׁתָא דָא, אָתָא לְקַמֵּיהּ ר' אֶלְעָזָר
בְּרֵיהּ, א"ל, נָדָב וַאֲבִיהוּא מַאי עֲבִידְתַּיְיהוּ בְּפִנְחָס. אִי לָא הֲוָה פִּנְחָס
בְּעָלְמָא כַּד מִיתוּ, וּבָתַר אָתָא לְעָלְמָא וְאַשְׁלִים דּוּכְתַּיְיהוּ שַׁפִּיר. אֲבָל
פִּנְחָס בְּעָלְמָא הֲוָה, וְנִשְׁמָתֵיהּ בֵּיהּ בְּקִיּוּמָא קָאֵי.

71. Rabbi Shimon was sitting and engaging in the study of this portion,
when his son, Rabbi Elazar, came to him and asked: How did it come about
that Nadab and Abihu were ABLE TO INCARNATE in Pinchas? Had Pinchas
not been in the world when they died, and had only come into the world
later, AND THEY WERE INCARNATED IN HIM, and he had perfected their
souls, it would have been fine. But Pinchas was alive AT THE TIME WHEN
NADAB AND ABIHU DIED, and his soul already existed in him, SO HOW

COULD THEY HAVE INCARNATED IN HIM?

72. א"ל בְּרִי, רָזָא עִלָּאָה הָכָא, וְהָכִי הוּא. דִּבְשַׁעֲתָא דְּאִסְתָּלָקוּ מִן עָלְמָא, לָא הֲווֹ מִתְטַמְּרָן תְּחוֹת גַּדְפֵּי טִנָרָא קַדִּישָׁא. מ"ט. בְּגִין דִּכְתִיב וּבָנִים לֹא הָיוּ לָהֶם, דְּאַזְעִירוּ דִּיּוּקְנָא דְּמַלְכָּא, דְּהָא אִינּוּן לָא אִתְחֲזוּן לְשַׁמְּשָׁא בִּכְהוּנָה רַבָּה.

72. He replied: My son, there is a divine secret here: When NADAB AND ABIHU left the world, they did not take shelter under the wings of the Holy Rock, WHICH IS MALCHUT. The reason for this is found in the verse: "And Nadab and Abihu...had no children" (Bemidbar 3:4). That is, they decreased the King's image, FOR THEY DID NOT PERFORM THE PRECEPT OF BEING FRUITFUL AND MULTIPLYING, PRODUCING CHILDREN IN THE IMAGE OF ELOHIM. For this reason they were not fitted to serve in the high priesthood.

73. בְּשַׁעֲתָא דְּקַנֵּי פִּנְחָס עַל בְּרִית קַדִּישָׁא, וְעָאל בְּגוֹ כַּמָּה אוּכְלוֹסִין, וְסָלִיק לוֹן, לְגַיְיפִין עַל רוּמְחָא, לְעֵינַיְיהוּ דְּכָל יִשְׂרָאֵל. כַּד חָמָא שִׁבְטָא דְּשִׁמְעוֹן בְּכַמָּה אַכְלוֹסִין דְּאָתוּ לְגַבֵּיהּ, פַּרְחָא נִשְׁמָתֵיהּ מִנֵּיהּ, וּתְרֵין נִשְׁמָתִין דַּהֲווֹ עַרְטִירָאִין בְּלָא דּוּכְתָּא, אִתְקְרִיבוּ בָּהּ, וְאִתְכְּלִילוּ כַּחֲדָא, וְאִתְהַדְּרַת נִשְׁמָתֵיהּ, כְּלִילָא רוּחָא, דְּאִתְכְּלִיל בִּתְרֵין רוּחִין, וְאִתָּקְפוּ בֵּיהּ, כְּדֵין רָוַוח דּוּכְתַּיְיהוּ, לְמֶיהֱוֵי כַּהֲנָא מַה דְּלָא אִתְחֲזֵי מִן קַדְמַת דְּנָא.

73. When Pinchas was zealous for the Holy Covenant and went in amongst the crowds and held up the adulterers on spear-point in the sight of all Yisrael, he saw the tribe of Shimon coming at him in large numbers, and Pinchas' soul fled out of him DUE TO FEAR. THEN the two souls that were naked, NAMELY THE UNAMENDED SOULS OF NADAB AND ABIHU, approached the soul of Pinchas and were joined together with it, and his soul THEN returned to him, including spirit, which comprehends two spirits, and they supported him. He then earned the right to priesthood in their place OF NADAB AND ABIHU, for which he had not previously been fit.

74. וע"ד כְּתִיב, זָכָר נָא מִי הוּא נָקִי אָבָד, דְּלָא אִתְאֲבִיד בְּהַהִיא

שַׁעְתָּא, וְלָא אָבִיד רוּחֵיהּ כַּד פַּרְחָה מִנֵּיהּ. וְאֵיפֹה יְשָׁרִים נִכְחָדוּ. אִלֵּין בְּנֵי אַהֲרֹן, דְּאִתְהַדְּרוּ לְעָלְמָא, מַה דְּאָבַד בְּחַיֵּיהוֹן. וע״ד כְּתִיב בֵּיהּ בְּפִנְחָס בֶּן בֶּן, תְּרֵי זִמְנֵי. פִּנְחָס בֶּן אֶלְעָזָר בֶּן.

74. And about this it is written: "Recall, now, who that was innocent ever perished?" (Iyov 4:7). THIS WAS SAID ABOUT PINCHAS, who did not perish at that moment, and did not lose his spirit when it fled from him. The same verse continues: "or where were the upright cut off?" This refers to the sons of Aaron, NADAB AND ABIHU, who returned to the world BY REINCARNATING IN PINCHAS AND that which they had lost in their lifetime WAS CORRECTED, NAMELY THE PERFACTING OF THE COVENANT. This is why the word son is used twice regarding Pinchas: "Pinchas the son of Elazar, the son of Aaron" (Bemidbar 25:11), TEACHING US ABOUT THE TWO SOULS THAT HAD INCARNATED IN HIM, NAMELY THE SONS OF AARON. THUS THE SON OF ELAZAR REFERS TO PINCHAS, AND THE SON OF AARON REFERS TO NADAB AND ABIHU.

75. מַה כְּתִיב לְעֵילָא מִפַּרְשָׁתָא דָא. וַיֹּאמֶר יְיָ' אֶל מֹשֶׁה קַח אֶת כָּל רָאשֵׁי הָעָם וְהוֹקַע אוֹתָם לַיְיָ' נֶגֶד הַשָּׁמֶשׁ. וְכִי עַל דְּקַטְלִין בְּלֵילְיָא, אוֹ עַל דְּקַטְלִין בִּימָמָא בְּיוֹמָא דְּעֵיבָא, כְּתִיב נֶגֶד הַשָּׁמֶשׁ. אָמַר ר' יְהוּדָה, דִּתְהֵא מִיתַתְהוֹן בְּאִתְגַּלְיָיא, כְּמָה דְּחָבוּ בְּאִתְגַּלְיָיא.

75. What does scripture say just before this chapter? – "And Hashem said to Moses: Take all the chiefs of the people, and hang them up before Hashem against the sun" (Bemidbar 25:4). HE ASKS: What about when they are killed at night or on a cloudy day? Scripture WARNS THAT THEY MUST BE KILLED against the sun. WHAT IS THE MEANING OF "AGAINST THE SUN." Rabbi Yehuda said: "AGAINST THE SUN" MEANS THAT just as their sin was in public so must their death be in public.

76. א״ר שִׁמְעוֹן, לָאו בְּגִין כַּךְ אִתְּמַר. אֶלָּא מֵהָכָא אוֹלִיפְנָא, בְּדַרְגָּא דְּחָב ב״נ לְקוּדְשָׁא בְּרִיךְ הוּא, לְהַהוּא אֲתָר אִצְטְרִיךְ לְמֶעְבַּד תְּקַנְתָּא לְנַפְשֵׁיהּ. אִינּוּן חָבוּ בִּבְרִית קַדִּישָׁא דְּאִקְרֵי שֶׁמֶשׁ. בְּגִין כַּךְ דִּינָא

וְתִקּוּנָא דִּילְהוֹן אִיהוּ כְּנֶגֶד הַשֶּׁמֶשׁ, וְלָאו בַּאֲתָר אַחֲרָא. מִכָּאן דְּלָא אִצְטְרִיךְ ב"נ לְתַקָּנָא נַפְשֵׁיה, אֶלָּא בְּהַהוּא אֲתָר דְּחָב לְגַבֵּיה וּמַאן דְּלָא יַעְבִּיד הָכִי, לֵית לֵיה תִּקּוּנָא לְעָלְמִין כַּדְקָא יָאוּת.

76. Rabbi Shimon said: This was not the reason why it said "AGAINST THE SUN," but from this we learn that at whatever level a man sins before the Holy One, blessed be He, he must make amends in his soul at that same level. They sinned in the Holy Covenant, which is called 'sun', and this is why their correction is against the sun, THE SECRET OF THE COVENANT, and not elsewhere. It follows that a man requires to remedy the misdeeds he has committed only in the place where he sinned, and that if he attempts to remedy them elsewhere BUT NOT WHERE HE SINNED he will never make it right properly.

77. רִבִּי חִיָּיא פָּתַח, יִשְׂבְּעוּ עֲצֵי יְיָ' אַרְזֵי לְבָנוֹן אֲשֶׁר נָטָע, מַה כְּתִיב לְעֵילָּא, וְיַיִן יְשַׂמַּח לְבַב אֱנוֹשׁ וְגו'. וְכִי מַאי הַאי לְהַאי. אֶלָּא הָכִי אוֹלִיפְנָא, דִּכְתִיב מַצְמִיחַ חָצִיר לַבְּהֵמָה וְגו'. וְכִי שְׁבָחָא דִּבְהֵמָה דְּאִית לָהּ חָצִיר אָתָא דָּוִד לְמֵימַר בְּרוּחַ קוּדְשָׁא. אֶלָּא מַצְמִיחַ חָצִיר, אִלֵּין אִינּוּן שִׁתִּין אֶלֶף רִבּוֹא דְּמַלְאָכִין, שְׁלִיחָן, דְּאִתְבְּרִיאוּ בְּיוֹמָא תִּנְיָינָא דִּבְרֵאשִׁית, וְכֻלְּהוּ אֶשָּׁא מְלַהֲטָא. אִלֵּין אִינּוּן חָצִיר. אֲמַאי חָצִיר. בְּגִין דְּצַמְחִין כְּחָצִיר דָּא בְּעָלְמָא, דְּכָל יוֹמָא וְיוֹמָא אִתְקְצִירוּ הַשָּׁתָּא, וּלְבָתַר צַמְחִין וּמְהַדְרִין כְּמִלְּקַדְמִין.

77. Rabbi Chiya began: "The trees of Hashem have their fill; the cedars of Lebanon which He has planted" (Tehilim 104:16), and before it, "Wine makes glad the heart of man, oil to brighten his face" (Ibid. 15). HE ASKS, What is the connection between these two matters? AND ANSWERS, We have learned as follows: "He causes the grass to spring up for the cattle..." (Ibid. 14). And did David really come with the Holy Spirit to speak the praises of cattle that has grass? HE ANSWERS, No, but "He causes the grass to spring up" refers to the sixty thousand times ten thousands of angels, messengers, who were created on the second day of Creation. All of them are of burning fire. It is they who are meant by grass. Why are they grass? It is because they grow in the world as does grass: one day it is cut short, but then it again grows as previously.

78. וְע"ד כְּתִיב מַצְמִיחַ חָצִיר לַבְּהֵמָה, הה"ד יוֹדֵעַ צַדִּיק נֶפֶשׁ בְּהֶמְתּוֹ, וְתָנֵינָן, אֶלֶף טוּרִין סַלְקִין לָהּ בְּכָל יוֹמָא וְיוֹמָא. וְכָל טוּרָא וְטוּרָא שִׁתִּין רִבּוֹא הֲוֵי, וְהִיא אָכְלָה.

78. And this is why the verse says: "He causes the grass to spring up for the cattle." THIS IS THE SECRET OF MALCHUT IN THE ASPECT OF YUD HEI VAV HEI, FULLY SPELLED WITH THE LETTER HEI'S, THAT HAS THE SAME NUMERICAL VALUE, 52, AS THE WORD *BEHEMAH* (ENG. 'CATTLE'), as it is written: "A Righteous man (YESOD) regards the life of his beast (MALCHUT)" (Mishlei 12:10). And we have learned that a thousand mountains rise up TO MALCHUT each day and each one of the mountains is sixty times ten thousands OF ANGELS WHO ARE CALLED 'GRASS', AS MENTIONED ABOVE, and MALCHUT devours them.

79. וְעֵשֶׂב לַעֲבוֹדַת הָאָדָם, אֵלֵין אִינּוּן נִשְׁמָתְהוֹן דְּצַדִּיקַיָּיא, דְּהַהוּא אָדָם דְּרָכִיב וְשָׁלִיט עַל בְּהֵמָה דָּא אָכִיל, וְאָעִיל לוֹן בְּגַוֵויהּ, וּבִזְכוּתְהוֹן אִתְּזָן כָּל עָלְמָא מֵהַהוּא אָדָם, דִּכְתִּיב בֵּיהּ, וְעַל דְּמוּת הַכִּסֵּא דְּמוּת כְּמַרְאֵה אָדָם וְגוֹ'. וְע"ד כְּתִיב הָאָדָם, הַהוּא דְּאִשְׁתְּמוֹדַע, בְּגִין לְהוֹצִיא לֶחֶם מִן הָאָרֶץ, לְאַפָּקָא מְזוֹנָא לְעָלְמָא מִן הָאָרֶץ קַדִּישָׁא.

79. "and plants for the service of (lit. 'the') man" (Tehilim 104:14). These are the souls of the righteous, for that man, NAMELY ZEIR ANPIN, who is riding on and controlling the beast, NAMELY MALCHUT, devours them and takes them into himself. THAT IS TO SAY, THE SOULS OF THE RIGHTEOUS RISE UP AND ARE INCORPORATED INTO ZEIR ANPIN IN THE SECRET OF MAYIN NUKVIN (lit. 'FEMALE WATERS'), IN ORDER TO UNITE ZEIR ANPIN AND MALCHUT. And it is to their credit that the whole world is fed from that man, WHO IS ZEIR ANPIN, FOR THEY CAUSE HIS UNION WITH MALCHUT, AND THE FOOD IS BESTOWED UPON MALCHUT, AND MALCHUT DISTRIBUTES IT TO THE WHOLE WORLD, as is written: "and upon the likeness of the throne was a likeness as the appearance of a man above upon it..." (Yechezkel 1:26). That is why it says "for the service of the man," WITH THE DEFINITE ARTICLE – THAT IS, THAT SPECIFIC MAN, NAMELY ZEIR ANPIN. And this is in order to "bring forth food out of the

earth" (Tehilim 104:14), NAMELY to bring forth provisions for the world from the holy earth, WHICH IS MALCHUT.

‏80. וְיֵין, דָּא חַמְרָא עַתִּיקָא דְּנָגִיד מִלְעֵילָא. יְשַׂמַּח לְבַב אֱנוֹשׁ, אֱנוֹשׁ: דָּא רָזָא דְּהַהוּא נַעַר, דְּסָלִיק לְסִיבוּ, וְאִתְהַדָּר כְּמִלְּקַדְמִין. וְעַ"ד כְּתִיב, אֱנוֹשׁ כֶּחָצִיר יָמָיו.

80. "and wine" is old wine drawn from above, NAMELY THE ILLUMINATION OF CHOCHMAH, WHICH IS DRAWN FROM BINAH. "makes glad the heart of man (Heb. *enosh*)." Enosh here refers to the secret of that youth who attained old age, and later returns TO BE A YOUTH as formerly. THIS IS METATRON, PRINCE OF THE WORLD, WHO SAYS: "I HAVE BEEN YOUNG, AND NOW AM OLD" (TEHILIM 37:25), WHICH IS IN THE SECRET OF "RAN AND RETURNED" (YECHEZKEL 1:14). WHEN HE "RAN" TO RECEIVE CHOCHMAH, HE IS OLD, AND WHEN HE IS IN THE SECRET OF "RETURNED," HE IS YOUNG. Scripture therefore says ABOUT HIM: "As for man (Heb. *enosh*), his days are like grass" (Tehilim 103:15), FOR HE IS LIKE GRASS WHICH IS CUT AND GROWS AGAIN. WHEN HE RETURNS TO YOUTH, HIS FIRST THREE UPPER SFIROT ARE CUT, BUT LATER HE AGAIN REACHES OLD AGE, NAMELY GROWS AGAIN, AND SO ON AND SO FORTH.

‏81. לְהַצְהִיל פָּנִים, אִלֵּין אִינּוּן פָּנִים: דְּאִקְרוּן אַנְפֵּי רַבְרְבֵי, וְאַנְפֵּי זוּטְרֵי. מִשָּׁמֶן: מִנְּגִידוּ דְּעָלְמָא דְּאָתֵי, מְשַׁח וּרְבוּ קַדִּישָׁא עִלָּאָה. וְלֶחֶם לְבַב אֱנוֹשׁ יִסְעָד, הַהוּא לֶחֶם דְּאָזִילוּ שְׁחָקִים, וְטַחֲנָן מַנָּא לְמֵיכְלָא דְּצַדִּיקַיָּיא סָתָמָא, וּמִתַּמָּן אִתְנְגִיד לְכַמָּה חַיָּילִין, דְּאִקְרוּן לְבַב אֱנוֹשׁ. וְכֹלָּא אָתָא מִנְּגִידוּ עִלָּאָה.

81. "to brighten his face" (Tehilim 104:15): these are the faces that are called 'large countenances' and 'small countenances'. THE COMPLETED FIRST THREE SFIROT OF MALE AND FEMALE ARE THE LARGE COUNTENANCES, AND THE FIRST THREE SFIROT OF THE SIX ENDS OF MALE AND FEMALE ARE THE SMALL COUNTENANCES. "(lit. 'from') oil" (Ibid.), means from the flowing of the World to Come, NAMELY OF BINAH, WHENCE oil derives, as well as supernal, holy greatness. "and bread which sustains the heart of man" (Ibid.), that is that bread upon which the skies,

WHICH ARE THE SECRET OF NETZACH AND HOD, bestow and mill the manna for the food of the righteous in general, WHICH IS THE SECRET OF YESOD AND MALCHUT, WHO ARE CALLED 'RIGHTEOUS' AND 'RIGHTEOUSNESS', AND WHO ACCEPT THE MAYIN NUKVIN THAT NETZACH AND HOD GRIND FOR THEM. FROM THERE it is drawn out to a number of hosts who are called "the heart of man." And everything comes from the supernal flow, FROM BINAH.

82. יִשְׂבְּעוּ עֲצֵי יְיָ', אִלֵּין אִינּוּן אִילָנִין עִלָּאִין פְּנִימָאִין. אַרְזֵי לְבָנוֹן אֲשֶׁר נָטָע, דְּהָא אִתְעֲקָרוּ וְנָטַע לוֹן קוּדְשָׁא בְּרִיךְ הוּא. מַאי בֵּין עֲצֵי יְיָ', לְאַרְזֵי לְבָנוֹן. עֲצֵי יְיָ', אִלֵּין עֵץ הַחַיִּים, וְעֵץ הַדַּעַת וְטוֹב וָרָע. אַרְזֵי לְבָנוֹן, אִלֵּין חַמְשִׁין תַּרְעִין, דְּאִקְרוּן חֲמֵשׁ מֵאוֹת שָׁנָה.

82. "The trees of Hashem have their fill" (Ibid. 16): these are the inernal supernal trees, NAMELY ZEIR ANPIN AND MALCHUT. "The cedars of Lebanon which He has planted" (Ibid.): They are ZEIR ANPIN AND MALCHUT, who are uprooted FROM THEIR PLACE. The Holy One, blessed be He, WHO IS THE EMANATOR, planted them IN PLACE OF BINAH. What is the connection between the trees of Hashem and the cedars of Lebanon? THE TREES OF HASHEM refer to the Tree of Life, WHICH IS ZEIR ANPIN, and the Tree of the Knowledge of Good and Evil, WHICH IS MALCHUT. The cedars of Lebanon are the fifty gates OF BINAH which He planted IN MALE AND FEMALE, which are called 'five hundred years', FOR THEY ARE THE SECRET OF BINAH, CHESED, GVURAH, TIFERET, NETZACH AND HOD, MALE AND FEMALE RISE UP TO AND COAT. IN TERMS OF ZEIR ANPIN, WHOSE SFIROT ARE IN TENS, THEY ARE FIFTY, WHILE IN TERMS OF BINAH, WHOSE SFIROT ARE COUNTED IN HUNDREDS, THEY ARE FIVE HUNDRED.

83. אֲשֶׁר נָטָע. אֲשֶׁר שָׁם צִפֳּרִים יְקַנֵּנוּ, בְּטוּלֵיהוֹן, מְקַנְּנָן נִשְׁמָתְהוֹן דְּצַדִּיקַיָּיא, וְכָל חַיָּילִין קַדִּישִׁין אִתְזָנוּ מִתַּמָּן. חֲסִידָה, בְּרַתֵּיהּ דְּאַבְרָהָם אָבִינוּ, דְּאִקְרֵי חָסִיד, וְעָבֵד חֶסֶד עִם כָּל בְּנֵי עָלְמָא, בְּג"כ אִקְרֵי חֲסִידָה. בְּרוֹשִׁים בֵּיתָהּ. בֵּין דְּרוֹעֵי עָלְמָא יִתְבָּא

ע"כ רעיא מהימנא

83. "which He has planted, where the birds make their nests" (Tehilim 104:16-17). In the shadow OF ZEIR ANPIN AND MALCHUT the souls of the righteous make their nests, and all the holy hosts are fed from there. The stork (Heb. *chasidah*) IS MALCHUT, that is the daughter of the Patriarch Abraham, who is called 'pious' (Heb. *chasid*), and who performed deeds of kindness (Heb. *Chesed*) for all people. This is why MALCHUT is called 'a stork'. "The cypress trees are her house" (Ibid. 17): this means that she is situated between the arms of the world, WHICH ARE CHESED AND GVURAH OF ZEIR ANPIN. THESE BECOME FOR HER CHOCHMAH AND BINAH, WHICH ARE HEADS (HEB. *RASHIM*), WHICH IS WHY HE SAYS, "THE CYPRESS TREES (HEB. *BEROSHIM*) ARE HER HOUSE" THAT IS TO SAY: HER HOUSE IS AT THE HEADS (HEB. *BERASHIM*).

End of Ra'aya Meheimna (the Faithful Shepherd)

13. "For the wind passes over it, and it is not"

A Synopsis
Rabbi Aba, Rabbi Yosi and Rabbi Chiya discuss the title verse, and we learn that "the wind" is the concealed and holy spirit that is hidden from everyone; this is the secret of Enoch who became Metatron.

The Relevance of this Passage
Here we are renewed in spirit and body. The life force grows strong within us and we are rejuvenated and made young again by the regenerative Light of *Binah*.

Those who have difficulty bearing children are hereby protected from the evil angel called Anger. They become unrecognizable to this negative entity, in the act of reading this passage. The angel called Anger is disoriented, causing him to pass over us and this world, forevermore, as he wanders into oblivion. Those who are barren are made fertile, indeed becoming fruitful child bearers.

Anger, the basis of illness, is banished from our being. Our bones, sinews, and flesh are healed and rejuvenated.

We are enveloped in a field of energy that protects us from the negativity and destructive forces in our environment. We attract Righteous souls into our lives, instead of negative people who constantly loot us of Light.

84. רִבִּי אַבָּא ור' יוֹסֵי, קָמוּ לְמִלְעֵי בְּאוֹרַיְיתָא בְּפַלְגוּת לֵילְיָא, עַד דַּהֲווֹ יַתְבֵי וְלָעָאן בְּאוֹרַיְיתָא. א"ר יוֹסֵי, הָא דא"ר חִיָּיא אֱנוֹשׁ כֶּחָצִיר יָמָיו שַׁפִּיר קָאָמַר. אֲבָל בְּמַאי אוֹקִימְנָא סוֹפֵיהּ דִּקְרָא, כִּי רוּחַ עָבְרָה בּוֹ וְאֵינֶנּוּ וְלֹא יַכִּירֶנּוּ עוֹד מְקוֹמוֹ. א"ל הָכִי הוּא וַדַּאי, אֱנוֹשׁ כֶּחָצִיר יָמָיו כְּמָה דְּאָמַר, כְּצִיץ הַשָּׂדֶה הַהוּא שָׂדֶה דְּאִשְׁתְּמוֹדַע. כֵּן יָצִיץ דְּאִתְחַדָּשׁ וְאִתְהַדָּר כְּמִלְּקַדְמִין.

84. Rabbi Aba and Rabbi Yosi rose at midnight to engage in Torah. They were still sitting and engaging in Torah, when Rabbi Yosi said: Rabbi Chiya's comment on THE VERSE "As for man, his days are like grass" (Tehilim 103:15) is fine, but what is taught about the end of the verse: "For

the wind passes over it, and it is not; and its place knows it no more" (Ibid. 16). He replied, it is certainly as follows: "As for man, his days are as grass" is as explained BY RABBI CHIYA. "like a flower of the field" (Ibid. 15) – this is the known field, NAMELY MALCHUT. "so he blooms" means that he is renewed and returns as formerly.

85. כִּי רוּחַ עָבְרָה בּוֹ וְאֵינֶנּוּ, דָּא הוּא רוּחָא עִלָּאָה טְמִירָא קַדִּישָׁא גְּנִיזָא מִכֹּלָּא, דְּכָלִיל לֵיהּ בְּגַוֵּיהּ. וּכְדֵין וְאֵינֶנּוּ. וְדָא הוּא רָזָא דַּחֲנוֹךְ, דִּכְתִיב בֵּיהּ וְאֵינֶנּוּ כִּי לָקַח אוֹתוֹ אֱלֹהִים, דָּא אֱלֹהִים עִלָּאָה. רוּחַ עִלָּאָה, רוּחַ גְּנִיזָא טְמִירָא. וְלָא יַכִּירֶנּוּ עוֹד מְקוֹמוֹ. דְּהָא אִתְכְּלִיל רוּחָא זְעֵירָא, בְּרוּחָא עִלָּאָה. מַה כְּתִיב בַּתְרֵיהּ, וְחֶסֶד יְיָ׳ מֵעוֹלָם וְעַד עוֹלָם וְעָאל לֵיהּ כַּהֲנָא רַבָּא לְגוֹ קֹדֶשׁ קָדָשִׁים. וְנָטִיל לֵיהּ, וְאוֹלִיד לֵיהּ כְּמִלְּקַדְמִין, וְאִתְחַדָּשׁ כְּנֶשֶׁר עוּלְמִין. וְאִתְהַדָּר אִיהוּ נַעַר.

85. "For the wind (spirit) passes over it and it is not." This is a heavenly concealed and holy spirit, which is hidden from all, NAMELY THE SPIRIT OF BINAH, which engulfs METATRON, who then "is not." And this is the secret of Enoch, about whom Scripture says: "and he was not, for Elohim took him" (Beresheet 5:24). The reference here is to the higher Elohim, NAMELY BINAH, who is an upper spirit, hidden and concealed. "and its place knows it no more": This is the small spirit OF METATRON that is engulfed by the upper spirit OF BINAH. And what is written further on? "But the steadfast love (Heb. Chesed) of Hashem is from everlasting to everlasting" (Tehilim 103:17). That means that the High Priest, WHO IS CHESED, introduces him into the Holy of Holies and takes him and has him born as before, he renews his youth like an eagle and becomes a youth again.

A Synopsis
Moses tells Rabbi Shimon that this explanation is incomplete because it doesn't say what "passes over it" means. Rabbi Shimon says this refers to Anger, and that the verse is to be applied to one who dies childless. Such a person must achieve a change of place, a change of name and a change of action. Because his countenance is so changed, the evil angel whose name is Anger will pass him over because he will not be recognizable. Rabbi Shimon advises anyone who lives in a city where he is unable to keep the commandments and where he is not studying the Torah successfully to move to a place where he can replant himself

among good people, sages of the Torah. Lastly we are reminded that the most important thing is not talking about the Torah but performing its precepts.

רעיא מהימנא

86. וּבְחִבּוּרָא קַדְמָאָה אָמַר רַעְיָא מְהֵימָנָא בּוּצִינָא קַדִּישָׁא, שַׁפִּיר אָמְרוּ ר' אַבָּא וְר' חִיָּיא וְר' יוֹסֵי, אֲבָל כִּי רוּחַ עָבְרָה בּוֹ וְאֵינֶנּוּ, הָכָא צָרִיךְ לְמִפְתַּח מִלִּין, מַאי עָבְרָה בּוֹ. דָּא עֶבְרָה וָזַעַם וְצָרָה. חַד מֵאִינּוּן מַלְאֲכִין רָעִים.

Ra'aya Meheimna (the Faithful Shepherd)

86. The Faithful Shepherd said: Holy Luminary, the commentary ABOVE of Rabbi Aba, Rabbi Chiya, and Rabbi Yosi ON THE VERSE "AS FOR MAN, HIS DAYS ARE AS GRASS" is very nice, but what about "The wind passes over it and it is not"? Here matters have to be developed. What is the meaning of "passes (Heb. *avrahi*) over it"? AND HE REPLIES, it refers to "anger (Heb. *evrah*), wrath and indignation" (Tehilim 78:49), where it is one of these evil angels, THE ONE CALLED 'ANGER', AND THIS IS THE MEANING OF THE VERSE "THE WIND PASSES OVER IT," WHICH SHOULD THEREFORE BE RENDERED 'THE SPIRIT OF ANGER IS IN HIM'. AND THE VERSE IS TO BE APPLIED TO ONE WHO DIES CHILDLESS, WHO INCARNATES.

87. דְּבְגִין דְּלָא יִשְׁתְּמוֹדְעוּ בֵּיהּ אִינּוּן מָארֵי חוֹבִין, צָרִיךְ לְמֶעְבַּד לֵיהּ שִׁנּוּי מָקוֹם, וְשִׁנּוּי הַשֵּׁם, וְשִׁנּוּי מַעֲשֶׂה. כְּגַוְונָא דְּאַבְרָהָם, דְּאִתְּמַר בֵּיהּ לֶךְ לְךָ מֵאַרְצְךָ וּמִמּוֹלַדְתְּךָ, הֲרֵי שִׁנּוּי מָקוֹם. וְלֹא יִקָּרֵא עוֹד שִׁמְךָ אַבְרָם, וְהָיָה שִׁמְךָ אַבְרָהָם, הֲרֵי שִׁנּוּי הַשֵּׁם. שִׁנּוּי מַעֲשֶׂה דְּאִשְׁתַּנֵּי מֵעוֹבָדִין בִּישִׁין דְּעָבַד בְּקַדְמֵיתָא, לְעוֹבָדִין טָבִין. אִיהוּ מִתְלָא. לְרוּחַ דְּהַהוּא דְּמִית בְּלָא בְּנִין. כְּגַוְונָא דָּא עָבֵד קוּדְשָׁא בְּרִיךְ הוּא לְאָדָם, כָּךְ תָּרִיךְ לֵיהּ מֵהַהוּא עָלְמָא, וְאַיְיתֵי לֵיהּ לְהַאי עָלְמָא. וְהָא אִתְּמַר לְעֵיל.

87. In order that the monitors of sins should not recognize him, WHO DIED CHILDLESS, it is necessary to perform for him a change of place, a change

of name, and a change of action. This is how it was with Abraham, as Scripture tells us. "Get you out of your country, and from your kindred" (Beresheet 12:1) is the change of place. "Neither shall your name anymore be called Abram, but your name shall be Abraham" (Beresheet 17:5) is the change of name. And there is also the change of action, for he changed from doing bad deeds, as he had at first, to doing good deeds. A similar thing happens to the spirit of the man who dies childless, for likewise, the Holy One, blessed be He does to the man in banishing him from that world BECAUSE HE DIED CHILDLESS, and brings him to this world IN A REINCARNATION INTO THE SON THAT IS BORN OUT OF HIS WIFE'S LEVIRATE MARRIAGE, and this has already been discussed above.

88. מְשַׁנֶּה פָּנָיו וַתְּשַׁלְּחֵהוּ, ובג״ד כִּי רוּחַ עָבְרָה בּוֹ, חַד מֵאִינוּן מַלְאָכִין רָעִים, כַּד חֲזֵי לֵיהּ מְשׁוּנֶּה, בְּזִמְנָא דְּאִעְרַע עִמֵּיהּ, שָׁאִלִין לֵיהּ שְׁאַר מַשְׁחִיתִין עָלֵיהּ, דָּא הוּא מָארֵי חוֹבָךְ. אִיהוּ עָנֵי לוֹן וְאָמַר, וְאֵינֶנּוּ.

88. "You change his countenance and send him away" (Iyov 14:20). BECAUSE HE CHANGES HIS COUNTENANCE WHEN HE BANISHES HIM FROM THE SUPERNAL WORLD, IT IS SAID: "The wind passes (Heb. *avrah*) over it," WHICH ALLUDES TO one of the evil angels WHOSE NAME IS anger (Heb. *evrah*) AS MENTIONED ABOVE. And when he sees that he has altered, when he meets him, and the other demons of destruction ask about him: "Is this your sinner?" he answers them and says: he "is not," FOR HE DOES NOT RECOGNIZE HIM, AND THIS IS THE SECRET OF THE VERSE "YOU CHANGE HIS COUNTENANCE."

89. כַּד אִתְתְּרַךְ מֵאַתְרֵיהּ, וְאִתְנְטַע בְּאֲתָר אַחֲרָא, אִתְּמַר בֵּיהּ וְלֹא יַכִּירֶנּוּ עוֹד מְקוֹמוֹ. בְּגִין דְּעָפָר אַחֵר יִקַּח וְטָח אֶת הַבַּיִת. וְדָא אִיהוּ רָזָא, וְנָתַץ אֶת הַבַּיִת אֶת אֲבָנָיו וְאֶת עֵצָיו, אִינּוּן גַּרְמִין וְגִידִין וּבִשְׂרָא דַּהֲוָה חָזַר עֲפָרָא. מַה כְּתִיב בֵּיהּ וְנָחַשׁ עָפָר לַחְמוֹ. בְּגִין דַּהֲוָה מְנוּגָּע. וּלְבָתַר וְעָפָר אַחֵר יִקַּח וְטָח אֶת הַבַּיִת, וּבְנֵי לֵיהּ גַּרְמִין וְגִידִין. וְאִתְחַדָּשׁ, כְּבַיִת יָשָׁנָה דְּעַבְדִין לֵיהּ חֲדָשָׁה. וַדַּאי אִיהוּ דְּאִתְחַדָּשׁ.

89. NOW HE EXPLAINS THE SECRET OF THE VERSE "AND SEND HIM AWAY." When he is banished from his place and implanted elsewhere,

NAMELY AFTER HE HAS ALREADY ENTERED A BODY IN THIS WORLD, it is said about him: "And its place knows it no more," for "and he shall take other mortar, and shall plaster the house" (Vayikra 14:42), NAMELY HE TOOK ANOTHER BODY OF DIFFERENT DUST, FOR BODY IS TERMED HOUSE. And this is the secret of, "And he shall break down the house, the stones of it, and its timber" (Ibid. 45), namely those bones, sinews, and flesh that he had PREVIOUSLY returned to the dust. What is written about it? "and dust shall be the serpent's food" (Yeshayah 65:25), FOR THE DUST THAT IS MADE UP OF THE DECEASED'S BODY IS OF THE ASPECT OF THE SERPENT, since it was afflicted BY IT. AND, THEREFORE, later "he shall take other mortar, and shall plaster the house," namely build for himself bones and sinews and be renewed, as an old house that is made new, which certainly is renovated.

90. וּמַאי דְּאָמַר וְלֹא יַכִּירֶנּוּ עוֹד מְקוֹמוֹ. עַל רוּחַ, דְּאִתְכְּלִיל רוּחָא זְעֵירָא, בְּרוּחָא עִלָּאָה. הַאי אִיהוּ מְתַלָא, לְאִילָן דְּלָא עָבֵיד אֵיבִין, נַטְלִין עַנְפִין דִּילֵיהּ, וּמַרְכִּיבִין לֵיהּ בְּעַנְפָּא דְּאִילָנָא אַחֲרָא עִלָּאָה, דְּעָבֵיד פֵּירִין, וְאִתְכְּלִיל דָּא בְּדָא, וְעָבֵיד פֵּירִין. בְּהַהוּא זִמְנָא אִתְּמַר בֵּיהּ, וְלֹא יַכִּירֶנּוּ עוֹד מְקוֹמוֹ.

90. What about "and its place knows it no more"? THIS IS SAID about HIS spirit, for his small spirit is engulfed in the Supernal Spirit. This is a parable to a tree that is not producing fruit. Its branches are taken and grafted onto a better quality tree that produces fruits, combining both into each other. NOW BOTH produce fruits. About this moment it is said, "and its place knows it no more" SINCE EVEN THE WHEREABOUT OF THE DEFECTIVE SPIRIT IS NOT RECOGNIZABLE.

91. אוֹף הָכִי בַּר נָשׁ דְּיָתִיב בְּקַרְתָּא דְּיַתְבִין בָּהּ אֲנָשִׁין בִּישִׁין, וְלָא יָכִיל לְקַיְּימָא פִּקּוּדִין דְּאוֹרַיְיתָא, וְלָא אַצְלַח בְּאוֹרַיְיתָא, עָבֵיד שִׁנּוּי מָקוֹם, וְאִתְעֲקַר מִתַּמָּן, וְאִשְׁתְּרָשׁ בַּאֲתָר דְּדַיְירִין בֵּיהּ גּוּבְרִין טָבִין, מָארֵי תוֹרָה, מָארֵי פִּקּוּדִין, דְּאוֹרַיְיתָא אִקְרֵי עֵץ. הה"ד, עֵץ חַיִּים הִיא לַמַּחֲזִיקִים בָּהּ. וּבַר נָשׁ הוּא עֵץ, דִּכְתִיב כִּי הָאָדָם עֵץ הַשָּׂדֶה. וּפִקּוּדִין דְּבָהּ, דַּמְיָין לְאֵיבָא, וּמַה כְּתִיב בֵּיהּ, רַק עֵץ אֲשֶׁר תֵּדַע כִּי לֹא עֵץ

מַאֲכָל הוּא אוֹתוֹ תַשְׁחִית וְכָרַתָּ. אוֹתוֹ תַשְׁחִית מֵעָלְמָא דֵּין, וְכָרַתָּ
מֵעָלְמָא דְאָתֵי. וּבְגִין דָא צָרִיךְ לְאַעְקְרָא מֵהַהוּא אֲתָר, וְיִתְנְטַע בַּאֲתָר
אַחֲרָא בֵּין צַדִּיקַיָּיא.

91. And so it is with a man who lives in a city where bad people dwell, and he is unable to keep the commandments of the Torah and is not successful with the Torah. He should change his place of residence and move from there, and settle somewhere with good people, sages of the Torah, who keep the precepts. This is because the Torah is called 'a tree', as it is written: "She is a tree of life to those who lay hold on her" (Mishlei 3:18). Man, too, is a tree, as it is written: "For man is a tree of the field" (Devarim 20:19), and the precepts of the Torah are like fruits. And what is written about it? "Only the trees which you know are not trees for food, you shall destroy and cut them down" (Devarim 20:20) That is to say, you shall destroy it from this world and cut it down from the World to Come. This is why he has to uproot HIMSELF from the place WHERE THERE ARE EVIL PEOPLE AND WHERE HE CAN NOT SUCCEED WITH THE TORAH AND THE PRECEPTS, and implant HIMSELF elsewhere, among righteous people, WHERE HE CAN SUCCEED WITH THE TORAH AND THE PRECEPTS.

92. מַה בַּר נָשׁ בְּלָא בְּנִין, אִתְקְרֵי עָקָר, וְאִתְּתֵיה עֲקָרָה. אוֹף הָכִי
אוֹרַיְיתָא בְּלָא פִּקוּדִין, אִתְקְרִיאַת עֲקָרָה, וּבְגִין דָא אוּקְמוּהָ, לָא
הַמִּדְרָשׁ הוּא הָעִיקָר אֶלָּא הַמַּעֲשֶׂה. אָתוּ חַבְרַיָּיא וְאִשְׁתְּטָחוּ קַמֵיה,
וְאָמְרוּ וַדַּאי כְּעַן אוֹלִיפְנָא חִדוּשָׁא, אֵיךְ אִתְכְּלִיל רוּחַ בְּרוּחַ, כְּמַאן
דְּחָזֵי מִלָה בְּעֵינָא וְאִתְבְּרִיר לֵיה. בְּקַדְמֵיתָא הֲוָה לָן קַבָּלָה, וּכְעַן בְּרִירוּ
דְּמִלָה.

92. As the childless man is called 'barren' and his wife 'barren', so also is the Torah when unaccompanied by precepts is considered barren. On this we have learned: 'Not the expounding of the Torah is the chief thing but the doing of it'. The companions came and prostrated themselves in front of him and said: We have certainly learned something new here – how one spirit can be incorporated in another, it is clear as one who sees something with his own eyes and it becomes clear to him. Before we had only a tradition ABOUT THESE MATTERS, but now they have been clearly explained.

14. Why is the righteous punished for the iniquity of his generation

A Synopsis

Rabbi Shimon says that the Other Side is content to control the Righteous because then it can afford to ignore the rest of the world. For this assertion we have the evidence of the story of Job, where the Satan's attention to Job enabled God to save the rest of his generation. If the righteous one is strong, and he bears his afflictions and overcomes the accuser, he can save the whole generation – indeed, this is how Moses became the Faithful Shepherd over Yisrael, and why he will control them in the World to Come. Moses asks Rabbi Shimon why one righteous person is affected while another is not, and the response is that God does only what is necessary: if one will suffice, He only afflicts one, but if the sins are widespread He will also afflict other righteous men. Moses talks about three types of righteous people, all of whom become a chariot for Adam and the patriarchs, and who acquire from them the strength to suffer and to protect the whole generation.

The Relevance of this Passage

A wealth of wisdom and healing forces pour out of this passage. We're told that Job and Moses were men of titanic spiritual strength who wrestled with and triumphed over Satan, preoccupying him in order to free their entire generation. Our reading resurrects their fortitude and might, luring Satan back into battle with these great spiritual warriors. The Zohar and the spirit of Job and Moses now bear the brunt of Satan's attack so that our entire generation is freed from the clutches of the Other Side. These great warriors secure their final victory over this age-old foe.

Moreover, in our meditation, we contribute to the demise of Satan, repaying the righteous who have fought so valiantly for us throughout the ages. The righteous souls among us here and now stop suffering on our behalf.

The final bell is rung and this cosmic conflict between life and death, good and evil, is ended at last, with Life and Goodness victorious.

The Zohar then expounds upon the spiritual function of the body's organs, including the liver, the spleen, the kidneys, the heart, and the lungs, and their relationship to sin, disease, and the patriarchs.

Disease originates in the liver, caused by the sins we commit, knowingly or unknowingly, this life or past.

When disease strikes, there must be bloodletting from the right arm in order to heal the entire body. Thus, here we invoke Abraham, who signifies the right arm, to spiritually bloodlet. Our bodies are now purified of disease as we cleanse our sins and the iniquities of our generation. Esau represents the liver and Ishmael represents the spleen. When reading this passage, negative blockages in our liver and spleen are purged while the destructive influences of Esau and Ishmael are dissolved into nothingness.

Our meditation invokes the greatness of Isaac, who represents the Left Arm side of judgment. Blood is herewith let from the *left arm,* generating healing and purifying all transgressions.

Our reading summons forth the power of Jacob, who represents the body. Blood is herewith let from both the right and left arms, arousing well-being and cleansing all trespasses.

Our heartfelt contemplation of these verses evoke Adam and all the patriarchs when disease, sickness, and sin are rampant in civilization. Blood is herewith let from the veins in the head, thus healing and regenerating the body's organs, bones, and blood, and cleansing this world of all of its sins, wiping out airborne diseases and all plagues.

Finally, the healing process and the regeneration of our cells and souls are sealed by Moses, whose name is rearranged into the *Mem Hei Shin*, one of the *72 Names of God,* that ignites health, well-being and restoration.

All these miraculous effects are achieved on account of the holiness of this book and the saintliness of the Patriarchs. Our acknowledgment and appreciation of this truth magnifies the healing effect exponentially with every set of eyes that fall upon these verses.

93. וְתוּ אִתְּמַר בְּחִבּוּרָא קַדְמָאָה, דְּהָא נִיחָא לֵיהּ לְסִטְרָא אַחֲרָא לְשַׁלְטָאָה עַל זַכָּאָה, יַתִּיר מִכֹּלָּא, וְלָא חַיִּישׁ כְּדֵין לְכָל עָלְמָא. אַדְהָכִי, הָא טוּלָא אִזְדְּמַן לְגַבַּיְיהוּ, וא"ל מִנָּלָן. מֵאִיוֹב. דְּחֲזָא קוּדְשָׁא בְּרִיךְ הוּא דְּדָרָא הֲווֹ מְחוּיָבִין כְּלָיָיה, וְאָתָא שָׂטָן לְקַטְרְגָא, אָמַר לֵיהּ קוּדְשָׁא בְּרִיךְ הוּא, הֲשַׂמְתָּ לִבְּךָ אֶל עַבְדִּי אִיּוֹב כִּי אֵין כָּמוֹהוּ בְּכָל הָאָרֶץ, לְאִשְׁתְּזָבָא בֵּיהּ דָּרָא. וְאִיהוּ מְתַלָּא לְרַעְיָא דְּאָתָא זְאֵב לְמִטְרַף עָאנֵיהּ, וּלְמֵיבַד לֵיהּ. מַה עָבֵד הַהוּא רַעְיָא דְּהֲוָה חַכִּימָא, יָהִיב לֵיהּ אִמְרָא

תַּקִּיפָא וּשְׁמֵנָה וְרַבְרְבָא מִכֻּלְּהוּ, הַהוּא דַּהֲווֹ מִתְנַהֲגִין אֲבַתְרֵיהּ כֻּלְּהוּ. וּבְרְעוּ לְשַׁלְטָאָה עַל הַהוּא אִמְּרָא טָבָא, שָׁבַק לְכֻלְּהוּ. מַה עֲבַד הַהוּא רַעְיָא, בְּשַׁעֲתָא דַּהֲוָה זְאֵב אִשְׁתָּדַּל בְּהַהוּא אִמְּרָא, בָּרַח רַעְיָא עִם עָאנָא וְשַׁוֵּי לוֹן בְּאַתְרֵיהוֹן. וּלְבָתַר תָּב לְאִמְּרָא, וְשֵׁזִיב לֵיהּ מִזְּאֵב.

93. Moreover, we learned in the first part of the compilation that the Other Side prefers to have control over the righteous more than anything else, because it does not then care for the rest of the world. While they were still discussing this, a shade came upon them, and asked: How do we know THAT IT PREFERS TO HAVE CONTROL OVER THE RIGHTEOUS TO CONTROL OVER THE WHOLE WORLD? We know this from Job. For the Holy One, blessed be He, saw that generation was deserving of annihilation, and when the Satan came to denounce, the Holy One, blessed be He, THEN said to him: "Have you considered My servant, Job, that there is none like him on earth" (Iyov 1:8), in order to save through him the whole generation. The matter can be likened to a shepherd when a wolf comes to devour his flock and destroy them. Being wise, what does the shepherd do? He gives the wolf a lamb that is stronger, fatter, and larger than the others, the leader of the flock, and the wolf, out of his desire to have control over the lamb, forgets about the rest of the flock. What does the shepherd do next? While the wolf is preoccupied with that lamb, he flees with the flock and brings them to safety. Later, he returns to the lamb and saves it from the wolf.

94. הָכִי עָבֵיד קוּדְשָׁא בְּרִיךְ הוּא עִם דָּרָא, יָהִיב קוּדְשָׁא בְּרִיךְ הוּא לַצַּדִּיק, בִּרְשׁוּ מְקַטְרְגָא, לְשֵׁזָבָא לְדָרָא בְּגִינֵיהּ. וְאִם הוּא תַּקִּיף כְּיַעֲקֹב, אִתְּמַר בֵּיהּ וַיֵּאָבֵק אִישׁ עִמּוֹ, כְּ"שׁ וכ"שׁ דְּנָצַח לֵיהּ, עַד דְּאָמַר שַׁלְּחֵנִי. אָמַר טוּלָא טוּלָא, הָכִי הוּא, זַכָּאָה חוּלָקֵיהּ דְּהַהוּא צַדִּיק, דְּאִיהוּ תַּקִּיף לְמִסְבַּל יִסּוּרִין, כְּ"שׁ מַאן דְּנָצַח בְּהוֹן לִמְקַטְרְגָא דִּילֵיהּ. דְּאִיהוּ שׁוּלְטָנוּתֵיהּ עַל כָּל דָּרָא, וְאִתְחֲשִׁיב לֵיהּ כְּאִילּוּ הוּא שֵׁזִיב לוֹן, וְקוּדְשָׁא בְּרִיךְ הוּא עֲבֵיד לֵיהּ רַעְיָא עֲלַיְיהוּ בְּאַתְרֵיהּ, וּבְגִין דָּא זָכָה רַעְיָא מְהֵימְנָא. לְמֶהֱוֵי רוֹעֶה עַל יִשְׂרָאֵל, וְלֹא עוֹד אֶלָּא דְּהָכִי אַשְׁלִיט לֵיהּ עֲלַיְיהוּ בְּעָלְמָא דְּאָתֵי. בְּגִין דְּשֵׁזִיב לוֹן דְּלָא אִתְאֲבִידוּ מִתַּמָּן, דְּאַנְהִיג לוֹן בְּאוֹרַיְיתָא וּבְעוֹבָדִין טָבִין.

94. This is exactly what the Holy One, blessed be He, did with the generation. He offered the righteous man for indictment in order to save the generation on his account. And if, like Jacob, THE RIGHTEOUS MAN is strong, the verse says of him: "and there a man wrestled with him" (Beresheet 32:25). This is even more the case when he overcomes THE ACCUSER until he says: "Let me go" (Ibid. 27). He said: O Shade, O Shade, that is just how it is. Happy is the portion of that righteous man who is strong in suffering afflictions, and how much more so the one who, by means of his AFFLICTIONS, manages to overcome his accuser who has SPREAD his control over the whole generation, and it is accounted to him as though he had saved them, and the Holy One, blessed be He, appoints him as shepherd over them in the place OF THE ACCUSER. This was how the Faithful Shepherd came to be the shepherd over Yisrael, and not only that, but he will control them in the World to Come. And this was because he saved them that they should not be lost TO THE WORLD TO COME, for he guided them in the Torah and good deeds.

95. אַדְהָכִי הָא רַעְיָא מְהֵימָנָא, אָמַר לוֹן, וַאֲמַאי לָקֵי דְּרוֹעָא יְמִינָא. דְּאוֹרַח כָּל מָארֵי אַסְוָותָא דַּאֲקִיזִין בְּקַדְמֵיתָא דְּרוֹעָא יְמִינָא, וְהָא דְּרוֹעָא שְׂמָאלָא אִיהוּ קָרִיב לְלִבָּא, אֲמַאי לָא אֲקִיזִין לֵיה. אָמַר לֵיה בְּגִין דְּקוּדְשָׁא בְּרִיךְ הוּא לָא בָּעֵי לְאַלְקָאָה יַתִּיר, דְּהָא בְּהַאי סַגֵּי, וְאִי אִתְיְקַר מַרְעָא עַל שַׁיְיפִין דְּגוּפָא, אָקִיז דְּרוֹעָא שְׂמָאלָא.

95. While they were yet talking, the Faithful Shepherd himself came and said to them: And why was the right arm afflicted? Because the way of all healers is to let blood first from the right arm? Since the left arm is the one that is nearer the heart, why is blood not let from it? OR, TO PUT THE QUESTION IN OTHER WORDS: WHY IS IT THAT ONE RIGHTEOUS MAN IS AFFLICTED AND ANOTHER IS NOT? He answered: Because the Holy One, blessed be He, does not want overly to strike, and one RIGHTEOUS MAN suffices. But if the illness is serious and spreads throughout the parts of the body, blood is let from the left arm ALSO, NAMELY OTHER RIGHTEOUS MEN ARE ALSO AFFLICTED.

96. א"ל, אִי לָא הֲווֹ תַּרְוַוְיְיהוּ בְּחַד זִמְנָא, יָאוּת אֲבָל אִית צַדִּיק הָכָא, וְאִית צַדִּיק הָכָא, לְדָא אִית מַרְעִין וּמַכְתְּשִׁין, וּלְדָא אִית טִיבוּ. אֲמַאי.

אִי אִתְיְיקַר בֵּיהּ מַרְעָא יַקִּיז לְתַרְוַויְיהוּ, דְּאִינּוּן תְּרֵין דְּרוֹעִין, לְמֵיהַב
אַסְוָותָא לְכָל שַׁיְיפִין, וְאִי לָא אִתְיְיקַר בֵּיהּ מַרְעָא עַל כָּל שַׁיְיפִין,
אֲמַאי אָקִיז לִדְרוֹעָא יְמִינָא, יַתִּיר מִשְּׂמָאלָא. אֶלָּא א״ל אֵימָא אַנְתְּ.

96. He said to him: If the two of them were not (afflicted) at the same time, that would be fine, but what about the case of the two righteous men, one of whom suffers from diseases and troubles, while the other is treated with kindness? Why is it that if the disease, NAMELY THE SINS OF THE GENERATION, spread, blood is let from both of them, NAMELY BOTH THE RIGHTEOUS PERSONS, who are the two arms, so that healing may be given to all parts OF THE BODY, NAMELY THE WHOLE OF THE GENERATION. And in the case where the illness does not become more serious, and does not spread throughout the parts of the body, why is more blood let from the right arm than from the left? WHY IS ONE MADE TO SUFFER AND NOT THE OTHER? He said to him: Why don't you give the answer?

97. אָמַר לֵיהּ, וַדַּאי גּוּפָא וּתְרֵין דְּרוֹעִין, אִינּוּן לָקֳבֵל אֲבָהָן. רֵישָׁא,
לָקֳבֵל אָדָם קַדְמָאָה. דְּרוֹעָא יְמִינָא, לָקֳבֵל אַבְרָהָם. דְּרוֹעָא שְׂמָאלָא,
לָקֳבֵל יִצְחָק. גּוּפָא, לָקֳבֵל יַעֲקֹב. וּמִלְגוֹ לְגוּפָא, כָּבֵד לִימִינָא. טְחוֹל
לִשְׂמָאלָא. עֵשָׂו וְיִשְׁמָעֵאל. לִבָּא יַעֲקֹב, בְּאֶמְצָעִיתָא. כַּנְפֵי רֵיאָה
וְכוּלְיָין, לָקֳבֵל אַבְרָהָם וְיִצְחָק. רֵיאָה מַיִם. דְּאִינּוּן שׁוֹאֲבִין כָּל מִינֵי
מַשְׁקִין. כּוּלְיָין אֶשָּׁא, דְּבָשִׁיל זֶרַע דְּנָחִית מִמּוֹחָא.

97. He said to him: Certainly the body and the two arms stand for the three patriarchs and the head for Adam. The right arm corresponds to Abraham and the left arm to Isaac, while the body represents Jacob. Within the body, the liver is on the right, the spleen to the left, THESE BEING THE TWO KLIPOT OF Esau and Ishmael. The heart is Jacob, between them. The lungs and kidneys represent Abraham and Isaac, the lung being water, HINTING AT CHESED, for THE LUNG draws in all sorts of potions, while the kidneys are fire, which cooks the seed that descends from the brain.

98. וּבְגִין דְּאַבְרָהָם אִיהוּ מַיִם, שַׁוֵּוי זַרְעֵיהּ בְּגָלוּתָא דֶּאֱדוֹם וּבְגִין דָּא
כָּבֵד לִימִינָא דְּאַבְרָהָם, וּמָרָה, דְּכָבֵד חֶרֶב דִּילֵיהּ, אִיהִי מָרָה, אִתְּמַר

בָּהּ וְאַחֲרִיתָהּ מָרָה כַלַּעֲנָה. וְאִי חוֹבִין מִתְרַבִּין בִּבְנוֹי דְּאַבְרָהָם דְּאִינּוּן
בְּגָלוּתָא דֶּאֱדוֹם, אִתְיְקַר בֵּיהּ מְרַע עָלַיְיהוּ מִסִּטְרָא דְּכָבֵד, דִּרְוֹעָא
יְמִינָא צָרִיךְ לְאַלְקָאָה לְאָקָזָא דָּמֵיהּ מִנֵּיהּ, דְּמַאן דְּנַטְלִין מִנֵּיהּ
מָמוֹנֵיהּ, כְּאִילּוּ שָׁפִיכוּ דָּמֵיהּ, וְאִשְׁתְּאַר עָנִי, דְּעָנִי חָשׁוּב כַּמֵּת.

98. And since Abraham is water, NAMELY CHESED, IF, THEREFORE, HIS OFFSPRING IMPAIRS CHESED, He places his offspring in the exile of Edom, WHICH IS THE WASTE MATTER OF GVURAH FROM THE LEFT, AND THERE THEY RECEIVE THEIR PUNISHMENT: BECAUSE OF THEM BEING THE OPPOSITE OF THEIR NATURE. This is why the liver and the gall that is in the liver are to the right of Abraham, NAMELY TO THE RIGHT OF THE BODY, his sword, NAMELY MALCHUT OF THE KLIPAH OF ESAU being the gall (Heb. *marah*). About this it is said: "But her end is bitter (Heb. *marah*) as wormwood" (Mishlei 5:4). And if the sins increase among the children of Abraham, NAMELY AMONG THOSE WHO EXTEND FROM THE SIDE OF CHESED, who are placed in the exile of Edom, and the disease spreads over them from the side of the liver, they have to be smitten and blood has to be let from the right arm, NAMELY FROM THOSE RIGHTEOUS WHO COME FROM THE SIDE OF CHESED, AND NOT FROM THOSE OF THE SIDE OF GVURAH, FOR THE BLEMISH IS IN THOSE OF THE SIDE OF CHESED. And 'whoever has his money taken is as though his blood was spilled', for he remains poor, and a poor man is considered as dead.

99. וְאִי חוֹבִין מִתְרַבִּין מִסִּטְרָא דִּבְנֵי יִצְחָק, דְּאִינּוּן בְּגָלוּתָא בֵּין
יִשְׁמָעֵאל, בֵּי מַרְעֵיהּ יִתְיְקַר מִסִּטְרָא דִּטְחוֹל לִשְׂמָאלָא, וְצָרִיךְ לְאָקָזָא
דִּרְוֹעָא שְׂמָאלָא, וְלָא יַתִּיר.

99. But if the sins increase among the children of Isaac, NAMELY THOSE WHO DESCEND FROM HIM IMPAIR THE QUALITY OF GVURAH, WHICH IS THE SECRET OF ISAAC, they are THEN put into exile among Ishmael, WHO ARE THE KLIPAH OF THE RIGHT, WHICH IS THE OPPOSITE OF THE NATURE OF THE CHILDREN OF ISAAC, IN ORDER TO INCREASE THEIR PUNISHMENT. The disease spreads from the side of the spleen, which is to the left OF THE BODY AND CONTROLS THE CHILDREN OF ISAAC WHO IMPAIRED THE NATURE OF THE LEFT. And blood has THEREFORE to be let from the left arm, THAT IS TO SAY, FROM THOSE RIGHTEOUS WHO COME

FROM THE SIDE OF GVURAH, and not from any others. THIS IS BECAUSE
THE IMPAIRED HERE ARE THOSE WHO COME NOT FROM ABRAHAM, THE
RIGHT ARM, BUT FROM ISAAC, THE LEFT ARM.

100. וְאִי חוֹבִין מִתְרַבִּין בִּבְנֵי יַעֲקֹב, דְּאִינוּן אֲחִידָן לִתְרֵין סִטְרִין,
דְּאִינוּן מְפוּזְרִים בִּבְנֵי עֵשָׂו וְיִשְׁמָעֵאל, הָא מַרְעָא אִתְּיקַר עַל גּוּפָא,
וּבָעֵי לְאָקֳזָא ב׳ דְּרוֹעִין. וְאִי כֻּלְּהוּ תְּלַת בְּמַרְעִין כַּחֲדָא. הָא מַרְעָא
סָלִיק לְרֵישָׁא, וּבָעֵי לְאָקֳזָא וְרִידִין דְּרֵישָׁא, וְאִלֵּין תְּלַת אִתְעֲבֵידוּ
מֶרְכָּבָה לְאָדָם קַדְמָאָה וְלַאֲבָהָן, וּבְהוֹן אִתְּתְקְפוּ לְמִסְבַּל יִיסוּרִין,
לְאַגָּנָא עַל דָּרָא לְאַרְבַּע סִטְרֵי דְעָלְמָא.

100. And if sins increase amongst the children of Jacob, NAMELY THOSE
WHO DESCEND FROM HIM IMPAIR HIS NATURE, WHICH INCLUDES BOTH
SIDES, CHESED AND GVURAH, who are scattered IN EXILE among the
children of Esau and Ishmael, NAMELY IN THE KLIPOT OF THE RIGHT AND
OF THE LEFT, then the disease spreads over the body, WHICH IS THE
ASPECT OF JACOB, and blood has to be let from both arms. But if all three
of them, NAMELY THOSE DRAWN FROM JACOB, FROM ISAAC, AND FROM
ABRAHAM, are diseased together, NAMELY ALL OF THEM HAVE BLEMISHED
THEIR OWN ROOTS, the disease then rises to the head, and blood has to be
let from the veins that are in the head. And these three TYPES OF
RIGHTEOUS PEOPLE, THOSE DESCENDED FROM ABRAHAM, ISAAC AND
JACOB, became a Chariot for Adam and the patriarchs, and acquire from
them strength to suffer torments and protect the generation throughout the
four winds of the world.

101. וַוי לֵיהּ לְדָרָא, דְּגַרְמִין דְּיִלְקוּן אֲבָהָן וְאָדָם קַדְמָאָה, וְאִלֵּין
צַדִּיקַיָּא דְּבֵינַיְיהוּ, דְּלֵית אַפְרְשׁוּתָא בֵּין אִלֵּין צַדִּיקַיָּא, לַאֲבָהָן וְאָדָם,
דְּאִינוּן נִשְׁמָתִין דִּלְהוֹן, וְדוֹחֲקָא וְצַעֲרָא וִיגוֹנָא דִּלְהוֹן, מָטֵי לַאֲבָהָן
וְאָדָם. כְּגַוְונָא דְיַמָּא, אִלֵּין נַחֲלִין דְּנַפְקִין מִתַּמָּן, אִי חוֹזְרִין עֲכוּרִין
וּמְלוּכְלְכִין לְיַמָּא, הָא יַמָּא נָטִיל מִן עֲכִירוּ וְלִכְלוּכָא דִּלְהוֹן. וּבְחֵילָא
דְיַמָּא דְּאִיהִי תַּקִּיפָא, לָא סָבִילַת לִכְלוּכָא דִּלְהוֹן, וּזְרִיקַת לֵיהּ לְבַר,
וְאִשְׁתְּאָרוּ נַחֲלִין צְלִילִין וְדַכְיָין מֵהַהוּא לִכְלוּךְ.

101. Woe to that generation that causes the patriarchs and Adam to be struck, and the righteous men amongst them as well, for there is no difference between the righteous OF A GENERATION and the patriarchs and Adam. This is because those RIGHTEOUS are their souls DRAWN FROM THEM and their distress, pain, and anguish reach to the patriarchs and Adam. It is like the sea when a number of rivers flow out of it and return to it, impure and dirty, and the sea receives their impurity and dirt. And because of the sea's strength, for it is strong, it does not hold their dirt, but throws it out, and the rivers remain clear and pure, without that dirt.

102. כְּגַוְונָא דְּאִימָא, דִּדְכִיאַת לְכְלוּכִין דִּבְנָהָא זְעִירִין, הָכִי אֲבָהָן מְדַכְּאִין חוֹבִין וְלִכְלוּכִין דִּבְנַיְיהוּ דְיִשְׂרָאֵל, כַּד אִשְׁתְּכָחוּ בְּהוֹן צַדִּיקַיָּיא בְּעוֹבָדֵיהוֹן, תַּקִּיפִין לְמִסְבַּל יִסּוּרִין עַל דָּרֵיהוֹן. בְּהַהוּא זִמְנָא לֵית אַפְרָשָׁא בְּהוֹן. אָתוּ כֻּלְּהוּ וּבָרִיכוּ לֵיהּ, וְאָמְרוּ לֵיהּ סִינַ"י סִינַ"י, דְּקוּדְשָׁא בְּרִיךְ הוּא וּשְׁכִינְתֵּיהּ מַלִּיל בְּפוּמוֹי, מַאן יָכִיל לְקָיְימָא קַמֵּיהּ בְּכֹלָּא. זַכָּאָה חוּלָקָנָא, דִּזְכֵינָא לְחַדְּשָׁא חִבּוּרָא קַדְמָאָה דָא בָּךְ, לְאַנְהָרָא שְׁכִינְתָּא בְּגָלוּתָא.

102. It can also be likened to a mother who cleans the dirt from her small children. In such a manner the patriarchs cleanse the sins and the dirt from their children, Yisrael, when there are among them people of righteous deeds who are strong enough to suffer torments for the sake of the generation. At that time there is no difference between them AND THE PATRIARCHS, FOR THEY CLEANSE THE SINS OF THE GENERATION LIKE THE PATRIARCHS. They all came and blessed him, THE FAITHFUL SHEPHERD, and said to him: Sinai, Sinai, through whose mouth the Holy One, blessed be He, and His Shechinah speak, who is able to confront him in any MATTER? Happy is our portion that we have merited to revise and refresh new matters in this first part of the compilation through you, to illuminate the Shechinah in exile.

103. אָמַר לוֹן, רַבָּנָן דְּכָל דָּרָא הֲוִיתוּ בְּזִמְנַיְיהוֹן, כ"ש בּוּצִינָא קַדִּישָׁא, דְּנָהִיר חָכְמָתֵיהּ בְּכָל דָּרִין דַּהֲווֹ אֲבַתְרֵיהּ, אַל תִּתְּנוּ דֶמִי לְקוּדְשָׁא בְּרִיךְ הוּא בְּאוֹרַיְיתָא, עַד יְעָרֶה עָלֵינוּ רוּחַ קַדְשָׁא דְּהָא לָא אִית רְשׁוּ לְאִשְׁתַּמְּשָׁא בִּמְטַטְרוֹ"ן שַׂר הַפָּנִים אֶלָּא לָךְ, דְּאַתְוָון דִּילֵיהּ רְמִיזִין בִּשְׁמָךְ.

103. He said to them: Sages of all generations during whose time you, have been OR WILL BE, and how much more so the Holy Luminary, THAT IS, RABBI SHIMON, whose wisdom will shine in all the generations that come after him: do not give the Holy One, blessed be He, quiet in the Torah until the Holy Spirit is poured out on us. (THERE APPEARS TO BE AN OMISSION IN THE TEXT HERE). For none but you may use Metatron the great prince, since your name is intimated in the initials of his, FOR THE INITIAL LETTERS OF THE WORDS METATRON THE GREAT PRINCE ARE *MEM SHIN HEI*, WHICH SPELL MOSES.

15. The patient's pulse in the exile of Edom

A Synopsis
The metaphor of Yisrael as a sick patient is used to show how the children of Yisrael are faring while in exile. With the description of the ten blowings of the Shofar we see how the length of the exile and the coming redemption are indicated.

The Relevance of this Passage
Each of us, individually, is Israel. The exile spoken of in the Zohar is our exile; namely, the lack of health, fulfillment, and joy in our life. Healing, redemption, and freedom begin here with the mighty and majestic blast of the Shofar. The duress that has marked our exile is hereby decimated, for the Redemption is now upon us. Our hearts are healed, spiritually and physically. Cardiovascular ailments are remedied. The pulse of man begins to beat strong and slowly like that of an Olympic champion.

The Zohar comments on an oath that concerns the Creator waging war with *Amalek*. *Amalek* signifies the doubts and uncertainties that blemish our hearts and disconnect us from the truth of the Light. *Amalek* is now slain by the laser-like beams of Light that shoot out from the Shofar. The song of freedom is heard around the world through the musical arrangement of the *Yud Hei Vav Hei*, the *72 Names,* and the pulsing, rhythmic reverberations of the ram's horn.

The Zohar reveals that the righteous suffer sickness to atone for the sins of their generation. Here, the Zohar plays the role of the Righteous, absorbing illnesses on our behalf. The Light of Healing is ignited by this phenomenon and we use it heal our ailments. But Light is limitless, endless. Therefore, a deadly surprise is in store for the Other Side: We now utilize this Light of Healing and shine it back upon the virtuous souls among us who suffer for our generation. And this is all blessedly ironic that we, the common reader, can now heal the Righteous, using *their own* Light and sharing it back with them in deep gratitude for their unconditional support.

In addition, this dramatic display of energy destroys all disease and sickness that exists in the collective body and soul of man. All sins – from the time of Adam until now – are atoned by the Light of these divinely inspired verses. They nullify the power of the Other Side.

104. וּכְעַן צָרִיךְ אַסְיָא, לְמִנְדַּע בְּכַמָּה דַּרְגִּין אִסְתַּלַּק דְּפִיקוּ דְּהַהוּא חוֹלֶה בְּגָלוּתָא דֶאֱדוֹם, דְּאִתְּמַר עָלֵיהּ שֶׁחוֹלַת אַהֲבָה אָנִי. דְּהָא כַּמָּה אַסְיָין אִתְכַּנְשׁוּ עָלֵיהּ, לְמִנְדַּע קֵץ דְּמַרְעָא דִּילֵיהּ, בְּאִלֵּין דְּפִיקִין, וְלָא הֲוָה חַד מִנַּיְיהוּ דְּאִשְׁתְּמוֹדַע בְּהוֹן, דִּדְפִיקוּ דְּהַהוּא חוֹלֶה, לָא כָּל אַסְיָא בָּקִי לְאִשְׁתְּמוֹדַע בֵּיהּ, דְּאִית דְּפִיקִין דְּקִשְׁרַ"ק קַשַׁ"ק קַרַ"ק, דְּאָמַר נָבִיא עָלַיְיהוּ כְּמוֹ הָרָה תַּקְרִיב לָלֶדֶת תָּחִיל תִּזְעַק בַּחֲבָלֶיהָ.

104. And now there is need of a doctor to know by how many degrees the pulse of the patient, YISRAEL, has increased in the exile of Edom, for it is said about him "that I am sick with love" (Shir Hashirim 5:8). For a number of doctors gathered over him to consider the pulse rate in order to know when his illness would come to an end, but not one of them could understand them, for no doctor is competent to read the pulse beats of this particular patient, for there are beats of T'kiah–Sh'varim–T'ruah–T'kiah, T'kiah Sh'varim T'kiah, T'kiah T'ruah T'kiah, as the prophet said about them: "Like as a woman with child, whose time of delivery draws near, is in pain and cries out in her pangs" (Yeshayah 26:17).

105. וְכֻלְּהוּ עֲשֶׂר שׁוֹפָרוֹת, כְּלִילָן בִּתְלַת, דְּאִינּוּן סִימָן קַשַׁ"ר, דְּאִיהוּ תְּקִיעָה שְׁבָרִים תְּרוּעָה. וּתְקִיעָה אַחְזֵי אֲרִיכוּ דְּגָלוּתָא, שְׁבָרִים קָרִיבוּ דְּגָלוּתָא. תְּרוּעָה בֵּיהּ יֵיתֵי פּוּרְקָנָא, דְּאַחְזֵי דּוֹחֲקָא בָּתַר דּוֹחֲקָא, וְלֵית רְוָוחָא בֵּין דָּא לְדָא, דְּוַדַּאי כֵּיוָן דִּשְׁאָר עַמִּין מְעַכְּבִין לוֹן לְיִשְׂרָאֵל בְּגָלוּתָא, דּוֹחֲקָא דִּלְהוֹן מְקָרֵב לוֹן פּוּרְקָנָא. אוּף הָכִי מְהִירוּ דִּדְפִיקוּ דָּא בָּתַר דָּא, בֵּיהּ נָפִיק נַפְשָׁא דב"ן, בָּתַר דְּלֵית רֵיוַח בֵּין דָּא לְדָא.

105. And all the ten Shofar blows, WHICH ARE T'KIAH SH'VARIM-T'RUAH T'KIAH, T'KIAH SH'VARIM T'KIAH, T'KIAH T'RUAH T'KIAH, are included in three T'kiah Sh'varim T'ruah. FOR THEY INCLUDE ONLY THESE THREE DIFFERENT VARIATIONS IN BLOWS. T'kiah stands for the length of the exile. Sh'varim TEACHES ABOUT the proximity of the exile, and T'ruah about the coming redemption, FOR THE SOUNDS OF THE T'RUAH teach about duress after duress with no respite between them. And clearly, since the other nations make Yisrael's exile more difficult, it is the duress that they suffer that brings the redemption closer. And so it is, too, in our case of

the patient's pulse: AS the beats come faster, one after the other, with no space between them, the man's soul leaves him.

106. קֶשֶׁר"ק קֶשׁ"ק קֶר"ק, אִיהוּ דְּשַׁוֵּי קֶשׁ"ר, תְּקִיעָה שְׁבָרִים תְּרוּעָה. דְּאִתְעַבָּר בֵּיהּ שֶׁקֶר מִן עָלְמָא, דְּבֵיהּ אוֹמָאָה, מִלְחָמָה לַיְיָ' בַּעֲמָלֵק. יִתְּעַר בְּעָלְמָא. שִׁיר פָּשׁוּט, וְכָפוּל, וּמְשׁוּלָשׁ, וּמְרוּבָּע. דְּאִיהוּ סָלִיק אַתְוָון דִּילֵיהּ, י', י"ה, יה"ו, יהו"ה, ע"ב. בְּהַהוּא זִמְנָא, וּבְכֵן צַדִּיקִים יִרְאוּ וְיִשְׂמָחוּ וִישָׁרִים יַעֲלוֹזוּ וַחֲסִידִים בְּרִנָּה יָגִילוּ. ו' תּוֹסֶפֶת, אֶלֶף שְׁתִיתָאָה. קוֹדֶם דִּילֵיהּ עֶ"ב, חָרַב בֵּי מַקְדְּשָׁא, וּלְבָתַר דִּילֵיהּ, עַד תַּשְׁלוּם רָעָב, יִהְיֶה עֶרֶב. הה"ד עֶרֶב וִידַעְתֶּם כִּי יְיָ' הוֹצִיא אֶתְכֶם וְגוֹ'. כִּי עַבְדְּךָ עָרַב אֶת הַנַּעַר וְגוֹ'.

ע"כ רעיא מהימנא

106. T'kiah Sh'varim-T'ruah T'kiah, T'kiah Sh'varim T'kiah, T'kiah T'ruah T'kiah, WHICH ARE THE SECRET OF THE EXILE'S BEATS, AS ABOVE, make Kof Shin Resh (Heb. *kesher* - Eng. 'tie'), the initials of T'kiah Sh'varim T'ruah, by which falsehood (Heb. *sheker*, Shin Kof Resh) is removed from the world. Concerning this was the oath: "Hashem will have war with Amalek" (Shemot 17:16), FOR THE REDEMPTION WILL COME BY THE BEATS HINTED AT T'KIAH SH'VARIM-T'RUAH T'KIAH, T'KIAH SH'VARIM T'KIAH, T'KIAH T'RUAH T'KIAH. AND THEN a simple, double, triple and quadruple song will arise in the world, where the letters OF THE YUD HEI VAV HEI will multiply AND JOIN TOGETHER. FIRST WILL COME Yud, THEN Yud-Hei, THEN Yud-Hei-Vav AND THEN Yud Hei Vav Hei, WHERE YUD IS THE SIMPLE SONG, YUD-HEI DOUBLE, YUD-HEI-VAV IS TRIPLE AND YUD HEI VAV HEI IS QUADRUPLE, AND THEIR NUMERICAL VALUE TOGETHER TOTALS 72. AT THE TIME OF THE REDEMPTION THIS NAME OF 72 WILL AWAKEN. At that time THE PRAYER WILL BE ANSWERED: 'And therefore (Heb. *uv'chen*) the righteous shall see and be glad, the upright exult and the pious rejoice in song'. THE NUMERICAL VALUE OF '*UV'CHEN*', IS 78, NAMELY 72 WITH THE ADDITION OF SIX, WHICH IS THE VALUE OF VAV. This added Vav REFERS TO the sixth millennium. The Second Temple was destroyed 172 years before THE FIFTH MILLENNIUM. THAT IS, THE DESTRUCTION OF THE TEMPLE CAME 172

YEARS EARLY, BEFORE THE FIFTH MILLENIUM. And after it IT WILL ARRIVE AFTER THE FIFTH MILLENNIUM at the end of Resh Ayin Bet (272) YEARS OF THE SIXTH MILLENNIUM. FOR THE EXILE IS SUPPOSED TO LAST 1,200 YEARS, TO FULFIL: "YOU, O SOLOMON, MAY HAVE THE THOUSAND, AND THOSE THAT KEEP ITS FRUIT TWO HUNDRED" (SHIR HASIRIM 8:12). WITH THE REVELATION OF THE NAME OF 72, IT AMOUNTS TO 1,272. THE 172 YEARS PRCEDING THE FIFTH MILLENIUM AMY OR MAY NOT BE PART OF THIS COUNT. HENCE IT SAYS "UNTIL THE COMPLETION OF 272...(HEB. *RA'AV* RESH, AYIN, BET)." As in the verse "At evening (Heb. *erev*, Ayin Resh Bet) and you shall know that Hashem has brought you out, etc." (Shemot 16:6), and, "For your servant became surety (Heb. *arav*, Ayin Resh Bet) for the lad" (Beresheet 44:32). You should know that all those dates mentioned in the Zohar refer to an awakening from above, which will occur at these times for redemption. But certainly it depends on the people actions and repentance.

End of Ra'aya Meheimna (the Faithful Shepherd)

A Synopsis
Rabbi Aba recalls a time when he asked Rabbi Shimon why the righteous are punished for the sins of a generation, and was told that this atones for the sins of the world. He had said that all mortals are parts of the one body. Rabbi Aba learned that usually one righteous man is sufficient to atone for everyone, but if there is too much sin then more righteous men are stricken. When the righteous die then everything is healed and atoned for.

107. עַד דַּהֲווֹ יַתְבֵי, חָמוּ חַד טוּלָא דְּקַיְימָא עֲלַיְיהוּ, אַזְלָא וְאַתְיָא, אַזְלָא וְאַתְיָא, בְּגוֹ בֵּיתָא. תַּוְוהוּ. א"ר אַבָּא, יוֹסֵי בְּנִי, אֵימָא לָךְ מַה דַּהֲוָה לִי עִם בּוּצִינָא קַדִּישָׁא. יוֹמָא חַד הֲוֵינָן אַזְלִינָן בְּבִקְעָתָא דְּאוֹנוֹ, וַהֲוֵינָן לָעָאן בְּאוֹרַיְיתָא, כָּל הַהוּא יוֹמָא, וּמִגוֹ תּוּקְפָּא דְּשִׁמְשָׁא אוֹתְבָנִין גַּבֵּי חַד טִינָרָא, בְּגוֹ נוּקְבָּא חֲדָא.

107. While they were still sitting, they saw a shade standing over them that came and went, hither and thither in the house. They were astonished. Rabbi Aba said: Yosi, my son, I shall tell you what happened to me when I was

with the Holy Luminary, THAT IS RABBI SHIMON, one day when we were walking in the Valley of Ono, and engaging in Torah the whole of that day, and because of the intensity of the sun's heat, we sat in a niche under a rock.

108. אֲמֵינָא לֵיהּ, מַאי הַאי, דְּבְכָל שַׁעֲתָא דְּחַיָּיבִין אַסְגִּיאוּ בְּעָלְמָא, וְדִינָא שַׁרְיָיא בְּעָלְמָא, זַכָּאִין דִּבְהוֹן לָקָאן עֲלַיְיהוּ. דְּהָכִי תְּנֵינָן, בְּחוֹבָא דְּדָרָא, קַדִּישַׁיָּיא וְצַדִּיקַיָּיא יִתְפְּסוּן. אֲמַאי, אִי בְּגִין דְּאִינּוּן דְּלָא מוֹכִיחִין לְעָלְמָא עַל עוֹבָדַיְיהוּ, כַּמָּה אִינּוּן דְּמוֹכִיחִין, וְלָא מְקַבְּלֵי מִנַּיְיהוּ, וְצַדִּיקַיָּיא אִתְכַּפְיָין קַמַּיְיהוּ. וְאִי בְּגִין דְּלָא הֲוֵי מַאן דְּיָגִין עַל עָלְמָא, לָא יֵהוֹן מֵתִין, וְלָא יִתָּפְסוּן בְּחוֹבַיְיהוּ, דְּהָא חֶדְוָוה אִיהוּ לְצַדִּיקַיָּיא בְּאֲבוּדָא דִּלְהוֹן.

108. I asked him to explain to me why it is that, whenever the number of wicked in the world increases and Judgment rests on the world, the righteous among them are smitten on their account. For this is what we have learned about the sins of the generations: that it is the holy and righteous who are punished. Why should this be so. Could it be because they do not admonish the world about their deeds? For there are many who do admonish, but they will not accept it from them so they are subdued before those WHO DO NOT LISTEN TO THEM. THUS WHY THEY ARE PUNISHED FOR THE SIN OF THE GENERATION. Or maybe it is because the world has no protector AND THE RIGHTEOUS ARE PUNISHED AND DIE SO THAT THE WICKED CAN EXIST ON THEIR MERIT? AND I ASKED HIM: Were the righteous not to die and not to be punished for the sins OF THE WICKED, BUT IF THE WICKED WERE TO PERISH, then would not this be a cause of joy for the righteous that the wicked should perish? AS WRITTEN "BUT WHEN THE WICKED PERISH, THERE IS JUBILATION" (MISHLEI 11:10).

109. א"ל, בְּחוֹבָה דְּדָרָא וַדַּאי מִתָּפְסִין צַדִּיקַיָּיא, וְהָא אוֹקִימְנָא הָנֵי מִילֵי. אֲבָל בְּשַׁעֲתָא דְּיִתָּפְסוּן צַדִּיקַיָּיא בְּמַרְעִין, אוֹ בְּמַכְתְּשִׁין, בְּגִין לְכַפְּרָא עַל עָלְמָא הֲוֵי, כְּדֵין יִתְכַּפְּרוּן כָּל חוֹבֵי דָּרָא, מְנָלָן, מִכָּל שַׁיְיפֵי גּוּפָא, בְּשַׁעֲתָא דְּכָל שַׁיְיפִין בְּעָאקוּ, וּמְרַע סַגִּי שַׁרְיָיא עֲלַיְיהוּ, שַׁיְיפָא חֲדָא אִצְטְרִיךְ לְאַלְקָאָה, בְּגִין דְּיִתָּסוּן כֻּלְּהוּ, וּמְנוּ. דְּרוֹעָא. דְּרוֹעָא

אַלְקֵי וְאַפִּיקוּ מִינֵיה דָּמָא, כְּדֵין הָא אַסְוָותָא לְכָל שַׁיְיפֵי גּוּפָא.

109. He said to me: The righteous are certainly caught for the sins of the generation, and we have already discussed these matters. But when the righteous are caught with diseases and pestilence, it is in order to atone for the sins of the world, for then atonement is effected for the sins of the generation, SINCE THE SIDE OF HOLINESS IS THEREBY UPLIFTED AND THE OTHER SIDE SURRENDERS. How do we know about this? We learn it from all the parts of the body, for when all parts of the body are in trouble and a serious illness prevails in them, one limb has to suffer so that all of them should be healthy. And which IS THE LIMB THAT IS TO SUFFER? It is of course the arm, from which blood is let, and then all parts of the body regain health.

110. אוֹף הָכִי בְּנֵי עָלְמָא אִינוּן שַׁיְיפִין הָא עִם דָּא. בְּשַׁעֲתָא דְּבָעֵי קוּדְשָׁא בְּרִיךְ הוּא לְמֵיהַב אַסְוָותָא לְעָלְמָא, אַלְקֵי לְחַד צַדִּיקָא בֵּינַיְיהוּ, בְּמַרְעִין וּבְמַכְתָּשִׁין, וּבְגִינֵיה יָהִיב אַסְוָותָא לְכֹלָּא. מְנָלָן. דִּכְתִיב וְהוּא מְחוֹלָל מִפְּשָׁעֵינוּ מִדֻּכָּא מֵעֲוֹנוֹתֵינוּ וְגו'. וּבַחֲבוּרָתוֹ נִרְפָּא לָנוּ. וּבַחֲבוּרָתוֹ, אֲקִזוּתָא דְּדָמָא, כְּמַאן דְּאָקִיז דְּרוֹעָא, וּבְהַהוּא חַבּוּרָא נִרְפָּא לָנוּ, אַסְוָותָא הוּא לָנָא לְכָל שַׁיְיפִין דְּגוּפָא.

110. And so it is that all people are body parts together. When the Holy One, blessed be He, wishes to grant healing to the world, He inflicts diseases and pestilence on one righteous man from among them, and, for his sake, gives healing to everyone. Where do we learn this from? From the verse: "But he was wounded because of our transgressions...and by his injury we are healed" (Yeshayah 53:5). "and by his injury": this refers to the letting of blood, as one who lets blood from the arm, for in that injury "we are healed," that is to say, we, all the parts of the body, find healing.

111. וּלְעוֹלָם לָא אַלְקֵי צַדִּיקָא, אֶלָּא לְמֵיהַב אַסְוָותָא לְדָרָא, וּלְכַפְּרָא עֲלַיְיהוּ. דְּהָא נִיחָא לְסִטְרָא אַחֲרָא דְּדִינָא שַׁלְטָא עַל זַכָּאָה יַתִּיר מִכֹּלָּא, דְּלָא חָיֵישׁ כְּדֵין לְכָל עָלְמָא, וְלָא אַשְׁגַּח בְּהוּ, מֵחֶדְוָה דְּשַׁלִּיט עֲלֵיה. וְהַהוּא זַכָּאָה זָכֵי לְשׁוּלְטָנָא עִלָּאָה, בְּהַאי עָלְמָא, וּבְעָלְמָא

דְּאָתֵי. צַדִּיק וְטוֹב לוֹ, דְּלָא חָיֵישׁ קוּדְשָׁא בְּרִיךְ הוּא לְכַפְּרָא עַל עָלְמָא.

111. And He never smites the righteous man unless it is in order to grant healing to the generation and to make atonement for their sins, for the Other Side prefers MORE THAN ANYTHING ELSE that Judgment should have control over the righteous, for he does not then consider the rest of the world important and he doesn't watch over them because of his great joy that he has control OVER THE RIGHTEOUS. And the righteous person WHO SUFFERS BECAUSE OF THE GENERATION merits heavenly rule, in this world and in the World to Come. And WHERE THERE IS a righteous man with whom things are going well, the explanation is that the Holy One, blessed be He, is not concerned to make atonement for the world.

112. אֲמֵינָא לֵיהּ, אִלּוּ לָא הֲווֹ בְּחַד זִמְנָא, יָאוּת. אֲבָל אִית צַדִּיק הָכָא, וְאִית צַדִּיק הָכָא, לְדָא אִית מַרְעִין וּמַכְתְּשִׁין, וּלְדָא אִית כָּל טִיבוּ דְעָלְמָא. אָמַר לִי, בְּחַד מִנַּיְיהוּ אוֹ תְּרֵין סַגֵּי, דְּלָא בָּעָא קוּדְשָׁא בְּרִיךְ הוּא לְאַלְקָאָה כֹּלָּא, כְּמָה דְּלָא אִצְטְרִיךְ אֶלָּא דְּרוֹעָא חֲדָא, לְאַלְקָאָה וּלְאַקֶּזָאָה לְמֵיהַב אַסְוָותָא לְכָל שַׁיְיפִין. אוֹף הָכָא, בְּחַד צַדִּיקָא סַגֵּי.

112. I said to him: BUT IF THERE ARE TWO RIGHTEOUS MEN, WHERE ONE OF THEM IS RIGHTEOUS WHO SUFFERS BADLY FOR HIM, WHILE THE OTHER IS RIGHTEOUS WHO FLOURISHES? If they do not live at the same time, THEN WHAT YOU HAVE SAID makes sense THAT IS, THAT THE RIGHTEOUS MAN WHO FLOURISHES LIVES AT A TIME WHEN THE HOLY ONE, BLESSED BE HE, IS NOT CONCERNED TO MAKE ATONEMENT FOR THE WORLD, WHILE THE RIGHTEOUS MAN WHO SUFFERS LIVES AT A TIME WHEN THE HOLY ONE, BLESSED BE HE, IS CONCERNED TO MAKE ATONEMENT FOR THE WORLD. But what about the case where there are two righteous men, one here and one here, both living AT THE SAME TIME, and the one suffers from diseases and pestilences while the other enjoys all the good things of the world? He said to me: One, or possibly two, righteous men are sufficient FOR THE ATONEMENT OF THE GENERATION, for the Holy One, blessed be He, does not need to smite all of them, just as it is unnecessary to smite and draw blood from more than one arm in order to

grant health to all parts OF THE BODY. Similarly, here too, one righteous man suffices.

113. וְאִי אִתְּקַף בֵּיהּ מְרַע, עַל כָּל שַׁיְיפִין, כְּדֵין אִצְטְרִיךְ תְּרֵין דְּרוֹעִין לְאַקֱזָאָה. אוּף הָכִי, אִי אַסְגִּיאוּ חוֹבִין יַקִּירִין עַל עָלְמָא, כְּדֵין כָּל זַכָּאִין אַלְקוּן, לְמֵיהַב אַסְוָותָא עַל כָּל דָּרָא. אֲבָל בִּזְמַן דְּלָא אַסְגִּיאוּ כָּל כַּךְ, כְּדֵין חַד זַכָּאָה אַלְקֵי, וּשְׁאָר צַדִּיקַיָּא בִּשְׁלָם, דְּהָא לָא אִצְטְרִיךְ עָלְמָא דִּילְקוּן כֻּלְּהוּ. אִתְּסִיאוּ עַמָּא. אִתְּסִיאוּ צַדִּיקַיָּא. וּלְזִמְנִין דְּכָל יוֹמֵיהוֹן קַיְימִין בְּמַרְעִין, לְאַגָּנָא עַל דָּרָא. מִיתוּ, הָא אִתְּסֵי כֹּלָּא, וְאִתְכַּפַּר. לְזִמְנִין דְּחוֹבִין אִינּוּן יַקִּירִין יַתִּיר.

113. But if the illness strikes all parts of the body, it is then necessary to let blood from both of the arms. So also in our case. If the number of serious sins in the world increases, then all the righteous have to be smitten in order to grant healing to the whole generation. But when they are not so many, then only one righteous man is smitten, and the other righteous live in peace, for the world is not in such need that all of them need to be smitten. And if the people are healed, the righteous are also healed, but it sometimes happens that THE RIGHTEOUS are inflicted with diseases throughout their lives in order to protect the generation, at a time WHEN THE SINS ARE HEAVIER. When THE RIGHTEOUS die, then everything is healed, and atoned for.

16. All nations do not sway – just Yisrael

A Synopsis
Rabbi Aba recounts Rabbi Shimon's explanation of why the children of Yisrael sway when they read the Torah. He learned that the spirit of man is the candle of God, and that light flickers and moves, swaying to and fro.

The Relevance of this Passage
We are told that Israel sways back and forth when learning Torah, whereas idol worshipping nations are in constant repose, frozen still, with no flaming Light of Torah upon them. All of us are *idol worshipping nations*, to one degree or another. *Idolatry* does not pertain to manmade statues and icons before which we bow down. An idol is defined as any material possession or external situation that controls our emotions and behavior. Our negative tendencies lead us to become worshippers of wealth and disciples of decadence. We are adorers of images – the images and icons of our culture, and the self-image we feel we must project to others.

Should any of these determine or influence our degree of contentment and joy of life, then we have surrendered control and severed our connection to the Light of the Creator, our source and fountainhead for true fulfillment.

We remove the power and allure of the "idols" that control us by invoking the liberating Light of the Creator through the mystical insights of Rabbi Shimon bar Yochai.

This great sage, we are told, cried as he revealed these hidden mysteries. His tears fall again, like fiery sparks of divinity that kindle the candle of the Creator – our souls – so that we flicker and sway, to and fro, with delight, as the secrets of the Torah radiate to the four corners of the world.

114. קַמְנָא וְאָזַלְנָא. וְתוּקְפָּא דְשִׁמְשָׁא הֲוָה יַתִּיר, וְדָחִיק לָן בְּאוֹרְחָא. חֲמֵינָן אִילָנִין בְּמַדְבְּרָא, וּמַיְין תְּחוֹתַיְיהוּ. יָתִיבְנָא תְּחוֹת חַד טוּלָא דְאִילָנָא דְמַדְבְּרָא. שָׁאִילְנָא לֵיהּ, מַאי הַאי דְּכָל עַמִּין דְּעָלְמָא לָא עַבְדִין נְעֲנוּעָא, אֶלָּא יִשְׂרָאֵל בִּלְחוֹדַיְיהוּ, דְּכַד לָעָאן בְּאוֹרַיְיתָא, מִתְנַעְנְעָן הָכָא וְהָכָא, בְּלָא לְמוּדָא דְּבַר נָשׁ בְּעָלְמָא, וְלָא יַכְלִין לְמֵיקַם בְּקִיּוּמַיְיהוּ.

114. We got up and walked on. The intensity of the sun's heat was excessively STRONG and made it difficult for us to continue. Then we saw some trees in the wilderness with water under them. We sat down in the shade of one of the trees in the wilderness, and I asked him, RABBI SHIMON: Can you explain to me why it is that of all the nations of the world the only one that sways is Yisrael? For when they study Torah they sway back and forth? And this is not something that they learned from anyone else, but they just can not stand still.

115. אָמַר לִי, אַדְכַּרְתָּן מִלְּתָא עִלָּאָה, וּבְנֵי עָלְמָא לָא יַדְעִין, וְלָא מַשְׁגִּיחִין. יָתִיב שַׁעֲתָא וּבָכָה, אָמַר, וַוי לִבְנֵי נָשָׁא דְּאַזְלִין כִּבְעִירֵי חַקְלָא, בְּלָא סוּכְלְתָנוּ. בְּמִלָּה דָּא בִּלְחוֹדוֹי אִשְׁתְּמוֹדְעָן נִשְׁמָתְהוֹן קַדִּישִׁין דְּיִשְׂרָאֵל, בֵּין נִשְׁמָתְהוֹן דְּעַמִּין עעכו"ם. נִשְׁמָתְהוֹן דְּיִשְׂרָאֵל אִתְגְּזָרוּ, מִגּוֹ בּוּצִינָא קַדִּישָׁא דְּדָלִיק, דִּכְתִיב נֵר יְיָ' נִשְׁמַת אָדָם. וְהַאי נֵר בְּשַׁעֲתָא דְּאִתְדְּלִיק מִגּוֹ אוֹרַיְיתָא דִּלְעֵילָּא, לָא שָׁכִיךְ נְהוֹרָא עֲלֵיהּ אֲפִילוּ רִגְעָא. וְרָזָא דָּא, אֱלֹהִים אַל דֳּמִי לָךְ. כְּגַוְונָא דָא כְּתִיב, הַמַּזְכִּירִים אֶת יְיָ' אַל דֳּמִי לָכֶם, לָא שָׁכִיכוּ לְכוֹן. נְהוֹרָא דְּשַׁרְגָּא כֵּיוָן דְּאִתְאַחֲדָא גּוֹ פְּתִילָה, הַהוּא נְהוֹרָא לָא שָׁכִיךְ לְעָלְמִין, אֶלָּא מִתְנַעְנְעָא נְהוֹרָא לְכָאן וּלְכָאן, וְלָא מִשְׁתְּכִיךְ לְעָלְמִין.

115. He said to me: You have reminded me of a heavenly matter, yet people do not know and do not pay attention. He sat down for a while and cried. Then he said: Woe to people who go around like the beasts of the field, without understanding. In this matter alone are the holy souls of Yisrael distinguished from the souls of the other peoples, worshippers of stars and constellations. The souls of Yisrael are derived from the holy burning candle, WHICH IS MALCHUT, as it is written: "The spirit of man is the candle of Hashem" (Mishlei 20:27). And when this candle is kindled from the higher Torah, WHICH IS ZEIR ANPIN, its light is not still for even a moment, and this is the secret of the verse: "Elohim, keep not silent" (Tehilim 83:2), WHICH IS WRITTEN ABOUT MALCHUT. And something similar is written ABOUT THE SOULS: "you that make mention of Hashem, keep you not silent" (Yeshayah 62:6), NAMELY you have no respite. Once the light of the candle has taken hold of the wick, that light will never rest, rather, the fire light sways to and fro, and never stays still.

116. כְּגַוְונָא דָא, יִשְׂרָאֵל, דְּנִשְׁמָתַיְיהוּ מִגּוֹ הַהוּא נְהוֹרָא דְּשַׁרְגָּא, כֵּיוָן דְּאָמַר מִלָּה חֲדָא דְּאוֹרַיְיתָא, הָא נְהוֹרָא דָּלִיק, וְלָא יַכְלִין אִינּוּן לְאִשְׁתַּכְּכָא, וּמִתְנַעְנְעָן לְכָאן וּלְכָאן, וּלְכָל סִטְרִין. כִּנְהוֹרָא דְּשַׁרְגָּא, דְּהָא נֵר יְיָ׳ נִשְׁמַת אָדָם כְּתִיב.

116. This is how it is with Yisrael, too, for their souls are of the light of the same candle, WHICH IS MALCHUT. Once one has raised one Torah subject, the light begins to burn, and they are unable to obtain respite, but sway hither and thither and from side to side, just as the flame of the candle flickers, for it is written: "The spirit of man is the candle of Hashem."

117. וּכְתִיב, אָדָם אַתֶּם, אַתֶּם קְרוּיִין אָדָם, וְלָא אוּמִין עכו"ם. נִשְׁמָתִין דְּעַמִּין עכו"ם, מִדְעִיכוּ דְקַשׁ, בְּלָא נְהוֹרָא דְּשָׁרֵי עֲלַיְיהוּ. וע"ד מִשְׁתַּכְּכִין, וְלָא מִתְנַעְנְעָן, דְּהָא לֵית לוֹן אוֹרַיְיתָא, וְלָא דַּלְקִין בָּהּ, וְלָאו נְהוֹרָא שַׁרְיָיא בְּהוֹן, אִינּוּן קַיְימִין כְּעֵצִים בְּגוֹ נוּרָא דְּדָלִיק, בְּלָא נְהוֹרָא דְּשַׁרְיָא עֲלַיְיהוּ, וע"ד מִשְׁתַּכְּכִין בְּלָא נְהוֹרָא כְּלָל. א"ר יוֹסֵי, דָּא אִיהוּ בְּרִירוּ דְּמִלָּה, זַכָּאָה חוּלָקִי דְּזָכֵינָא לְהַאי, לְמִשְׁמַע דָּא.

117. And it is written: "But you...are men" (Yechezkel 34:31). This means that you, and not the nations of the world, are called 'men'. The souls of the idol worshipping peoples are of extinguished straw, with no light resting on them. This is why they are in repose and do not sway, for they have no Torah by which to be enflamed and no light rests on them. THIS IS WHY they stand like trees in a blaze, burning without a light resting on them, and so they are still without any light at all. Rabbi Yosi said: So this is the explanation of the matter. Happy is my lot that I deserved to hear this matter.

17. "Let Yisrael rejoice in Him who made him"

A Synopsis
We learn why people must involve God and His Shechinah in their rejoicing.

The Relevance of this Passage
The Light of the Holy One participates in our rejoicing by virtue of our meditative read of this passage. The negative force called (do not pronounce this name) *Samael* and all his band are banished eternally from this world. The *Shechinah,* on one level of understanding, is connected to our immune system and to the ozone layer of the planet. Hence, here we evoke the presence of the *Shechinah* to filter out and ward off harmful entities (*Samael* and his band) that bring sickness, airborne diseases and destruction to our midst. Our personal and global immune systems are fortified forevermore. The protective energy that our parents naturally imbue to us is resurrected here, even if our parents are watching over us from the next world.

118. קוּם ר' אַבָּא, לְחַדְּשָׁא מִילִין דְּאוֹרַיְיתָא, דְּאַמְרַת בְּחִבּוּרָא קַדְמָאָה. פָּתַח ר' אַבָּא וְאָמַר, שִׁירוּ לַיְיָ' שִׁיר חָדָשׁ תְּהִלָּתוֹ מִקְצֵה הָאָרֶץ וְגוֹ'. כַּמָּה חֲבִיבִין יִשְׂרָאֵל קַמֵּי קוּדְשָׁא בְּרִיךְ הוּא, דְּחֶדְוָה דִּלְהוֹן וְתוּשְׁבַּחְתָּא דִּלְהוֹן לָאו אִיהוּ, אֶלָּא בֵּיהּ דְּהָכָא תָּנֵינָן, כָּל חֶדְוָה דְּיִשְׂרָאֵל דְּלָא מִשְׁתַּתְּפֵי בָּהּ לְקוּדְשָׁא בְּרִיךְ הוּא, לָאו אִיהוּ חֶדְוָה. וְזַמִּין אִיהוּ סָמָאֵל וְכָל סִיַּיעְתָּא דִּילֵיהּ לְקַטְרְגָא לְהַהוּא חֶדְוָה, וְאִשְׁתְּאָר בְּצַעֲרָא וּבִכְיָה, וְקוּדְשָׁא בְּרִיךְ הוּא לָא אִשְׁתְּתַּף בְּהַהוּא צַעֲרָא.

118. Arise, Rabbi Aba, to expound and refresh new matters in the Torah, as you said in the compilation of the first part! Rabbi Aba began: "Sing to Hashem a new song, and His praise from the end of the earth..." (Yeshayah 42:10). How beloved are Yisrael before the Holy One, blessed be He, for their rejoicing and their praises are only in Him! For so we have learned that any rejoicing of Yisrael in which they do not involve the Holy One, blessed be He, is no rejoicing at all. And in the future Samael and all his band will denounce that rejoicing, and they will be left with sorrow and weeping, and the Holy One, blessed be He, will not partake of that sorrow.

119. אֲבָל מַאן דְּשָׁתִּיף קוּדְשָׁא בְּרִיךְ הוּא וּשְׁכִינְתֵּיהּ בְּחֶדְוָה דִּילֵיהּ, אִם יֵיתֵי מְקַטְרְגָא לְקַטְרְגָא בְּהַהִיא חֶדְוָה. קוּדְשָׁא בְּרִיךְ הוּא וּשְׁכִינְתֵּיהּ מִשְׁתַּתֵּף בְּהַהוּא צַעֲרָא. מַה כְּתִיב בֵּיהּ בְּכָל צָרָתָם לֹא צָר. וּבְמַאי. בְּגִין דְּעִמּוֹ אָנֹכִי בְצָרָה.

119. But whoever involves the Holy One, blessed be He, and His Shechinah in his rejoicing, if the accuser should come to denounce that rejoicing, the Holy One, blessed be He and His Shechinah participate in that sorrow. For does not Scripture say: "In all their affliction He was afflicted" (Yeshayah 63:9)? And how is this? Because THE VERSE SAYS: "I will be with him in trouble" (Tehilim 91:15).

120. וּמְנָלָן, דְּאִית לוֹן לְיִשְׂרָאֵל לְשַׁתְּפָא לְקוּדְשָׁא בְּרִיךְ הוּא וּשְׁכִינְתֵּיהּ בְּחֶדְוָה דִּלְהוֹן. דִּכְתִּיב יִשְׂמַח יִשְׂרָאֵל בְּעוֹשָׂיו. הַהִיא חֶדְוָה דְּיִשְׂרָאֵל לָאו אִיהוּ, אֶלָּא בְּעוֹשָׂיו. בְּעוֹשָׂיו, בְּעוֹשׂוֹ מִבָּעֵי לֵיהּ. אֶלָּא אִלֵּין קוּדְשָׁא בְּרִיךְ הוּא וּשְׁכִינְתֵּיהּ, וְאָבִיו וְאִמּוֹ, דְּאַף עַל גַּב דְּמִיתוּ, קוּדְשָׁא בְּרִיךְ הוּא אַעֲקַר לוֹן מג"ע, וְאַיְיתֵי לוֹן עִמֵּיהּ לְהַהוּא חֶדְוָה, לְנַטְלָא חוּלָקָא דְּחֶדְוָה עִם קוּדְשָׁא בְּרִיךְ הוּא וּשְׁכִינְתֵּיהּ. כד"א הָעוֹשׂוֹ יַגֵּשׁ חַרְבּוֹ.

120. And how do we know that Yisrael have to involve the Holy One, blessed be He, and His Shechinah, in their rejoicing? It is as is written: "Let Yisrael rejoice in Him (lit. 'they') who made him" (Tehilim 149:2), THE MEANING OF WHICH IS THAT Yisrael has no rejoicing but with them who made him. HE ASKS, Why "them who made him" when it should be "He"? HE ANSWERS THAT this refers to the Holy One, blessed be He, and His Shechinah, and a person's father and his mother. For, even if the latter be dead, the Holy One, blessed be He, uproots them from the Garden of Eden and brings them with Him to that rejoicing, so that they can participate in the rejoicing with the Holy One, blessed be He and His Shechinah. AND THE MEANING OF "THEM WHO MADE HIM" IS as in the verse: "let Him that made him bring near His sword to him" (Iyov 40:19).

18. Three craftsmen: heaven, earth and water

A Synopsis

Rabbi Aba says that a person is made by the partnership between his father, his mother and God. He then refers to the three craftsmen made by God – the heaven, the earth and the water – and with whom He produced the world. When these three were finished God commanded them to produce the body of man, and He provided the soul. When a person rejoices he is rejoicing with his parents, even though they may already have passed to the World to Come, and also with God.

The Relevance of this Passage

Water is the lifeblood of man and this planet. We are born in water inside the womb of our mother, and water is our primary substance, comprising over 65% of our body. The cleansing and healing power of water flows to us and washes away the stains on our souls, the seeds of all sickness.

The nurturing influences of our father and mother and our supernal Creator fill us with well-being and with the primordial energy of Creation. The life force within us intensifies.

We have learned that when we rejoice in this world, our parents in the next world rejoice with us if our hearts are filled with love for the Creator. However, when we experience distress, our parents are not informed. The words that speak these spiritual truths eliminate distress from our lives and our world so that only joy and celebration fill all existence.

121. ד״א בְּעוֹשָׂיו, בְּגִין דב״נ אִתְעֲבֵיד בְּשׁוּתָּפוּת, גַּבְרָא וְאִתְּתָא, וְקוּדְשָׁא בְּרִיךְ הוּא. וְעַל רָזָא דָא כְּתִיב, נַעֲשֶׂה אָדָם, בְּשׁוּתָפוּ. דְּתָנֵינָן, תְּלַת אוּמָנִין עָבֵד קוּדְשָׁא בְּרִיךְ הוּא, לְאַפָּקָא מִנְּהוֹן עָלְמָא, וְאִלֵּין אִינוּן: שְׁמַיָּא, וְאַרְעָא, וּמַיָּא. וְכָל חַד שַׁמֵּשׁ חַד יוֹמָא, וְאָהֲדְרוּ כְּמִלְּקַדְמִין.

121. An alternative explanation of "they who made him" IS THAT IT REFERS TO THE HOLY ONE, BLESSED BE HE, AND THE PERSON'S FATHER AND MOTHER, since man is made in partnership between man, his wife, and the Holy One, blessed be He. And about this secret it is written:

"Let Us make man" (Beresheet 1:26), "Us," implying a partnership WITH HIS FATHER AND HIS MOTHER. For we have learned that the Holy One, blessed be He, made three craftsmen with whom to produce the world, namely, heaven, earth and water, and each one of them served for one day, AND THEN LATER each served FOR A SECOND DAY, as previously.

122. יוֹמָא קַדְמָאָה, אַפִּיק שְׁמַיָא אוּמָנוּתָא דִילֵיהּ, דִּכְתִּיב וַיֹּאמֶר אֱלֹהִים יְהִי אוֹר וַיְהִי אוֹר. יוֹמָא תִּנְיָינָא, אַפִּיקוּ מַיָא אוּמָנוּתָא לְעֲבִידְתָּא, דִּכְתִּיב וַיֹּאמֶר אֱלֹהִים יְהִי רָקִיע בְּתוֹךְ הַמַּיִם וְגוֹ'. אִסְתְּלָקוּ פְּלָגָא מַיָיא לְעֵילָא, וּפְלָגָא מַיָיא לְתַתָּא אִשְׁתְּאָרוּ. וְאִלְמָלֵא כַּךְ דְּמַיָא אִתְפְּרָשׁוּ, עָלְמָא לָא הֲוָה קָאֵים. יוֹמָא תְּלִיתָאָה, עֲבִידַת אַרְעָא וְאַפִּיקַת כְּמָה דְּאִתְפַּקְדַת, דִּכְתִּיב וַיֹּאמֶר אֱלֹהִים תַּדְשֵׁא הָאָרֶץ דֶּשֶׁא עֵשֶׂב, וּכְתִיב וַתּוֹצֵא הָאָרֶץ דֶּשֶׁא וְגוֹ'.

122. On the first day heaven produced its craft, as it is written: "And Elohim said, Let there be light: and there was light" (Beresheet 1:3). On the second day water gave of its craft, as it is written: "And Elohim said, Let there be a firmament in the midst of the waters..." (Ibid. 6), where half the waters ascended on high and half remained below; and had the waters not divided there would have been no world. On the third day the earth did as it was commanded, as it is written: "Let the earth bring forth grass... And the earth brought forth grass" (Ibid. 11-12).

123. עַד הָכָא כָּל אוּמָנָא מֵאִלֵּין תְּלָתָא, אַפִּיק אוּמָנוּתָא דִּילֵיהּ, וְעַבְדוּ מַה דְּאִתְפַּקְדוּ. אִשְׁתְּאָרוּ תְּלַת יוֹמִין אַחֲרָנִין. יוֹמָא ד', אִתְפְּקַד אוּמָנָא קַדְמָאָה לְמֶעֱבַד אוּמָנָא דִּילֵיהּ, דִּכְתִּיב וַיֹּאמֶר אֱלֹהִים יְהִי מְאֹרֹת וְגוֹ', וְהַיְינוּ שָׁמַיִם. בְּיוֹמָא חֲמִשָׁאָה, אַפִּיקוּ מַיָא דְּאִיהוּ אוּמָנָא אָחֳרָא, דִּכְתִּיב וַיֹּאמֶר אֱלֹהִים יִשְׁרְצוּ הַמַּיִם וְגוֹ'. בְּיוֹמָא שְׁתִיתָאָה, עֲבַדַת אַרְעָא אוּמָנוּתָא דִּילָהּ, דִּכְתִּיב וַיֹּאמֶר אֱלֹהִים תּוֹצֵא הָאָרֶץ נֶפֶשׁ חַיָּה וְגוֹ'.

123. So far each OF THE THREE CRAFTSMEN had produced of its craft and they had done what they had been commanded to do. Three other days remained IN THE ACT OF CREATION. On the fourth day, the first craftsman, HEAVEN, was commanded to do its craft, as it is written: "And Elohim said,

Let there be lights in the firmament of the heaven..." (Ibid. 14), and so we have the skies. On the fifth day it was again the turn of the second craftsman, water, as it is written: "And Elohim said, Let the waters swarm..." (Ibid. 20). On the sixth day the earth again produced its craft, as it is written: "And Elohim said, Let the earth bring forth living creatures" (Ibid. 24).

124. כֵּיוָן דְּתְלַת אוּמָנִין אִלֵּין אַשְׁלִימוּ עוֹבָדַיְיהוּ. אָמַר לוֹן קוּדְשָׁא בְּרִיךְ הוּא, אוּמָנוּתָא חֲדָא אִית לִי לְמֶעְבַּד, וְאִיהוּ אָדָם. אִתְחַבָּרוּ כַּחֲדָא, וַאֲנָא עִמְכוֹן, נַעֲשֶׂה אָדָם, גּוּפָא דִּלְכוֹן, וַאֲנָא אֱהֵא שׁוּתָּפוּ עִמְכוֹן, וְנַעֲשֶׂה אָדָם. כְּמָה דִּבְקַדְמֵיתָא הֲוָה בְּשׁוּתָּפוּ, הָכִי נָמֵי לְבָתַר. אַבָּא, דְּבֵיהּ עָבֵיד עֲבִידְתָּא דִּשְׁמַיָּא, וַעֲבִידְתָּא דְּמַיָּא. וְאִתְּתָא, דְּאִיהִי אוּמָנָא תְּלִיתָאָה, כְּגַוְונָא דְּאַרְעָא. וְקוּדְשָׁא בְּרִיךְ הוּא דְּאִשְׁתָּתַּף בַּהֲדַיְיהוּ. וְעַל רָזָא דָּא כְּתִיב בְּעוֹשָׂיו.

124. These three craftsmen having finished their tasks, the Holy One, blessed be He, said to them: I have one more creation to make, namely Man. Join yourselves together and let us, I with you, make Man. The body shall be made by you, but I will be a partner with you BY GIVING THE SOUL, and we shall make Man. And just as formerly the three craftsmen worked in a partnership IN THE ACT OF CREATION, so also was it subsequently WITH THE CREATION OF MAN. There is the father, with whom He made the works of heaven and the works of the water, FROM WHOM COMES THE WHITENESS IS IN MAN; and the woman, who is the third craftsman, like the earth, FROM WHOM COMES THE REDNESS IN THE BABY. And then there is the Holy One, blessed be He, who participated with them, FROM WHOM COMES THE SOUL. And in respect of this secret, the text has "they who made him" IN REFERENCE TO THE HOLY ONE, BLESSED BE HE, A PERSON'S FATHER AND HIS MOTHER.

125. וְאַף עַל גַּב דְּאַבָּא וְאִמָּא אִתְפָּרְשׁוּ מֵהַאי עָלְמָא, חֶדְוָה בְּכָל שׁוּתָּפוּתָא הֲוֵי. דִּתְנֵינָן, בְּשַׁעֲתָא דְּבַר נָשׁ שָׁתִּיף לְקוּדְשָׁא בְּרִיךְ הוּא לְחֶדְוָוה דִּילֵיהּ, קוּדְשָׁא בְּרִיךְ הוּא אָתֵי לְגִנְתָּא דְּעֵדֶן, וְאַעֲקַר מִתַּמָּן לַאֲבוּהִי וְאִמֵּיהּ, דְּאִינּוּן שׁוּתָּפִין בַּהֲדֵיהּ, וְאַיְיתֵי לוֹן עִמֵּיהּ לְהַהוּא

חֶדְוָוה, וְכֻלְהוּ זְמִינִין תַּמָּן, וּבְנֵי נָשָׁא לָא יַדְעִין. אֲבָל בְּעָקוּ דב"נ,
קוּדְשָׁא בְּרִיךְ הוּא זַמִּין לְגַבֵּיה בִּלְחוֹדוֹי, וְלָא אוֹדַע לַאֲבוּהִי וּלְאִמֵּיה,
הה"ד בַּצַּר לִי אֶקְרָא יְיָ' וְאֶל אֱלֹהַי אֲשַׁוֵּעַ וְגוֹ'.

125. And even though his father and his mother might have departed from this world, a man rejoices with all the three partners of his making, as we have learned: When a man involves the Holy One, blessed be He, in his rejoicing, the Holy One, blessed be He, comes to the Garden of Eden, and takes his father and mother from there, for they are partners with Him, and brings them with Him to that rejoicing, and all of them are there together but people do not know it. When, on the other hand, a man is in trouble, the Holy One, blessed be He, is there with him alone, and He does not inform his father and mother, as it is written: "In my distress I called upon Hashem, and cried to my Elohim" (Tehilim 18:7).

19. Three partners: The Holy One, Blessed Be He, one's father and one's mother

A Synopsis

We learn how many partners are responsible for creating and sustaining a person, including God and His Shechinah, one's mother and father, the angels, the sun and moon, the living creatures, the trees and the seed of the earth. At the time of the redemption all will come together and rejoice.

The Relevance of this Passage

The body and soul of man are cleansed, healed and redeemed through this powerful passage that explicates upon the creation of a man and the Final Redemption. Healing begins with our eyes, bones, sinews, brain, flesh, and skin.

Our supernal parents; the Patriarchs Abraham, Isaac, and Jacob; and the Matriarchs Sarah, Rivkah, Rachel, and Leah; along with our own parents if they dwell in the world beyond, come forth at the behest of the Creator to commence the ultimate rejoicing. This rejoicing is the Final Redemption; and as the Zohar states, there is no rejoicing like that of the Redemption.

The Light that will resurrect the dead and summon the souls from Eden to animate the risen bodies shines forth as we visually embrace these verses. And because all of this is ignited by the Zohar, the process is quick, merciful, and pleasant.

רעיא מהימנא

126. אָמַר קוּדְשָׁא בְּרִיךְ הוּא, אֲנָא וּשְׁכִינְתִּי שׁוּתָּפוּתָא דְּנִשְׁמְתָא, וַאֲבוֹי וְאִמֵּיהּ שׁוּתָּפוּתָא דְּגוּפָא, דַּאֲבוֹי מַזְרִיעַ לוֹבֶן, דְּעַיְינִין, וּדְגַרְמִין, וְגִידִין, וּמוֹחָא. וְאִתְּתָא שְׁחוֹר דְּעַיְינִין, וְשַׂעֲרָא, וּבִשְׂרָא, וּמַשְׁכָא. וְאוֹף הָכִי שְׁמַיָּא וְאַרְעָא. וְכָל חַיָּילִין דִּלְהוֹן, אִשְׁתַּתָּפוּ בִּיצִירָתֵיהּ. מַלְאָכִין, מִנְּהוֹן יֵצֶר הַטּוֹב וְיֵצֶר הָרָע לְמֶהֱוֵי מְצוּיָּיר מִתַּרְוַויְיהוּ. שִׁמְשָׁא וְסִיהֲרָא, לְאַנְהֲרָא לֵיהּ בִּימָמָא וְלֵילְיָא. חֵיוָן וּבְעִירָן וְעוֹפִין וְנוּנִין, לְאִתְפַּרְנְסָא מִנְּהוֹן. כָּל אִילָנִין וְזַרְעִין דְּאַרְעָא, לְאִתְפַּרְנְסָא מִנְּהוֹן.

Ra'aya Meheimna (the Faithful Shepherd)

126. Said the Holy One, blessed be He: 'I and My Shechinah are the partners in the soul, a person's father and mother are the partners in the body, for his father injects the whiteness IN THE BABY, namely the white of the eyes, bones, sinews, and brain, and the woman SUPPLIES the black of the eyes, hair, flesh, and skin. The heavens, the earth, and all their hosts also participate in MAN'S creation. The angels, TOO, TAKE PART, FOR from them COME the Good Inclination and the Evil Inclination, THAT MAN should be portrayed in both of them. THE PART OF the sun and the moon is to give him light by day and by night, and even the beasts, cattle, birds, and fish PARTICIPATE IN MAN, for he makes a living from them. The trees and the seed of the earth PARTICIPATE IN HIM to sustain and nourish him'.

127. מַה עָבֵד קוּדְשָׁא בְּרִיךְ הוּא, אַעֲקַר לַאֲבוּי וּלְאִמֵּיה מִגִּנְתָּא דְּעֵדֶן, וְאַיְיתֵי לְהוּ עִמֵּיה, לְמֶהֱוֵי עִמֵּיה בְּחֶדְוָה דִּבְנוֹי, וְלֵית חֶדְוָה כְּחֶדְוָה דְּפוּרְקָנָא, דִּכְתִיב בָּה, יִשְׂמְחוּ הַשָּׁמַיִם וְתָגֵל הָאָרֶץ וַיֹּאמְרוּ בַגּוֹיִם יְיָ מָלָךְ. אָז יְרַנְּנוּ עֲצֵי הַיָּעַר מִלִּפְנֵי יְיָ כִּי בָא לִשְׁפּוֹט אֶת הָאָרֶץ.

ע"כ רעיא מהימנא

127. What does the Holy One, blessed be He, do? He uproots his father and mother from the Garden of Eden and brings them with Him so that they should be with Him at the rejoicing of their children. AND SO IT IS AT THE TIME OF THE REDEMPTION, for there is no rejoicing like that of the Redemption, about which it is written: "Let the heavens be glad, and let the earth rejoice: and let it be said among the nations, Hashem reigns... Then shall the trees of the wood sing for joy before Hashem, because He comes to judge the earth" (I Divrei Hayamim 16:31-33), FOR THEN THE HOLY ONE, BLESSED BE HE, BRINGS THE PATRIARCHS AND MATRIARCHS OF YISRAEL TO BE AT THEIR REJOICING.

End of Ra'aya Meheimna (the Faithful Shepherd)

20. "Behold, I give to him My covenant of peace"

A Synopsis

We learn about two alphabets, the large letters belonging to the World to Come and the small letters belonging to this world. As the Yud was added to the name of Pinchas the explanation becomes clear that God asked Moses to give His Shechinah to Pinchas. Next we realize that the shade of the departed Rabbi Pinchas ben Yair has been with the rabbis in their discussions, for he had spoken of those same matters while he was still alive.

The Relevance of this Passage

The Light of *Binah* – signified by the large letters of the alphabet – denotes the next world of immortality, paradise, and joy. This great Light shines forth the moment we meditate upon the alphabet depicted in this mystical text. Hence, the next world now becomes our world, for darkness and death cannot prevail in the presence of *Binah's* Light.

A person bearing a single candle can provide illumination to his friend without diminishing his own light. Similarly, the awesome spiritual Light awarded to Moses and Pinchas by virtue of their mighty spiritual deeds, now shines upon us. In addition, the Light we generate through our own visual connection is shared with all mankind. This natural and wondrous effect extends to everyone who embraces this book. Hence, spiritual Light expands *exponentially* in the world, extinguishing the darkness and death that have cursed our existence far too long.

Finally, the secrets of the Torah, revealed by the sages all through time, are revealed everywhere as these holy men revisit our realm to unleash this hidden Light to all mankind.

128. אַהֲדָר הַהוּא טוּלָא דְמִלְּקַדְמִין, וְאָזְלָא גּוֹ בֵּיתָא, כְּמוֹ דִּיּוּקְנָא דב"נ. נָפַל עַל אַנְפּוֹי ר' אַבָּא. אָמַר רִבִּי יוֹסֵי, אַדְכַּרְנָא דְּבַהַאי אַתְרָא חֲמֵינָא לֵיהּ לר' פִּנְחָס בֶּן יָאִיר, יוֹמָא חַד הֲוָה קָאִים בְּהַאי דּוּכְתָּא, וַהֲוָה אָמַר הָכִי, פִּינְחָס בֶּן אֶלְעָזָר בֶּן אַהֲרֹן הַכֹּהֵן, בָּאת י' זְעֵירָא.

128. The same shade returned again and walked around the house like an image of a man. Rabbi Aba fell on his face. Rabbi Yosi said: I recall that in this spot I saw Rabbi Pinchas ben Yair. One day he was standing on this

spot and asked as follows: In the verse "Pinchas, the son of Elazar, the son of Aaron the priest" (Bemidbar 25:11): WHY IS PINCHAS HERE SPELLED with the addition of the small letter Yud?

129. בְּגִין דִּתְרֵין אַלְפִין בֵּיתִין רְשִׁימִין, אַלְפָא בֵּיתָא דְּאַתְוָון רַבְרְבָן, וְאַלְפָא בֵּיתָא דְּאַתְוָון זְעִירָן. אַתְוָון רַבְרְבָן, אִינּוּן בְּעָלְמָא דְּאָתֵי. וְאַתְוָון זְעִירָן, אִינּוּן בְּעָלְמָא תַּתָּאָה. י' זְעֵירָא, בְּרִית קַיָּימָא קַדִּישָׁא. כֵּיוָן דְּקַנֵּי פִּנְחָס עַל בְּרִית דָּא, אִתּוֹסַף בֵּיהּ י' זְעֵירָא, רָזָא דִּבְרִית דָּא.

129. AND HE ANSWERS, because there are two sets of recorded alphabets, one alphabet of large letters and one of small letters. AND HE EXPLAINS: the large letters belong to the World to Come AND ARE IN THE ASPECT OF BINAH, WHICH IS CALLED 'THE WORLD TO COME', while the small letters belong to this world AND ARE OF THE ASPECT OF MALCHUT, WHICH IS CALLED 'THIS WORLD'. HERE LIES THE REASON FOR the small letter Yud, which is a sign of the Holy Covenant, NAMELY MALCHUT. Since Pinchas was zealous for this Covenant, a small Yud was added to him, which is the secret of this Covenant, NAMELY MALCHUT.

130. בְּהַהוּא שַׁעֲתָא, אָמַר קוּדְשָׁא בְּרִיךְ הוּא, מָה אַעְבִּיד עִם מֹשֶׁה, בְּרִית דָּא מִמֹּשֶׁה הֲוֵי, וְכַלָּה דִּילֵיהּ הֲוֵי. גְּנַאי הוּא לְמֵיהַב לֵיהּ לְאַחֲרָא, בְּלָא דַּעְתָּא וּרְעוּתָא דְּמֹשֶׁה, לָאו יָאוּת הוּא. שָׁארֵי קוּדְשָׁא בְּרִיךְ הוּא וְאָמַר לְמֹשֶׁה, מֹשֶׁה, פִּנְחָס בֶּן אֶלְעָזָר בֶּן אַהֲרֹן הַכֹּהֵן. א"ל מֹשֶׁה, רבש"ע מַהוּ. א"ל, אַנְתְּ הוּא דִּמְסָרַת נַפְשָׁךְ עַל יִשְׂרָאֵל דְּלָא יִשְׁתֵּצוּן מִן עָלְמָא בְּכַמָּה זִמְנִין, וְאִיהוּ הֵשִׁיב אֶת חֲמָתִי מֵעַל בְּנֵי יִשְׂרָאֵל וְגו'. אָמַר מֹשֶׁה מַה אַתְּ בָּעֵי מִנִּי, הָא כֹּלָּא דִּידָךְ.

130. At that time, the Holy One, blessed be He, said: What can I do with Moses, for this Covenant came from Moses, and the bride, WHO IS MALCHUT, is his. It is not nice to give her, MALCHUT, to another, unless Moses knows about it and desires it. It is not proper. The Holy One, blessed be He, started by saying to Moses: 'Moses, "Pinchas, the son of Elazar, the son of Aaron the priest."' Moses asked Him: Master of the Universe, what of him? THE HOLY ONE, BLESSED BE HE, answered him: 'You are the

one who has given your soul for Yisrael a number of times so that they should not disappear from the world, while he, PINCHAS, "has turned My wrath away from the children of Yisrael"(Bemidbar 25:11). Moses said: What do You want of me? Is not everything Yours? AND IF YOU WANT TO CAUSE MALCHUT TO REST ON HIM, WHO CAN TELL YOU WHAT YOU SHOULD DO?

131. א״ל, הָא כֹּלָא דִּידָךְ הִיא, אֵימָא לֵיה דְּתִשְׁרֵי בְּגַוֵּיה. אָמַר מֹשֶׁה, הָא בְּלִבָּא שְׁלִים תְּהֵא לְגַבֵּיה. א״ל אֵימָא אַנְתְּ בְּפוּמָךְ, וְאָרִים קָלָךְ, דְּאַנְתְּ מָסַר לֵיה בִּרְעוּתָא, בְּלִבָּא שְׁלִים. הה״ד, לָכֵן אֱמֹר, אַתְּ אֵימָא בִּרְעוּתָא, הִנְנִי נוֹתֵן לוֹ אֶת בְּרִיתִי שָׁלוֹם. מֹשֶׁה הֲוָה אָמַר הִנְנִי נוֹתֵן לוֹ וְגוֹ', דְּאִילּוּ קוּדְשָׁא בְּרִיךְ הוּא, ה״ל לְמֵימַר לָכֵן אֱמֹר לוֹ הִנְנִי נוֹתֵן לוֹ אֶת בְּרִיתִי שָׁלוֹם, אֲבָל לָא כְּתִיב אֶלָּא לָכֵן אֱמֹר. וְאִי תֵּימָא, דְּאִתְעַבְּרַת מִן מֹשֶׁה. לָא. אֶלָּא כְּבוּצִינָא דָּא דְּאַדְלִיקוּ מִינָּה, דָּא יָהִיב וְאַהֲנֵי, וְדָא לָא אִתְגְּרַע מִנָּה.

131. Said THE HOLY ONE, BLESSED BE HE, TO MOSES: 'Here: it is all yours! You tell PINCHAS THAT MY SHECHINAH will rest within him.' Moses said: In all sincerity, let MALCHUT be with him. Said THE HOLY ONE, BLESSED BE HE, 'You tell him yourself, and in a loud voice, that you are handing THE SHECHINAH over to him, willingly and sincerely. Thus the verse "Wherefore say" – you say it willingly – "Behold, I give to him My covenant of peace" (Ibid. 12). Moses started to say: "Behold I give to him..." For if IT WAS REFERRING TO the Holy Blessed One, what should have been said was: 'Wherefore say to him, Behold, I give to him my covenant of peace'. But this is not written, but rather "Wherefore say" WITHOUT 'TO HIM', THE MEANING BEING THAT MOSES WAS COMMANDED TO SAY IT. Should you suggest that THE SHECHINAH was completely removed and taken away from Moses AND GIVEN TO HIM, you would be wrong, for it is like a candle that is used to light something else. The one gains the benefit of the light, while the other does not diminish.

132. אָתָא הַהוּא טוּלָא, וְיָתִיב, וְנָשִׁיק לֵיה. שָׁמְעוּ חַד קָלָא דַּהֲוָה אָמַר, פְּנוּן אֲתָר, פְּנוּן אֲתָר לר' פִּנְחָס בֶּן יָאִיר, דְּאִיהוּ גַּבַּיְיכוּ. דְּתָנִינָן, דְּכָל אֲתָר דְּצַדִּיקָא אִתְחַדַּשׁ בֵּיה מִלֵּי דְּאוֹרַיְיתָא, כַּד אִיהוּ בְּהַהוּא

עָלְמָא, פָּקִיד לְהַהוּא אֲתָר, וְאָתֵי לֵיהּ לְגַבֵּיהּ. וכ״ש כַּד שָׁרָאן בְּגַוַּויְיהּ
צַדִּיקַיָּיא אַחֲרָנִין. לַחְדַּתָּא בְּהַהוּא אֲתָר, דְּאַמְרִין מִלֵּי דְּאוֹרַיְיתָא.
כְּגַוְונָא דָּא דַּהֲוָה אָתֵי ר' פִּנְחָס בֶּן יָאִיר לְמִפְקַד לְאַתְרֵיהּ, וְאַשְׁכַּח
אִלֵּין צַדִּיקַיָּיא מְחַדְּתִּין מִלִּין דְּאוֹרַיְיתָא, וְאִתְחַדָּשׁ כְּמִלְּקַדְמִין, הַהוּא
מִלָּה דר' פִּנְחָס בֶּן יָאִיר קַמֵּיהּ.

132. The same shade came, sat down, and kissed him. They heard a certain voice saying: Make room, make room for Rabbi Pinchas ben Yair, for he is among you. As we have learned: in every place where a righteous man made a new interpretation of a matter in the Torah while he was in this world, he comes from the World to Come and visits that place. And this is even more likely when there are other righteous men in that place, deriving new interpretations and speaking about the Torah. And so it was that Rabbi Pinchas ben Yair came to visit his place and found there a number of righteous men revealing new interpretations of the Torah, and that matter was renewed again in the presence of Rabbi Pinchas ben Yair. IN OTHER WORDS, THAT SAME TORAH MATTER THAT RABBI PINCHAS HAD SPOKEN OF WAS REESTABLISHED IN HIS PRESENCE WHEN YOU MENTIONED IT IN HIS NAME.

133. א״ר אַבָּא, יָאוּת מִלָּה דְּרַבִּי פִּנְחָס בֶּן יָאִיר, דְּהָא לָא כְּתִיב לָכֵן
הִנְנִי נוֹתֵן, אֶלָּא לָכֵן אֱמוֹר הִנְנִי נוֹתֵן לוֹ. וְכִי מִלָּה דָּא הֲוָה גְּנִיזָא
מֵחֲסִידָא דָּא תְּחוֹת יְדָךְ, וְלָא הֲוֵית אָמַר. זַכָּאָה חוּלָקָנָא, דְּזָכֵינָא
לְמֶהֱוֵי בְּסִיַּעְתָּא דְּטוּלָא קַדִּישָׁא הָכָא.

133. Rabbi Aba said: This interpretation of Rabbi Pinchas ben Yair is very nice, for it is indeed not written: 'Wherefore I give', but "Wherefore say, Behold, I to give to him," MEANING THAT MOSES WAS COMMANDED TO SAY TO HIM, AS NOTED ABOVE. And just to think that this matter was hidden with you from that devout man, and you said nothing UNTIL NOW. Happy is our portion that we were privileged to be here with the help of the holy shade.

21. "Whatever your hand finds to do, do it with your strength"

A Synopsis

Rabbi Aba says that righteous men draw their strength from the power of God when they undertake to do His will. By awakening ourselves we awaken the holy and divine power, thus shattering any power that the Other Side may have had over us. Rabbi Aba tells us that the strength that includes deed and speech and knowledge and wisdom does not exist at all in Sheol. We hear that all men actually go to Sheol, but the righteous rise up again immediately, having gone there to bring up with them anyone who considered repentance but was unable to repent before he died.

The Relevance of this Passage

Reading these verses with great passion and effort is akin to performing spiritual deeds (the will of our Master) in this world with great strength. Correspondingly, Satan and the dark side of our nature are shattered by the force of the Creator, liberating us eternally from their influence. All of our own sins are cleansed by virtue of the Righteous so that none of us face the fate of Hell. *Sheol*, one of Hell's levels, is condemned and shut down permanently. But a moment before this occurs, the repenting wicked residing down there ascend out of this dimension through the virtue of the Righteous and our own efforts extended here.

In paragraph 134, the Zohar text says:

HIS VERDICT OF SEVENTY YEARS IS TORN UP.

This verse means that a man's judgments are abolished from his life. Here guilty verdicts procured against us in the Upper Worlds are torn up. Judgments are repealed, for us and all mankind.

134. אוֹף הוּא פָּתַח וְאָמַר, מִשְׁמֵיה דר' פִּנְחָס כֹּל אֲשֶׁר תִּמְצָא יָדְךָ
לַעֲשׂוֹת בְּכֹחֲךָ עֲשֵׂה וְגוֹ', כַּמָה יָאוּת לֵיה לב"נ בְּעוֹד דְּבוּצִינָא דָּלִיק
וְשַׁרְיָא עַל רֵישֵׁיה, לְאִשְׁתַּדְּלָא וּלְמֶעְבַּד רְעוּתָא דְמָארֵיה. בְּגִין דְּהַהוּא
נְהוֹרָא דְּבוּצִינָא, אִיהִי כֹּ"ח דְּשַׁרְיָא עֲלֵיה. וע"ד כְּתִיב, יִגְדַּל נָא כֹּח
יְיָ'. כֹּח יְיָ', דָּא הוּא כֹּח, דְּשַׁרְיָא עַל רֵישֵׁיהוֹן דְּצַדִּיקַיָּיא, וְכָל אִינוּן
דְּמִשְׁתַּדְּלִין בִּרְעוּתָא דְמָארֵיהוֹן. וְעַל דָּא תָּנֵינָן, כָּל הָעוֹנֶה אָמֵן יְהֵא
שְׁמֵיה רַבָּא מְבָרַךְ בְּכָל כֹּחוֹ.

134. Then he began and said in the name of Rabbi Pinchas: "Whatever your

hand finds to do, do it with your strength" (Kohelet 9:10). How good it is for a man to try to fulfill the will of his Master while the flame is yet burning and resting on his head. For the light of that flame is strength resting upon him, and so is it written: "let the power of my Hashem be great" (Bemidbar 14:17). "the power of Hashem" – this is the power that rests on the head of the righteous and of all those who willingly undertake the will of their Master, WHICH IS THE SHECHINAH. And about this we have already learned: 'Whoever responds with all his power: 'Amen. May His great name be blessed...' - HIS VERDICT OF SEVENTY YEARS IS TORN UP'.

135. וַדַּאי אִצְטְרִיךְ לְאִתְּעָרָא כָּל שַׁיְיפוֹי בְּחֵילָא תַּקִיף בְּגִין דִּבְאִתְּעָרוּתָא תַּקִיף דְּאַתְקַף, אִתְּעַר הַהוּא כֹּח קַדִּישָׁא עִלָּאָה, וְאִסְתַּלָּק גּוֹ קוּדְשָׁא וְאִתְּבַּר חֵילָא וְתוּקְפָּא דְּסִטְרָא אַחֲרָא. וע״ד בְּכָחֲךָ, אִצְטְרִיךְ לְמֶעְבַּד רְעוּתָא דְּמָארָךְ.

135. He surely has to awaken all his body parts with great power IN THE WORSHIP OF THE HOLY ONE, BLESSED BE HE, for by means of this powerful awakening that he summons up, he also awakens that holy and supernal power, WHICH IS MALCHUT, and he is uplifted in holiness and shatters the power and hold of the Other Side. Hence IT IS WRITTEN: "WHATEVER YOUR HAND FINDS TO DO, DO IT WITH YOUR STRENGTH," FOR IT IS with your own strength that you must perform the will of your Master.

136. כִּי אֵין מַעֲשֶׂה וְחֶשְׁבּוֹן וְגוֹ', בְּגִין דִּבְהַהוּא כֹּח אִית מַעֲשֶׂה, אִשְׁתַּדְּלוּתָא לְאִשְׁתַּדְּלָא בְּהַאי עָלְמָא דְּאִקְרֵי מַעֲשֶׂה, עָלְמָא דְּעוֹבָדָא, לְמִשְׁלַם סוֹפָא דְּמַחֲשָׁבָה. וְחֶשְׁבּוֹן, דָּא הוּא עָלְמָא, דְּתַלְיָא בְּדִבּוּרָא, דְּהָא חֶשְׁבּוֹן בְּדִבּוּרָא תַּלְיָיא. וע״ד, כָּל גִּימַטְרִיאוֹת, וּתְקוּפִין, וְעִבּוּרִין דְּעָלְמָא, בְּסִיהֲרָא הֲווֹ. וְדַעַת, דָּא אִיהוּ רָזָא דְּשִׁית סִטְרִין, דְּתַלְיָין בְּמַחֲשָׁבָה, וְאִקְרוּן עָלְמָא דְּהַהוּא מַחֲשָׁבָה. וְחָכְמָה, דְּכֹלָּא תַּלְיָיא מִנֵּיהּ.

136. "for there is not work, nor device, nor knowledge, nor wisdom in Sheol, whither you go" (Ibid.). For it is in this power, that there is deed;

namely, the effort to engage in this world is called 'deed', namely the world of action, to complement the end of the thought. Device refers to the world that depends on speech, NAMELY MALCHUT, WHICH IS CALLED 'SPEECH', for a calculation of device depends on speech, and this is why all the numerology and the solstices and equinoxes are based on the moon, WHICH IS MALCHUT. "knowledge" refers to the secret of the six ends, WHICH IS ZEIR ANPIN, which are dependent on thought, and are called the world of that thought, WHICH IS BINAH. "wisdom" REFERS TO CHOCHMAH, on which everything is dependent, AS IT IS SAID: "IN WISDOM HAVE YOU MADE THEM ALL" (TEHILIM 104:24).

137. וְכָל אִלֵּין כְּלִילָן בְּהַהוּא כֹּחַ, מַה דְּלָאו הָכִי בְּסִטְרָא דִּשְׁאוֹל, דַּרְגָּא דְּגֵיהִנָּם. דְּהָא כָּל בַּ"ן דְּלָא אִשְׁתַּדַּל בְּהַאי כֹּ"חַ, בְּהַאי עָלְמָא, לְאַעֲלָאָה בֵּיהּ, בְּמַעֲשֶׂה וְחֶשְׁבּוֹן וְדַעַת וְחָכְמָה, סוֹפֵיהּ לְאַעֲלָאָה בִּשְׁאוֹל, דְּלֵית בֵּיהּ מַעֲשֶׂה וְחֶשְׁבּוֹן וְדַעַת וְחָכְמָה. דְּהָא סִטְרָא אָחֳרָא, אֹרַח שְׁאוֹל אִיהִי, דִּכְתִיב, דַּרְכֵי שְׁאוֹל בֵּיתָהּ. מָאן דְּאִתְרְפֵי מֵהַאי כֹּ"חַ קַדִּישָׁא, אַתְקַף בֵּיהּ סִטְרָא אָחֳרָא, דִּשְׁאוֹל בֵּיתָהּ.

137. And all of them, THE DEED, OR CALCULATION, DEVICE, KNOWLEDGE, AND WISDOM, are included in that same strength, WHICH IS THE SHECHINAH THAT RESTS ON THE HEAD OF THE RIGHTEOUS. This is not the case on the side of Sheol, which is a level of Gehenom. For the end of everyone who does not try with this strength to enter it by means of deed, accounting device, knowledge, and wisdom in this world will eventually arrive in Sheol, where there is no deed, nor accounting device, nor knowledge, nor wisdom. For the Other Side is the way to Sheol, as it is written: "Her house is the way to Sheol" (Mishlei 7:27). Whoever becomes listless in relation to that holy strength is attacked by the Other Side, whose house is Sheol.

138. אֲשֶׁר אַתָּה הוֹלֵךְ שָׁמָּה, וְכִי כָּל בְּנֵי עָלְמָא אָזְלֵי לִשְׁאוֹל. אִין. אֲבָל סַלְקִין מִיָּד, דִּכְתִיב, מוֹרִיד שְׁאוֹל וַיָּעַל. בַּר אִינּוּן חַיָּיבִין, דְּלָא הִרְהֲרוּ תְשׁוּבָה לְעָלְמִין, דְּנַחְתִּין וְלָא סַלְקִין. וַאֲפִילוּ צַדִּיקִים גְּמוּרִים נַחְתִּין תַּמָּן. אֲמַאי נַחְתִּין. בְּגִין דְּנַטְלִין כַּמָה חַיָּיבִין מִתַּמָּן, וְסַלְקִין לוֹן לְעֵילָּא. וּמָאן אִינּוּן. אִינּוּן דְּהִרְהֲרוּ בִּתְשׁוּבָה בְּהַאי עָלְמָא, וְלָא יָכִילוּ,

וְאִסְתְּלָקוּ מִן עָלְמָא. וְצַדִּיקַיָּיא נַחְתִּין בְּגִינֵיהוֹן דְּחַיָּיבִין גּוֹ שְׁאוֹל,
וְנַטְלִין לוֹן, וְסַלְּקִין לוֹן מִן תַּמָּן.

138. "whither you go": HE ASKS, Do, indeed, all men go there to Sheol?
HE ANSWERS, yes, but THE RIGHTEOUS rise up again immediately, as it is
written: "He brings down to Sheol, and brings up" (I Shmuel 2:6). This
verse, however, is not to be applied to the wicked who never for a moment
considered repentance, for they go down TO SHEOL and do not ascend
again. Even the completely righteous go down there. Why should this be? It
is because they take from there a number of wicked and bring them up from
there. Who are the ones THAT THEY BRING UP? They who considered
repentance in this world, but were unable to repent for they died. And it is
for these wicked people that the righteous go down to Sheol and take them
and bring them up from there.

22. "Your eyes like the pools in Cheshbon"

A Synopsis

Rabbi Yosi is prompted by the shade of Rabbi Pinchas ben Yair to remember the esoteric explanation of the accounting of the numerical values of letters.

The Relevance of this Passage

Both science and Kabbalah understand that mathematical numbers are interwoven into the fabric of reality. Moreover, letters and their alphabetic structure are also an integral part of reality. For instance, the DNA in our cells consist of four chemical letters – A, T, C, and G – which refer to four different nucleotides. These four nucleotides combine to create 20 amino acids, which produce the "words" and "sentences" composing the genetic code of every individual. This alphabetic structure extends to all physical matter. Just as letters combine to form words, atoms combine to create more complicated structures such as molecules. Just as words combine to form sentences, molecules combine to create various kinds of matter.

Here we connect to the metaphysical DNA level of reality – the letters of the Hebrew Alphabet. We link up with the dimension of Chochmah and Binah causing sparkling pools of Light to fill our existence. The concept of counting, according to Kabbalah, indicates control. Thus, here we attain control over the stars and planets, altering our fate to secure an immediate and sweet Final Redemption.

139. אָמַר ר' יוֹסֵי, כְּתִיב אַחַת לְאַחַת לִמְצֹא חֶשְׁבּוֹן. חֶשְׁבּוֹן דְּגִימַטְרִיָּיאוֹת דְּקַיְּימָן בְּסִיהֲרָא, בְּאָן דַּרְגָּא דִּילָה אִינּוּן. לָא אָתִיב לֵיהּ. אָמַר, שְׁמַעְנָא, וְלָא אַדְכַּרְנָא מִלָּה. קָם הַהוּא טוּלָא, וּבָטַשׁ בְּעֵינוֹי דר' אַבָּא, נָפַל עַל אַנְפּוֹי מִגּוֹ דְּחִילוּ. עַד דַּהֲוָה נָפַל עַל אַנְפּוֹי, נָפַל קְרָא בְּפוּמֵיהּ, דִּכְתִיב, עֵינַיִךְ בְּרֵכוֹת בְּחֶשְׁבּוֹן עַל שַׁעַר בַּת רַבִּים. וְאִלֵּין עַיְינִין דִּילָה, פַּרְפְּרָאוֹת לְגוֹ חָכְמָה עִלָּאָה, דְּאִתְמַשְּׁכָא מִלְּעֵילָּא, וּמִגּוֹ חֶשְׁבּוֹן וּתְקוּפִין וְעִבּוּרִין אִתְמַלְּיָין, וְאִתְעֲבִידוּ בְּרֵיכוֹת, דְּנָפְקוּ מִיָּמִין, לְכָל סִטְרִין, עַד דְּאִתְפַּקְדָן לְכָל חוּשְׁבָּן וְעִבּוּרִין דְּסִיהֲרָא דִּלְבַר, וְכֹכְבִין וּמַזָּלֵי לְמֶעְבַּד חֶשְׁבּוֹן, וְדָא אִיהוּ עַל שַׁעַר בַּת רַבִּים, דָּא אִיהִי סִיהֲרָא דִּלְבַר.

139. Rabbi Yosi said: It is written: "counting one thing to another, to find out the sum (Heb. *cheshbon*)" (Kohelet 7:27), AND HE ASKED: the calculation (Heb. *chesbon*) of numerical value pertains to the moon, WHICH IS MALCHUT, but in which of her levels? He did not answer, but said: I have heard this matter, but do not remember it. That shade arose and hit Rabbi Aba in the eyes. He fell on his face out of fear, and while he was still lying on his face, a verse came to him, that is written: "Your eyes like the pools in Heshbon, by the gate of Bat-rabbim" (lit. 'daughter of many')" (Shir Hashirim 7:5). THE EXPLANATION IS: This refers to the eyes OF MALCHUT, NAMELY HER CHOCHMAH WHICH IS CALLED 'EYES', and they are appetizers, NAMELY DELICACIES to the divine Chochmah which is drawn from above, FROM BINAH, AND HER EYES are filled by reckoning and solstices, equinoxes and intercalation of the moon and become pools flowing out from the right in all directions until they are counted in every account and intercalation of the moon from the outside, NAMELY OF THE EXTERNAL PARTS OF MALCHUT, also of the stars and the constellations – in order to reach a sum. And this is "by the gate of Bath-rabbim," which is the moon, WHICH IS MALCHUT, from the outside.

23. "in the evening she would go, and on the morrow she would return"

A Synopsis
Rabbi Aba again goes over the matter of God persuading Moses to give His holy covenant of peace to Pinchas. We learn that Malchut has permission from Zeir Anpin to live among the righteous in the world. If Pinchas had not been given Malchut he would never have been able to attain the high priesthood.

The Relevance of this Passage
The Zohar expounds upon *Zeir Anpin*, which is the Upper World. It relates truths about the Right and Left Columns, which are Mercy and Judgment, respectively. In doing so, the Zohar balances and corrects our realm of *Malchut*.

We behold verses that tell of Pinchas's possession of *Malchut,* his attainment of the priesthood, and the secret of the covenant being an aspect of our world of *Malchut* when she cleaves to the Upper Right, which is *Chesed* of *Zeir Anpin*. This Upper Right will, in the future, construct the Holy Temple.

As we meditate upon these texts, we are actually rebuilding two Temples: Each of us is a microcosm of the Temple. Hence, construction of the Temple takes place within our own physical body, creating a place where the Light of the Creator can rest upon us; and we erect the Temple in Jerusalem, spiritually speaking, where the Light nourishes the entire world, initiating our Final Redemption. *Malchut,* which not only represents our world but all mankind, then rises and attaches to *Zeir Anpin,* uniting in a celebration of Light.

140. א"ר אַבָּא לר' יוֹסֵי, הַהוּא מַרְגְּלָא קַדִּישָׁא דַּהֲוָה תְּחוֹת יְדָךְ, מִגּוֹ סִיַּעְתָּא דַּחֲסִידָא קַדִּישָׁא דְּאִיהוּ גַּבָּן, כַּמָּה שַׁפִּיר אִיהוּ, וְאַהֲדַרְנָא בֵיהּ. דְּהָא וַדַּאי לָא אִצְטְרִיךְ לְאַפָּקָא אִתְּתָא, לְמִשְׁרֵי בַּאֲתַר אַחֲרָא, עַד דְּבַעְלָהּ יָפְקַד לָהּ וְיָהִיב לָהּ רְשׁוּ לְמֶהַךְ. וְאוֹדְעִין לְבַעְלָהּ בְּקַדְמֵיתָא, וּמְפַיְּיסִין לֵיהּ, דְּהוּא יָפְקַד לָהּ, וְיָהִיב לָהּ רְשׁוּ לְמֵיהַךְ לְהַהוּא אֲתַר. כַּךְ קוּדְשָׁא בְּרִיךְ הוּא פַּיִּיס לְמֹשֶׁה, וְעַד דְּיָהַב לֵיהּ רְשׁוּ, וַא"ל אֵימָא אַנְתְּ, הִנְנִי נוֹתֵן לוֹ אֶת בְּרִיתִי שָׁלוֹם, לְמִשְׁרֵי בְּגַוֵּויהּ, וְעַד דְּיָהַב לָהּ

רְשׁוּ לְמֵהַךְ תַּמָּן, לָא אַזְלַת.

140. Rabbi Aba said to Rabbi Yosi: That holy pearl that was in your possession with the help of the holy pious one who visited us, NAMELY THE REPORT FROM RABBI PINCHAS BEN YAIR, WITH HIS HELP BY COMING TO US – it is so beautiful that I must go over it again. For it is certainly unnecessary to take out a wife to another place unless her husband so commands and gives her permission to go. ACCORDINGLY, one first of all informs her husband and placates him so that he should command her and give her permission to go to that place. So the Holy One, blessed be He, placated Moses until he gave his permission. Then He said to him: 'You say it – "Behold, I give to him My covenant of peace"' (Bemidbar 25:12), so She would abide in PINCHAS, and so long as he had not given Her permission to go, She did not go.

141. מְנָלָן. מִצַּדִּיקוֹ שֶׁל עוֹלָם, דִּיָהִיב לָהּ רְשׁוּ, לְמִשְׁרֵי גּוֹ צַדִּיקֵי בְּהַאי עָלְמָא. וְיָתְבָא עִמְּהוֹן, כְּכַלָּה גּוֹ קִשׁוּטָהָא. וְצַדִּיקָא דְעָלְמָא חָמֵי, וְחַדֵּי בְּהַאי. אֲבָל בֵּין דְּרוֹעֵי דְּבַעֲלָהּ שְׁכִיבַת, וְאִתְהַדְּרַת לְמֶהֱוֵי בַּהֲדַיְיהוּ, וְתָבַת לְבַעֲלָהּ. כד"א, בָּעֶרֶב הִיא בָאָה וּבַבֹּקֶר הִיא שָׁבָה. בָּעֶרֶב הִיא בָאָה, לְגַבֵּי בַעֲלָהּ. וּבַבֹּקֶר הִיא שָׁבָה, לְגַבֵּי צַדִּיקַיָּיא דְּעָלְמָא. וְכֹלָּא בִּרְשׁוּתָא דְּבַעֲלָהּ.

141. How do we know this? From the Righteous of the world, WHICH IS YESOD OF ZEIR ANPIN, who gave MALCHUT permission to abide among the righteous in this world, and she dwells among them as a bride in all her jewelry, and the Righteous of the world sees it, and is happy. But she lies in the arms of her husband, WHICH IS THE SECRET OF THE RIGHT COLUMN AND THE LEFT COLUMN, WHICH ARE CHESED AND GVURAH OF ZEIR ANPIN, and returns from there to be with the righteous, then returning to her husband, as it is written: "in the evening she would go, and on the morrow she would return" (Ester 2:14). "in the evening she would go" to her husband, NAMELY AT MIDNIGHT, FOR THEN IS THE UNION OF THE LEFT; "and on the morrow" WHEN SHE IS FULL OF CHASSADIM FROM THE UNION OF THE RIGHT, "she would return" to be among the righteous of the world, everything being done with the permission of her husband, ZEIR ANPIN.

142. וּמֹשֶׁה כָּךְ אָמַר, הִנְנִי נוֹתֵן לוֹ אֶת בְּרִיתִי, כְּמָה דְצַדִּיק דִּלְעֵילָּא
נוֹתֵן, אוֹף אֲנָא הִנְנִי נוֹתֵן, מַתָּנָה לְמֶהְדַּר מַתָּנָה אִיהִי. וּבְגִין בְּרִית דָּא,
רָוַח כְּהוּנָה עִלָּאָה. וְאִי לָא תְּהֵא בַּהֲדֵיהּ, לָא אִתְקְשַׁר פִּנְחָס בְּדַרְגָּא
דִּכְהוּנָה עִלָּאָה, דְּהָא בְּרִית דַּבְקָא אִיהוּ תָּדִיר בִּימִינָא עִלָּאָה. וִימִינָא
עִלָּאָה דָּא, זַמִּין לְמִבְנֵי בֵּי מַקְדְּשָׁא, דְּאִיהוּ בְּרִית.

142. What Moses said was: "Behold I give to him My Covenant," WHICH IS THE SECRET OF MALCHUT. Just as the Righteous on high gives, so also do I give a present, on condition that the present be returned, NAMELY JUST AS THE RIGHTEOUS ON HIGH GIVES ON CONDITION THAT IT BE RETURNED. AS "IN THE EVENING SHE WOULD GO AND ON THE MORROW SHE WOULD RETURN," AS EXPOUNDED ABOVE, SO ALSO WITH MOSES. And because of this covenant, he earned the high priesthood, WHICH IS THE SECRET OF CHESED, and if he had not had MALCHUT with him, Pinchas could not have risen to the level of the high priesthood, for the covenant IS AN ASPECT OF MALCHUT, when she is always cleaving to the upper right, WHICH IS CHESED of ZEIR ANPIN. And this upper right will, in the future, construct the Temple, which is the covenant, NAMELY MALCHUT.

24. A third Temple is not mentioned in the Torah

A Synopsis

We hear how a gentile told Rabbi Eliezer that Yisrael were not close to God, citing various kinds of evidence, whereupon the Rabbi turned him into a heap of bones. Rabbi Eliezer recounts the answers that Elijah once gave him when he raised the same issues as the gentile. We hear an explanation of the First and Second Temples, and how God will reveal the Temple at the time of the final redemption.

The Relevance of this Passage

The final Temple will not be a physical structure erected by the hand of man. Rather, it's a spiritual and physical Temple actualized by the will of God in the moment we complete our correction. Any structure in our world that does not include the workmanship and Light of God is doomed to destruction.

This dissertation imbues all of our endeavors, all that we build, with the sacred craftsmanship of the Creator. The spiritual foundation, columns, and pillars of the Temple rise up in this passage. And although our eyes do not observe its construction, the Light generated by its presence illumines the planet, banishing forces of darkness, sin, death, and destruction. The Final Redemption unfolds with great kindness, for this ancient book is a book of kindness; and its every page bespeaks compassion, mercy, and leniency.

143. אָמַר רִבִּי אַבָּא, אִדְכַּרְנָא מִלָּה חֲדָא, דְּשָׁמַעְנָא מִבּוּצִינָא קַדִּישָׁא, דְּשָׁמַע מִשְּׁמֵיהּ דְּרִבִּי אֱלִיעֶזֶר. יוֹמָא חַד, אָתָא לְקַמֵּיהּ חַד חַכִּים גּוֹי, אֲ"ל סָבָא סָבָא, תְּלַת בַּעֲיָין בָּעֵינָא לְמִתְבַּע מִנָּךְ. חַד, דְּאַתּוּן אַמְרִין דְּיִתְבְּנֵי לְכוּ בֵּי מַקְדְּשָׁא אָחֳרָא, וְהָא לָא הֲווֹ לְמִבְנֵי אֶלָּא תְּרֵי זִמְנִין, בַּיִת רִאשׁוֹן וּבַיִת שֵׁנִי, בַּיִת שְׁלִישִׁי לָא תִּשְׁכַּח בְּאוֹרַיְיתָא, וְהָא מַה דַּהֲוָה לֵיהּ לְמִבְנֵי, כְּבָר אִתְבְּנוּן, וּלְעוֹלָם לֵית בֵּיהּ יַתִּיר, דְּהָא תְּרֵי בָּתֵּי יִשְׂרָאֵל קָרָא לוֹן קְרָא. וּכְתִיב, גָּדוֹל יִהְיֶה כְּבוֹד הַבַּיִת הַזֶּה הָאַחֲרוֹן מִן הָרִאשׁוֹן.

143. Rabbi Aba said: I have remembered a certain matter I heard from the Holy Luminary, RABBI SHIMON, who heard it said in the name of Rabbi

Eliezer. One day a clever gentile came and said to him: Old man, old man, I have three questions that I want to put to you. The first is: You say that another Temple will be built for you, but the Temple is not to be built more than twice. The First Temple and the Second Temple ARE MENTIONED, but you will not find a Third Temple in the Torah, and that which you had to build has already been built, and there will never be another one, for Scripture has referred to the two Temples of Yisrael, AND ABOUT THE SECOND TEMPLE it is written: "The glory of this latter house shall be greater than that of the former" (Chagai 2:9).

144. וְתוּ, דְּאַתּוּן אֲמָרִין, דְּאַתּוּן קְרֵבִין לְמַלְכָּא עִלָּאָה, יַתִּיר מִכָּל שְׁאַר עַמִּין, מַאן דְּמִתְקְרִיב לְמַלְכָּא, אִיהוּ חַדֵּי תָּדִיר, בְּלָא צַעֲרָא, בְּלָא דְּחִילוּ, וּבְלָא דְּחִיקוּ. וְהָא אַתּוּן בְּצַעֲרָא וּבְדֹחֲקָא וּבְיגוֹנָא תָּדִיר, יַתִּיר מִכָּל בְּנֵי עָלְמָא. וַאֲנָן לָא אִתְקְרִיב לָן צַעֲרָא וְדֹחֲקָא וִיגוֹנָא כְּלָל. אֲנָן קְרִיבִין לְמַלְכָּא עִלָּאָה, וְאַתּוּן רְחִיקִין מִנֵּיהּ, וע״ד אִית לְכוּ צַעֲרָא וְדֹחֲקָא אֲבְלָא וִיגוֹנָא, מַה דְּלָא אִית לָן.

144. Also, you say that you are closer to the supernal King than all other peoples. Whoever is close to the King is forever rejoicing, without pain, without fear, without troubles. But you are perpetually in pain, trouble and agony, more than anyone else. Look at us – no pain, trouble nor agony approaches us at all, from whence it follows that we are close to the supernal King and you are far from Him, and this is why you have pain and trouble and sorrow and agony, which we do not have.

145. וְתוּ, דְּאַתּוּן לָא אָכְלֵי נְבֵלָה וּטְרֵפָה, בְּגִין דִּתְהֱווֹן בְּרִיאִין, וְגוּפָא דִּלְכוֹן לֶהֱוֵי בְּבְרִיאוּתָא. אֲנָן אָכְלִינָן כָּל מַה דְּבָעֵינָן, וַאֲנָן תַּקִּיפִין בְּחֵילָא בִּבְרִיאוּתָא, וְכָל שַׁיְיפוֹן דִּילָן בְּקִיּוּמַיְיהוּ. וְאַתּוּן דְּלָא אַכְלִין, חַלָּשִׁין כֻּלְּכוּ בְּמַרְעִין בִּישִׁין, וּבִתְבִירוּ יַתִּיר מִכָּל שְׁאַר עַמִּין. עַמָּא דְּסָנֵי לְכוֹן אֱלָהֲכוֹן בְּכֹלָא. סָבָא סָבָא, לָא תֵּימָא לִי מִדִּי, דְּלָא אַשְׁמְעִינָךְ, וְלָא אֲקַבֵּל מִנָּךְ. זָקִיף עֵינוֹי ר' אֱלִיעֶזֶר, וְאַשְׁגַּח בֵּיהּ, וְאִתְעֲבֵיד תְּלָא דְּגַרְמֵי.

145. Further: You do not eat of an animal found dead or an animal not

-118-

ritually slaughtered so that you will be healthy and your body healthy. We eat anything we want and we are physically strong and healthy and all our limbs are fit. You do not eat and all are sick with bad illnesses and broken more than all other peoples. You are a people whom Hashem hates above all. Old man, old man, do not say anything to me because I shall not listen to you, nor accept it from you. Rabbi Eliezer lifted up his eyes, looked at him, and turned him into a heap of bones.

146. כֵּיוָן דְּנָח רוּגְזֵיהּ, אַהֲדָר רֵישֵׁיהּ וּבָכָה, וְאָמַר, יְיָ' אֲדוֹנֵנוּ מָה אַדִּיר שִׁמְךָ בְּכָל הָאָרֶץ. כַּמָּה תַּקִּיף חֵילָא דִּשְׁמָא קַדִּישָׁא, תַּקִּיפָא בְּכָל אַרְעָא, וְכַמָּה חֲבִיבִין מִלֵּי דְּאוֹרַיְיתָא, דְּלֵית לָךְ מִלָּה זְעֵירָא דְּלָא תִּשְׁכַּח לָהּ בְּאוֹרַיְיתָא, וְלֵית מִלָּה זְעֵירָא דְּאַתְיָא בְּאוֹרַיְיתָא, דְּלָא נָפְקַת מִפּוּמֵיהּ דְּקוּדְשָׁא בְּרִיךְ הוּא. מִלִּין אִלֵּין דְּשָׁאַל הַהוּא רָשָׁע, אֲנָא שָׁאֵלְנָא יוֹמָא חַד לְאֵלִיָּהוּ, וְאָמַר דְּהָא בִּמְתִיבְתָּא דִּרְקִיעָא, אִתְסָדָרוּ קַמֵּיהּ דְּקוּדְשָׁא בְּרִיךְ הוּא, וְהָכִי הוּא.

146. When his anger had subsided, he looked back, cried, and said: "Hashem, our Master, how majestic is Your name in all the earth" (Tehilim 8:2). How strong is the power of the Holy Name that is strong in all the earth, and how beloved are the words of the Torah, for nothing is so minor that it will not be found in the Torah, and even the smallest thing in the Torah issued from the mouth of the Holy One, blessed be He. Those matters that that wicked one asked, I too, once asked of Elijah, and he replied that in the Yeshivah of the firmament THESE VERY MATTERS were laid out before the Holy One, blessed be He, as follows:

147. דְּכַד נָפְקוּ יִשְׂרָאֵל מִמִּצְרַיִם, בָּעָא קוּדְשָׁא בְּרִיךְ הוּא לְמֶעְבַּד לוֹן בְּאַרְעָא, כְּמַלְאָכִין קַדִּישִׁין לְעֵילָּא, וּבָעָא לְמִבְנֵי לוֹן בֵּיתָא קַדִּישָׁא, וּלְנַחְתָּא לֵיהּ מִגּוֹ שְׁמֵי רְקִיעִין, וּלְנַטְעָא לוֹן לְיִשְׂרָאֵל, נְצִיבָא קַדִּישָׁא, כְּגַוְונָא דְּדִיּוּקְנָא דִּלְעֵילָּא. הה"ד תְּבִיאֵמוֹ וְתִטָּעֵמוֹ בְּהַר נַחֲלָתְךָ. בְּאָן אֲתַר בְּמָכוֹן לְשִׁבְתְּךָ פָּעַלְתָּ יְיָ'. בְּהַהוּא דְּפָעַלְתָּ אַנְתְּ יְיָ', וְלָא אַחֲרָא. מָכוֹן לְשִׁבְתְּךָ פָּעַלְתָּ יְיָ', דָּא בֵּית רִאשׁוֹן. מִקְּדָשׁ יְיָ' כּוֹנְנוּ יָדֶיךָ, דָּא בֵּית שֵׁנִי. וְתַרְוַויְיהוּ, אוּמָנוּתָא דְּקוּדְשָׁא בְּרִיךְ הוּא אִינּוּן.

147. When Yisrael came out of Egypt, the Holy One, blessed be He, wanted to establish them in the country as are the holy angels on high, and He wanted to build a Temple for them, bring it down from the upper heavens, and plant Yisrael in the land as a holy planting, after the pattern of the heavenly form, as it is written: "You shall bring them in, and plant them in the mountain of Your inheritance" (Shemot 15:17). And where would that be? "in the place, Hashem, which You have made for You to dwell in" (Ibid.). In that PLACE which You, Hashem, have made, and in no other. "The place, Hashem, which You have made for You to dwell in" refers to the First Temple, and the continuation of the verse, "in the sanctuary, Hashem, which Your hands have established," refers to the Second Temple. Both of them are the work of the Holy One, blessed be He.

148. וּמִדְּאַרְגִּיזוּ קַמֵּיהּ בְּמַדְבְּרָא, מִיתוּ, וְאַכְנָס לוֹן קוּדְשָׁא בְּרִיךְ הוּא לִבְנַיְיהוּ בְּאַרְעָא. וּבֵיתָא אִתְבְּנֵי עַל יְדָא דְּבַר נָשׁ, וּבְגִין כָּךְ לָא אִתְקַיָּים. וּשְׁלֹמֹה הֲוָה יָדַע, דִּבְגִין דְּהַאי עוֹבָדָא דְּבַר נָשׁ לָא יִתְקַיָּים, וְעַל דָּא אָמַר, אִם יְיָ' לֹא יִבְנֶה בַיִת שָׁוְא עָמְלוּ בוֹנָיו בּוֹ, דְּהָא לֵית לֵיהּ בֵּיהּ קִיוּמָא. בְּיוֹמוֹי דְּעֶזְרָא, גָּרַם חֲטָאָה, וְאִצְטָרְכוּ אִינּוּן לְמִבְנֵי, וְלָא הֲוָה בֵּיהּ קִיוּמָא. וְעַד כְּעַן, בִּנְיָינָא קַדְמָאָה דְּקוּדְשָׁא בְּרִיךְ הוּא, לָא הֲוָה בְּעָלְמָא, וּלְזִמְנָא דְּאָתֵי כְּתִיב, בּוֹנֵה יְרוּשָׁלַם יְיָ', אִיהוּ וְלָא אָחֳרָא. וּבְנְיָינָא דָּא אֲנָן מְחַכָּאן, וְלָא בִּנְיָינָא דְּבַר נָשׁ, דְּלֵית בֵּיהּ קִיוּמָא כְּלַל.

148. But when they angered Him in the wilderness, they died, and the Holy one. blessed be He, brought their children into the land, and the Temple was constructed by man, which is why it did not last. FOR THE BUILDING HAS TO BE THE WORK OF THE HOLY ONE, BLESSED BE HE. King Solomon knew that the Temple that he built was built by man and would not therefore last, which is why it is written: "Unless Hashem builds the house, they who build it labor in vain" (Tehilim 127:1) And indeed it no longer exists. In the days of Ezra, because of the sin, they had to rebuild THE TEMPLE, which is why it had no lasting existence. And up until now the first building of the Holy One, blessed be He, has not been placed in the world, but concerning the future it is written: "Hashem builds Jerusalem" (Tehilim 147:2). He WILL BUILD and no other. It is for this building that we are waiting, and not for a man made structure which has no permanence.

149. בֵּית רִאשׁוֹן, וּבֵית שֵׁנִי, יָחִית לוֹן קוּדְשָׁא בְּרִיךְ הוּא כַּחֲדָא מִלְּעֵילָא. בֵּית רִאשׁוֹן בְּאִתְכַּסְיָא, וּבֵית שֵׁנִי בְּאִתְגַּלְיָא. הַהוּא בֵּית לֶהֱוֵי בְּאִתְגַּלְיָא, דְּאִתְקְרֵי בֵּית שֵׁנִי, דְּיִתְחֲזֵי לְכָל עָלְמָא אוּמָנוּתָא דְּקוּדְשָׁא בְּרִיךְ הוּא. חֶדְוָה שְׁלִים, וּרְעוּתָא דְּלִבָּא בְּכָל קִיּוּמָא.

149. The Holy One, blessed be He, will bring down the First Temple and the Second Temple from on high simultaneously. The First Temple, WHICH IS EQUIVALENT TO BINAH, will be concealed, and the Second Temple, WHICH IS PARALLEL TO MALCHUT, will be in the open. That house that is called 'the Second Temple' will be in the open so that the art of the Holy One, blessed be He, will be visible to the whole world. AND THEN THERE WILL BE perfect rejoicing, and goodwill in all its existence.

150. הַהוּא בֵּית רִאשׁוֹן בְּאִתְכַּסְיָא, אִסְתְּלַק לְעֵילָא, עַל גַּבּוֹי דְּהַהוּא דְּאִתְגַּלְיָא. וְכָל עָלְמָא יֶחֱמוּן, עֲנָנֵי יְקָר דְּסָחֲרָן עַל גַּבֵּי דְּהַהוּא דְּאִתְגַּלְיָיא, וּבְגוֹ דְּאִינּוּן עֲנָנִין, הֲוֵי בֵּית רִאשׁוֹן, בְּעוֹבָדָא טְמִירָא, דְּסָלִיק עַד רוּם יְקָר שְׁמַיָּיא, וּבִנְיָינָא דָּא אֲנָן מְחַכָּאן.

150. The First Temple THAT WILL BE concealed ascends on high over THE SECOND TEMPLE that is revealed, and the whole world will see the clouds of glory that surround the Temple that is revealed, and within those clouds will be the First Temple in a hidden action, rising to the height of the glory of the heavens, WHICH IS BINAH, and this is the building for which we are waiting.

151. וְעַד כְּעַן, לָא הֲוָה בְּעָלְמָא, דַּאֲפִילוּ קַרְתָּא דִּירוּשְׁלֵם לָא לֶיהֱוֵי אוּמָנוּתָא דב״נ, דְּהָא כְּתִיב, וַאֲנִי אֶהְיֶה לָהּ נְאֻם יְיָ' חוֹמַת אֵשׁ סָבִיב וְגוֹ'. אִי לְקַרְתָּא כְּתִיב הָכִי, כָּל שֶׁכֵּן בֵּיתָא, דְּאִיהוּ דִּיּוּרָא דִּילֵיהּ. וְעוֹבָדָא דָּא, הֲוֵי אִתְחֲזֵי לְמֶהֱוֵי בְּרֵישָׁא, כַּד נַפְקוּ יִשְׂרָאֵל מִמִּצְרַיִם, וְאִסְתְּלַּק עַד לְסוֹף יוֹמִין, בְּפוּרְקָנָא בַּתְרָאָה.

151. So far this has not happened in the world, for even the city of Jerusalem will not be the result of man's skills, for it is written: "for I, says

Hashem, will be to her a wall of fire round about, and will be the glory in the midst of her..." (Zecharyah 2:9). If this is what is written about the city, how much more so will this be the case for the Temple, which is His dwelling place. And this action OF THE HOLY ONE, BLESSED BE HE, should have been seen at the beginning, when Yisrael came out of Egypt, but it was delayed for the End of Days, for the final Redemption.

25. Why Yisrael are in more trouble than other peoples

A Synopsis

We are told that Yisrael is the heart of the whole world, and the heart is the only part of the body that knows pain and trouble because it incorporates existence and intelligence. Thus it is the only part that is close to God at all.

The Relevance of this Passage

The Light of healing flows to our heart and to the entire cardiovascular system. Moreover, this Light warms and heals our spiritual heart, transforming us into kind, compassionate, and loving people. The Light energy generated here is the lifeblood of humanity. And just as the heart furnishes the body with blood, this Light flows to the collective body of man – the nations of the world – nourishing their souls with divinity to melt away the barriers of religious and social intolerance. The suffering and pain endured by the heart ceases, replaced with gladness and joy. And the knowledge of the Creator permeates the land, bringing peace and love to all civilization.

152. שְׁאֶלְתָּא אַחֲרָא, דְּוַדַּאי אֲנָן קְרֵבִין לְמַלְכָּא עִלָּאָה, יַתִּיר מִכָּל שְׁאַר עַמִּין. וַדַּאי הָכִי הוּא, דְּיִשְׂרָאֵל עֲבַד לוֹן קוּדְשָׁא בְּרִיךְ הוּא לִבָּא דְּכָל עָלְמָא. וְהָכִי אִינּוּן יִשְׂרָאֵל בֵּין שְׁאַר עַמִּין, כְּלִבָּא בֵּין שַׁיְיפִין, כְּמָה דְּשַׁיְיפִין לָא יַכְלֵי לְמֵיקַם בְּעָלְמָא אֲפִילוּ רִגְעָא חֲדָא בְּלָא לִבָּא, הָכִי עַמִּין כֻּלְּהוּ, לָא יַכְלִין לְמֵיקַם בְּעָלְמָא, בְּלָא יִשְׂרָאֵל. וְאוֹף הָכִי יְרוּשְׁלֵם בְּגוֹ שְׁאַר אַרְעָאן, כְּלִבָּא בְּגוֹ שַׁיְיפִין. וְעַל דָּא אִיהִי בְּאֶמְצָעִיתָא דְּכוּלֵי עָלְמָא. כְּלִבָּא גוֹ שַׁיְיפִין.

152. The second question ASKED BY THAT GENTILE, IS THUS: FOR surely we are closer to the Supernal King than any of the other peoples. This must be so for the Holy One, blessed be He, made Yisrael the heart of the whole world, and the relationship of Yisrael to the other nations is as that of the heart to other parts of the body. And just as the other parts of the body do not last, even for a moment, without the heart, so it is that none of the other peoples can exist in the world without Yisrael. Jerusalem, too, has the same relationship with the other countries, being as the heart to the parts of the body, which is why it is in the center of the whole world just as the heart is in the center of the limbs.

153. וְיִשְׂרָאֵל מִתְנַהֲגָן גּוֹ שְׁאַר עַמִּין, כְּגַוְונָא דְלִבָּא גּוֹ שַׁיְיפִין. לִבָּא
אִיהִי רָכִיךְ וְחָלָשׁ, וְאִיהוּ קִיּוּמָא דְּכָל שַׁיְיפִין, לָא יָדַע מִצַּעֲרָא וְעָקָא
וִיגוֹנָא כְּלָל אֶלָּא לִבָּא, דְּבֵיהּ קִיוּמָא, דְּבֵיהּ סוּכְלְתָנוּ, שְׁאַר שַׁיְיפִין לָא
אִתְקְרִיב בְּהוּ כְּלָל, דְּהָא לֵית בְּהוּ קִיוּמָא, וְלָא יַדְעִין מִדִּי. כָּל שְׁאַר
שַׁיְיפִין לָא קְרִיבִין לְמַלְכָּא, דְּאִיהוּ חָכְמְתָא וְסוּכְלְתָנוּ, דְּשַׁרְיָא בְּמוֹחָא,
אֶלָּא לִבָּא. וּשְׁאַר שַׁיְיפִין, רְחִיקִין מִנֵּיהּ, וְלָא יַדְעִין מִנֵּיהּ כְּלָל. כַּךְ
יִשְׂרָאֵל, לְמַלְכָּא קַדִּישָׁא קְרִיבִין, וּשְׁאַר עַמִּין רְחִיקִין מִנֵּיהּ.

153. And Yisrael's conduct amongst the other nations is as that of the heart amongst the limbs. The heart is soft and weak, but gives existence to all the limbs, AND ALL THE LIMBS do not know pain, trouble and agony at all, but only the heart does, for in it is existence and intelligence. PAIN AND ANGUISH come nowhere near the other limbs, for they have no existence and know nothing. None of the other limbs comes near to the King, who is wisdom and intelligence that reside in the brain; the heart is the only exception. The other limbs are far from Him and know nothing about Him. Thus it is that Yisrael are near to the Holy King while the other peoples are far from Him.

26. Why Yisrael, who do not partake of animals found dead or not ritually slaughtered, are weak

A Synopsis

Elijah teaches that the heart takes for its nourishment only the clearest and purest of the blood, and this food is softer and weaker than the rest of the food.

The Relevance of this Passage

The purifying influences emitted here cleanse our blood of toxins and poisons. Vital salts are balanced. Fat, cholesterol, and wastes are extracted from the blood. Ailments of the heart and blood are treated and remedied by the Light. Afflictions of the skin are healed. The spiritual roots of all heart and blood ailments are exterminated. These are the personal physical effects achieved here.

Globally, toxins and poisons in the air and in our foods are extracted from our environment. Spiritually, the bonds among peoples of all faith are unblocked and cleared. Hatred, bigotry, and intolerance are purged out of the metaphysical arteries that interconnect the people of the world. Light and love are free to flow, harmonize, and regenerate the collective body of civilization.

154. שְׁאֶלְתָּא אַחֲרָא, דְּיִשְׂרָאֵל לָא אָכְלֵי נְבֵלוֹת וּטְרֵפוֹת, וְטִנּוּפָא וְלִכְלוּכָא דִּשְׁקָצִים וּרְמָשִׂים כִּשְׁאַר עַמִּין, הָכִי הוּא, דְּהָא לִבָּא דְּאִיהוּ רָכִיךְ וְחַלָּשׁ, וּמַלְכָּא וְקִיּוּמָא דְּכָל שְׁאַר שַׁיְיפִין, לָא נָטִיל לִמְזוֹנֵיהּ, אֶלָּא בְּרִירוּ וְצַחוּתָא דְּכָל דָּמָא, וּמְזוֹנֵיהּ נָקִי וּבְרִירָא, וְאִיהוּ רָכִיךְ וְחַלָּשׁ מִכֹּלָּא, וּשְׁאַר פְּסוֹלֶת אֲנָח לְכָל שַׁיְיפִין, וְכָל שְׁאַר שַׁיְיפִין לָא מַשְׁגִּחִין בְּהַאי, אֶלָּא כָּל כָּל פְּסוֹלֶת וּבִישׁ דְּכֹלָּא נַטְלִין, וְאִינוּן בְּתַקִּיפוּ כְּמָה דְּאִתְחֲזֵי לוֹן.

154. The other question POSED BY THAT GENTILE was that Yisrael do not partake of animals found dead or those not ritually slaughtered, nor of the filth and dirt of reptiles and insects as do the other peoples, BUT ARE NEVERTHELESS WEAKER THAN THEY ARE. This is how it is. For the heart, which is soft and weak and is the king and the sustenance of the other limbs, does not take FROM MAN'S FOOD for its nourishment other than from the clearest and purest of all the blood THAT IS MADE FROM FOOD, and its food

is clean and clear and is softer and weaker than all the rest. And it leaves the remaining waste matters OF THE BLOOD for the other limbs, and the other limbs are not concerned AS TO THE CLEANLINESS OF THEIR FOOD, but take all the waste matters, even the worst, and they are strong as befits them.

155. וְעַל דָּא בְּכָל שְׁאַר שַׁיְיפִין אִית אֲבַעְבּוּעִין, שְׂאֵת אוֹ סַפַּחַת, סְגִירוּ דְצָרַעַת. לְלִבָּא, לָאו מִכָּל הָנֵי כְּלוּם, אֶלָּא אִיהוּ נָקִי בְּרִירָא מִכֹּלָּא, לֵית בֵּיה מוּמָא כְּלָל. כַּךְ קוּדְשָׁא בְּרִיךְ הוּא נָטִיל לֵיה לְיִשְׂרָאֵל דְּאִיהוּ נָקִי וּבְרִירוּ דְלֵית בֵּיה מוּמָא עַל דָּא כְּתִיב, כֻּלָּךְ יָפָה רַעְיָתִי וּמוּם אֵין בָּךְ. אָתָא רִבִּי יוֹסֵי, נָשִׁיק יְדוֹי, אָמַר, אִילוּ לָא אֲתֵינָא לְעָלְמָא, אֶלָּא לְמִשְׁמַע דָּא, דַּיִי.

155. This is why all the other limbs have skin eruptions and scabs, bright spots and leprous boils, and the heart has none of them, for it is clean and clear, and has no blemish whatsoever. Thus the Holy One, blessed be He, took Yisrael, who is clean, clear, and without blemish, for Himself, as scripture says: "You are all fair, my love; there is no blemish in you" (Shir Hashirim 4:7). Rabbi Yosi came, kissed his hands, and said: If I had come into the world just to hear this, it would have been sufficient.

27. "Now the name of the man of Yisrael that was slain"

A Synopsis
Rabbi Eliezer tells Rabbi Yitzchak that the title verse does not say who killed the man because Pinchas had by then achieved priesthood, and it was not appropriate to mention a priest in connection with any killing.

The Relevance of this Passage
By virtue of Pinchas's priesthood and God's unending compassion, we are absolved of our sins and elevated to greater heights of holiness as repentance stirs in our souls. Our names are stricken from the prosecuting attorney's records so that judgments can no longer be set forth against us.

156. וְשֵׁם אִישׁ יִשְׂרָאֵל הַמֻּכֶּה וְגו'. אָמַר ר' יִצְחָק, הַאי קְרָא הָכִי הֲוָה לֵיהּ לְמִכְתַּב, וְשֵׁם אִישׁ יִשְׂרָאֵל אֲשֶׁר הִכָּה פִּנְחָס, וְלֹא הַמֻּכֶּה אֲשֶׁר הֻכָּה, לָא נֶאֱמַר אֶלָּא בְּאֹרַח סָתִים.

156. "Now the name of the man of Yisrael that was slain" (Bemidbar 25:14). Rabbi Yitzchak said: This verse should have been written so: 'Now the name of the man of Yisrael whom Pinchas slew', and not "that was slain, that was slain," simply WITHOUT EVEN MENTIONING THE ONE WHO DID THE SLAYING.

157. אֶלָּא הָכִי אָמַר ר' אֶלְעָזָר, כֵּיוָן דְּסַלְּקֵיהּ קוּדְשָׁא בְּרִיךְ הוּא לְפִנְחָס לְכַהֲנָא רַבָּא, לָא בָּעָא לְאַדְכְּרָא לֵיהּ לְפִנְחָס בְּקַטְלָנוּתָא דְּבַר נָשׁ. דְּהָא לָא אִתְחֲזֵי לְכַהֲנָא רַבָּא. עַד לָא סַלְּקֵיהּ לְכַהֲנָא רַבָּא, אַדְכַּר לֵיהּ, וְאָמַר וַיַּרְא פִּנְחָס וַיִּקַּח רֹמַח וְגו', וַיִּדְקֹר אֶת שְׁנֵיהֶם וְגו'. כֵּיוָן דְּסַלְּקֵיהּ לְכַהֲנָא רַבָּא לָא אַדְכַּר שְׁמֵיהּ בְּקַטְלָנוּתָא, דְּלָא אִתְחֲזֵי לֵיהּ, וְחָס עָלֵיהּ יְקָרָא דְקוּדְשָׁא בְּרִיךְ הוּא, דְּכַהֲנָא רַבָּא לָא אִתְחֲזֵי לְאַדְכְּרָא בְּקַטְלָנוּתָא. וְשֵׁם הָאִשָּׁה הַמּוּכָּה, אוּף הָכִי.

157. HE ANSWERS: this is how Rabbi Eliezer put it: Since the Holy One, blessed be He, had raised Pinchas to the level of High Priest, He did not want to mention Pinchas in the context of a man slaying, for this is not

fitting for a High Priest. Before He elevated him to the high priesthood, He did mention him, and said: "And when Pinchas...saw...and took a spear...and thrust both of them through..." (Ibid. 7-8). But once he was elevated to the high priesthood, his name is not mentioned in the context of killing, for this is unbefitting, and the honor of the Holy One, blessed be He, had compassion on him because it is not right for a High Priest to be mentioned in the context of a killing. "And the name of the Midianite woman that was slain" (Ibid. 15) IS also GIVEN WITHOUT STATING WHO THE SLAYER WAS, FOR THE SAME REASON.

28. What is now first will be last at the resurrection of the dead

A Synopsis
Rabbi Pinchas ben Yair explains that God will reconstruct a man in the opposite order that the body disintegrates, for now the body is first stripped of spirit, and then the skin, flesh, sinews and bones rot.

The Relevance of this Passage
In the act of describing the order of the death process in this sacred book, Pinchas is, essentially, launching a death blow to the Angel of Death himself, paving the way for the Resurrection of the Dead and for Immortality. If the force of Death lurks anywhere within our own body, the rays of Light launched by Pinchas eliminate it completely.

158. רִבִּי שִׁמְעוֹן הֲוָה אָזִיל מִקַּפּוֹטְקְיָא לְלוֹד, ור' יְהוּדָה אָזִיל עִמֵּיהּ, עַד דַּהֲווֹ אָזְלֵי פָּגַע בְּהוּ ר' פִּנְחָס בֶּן יָאִיר, וּתְרֵין גּוּבְרִין טוֹעֲנִין אֲבַתְרֵיהּ. שָׁכִיךְ חֲמָרֵיהּ דר' פִּנְחָס. טָעִינוּ לֵיהּ, וְלָא אָזִיל. אָמַר ר' פִּנְחָס, שִׁבְקוּ לֵיהּ, דְּהָא רֵיחָא דְּאַנְפִּין חַדְתִּין קָא אָרַח, אוֹ נִסָּא אִתְעֲבֵיד לָן הַשְׁתָּא. עַד דְּאִינּוּן תַּמָּן, נָפַק ר' שִׁמְעוֹן מִבָּתַר חַד טִנָּרָא. נָטַל חֲמָרָא וְאָזִיל, אָמַר ר' פִּנְחָס, וְלָא אֲמָרִית לְכוּ, דְּהָא רֵיחָא דְּאַנְפִּין חַדְתִּין קָא אָרַח.

158. Rabbi Shimon was traveling from Cappadocia to Lod, and Rabbi Yehuda was going with him. While they were en route, they were met by Rabbi Pinchas ben Yair and two donkey drivers following him. Rabbi Pinchas' donkey stopped. He prodded him WITH A SPUR THAT HE SHOULD CONTINUE, but he did not do so. Rabbi Pinchas said TO THE DONKEY DRIVERS: Leave him be, for he can discern the smell of new countenances APPROACHING US, or a miracle will happen to us. While they were still there, Rabbi Shimon appeared from behind one of the rocks, and the donkey continued on. Rabbi Pinchas said, Did I not tell you that he discerned the smell of new countenances?

159. נָחַת וְגָפִיף לֵיהּ ר' פִּנְחָס, וּבְכָה, אָמַר לֵיהּ, חֲמֵינָא בְּחֶלְמִי, דְּאַתְיָא שְׁכִינְתָּא לְגַבִּי, וְיָהֲבַת לִי נְבִזְבְּזָן רַבְרְבָן, וְחַדִּינָא בָּהּ. הַשְׁתָּא כְּמָה דַּחֲמֵינָא. אָמַר ר' שִׁמְעוֹן, מִקָּל פַּרְסֵי דַּחֲמָרָךְ, יָדַעְנָא דְּאַנְתְּ הוּא.

הַשְׁתָּא חֶדְוָה שְׁלִים. אָמַר ר' פִּנְחָס, נְתִיב בְּדוּךְ חַד, דְּמִלֵּי דְּאוֹרַיְיתָא אִצְטְרִיךְ צָחוּתָא. אַשְׁכְּחוּ עֵינָא דְּמַיָּיא, וְאִילָנָא, יָתְבוּ.

159. Rabbi Pinchas dismounted FROM HIS DONKEY, embraced RABBI SHIMON, and cried. He said to him, I saw in my dream that the Shechinah had come to me, and given me great presents, and I had rejoiced with Her. And now what I saw HAS COME TO PASS. Rabbi Shimon said: I knew that it was you from the sound of your donkey's footsteps. Now the rejoicing is complete. Rabbi Pinchas said, Let us sit down somewhere, as a Torah discussion has to be lucid. They found a well of water and a tree and sat down.

160. אָמַר ר' פִּנְחָס, מִסְתַּכֵּל הֲוֵינָא דְּהָא לִתְחִיַּית הַמֵּתִים, בְּאָרְחָא אָחֳרָא יַעֲבִיד לוֹן קוּדְשָׁא בְּרִיךְ הוּא, וּמַה דַּהֲוָה הַשְׁתָּא קַדְמָאָה, לִיהֱוֵי כְּדֵין בַּתְרָאָה. מְנָלָן. מֵאִינּוּן עֲצָמוֹת, הַנְהוּ גַּרְמִין דְּאַחֲיָא לוֹן קוּדְשָׁא בְּרִיךְ הוּא עַל יְדֵי יְחֶזְקֵאל, דִּכְתִיב וַתִּקְרְבוּ עֲצָמוֹת עֶצֶם אֶל עַצְמוֹ בְּקַדְמֵיתָא, וּלְבָתַר כְּתִיב וְרָאִיתִי וְהִנֵּה עֲלֵיהֶם גִּידִים וּבָשָׂר עָלָה וְגוֹ'. וַיִּקְרַם עֲלֵיהֶם עוֹר מִלְמַעְלָה וְרוּחַ אֵין בָּהֶם. דְּהָא מַה דְּאַפְשִׁיט בְּקַדְמֵיתָא, לִיהֱוֵי בַּתְרָאָה. בְּקַדְמֵיתָא אַפְשִׁיט מֵרוּחָא, וּלְבָתַר עוֹר, וּלְבָתַר בָּשָׂר, וּלְבָתַר עֲצָמוֹת.

160. Rabbi Pinchas said, I observed that the resurrection of the dead would be performed on us by the Holy One, blessed be He, in one way, and that what is now first to leave will be the last AT THE RESURRECTION. How do we know this? From those bones, the ones into which the Holy One, blessed be He, breathed life at the hands of Ezekiel. At the beginning it is written: "And the bones came together, bone to its bone" (Yechezkel 37:7), and later it is written: "And as I beheld, and, lo, there were sinews upon them, and flesh came up" (Ibid. 8). AND THE SAME VERSE CONTINUES: "and skin covered them above: but there was no breath in them." From here, too, we can learn that what A PERSON takes off first will be the last to be put on again. Initially, man is stripped of spirit, and then his skin ROTS, followed by the flesh, THEN THE SINEWS, and finally the bones. AT THE RESURRECTION IT WILL BE THE OTHER WAY AROUND: INITIALLY THE BONES, THEN THE SINEWS, FOLLOWED BY THE FLESH, AND LASTLY THE SKIN.

29. The resurrection of the dead

A Synopsis

Rabbi Shimon says that at the time of resurrection God will re-make a person from the remaining bone that has not disintegrated. We learn that all the souls of the righteous are concealed under God's throne, Malchut, and that the throne protects them so they can be returned. Rabbi Shimon says that wherever scripture does not explicitly state Hashem, the reference is always to Malchut.

The Relevance of this Passage

The Zohar's discourse on the deep mysteries surrounding the Resurrection of the Dead sends forth a mystical energy force when our eyes behold these verses. The regeneration of our body, our soul, our cells, and our spirit transpires. The illusion of death is now pierced, ending the greatest fraud ever to be perpetrated against the human race. The notion of dying loses power as the truth of immortality begins to take hold in our consciousness, setting into motion the Final Redemption and the reality of Heaven on Earth.

Moses, the Faithful Shepherd, guards and protects us from the Evil forces of the night which rise out of hell each evening. The gates to Hell are herewith locked forever, while the gateway to Eden opens wide.

161. אר"ש, בְּדָא אַקְשָׁן קַדְמָאֵי, אֲבָל גַּרְמִין אִלֵּין דְּאַחְיָא קוּדְשָׁא בְּרִיךְ הוּא, נִסִּין וְאָתִין מְשַׁנְיָין, עֲבַד בְּהוּ קוּדְשָׁא בְּרִיךְ הוּא. ת"ח מַה כְּתִיב, זְכָר נָא כִּי כַחוֹמֶר עֲשִׂיתָנִי וְאֶל עָפָר תְּשִׁיבֵנִי. מַה כְּתִיב בַּתְרֵיהּ, הֲלֹא כֶחָלָב תַּתִּיכֵנִי וְכַגְּבִינָה תַּקְפִּיאֵנִי, עוֹר וּבָשָׂר תַּלְבִּישֵׁנִי וּבַעֲצָמוֹת וְגִידִים תְּסוֹכְכֵנִי. זַמִּין קוּדְשָׁא בְּרִיךְ הוּא, לְבָתַר דְּיִתְבְּלֵי ב"נ בְּעַפְרָא, וּמָטֵי זִמְנָא דִּתְחִיַּית הַמֵּתִים, דְּהַהוּא גַּרְמָא דְּיִשְׁתְּאַר. לְמֶעְבַּד לֵיהּ כְּעִסָּה דָּא, וְכַגְּבִינָה דְּחָלָב, וּנְבִיעַ דְּחָלָב, דְּהוּא נְבִיעוּ נָקִי מְצוּחְצַח בְּצַחוּתָא. יִתְעָרַב הַהוּא גַּרְמָא וְיִתְמְחֵי כְּחָלָבָא, וּלְבָתַר יַקְפִּיא לֵיהּ, וְיִתְצַיֵּיר בְּצִיּוּרָא כַּגְּבִינָה בִּקְפִיאוּתָא, וּלְבָתַר יִתְמְשַׁךְ עֲלֵיהּ עוֹר וּבָשָׂר וַעֲצָמוֹת וְגִידִים.

161. Rabbi Shimon said: The earlier teachers had difficulties with this

passage, but the truth is that the Holy One, blessed be He, performed strange miracles and signs with these bones into which He breathed life. Come and see: "Remember, I beseech You, that You have fashioned me like clay; and will You bring me back to dust" (Iyov 10:9). And then, in the next verses: "Have You not poured me out as milk, and curdled me like cheese? You have clothed me with skin and flesh, and have knit me together with bones and sinews." When a person has rotted in the dust, and the time of the resurrection of the dead has arrived, the Holy One, blessed be He, will re-make him from the remaining bone THAT DOES NOT ROT, make it like dough and as cheese from milk and as flowing as a stream of pure clear milk. For the bone will be refined, BECOMING VERY THIN, and polished as milk, curdled, and fashioned into a shape, like curdled cheese. After this structure is done He will create anew the skin, veins and bones.

162. הה"ד הֲלֹא כֶחָלָב תַּתִּיכֵנִי וְכַגְּבִינָה תַקְפִּיאֵנִי. הִתְכַּתָּנִי לָא כְּתִיב, אֶלָּא תַתִּיכֵנִי. הִקְפִּיתָנִי לָא כְּתִיב, אֶלָּא תַקְפִּיאֵנִי. הִלְבַּשְׁתָּנִי לָא כְּתִיב, אֶלָּא תַּלְבִּישֵׁנִי. סוֹכַכְתָּנִי לָא כְּתִיב, אֶלָּא תְּסוֹכְכֵנִי. כֻּלְּהוּ לְבָתַר זִמְנָא מַשְׁמַע.

162. Hence "Have You not poured me out as milk, and curdled me like cheese? You have clothed me with skin and flesh": all the verbs are in fact in the future tense. Not 'Have You not poured me out', but 'Will You not pour me out'. Not 'Have You not clothed me with skin and flesh', but 'Will You not clothe me with skin and flesh...'. This is because the reference throughout is to a future time, THAT OF THE RESURRECTION.

163. וּלְבָתַר מַה כְּתִיב, חַיִּים וָחֶסֶד עָשִׂיתָ עִמָּדִי, דָּא רוּחָא דְּחַיֵּי. וְאִי תֵּימָא עָשִׂיתָ עִמָּדִי כְּתִיב, וְלָא כְּתִיב תַּעֲשֶׂה. אֶלָּא הָכִי אָמַר, חַיִּים וָחֶסֶד עָשִׂיתָ עִמָּדִי. בְּהַהוּא עָלְמָא שָׁדִית בִּי רוּחָא דְּחַיִּים, אֲבָל וּפְקוּדָּתְךָ, דְּמַטְרוֹנִיתָא דְּמַלְכָּא, שָׁמְרָה רוּחִי, אִיהִי נַטְרַת לְרוּחִי, בְּהַהוּא עָלְמָא. מַאי וּפְקוּדָּתְךָ, דְּאַתְּ זַמִּין לְפַקְּדָא לָהּ בְּקַדְמֵיתָא.

163. And what is written afterwards? "You have granted me life and favor" (Iyov 10:12). This is the spirit of life. But you may say: But it is written "have granted" IN THE PAST TENSE and not 'will grant'. HE ANSWERS

THAT he said: "You have granted me life and favor," for in that world You have given me the spirit of life. But, the verse continues, "and Your providence," namely that of the King's Matron, MALCHUT, "has preserved my spirit," namely guards my spirit in that world. And why DOES HE REFER TO MALCHUT AS "Your providence"? BECAUSE You will in the future visit her first. THEREFORE, HE REFERS TO HER AS HIS ASSIGNED ORDER AND COMMAND.

164. וְרָזָא דְּמִלָּה דָּא, כָּל נַפְשִׁין דְּצַדִּיקַיָּיא, גְּנִיזִין וּטְמִירִין תְּחוֹת כֻּרְסְיָיא דְּמַלְכָּא, וְאִיהִי נַטְרָא לוֹן, לְאָתָבָא לוֹן לְדוּכְתַּיְיהוּ, הה"ד וּפְקוּדָתְךָ שָׁמְרָה רוּחִי. מַאי וּפְקוּדָתְךָ. כד"א, פְּקוּדָתוֹ יִקַּח אַחֵר. פְּקוּדָתְךָ, דָּא מַטְרוֹנִיתָא דְּמַלְכָּא, דְּכָל רוּחִין אִינוּן פִּקְדוֹנִין בִּידָהָא, הה"ד בְּיָדְךָ אַפְקִיד רוּחִי וְגו', וְאִיהִי נַטְרָא לוֹן, בְּגִין דָּא שָׁמְרָה רוּחִי, וְאִיהִי נַטְרַת לָהּ.

164. And the secret of this matter is that all the souls of the righteous are hidden and concealed under the King's throne, WHICH IS MALCHUT, WHICH IS CALLED 'A THRONE', and it protects them so that they can be returned to their place, as it is written: "and Your providence has preserved my spirit." What is "Your providence (Heb. *pkudatcha*)"? It is as in the verse: "and let another take his possessions (Heb. *pkudato*)" (Tehilim 109:8). "Your providence" refers to the King's Matron, NAMELY MALCHUT, for all the spirits are pledges in her hands, as it is written: "Into Your hand I commit (Heb. *afkid*) my spirit" (Tehilim 31:6), and she protects them. Thus IS IT WRITTEN "has preserved my spirit," (Iyov 10:12) for she preserves it.

165. כְּגַוְונָא דָּא אָמַר דָּוִד, שָׁמְרָה נַפְשִׁי כִּי חָסִיד אָנִי. שָׁמְרָה: דָּא מַטְרוֹנִיתָא דְּמַלְכָּא. דְּאִיהִי נַטְרָא נַפְשִׁי, בְּגִין כִּי חָסִיד אָנִי. וּבְכָל אֲתָר דִּכְתִיב סְתָם, דָּא מַטְרוֹנִיתָא. כד"א, וַיִּקְרָא אֶל מֹשֶׁה. וַיֹּאמֶר אִם שָׁמוֹעַ תִּשְׁמַע בְּקוֹל יְיָ' אֱלֹהֶיךָ.

165. David said something similar: "Preserve my soul; for I am pious" (Tehilim 86:2). "Preserve" refers to the King's Matron, for she has preserved my soul because I am pious. And as a general rule, whenever

scripture is vague AND DOES NOT EXPLICITLY STATE HASHEM, the reference is to the Matron WHO IS MALCHUT. As for example, in the verse: "And He called to Moses" (Shemot 24:16), WHERE HASHEM IS NOT MENTIONED BY NAME, or "He said: If you will diligently hearken to the voice of Hashem your Elohim" (Shemot 15:26), WHERE THE SPEAKER AGAIN IS NOT NAMED AND THE REFERENCE IS TO MALCHUT.

166. בָּכָה ר' פִּנְחָס, וְאָמַר, וְלָאו אֲמָרִית לָךְ דִּשְׁכִינְתָּא יָהֲבַת לִי נִבְזְבְּזָן וּמַתְּנָן, זַכָּאָה חוּלָקִי דְּזָכֵינָא לְמֶחֱמֵי לָךְ, וְשָׁמַעְנָא דָּא. א"ל, בְּהַהוּא זִמְנָא, תִּינַח הַהוּא גַּרְמָא, שְׁאַר גַּרְמִין דְּיִשְׁתַּכְּחוּן מַה יִתְעֲבִיד מִנְּהוֹן. א"ל, כֻּלְּהוּ יִתְכְּלִילוּ בְּהַהוּא דְּהַאי גַּרְמָא, וְיִתְכְּלִילוּ בַּהֲדֵיהּ, וְיִתְעֲבִיד כֹּלָּא עִסָּה חֲדָא, וְתַמָּן יִתְצַיַּיר צִיּוּרָא, כְּמָה דְּאִתְּמַר. הה"ד, וְעַצְמוֹתֶיךָ יַחֲלִיץ. מַאי יַחֲלִיץ. כד"א חָלַץ מֵהֶם. כֻּלְּהוּ יִתְעַבְּרוּן מִקִּיּוּמַיְיהוּ, וְיִתְכְּלִילוּ בְּהַאי גַּרְמָא, לְמֶהֱוֵי עִסָּה חֲדָא. וּכְדֵין וְהָיִיתָ כְּגַן רָוֶה וּכְמוֹצָא מַיִם וְגו'.

166. Rabbi Pinchas cried and said, And did I not tell you that IN MY DREAM the Shechinah had given me great offerings and gifts? THE MEANING WAS THESE SAYINGS OF RABBI SHIMON. Happy is my portion that I have merited seeing you and hearing this. He said to him: WHAT YOU HAVE SAID CONCERNING that time OF THE RESURRECTION is correct regarding the one bone THAT DOES NOT ROT, but what happens to the other bones that are there? He said to him: They will all be included in the flow of that bone and will be incorporated with it and they will all be made into one dough, out of which MAN will be formed, as they said in the verse: "and make strong (Heb. *yachlitz*) your bones" (Yeshayah 58:11). What is the meaning of *yachlitz*? It is as in the verse: "He has withdrawn (Heb. *chalatz*) Himself from them" (Hoshea 5:6). In other words, they will all be withdrawn from their place and incorporated in this bone, making one dough, and then "you shall be like a watered garden, and like a spring of water" (Yeshayah 58.11).

A Synopsis

Moses gives a warning to people whose hearts are blocked off and whose eyes are closed, for the forces of the evil inclination will enter into them. He says that all the lights in the eyes issue from the heart.

רעיא מהימנא

167. אָמַר רַעְיָא מְהֵימָנָא, וַוי לוֹן לִבְנֵי נָשָׁא, דְּאִינּוּן אֲטִימִין לִבָּא, סְתִימִין עַיְינִין, דְּלָא יַדְעִין דְּכַד אָתֵי לֵילְיָא, תַּרְעִין דְּגֵיהִנָּם אִתְפְּתָחוּ, דְּאִיהִי מָרָה. וַעֲשָׁנִין דִּילָהּ, דְּמִתְפַּשְׁטִין סַלְקִין עַד מוֹחָא. וְכַמָּה חַיָּילִין דְּיֵצֶר הָרָע, מִתְפַּשְׁטִין בְּכָל אֶבְרִין דְּגוּפָא. וְתַרְעִין דְּג"ע, דְּאִיהוּ עַיְינִין דְּלִבָּא, מִסְתַּתְּמִין וְלָא מִתְפַּתְּחִין. דְּכָל נְהוֹרִין דְּעַיְינִין, מִלִּבָּא נָפְקִין.

Ra'aya Meheimna (the Faithful Shepherd)

167. The Faithful Shepherd said, Woe to those people whose hearts are blocked off and whose eyes are closed, for they do not know that when the night comes the gates of Gehenom are opened, which is CALLED 'gall', and the odors that spread from it rise up to the brain. And a number of forces of the Evil Inclination spread throughout the parts of the body. And the gates of the Garden of Eden which are the eyes of the heart are blocked off and not opened, for all the lights that are in the eyes issue forth from the heart.

30. "Into Your hand I commit my spirit"

A Synopsis

Moses goes on to say that the lights of the heart are angels that spread throughout the limbs like the branches of a tree. He tells us about the evil effect of shutting off the lights, and says that an ignorant man cannot be pious because unless he has studied the Torah he cannot join Zeir Anpin and Malchut.

The Relevance of this Passage

All forms of negativity and sin are purged from our body, purifying our souls as the Light of the Garden of Eden shines in our hearts and shoots out from our eyes. All evil spirits, such as *Lilit*, are liquidated as darkness is decimated by a flood of Light.

This lustrous Light heals ailments of the heart and cures sicknesses of the eyes.

Our dreams of the night are now of Eden only, as nightmares become extinct. David's name, invoked by the Zohar, imbues us with piety to preserve our soul and to annul all judgments. *Malchut* joins with *Zeir Anpin,* our world with the Upper World, completing and perfecting all existence, all by the redeeming hand of the Creator and upon the merit of a king named David.

168. וְתַרְעִין דְּלִבָּא, אִינוּן עַיְינִין מִסְתַּתְּמִין, בְּגִין דְּלָא מִסְתַּכְּלִין בְּאִלֵּין מַזִּיקִין, דְּאִינוּן לִילִית. וְלָא שַׁלְטִין בִּנְהוֹרִין דְּלִבָּא, דְּאִינוּן מַלְאָכִים דְּמִתְפַּשְּׁטִין בְּכָל אֲבָרִים, כְּעַנְפִין דְּאִילָנָא לְכָל סִטְרָא. בְּהַהוּא זִמְנָא אִינוּן כֻּלְּהוּ נְהוֹרִין סְתִימִין בְּלִבָּא, וּמִתְכַּנְּשִׁין לְגַבֵּיה, כְּיוֹנִים אֶל אֲרֻבּוֹתֵיהֶם. כְּנֹחַ וְאִתְּתֵיה, וְכָל מִין וּמִין, דְּעָאלוּ עִמֵּיה בַּתֵּיבָה.

168. And the gates of the heart, which are the eyes, are blocked off so that they should not view the evil spirits, that are Lilit. And thus they do not control the lights of the heart, which are angels, that spread throughout all the limbs as the branches of a tree in every direction. At that time all the lights are shut off in the heart, and they gather to it as doves into their dovecotes, as Noah and his wife and all the species who entered with him into the ark.

169. וּמַזִּיקִין דְּמִתְגַּבְּרִין עַל כָּל אֲבָרִים דְּגוּפָא, כְּמֵי טוֹפָנָא דְּגָבְרוּ

עֲלֵיהּ ט״ו אָמַר, בְּגִין דְּחָב בְּיָ״ה, וְאִסְתַּלָּק יָ״ה מִן גּוּפָא, וְאִשְׁתְּאַר
אִלֵּם, בְּלָא רְאִיָּה וּשְׁמִיעָה וְרֵיחָא וְדִבּוּר. וְרָזָא דְּמִלָּה, נֶאֱלַמְתִּי דוּמִיָּה,
דוּמִיָּ״ה: דּוֹ״ם יָ״ה. כְּהַהוּא זִמְנָא, חֲמֵשׁ עֶשְׂרֵה אַמָּה, גָּבְרוּ מַזִּיקִין עַל
גּוּפָא. וְאִינּוּן כְּבִסְלָא לְעוּגְיָא.

169. And the evil spirits that overcome all the parts of the body are like the waters of the flood, which prevailed over them fifteen cubits. This is because he had sinned in the matter of Yah (= 15), and Yah had left the body. THAT IS TO SAY, YUD-HEI HAD LEFT ELOHIM (ALEPH LAMED HEI YUD MEM), and He remained a mute (Heb. *ILEM*, ALEPH LAMED MEM), without sight, hearing, smell or speech. And the secret of the matter is to be found in the verse: "I was dumb (Heb. *ilem*) with silence (Heb. *dumiyah*)" (Tehilim 39:3). *Dumiyah* IS SPELLED DALET VAV MEM YUD HEI, WHICH CAN BE READ AS TWO WORDS: Silence (Heb. *dom*) of Yud Hei. IN OTHER WORDS, at that time OF THE FLOOD, the evil spirits prevailed for fifteen cubits over the body, and they ENCOMPASSED THE BODY as a furrow SURROUNDS THE DITCH OF the flower-bed.

170. וּכְגַוְונָא דְּנֹחַ, שָׁלַח אֶת הַיּוֹנָה בִּשְׁלִיחוּתֵיהּ. אוּף הָכִי שָׁלַח
נִשְׁמְתָא בְּאָדָם. רוּחֵיהּ בִּשְׁלִיחוּתֵיהּ. וּבְגִין דָּא צָרִיךְ בַּ״נ לְפַקְדָּא לָהּ
בְּמַטְרוֹנִיתָא. הה״ד בְּיָדְךָ אַפְקִיד רוּחִי. וְאִם הִיא אֲסִירָא בְּחוֹבוֹי
דְּגוּפָא, בִּידָא דְּחַיָּילִין דְּיֵצֶר הָרָע, מַה כְּתִיב, בְּיָדְךָ אַפְקִיד רוּחִי פָּדִיתָ
אוֹתִי יְיָ׳ אֵל אֱמֶת.

170. Just as Noah sent the dove out on his mission, so also does the soul of man send out HIS SPIRIT on its mission, and for this reason a man must commit his spirit with the Matron, WHO IS MALCHUT, as it says: "Into Your hand I commit my spirit" (Tehilim 31:6). But if it is imprisoned by the powers of the Evil Inclination because of sins of the body, what does Scripture have to say? "Into Your hand I commit my spirit; You have redeemed me, Hashem, the El of truth" (Ibid.) FOR THE HOLY ONE, BLESSED BE HE, REDEEMS HIM FROM THEIR HAND.

171. וְעוֹד בְּזִמְנָא דְּאִיהִי חַיֶּיבֶת, מַה כְּתִיב בְּרוּחֵיהּ, יָד לְיָד לֹא יִנָּקֶה
רָע. דְּאָזִיל מִיָּד לְיָד, בְּמַשִׁרְיָין דְּיֵצֶר הָרָע, דְּשַׁרְיָין עֲלֵיהּ בְּחוֹבִין

דִּילֵיהּ, וְזָרְקִין לֵיהּ מֵאֲתָר לַאֲתָר. וְהַאי אִיהוּ דְּאַחְזֵי גַּרְמֵיהּ בִּמְדִינָה
אַחֶרֶת, אוֹ בְּמַלְכוּ אַחֲרָא, וּלְזִמְנִין בְּאַשְׁפָּה, כְּפוּם חוֹבוֹי. וְאִי אִיהוּ
זַכָּאָה, כָּל מַשִׁרְיָין דְּיֵצֶר טוֹב כֻּלְּהוּ, וּפְנֵיהֶם וְכַנְפֵיהֶם פְּרוּדוֹת, לְקַבְּלָה
רוּחֵיהּ, וְסַלְקִין לֵיהּ לְעֵילָּא, לַאֲתָר דְּחֵיוָון דְּכָרְסַיָּיא, וְתַמָּן חֲזֵי, כַּמָה
חֶזְיוֹנוֹת, דְּמִיוֹנוֹת, וּמַרְאוֹת דִּנְבוּאָה. וּבְגִין דָּא אוּקְמוּהָ רַבָּנָן, דַּחֲלוֹם
אֶחָד מִשִׁשִׁים בַּנְבוּאָה.

171. And during the time that THE SOUL is guilty, what is said about his
spirit? "They who join hands for wicked ends shall not go unpunished."
(Mishlei 11:21), for it goes from hand to hand in the camps of the Evil
Inclination, which rest upon it in its sins and cast him out from place to
place. It is this that is happening when A MAN sees himself IN HIS DREAM in
another country or another kingdom, and sometimes in the refuse, all
depending on his sins. But if he is righteous, then all of the camps of the
Good Inclination, ABOUT WHOM IT IS SAID "Thus were their faces; and
their wings were divided upwards" (Yechezkel 1:11) in order to accept his
spirit, raise it upward to the place of the living creatures, THE BEARERS of
the throne, WHICH IS MALCHUT, and there he sees a number of visions,
likenesses and prophetic revelations. And this is why the sages taught "The
dream is one-sixtieth of prophecy."

172. וְעוֹד שָׁמְרָה נַפְשִׁי כִּי חָסִיד אָנִי, אֶלָּא הָכִי אוּקְמוּהָ רַבָּנָן. וְלֹא
עַם הָאָרֶץ חָסִיד. דְּאוֹרַיְיתָא אִתְיְהִיבַת מִיַּמִינָא דְּקוּדְשָׁא בְּרִיךְ הוּא,
דְּאִיהוּ חֶסֶד. וּבְגִין דָּא, מַאן דְּאִתְעַסַּק בְּאוֹרַיְיתָא, אִתְקְרֵי חָסִיד. בְּגִין
דָּא, אֲמֵינָא לְקוּדְשָׁא בְּרִיךְ הוּא, שָׁמְרָה נַפְשִׁי, וְלָא תִּדוּן לָהּ כְּעוֹבָדֵי
אִלֵּין עַמֵּי הָאֲרָצוֹת, דְּאִתְּמַר בְּהוּ וְלֹא עַם הָאָרֶץ חָסִיד. וְאִי תֵּימָא,
כַּמָה עַמֵּי הָאֲרָצוֹת אִינּוּן דְּעַבְדוּ חֶסֶד. אֶלָּא הָכִי אוּקְמוּהָ, אִי זֶהוּ
חָסִיד, זֶה הַמִּתְחַסֵּד עִם קוֹנוֹ. כְּגוֹן דָּוִד דַּהֲוָה מְחַבֵּר. וּמַאי הֲוָה מְחַבֵּר.
אוֹרַיְיתָא דִּלְעֵילָּא, הֲוָה מְחַבֵּר עִם קוּדְשָׁא בְּרִיךְ הוּא. וּבְגִין דָּא, שָׁמְרָה
נַפְשִׁי כִּי חָסִיד אָנִי.

172. Furthermore: "Preserve my soul; for I am pious" (Tehilim 86:2). But so
did the sages teach: 'An ignorant man can not be pious.' For the Torah was

given from the right side of the Holy One, blessed be He, which is Chesed. For this reason, one who engages in Torah is called 'pious', and therefore I say to the Holy One, blessed be He: "Preserve my soul," and do not judge it according to the deeds of these ignorant ones, about whom it is said: 'An ignorant man can not be pious.' And should you ask about the many ignorant people who act with piety, I would refer you to the teaching: 'Who is a pious man? He who behaves piously with his Maker,' like David, who is joining together, what did he join together? The heavenly Torah, WHICH IS ZEIR ANPIN, with the Holy One, blessed be He, WHO IS MALCHUT, AND THIS IS WHAT IS MEANT BY 'BEHAVING PIOUSLY WITH HIS MAKER': THAT HE UNITED THE HOLY ONE, BLESSED BE HE, AND HIS SHECHINAH. This is why, "Preserve my soul; for I am pious."

31. Two visions

A Synopsis
The Faithful Shepherd talks about the two visions – one for the soul in this world, and one for the soul in the World to Come. We learn that God created man with two countenances, and that when the soul leaves the body the soul goes to the two Gardens.

The Relevance of this Passage
More secrets of the resurrection are revealed to ensure that it unfolds speedily in *our* day, with great mercy and soft-heartedness.

The 248 bone segments and the 365 sinews of the body receive the energy of healing and regeneration.

Rabbi Shimon informs the Faithful Shepherd Moses that he merited in his lifetime what the righteous will merit *after* their lifetime. These poetic verses elevate us spiritually on the wings of Moses. We therefore merit what Moses merits, ensuring for us a gentle, Light-filled transition from this world to the next.

173. וְכַד ב״נ מִית, מַה כְּתִיב בָּה בְּהַאי נֶפֶשׁ בְּהִתְהַלֶּכְךָ תַּנְחֶה אוֹתָךְ בְּשָׁכְבְּךָ תִּשְׁמוֹר עָלֶיךָ, וַהֲקִיצוֹתָ לִתְחִיַּית הַמֵּתִים, הִיא תְשִׂיחֶךָ. דָּא לִתְחִיַּית הַמֵּתִים שַׁפִּיר, דְּיוֹקִים לֵיהּ לב״נ, אֲבָל לְאַגְרָא לְנִשְׁמָתָא בְּעָלְמָא דְּאָתֵי, מַאי הֲוִי.

173. When a man dies, what is written about his soul? "When you walk, it will lead you; when you lie down, it shall keep you; and when you awake" at the resurrection of the dead, it shall talk with you" (Mishlei 6:22). HE INQUIRES: this is fine as far as the resurrection of the dead is concerned, that it should awaken THE BODY OF MAN AT THE RESURRECTION OF THE DEAD, but what will be the reward of the soul in the World to Come?

174. אֶלָּא קוּדְשָׁא בְּרִיךְ הוּא מַלְבִּישׁ לָהּ כְּקַדְמֵיתָא בַּעֲנָנֵי כָּבוֹד. כְּקַדְמֵיתָא תֵּיעוּל בְּמַרְאָה, דְּאִיהוּ כְּגַוְונָא דְּגוּפָא, כָּלִיל ברמ״ח אֵיבָרִים. אוּף הָכִי תֵּיעוּל בַּמַרְאָה, כָּלִיל בְּמָאתַיִם וְאַרְבָּעִים וּשְׁמֹנָה נְהִירִין דְּמִתְפָּרְשָׁן מֵהַהוּא מַרְאָה. דְּאִתְּמַר בֵּיהּ, וַיֹּאמֶר אִם יִהְיֶה נְבִיאֲכֶם יְיָ' בַּמַרְאָה אֵלָיו אֶתְוַדָּע. וּבִלְבוּשִׁין דַּעֲנָנֵי כָּבוֹד וּרְאִיתִיהָ

לִזְכּוֹר בְּרִית עוֹלָם, דָּא אַסְפַּקְלַרְיָאָה הַמְּאִירָה. בַּחֲלוֹם אֲדַבֶּר בּוֹ, דָּא אַסְפַּקְלַרְיָאָה דְּלָא נַהֲרָא. כָּלִיל משס״ה נְהִירִין, כְּחֻשְׁבַּן יְשֵׁנָה. וְהַיְינוּ אֲנִי יְשֵׁנָה. חַד בְּעָלְמָא הֵין. וְחַד בְּעָלְמָא דְּאָתֵי. וְאִינוּן בְּעוֹבָדֵי יְדוֹי דְּקוּדְשָׁא בְּרִיךְ הוּא.

174. He answers, The Holy One, blessed be He, dresses THE SOUL as formerly in clouds of glory, and as formerly it enters into a vision. In the same sort of way that the body has 248 parts, it will also be in a vision including 248 lights that spread forth from that vision, FOR THE NUMERICAL VALUE OF THE LETTERS OF "*BEMAR'AH*" IS 248, as it is said about it: "If there be a prophet among you, I, Hashem, make myself known to him in a vision (Heb. *bemar'ah*)" (Bemidbar 12:6), and it will have the apparel of clouds of glory. IT IS SAID ABOUT IT: "and I shall look upon it, that I may remember the everlasting covenant" (Beresheet 9:16). This is the shining vision. "and speak to him in a dream" (Bemidbar 12:6): this is the vision (Heb. *mar'ah*) that does not shine, being made up of 365 lights, corresponding to the numerical value of '*yeshenah*' (lit. 'sleep'), as in the verse: "I sleep" (Shir Hashirim 5:2). One VISION, therefore, is FOR THE SOUL in this world, and the other VISION IS FOR THE SOUL in the World to Come, and they GIVE LIGHT to the work of the hands of the Holy One, blessed be He, NAMELY, THE SOULS.

175. וְרָזָא דִּלְהוֹן, זֶה שְׁמִי לְעוֹלָם. יָ״ה עִם שְׁמִי, שָׁלֹשׁ מֵאוֹת וַחֲמִשָּׁה וְשִׁשִּׁים. ו״ה עִם זִכְרִי, מָאתַיִם וּשְׁמֹנָה וְאַרְבָּעִים. וְכָרוֹזִין נַחְתִּין וְסַלְּקִין קַמֵּיהּ, הָבוּ יְקָר לִדְיוּקְנָא דְּמַלְכָּא.

175. And their secret is to be found in the verse: "this is My name for ever" (Shemot 3:15). THE NUMERICAL VALUE OF 'Yud Hei' and 'My name' (Heb. *shmi*) is together 365. "AND THIS IS MY MEMORIAL (HEB. *ZICHRI*) TO ALL GENERATIONS" (IBID.). THE NUMERICAL VALUE OF Vav Hei together with *zichri* is 248. And heralds descend and ascend before Him, proclaiming: 'Give honor to the likeness of the King', NAMELY TO THE SOUL.

176. וְהַיְינוּ וַיִּבְרָא אֱלֹהִים אֶת הָאָדָם בְּצַלְמוֹ בְּצֶלֶם אֱלֹהִים בָּרָא אוֹתוֹ.

וְהוּא דְּעֲבַד לֵיהּ בִּתְרֵין דְּיוּקְנִין, בִּתְרֵין פָּנִים דְּאִתְּמַר עָלָהּ כִּי לֹא
רְאִיתֶם כָּל תְּמוּנָה. וְעַל שְׁאָר דְּיוּקְנִין כְּתִיב, תְּמוּנַת כָּל וְגוֹ'. וּתְמוּנַת
יְיָ' יַבִּיט. וּתרי"ג מַלְאָכִין סַלְקִין לָהּ לְנִשְׁמָתָא. בְּאִלֵּין דְּיוּקְנִין, כֻּלְּהוּ
וּפְנֵיהֶם וְכַנְפֵיהֶם פְּרוּדוֹת, לְקַיֵּים קְרָא דִּכְתִיב בְּהוֹן וָאֶשָּׂא אֶתְכֶם עַל
כַּנְפֵי נְשָׁרִים וָאָבִיא אֶתְכֶם אֵלָי.

176. And this is the meaning of the verse: "So Elohim created man in His own image, in the image of Elohim He created him" (Beresheet 1:27). In other words, He created him in two forms: ONE, "IN HIS OWN IMAGE"; AND THE OTHER, "IN THE IMAGE OF ELOHIM," NAMELY with two countenances. 1) is as it is said: "for you saw no manner of form" (Devarim 4:15), and regarding the other FORBIDDEN forms it is written, "the similitude of any figure" (Devarim 4:16). 2) "and the similitude of Hashem does he behold" (Bemidbar 12:8). And 613 angels raise up the soul in these forms, all of them with "Thus were their faces; and their wings were divided upwards" (Yechezkel 1:11), to establish the verse that is said about them: "I bore you on eagles' wings, and brought you to Myself" (Shemot 19:4).

177. כְּגַוְונָא דְּנַפְקוּ מִמִּצְרַיִם, וְאַזְלוּ בַּעֲנָנֵי כָּבוֹד, וּבְכָל הַהוּא יְקָר,
כְּהַהוּא גַּוְונָא תְּהֵא מַפְקָנוּתָא דְּנִשְׁמָתָא, מִגּוּפָא דְּטִפָּה סְרוּחָה, לְמֵיזַל
לִתְרֵין גַּנִּים, דְּאִתְבְּרֵי שְׁמַיָּא וְאַרְעָא דִּלְהוֹן בְּשֵׁם יְיָ'. וּבְגִינֵיהּ אִתְּמַר,
יִשְׂמְחוּ הַשָּׁמַיִם וְתָגֵל הָאָרֶץ. בְּהַהוּא זִמְנָא יִתְקַיֵּים בב"נ וְלֹא יִכָּנֵף עוֹד
מוֹרֶיךָ לְגַבָּךְ, בְּשַׁתְּיִם יְכַסֶּה פָּנָיו, אֶלָּא וְהָיוּ עֵינֶיךָ רוֹאוֹת אֶת מוֹרֶיךָ.
וּמִסְטְרָא דְּאִלֵּין מַרְאוֹת, זָכָה מרע"ה, רַבָּן שֶׁל נְבִיאִים וַחֲכָמִים. אָמַר
בּוּצִינָא קַדִּישָׁא, אַנְתְּ הוּא דְּזָכִית בְּחַיָּיךְ, לָמָה דְּיִזְכּוּן צַדִּיקַיָּא בָּתַר
חַיֵּיהוֹן, זַכָּאָה חוּלָקֵךְ.

177. Just as they came out of Egypt and went with clouds of glory and all that honor, so, too, is the exit of the soul from its body – that "putrid drop": the soul goes to the two gardens, THE UPPER GARDEN OF EDEN AND THE LOWER GARDEN OF EDEN, whose heavens and earth were created by the Name of Yud Hei Vav Hei, for whose reason it was said: "Let the heavens be glad and the earth rejoice" (Tehilim 96:11). At that time the verse will be

fulfilled in man: "yet your teacher shall not withdraw himself any more" (Yeshayah 30:20) from you. "WITHDRAW HIMSELF" IS AS WRITTEN: "with two he covered his face..." (Yeshayah 6:2), nevertheless "but your eyes shall see your teacher" (Yeshayah 30:20). And Moses our Master, may peace be upon him – the master of the prophets and sages – is worthy in the aspect of these TWO visions. The Holy Luminary, THAT IS RABBI SHIMON, said TO THE FAITHFUL SHEPHERD, You are the one who merited in your lifetime what the righteous will merit after their lives. Happy is your portion!

32. 'Aleph Nun Yud', and 'Vav Hei Vav'

A Synopsis

We hear another interpretation of "Preserve my soul, for I am pious," where the esoteric meaning rests on the words 'I' and 'and He', and whereby we see how essential it is to refrain from separating Zeir Anpin and Malchut. This is because I and He are one, without distinction. We learn that the Left and Right Columns are united in the Central Column, Tiferet.

The Relevance of this Passage

The letters *Aleph Nun Yud* אני and *Vav Hei Vav* והו ignite tremendous forces of energy that accomplish many wonderful things for us.

All the worlds – the Upper and Lower – are connected and united into one. The Three Columns – Right, Left and Central – are unified into one harmonious whole.

This unification, which occurs through the power of the Central Column, eradicates our selfish impulses and desires. Opposite forces are now able to unite for the following reason: Our Desire to Receive is subjugated and then transformed into the *Desire to Receive for the Sake of Sharing*. Thus, our Receiving is given the form of sharing, which is identical to the imparting nature of the Light. In spiritual matters, *like attracts like;* and thus, we (and all the worlds) unite into a resplendent oneness, bringing healing and immortality to all existence.

178. ד"א שָׁמְרָה נַפְשִׁי כִּי חָסִיד אָנִי, אֲמַאי. כְּדֵי שֶׁאֶתְחַסֵּד עִם אֲנִ"י. דְּאִתְּמַר בֵּיהּ אֲנִ"י וָה"וּ. וַוי לֵיהּ לְמַאן דְּאַפְרִישׁ אֲנִי מִן הוּא. דְּאִתְּמַר הוּא עָשָׂנוּ וְלֹא אֲנַחְנוּ. דְּכֹלָּא חַד בְּלָא פֵּרוּדָא. הה"ד, רְאוּ עַתָּה כִּי אֲנִי אֲנִי הוּא אֲנִי אָמִית וַאֲחַיֶּה מָחַצְתִּי וַאֲנִי אֶרְפָּא וְאֵין מִיָּדִי מַצִּיל. אֲנִי יְדֹוָ"ד, אֲנִי הוּא וְלֹא אַחֵר. וְדָא אֲנִי מִן אֲדֹנָ"י. יְדֹוָד עַמּוּדָא דְּאֶמְצָעִיתָא.

178. Another interpretation of the verse "Preserve my soul; for I am pious" (Tehilim 86:2) is as follows: Why should He preserve my soul? So that I should behave piously with 'I', NAMELY THAT I SHOULD UNITE WITH AND BRING THE CHESED FROM YUD HEI VAV HEI WHICH IS ZEIR ANPIN TO

'I', WHICH IS MALCHUT, for it has been said about it: I and He, WHERE 'ALEPH-NUN-YUD (ENG. 'I')' IS MALCHUT AND 'VAV-HEI-VAV (ENG. 'AND HE')' IS ZEIR ANPIN. Woe to anyone who separates 'I' from 'He', NAMELY TO ANYONE WHO CAUSES A SEPARATION BETWEEN ZEIR ANPIN AND MALCHUT, as it is said: "it is He who made us, and we belong to Him" (Tehilim 100:3), WHERE 'HE' STANDS FOR ZEIR ANPIN. This is because everything is one, NAMELY I AND HE ARE ONE, without division. This is what is said: "See now that I, even I am He... I kill and I make alive, I wound, and I heal: neither is there any that can deliver out of my hand" (Devarim 32:39). I am Hashem, I am He, and no other. And this 'I' is derived from Adonai, NAMELY THE LETTERS OF 'ANI' (I) ARE FOUND IN ADONAI. Yud Hei Vav Hei is the Central Column, NAMELY ZEIR ANPIN.

179. וּבְגִין דְּיִדוֹ"ד אִיהוּ לִימִינָא דְּאִיהִי חֶסֶד, אָמַר, שָׁמְרָה נַפְשִׁי דְּאִתְחַסֵּד בָּךְ עִם אֲנִי, וְאִיהוּ אֲדֹנָ"י לַגְּבוּרָה. וּבְתִפְאֶרֶת, אִתְחַבְּרָן תְּרֵין שְׁמָהָן יאהדונה"י. וְרָזָא דְּמִלָּה בְּחֶסֶד וּבִגְבוּרָה, וּפְנֵיהֶם וְכַנְפֵיהֶם פְּרוּדוֹת מִלְמַעְלָה וּבְתִפְאֶרֶת, דְּאִתְקְרֵי יְדֹוָ"ד אִישׁ מִלְחָמָה, מַה כְּתִיב שְׁתַּיִם חוֹבְרוֹת אִישׁ, תַּרְתֵּין שְׁמָהָן מִתְחַבְּרָן בֵּיהּ כַּחֲדָא. וּשְׁתַּיִם מְכַסּוֹת אֶת גְּוִיּוֹתֵיהֶנָה. תִּפְאֶרֶת אִתְקְרֵי גּוּף, וּגְוִיָּתוֹ כְתַרְשִׁישׁ יאההויה"ה.

179. And because Yud Hei Vav Hei, WHICH IS ZEIR ANPIN, is on the right, namely Chesed, he said: "Preserve my soul, FOR I AM PIOUS (HEB. CHASID)," meaning that I shall behave piously towards You and with 'I' which is Adonai, which is Gvurah. THAT IS TO SAY, I SHALL UNITE YUD HEI VAV HEI, WHICH IS CHESED, WITH ADONAI, WHICH IS GVURAH, SO CHASSADIM WILL BE DRAWN DOWN FROM YUD HEI VAV HEI TO ADONAI, AND IT, TOO, WILL BE CHESED. And both the names, YUD HEI VAV HEI AND ADONAI, combine together in Tiferet, WHICH IS THE CENTRAL COLUMN, AND COME TOGETHER THUS; Yud Aleph Hei Dalet Vav Nun Hei Yud. FOR IT IS THE CENTRAL COLUMN THAT COMBINES CHESED, WHICH IS THE SECRET OF YUD HEI VAV HEI WITH GVURAH, WHICH IS THE SECRET OF ADONAI. And the inner meaning of the matter is with Chesed and Gvurah, WHICH ARE THE RIGHT AND LEFT COLUMNS, ABOUT WHICH IT IS SAID: "Thus were their faces: and their wings were divided upwards" (Yechezkel 1:11), SINCE 'THEIR FACES' IS THE SECRET

OF CHOCHMAH, BINAH AND DA'AT, AND THE TWO COLUMNS, THE RIGHT AND THE LEFT, WHICH ARE CHOCHMAH AND BINAH, ARE DIVIDED. AND SO WITH THE TWO WINGS, THE SECRET OF THE RIGHT AND LEFT COLUMNS, WHICH ARE DIFFERENT FROM EACH OTHER, AND ARE THEREFORE DIVIDED. And in Tiferet, WHICH IS THE CENTRAL COLUMN, that is called: "Hashem is a man (Heb. *ish*) of war" (Shemot 15:3), BECAUSE HE FIGHTS WITH THE LEFT COLUMN, AND MAKES IT SMALLER IN ORDER TO BRING IT TOGETHER IN UNITY WITH THE RIGHT, it is written: "two wings of everyone (Heb. *ish*) were joined one to another" (Yechezkel 1:11), for the two names, YUD HEI VAV HEI AND ADONAI were joined together in it, AND THUS "and two covered their bodies" (Ibid.), FOR THE TWO WINGS JOINED THE BODY AND BECAME AS ONE. And Tiferet is called 'body', THIS BEING THE INNER MEANING OF THE VERSE: "his body was like beryl" (Daniel 10:6). AND SO IT IS WITH THE TWO COLUMNS, RIGHT AND LEFT OF THE FIRST THREE SFIROT WHICH ARE CHOCHMAH AND BINAH, THAT ARE THE TWO NAMES, YUD HEI VAV HEI AND EHEYEH, ABOUT WHICH IT IS SAID "THEIR FACES...DIVIDED UPWARDS." THEY JOIN TOGETHER AND COMBINE BY THE CENTRAL COLUMN, WHICH IS THE SECRET OF DA'AT. AND THEY COME TOGETHER THUS: Yud-Aleph-Hei-Hei-Vav-Yud-Hei-Hei.

33. Three times was David made a servant

A Synopsis

We are told the three ways that a man must make himself a servant in terms of worship.

The Relevance of this Passage

David, the Three Patriarchs, and Moses instill within us the three ways of being a servant in worship.

In truth, our only free will in this world is to choose who will be our master – the Light of the Creator or the Satan himself. Our thoughts and our desires originate from one or the other. Our only choice is to choose which voice we shall heed.

Here we choose the Light.

Just as a man's hands act synchronously with the thoughts that direct it, our actions become synchronous with the will of the Creator. Our thoughts, ideas, decisions, and actions derive solely from the Light (our soul), which leads us to endless fulfillment. This effect is extended to all mankind, so that civilization transforms into a vision and model of the Creator's radiance.

180. הוֹשַׁע עַבְדְּךָ אַתָּה אֱלֹהַי שַׂמֵּחַ נֶפֶשׁ עַבְדֶּךָ תְּנָה עֻזְּךָ לְעַבְדֶּךָ. תְּלַת זִמְנִין אִתְעֲבֵיד דָּוִד עֶבֶד בִּתְהִלָּה דָּא, לָקֳבֵל ג' זִמְנִין, דְּאוֹקְמוּהָ מָארֵי מַתְנִיתִין, דְּבָעֵי ב"נ לְמֶהֱוֵי עַבְדָּא בִּצְלוֹתָא. בְּבִרְכָאן קַדְמָאִין, כְּעֶבֶד דִּמְסַדֵּר שְׁבָחוֹי קַמֵּי רַבֵּיהּ. בְּאֶמְצָעִיּוֹת, כְּעַבְדָּא דְּבָעֵי פְּרָס מֵרַבֵּיהּ. בַּאֲחֲרוֹנוֹת, כְּעֶבֶד דְּמוֹדֶה קָדָם רַבֵּיהּ, בַּפְּרָס דְּקַבִּיל מִינֵּיהּ, וְאָזִיל לֵיהּ.

180. It is written: "O You, My Elohim, save Your servant... Rejoice the soul of Your servant...give Your strength to Your servant" (Tehilim 86:2,4,16). David is thrice referred to as a servant in this psalm, which parallels the three times that a man has to be as a servant in the Amidah prayer, as taught by the sages of the Mishnah: 'In the first blessings, A MAN SHOULD BE as a servant arranging praises before his Master; in the intermediate ones, as a servant asking for a favor of his Master; and in the last BLESSINGS, a man should be as a servant thanking his Master for a favor received, and going on his way'.

181. וּתְלַת זִמְנִין דְּבָעֵי לְמֶעֱבַד עֶבֶד, מִסְּטְרָא דַּעֲבוֹדָה. דְּאוֹקְמוּהָ

-147-

מָארֵי מַתְנִיתִין, דְּלֵית עֲבוֹדָה אֶלָּא תְּפִלָּה. וּתְלַת אֲבָהָן, אִתְקְרִיאוּ עֲבָדִים מִסִּטְרָהָא, ע"ש שְׁכִינְתָּא, דְּאִיהִי עֲבוֹדַת יְיָ'. וְאוֹף הָכִי מֹשֶׁה עֶבֶד יְיָ'. וּבג"ד, כִּי לִי בְּנֵי יִשְׂרָאֵל עֲבָדִים. אֲבָל לְגַבֵּי אַחֲרָנִין, כָּל יִשְׂרָאֵל בְּנֵי מְלָכִים הֵם, מִסִּטְרָא דְּמַלְכוּת. וְאִיהִי אֲמַאי אִתְקְרִיאַת עֲבוֹדָה. כְּאוֹרַח דְּאִתְּתָא לְמִיפְלַח לְבַעֲלָה, וְאוֹרַח בְּנִין, לְמִפְלַח לַאֲבוּהוֹן.

181. And these are the three occasions that A MAN has to make himself as though a servant in terms of worship. And the sages of the Mishnah taught: There is no worship but prayer. And the three patriarchs are called 'servants' by the aspect of her, namely in the name of the Shechinah, which is the worship of Hashem. And so also is Moses REFERRED TO AS the servant of Hashem, which explains "For to Me the children of Yisrael are servants" (Vayikra 25:55). But in terms of the other QUALITIES IN HER, all Yisrael are called 'the children of kings' from the point of view of Malchut IN THEM. And why should MALCHUT be termed worship? It can be likened to the way of a wife who serves her husband, or children who serve their father.

34. David made himself poor, pious and a servant

A Synopsis

We learn how David's correction of the three Columns was effected through making himself as if poor, a servant, and pious. We are told that except for Moses, there has never been anyone who could access the highest understanding, and it is even more impossible to access the highest wisdom, for it is said that a wise man is preferable to a prophet.

The Relevance of this Passage

Meditating upon the letters *Aleph Chet Dalet* אחד and David's name דוד imbues our souls with a feeling of spiritual poverty. This action corrects our Left Column, the selfish *Desire to Receive for the self alone*. Moreover, David made himself a pious servant in order to correct the Right and Central columns, respectively. Thus, our own three Columns are rectified, freeing us eternally from the influence of the Other Side.

The Light of *Binah*, a realm that only Moses attained, illumines our souls. This Light bespeaks the eternal *World To Come;* therefore, restoration and immortality now permeate our body and soul. Darkness and disease are banished as Binah's Light gleams throughout existence. The *World to Come* is now!

182. וְדָוִד, אִתְעֲבֵיד עָנִי, חָסִיד, וְעֶבֶד. הה"ד, תְּפִלָּה לְדָוִד הַטֵה אֲדֹנָי אָזְנְךָ עֲנֵנִי כִּי עָנִי וְאֶבְיוֹן אָנִי. שָׁמְרָה נַפְשִׁי כִּי חָסִיד אָנִי. הוֹשַׁע עַבְדְּךָ אַתָּה אֱלֹהַי הַבּוֹטֵחַ אֵלֶיךָ. אִתְעֲבֵיד עָנִי לְתַרְעָא דְּמַלְכָּא, דְּאִתְּמַר בָּהּ, אֲדֹנָי שְׂפָתַי תִּפְתָּח. אדנ"י היכ"ל, אִתְעֲבֵיד עָנִי לְתַרְעָא דְּהֵיכָלָא דְּמַלְכָּא. וּמַה כְּתִיב. הַטֵה אֲדֹנָי אָזְנְךָ עֲנֵנִי וְדָא שְׁכִינְתָּא תַּתָּאָה. דְּאִיהוּ אֹזֶן לְקַבְּלָא צְלוֹתִין וּלְמִשְׁמַע לוֹן. כְּדִכְתִיב, כִּי לֹא בָזָה וְלֹא שִׁקַץ עֱנוּת עָנִי וְלֹא הִסְתִּיר פָּנָיו מִמֶּנּוּ וּבְשַׁוְּעוֹ אֵלָיו שָׁמֵעַ.

182. And David made himself poor, pious and a servant, as it is written: "A prayer of David. Incline Your ear, Hashem, hear me: for I am poor and needy. Preserve my soul; for I am pious: O You, my Elohim, save Your servant, who trusts in You" (Tehilim 86:1-2). He became poor at the gate of the King, WHICH IS MALCHUT, about which it is said: "Adonai, open my

lips" (Tehilim 51:17). Adonai is the palace, and he became poor at the gate of the king's palace, WHICH IS ADONAI, namely MALCHUT. And what does it say? "Incline Your ear, Hashem, hear me." And this is the lower Shechinah, WHICH IS MALCHUT, which is an ear to receive and listen to prayers, as it is written: "For He has not despised nor abhorred the affliction of the afflicted; nor has He hid His face from him: but when he cried to Him, He heard" (Tehilim 22:25).

183. דְּאִיהוּ אִתְעֲבֵיד עָנִי וְדָל, מִסִּטְרָא דְּאָת ד' מִן אֶחָד, לְמִשְׁאַל מִן
א"ח, דְּאִיהוּ עַמּוּדָא דְּאֶמְצָעִיתָא. לְקַיְּימָא בֵּיהּ, דַּלּוֹתִי וְלִי יְהוֹשִׁיעַ,
דְּלָא יְמוּת מָשִׁיחַ בֶּן אֶפְרַיִם. וְשָׁאִיל מִנֵּיהּ בְּהַהוּא תַּרְעָא, בְּגִין יִשְׂרָאֵל
הָעֲנִיִּים, לְקַיֵּים בְּהוּ וְאֶת עַם עָנִי תּוֹשִׁיעַ.

183. For he became "poor and needy" in respect of the letter Dalet of (the word) 'Echad' (Aleph-Chet-Dalet) (= 1), WHICH IS THE SECRET OF MALCHUT, IN THE FIRST STATE, WHEN SHE IS RECEIVING FROM THE LEFT COLUMN, FOR SHE IS THEN NEEDY, AS THE LETTER 'DALET' TEACHES US OF HER POVERTY (HEB. DALAH). Then he requests HELP from Aleph-Chet OF ECHAD. AND THIS IS THE SECRET OF ZEIR ANPIN WHICH, IN THIS STATE IS MALCHUT, IS CALLED 'BROTHER' (ALEPH-CHET), AND MALCHUT SISTER, BEING THEN AT THE SAME LEVEL EVOLVING FROM BINAH, AS A BROTHER AND SISTER. This is the Central Column, NAMELY ZEIR ANPIN, with which to fulfill the verse: "I was brought low, and He saved me" (Tehilim 116:6), so that Messiah son of Ephraim should not die. FOR MESSIAH SON OF EPHRAIM IS DRAWN FROM MALCHUT WHEN THE LATTER IS FEEDING FROM THE LEFT, AND IS FULL OF JUDGMENT. And DAVID FURTHER requested of Him at this gate on behalf of Yisrael, who are poor, that the verse "And the afflicted people You will save" (II Shmuel 22:28) be fulfilled in them, AND THIS IS WHY HE MADE HIMSELF POOR, FOR IT IS THE SECRET OF THE LEFT COLUMN.

184. וּלְבָתַר שָׁאִיל בְּגִין כַּהֲנַיָּא, דְּיַחֲזוֹר עֲבוֹדָה לִמְקוֹמָהּ, וְאִתְעֲבֵיד
עֶבֶד. וּלְבָתַר דְּיָהִיב לוֹן אוֹרַיְיתָא מִסִּטְרָא דְּחֶסֶד, לְמֶעְבַּד גְּמוּל עִם
דְּלֵי"ת מִן אוֹרַיְיתָא, וּבְגִין דָּא אִתְעֲבֵיד חָסִיד. כַּךְ מָטָא לַג' סְפִירָאן
עִלָּאִין, פָּתַח וְאָמַר יְיָ' לֹא גָבַהּ לִבִּי וְלֹא רָמוּ עֵינַי וְלֹא הִלַּכְתִּי

בִּגְדוֹלוֹת וּבְנִפְלָאוֹת מִמֶּנִּי.

184. And afterwards he requested for the sake of the priests, THE SECRET OF THE RIGHT COLUMN, CHESED, that the worship be returned to its place, and he made himself a servant. And later He gave them the Torah from the side of Chesed, to give a reward (Heb. *gemul*) to the letter 'Dalet' of the Torah. IN OTHER WORDS, THE TORAH, WHICH IS THE SECRET OF ZEIR ANPIN, THE CENTRAL COLUMN, UNITES THE CHESED OF THE RIGHT COLUMN WITH THE GVURAH OF THE LEFT COLUMN, AND THEN GIVES A REWARD TO THE DALET, WHICH IS THE SECRET OF MALCHUT RECEIVING CHASSADIM AND BECOMING RICH, IN THE SECRET OF THE TWO LETTERS 'GIMEL' AND 'DALET' THAT FOLLOW EACH OTHER IN THE ORDER OF THE ALPHABET. And this is why he became pious. HE THEREBY CORRECTED THE SECRET OF THE THREE COLUMNS, CHESED, GVURAH AND TIFERET. HE MADE HIMSELF POOR TO CORRECT THE LEFT COLUMN. HE MADE HIMSELF A SERVANT TO CORRECT THE WORSHIP OF THE PRIESTS, WHICH ARE THE RIGHT COLUMN, AND HE MADE HIMSELF PIOUS TO CORRECT THE CENTRAL COLUMN, SO IT WOULD BESTOW CHESED UPON MALCHUT. SUBSEQUENTLY HE CORRECTED THE THREE COLUMNS CHESED, GVURAH AND TIFERET, and when he reached the three upper Sfirot, CHOCHMAH, BINAH AND DA'AT, he began to say: "Hashem, my heart is not haughty, nor my eyes lofty: nor do I exercise myself in great matters, or in things too high for me" (Tehilim 131:1), NAMELY HE DID NOT TOUCH THEM.

185. שְׁלֹמֹה אָמַר, הָא בִּינָה אִיהִי דְּמֹשֶׁה, אֶשְׁאַל בְּחָכְמָה עִלָּאָה, דְּאִיהִי לְעֵיל מִדַּרְגֵּיה. מַה כְּתִיב, אָמַרְתִּי אֶחְכָּמָה וְהִיא רְחוֹקָה מִמֶּנִּי. וְהָא כְּתִיב וַיְיָ' נָתַן חָכְמָה לִשְׁלֹמֹה. חָכְמָה זְעֵירָא. וּבָעָא לְסַלְקָא מִתַּתָּא לְעֵילָא, דְּאִתְרְחִיקַת מִנֵּיהּ. בְּגִין דַּאֲפִילוּ לַבִּינָה לֵית בַּר נָשׁ בְּעָלְמָא דְּיָכִיל לְסַלְקָא, בַּר מִמֹּשֶׁה, כְּ"שׁ לְעֵילָא מִנֵּיהּ, דְּאִיהוּ חָכְמָה עִלָּאָה, מִסִּטְרָא דִּילָהּ חָכָם עָדִיף מִנָּבִיא. וְאע"ג דְּאוּקְמוּהָ בְּאֹרַח דְּרָשָׁא, עַל פָּרָה אֲדוּמָה. שִׁבְעִים פָּנִים לַתּוֹרָה.

185. Solomon said, Since Binah belongs to Moses, I shall ask for upper Chochmah, which is above the level OF MOSES. It is written: "I said, I will be wise; but it was far from me" (Kohelet 7:23), FOR UPPER CHOCHMAH

WAS NOT GIVEN TO HIM. HE ASKS, but what about the verse: "And Hashem gave Solomon wisdom" (I Melachim 5:26)? HE ANSWERS, this refers to lower wisdom, WHICH IS MALCHUT. And he wanted to ascend upwards from below, NAMELY FROM LOWER CHOCHMAH HE WANTED TO ATTAIN UPPER CHOCHMAH, but it drew away from him. This is because there is no man in the world, apart from Moses, who can ascend to Binah, and how much truer is this for upper Chochmah, which is above BINAH. In its terms, 'a wise man is better than a prophet'. And even though THE VERSE "I SAID: I WILL BE WISE, BUT IT WAS FAR FROM ME" was applied homiletically to a red heifer, WHOSE REASON HE COULD NOT UNDERSTAND, 'there are seventy possible interpretations of Torah', THIS, TOO, BEING A TERM IN THE SECRET OF SCRIPTURE.

35. The allusions of Elazar, Yosi, Yehuda, Yudai, Aba and Rabbi Shimon and his friends

A Synopsis
Moses speaks to each of the rabbis inviting their interpretations and telling each one what his name means.

The Relevance of this Passage
For millennia, the full measure of mystical power and magic embedded into the letters of the names above have remained bottled up inside this sacred book, waiting for the eyes of man to shine upon it and thus release into the cosmos.

That time is now. Light bursts forth, full throttle, in this dynamic and highly potent passage. Supernal matings take place, angelic forces spill down upon Creation, and all the worlds are corrected and unified. The result is untold merciful transformation and compassionate correction in our lives.

186. ר' אֶלְעָזָר, קוּם לְחַדְּשָׁא מִלִּין קַמֵּי שְׁכִינְתָּא, דִּי תְּהֵא עֵזֶר לְאָבִיךָ, דִּשְׁמָא גָּרִים, עֵזֶר אֵל, אֵל מִימִינָא, עֵזֶר מִשְּׂמָאלָא. הה"ד, אֶעֱשֶׂה לּוֹ עֵזֶר כְּנֶגְדּוֹ. בְּמַאי. בְּזֶרַע שַׁפִּיר, דְּאִיהוּ הֵפֶךְ עֵזֶר.

186. THE FAITHFUL SHEPHERD SAID, Rabbi Elazar, Rise up and say some new interpretations before the Shechinah, so that you may be of help (Heb. *ezer*) to your father, as your name requires, FOR THE LETTERS OF 'ELAZAR' MAKE UP THE TWO WORDS '*ezer*' '*El*', NAMELY '*El*' from the right, WHICH IS THE SECRET OF CHESED, AND '*Ezer*' from the left, WHICH IS THE SECRET OF GVURAH. This is what is written: "I will make him a help (Heb. *ezer*) to match him" (Beresheet 2:18), FOR MALCHUT, WHICH IS BUILT UP FROM THE LEFT, IS REFERRED TO AS A HELPMATE FOR HIM. In what way DOES IT BECOME A HELP TO HIM? With good seed (Heb. *ZERA*), which are the letters of '*ezer*' in a different order.

187. וְיֵקוּם ר' יוֹסֵי עִמָּךְ, דְּאִיהוּ כֻּרְסְיָיא שְׁלֵימָתָא לְמָארֵיהּ, דְּהָכִי סָלִיק יוֹסֵי, לְחֻשְׁבּוֹן הַכִּסֵּ"א, אֱלֹהִים בְּחוּשְׁבָּן. וְיֵקוּם עֲמֵיהּ ר' יְהוּדָה, דְּבֵיהּ הוֹ"ד, וּבֵיהּ יָ"ה, וּבֵי יְדוֹדָ ד', ד' חִיּוָן. וּפְנֵיהֶם וְכַנְפֵיהֶם פְּרוּדוֹת, כֻּלְּהוּ, לְקַבְּלָא לֵיהּ. וּמִנֵּיהּ דָּוִד, דְּהוֹדָה לְקוּדְשָׁא בְּרִיךְ הוּא, דַּרְגָּא

בְּהוֹדָאוֹת דְּאִיהוּ מִצַּד הוֹד. וְיֵקוּם עֲמֵיהּ ר' אֶלְעָאי, בְּגִי' יַבַּ"ק, בָּקִי בְּהִלְכְתָא.

187. And let Rabbi Yosi rise up with you, for he is a perfect throne for his Master, for the numerical value of Yosi is the same as that of the throne (Heb. *hakisse*) and that of Elohim. And let Rabbi Yehuda rise up with him, for in him are THE TWO WORDS *Hod* and *Yah*, THE LATTER OF WHICH INSTRUCTS US ABOUT THE FIRST STAGE OF MALCHUT, WHICH IS THEN THE FIRST THREE SFIROT. In him are contained THE LETTERS Yud Hei Vav Hei plus Dalet. THAT INDICATES ZEIR ANPIN, CALLED YUD HEI VAV HEI, AND MALCHUT, CALLED DALET, PRIOR TO HER BEING JOINED IN A MATING WITH YUD HEI VAV HEI. IT IS THE SECRET OF the Dalet (= 4) living creatures, ABOUT WHOM IT IS SAID: "Thus were their faces; and their wings were divided" (Yechezkel 1:11). THIS REFERS TO all of them, FOR THEY DO NOT YET HAVE THE UNITY OF RIGHT AND LEFT OR ARE READY to receive THE CENTRAL COLUMN THAT WILL UNITE THEM. THEREFORE, THEY ARE THE FOUR LIVING CREATURES, FOR AFTER THE UNIFICATION OF RIGHT AND LEFT, THEY ARE CONSIDERED AS THREE LIVING CREATURES, WHICH IS THE SECRET OF THE THREE COLUMNS, EACH ONE OF WHICH HAS FOUR COUNTENANCES. And from him, FROM JUDAH, CAME David, who gave thanks to the Holy One, blessed be He, at the level of thanksgivings (Heb. *hodaot*), which is from the side of Hod. And let Rabbi Elai rise up with him, for the numerical value of the letters of Elai is 112, the same as that of *Yud-Bet-Kof*, WHICH, IN A DIFFERENT ORDER, SPELL *BAKI* (LIT. 'ERUDITE'), FOR HE IS erudite in the Halachah.

188. וְיֵקוּם עֲמֵיהּ ר' יוּדָאי, דְּחוּשְׁבָּנֵיהּ אֵ"ל. כְּגוֹן מִיכָאֵל, מַלְאָכִין רְשִׁימִין בְּאֵל. כְּגוֹן יֵשׁ לְאֵל יָדִי. וְרָזָא דְּאֵל, אִ' דְּמוּת אָדָם. ל' תְּלַת חֵיוָן, דְּאִינּוּן ד' אַנְפִּין לְכָל חַד, דִּרְמִיזִין תְּלַת יוֹדִין, הָעוֹלִים ל'. וְאִינּוּן בְּרָאשֵׁי תְּלַת אַזְכָּרוֹת, דְּאִינּוּן יְיָ' מֶלֶךְ, יְיָ' מָלַךְ, יְיָ' יִמְלוֹךְ לְעוֹלָם וָעֶד. וְיֵקוּם ר' אַבָּא עִמְּהוֹן, דְּאִיהוּ חוּשְׁבָּנֵיהּ ד', ד' חֵיוָן.

188. And let Rabbi Yudai rise up with him, for the numerical value of the letters of Yudai is the same as that of El, and he is like the angels, Michael

and the others, who have the letters of 'El' in their names. It is as IN THE MEANING OF the expression: "It is in the power (Heb. *el*) of my hand" (Beresheet 31:29), WHERE THE WORD CONNOTES STRENGTH. And the secret of '*El*' (*Aleph-Lamed*) is as follows: the Aleph is the likeness of a man, FOR THE LETTER HAS THE FORM OF A BODY WITH TWO ARMS, and the Lamed is the secret of the three living creatures, EACH ONE OF which is with four countenances, and THE THREE LIVING CREATURES are intimated in the three Yuds that amount to Lamed, which are at the beginning of the three recited Yud Hei Vav Hei's which are 'Hashem reigns, Hashem reigned, Hashem will reign forever'. IN OTHER WORDS: THE THREE YUDS AT THE HEAD OF EACH YUD HEI VAV HEI HINT AT THE THREE LIVING CREATURES, EACH OF WHICH HAS FOUR COUNTENANCES, FOR IN EACH NAME ARE THE FOUR LETTERS OF YUD HEI VAV HEI. AND THIS IS THE SECRET OF THE LETTER LAMED OF '*EL*'. And let Rabbi Aba rise up with them, for the numerical value of his name is four, NAMELY the four living creatures.

189. רִבִּי שִׁמְעוֹן אִיהוּ כְּאִילָנָא, ור' אֶלְעָזָר בְּרֵיה וְחַבְרוֹי, דְּאִינּוּן חֲמִשָׁה דְּאַדְכַּרְנָא, כַּעֲנָפִין דְּאִילָנָא רַבְרְבִין דְּדַמְיָין לִדְרוֹעִין וְשׁוֹקִין.

189. Rabbi Shimon is like a tree, and Rabbi Elazar his son and his friends, the five that we have just mentioned, are like large branches COMING OUT of the tree, similar to arms and legs, WHERE ARMS ARE CHESED AND GVURAH, AND LEGS ARE NETZACH AND HOD.

36. To the chief musician, Give thanks, Rejoice O you righteous, Praise, Melody, Tune, Song, Blessing...

36. To the chief musician, Give thanks, Rejoice O you righteous, Praise, Melody, Tune, Song, Blessing...

A Synopsis

Rabbi Shimon equates the kinds of music and praise to the various Sfirot. After a question from the Faithful Shepherd, Rabbi Shimon challenges him to show why, if he was at the level of Binah, scripture says that God gave Hod (honor) to him. Moses' answer includes a description of the study of the divine Chariot, and we hear that this work can never be expounded upon by one person alone unless he is a sage who has merited Chochmah, Binah and Da'at.

The Relevance of this Passage

A pure melody sings out from the Heavens to bespeak the final victory of the Light over the forces of Evil, and the demise of the wicked. The Letters *Mem* מ *and Lamed* ל, the Sfirot, *Netzach* and *Hod,* and the *72 Names* light our souls with pleasure evermore!

In paragraph 195, Moses (the Faithful Shepherd) reveals a secret concerning the "fifty Gates of Binah." These fifty Gates correspond to the spiritual path of man, via Kabbalah, and Binah is the World to Come. The World to Come denotes the bliss, perfection, and ultimate fate of humanity. Thus, here we bring the Light of Binah into the present day so that our world is immediately corrected and filled with bliss.

190. קוּם ר״ש, וְיִתְחַדְּשׁוּן מִלִּין מִפּוּמֶךָ, בְּהַאי קְרָא דִּמְלְקַדְמִין. לַמְנַצֵּחַ, תַּמָּן נֶצַח, נִגּוּן צַח. וּבֵיהּ אִתְקְרֵי יְדֹוָד מָארֵי נָצְחָן קְרָבִין, לְגַבֵּי אוּמִין עכו״ם דְּעָלְמָא, וְרַחֲמִין וְדִינָא לְיִשְׂרָאֵל. וְרָזָא דְּמִלָּה, וּבַאֲבוֹד רְשָׁעִים רִנָּה. מ״ל, שַׁבְעִין שְׁמָהָן אִית לֵיהּ, וְעִם נֶצַח וְהוֹד, ע״ב, כְּחוּשְׁבַּן חֶסֶ״ד, וְרָזָא דְּמִלָּה, נְעִימוֹת בִּימִינְךָ נֶצַח.

190. Rise, Rabbi Shimon, and let us hear new matters from your mouth on this verse: "TO THE CHIEF MUSICIAN UPON SHUSHAN-EDUT, A WRIT OF DAVID TO TEACH" (TEHILIM 60:1). IT first SAYS "To the chief musician (Heb. *lamnatze'ach*)." It contains THE LETTERS OF Netzach, THE MEANING OF WHICH IS *nigun tzach* (lit. 'pure melody'), and by it Hashem is called a man of war towards the nations of the world, but of Mercy and Judgment

towards Yisrael. And the secret of the matter is contained in: "And when the wicked perish, there is joy" (Mishlei 11:10). THUS, WHEN HASHEM IS VICTORIOUS (Heb. *MENATZEACH*) OVER THE WICKED, THERE IS A PURE MELODY. Mem and Lamed OF THE WORD *LAMNATZE'ACH* are the secret of the seventy names that He has. Together with Netzach and Hod, they come to 72, which is the numerical value of Chesed. And the secret of the matter IS IN THE VERSE: "at Your right hand are pleasures (Heb. *Netzach*) for evermore" (Tehilim 16:11), FOR NETZACH IS TO THE RIGHT, WHICH IS CHESED.

191. הוֹד, בֵּיהּ הוֹדוּ לַיְיָ'. צַדִּיק, בֵּיהּ רַנְּנוּ צַדִּיקִים בַּיְדֹוָד. וּבֵיהּ רָנּוּ לְיַעֲקֹב שִׂמְחָה. תִּפְאֶרֶת, בֵּיהּ הַלְלוּ אֵל. הַלְלוּיָהּ, הַלְלוּ יָהּ. דְּתַמָּן יָדוּ"ד. בְּנִגּוּן וּבְזֶמֶר, חֶסֶד וּגְבוּרָה. בְּשִׁיר וּבִבְרָכָה, חָכְמָה וּבִינָה. בְּאַשְׁרֵי, כֶּתֶר. בִּתְהִלָּה, מַלְכוּת.

191. HAVING CLARIFIED THAT *LAMNATZE'ACH* IS THE SECRET OF THE SFIRAH NETZACH, HE CONTINUES: about Hod IT IS SAID, "Give thanks (Heb. *hodu*) to Hashem" (I Divrei Hayamim 16:8). Of the righteous, WHICH IS YESOD, it is written: "Rejoice in Hashem, O you righteous" (Tehilim 33:1), and also: "Sing with gladness for Jacob" (Yirmeyah 31:6), WHICH IS AN INDICATION OF UNITY OF TIFERET, YESOD AND MALCHUT. FOR 'SING' IS YESOD, IN WHICH THERE IS SINGING. JACOB IS TIFERET AND GLADNESS IS MALCHUT. Of Tiferet it is said: "Praise (Heb. *halelu*) El" (Tehilim 150:1), "Haleluyah," "Praise Yah" and the name of Yud Hei Vav Hei, SINCE YUD HEI VAV HEI IS A NAME FOR TIFERET. Of melody and tune: these are Chesed and Gvurah, MELODY BEING CHESED, AND TUNE GVURAH; Of song and blessing: they are Chochmah and Binah, SONG BEING CHOCHMAH, AND BLESSING BINAH. Happy IS Keter and praise is Malchut.

192. מִזְמוֹר, בֵּיהּ רָ"ז, וּבֵיהּ מוּ"ם. מִסִּטְרָא דְּזֶמֶר דְּאוֹרַיְיתָא וְזֶמֶר דִּצְלוֹתָא. זֶמֶר מִסִּטְרָא אַחֲרָא, אִיהִי מוּ"ם זָ"ר. זִמְרָא בְּבֵיתָא, חָרְבָּא בְּבֵיתָא. נִדָּה שִׁפְחָה בַּת עכו"ם זוֹנָה. וְדָא אַתְוָון מִזמוֹ"ר. נְגוּ"ן, תַּמָּן גַּ"ן. הָכִי שַׁפִּירוּ דְּנִגּוּנָא, בֵּיהּ הַלֵּל. כְּגוֹן לֵיל שִׁמּוּרִים הוּא לַיְיָ' לְהוֹצִיאָם מֵאֶרֶץ מִצְרָיִם. אַשְׁרֵי דְּבֵיהּ שָׁרֵי עָלְמָא מְשַׁבְּחִין, אַשְׁרֵי הָעָם

שֶׁכְּכָה לוֹ. בִּבְרָכָה, אֲבָרְכָה אֶת ה' בְּכָל עֵת. בַּתְּהִלָּה, תָּמִיד תְּהִלָּתוֹ בְּפִי.

192. AND HE ELUCIDATES, A psalm (Heb. *mizmor*), WHICH IS GVURAH, that has in it THE LETTERS OF Raz (lit. 'secret') and THE LETTERS OF Mum (lit. 'blemish') from the side of the tune (Heb. *zemer*) of the Torah and the tune of prayer. FOR WHEN THE LEFT COLUMN HAS CONTROL BY ITSELF, LIGHT TURNS INTO A SECRET, WHICH IS THE BACK PART OF THE LIGHT. AND THEREFORE IT HAS IN IT A BLEMISH, CONTAINING A HOLD FOR THE EXTERNAL FORCES, AND ALL OF THIS IS FROM THE SIDE OF HOLINESS. THE PSALM (HEB. *MIZMOR*) THAT IS SUNG BY a tune of the Other Side contains THE PHONEMES *mum zar* (Eng. 'a foreign blemish'). AND THIS IS WHY THEY SAID 'a tune (Heb. *zemer*) in the house is destruction in the house', AND IT IS FROM THE ASPECT OF a menstruating woman, handmaid, daughter of idol worshippers, prostitute. And these are the letters of Mizmor, NAMELY '*MUM ZAR*'. Melody (Heb. *nigun*) IS CHESED, containing THE LETTERS OF Gan (Eng. 'garden'), WHICH IS MALCHUT. And such is the beauty of the melody, which has in it *Halel* (Eng. 'praise'), like THE *HALEL* in "It is a night of watchfulness to Hashem for bringing them out of the land of Egypt" (Shemot 12:42). IN OTHER WORDS, NOT THE WHOLE MELODY IS CHESED, BUT ONLY THE BEAUTY OF THE MELODY TENDS TOWARDS CHESED, WHICH IS THE SECRET OF THE *HALEL* OF THE EXODUS FROM EGYPT, WHICH INCLINES TOWARDS CHESED. 'Happy', with which everyone begins to offer praises, IS KETER, SINCE LIKE KETER, IT IS THE BEGINNING OF THE SFIROT, NAMELY, "Happy is that people, that is in such a case" (Tehilim 144:15). Of blessing, it is as in "I will bless Hashem at all times" (Tehilim 34:2), WHICH IS BINAH, FOR THE BOUNTY OF BINAH IS UNCEASING; of praise IS MALCHUT, as in "His praise shall continually be in my mouth" (Ibid.), FOR MOUTH INTIMATES MALCHUT.

193. עַל שׁוּשַׁן עֵדוּת, דָּא הוֹד. דְּאִיהוּ שׁוּשַׁן, סוּמָק שַׁלִּיט עַל חִוָּור, דְּנֶצַח שַׁלִּיט אִיהוּ חִוָּור עַל סוּמָק. מַאי עֵדוּת. דָּא צַדִּיק. אִיהוּ בְּרִית, דְּאִיהוּ אָחִיד לִשְׁמַיָּא וְאַרְעָא. הה"ד הַעִידוֹתִי בָכֶם הַיּוֹם אֶת הַשָּׁמַיִם וְאֶת הָאָרֶץ. מַאי מִכְתָּם. מָ"ךְ תָּ"ם מָךְ, אִיהוּ צַדִּיק. תָּם, עַמּוּדָא דְּאֶמְצָעִיתָא, דַּרְגָּא דְּיַעֲקֹב. אִישׁ תָּם. גּוּף וּבְרִית חַשְׁבִּינָן חַד. לְלַמֵּד, חֶסֶד וּגְבוּרָה, דְּמִתַּמָּן אוֹרַיְיתָא אִתְיְהִיבַת, לִלְמוֹד וּלְלַמֵּד.

193. RETURNING NOW TO THE VERSE: "TO THE CHIEF MUSICIAN UPON SHUSHAN-EDUT, A WRIT OF DAVID TO TEACH" (TEHILIM 60:1), IT HAS BEEN EXPLAINED THAT "*LAMNATZE'ACH*" IS NETZACH. AND HE CONTINUES "upon *Shushan-edut*" is Hod, that is *Shoshan* (Eng. 'rose') in which the red controls the white, while with Netzach the white controls the red. But what is *Edut* (Eng. 'testimony')? This is the Righteous who is the Covenant, NAMELY YESOD, which holds the heaven and the earth WHICH ARE ZEIR ANPIN AND MALCHUT. This is as it is written: "I call heaven and earth to witness against you this day" (Devarim 4:26), WHICH IMPLIES THE UNITY OF TIFERET, YESOD AND MALCHUT, FOR 'I CALL TO WITNESS' IS YESOD, WHILE THE HEAVEN AND EARTH ARE TIFERET AND MALCHUT. What is "writ" (Heb. *michtam*)? It forms the two words *mach* and *tam*; *mach* (Eng. 'humble') is the Righteous, NAMELY YESOD, while *tam* (Eng. 'complete') is the Central Column, NAMELY TIFERET, WHICH IS THE SECRET OF THE BODY, on the level of "Jacob was a plain (Heb. *Tam*) man" (Beresheet 25:27). We count the body and the covenant, WHICH ARE TIFERET AND YESOD, as one, WHICH IS WHY *MACH* AND *TAM* ARE WRITTEN AS ONE WORD: *MICHTAM*. "to teach": This is Chesed and Gvurah, for from there was the Torah given 'to study and to teach'.

194. א״ל שַׁפִּיר קָאַמְרַת, אֲבָל לַמְנַצֵּחַ עַל הַשְּׁמִינִית, דְּלָא תָּזוּז נֶצַח מִן הוֹד, דְּאִיהִי סְפִירָה ח׳, אָמַר לַמְנַצֵּחַ עַל הַשְּׁמִינִית. אָמַר בּוּצִינָא קַדִּישָׁא, אִי הָכִי, בִּינָה דַּרְגָּא דִּילָךְ, וַאֲמַאי אוֹקְמוּהָ וְנָתַן הַהוֹד לְמֹשֶׁה, שֶׁנֶּאֱמַר וְנָתַתָּה מֵהוֹדְךָ עָלָיו.

194. THE FAITHFUL SHEPHERD said to him: What you say is all very well, but SCRIPTURE SAYS: "To the chief musician upon the Shminit (Eng. 'eighth')" (Tehilim 12:1). THIS MEANS that Netzach should not move from Hod, which is the eighth Sfirah, and that is why he says: "To the chief musician (Heb. lamnazte'ach) upon the eighth," RATHER THAN "TO THE CHIEF MUSICIAN UPON SHUSHAN," AS YOU HAVE IT. The Holy Luminary, RABBI SHIMON, responded: If that is so, IF YOU WANT TO BE SO PEDANTIC, ONE CAN ASK AN EVEN MORE PROFOUND QUESTION. Your level is that of Binah; why, then, was it taught that He gave Hod to Moses, as it is written: "And you shall put some of your honor (Heb. hod) upon him" (Bemidbar 27:20)?

195. א"ל, שַׁפִּיר קָא שָׁאֵלְתָּ. ה' סַלְקָא בְּאָת י', חֲמֵשׁ זִמְנִין עֶשֶׂר, לַחֲמִשִׁין תַּרְעִין דְּבִינָה, וְאִתְפַּשְׁטוּתָא דִּלְהוֹן מֵחֶסֶד עַד הוֹד, הֵן חָמֵשׁ עֶשְׂרָה בְּכָל סְפִירָה, אִינּוּן חַמְשִׁין. וּבְגִין דָּא, מִבִּינָה עַד הוֹד, כֹּלָּא אִתְפַּשְׁטוּתָא חֲדָא. לְבָתַר אָתָא צַדִּיק, וְנָטִיל כָּל חַמְשִׁין תַּרְעִין בִּלְחוֹדוֹי, לְמֶהֱוֵי שָׁקִיל לְכָל חָמֵשׁ, וְאִתְקְרֵי כָּל, דְּנָטִיל כָּל חַמְשִׁין תַּרְעִין. וְאוֹף הָכִי כַּלָּה, נְטִילַת לְהוּ כֻּלְּהוּ. אָמַר, כְּעַן וַדַּאי אִתְיַישַּׁב מִלָּה עַל בּוּרְיֵיהּ.

195. THE FAITHFUL SHEPHERD replied: That is a good question that you have asked. THE REASON IS THAT the letter Hei OF YUD HEI OF THE YUD HEI VAV HEI increases AND IS MULTIPLIED by the Yud OF YUD-HEI, making five times ten, which are the fifty gates of Binah, whose extension is from Chesed to Hod, namely five SFIROT. And in each of the Sfirot there are ten, making fifty SFIROT, THAT RECEIVE THE FIFTY GATES OF BINAH, and there is, therefore, just one extension from Binah to Hod; SO, WHEN MENTIONING HOD THEN BINAH IS INCLUDED. Then comes the Righteous, WHICH IS YESOD, and by himself takes all fifty gates OF BINAH, he is equivalent to all five, SINCE YESOD INCORPORATES ALL FIVE SFIROT: CHESED, GVURAH, TIFERET, NETZACH AND HOD. And he is called 'all', (Heb. *kol* = fifty) because he takes all fifty gates. And so also does the bride (Heb. *kalah*), WHICH IS MALCHUT, take all FIFTY GATES, WHICH IS WHY SHE IS CALLED 'KALAH', NAMELY *KOL*, AS YESOD, HINTING AT THE FIFTY GATES, WITH THE ADDITION OF HEI, SHE BEING FEMININE. Said RABBI SHIMON: Now surely everything is falling into place.

196. וְעוֹד לַמְנַצֵּחַ, תַּמָּן מ"ל עִם נֶצַח. וְדָא מ"ל מִן חַשְׁמַ"ל. מִן ח"שׁ, הוֹד וְנֶצַח, אִינּוּן לָקֳבֵיל תְּרֵין שִׁפְוָון. וּבג"ד אִתְקְרִיאוּ שִׁפְוָון, חֵיוָן אֵשָּׁא מְמַלְּלָא. וּבַחֲגִיגָה עַד הֵיכָן מַעֲשֵׂה מֶרְכָּבָה, וְאוֹקְמוּהָ מִן וָאֵרָא עַד חַשְׁמַל. דְּמִסִּטְרָא דִּגְבוּרָה אִתְקְרִיאוּ חֵיוָן אֵשָּׁא. וְנָהָר דְּנָפִיק מְזֵיעָן דִּלְהוֹן, יְסוֹד. כֻּלְּהוּ תְּלַת אִינּוּן מֶרְכָּבָה לְתִפְאֶרֶת, אָדָם.

196. Moreover, THE LETTERS OF *Lamnatze'ach* can be re-arranged as *mal* with *Netzach*. And that *mal* is MEM AND LAMED of *Chashmal* (Eng.

'electrum'), WHEN REMOVING MEM AND LAMED from Chet Shin, WHICH ARE THE FIRST AND LAST LETTERS OF *CHAYOT ESH* (ENG. 'LIVING CREATURES OF FIRE'). And these are Hod and Netzach, which correspond to the two lips, NETZACH BEING THE UPPER AND HOD THE LOWER LIP. Therefore the lips are called 'muttering living creatures of fire'. And in Chagigah the question is asked: 'Until where is the study of the divine Chariot?' And the answer was given: From "And I looked" (Yechezkel 1:4) until "*electrum*" (Yechezkel 1:27), WHERE THE WORD *CHASHMAL* (CHET SHIN MEM LAMED) FORMS THE INITIALS OF *CHAYOT ESH MEMALELOT* (ENG. 'MUTTERING LIVING CREATURES OF FIRE'). For from the side of Gvurah, NETZACH AND HOD are called 'living creatures of fire', and the river that flows from the sweat of these LIVING CREATURES OF FIRE is Yesod. All three of them, THAT IS NETZACH, HOD AND YESOD, form a Chariot for the splendor (Heb. *Tiferet*) of man, WHICH IS ZEIR ANPIN.

197. מַעֲשֵׂה מֶרְכָּבָה, דָּא מַלְכוּת. וּבִתְלַת אִלֵּין, אִיהוּ חָכְמָה וּבִינָה וָדַעַת. וּבג"ד אוּקְמוּהָ מָארֵי מַתְנִיתִין, דְּאֵין דּוֹרְשִׁין בְּמַעֲשֵׂה מֶרְכָּבָה בְּיָחִיד, אא"כ הוּא חָכָם וּמֵבִין מִדַּעְתּוֹ.

197. The study of the divine Chariot is Malchut, INASMUCH AS IT IS MADE BY THE CHARIOT THAT IS NETZACH, HOD AND YESOD, and in these three (NETZACH, HOD, and YESOD) are Chochmah, Binah, and Da'at OF MALCHUT, FOR CHOCHMAH, BINAH AND DA'AT of MALCHUT ARE MADE FROM THE HEADS of NETZACH, HOD AND YESOD OF ZEIR ANPIN. For this reason the sages of the Mishnah taught: 'The study of the divine Chariot may not be expounded by one alone, unless he is a sage who understands of his own knowledge'. THIS REFERS TO ONE WHO HAS MERITED CHOCHMAH, BINAH, AND DA'AT, SINCE A SAGE PERTAINS TO CHOCHMAH, 'WHO UNDERSTANDS' PERTAINS TO BINAH, AND 'OF HIS OWN KNOWLEDGE IS DA'AT'.

37. The Chariot of Metatron

A Synopsis

We hear the esoteric explanation of the chariot below Zeir Anpin, that is Metatron, who is also known as the small man. This includes a description of the great and powerful flow of the waters of Chochmah that run from the sea of Torah, and from which three of the four rabbis were unable to emerge in peace. Lastly, it is shown how the first nine letters of the alphabet correspond to the nine Sfirot.

The Relevance of this Passage

Much supernal wisdom is distilled here. The forces of judgment that reside in water (which gives water the potential to destroy through flood or drowning) are extracted from this sacred liquid. Water, the lifeblood of Earth and humanity, is now restored to its original state of healing and rejuvenation.

The spiritual influences of water arise to cleanse, purify, and renew us. The name of Metatron arouses immortality and reversal of the aging process, for Metatron embodies eternal youth. Thus, the waters in our cells are purified, causing our cells to regenerate and flourish.

198. וְאִית מֶרְכָּבָה לְתַתָּא מִזְעֵיר אַנְפִּין, דְּאִיהוּ מְטַ״טְרוֹן. אָדָם הַקָּטָן. דְּבַמֶרְכָּבָה דִּילֵיהּ דְּאִיהוּ פַּרְדֵּס, רְדִיפֵי מַיָּא דְאוֹרַיְיתָא, דְּנָפִיק מִגּוֹ פַּרְדֵּס דִּילֵיהּ, לִתְלַת מֵאַרְבַּע, דְּאִתְּמַר עָלַיְיהוּ, אַרְבְּעָה נִכְנְסוּ לַפַּרְדֵּס. וְהָא אִתְּמַר.

198. And there is a Chariot below NETZACH, HOD and YESOD OF Zeir Anpin, which is Metatron, ALSO KNOWN AS the small man. And in his Chariot, which is an orchard (Heb. *pardes*), the water of the Torah rush, LIKE A RIVER WHOSE WATERS ARE FLOWING WITH GREAT SPEED AND FORCE TOWARDS THE SEA, flowing out of his orchard, to the three of the four, about whom it was said that four entered the orchard, NAMELY: BEN AZZAI AND BEN ZOMA, ELISHA BEN ABUYAH AND RABBI AKIVA. THE FIRST THREE WERE INJURED BY THE FORCE OF THE FLOW OF THE WATERS OF CHOCHMAH, WHICH ARE CALLED 'AN ORCHARD', AND ONLY RABBI AKIVA ENTERED IN PEACE AND LEFT IN PEACE. And we have already learned this.

199. דְּאִיהוּ צִפָּרָא דְּחָזָא רַבָּה בַּר בַּר חַנָּה, לְכֵיף יַמָּא דְּאוֹרַיְיתָא,
דְיַמָּא מָטֵי עַד קוּרְסוּלוֹי. וְרֵישֵׁיהּ מָטֵי עַד צֵית שְׁמַיָּא, וְלָא אַכְשִׁילוּ
תְּלַת בֵּיהּ, מִשּׁוּם דִּנְפִישֵׁי מַיָּא דִּילֵיהּ, אֶלָּא מִשּׁוּם דִּרְדִיפֵי מַיָּא
וְאוֹקְמוּהָ.

199. For he, METATRON, is the bird who was seen by Raba bar bar Channah
on the beach of the sea of the Torah when the sea, WHICH IS THE SECRET
OF MALCHUT, ROSE AND reached his ankles, NAMELY TO THE END OF HIS
NETZACH AND HOD, CALLED 'ANKLES', and his head reached to the top of
the heavens, WHICH IS ZEIR ANPIN. AND THE THREE OF THEM THAT
WERE FAULTED IN IT, THE SECRET OF THE *PARDES*, AS ABOVE: these
three did not fail by it because it contains much waters OF CHOCHMAH, but
because of the force of the flow of the waters OF CHOCHMAH IN IT. THAT
IS TO SAY THAT THEY ARE SHARP AND FORCEFUL WITH JUDGMENTS, and
so we have learned.

200. אבג כָּלִיל לוֹן דְּסַלְקִין לְשִׁית, לְקַבֵּל אַתְוָון מְטַטְרוֹ״ן. רְבִיעָאָה
ד׳, קוֹל דְּמָמָה דַקָּה, דְּתַמָּן אָתֵי מַלְכָּא. וְאִיהוּ אָדָם לְשֶׁבֶת עַל הַכִּסֵּא.

200. THE LETTERS Aleph, Bet and Gimel include them, THE CHARIOT OF
METATRON, FOR THE NUMERICAL VALUE OF THESE THREE LETTERS
amounts to six, which is the number of letters IN THE NAME Metatron. The
fourth LETTER OF THE ALPHABET, Dalet, IS THE SECRET OF "a still small
voice" (I Melachim 19:12), WHICH IS THE SECRET OF MALCHUT. For the
King comes there, for it is a man to sit on the throne, SINCE MALCHUT IS
THE SECRET OF A MAN WHO SITS ON THIS THRONE OF METATRON.

201. א י״י, מַיִם עֶלְיוֹנִים, וּמַיִם תַּחְתּוֹנִים. דְּלֵית בֵּינַיְיהוּ אֶלָּא כְּמְלֹא
נִימָא, דְּאִיהוּ ו׳, נָטוּי בֵּינַיְיהוּ, בָּרְקִיעַ דְּאִיהוּ מַבְדִּיל בֵּין מַיִם לְמַיִם,
דְּיְהֵא הַבְדָּלָה בֵּין נוּקְבָּא לִדְכוּרָא. בג״ד וִיהִי מַבְדִּיל וְרָזָא דְּמִלָּה,
יאהדונהי. מַיִם עֶלְיוֹנִים זְכָרִים י׳ עִלָּאָה, מַיִם תַּחְתּוֹנִים נְקֵבוֹת, י׳
תַּתָּאָה. שִׁית אַתְוָון בֵּינַיְיהוּ, כְּחוּשְׁבַּן ו׳, דָּא מְטַטְרוֹן, דְּאִיהוּ בֵּין א.

201. The two Yud's in THE SHAPE OF the Aleph א: THE UPPER YUD

STANDS FOR the upper waters, WHICH IS THE SECRET OF ZEIR ANPIN, and THE LOWER YUD FOR the lower waters, WHICH IS THE SECRET OF MALCHUT, between them is but a hairsbreadth, which is Vav WRITTEN LIKE THE LINE IN THE MIDDLE OF THE ALEPH. It is a slant line between THE TWO. YUD IS IN THE SECRET OF the firmament WHICH IS THE SECRET OF THE CURTAIN that "divide water from water" (Beresheet 1:6). Thus there should be a division between female and male, and that is why IT IS WRITTEN "and let it divide..." (Idib.). And the inner meaning of the matter is the permutation YUD HEI VAV HEI AND ADONAI, *Yud-Aleph-Hei-Dalet-Vav Nun-Hei-Yud* WHICH IS A COMBINATION OF THE TWO NAMES. The upper Yud OF THE COMBINATION is the upper, male waters and the lower Yud OF THE COMBINATION is the lower, female waters. The six letters ALEPH HEI DALET VAV NUN HEI, which come between THE TWO YUD'S have the same are numerical value as Vav (= 6), who is THE SECRET OF Metatron, which is THE VAV between THE TWO YUD'S IN THE FORM OF the Aleph.

202. וְעוֹד, יוֹד נְקוּדָה. ו' גַּלְגַּל. וְלֵית תְּנוּעָה בְּגַלְגַּל בְּשִׁית סְטְרִין כְּחוּשְׁבַּן ו', אֶלָּא בְּהַהִיא נְקוּדָה. וְהַהוּא נְקוּדָה אִיהוּ יְחוּדָא דְכֹלָּא, וְאַסְהִידַת עַל הַהוּא יָחִיד, דְּלֵית לֵיהּ שֵׁנִי, דְּאוֹקְמוּהָ עֲלֵיהּ רַבָּנָן, שֶׁצָּרִיךְ לְיַחֵדוּ כְּדֵי שֶׁתַּמְלִיכֵהוּ עַל הַשָּׁמַיִם וְעַל הָאָרֶץ, וְעַל ד' רוּחוֹת עָלְמָא. ב', שָׁמַיִם וָאָרֶץ. ג', עַמּוּדָא סָבִיל לוֹן. ד', אַרְבַּע חֵיוָן. ה' כְּרְסַיָּיא. ו', שִׁית דַּרְגִּין לְכָרְסַיָּיא. וְעוֹד, א ב ג ד ה ו ז ח ט: אָדָם. י' יִיחוּד דִּילֵיהּ, מַלְכוּת, עֲשִׂירָאָה דְאָדָם. תֵּשַׁע, אִיהוּ לָקֳבֵל תֵּשַׁע אַתְוָון. זַכָּאִין אִינוּן יִשְׂרָאֵל, דְּיַדְעִין רָזָא דְמָארֵיהוֹן.

202. Furthermore, Yud is a point, WHICH IS THE SECRET OF SUPERNAL CHOCHMAH. Vav is THE SECRET OF a wheel, WHICH REVOLVES IN THE SIX SFIROT: CHESED, GVURAH, TIFERET, NETZACH, HOD AND YESOD. And there is no movement in the wheel at the six extremities, as the numerical value of Vav, except at the point, FOR IT RECEIVES EVERYTHING THAT IS IN CHESED, GVURAH, TIFERET, NETZACH, HOD AND YESOD FROM THIS YUD. And this point is the unity of everything, and is witness to that unity, WHICH IS THE ENDLESS LIGHT, who has no second, and about whom the sages taught that one has to proclaim His unity in order to establish His kingship over the heavens and the earth and the four directions

of the compass. THIS IS THE SECRET OF THE ALEPH (= 1). Bet (= 2) is THE SECRET OF heaven and earth, WHICH ARE ZEIR ANPIN AND MALCHUT. Gimel (= 3) is THE SECRET OF the pillar that bears them, WHICH IS THE SECRET OF YESOD. Dalet (= 3) is THE SECRET OF the four living creatures OF THE CHARIOT. Hei (= 5) is THE SECRET OF the throne , WHICH IS MALCHUT. Vav is THE SECRET OF the six steps up to the throne, WHICH ARE CHESED, GVURAH, TIFERET, NETZACH, HOD AND YESOD. Moreover, Aleph, Bet, Gimel, Dalet, Hei, Vav, Zayin, Chet, Tet are THE SECRET OF man, NAMELY THE FIRST NINE SFIROT OF ZEIR ANPIN. Yud is His Unity, NAMELY Malchut, WHICH IS the tenth SFIRAH of ZEIR ANPIN WHO IS CALLED '*Adam*' (lit. 'man'). THIS IS THE SECRET OF THE YUD HEI VAV HEI, FULLY SPELLED WITH ALEPHS, MAKING THE NUMERICAL VALUE OF ADAM. The nine SFIROT OF ZEIR ANPIN correspond to the nine letters. Happy are those of Yisrael who know the secret of their Master!

38. Smoke and Fragrance and Incense

A Synopsis
Rabbi Yehuda, Rabbi Shimon and the Faithful Shepherd discuss the smoke that emerged from the left nostril and the fragrance that was drawn into the right nostril, and we learn that these are Judgment and Mercy. Incense corrects the two and removes death from the world.

The Relevance of this Passage
We now offer our negative, self-destructive traits as a sacrifice through the verses that speak the mysteries of the burnt offerings and incense. This action has a profound effect upon our lives as revealed by the Zohar:

"...nothing is as effective as incense for doing away with death in the world, for incense is the connecting of Judgment with Mercy with the sweet savor in the nostrils."

This passage lights the sticks of incense on our behalf in the following manner: Smoke, we are told, denotes judgment, which correlates to the left nostril. Our repentant reading of this passage repeals all judgments decreed against us and our neighbors.

Fragrance correlates to the right nostril, bringing Mercy into the body instead of Judgment. Thus, here we arouse great Mercy in the world.

Judgment and Mercy then combine together. Smoke and fragrance blend together to generate a sweet incense that slays the Angel of Death, forever banishing the force of death from our body and civilization.

203. ד״א, צַו אֶת בְּנֵי יִשְׂרָאֵל וְאָמַרְתָּ אֲלֵיהֶם אֶת קָרְבָּנִי לַחְמִי לְאִשַּׁי רֵיחַ נִיחֹחִי. ר׳ יְהוּדָה אָמַר, בְּקָרְבָּנָא אִית עָשָׁן, וְאִית רֵיחַ, וְאִית רֵיחַ נִיחֹחַ. עָשָׁן אִיהוּ מִסִּטְרָא דְּדִינָא, הה״ד, כִּי אָז יֶעְשַׁן אַף יְיָ'. עָלָה עָשָׁן בְּאַפּוֹ וְאֵשׁ מִפִּיו תֹּאכֵל. רֵיחַ נִיחֹחִי, רַחֲמֵי. וְרֵיחַ אַפֶּךְ כַּתַּפּוּחִים.

203. Another explanation: "Command the children of Yisrael, and say to them, My offerings, the provision of My sacrifices made by fire, of a sweet savor to Me" (Bemidbar 28:2). Rabbi Yehuda said: With an offering there is smoke and there is fragrance and there is a sweet savor. Smoke is from the side of Judgment, as it is said: "But then the anger (also: 'nose') of Hashem

shall smoke" (Devarim 29:19), "There went up a smoke out of His nostrils, and fire out of His mouth devoured" (Tehilim 18:9). Sweet savor is Mercy, as it is said: "and the scent of your countenance (lit. 'nose') like apples" (Shir Hashirim 7:9).

204. אָמַר רַעְיָא מְהֵימָנָא, וְהָא תַּרְוַויְיהוּ עָשָׁן וְרֵיחַ, אִינּוּן בְּאַף, וְקַרְאִין סַהֲדִין. חַד, עָלָה עָשָׁן בְּאַפּוֹ. וְתִנְיָינָא, וְרֵיחַ אַפֵּךְ כַּתַּפּוּחִים. וַאֲמַאי אִתְקְרֵי חַד עָשָׁן דִּינָא וְתִנְיָינָא רַחֲמֵי. אֶלָּא, בְּחוֹטָמָא אִית תְּרֵין חַלּוֹנִין, וְאִתְּמַר בִּשְׂמָאלָא, עָלָה עָשָׁן בְּאַפּוֹ, מַאי עָלָה. אֶלָּא מִלְּבָא דְּאִיהוּ בִּשְׂמָאלָא, לָקֳבֵל גְּבוּר. מִימִינָא נָחִית רוּחָא לְגַבֵּיהּ, לְקָרְרָא לֵיהּ, וּלְשַׁכְּכָא רוּגְזֵיהּ, מִסִּטְרָא דְּחֶסֶד, דְּתַמָּן מוֹחָא. חָכְמָה לִימִינָא, הָרוֹצֶה לְהַחְכִּים יַדְרִים. בִּינָה בְּלִבָּא, כְּלַפֵּי שְׂמָאלָא, הָרוֹצֶה לְהַעֲשִׁיר יַצְפִּין. ובג"ד עָלָה עָשָׁן בְּאַפּוֹ, מִן בִּינָה לְגַבֵּי חָכְמָה, דְּאִיהִי לִימִינָא, וּמְקַבֵּל לֵיהּ בְּחֶדְוָה, בְּנִגּוּנָא דְּלֵיוָאֵי.

204. The Faithful Shepherd said, Both of them, smoke and fragrance, are in the nose, and are called 'witnesses'. The former IS IN THE NOSE, AS IT IS WRITTEN: "There went up a smoke out of His nostrils," and the latter, AS IT IS SAID: "and the scent of your countenance (lit. 'nose') like apples." If that is so, then why is the former, smoke, called 'Judgment', and the latter, FRAGRANCE, called 'Mercy'? HE ANSWERS THAT in the nose there are two windows, EACH OF WHICH IS A NOSTRIL. "There went up a smoke out of His nostrils" is said about the left-hand NOSTRIL, WHICH IS JUDGMENT. What is the meaning of "went up"? It is THAT THE SMOKE ROSE UP from the heart, which is on the left and is parallel to Gvurah. And from the right a breeze descends to cool it and quiet its anger from the side of Chesed, which is where the brain is; namely Chochmah, which is to the right, 'He who wishes to acquire wisdom, let him turn south'. And Binah, WHICH IS THE SECRET OF CHOCHMAH OF THE LEFT, is in the heart, opposite the left, 'and he who wishes to enrich let him turn north'. And this is why "There went up a smoke out of His nostrils," namely from Binah, WHICH IS ON THE LEFT, to Chochmah, which is on the right. And CHOCHMAH welcomes it with rejoicing to the accompaniment of the music of the Levites.

205. וְהַאי עָשָׁן לָא סָלִיק, אֶלָּא ע"י אֵשׁ, דְּאַדְלִיק בְּעֵצִים, דְּאִינּוּן

אֵבָרִים מַלְיָין פִּקּוּדִין, עֲצֵי עוֹלָה. מָארֵי תּוֹרָה, אוֹרַיְיתָא דְּאִיהִי
אַדְלִיקַת בְּהוֹן, אֵשׁ בְּתוּקְפָּא דִּגְבוּרָה, וְעָלָה עָשָׁן בְּהוֹן. בְּבִינָה עָשָׁן
הַמַּעֲרָכָה.

205. And this smoke only rises up with fire that is kindled with pieces of
wood that are limbs filled with the precepts, which are CALLED "the wood
for the burnt offering" (Beresheet 22:3). And the Torah of Torah scholars is
enkindled by THE PRECEPTS, their fire is by virtue of Gvurah, and the
smoke rising up in them, in Binah, IS CALLED 'the smoke' of the set order
on the altar.

206. וּמִדְּסָלִיקַת לְאַף, אִתְקְרֵי קְטֹרֶת, הֲה"ד, יָשִׂימוּ קְטוֹרָה בְּאַפֶּךָ.
וְלֵית דְּבָטִיל מוֹתָנָא בְּעָלְמָא, כַּקְטֹרֶת, דְּאִיהוּ קְשׁוּרָא דְּדִינָא בְּרַחֲמֵי,
עִם רֵיחַ נִיחוֹחַ בְּאַף. תַּרְגּוּם דְּקֶשֶׁר קְטִירוּ. א"ר יְהוּדָה, זַכָּאָה חוּלָקָנָא
דְּרַוַוחְנָא מִלִּין סְתִימִין בְּאִתְגַּלְיָיא. עוֹד אָמַר בּוּצִינָא קַדִּישָׁא, דְּבָתַר
דִּצְלוֹתָא אִיהִי כְּקָרְבְּנָא, מַאן דְּיֵימָא פִּטוּם הַקְּטֹרֶת, בָּתַר תְּהִלָּה לְדָוִד,
בָּטִיל מוֹתָנָא מִבֵּיתָא.

206. And when the smoke has arisen to the nose, it is called "incense," as it
is written: "They shall put incense in your nostrils." (Devarim 33:10). And
nothing is as effective as incense for doing away with death in the world, for
incense is the connecting of Judgment with Mercy with the sweet savor in
the nostrils. For 'connect' is in Aramaic 'ktiru', AND HENCE INCENSE
(HEB. KTORET) MEANS CONNECTION. Rabbi Yehuda said, Happy is our
portion that we have gained hidden matters and can understand them
openly. The Holy Luminary added, Since prayer is like a sacrifice, anyone,
therefore, who says the prayer 'Compounding of the Incense' after "A
praise of David" (Tehilim 145:1) does away with death from the house.

39. The three prayers

A Synopsis
The Faithful Shepherd tells us how the three prayers were instituted to parallel the sacrifices.

The Relevance of this Passage
Some of the most significant spiritual insights into the physiology of heart disease are revealed in this essential passage of Zohar. Therefore, a more detailed discussion is warranted. We begin with the ancient ritual of sacrifice.

As we visually connect to these verses with repentance in our hearts, the sacrifices and burnt offerings that were made three times daily during the time of the Temple are now executed on our behalf.

The effect of this action is deeply profound and vitally important.

The power of the morning prayer is summoned forth, which denotes the lone lamb sacrificed during the early dawn. This corresponds to Abraham, and the prayer now awakens untold mercy in our world. Abraham was a deeply sharing individual, who offered unconditional kindness to both friends and strangers. For this reason, the name of Abraham arouses mercy.

The afternoon prayer manifests the sacrificial lamb that is offered towards evening, which connects to Isaac. This action silences judgments that are due to us as a result of our negative behavior.

The evening prayer concerns the fat that's "devoured all night," and these fats are herewith burned by our efforts extended here. This sacrifice appeases evil forces and removes illnesses from our bodies.

These sacrifices are intimately tied to the organs of the body.

Rabbi Pinchas, utilizing the cryptic language of the Zohar, explains that the brain controls the heart, while the heart controls the liver. The brain is the domain of our consciousness and emotions. If we allow the Other Side, our ego, to control our thoughts and states of mind, there will inevitably be anger, hostility, and fury in our hearts. This ill will is then transferred to the liver.

The liver, we're told, is the physical manifestation of the negative entities (do not pronounce this name) *Samael* and the Serpent, intertwined as one. Our anger and fury feed these evil entities, allowing them to grow stronger in our bodies. Thus, the Zohar states:

> "And from the liver, WHICH REPRESENTS (do not pronounce this name) *SAMAEL*, come all the diseases and

illnesses to all parts of the body…"

However, Rabbi Shimon explains that these evil beings will "devour" the fat and waste that we sacrifice during our evening prayer. Thus, the fat offering becomes an appeasement, a token feed, to keep these wicked forces at bay. This will be reflected in the liver, and our illnesses are kept at a distance. On a practical level, the fat that is sacrificed correlates to our personal selfish traits. Our recognition and acknowledgment of our own disdainful qualities is the ultimate meaning of the sacrifice.

A remarkable revelation concerning heart disease and the liver is made by the Zohar in this passage, 2000 years before modern medicine. Just as the liver absorbs and digests fats and filters toxins from the blood on a physical level, the prayer and sacrifice burn away the spiritual fats and toxins of anger and negativity.

In other words, the evening prayer allows us to metaphysically sacrifice the fat – our negative character traits – which is the key to healthy liver function.

According to medical science, the human liver produces approximately 1,000 milligrams of cholesterol a day. Cholesterol is used to produce the bile we need for the digestion and absorption of fats. The bile also removes wastes and toxic matter from the blood.

Cholesterol levels can be high if the conversion of cholesterol to bile is impaired. If so, low bile acid levels send a powerful signal to the liver to provide *more* cholesterol.

High levels of cholesterol and fatty substances in the bloodstream are primary causes of atherosclerosis (clogging of the arteries) and coronary heart disease!

Excess fat collects in heart cells, killing the cells and eventually damaging the heart muscle, causing seizures of the heart.

Thus, low blood cholesterol and low fat is key to a healthy cardiovascular system. A healthy, full-functioning liver delivers clean, low-fat, toxic-free blood to the heart, which then pumps the purified blood to the rest of the body.

This physiological truth is found in the following Zohar verse:

> "…their [the evil angels'] receiving is that they devour the fatty parts and the fat for the sacrifice, as it is written: 'and the fat that is upon them.' And then everything is offered to the heart."

What is "offered to the heart" spiritually is mercy and gladness – the Light of the Creator.

What is "offered to the heart" physically is purified blood, low in fat, toxins, wastes, and cholesterol – the key for healthy cardiovascular function.

Thus, a healthy body begins with spiritual soundness of mind, heart, and liver.

Here we ignite the power of the sacrifices and the three daily prayers. The influences of the evil angels and ailments of the liver and heart are abated. Our brain, which bears our consciousness, is liberated from the sway of the Other Side. Our blood is purified, as anger and judgment are expunged from our hearts and livers. The cardiovascular system is cleansed, healed, and renewed.

In addition, the widespread revelation of these ancient secrets, for the first time in history, generates an artillery of Light that thwarts cardiovascular and liver diseases *eternally* by exterminating their deep-seated spiritual roots – the negative angels *Lilit* and (do not pronounce this name) *Samael*.

207. אָמַר רַעְיָא מְהֵימָנָא, כְּעַן בָּעֵי לְמִנְדַּע, אֵיךְ אַתְקִינוּ צְלוֹתִין לָקֳבֵל קָרְבְּנִין. אֶלָּא תְּלַת צְלוֹתִין, לְקַבֵּל אֶת הַכֶּבֶשׂ הָאֶחָד תַּעֲשֶׂה בַבֹּקֶר, דָּא צְלוֹתָא דְּשַׁחֲרִית, דְּאִתְּמַר בָּהּ, וַיַּשְׁכֵּם אַבְרָהָם בַּבֹּקֶר אֶל הַמָּקוֹם אֲשֶׁר עָמַד שָׁם אֶת פְּנֵי יְיָ. וְאוֹקְמוּהָ רַבָּנָן, דְּלֵית עֲמִידָה אֶלָּא צְלוֹתָא. וְאֶת הַכֶּבֶשׂ הַשֵּׁנִי תַּעֲשֶׂה בֵּין הָעַרְבַּיִם, לְקַבֵּל צְלוֹתָא דְּמִנְחָה, דְּתַקִּין לָהּ יִצְחָק. הה"ד, וַיֵּצֵא יִצְחָק לָשׂוּחַ בַּשָּׂדֶה לִפְנוֹת עָרֶב. וְלֵית שִׂיחָה, אֶלָּא צְלוֹתָא. צְלוֹתָא דְּעַרְבִית, לְקַבֵּל אֵמוּרִין וּפְדָרִין דְּמִתְאַכְּלִין כָּל הַלַּיְלָה. הה"ד, וַיִּפְגַּע בַּמָּקוֹם וַיָּלֶן שָׁם כִּי בָא הַשָּׁמֶשׁ. וְלֵית פְּגִיעָה, אֶלָּא צְלוֹתָא.

207. The Faithful Shepherd said, One has to know how the prayers were instituted to parallel the sacrifices. For there are prayers are three. Shacharit (the morning prayer) parallels "The one lamb you shall offer in the morning" (Shemot 29:39 and Bemidbar 28:4), as it is said: "And Abraham went early in the morning to the place where he had stood before Hashem" (Beresheet 19:27), and the sages have taught that standing means prayer. "and the other lamb you shall offer towards evening" (Shemot 29:39 and

Bemidbar 28:4) parallels Minchah (the afternoon prayer), which was set by Isaac, as it is said: "And Isaac went out to meditate in the field at the eventide" (Beresheet 24:63), and there is no meditation that is not prayer. Arvit (the evening prayer) parallels the parts and the fat which are devoured all night. And it is said, "And he lighted on a certain place, and tarried there all night, because the sun was set" (Beresheet 28:11). Lighting upon refers to nothing else than prayer.

208. אַדְהָכִי דַאֲנָן בַּאֲתָר דָא, אַמַּאי כְּתִיב וַיִּקַח מֵאַבְנֵי הַמָּקוֹם וַיָּשֶׂם מְרַאֲשׁוֹתָיו וַיִּשְׁכַּב בַּמָּקוֹם הַהוּא, וְכִי לָא הֲווֹ לֵיהּ כָּרִים וּכְסָתוֹת לְמִשְׁכַּב. אֶלָּא הוֹאִיל וְאָתָא חָתָן לְגַבֵּי כַּלָּה, אע"ג דְּלָא הֲוָה אָרְחוֹי לְמִשְׁכַּב אֶלָּא בְּכָרִים וּכְסָתוֹת, וְאִיהִי יְהִיבַת לֵיהּ אֲבָנִים לְמִשְׁכַּב, יְקַבֵּל כֹּלָּא בִּרְעוּתָא דְלִבָּא, וְהָא אִתְּמַר. וְאוֹף הָכִי אִתְּמַר בְּחִבּוּרָא קַדְמָאָה. מ"ד וַיֹּאמֶר יַעֲקֹב כַּאֲשֶׁר רָאָם, אר"ש תִּיב. וְאֵימָא קְרָא.

ע"כ רעיא מהימנא

208. Since we have referred to the story in our discussion, THERE IS A POINT IN ASKING why scripture says, "and he took of the stones of that place, and put them under his head, and lay down in that place to sleep" (Beresheet 28:11). Did he not have pillows and cushions to lie ON? AND HE ANSWERS: When the groom comes to the bride, even if he is used to lying on pillows and cushions, should she give him stones to lie on, he should accept everything willingly. And we have already learned this, and it is also stated in the first compilation. With respect to the verse: "And when Jacob saw them, he said" (Beresheet 32:3), Rabbi Shimon said: Sit down. And scripture says...CONTINUES ON PARAGRAPH 238 .

End of Ra'aya Meheimna (the Faithful Shepherd)

A Synopsis
Rabbi Pinchas has been thinking about the meaning of 'keeping' and 'remembering', and he opens the topic of the role of the liver in the sacrifice. Rabbi Shimon furthers the explanation, telling how the heart receives the confession and offers it to the brain. He closes by saying that all ills come from the liver and all goodness comes from the heart.

209. אָמַר רִבִּי פִּנְחָס, מִסְתַּכֵּל הֲוֵינָא, שְׁמִירָה בַּלֵב אִיהוּ וַדַּאי, וע"ד שָׁמוֹר בַּלֵב, וְלָאו בַּאֲתַר אַחֲרָא. זְכִירָה בַּזָּכָר, בְּמוֹחָא, דְּרָכִיב וְשַׁלִּיט עַל הַלֵב. וְלֵית זְכִירָה אֶלָּא בְּמוֹחָא. וע"ד זָכוֹר לְזָכָר וְשָׁמוֹר לִנְקֵבָה. מוֹחָא דְּאִיהוּ דְּכוּרָא, רָכִיב וְשַׁלִּיט עַל הַלֵב. לֵב שַׁלִּיט וְרָכִיב עַל הַכָּבֵד. כָּבֵד סָמָאֵל וְנָחָשׁ דָּא בְּדָא, וְאִיהוּ חַד. יוֹתֶרֶת הַכָּבֵד וְכָבֵד. וע"ד בְּקוֹרְבָּנָא, יוֹתֶרֶת הַכָּבֵד, דָּא נָחָשׁ. כָּבֵד מֵיכְלָא דִּדְכוּרָא, רָזָא דְּסָמָא"ל.

209. Rabbi Pinchas said, I have been thinking: Keeping certainly is in the heart, which is why it is written: "Keep" (Devarim 5:12), of the heart, WHICH IS MALCHUT, and of nowhere else. 'Remembering' (Heb. zechirah) is a matter of the male (Heb. zachar), namely in the brain, WHICH IS ZEIR ANPIN, that rides and controls the heart. Remembering pertains to the brain alone and it is therefore written: "Remember THE SHABBAT DAY" (Shemot 20:8), for the male, WHICH IS ZEIR ANPIN, while "Keep THE SHABBAT DAY" (Devarim 5:12) is for the female, WHICH IS MALCHUT. The brain, which is the male, ZEIR ANPIN, mounts and controls the heart, WHICH IS MALCHUT. The heart controls and mounts the liver, and liver is Samael and Serpent intertwined, and they are one. And they are the lobe of the liver and the liver, and so it is with the sacrifice. The lobe of the liver is Serpent, and the liver is food for the male, the male, who is the secret of Samael.

210. אָמַר ר"ש, וַדַּאי כַּךְ הוּא, וְיָאוּת הוּא. וּבְרִירָא דְּמִלָּה, וְרָזָא וְסִתְרִין דְּקָרְבָּן, הָכִי הוּא. כָּבֵד נָטִיל בְּקַדְמֵיתָא, הוּא וְיוֹתֶרֶת דִּילֵיהּ, סָמָאֵל וּבַת זוּגוֹ. וְכָל אִינּוּן עַרְקִין דְּכַבְדָּא. חַיָּילִין וּמַשְׁרְיָין דִּלְהוֹן. וּנְטִילוּ דִּלְהוֹן, דְּאַכְלִין חֲלָבִין שַׁמְנִינוּ דְּקָרְבְּנָא. הה"ד, וְאֶת הַחֵלֶב אֲשֶׁר עֲלֵיהֶם. וּכְדֵין קָרִיב כֹּלָּא לְגַבֵּי לֵב.

210. Rabbi Shimon said: That is certainly how it is, and it is good, and it is a clarification of the matter and thus are the secret of the hidden matters of the sacrifice. The liver receives FIRST, together with its lobe, which are Samael and SERPENT his mate, and all those arteries that are in the liver are their hosts and encampments, and their receiving is that they devour the fatty parts and the fat of the sacrifice, as it is written: "and the fat that is upon them" (Shemot 29:22). And then everything is offered to the heart.

211. וְלֵב לָא נָטִיל מִכֹּלָא. אֶלָּא וִדוּי דְּאִתְעֲבֵיד בֵּיה, וְסָלִיק בְּהַהוּא תְּנָנָא וּצְלוֹתָא דְּאִתְעֲבֵיד עֲלֵיה דְּקָרְבְּנָא. לֵב קָרִיב לְגַבֵּי מוֹחָא, רְעוּתָא דְּיִחוּדָא דְּכַהֲנָא בֵּיה, וְחֶדְוָותָא דְּלֵיוָאֵי. מוֹחָא דָּא, נְהוֹרָא דְּאַתְיָא מִמּוֹחָא עִלָּאָה. מוֹחָא קָרִיב לְגַבֵּיה טָמִיר מִכֹּלָא, דְּלָא אִתְיְדַע כְּלָל. וְכֹלָּא אִתְקְשַׁר דָּא בְּדָא. וּמוֹחָא קָרִיב נַחַת רוּחַ דְּכֹלָּא.

211. And the heart does not receive from the whole of the sacrifice, but only from the confession made with it, which ascends with the smoke and the prayer that is made over the sacrifice. SUBSEQUENTLY, the heart offers to the brain the desire of the unification of the priests in it and the rejoicing of the Levites. This brain, WHICH IS ZEIR ANPIN, is the light that comes from the supernal Brain, WHICH IS ABA AND IMA, and the SUPERNAL Brain offers to the All-Hidden who is completely unknown, THAT IS, KETER, and everything is interconnected. And the brain, WHICH IS ZEIR ANPIN, offers pleasure to all, TO ALL THE UPPER BEINGS.

212. עַרְקִין דְּכַבְדָּא, אִלֵּין אִישִׁים, וְכָל אִינּוּן חַיְילֵיהוֹן. כָּבֵד, כְּמָה דְּאִתְּמַר. יוֹתֶרֶת נְקֵבָה, נוּקְבָּא דִּילֵיה. אֲמַאי יוֹתֶרֶת. דְּלָא אִתְחַבְּרַת בִּדְכוּרָא. אֶלָּא כַּד אַשְׁאָרַת לָה שַׁעֲתָא, לְבָתַר דְּעַבְדַת נְאוּפָהָא, וְשָׁבְקָא לֵיה. תּוּ, יוֹתֶרֶת נְקֵבָה, דְּכַד בַּעְיָא לְאִתְחַבְּרָא בב״נ, אִתְעֲבֵידַת לְגַבֵּיה שִׁיּוּרִין, דְּלָא אִתְחֲשָׁבַת כְּלָל. לְבָתַר אִיהִי אִתְקָרְבַת זְעֵיר זְעֵיר לְגַבֵּיה, עַד דְּאִתְעֲבֵידָא לֵיה חִבּוּרָא חֲדָא. וּמֵאִלֵּין עַרְקִין דְּכַבְדָּא, מִתְפַּשְּׁטָן אָחֳרָן זְעִירִין, לְכַמָּה זַיְינִין, וְכֹלָּא נַטְלִין אֵמוּרִין וּפְדָרִין. וְכֻלְּהוּ כְּלִילָן בַּכָּבֵד.

212. The arteries that are in the liver, are Ishim, NAMELY THE ANGELS OF THE EVIL FORCES, and all these are their hosts. The liver is as we said, THAT IS SAMAEL, while the lobe OF THE LIVER, which is feminine, is his female. And why IS IT CALLED 'lobe' (Heb. *yoteret*, derived from left-over)? It is because she does not join together with the male, WHICH IS SAMAEL, unless she has some spare time left over after the prostitution in which she engages, and after she leaves him. *YOTERET* MEANS LEFT OVER, FOR SHE LEAVES THE MALE, AND MAKES HIM INTO A LEFT-OVER, AFTER

ALL HER FORNICATIONS. Again, the female is, therefore, CALLED '*yoteret*', for when she wants to join together with a man TO MAKE HIM SIN, she first of all becomes for him as left-overs, without any importance, NAMELY WITHOUT THE POWER TO RULE OVER MAN, FOR AT FIRST A SIN IS AS THE BREADTH OF A HAIR. Later she draws close to him, little by little, until she is in one union with him, AND HE CAN NO LONGER SEPARATE HIMSELF FROM HER. And from those arteries that are in the liver, other forces of a number of types spread out, and they all take the limbs and the fats THAT ARE BURNT ON THE ALTAR AT NIGHT, and all of them are included in the liver, WHICH IS SAMAEL.

213. לֵב דְּאִיהוּ עִקָּרָא בִּקְדוּשָׁה, נָטִיל וּמַקְרִיב לְמוֹחָא כְּמָה דְאִתְּמַר. לֵב שַׁרְיָא עַל תְּרֵין כּוּלְיָין, וְאִינּוּן תְּרֵין כְּרוּבִין. יָהֲבִין עֵיטָא. וְאִינּוּן רְחִיקִין קְרִיבִין, יְמִינָא וּשְׂמָאלָא. וְכֻלְּהוּ נַטְלִין וְאָכְלִין כָּל חַד כַּדְקָא יָאוֹת, עַד דְּאִתְקְשַׁר כֹּלָּא כַּחֲדָא.

213. And the heart, which is the main thing in holiness, NAMELY MALCHUT, takes and offers to the brain as we have learned. The heart rests over the two kidneys, WHICH ARE NETZACH AND HOD, and they are two Cherubs, who are advisers, IN THE SECRET OF THE ADVISING KIDNEYS. THAT IS TO SAY THEY ARRANGE THE BOUNTY THAT DESCENDS FROM ZEIR ANPIN AND MALCHUT IN THE SECRET OF THE HEAVENS THAT GRIND THE MANNA FOR THE RIGHTEOUS, WHICH ARE RIGHTEOUS AND RIGHTEOUSNESS, NAMELY YESOD AND MALCHUT. And they are far and near, right and left. FOR WHEN NETZACH, WHICH IS RIGHT, IS IN CONTROL THEY ARE NEAR, BUT WHEN HOD, WHICH IS LEFT, IS IN CONTROL THEY ARE FAR. And all of them take and eat FROM THE LIGHT OF THE UNION AFFECTED BY THEIR SACRIFICE, each one as befits it, until everything is connected together as one.

214. זִבְחֵי אֱלֹהִים רוּחַ נִשְׁבָּרָה, דָּא מִתְקָרִיב לַלֵּב, רוּחַ נִשְׁבָּרָה, וְדוּי וּצְלוֹתָא. דְּהָא וַדַּאי וְהָרוּחַ תָּשׁוּב אֶל הָאֱלֹהִים אֲשֶׁר נְתָנָהּ. וְכָבֵד מַקְרִיב לֵיהּ לְגַבֵּיהּ לֵב, דְּאִיהוּ סַנֵּיגוֹרָא עֲלֵיהּ, וְכֹלָּא קְשׁוּרָא כַּחֲדָא בְּקוּרְבְּנָא.

214. "The sacrifices of Elohim are a broken spirit" (Tehilim 51:19). This,

namely a broken spirit, confession, and prayer is an approach offered to the heart. For it is certain that: "and the spirit returns to the Elohim who gave it" (Kohelet 12:7), NAMELY A BROKEN SPIRIT ASCENDS TO ELOHIM WHO IS MALCHUT THAT IS CALLED 'HEART'. And the liver, WHICH IS SAMAEL, offers it closer to the heart, for it HAS BECOME a good advocate for it. And everything is one bond in the sacrifice.

215. מִן כָּבֵד, נָפְקִין כָּל מַרְעִין, וְכָל מַכְתְּשִׁין, לְכָל שַׁיְיפֵי גוּפָא, וּבֵיהּ שַׁרְיָין. לֵב, אִיהוּ זָכִיךְ מִכֹּלָּא. מִנֵּיהּ נָפְקִין כָּל טַב, וְכָל בְּרִיאוּתָא דְּשַׁיְיפִין כֻּלְּהוּ, וְכָל תּוּקְפָּא, וְכָל חֶדְוָה, וְכָל שְׁלִימוּ דְּאִצְטְרִיךְ לְכָל שַׁיְיפִין.

215. And from the liver, WHICH REPRESENTS SAMAEL, come all the diseases and illnesses to all parts of the body, and they rest in it. But the heart, WHICH REPRESENTS MALCHUT, is the purest of all THE PARTS OF THE BODY, and from it are derived all goodness, all health of all the parts, and all the strength and all the joy and all the perfection needed by all the parts.

40. The sacrifices

A Synopsis

The Faithful Shepherd says that the purpose of the sacrifices is to remove the impure sides and bring the holy sides near. Rabbi Shimon argues that God distributes the food of the sacrifices as appropriate – He gives the nourishment of the Torah to those on the side of holiness, and he gives ordinary food to those on the Other Side. God takes nothing from the sacrifice other than the desire and remorse of the heart. Rabbi Shimon says that the priest is the brain, the Levite is the heart, and Yisrael is the body. The Faithful Shepherd continues the discussion with a higher explanation of the union effected by the sacrifices, and we learn that those who are like animals were commanded to sacrifice animals for atonement, but that those who are like angels offer up their good deeds instead. Moses talks about the Prime Cause, Ein Sof, saying that the four elements have no proximity to one another except when He is among them, and saying that the sacrifices draw them close to Him.

The Relevance of this Passage

Once again we have a passage that presents consequential findings in regards to the underlying cause of coronary heart disease and other chronic ailments. As such, we will explore each topic one at a time:

The Liver and Bile. In paragraph 216, we learn the human liver and all of its arteries are the abode of evil angels. The ancient sacrifices serve the same function as the liver: Evil angels devour the fat of the sacrifice just as the liver's bile digests the fat in our blood. Remarkably, it took another 1800 years for medical science to learn this Kabbalistic truth, when, in the 18th century, Swiss biologist Albrecht von Haller discovered that bile helps to digest fats.

Spiritually, the fat that is sacrificed correlates to our negative characteristics born of ego. Accordingly, we must meditate to sacrifice and cleanse away these immoral traits from our nature as we read this section. This action engenders healing and wellness of the heart.

We arouse the spiritual influences of the ancient sacrifices to remove poisons, toxins and fat from our cardiovascular system. Furthermore, this action devours toxins and wastes from the spiritual atmosphere.

Our Accuser (the Satan) is hereby relieved of his duties as prosecutor, thus rendering any pending judgments null and void.

The Light we kindle imbues us with holiness so that we may now merit peace in this world and the next. Just as high blood cholesterol and fat eventually harden a man's arteries and destroy his heart, we now turn the tables on the demons as the Light devours their heart and kills off the evil angels.

The Liver, Blood, and Heart. Next, the Zohar reveals remarkable insights into the function of the blood, liver, and the heart. The Zohar speaks of a man's death, stating that "an image of a dog descends" at the time of death if a man is not worthy. The Hebrew word for *dog* is *kelev*. This word conceals another word within it – the Hebrew word for *heart,* which is *lev* (*ke*l*ev* כ-ל-ב).

Dog is therefore a code word for the human heart. Thus, the verse refers to a man's death caused by heart ailments if he is not "meritorious" or worthy. "Not meritorious" means a man is disconnected from the Light of the Creator, enslaved to the will of his ego, ruled by the anger and hostility borne of rash behavior. This, and nothing else, is the root cause of all illness, for it causes darkness on the spiritual level and liver dysfunction on a physical level. This darkness creates an opening for the evil angels to bring sickness upon us, through our liver. The foods we eat are merely an effect and not the ultimate causative factors behind heart disease or other illnesses. They are simply the tools used by negative forces to physically *manifest* the spiritual darkness caused by our wrongful and insensitive behavior. Moreover, these negative angels deceive us into believing that the disease is caused by physical effects alone, and not the cumulative effect of our reactive emotions, selfish behavior, and rude actions towards others.

Conversely, the Zohar says that if a man is meritorious, then when he leaves this world "the image of a lion descends to welcome his soul." When a man is spiritually aware and accountable for all of his negative behavior during life, then the first image that greets him upon his death is that of a lion.

The lion represents the Sfirah of *Chesed*, which is Mercy. The lion also signifies King David, over whom the Angel of Death has absolutely no control. Moreover, the lion and the heart embody the concept of a king. A King wears a crown signifying the *Sfirah* of *Keter*, the highest spiritual dimension. While scanning this passage we are receiving spiritual energy from *Keter,* which offers us untold mercy and complete refuge from the Angel of Death.

These awesome positive forces now cause the World to Come to

become our world in a kindhearted and merciful manner. These sublime secrets reveal Light which heals our hearts, purges any traces of the death force from our body, and deals a final death blow to the Angel of Death himself. And because the concept of immortality is a difficult one for us to believe, these verses strengthen our consciousness so that we perceive death's illusions and liberate our minds from the prison of skepticism and doubt.

These benefits are realized only through the power of the sacrifices spoken of herein. What are these sacrifices on a practical level? The Zohar says they are:

"a broken spirit; a broken and contrite heart..."

Namely, we must scan and meditate upon these words with repentance in our soul for the indignities we have shown to others; a broken heart for the disrespect and incivility we have inflicted upon friends and family; and deep remorse and acknowledgement of our discourteous and abusive behavior.

This is our sacrifice, and with it we become clean and purified, having attained all the goodness, Light, and healing that are expounded upon in this powerful passage.

Two Kinds of Fat. In paragraph 220, the Zohar first speaks about the priest as the "brain," then segues into a discussion on the Central Column, and immediately thereafter proceeds to reveal an astonishing truth concerning fat, the liver, the heart, and the arteries.

We're told that there are two kinds of fat – pure and impure, as stated in the verse:

"...in the body there are pure and impure fatty parts, clean blood without waste matter and blood contaminated with waste matter..."

The pure fats, the Zohar says, are associated with a healthy heart and arteries, whereas impure fats are dangerous, used by the evil angel (do not pronounce this name) *Samael,* who's connected with our liver, to cause ailments of the heart and brain. The brain is the priest that works to overcome the control of *Samael* over the heart. This secret is concealed in the following verse:

"And if the liver, WHICH IS SAMAEL, wishes to offer fatty parts that are ritually impure to the heart, he takes only the fat of a ritually pure fatty part."

Remarkably, 2000 years later, medical science confirmed this ancient observation:

40. The sacrifices

Science now understands that the human liver synthesizes cholesterol for the body. Cholesterol is, essentially, a fatty substance ("fatty parts"); and there are, in fact, two kinds of cholesterol – good and bad, pure and impure.

• Good cholesterol is known as HDL (high-density lipoproteins).

• Bad cholesterol is termed LDL (low-density lipoproteins).

An overabundance of *bad cholesterol* clogs the arteries. It helps form plaque, which narrows the arteries and decreases blood flow to the heart and brain. With less blood, the heart receives less oxygen. A lack of oxygen can cause chest pain, called "angina." With a lesser flow of oxygen, one becomes much more susceptible to heart attacks, and strokes. Buildup of bad cholesterol is the most common cause of heart disease. Yet this buildup occurs so slowly, we are not even aware of the increasing danger.

In the language of Zohar, bad cholesterol is referred to as the "fatty parts" that are "ritually impure" and "offered" to the heart by the liver, "Samael."

Good cholesterol removes bad cholesterol from the bloodstream. It contains an enzyme that helps break down deposits and takes bad cholesterol away from coronary arteries back to the liver, where is it turned into bile, which absorbs and digests the fats; and it is then excreted from the body. Good cholesterol does not collect or stick to the inner linings of the arteries. High levels of good cholesterol reduce the risk of heart disease and strokes.

The Zohar refers to the good cholesterol as "pure fatty parts," the "clean blood without waste matter."

Good and bad cholesterol levels are inversely connected. When one increases, the other decreases. That is, a constant cholesterol level with an increase in the level of good cholesterol will automatically lower the level of bad cholesterol, and, in turn, reduce the risk of coronary heart disease and stroke.

Scientists use the ratio between good and bad cholesterol (LDL/HDL ratio) as a predictor of heart disease and stroke risk.
Ratio and balance are the key. This medical truth is found in the Zohar's discussion on the "Central Column." The Central Column balances the Right and Left Columns ("pure" and "impure," respectively) in the appropriate and proper measure.

A malfunctioning liver can cause a dangerous imbalance between the good and bad cholesterols, coronary heart disease, immune dysfunction, and blood sugar problems.

The Zohar then reveals the ultimate cause behind heart disease and liver dysfunction when it speaks of "Evil Inclination" and "Good Inclination," which, we are told, are rooted in the arteries of the liver and heart, respectively. This is a very profound insight.

Our behavior towards others, our manner of living, be it spiritual or physical, is the ultimate determining factor that decides between health and sickness, according to the Zohar. Disease is not the result of eating habits or other external factors. They are merely the weapons, used by the negative forces, to inflict judgment and manifest the spiritual darkness we have created.

If our consciousness and our behavior are rooted in our Evil Inclination, our liver will discharge impure fats into the arteries because the negative angel (do not pronounce this name) *Samael* seizes the pure fat, as stated in the verse: "...he takes only the fat of a ritually pure fatty part" and offers "fatty parts that are ritually impure to the heart." Again, we have a verse of Zohar that is profoundly insightful, worthy of deep reflection.

If we choose a life of spirituality, sacrificing our selfish impulses in favor of our Good Inclination, the evil being *Samael* relinquishes control. Clean, purified blood courses through our veins. Liver function is sound, reflecting the well-being of our spiritual state of mind.

This profound insight is further reinforced in the following verse:

> "...there are two types of people: Yisrael, WHO IS LIKE THE ARTERIES OF THE HEART, and the other nations of the world, WHO ARE LIKE THE ARTERIES OF THE LIVER."

Yisrael refers to the spiritual individual – he who embraces the wisdom of Kabbalah and becomes accountable for all of his actions and their consequences. The term "other nations" refers to those of us who live according to the whims of egocentricity, who are guided by intellect alone, neglecting the needs and the will of the soul.

The Light of this paragraph destroys the negative angel *Samael* and his army, and their destructive influence over our mind and the world. This spiritual energy balances our blood cholesterol levels in favor of the good cholesterol (HDL). Arteries are unclogged and cleansed. We receive healing of the liver, the brain, and entire cardiovascular system. Most importantly, we receive healing of the soul so that we now triumph over the Evil Inclination, once and for all, and bring immortality and joy to the world.

Of Angels, Supernal Worlds, and other Lofty things. The remainder of this passage speaks in deeply obscured prose concerning angels, sacrifices, supernal worlds, matings, the

Tetragrammaton יהוה, different classes of souls, and other sublime matters. Most relevant to us is the Light that is cast from this narrative. This Light ignites the pertinent ancient sacrifices on our behalf. We are cleansed of sin. Supernal worlds are aligned, then connected, allowing divine Energy to cascade downward upon creation. The Energy of the Faithful Shepherd – Moses – becomes a beacon of Light for all mankind, leading us to our Final Redemption, only through peace and kindness.

רעיא מהימנא

216. אָמַר רַעְיָא מְהֵימָנָא, לֵית קַרְבְּנִין, אֶלָּא לְרַחֲקָא סִטְרִין מְסָאֲבִין, וּלְקָרְבָא דַּרְגִּין קַדִּישִׁין. וְאִתְּמַר בְּחִבּוּרָא קַדְמָאָה, דִּלְהוֹן, עַרְקִין דְּכַבְדָּא, אִית מִנְהוֹן רַבְרְבִין, אִית מִנְהוֹן רַבְרְבִין וּזְעֵירִין, וּמִתְפַּשְּׁטִין מִנְהוֹן לְכַמָּה סִטְרִין. וְאִלֵּין נַטְלִין אֵבָרִין וֶאֱמוּרִין וּפְדָרִין דְּמִתְאַכְּלִין כָּל הַלַּיְלָה, דְּהָא קָרְבָּן כֹּלָּא לַיְיָ'.

Ra'aya Meheimna (the Faithful Shepherd)

216. The Faithful Shepherd said: THE PURPOSE OF the sacrifices is to remove the impure aspects and bring the holy aspects near. And we learned in the first compilation that among the arteries of the liver, WHICH ARE THE FORCES OF SAMAEL, AS ABOVE, there are large ones and there are those that are both large and small, and they spread out from there in a number of directions, and they take the parts and the pieces and fats that are consumed on the altar the whole night, for the whole of the sacrifice belongs to Hashem, AND THE OTHER SIDE TAKES ONLY THE PARTS AND THE FATS.

217. אָמַר בּוּצִינָא קַדִּישָׁא, רַעְיָא מְהֵימָנָא, וַהֲלֹא אָמַרְת לְעֵיל דְּקָרְבְּנִין דְּקוּדְשָׁא בְּרִיךְ הוּא לָאו אִינּוּן אֶלָּא לְקָרְבָא י' בה' ו' בה'. אֶלָּא, אע"ג דְּכָל קָרְבָּנִין צְרִיכִין לְקָרֵב קַמֵּיה, אִיהוּ פָּלִיג לְכָל מַשִׁרְיָין, מַאֲכָלִין דְּקָרְבָּנִין, לְכָל חַד כַּדְקָא חֲזֵי לֵיה, לְשִׁכְלַיִּים, מְזוֹנֵי דְּאוֹרַיְיתָא, וּמִשְׁתַּיָּיא דַּיְינָא וּמַיָּא דְּאוֹרַיְיתָא. לְטִבְעַיִּים, דְּאִינּוּן שֵׁדִים דְּאִינּוּן כִּבְנֵי אָדָם, יָהִיב לוֹן אִלֵּין מַאֲכָלִין טִבְעַיִּים, דְּנַחֲתִית אֶשָׁא דִּלְהוֹן, לְמֵיכַל לוֹן.

217. The Holy Luminary, THAT IS, RABBI SHIMON, said, O, Faithful Shepherd, did you not say before that the only purpose of the sacrifices of the Holy One, blessed be He, is to draw close the Yud to the Hei and the Vav to the Hei? Nevertheless, although all the sacrifices have to be offered before Him, BEFORE THE HOLY ONE, BLESSED BE HE, He distributes the foodstuffs of the sacrifices to all the various camps, to each as befits it. To the mental ones, NAMELY ON THE SIDE OF HOLINESS, HE GIVES the nourishment of the Torah, and drinks of the wine and water of the Torah, WHICH IS THE SECRET OF THE CENTRAL COLUMN THAT IS CALLED 'TORAH', BY WHICH ALL THE LIGHTS ARE CORRECTED. To the natural ones, which are the demons who are like people, NAMELY THE OTHER SIDE, He gives them natural foodstuffs, and their fire descends to devour them, NAMELY THE ILLUMINATIONS COMING FROM THE LEFT COLUMN OF SEPARATION, WITHOUT THE RECONCILING OF THE CENTRAL COLUMN THAT IS CALLED 'TORAH'.

218. כְּמָה דְּאוּקְמוּהָ רַבָּנָן, אִי זָכוּ, הֲוָה נָחִית כְּמוֹ אַרְיֵה דְּאֶשָּׁא לְמֵיכַל קָרְבְּנִין. וְאִי לָא, הֲוָה נָחִית תַּמָּן כְּמִין כַּלְבָּא דְּאֶשָּׁא. וְאוֹף הָכִי כַּד מִית ב״נ, אִי זָכֵי, נָחִית בִּדְמוּת אַרְיֵה, לְקַבְּלָא נַפְשֵׁיהּ. וְאִי לָאו בִּדְמוּת כֶּלֶב, דְּאָמַר דָּוִד עֲלֵיהּ, הַצִּילָה מֵחֶרֶב נַפְשִׁי מִיַּד כֶּלֶב יְחִידָתִי.

218. And this is as the sages taught. If Yisrael are meritorious, He would descend like a lion of fire to devour the sacrifices, but if they were not meritorious, He would descend like a dog of fire. Likewise, when a man dies, if he has been meritorious, the image of a lion descends to welcome his soul, but if he has not BEEN MERITORIOUS, an image of a dog descends, concerning which David said: "Deliver my soul from the sword; my only one from the power of the dog" (Tehilim 22:21).

219. וּבְגִין לְשֵׁיזָבָא קוּדְשָׁא בְּרִיךְ הוּא גּוּפֵיהוֹן דְּיִשְׂרָאֵל מִנְּהוֹן וְנַפְשֵׁהוֹן. מָנֵי, לְקָרֵב קָרְבְּנִין דִּבְעֵירָן וְגוּפָן בְּאַתְרַיְיהוּ, לְקַיֵּם אִם רָעֵב שׂוֹנַאֲךָ הַאֲכִילֵהוּ לָחֶם וְאִם צָמֵא הַשְׁקֵהוּ מָיִם. אֲבָל קוּדְשָׁא בְּרִיךְ הוּא, לָא נָטִיל אֶלָּא רְעוּתָא דְּלִבָּא, וּתְבִירוּ דִּילֵיהּ. הה״ד, זִבְחֵי אֱלֹהִים רוּחַ נִשְׁבָּרָה לֵב נִשְׁבָּר וְנִדְכֶּה אֱלֹהִים לֹא תִבְזֶה. כְּגַוְונָא דִּכְלֵי חֶרֶס, דְּאִתְּמַר בְּהוֹן נִשְׁבָּרוּ נִטְהָרוּ.

219. And since the Holy One, blessed be He, desired to save the bodies of Yisrael from them, and their souls, too, He commanded that sacrifices be offered of beasts and bodies in their stead, SO THAT THE OTHER SIDE SHOULD NOT HAVE CONTROL OVER THEM, BUT SHOULD ENJOY THEM (THE SACRIFICED ANIMALS). This fulfills the verse: "If your enemy be hungry, give him bread to eat, and if he be thirsty give him water to drink" (Mishlei 25:21). AND THUS WILL THE ACCUSER BECOME COUNSEL FOR THE DEFENSE. But the Holy One, blessed be He, takes nothing FROM THE SACRIFICE except the wish of the heart and the bearking of the heart, as it is written: "The slaughtered sacrifices for Elohim are a broken spirit; a broken and contrite heart, Elohim, You will not despise" (Tehilim 51:19). They are like earthenware vessels, about which it is said: 'After they are broken, they become clean'.

220. כַּהֲנָא מוֹחָא. לֵוִי לִבָּא. גּוּפָא יִשְׂרָאֵל. וְאִתְּמַר בְּהוֹן, כֹּהֲנִים בַּעֲבוֹדָתָם, וּלְוִיִּם בְּדוּכְנָם, וְיִשְׂרָאֵל בְּמַעֲמָדָם. וְאִי כָּבֵד בָּעֵי לְקָרְבָא לְגַבֵּי דְלִבָּא, חֶלְבֵּיה דְּאִינּוּן מְסָאֲבִין, אִיהוּ לָא נָטִיל. אֶלָּא שַׁמְנוּנוּ דַּחֲלֵב טָהוֹר. כְּגַוְונָא דְאִית בְּגוּפָא, חֵלֶב טָהוֹר וְחֵלֶב טָמֵא, דָּם צָלִיל בְּלָא פְּסוֹלֶת, וְדָם עָכוּר בִּפְסוֹלֶת. וְעָרְקִין דְּלִבָּא, חַיָּילִין קַדִּישִׁין. וְעָרְקִין דְּכָבֵד, חַיָּילִין מְסָאֲבִין. אוֹף הָכִי אִינּוּן מַשִׁרְיָין דְּיֵצֶר הָרָע, וּמַשִׁרְיָין דְּיֵצֶר הַטּוֹב, אִלֵּין מְמָנָן עַל עָרְקִין דְּלִבָּא, וְאִלֵּין מְמָנָן עַל עָרְקִין דְּכַבְדָּא. אוֹף הָכִי תְּרֵי אוּמֵּי, יִשְׂרָאֵל, וְאוּמִין דְּעָלְמָא עכו״ם.

220. The priest is the brain, STANDING FOR ZEIR ANPIN, WHICH IS RIGHT. Levi is the heart, STANDING FOR MALCHUT, WHICH IS ON THE LEFT. Yisrael is the body, NAMELY THE CENTRAL COLUMN, FOR WHEN THE SOULS OF YISRAEL RISE UP TO MAYIN NUKVIN (LIT. ' FEMALE WATERS'), THEY BECOME THE CENTRAL COLUMN, BETWEEN ZEIR ANPIN AND MALCHUT. And it is said about them: 'The priests at their service, the Levites at their stand, and Yisrael at their post'. And if the liver, WHICH IS SAMAEL, wishes to offer fatty parts that are ritually impure to the heart, it receives only the fat of a ritually pure fatty part. For just as in the body there are pure and impure fatty parts, clean blood without waste matter and blood contaminated with waste matter, as the arteries of blood in the heart, WHICH IS MALCHUT, are the holy hosts, while the arteries of the

liver, WHICH IS SAMAEL, are the impure hosts. Here also, there are camps of the Evil Inclination and camps of the Good Inclination. The latter are appointed over the arteries of the heart and the former over the arteries of the liver. Similarly, too, there are two types of people: Yisrael, WHO ARE LIKE THE ARTERIES OF THE HEART, and the other nations of the world, WHO ARE LIKE THE ARTERIES OF THE LIVER.

221. אָמַר לֵיהּ רַעְיָא מְהֵימָנָא, שַׁפִּיר קָא אַמְרַת בְּכֹלָּא, אֲבָל אֲפִילוּ יִשְׂרָאֵל לָאו כֻּלְּהוּ שָׁוִין, דְּאִית בְּהוֹן בְּנֵי מַלְכוּת, מִסִּטְרָא דְּמַלְכוּת קַדִּישָׁא, כְּלִילָא מֵעֲשַׂר סְפִירָאן, וּמִכָּל הֲוַויִין וְכִנּוּיִין. וְאִית מִנְּהוֹן עַבְדִּין, מִסִּטְרָא דְּעֶבֶד, דְּאִיהוּ עַבְדּוֹ זְקַן בֵּיתוֹ. וְאִית מִנְּהוֹן כִּבְעִירָן, וְאִתְּמַר בְּהוֹן, וְאַתֵּן צֹאנִי צֹאן מַרְעִיתִי אָדָם אַתֶּם. וְאִינּוּן דְּדַמְיָין לְעָנָא, קוּדְשָׁא בְּרִיךְ הוּא מָנֵי לְקָרְבָא בְּעִירָן בְּאַתְרַיְיהוּ, לְכַפְּרָא עֲלַיְיהוּ. וְאִינּוּן דְּדַמְיָין לְמַלְאָכִין, קָרְבְּנִין דִּלְהוֹן אִינּוּן עוֹבָדִין טָבִין, דִּמְמָנָן עֲלַיְיהוּ מַלְאָכִים, דִּמְקָרִיבִין לְקוּדְשָׁא בְּרִיךְ הוּא בְּאַתְרַיְיהוּ.

221. The Faithful Shepherd said to him: What you have said is altogether beautiful, but even Yisrael are not all equal, for there are among them the children of royalty, from the side of the holy Malchut that is composed of ten Sfirot and all the names of Yud Hei Vav Hei and their titles. And there are those that are like slaves, from the side of the servant, METATRON, who is "the eldest servant of his house" (Beresheet 24:2), NAMELY OF MALCHUT. There are also those who are like animals, about whom it is said: "And you, My flock, the flock of My pasture, are men" (Yechezkel 34:31). And the Holy One, blessed be He, commanded those who are like sheep to sacrifice animals in their stead, to make atonement for them. But the sacrifices of those who are like angels are the good deeds, over which are appointed angels who offer the good deeds before the Holy One, blessed be He, in their stead.

222. וְאִינּוּן דַּהֲווֹ בְּנִין לַיְדֹוָד, הה"ד בָּנִים אַתֶּם לַיְיָ' אֱלֹהֵיכֶם. בְּחוֹבִין דִּלְהוֹן מִתְפָּרְדֵי אַתְוָון, וְתִקּוּנָא דִּלְהוֹן הוּא אוֹרַיְיתָא, דְּאִיהוּ שֵׁם יְדֹוָד, לְקָרְבָא אַתְוָון, י' בְּה', ו' בְּה', בְּקָרְבְּנָא דִּלְהוֹן.

222. And there are those who are the children of Yud Hei Vav Hei, about

whom it is written: "You are the children of Hashem your Elohim" (Devarim 14:1). It is because of their sins that the letters OF YUD HEI VAV HEI become separated, FOR THERE IS NO SUPERNAL UNION OF YUD-HEI, AND THERE IS NO UNION OF ZEIR ANPIN AND MALCHUT, WHICH ARE VAV-HEI. And their correction lies in the Torah, which is the name of Yud Hei Vav Hei, to bring the letters together by means of their sacrifice: Yud with Hei, WHICH IS THE SECRET OF THE UNION OF ABA AND IMA, and Vav with Hei, WHICH IS THE SECRET OF THE UNION OF ZEIR ANPIN AND MALCHUT.

223. הֲרֵי בְּכָל קָרְבְּנִין, בֵּין דִּבְעִירֵי, בֵּין דְּמַלְאָכִין דִּמְמָנָן עַל פְּקוּדִין, בֵּין בְּמַלְכוּתָא, בֵּין בִּשְׁמֵיהּ. כֹּלָּא צָרִיךְ לְקָרְבָא לְקוּדְשָׁא בְּרִיךְ הוּא בְּאַתְוָון קַדִּישִׁין. וְאִיהוּ רָכִיב בְּאַרְבַּע חֵיוָן דְּמַלְאָכִים. וְאִיהוּ רָכִיב בְּאַרְבַּע יְסוֹדִין, דְּמִנְּהוֹן אִתְבְּרִיאוּ אַרְבַּע חֵיוָן טִבְעִיִּים. וְאִיהוּ הוּא דִּמְקָרֵב מַיָּא בְּאֶשָּׁא, וְרוּחָא בְּעַפְרָא. הה"ד, עוֹשֶׂה שָׁלוֹם בִּמְרוֹמָיו. וְאוֹף הָכִי הוּא מְקָרֵב מִיכָאֵל דְּאִיהוּ מַיִם שִׂכְלִיִּים, עִם גַּבְרִיאֵל. דְּהוּא אֵשׁ שִׂכְלִי. וְאִיהוּ מְקָרֵב אוּרִיאֵל, דְּאִיהוּ אַוִּיר. דְּהַיְינוּ רוּחַ שִׂכְלִי. עִם רְפָאֵל, דְּאִיהוּ אֵפֶר, דְּהַיְינוּ עָפָר שִׂכְלִית. דְּמִיָּד דְּאִסְתַּלָּק קוּדְשָׁא בְּרִיךְ הוּא מִבֵּינַיְיהוּ, לֵית בְּהוֹן חֵילָא.

223. And in all the sacrifices, whether OF THOSE WHO ARE animal-LIKE, or those who are like the ASPECTS OF angels appointed over the precepts, or of those WHO ARE OF THE ASPECT of Malchut, or OF THOSE WHO ARE of the name OF THE YUD HEI VAV HEI, in all cases THE SACRIFICE has to offer them all to the Holy One, blessed be He, THE UNION OF THE FOUR holy letters OF THE YUD HEI VAV HEI. AND THE HOLY ONE, BLESSED BE HE, mounts WITH THE FOUR LETTERS OF THE YUD HEI VAV HEI on the four living creatures of the angels, MICHAEL, GABRIEL, URIEL AND RAPHAEL, WHICH ARE THE CHARIOT THAT IS IN BRIYAH. AND THE HOLY ONE, BLESSED BE HE rides, WITH THE FOUR LETTERS OF THE YUD HEI VAV HEI, on the four elements OF FIRE, WIND, WATER AND EARTH, WHICH ARE THE SECRET OF CHESED AND GVURAH, TIFERET AND MALCHUT, THAT ARE IN YETZIRAH, WHICH ARE THE ASPECT OF YESOD. From them were created the four natural beings, NAMELY CHESED, GVURAH, TIFERET AND MALCHUT, THAT ARE IN THE WORLD OF ASIYAH.

AND THE HOLY ONE, BLESSED BE HE, Himself brings water close to fire, WHICH IS THE SECRET OF THE TWO COLUMNS CHESED AND GVURAH AND ARE THE SECRET OF YUD-HEI, and of wind to the earth NAMELY TIFERET, THAT IS CALLED 'WIND', TO MALCHUT, THAT IS CALLED 'EARTH', THIS BEING THE SECRET OF VAV-HEI. And this is as it is written: "He makes peace in His high places" (Iyov 25:2). And so also, He brings together THE FOUR LIVING CREATURES OF THE ANGELS, NAMELY: Michael, who is considered mental water, with Gabriel, who is mental fire, WHICH IS THE SECRET OF RIGHT AND LEFT, AND THE PRINCIPLE OF YUD-HEI; and He also brings close Uriel, who is air, namely the mental wind, with Raphael, dust, who is mental earth, WHICH IS THE SECRET OF VAV-HEI. For the moment the Holy One, blessed be He, departs from among them, they have no strength.

224. וְאִי תֵּימָא, הָא כְּתִיב בְּכָל קָרְבְּנִין לַיְדֹוָ״ד, וְאֵיךְ אָמַרְנָא דְאִית פֵּרוּדָא בְּאַתְוָון. אֶלָּא הַאי אִתְּמַר, בְּדַרְגִּין דְּאִתְבְּרִיאוּ וְאִתְקְרִיאוּ בִּשְׁמֵיה. וְלָא דְּאִינּוּן אִיהוּ מַמָּשׁ. הַהַ״ד, כֹּל הַנִּקְרָא בִשְׁמִי וְלִכְבוֹדִי בְּרָאתִיו יְצַרְתִּיו אַף עֲשִׂיתִיו. דְּאִית אַתְוָון דִּיְדֹוָ״ד בַּאֲצִילוּת, דְּלֵית בְּהוֹן פֵּרוּדָא וְהַפְסָקָה, דְּאִינּוּן כְּמַבּוּעִין לְגַבַּיְיהוּ, דְּאַשְׁקְיָין לְאִילָנִין. וּבְגִין אִלֵּין דְּאִתְבְּרִיאוּ, אַדְמְיָין י׳ לְרֵישָׁא, ו׳ לְגוּפָא, ה׳ ה׳ לְעֶשֶׂר אֶצְבְּעָן.

224. You might suggest that since it is written that all the sacrifices are to Yud Hei Vav Hei, and ask how, therefore, it can be said that there is a separation of the letters OF YUD HEI VAV HEI, AND THAT THE SACRIFICE NOW COMES TO UNITE THEM. HE ANSWERS, This is said about those stages that were created and called by His name and not that they are He Himself, as it is written: "every one that is called by My name: for I have created him for My glory; I have formed him; yea, I have made him" (Yeshayah 43:7). And there are the four letters of Yud Hei Vav Hei in Atzilut, containing no separation nor cessation, for they are as fountains FOR ALL THE WORLDS, watering the trees. And regarding those that were created, NAMELY VIS-A-VIS THE YUD HEI VAV HEI ATTIRED IN THE WORLD OF CREATION, THE FOUR LETTERS OF ATZILUT are likened, the Yud to a head, the Vav to a body, while the two Hei's ARE LIKENED to ten fingers.

225. אֲבָל עִלַּת הָעִלּוֹת עַל כֹּלָּא, דְּאִתְקְרֵי יְדֹוָ"ד, אִתְּמַר בֵּיהּ, וְאֶל מִי תְּדַמְּיוּנִי וְאֶשְׁוֶה יֹאמַר קָדוֹשׁ. וְאֶל מִי תְּדַמְּיוּן אֵל וּמַה דְּמוּת תַּעַרְכוּ לוֹ. אֲנִי יְיָ' לֹא שָׁנִיתִי. לָא מָטֵי בֵּיהּ חוֹבִין לְאַפְרְשָׁא אַתְווֹי, יְ' מֵהֵ', וְ' מֵהֵ', דְּלֵית בֵּיהּ פְּרוּדָא. וְעָלֵיהּ אִתְּמַר, לֹא יְגוּרְךָ רָע. אִיהוּ שַׁלִּיט עַל כֹּלָּא, וְלֵית מַאן דְּשַׁלִּיט בֵּיהּ. אִיהוּ תָּפִיס בְּכֹלָּא, וְלֵית מַאן דְּתָפִיס בֵּיהּ. וְאִיהוּ לָא אִתְקְרֵי יְדֹוָ"ד, וּבְכָל שְׁמָהָן, אֶלָּא בְּאִתְפַּשְׁטוּת נְהוֹרֵיהּ עֲלַיְיהוּ. וְכַד אִסְתְּלִיק מִנַּיְיהוּ, לֵית לֵיהּ מִגַּרְמֵיהּ שֵׁם כְּלָל מִנְּהוֹן. עָמוֹק עָמוֹק מִי יִמְצָאֶנּוּ.

225. But the Cause of Causes, NAMELY THE ENDLESS LIGHT, BLESSED BE HE, who is over everything, who is called Yud Hei Vav Hei, THAT IS, ITS LIGHT IS ATTIRED IN THE YUD HEI VAV HEI, about Him it is said: "To whom then will you liken Me, that I should be equal? says the Holy One" (Yeshayah 40:25). "To whom then will you liken El, or what likeness will you compare to Him?" (Ibid. 18) "For I am Hashem, I do not change" (Malachi 3:6). The sins of the creatures BELOW do not touch Him, nor separate in Him the letter Yud from the letter Hei, nor the Vav from the Hei. For there is no separation in Him and it is said about Him, "nor shall evil dwell with You" (Tehilim 5:5). He rules over all and there is none who rules over Him. He comprehends all and there is none who comprehends Him. And He is not called by Yud Hei Vav Hei, nor by all the other names, but is known by His light that spreads over them, OVER THE LEVELS THAT ARE IN THE FOUR WORLDS, ATZILUT, BRIYAH, YETZIRAH AND ASIYAH. And when He departs from them, He has, of Himself, no name at all. "exceeding deep, who can find it?" (Kohelet 7:24).

226. לֵית נְהוֹרָא יָכִיל לְאִסְתַּכְּלָא בֵּיהּ, דְּלָא אִתְחַשְׁכַת. אֲפִילוּ כֶּתֶר עֶלְיוֹן, דְּאִיהוּ נְהוֹרֵיהּ תַּקִּיף עַל כָּל דַּרְגִּין, וְעַל כָּל חֵילֵי שְׁמַיָּא, עִלָּאִין וְתַתָּאִין, אִתְּמַר עָלֵיהּ, יָשֶׁת חֹשֶׁךְ סִתְרוֹ. וְעַל חָכְמָה וּבִינָה, עָנָן וַעֲרָפֶל סְבִיבָיו. כְּמ"שׁ שְׁאָר סְפִירָאן. כְּמ"שׁ חַיָּון. כְּמ"שׁ יְסוֹדִין, דְּאִינּוּן מֵתִים. אִיהוּ סוֹבֵב עַל כָּל עָלְמִין, וְלֵית סוֹבֵב לוֹן לְכָל סִטְרָא, עֵילָּא וְתַתָּא, וּלְאַרְבַּע סִטְרִין, בַּר מִנֵּיהּ. וְלֵית מַאן דְּנָפִיק מֵרְשׁוּתֵיהּ לְבַר. אִיהוּ מְמַלֵּא כָּל עָלְמִין. וְלֵית אוֹחֲרָא מְמַלֵּא לוֹן.

226. And there is no light that can withstand His radiance without appearing dark, even upper Keter OF ATZILUT, whose light is stronger than all of the levels and all the hosts of the upper and lower heavens, and it is said about it, IN RELATION TO HIMSELF: "He made darkness His secret place" (Tehilim 18:12). Concerning Chochmah and Binah, IT IS SAID, "cloud and mist are round about Him" (Tehilim 97:2). How much more is it so for the other Sfirot and for the celestial beings, and the elements that are dead, WITHOUT LIFE. He surrounds all the worlds, and none but He surrounds them in any direction, up or down or to the four corners of the world, and no one has left His domain for the outside, for He fills all the worlds and there is no other that fills them.

227. אִיהוּ מְחַיֶּה לוֹן וְלֵית עֲלֵיהּ אֱלָהָא אַחֲרָא, לְמֵיהַב לֵיהּ חַיִּין. הה"ד, וְאַתָּה מְחַיֶּה אֶת כּוּלָם. וּבְגִינֵיהּ אָמַר דָּנִיֵּאל, וְכָל דָּאֲרֵי אַרְעָא כְּלָא חֲשִׁיבִין וּכְמִצְבְּיֵיהּ עָבֵיד בְּחֵיל שְׁמַיָּא. אִיהוּ מְקַשֵּׁר וּמְיַחֵד זִינָא לְזִינֵיהּ, עֵילָא וְתַתָּא. וְלֵית קוּרְבָא לְהוּ בַּד' יְסוֹדִין, אֶלָּא קוּדְשָׁא בְּרִיךְ הוּא כַּד אִיהוּ בֵּינַיְיהוּ.

227. He grants life TO ALL THE WORLDS, and there is no other Eloha above Him to give Him life, as it is said: "and You do preserve them all" (Nechemyah 9:6), and for Him Daniel said: "and all the inhabitants of the earth are reputed as nothing: and He does according to His will in the host of heaven" (Daniel 4:32). He joins together and unites members of each species above and below, and the four elements have no proximity TO EACH OTHER apart from when the Holy One, blessed be He, is among them.

228. מִיַּד דְּחָבוּ, אִלֵּין דְּאִתְקְרִיאוּ בָּנִים אַתֶּם לַיְדֹוָד אֱלֹקֵיכֶם, אִסְתְּלַק מִן אַתְוָון, אִשְׁתְּאָרוּ בְּפֵרוּדָא. וּמַאי תִּקּוּנֵיהּ, לְקָרְבָא אַתְוָון בְּקוּדְשָׁא בְּרִיךְ הוּא, י' בְּה', ו' בְּה'. אוֹף הָכִי אִינּוּן עוֹבְדִין דִּילֵיהּ, מִסְּטְרָא דְּחַיָּון. בְּחוֹבִין דִּלְהוֹן גָּרְמוּ לֵיהּ, לְאִסְתַּלְּקָא מִנְהוֹן. מַאי תַּקַנְתָּא דִּלְהוֹן. לְנַחְתָּא קוּדְשָׁא בְּרִיךְ הוּא עֲלַיְיהוּ, לְקָרְבָא לוֹן. אוֹף הָכִי אִינּוּן דַּהֲווֹ מֵאַרְבַּע יְסוֹדִין, דְּאִינּוּן עָאנָא דְּקוּדְשָׁא בְּרִיךְ הוּא, דְּגָרְמוּ לְסַלְּקָא קוּדְשָׁא בְּרִיךְ הוּא מִנַּיְיהוּ. מַאי תַּקָּנָה. לְקָרְבָא לוֹן לְקוּדְשָׁא בְּרִיךְ הוּא.

228. Immediately, when those who are called "You are the children of Hashem your Elohim" (Devarim 14:1), WHO ARE FROM THE SIDE OF THE YUD HEI VAV HEI, sinned, He removes Himself from the letters OF THE YUD HEI VAV HEI, which are left separated from each other. How is this to be corrected? By bringing together the letters in the Holy One, blessed be He, Yud to Hei, WHICH IS THE UNION OF CHOCHMAH AND BINAH, Vav to Hei, WHICH IS THE UNION OF TIFERET AND MALCHUT. So also: those who are His servants, WHO ARE FROM THE SIDE OF METATRON, AND ARE from the side of the living creatures MICHAEL, GABRIEL, URIEL AND RAPHAEL, whose sins caused HIS DIVINITY to leave them, how are they to be corrected? By AGAIN bringing the Holy One, blessed be He, down to them, and to bring them close TO EACH OTHER. So also with those who are from the four elements, FIRE, WIND, WATER AND EARTH, which are CALLED 'the flock of the Holy One, blessed be He', who, BY THEIR SINS, cause the Holy One, blessed be He, to ascend from them, what is their correction? It is to draw them close to the Holy One, blessed be He.

229. וּבְגִין דָּא בְּכֻלְּהוּ מָנֵי, קָרְבָּן לַיְדֹוָד, אֶת קָרְבָּנִי לַחְמִי לְאִשַּׁי. אוֹף אֶת הַכֶּבֶשׂ אֶחָד תַּעֲשֶׂה בַבֹּקֶר וְאֶת הַכֶּבֶשׂ הַשֵּׁנִי תַּעֲשֶׂה בֵּין הָעַרְבָּיִם. וּכְתִיב שְׁתֵּי תוֹרִים אוֹ שְׁנֵי בְנֵי יוֹנָה, כָּל זִינָא אָזִיל לְזִינֵיהּ. וְקוּדְשָׁא בְּרִיךְ הוּא מְקָרֵב כֹּלָּא בַּאֲתָר דָּא, אִיהוּ עִלַּת עַל כֹּלָּא, דְּלֵית אֱלָהָא בַּר מִנֵּיהּ. וְלֵית מַאן דְּיָכִיל לְקָרְבָא חֵילִין, בַּר מִנֵּיהּ.

229. And this is why He commanded for all of them a sacrifice to Yud Hei Vav Hei, NAMELY IN ORDER TO UNITE THE LETTERS OF THE YUD HEI VAV HEI, THAT WERE SEPARATED AND REMOVED, AS EXPLAINED ABOVE. "My offerings, the provisions of My sacrifices made by fire" (Bemidbar 28:2). Also: "The one lamb you shall offer in the morning and the other lamb you shall offer towards evening" (Ibid. 4), and: "two turtledoves, or two young pigeons" (Vayikra 5:7). One goes after its own kind, AND JOINS IT. And the Holy One, blessed be He, brings all together in this place, for He is the cause of all; there is no Eloha beside Him, and none but He is able to bring the forces together.

230. אֲבָל חֵילִין דְּאוּמִין דְּעעכו"ם, אִינּוּן מִסִּטְרָא דִּפְרוּדָא. וַוי לְמַאן דְּגָרִים בְּחוֹבוֹי, לְאַעֲלָא אַתְוָון וְחֵיוָן וִיסוֹדִין. דְּמִיָּד אִסְתַּלָּק קוּדְשָׁא

בְּרִיךְ הוּא מִיִּשְׂרָאֵל. וְיֵיעָלוּן אוּמִין עעכו״ם בֵּינַיְיהוּ. לֵית לוֹן קְרִיבוּת
בְּקוּדְשָׁא בְּרִיךְ הוּא, דְּלֵית קוֹרְבְּנִין בְּחוּצָה לָאָרֶץ. ובג״ד אוּקְמוּהָ
רַבָּנָן, הַדָּר בְּחוּצָה לָאָרֶץ דּוֹמֶה כְּמִי שֶׁאֵין לוֹ אֱלוֹהַ. בְּהַהוּא זִמְנָא
דְּאָמַר מִלִּין אִלֵּין, נַחְתּוּ כָּל אַתְוָון קַדִּישִׁין, וְחֵיוָן קַדִּישִׁין, וד׳ יְסוֹדִין,
לְגַבֵּיה, וּבְרִיכוּ לֵיהּ וְאָמְרוּ, עַל יְדָךְ רַעְיָא מְהֵימְנָא, נָחִית עֲלָן קוּדְשָׁא
בְּרִיךְ הוּא, וּמִתְקָרְבִין זִינָא לְזִינֵיהּ, בְּרִיךְ אַנְתְּ לְקוּדְשָׁא בְּרִיךְ הוּא,
בְּאַרְבַּע יְסוֹדִין. כְּעַן אִתְבְּרִיר כֹּלָּא עַל בּוּרְיֵיהּ.

ע״כ רעיא מהימנא

230. But the forces of the idol-worshipping nations are from the side of Separation. Woe to him who by his sins brings SEPARATION to the letters, living creatures and elements, for the Holy One, blessed be He, immediately removes Himself from Yisrael, and the idol-worshipping nations come in among them. THE IDOL-WORSHIPPERS have no proximity to the Holy One, blessed be He, since there are no sacrifices outside the Land of Yisrael, WHERE THE IDOL-WORSHIPPERS DWELL. In this context, the sages taught: 'He who lives outside the Land of Yisrael is comparable to one has no Eloha'. As THE FAITHFUL SHEPHERD said these things, all the holy letters FROM ATZILUT, and the holy living creatures FROM BRIYAH, and the four elements IN YETZIRAH AND ASIYAH came down to him, blessed him, and said: "By your doing, O Faithful Shepherd, did the Holy One, blessed be He, descend upon us, and each kind was drawn close to its own kind. You are blessed to the Holy One, blessed be He, by the four elements. Now everything has been clarified in its rightful place."

End of Ra'aya Meheimna (the Faithful Shepherd)

41. "Delight yourself also in Hashem"

A Synopsis

Rabbi Shimon talks about the scripture that begins with "Trust in Hashem, and do good; dwell in the land, and enjoy security." He once more reminds us why, after his promotion to the office of high priest, Pinchas is not named in the killing of Zimri.

The Relevance of this Passage

In this particular portion of Zohar, the concept of doing "good" concerns the goal of correcting our sexual sins, past and present, and the original root of all sins, which will be explained shortly. This correction is referred to by the Zohar as the "Holy Covenant." The reader however, should make no mistake; the Zohar is in no way implying a moralistic, Puritan, or Victorian attitude towards sexual intercourse. On the contrary, sex is sacred, according to the Kabbalist, and it is a powerful vehicle to connect to the Light of the Creator and imbue our plane of existence with an abundance of positive spiritual energy.

Sexual connections between a wife and husband cause the lower world (female) to rise and join the Upper World (male). Thus, through the love we make, we can contribute to the elevation of our souls and the ascent of the entire world.

But it is not enough to merely turn on. Animals are capable of physical arousal without any forethought or consideration of the divine aspects of sexual relations. One must have the courage, intent and focus to tune in to the spiritual dimension and purpose of intimate relations between a man and wife.

First, we must ask, what constitutes a sexual sin?

Sex that is divorced from our inner self, and from our partner, prevents us from experiencing the kind of connections that evoke a sense of Heaven here on Earth. Sexual relations that are devoid of divine intent, that are self-serving and self-indulgent, are likened to an electrical short-circuit. There is an enormous but brief spark of energy, which is then followed by darkness.

When we resist selfishness and animal lust, striving to share with our mate, putting their needs and desires ahead of our own, meditating to connect to the divine aspects of sex, a circuit of energy is established. This act of resisting our primal urges equates to the resisting function of a filament in a light bulb. A filament resists electrical current, which then generates light.

Without a filament (resistance), the surge of electricity flowing

between the plus and minus poles is far too intense for the bulb to handle. A short circuit erupts in a blinding burst of light, followed by a burnt-out bulb and darkness. Likewise, selfish, wanton sex is tempting, for it delivers a burst of pleasure. However, this is the metaphysical version of a short-circuit. We burn out, and darkness inevitably ensues. This resulting darkness creates an opening for negative energy and ailments (often associated directly or indirectly with the sexual organs) to enter into our lives.

These self-centered urges have their origin in a consequential event that took place *prior* to the creation of physical man. It is this event that corresponds to the Holy Covenant.

THE GENESIS STORY

Before the creation of the world, Adam and Eve were spiritual beings who comprised all the souls of humanity. Each of us was like cells that formed the body of these supernal beings. Adam and Eve, collectively, are known as the Vessel.

In the traditional Biblical story of Creation, we are told that after creating the other living things of the earth, God created Adam, the first man. But not wanting Adam to be alone, God made a partner, taken from Adam's rib. This was Eve, the first woman. God left the couple in the Garden of Eden with the instruction that while they could partake of all the delights they found there, including fruit from the Tree of Life, they were forbidden to eat from the Tree of Knowledge of Good and Evil, for the fruits were unripe and they would surely die.

But someone else happened to be in the Garden – the infamous serpent (the angel Satan, also known as *Samael*).

Urged on by the seductive encouragement of the snake, Eve disobeyed. She plucked an apple from the forbidden tree and ate it. Then, she offered the apple to Adam, enticing him to eat it along with her. He did, and with that, their fleeting age of innocence was over.

DECONSTRUCTING GENESIS

Adam and Eve's bite of the fruit, on another level of spiritual understanding, indicates a sexual connection between the original vessel and the serpent. In other words, the act of succumbing to the deceptive prodding of the serpent also denotes a sexual union between them. The negative angel (do not pronounce her name) *Lilit* copulated with Adam and the angel (do not pronounce his name) *Samael* copulated with Eve. In deeper spiritual terms, this implies

that the consciousness of Adam and Eve was lowered and tainted by the negative angels.

Moreover, this sexual union, or lowering of consciousness, mutated the nature of the Vessel. In the language of genetics, the act of sexual connection between the Vessel and the serpent altered the Vessel's DNA from *Desire to Receive*, into a more selfish *Desire to Receive for the Self Alone*. Consequently, every cell (our souls) in the cosmic body of Adam and Eve had its DNA recombined with the DNA (consciousness) of the serpent.

The Vessel (Adam and Eve) then shattered into individual souls. These countless sparks of souls descended into this physical world and assumed the garment of physical bodies. They were then empowered with the task of eradicating the negative consciousness from their nature and reuniting all the scattered halves of the one fractured soul into one unified whole.

Thus, the dark and egocentric aspect of human nature was born from this sexual union between the Vessel and the serpent. All of our negative behavior, egoistic character traits, jealousies, etc., are rooted in this original sin.

Correcting this seed of all sins is the Holy Covenant that *Pinchas* was zealous for.

THE ZOHAR CONNECTION

In this passage, the Zohar refers to a particular Torah portion involving *Pinchas,* which correlates to the Holy Covenant. The Torah tells a story (Numbers 25:1) in which Yisrael begin committing ritualistic sexual acts and orgies with the "daughters of Moab" to connect to powerful, dark forces. Namely, they were using the divine act of sex to draw down energy for destructive purposes. For instance, the energy of the atom can be used in a positive fashion by generating the nuclear power that provides energy for an entire city. Conversely, atomic energy can be used destructively by a terrorist nation in the form of nuclear weapons.

In this Torah story, a man named *Zimri* and a woman named *Cozbi* began engaging in sex in front of Moses and the nation of Yisrael. Pinchas understood the laws of spiritual energy. He knew that negative forces and darkness would engulf our world as a result of this act. Therefore, in the story, he killed both of them to save the rest of the world from deadly plagues that would have decimated all mankind.

We've learned that the negative angels (do not pronounce their names)

Samael and *Lilit* are the underlying cause behind all of our negative selfish sexual impulses.

Thus, the deeper meaning behind the slaughter of Zimri and Cozbi concerns Pinchas's destruction of the two negative angels. This, in effect, corrects the Holy Covenant!

By correcting this sin (The Holy Covenant), the Zohar reveals that the Creator "shall give you the desires of your heart." Thus, all of our desires can now be fulfilled. Moreover, eternal peace and fulfillment are now attained for the entire world; for the Zohar states:

"...once the covenant is corrected, everything is corrected."

This ultimate correction now paves the way for eternal Light to illuminate our generation, for the Zohar quotes Pinchas and says:

"Happy is the generation that hears your interpretations of Torah...."

This is, clearly, our generation; for you, the reader, are now privy to this interpretation from this splendid book of Zohar.

Thus, here we receive the Light to destroy the angels *Samael* and *Lilit* externally and within ourselves. We correct the original sin of the Vessel (Adam and Eve) and our own sins (selfish sexual deeds). This action merits the reader the same destiny as *Pinchas,* which is happiness and attachment to the "first Light" that God created. This is the same Light that Abraham enjoyed, and it now shines in the souls of all mankind.

Any kind of ailment associated directly or indirectly with the sexual reproductive organs receives the Light zof healing and is purged from the world. These include cancers of the prostate, testicles, ovaries, uterus, fallopian tubes, and breasts; as well as AIDS and all forms of venereal disease.

All this radiant Light of healing and restoration ignites the moment we choose to become more sharing, caring and considerate. Choose it now, then meditate upon this passage, and everything that is Pinchas's becomes yours.

231. פָּתַח וְאָמַר, בְּטַח בַּיְיָ' וַעֲשֵׂה טוֹב שְׁכָן אֶרֶץ וּרְעֵה אֱמוּנָה. בְּטַח בַּיְיָ', כַּדְקָא יָאוּת. וַעֲשֵׂה טוֹב, תִּקוּנָא דִּבְרִית קַדִּישָׁא. דִּתְהֵא מְתַקֵּן לֵיהּ, וְנָטִיר לֵיהּ כַּדְקָא יָאוּת. וְאִי תַּעֲבִיד דָּא, אַנְתְּ תְּהֵא הָכָא בְּאַרְעָא, וְיִתְּזָן מִנָּךְ, וְיִתְפַּרְנֵס מִנָּךְ, הַהִיא אֱמוּנָה דִּלְעֵילָא.

231. He began by quoting: "Trust in Hashem, and do good; dwell in the land, and enjoy security" (Tehilim 37:3). "Trust in Hashem." This is as it should be. "And do good," THAT IS, UNDERTAKE the correction of the Holy Covenant, that you should correct it and keep it properly. And if you do this, you will be here in the land, NAMELY "DWELL IN THE LAND," and it will receive nourishment at your hand, and will flourish at your hand, namely that upper faitht WHICH IS MALCHUT, THIS BEING THE MEANING OF "ENJOY SECURITY (ALSO: 'CHERISH FAITH')."

232. וְתוּ, תִּתְעַנַּג עַל יְיָ' וְיִתֶּן לְךָ מִשְׁאֲלוֹת לְבֶּךָ. כָּל דָּא אִתְתְּקָנַת בְּתִקּוּנָא דִּבְרִית. כֵּיוָן דְּאִתְתַּקְנַת בְּרִית, אִתְּקַן כֹּלָּא. פִּנְחָס בְּגִין דְּקַנֵּי עַל בְּרִית דָּא, זָכָה לְכֹלָּא. וְלֹא עוֹד אֶלָּא דְּאָגִין עַל כָּל יִשְׂרָאֵל, וּבֵיהּ אִתְקַיָּים וְהִתְעַנַּג עַל יְיָ'. דְּהָא סָלִיק וְאִתְקְשַׁר לְעֵילָּא, בְּאוֹר קַדְמָאָה דְּבָרָא קוּדְשָׁא בְּרִיךְ הוּא, וְגָנִיז לֵיהּ. בְּהַהוּא אוֹר דְּאִתְהֲנֵי אַבְרָהָם מִנֵּיהּ, וְאַהֲרֹן כַּהֲנָא אִתְקְשַׁר בֵּיהּ.

232. And the following verse: "Delight yourself also in Hashem; and He shall give you the desires of your heart" (Ibid. 4). All this is remedied with the correction of the covenant, for once the covenant is corrected, everything is corrected. And Pinchas, because he was zealous for this covenant, merited everything. And not only that but he was protector of all Yisrael, and the verse "You shall delight yourself in Hashem" was upheld in him, for he ascended and made contact above, with the first light that the Holy One, blessed be He, created and then concealed, that same light that Abraham enjoyed and with which Aaron the priest was bound.

233. לְבָתַר דְּאִסְתַּלָּק לְכַהֲנָא רַבָּא, לָא אַדְכַּר לֵיהּ קַטְלָנוּתָא דְּזִמְרִי, וְלָא יָאוּת בְּגִין דְּלָא יִתְאֲחַד כְּלָל בְּעַנְפּוֹי דְּסִטְרָא אַחֲרָא, וְלָא אִתְחֲזֵי לְאַדְכְּרָא עֲלֵיהּ. דְּכָל מַאן דְּקַטִיל, עַנְפִּין דְּסִטְרָא אָחֳרָא אִית בֵּיהּ. וּפִנְחָס הָא מִתְאֲחִיד בִּימִינָא, וְלֵית לֵיהּ חוּלָק בְּסִטְרָא אָחֳרָא כְּלָל, וְעַל דָּא לָא אַדְכַּר הָכָא. מַה דְּאִתְחֲזֵי שְׁבָחָא, אִיהוּ גְּנַאי לֵיהּ, וּנְחִיתוּ מִדַּרְגָּא עִלָּאָה דְּאִתְאֲחִיד בֵּיהּ. וע"ד כְּתִיב הַמּוּכֶּה אֲשֶׁר הוּכָּה סְתָם, וְשֵׁם הָאִשָּׁה הַמּוּכָּה, וְלָא אַדְכַּר עַל יְדָא דְּמַאן.

233. After PINCHAS was promoted to the office of High Priest, the killing of Zimri is not mentioned in connection with him, for it is not fitting, in order that he should not be caught up in the tentacles of the Other Side, and it is indeed not proper to mention the killing in connection with him. Everyone who kills has branches of the Other Side in him, but Pinchas had already become united with the right, WHICH IS THE PRIESTHOOD, and had no portion whatsoever in the Other Side, which is why HIS NAME is not mentioned here. What might have seemed praiseworthy is really a matter of disgrace for him, for it would mean a descent from the upper level with which he was united. It is, therefore, written: "Now the name of the man of Yisrael that was slain, that was slain... And the name of the Midianite woman that was slain..." (Bemidbar 25:14-15), without mentioning by whom.

234. א״ר פִּנְחָס, זַכָּאָה דָּרָא דְּשַׁמְעִין מִילָךְ בְּאוֹרַיְיתָא, וְזַכָּאָה חוּלָקִי דְּזָכֵינָא לְכַךְ. אָמַר רִבִּי שִׁמְעוֹן, זַכָּאָה דָּרָא, דְּאַנְתְּ וַחֲסִידוּתָךְ אִשְׁתְּכַח בְּגַוֵויה. עַד דַּהֲווֹ יַתְבִין וּמְפַיְיסִין דָּא לְדָא, אָתָא רִבִּי אֶלְעָזָר בְּרֵיה דר״ש, וְאַשְׁכַּח לוֹן תַּמָּן. א״ר פִּנְחָס, וַדַּאי דִּכְתִּיב וַיֹּאמֶר יַעֲקֹב כַּאֲשֶׁר רָאָם מַחֲנֵה אֱלֹהִים זֶה. א״ל ר״ש, אֶלְעָזָר בְּרִי, תִּיב בְּרִי, וְאֵימָא קְרָא. יָתִיב רִבִּי אֶלְעָזָר.

234. Rabbi Pinchas said, Happy is the generation that hears your interpretations of Torah, and happy is my portion that I have so merited. Rabbi Shimon replied TO RABBI PINCHAS, Happy is the generation in which you and your piety exist. While they were still sitting appeasing and enjoying each other's company, Rabbi Elazar, the son of Rabbi Shimon, came and found them there. Rabbi Pinchas commented, this is certainly in fulfillment of the verse: "And when Jacob saw them, he said: This is Elohim's camp" (Beresheet 32:3). Rabbi Shimon said, Elazar, my son, sit you down, my son, and expound to us this verse, and Rabbi Elazar sat down.

42. Lighting upon means words of reconciliation

A Synopsis
Rabbi Elazar gives his interpretation of the time that Jacob was on his way and was met by angels of Elohim.

The Relevance of this Passage
The divine energy that erupts during the evening prayer flows from the letters that compose this passage to correct our world of *Malchut*. This energy arouses atonement in our hearts, for conciliation is the only way to conjoin our world with the Upper World, just as a man appeases his wife before he joins in sexual union with her. This gift of correction is given to us courtesy of Jacob.

235. פָּתַח וְאָמַר, וְיַעֲקֹב הָלַךְ לְדַרְכּוֹ וַיִּפְגְּעוּ בוֹ מַלְאֲכֵי אֱלֹהִים. מַאי וַיִּפְגְּעוּ בוֹ. אֶלָּא אִית פְּגִיעָה לְטַב. וְאִית פְּגִיעָה לְבִישׁ. וְאִית פְּגִיעָה לִצְלוֹתָא. אֶלָּא בְּשַׁעֲתָא דַּהֲוָה אָזִיל לְחָרָן, מַה כְּתִיב. וַיִּפְגַּע בַּמָּקוֹם, צְלוֹתָא דְּעַרְבִית הֲוָה דְּצַלֵּי בְּהַהוּא מָקוֹם. כד"א, הִנֵּה מָקוֹם אִתִּי. וּצְלוֹתָא דְּעַרְבִית בְּהַהוּא אֲתָר אִתְחֲזֵי.

235. He began: "And Jacob went on his way, and angels of Elohim met him" (Beresheet 32:2). HE ASKS, What is the meaning of "met him?" AND ANSWERS THAT there is a meeting for good, a meeting for evil and a meeting for prayer. When Jacob was on his way to Haran, what does scripture tell us? "And he came upon the place" (Beresheet 28:11), for he prayed the evening service at that place, WHICH IS MALCHUT THAT IS CALLED 'PLACE', as it is written: "Behold, there is a place by Me" (Shemot 33:21). For the evening prayer is proper for that place; THAT IS, THE EVENING PRAYER IS THE ASPECT OF CORRECTION OF MALCHUT, AND THIS IS IN ACCORD WITH WHAT WAS SAID ABOVE: "MEETING IS NONE OTHER THAN PRAYER."

236. תּוּ וַיִּפְגַּע בַּמָּקוֹם, מִלֵּי פִיּוּסִין אִיהוּ. דְּאָתָא שִׁמְשָׁא קַדִּישָׁא לְגַבֵּי סִיהֲרָא, בַּעֲלָהּ לְגַבֵּי אִתְּתָא. מִכָּאן דְּלָא יָאוֹת לַבַּעַל לְמֵיתֵי לְגַבֵּי אִתְּתָא, אִי לָא הֲוֵי בְּמִלֵּי פִיּוּסִין לְפַיְיסָא לָהּ. דִּכְתִיב וַיִּפְגַּע בַּמָּקוֹם,

-198-

וּלְבָתַר וַיָּלֶן שָׁם. כַּד הֲוָה אָתֵי יַעֲקֹב מֵחָרָן, מַה כְּתִיב, וַיִּפְגְּעוּ בּוֹ, שַׁדְרַת הִיא לְפַיְיסָא לֵיהּ, לְמֵיתֵי לְגַבָּהּ.

236. Again. "And he lighted on a certain place" (Beresheet 28:11). This means that he spoke words of conciliation, NAMELY AS HE HAS ALREADY NOTED: THERE IS NO MEETING THAT IS NOT CONCILIATION. "because the sun was set" (Ibid.), the holy one, WHICH IS ZEIR ANPIN, comes to the moon, WHICH IS MALCHUT, the husband to the wife. It follows that it is not right for a husband to come to his wife without words of appeasement to placate her, for it is written: "And he lighted on a certain place," WHICH MEANS THAT HE ADDRESSED HER WITH WORDS OF APPEASEMENT. And afterwards: "And he stayed there the night" (Ibid.). But what does scripture tell us about his return from Haran? "met him" (Beresheet 32:2), NAMELY MALCHUT sent messengers to placate him, so that he would come in to her.

237. וַיֹּאמֶר יַעֲקֹב כַּאֲשֶׁר רָאָם. מַאי כַּאֲשֶׁר רָאָם. אִלֵּין מַלְאָכִין דְּיוֹם, וּמַלְאָכִין דְּלַיְלָה הֲווֹ, וְאִתְכַּסִּיאוּ מִנֵּיהּ, וּלְבָתַר אִתְגַּלְיָין לֵיהּ. וְעַ"ד כַּאֲשֶׁר רָאָם, כְּתִיב מַחֲנֵה אֱלֹהִים זֶה. מֶהָכָא דַּהֲווֹ אִלֵּין דִּימָמָא, וְאִלֵּין דְּלֵילְיָא. אִינּוּן דְּלֵילְיָא כְּתִיב בְּהוּ, מַחֲנֵה אֱלֹהִים, וְאִינּוּן דִּימָמָא, כְּתִיב בְּהוּ, זֶה. וְעַ"ד וַיִּקְרָא שֵׁם הַמָּקוֹם הַהוּא מַחֲנָיִם. תְּרֵין מַשְׁרְיָין. וְהַשְׁתָּא מַשְׁרְיָין קַדִּישִׁין חֲמֵינָא הָכָא. זַכָּאָה אָרְחִי דְּאָתֵינָא הָכָא.

237. "And when Jacob saw them, he said" (Ibid. 3). HE ASKS, What is the meaning of "when Jacob saw them"? AND HE ANSWERS THAT they were the daytime angels OF ZEIR ANPIN, WHO IS CALLED 'DAY', and the night time angels OF MALCHUT, WHO IS CALLED 'NIGHT'. They were hidden from him and subsequently revealed to him, which is why: "when Jacob saw them," it is written: "This is Elohim's camp." From here we know that there were those of the day and those of the night. Concerning those of the night, it is written "Elohim's camp" FOR MALCHUT IS CALLED 'ELOHIM', and concerning those of the day, it is written: "This," FOR ZEIR ANPIN IS CALLED "THIS." And thus the verse continues: "and he called the name of that place *Machanaim* (lit. 'two camps')." And now I see here holy camps, NAMELY THE CAMP OF RABBI SHIMON AND THE CAMP OF RABBI PINCHAS. Happy is my path that brought me here!

43. lighting on me as appeasement

A Synopsis
From the words of Rabbi Shimon and Moses as they continue speaking about Jacob's encounter with the angels, we come to understand that there were two camps, the daytime angels and the night time angels, and that Jacob could not see them at night. We also learn the difference between 'coming upon', meaning appeasement, and 'lighting on', meaning union. In the evening prayer a person seeks for Adonai, the Shechinah, with entreaties, and he seeks for mercy from God.

The Relevance of this Passage
Sexual connections between husband and wife are imbued with spiritual purpose and Light. The Upper and Lower worlds are wedded, allowing mercy and Light to permeate our existence. The Evil Inclination and the influences of wicked angels are abated. We can meditate to cleanse the world of negativity caused by improper sexual relationships, which are those that lack the correct spiritual intent. Moreover, we can meditate to awaken all the Light that has been generated by the intimate relations that took place between the great sages and their soulmates throughout history. This Light embodies the mystical forces associated with the evening prayer and now corrects the physical world of *Malchut*.

רעיא מהימנא

238. אֶלָּא פְּגִיעָה אִיהִי פִּיּוּסָא, דְּכַד יֵיתֵי חָתָן לְגַבֵּי כַּלָּה, לֵית אֹרַח לְחָתָן לְייַחֲדָא בְּכַלָּה, אֶלָּא בְּפִיּוּסָא. וּלְבָתַר יַעֲבֵד עִמָּה לִינָה. וְהַיְינוּ כִּי בָא הַשֶּׁמֶשׁ.

Ra'aya Meheimna (the Faithful Shepherd)

238. (THIS IS THE CONTINUATION OF RABBI SHIMON'S WORDS, PARAGRAPH 208) But 'coming upon' means words of appeasement. When the groom comes to the bride, the groom does not unite with the bride without words of appeasement, and afterwards he spends the night with her. This is the meaning of "because the sun was set" (Beresheet 38:11).

239. אָמַר רַעְיָא מְהֵימָנָא, אִי הָכִי מַאי נִיהוּ כִּי בָא הַשֶּׁמֶשׁ דְּהָא אֹרַח

דְּרְשָׁא אוּקְמוּהָ, לְשׁוֹן כְּבִיָּיה, וְהַיְינוּ כִּי בָא הַשֶּׁמֶשׁ. אֶלָּא מֵהָכָא
אוֹלִיפְנָא, מַאן דִּמְיַיחֵד בְּאִתְּתֵיה, צָרִיךְ בְּלֵילְיָא לְמִכְבֵּי שְׁרָגָא,
וּבִימָמָא לָאו אֹרַח דְּרַבָּנָן לְשַׁמֵּשׁ מִטָּתָן, אֶלָּא בַּלַּיְלָה, אֹרַח צְנִעָא.
וּבְגִין דָּא, מָתַי אִתְעֲבֵיד לֵינָה. כִּי בָא הַשֶּׁמֶשׁ, דְּאִתְפְּנֵי שִׁמְשָׁא
מֵעָלְמָא.

239. The Faithful Shepherd said: If this is so, what is the meaning of "because the sun was set (Heb. *ki va*)," which is here explained homiletically, THAT '*KI VA*' IS derived from extinguishing (Heb. *kviyah*), and so "because the sun was set" MEANS WHEN THE LIGHT OF THE SUN WAS EXTINGUISHED. However, what we can learn from this is that whoever unites with the wife must extinguish the lights at night, and that the sages do not advocate sexual intercourse by the light of day, but only by night, with modesty. When, therefore, does one stay overnight? SCRIPTURE SAYS: When the sun has set, namely after the light of the sun has turned away from the world.

240. וּבְגִין דָּא, אוֹף הָכִי דְּצָרִיךְ לְאִתְכַּסְיָיא מִן שִׁמְשָׁא, וְהָכִי צָרִיךְ
לְאִתְכַּסְיָיא מֵאִלֵּין מַלְאֲכִין, דְּאִינּוּן מִיֵּצֶר הַטּוֹב מִימִינָא, בְּכַמָּה
מַשְׁרְיָין. וּמִיֵּצֶר הָרָע, דְּאָזִיל לִשְׂמָאלָא בְּכַמָּה מַשְׁרְיָין. וּבְגִין דָּא, בָּתַר
דְּאָתָא צַפְרָא, אָמַר כַּאֲשֶׁר רָאָם. וּמִסְטְרָא דְּיַעֲקֹב דַּהֲוָה אִישׁ תָּם, לָא
הֲוָה עִמֵּיה אֶלָּא חַיָּילִין דְּמַלְכָּא וּמַטְרוֹנִיתָא. וּבְגִין דָּא וַיִּקְרָא שֵׁם
הַמָּקוֹם הַהוּא מַחֲנָיִם. אִינּוּן מַלְאֲכִין דִּימָמָא כְּתִיב. כַּאֲשֶׁר רָאָם מַחֲנֵה
אֱלֹהִים זֶה. וְכַד אָתוּ מַלְאָכִים דְּלֵילְיָא, דְּאִתְכְּנָשׁוּ בַּהֲדֵיה, לְנַטְרָא לֵיה
אָמַר וַיִּקְרָא שֵׁם הַמָּקוֹם הַהוּא מַחֲנָיִם.

240. For this reason, just as one has to cover oneself up from the sun, so does one have to cover oneself from the angels who are from the Good Inclination on the right in a number of camps, AS WELL AS FROM THE ANGELS WHO ARE from the Evil Inclination that goes on the left in a number of camps. And so it was that after the morning had dawned, Jacob spoke when he saw the angels, FOR AT NIGHT HE DID NOT SEE THEM. And there was no one with Jacob, the plain man, WHO IS THE CENTRAL COLUMN except for the camps of the King and the Queen, WHO ARE

CALLED 'THE DAYTIME ANGELS' AND 'THE NIGHTTIME ANGELS'. This is why "And he called the name of that place *Machanaim* (lit. 'two camps')" (Beresheet 32:3). About the daytime angels, WHO ARE OF ZEIR ANPIN, WHO IS CALLED 'DAY', it is written: "And when Jacob saw them, he said: This is Elohim's camp" (Ibid.), FOR ZEIR ANPIN IS CALLED 'THIS'. And when the nighttime angels came, NAMELY THOSE OF MALCHUT WHO IS CALLED 'NIGHT', who gathered around him to protect him, it is said: "And he called the name of that place *Machanaim* (lit. 'two camps')." AND THERE IS NO DIFFICULTY HERE, FOR THE VERSE "WHEN JACOB SAW THEM" IS WRITTEN ABOUT THE TIME AFTER HE HAD RETURNED FROM LABAN, FOR 'THE TORAH IS OT IN CHRONOLOGICAL ORDER'.

241. בְּגִין דִּצְלוֹתָא אִיהִי כַּלָּה, הה"ד אִתִּי מִלְבָנוֹן כַּלָּה אִתִּי וְגוֹ'. אִתְקְרֵי הָכָא אִתִּי. וּבְאוֹרַיְיתָא דִּבְכְתָב אִתְּמַר עָלָה, הִנֵּה מָקוֹם אִתִּי. וּבְגִין דְּאִיהִי אִתְקְרִיאַת מָקוֹם בְּעָלְמָא דֵין, אִתְּמַר בָּה וַיִּפְגַּע בַּמָּקוֹם וַיָּלֶן שָׁם.

241. THE AUTHOR HERE WISHES TO RECONCILE WHAT HE SAID INITIALLY ON "AND HE LIGHTED ON A CERTAIN PLACE," THAT "THERE IS NO 'COMING UPON' THAT IS NOT PRAYER" AND WHAT HE SAID LATER, NAMELY THAT 'COMING UPON' MEANS APPEASEMENT WHEN A GROOM COMES TO A BRIDE...ACCORDING TO WHICH "AND HE LIGHTED ON A CERTAIN PLACE" MEANS THE UNITY OF BRIDE AND GROOM. AND THIS IS WHAT HE SAYS: Since prayer is a bride, NAMELY MALCHUT, as it is said: "Come with me from Lebanon, my bride, with me from Lebanon" (Shir Hashirim 4:8), THUS MALCHUT is here called "with me" (Heb. *iti*). And in the written Torah, it is said about her: "Behold, there is a place by Me (Heb. *iti*)" (Shemot 33:21). HENCE 'A PLACE' IS MALCHUT, AS IS 'WITH ME'. And since MALCHUT is called 'a place' in this world, it is said about her: "And he lighted on a certain place, and tarried there all night" (Beresheet 28:11).

242. ובג"ד אִיהִי אָמְרַת, מִי יִתְּנֵנִי בַמִּדְבָּר מְלוֹן אוֹרְחִים. דַּהֲוַת רְשׁוּ בִּפְנֵי עַצְמָה, וְלָאו עִם אִינוּן דְּקַבְעִין לָהּ חוֹבָה עִמְּהוֹן, בְּלָא חָתָן דִּילָה. וּבְכָל שַׁעֲתָא דב"נ מְצַלֵּי, קוּדְשָׁא בְּרִיךְ הוּא אַקְדִּים וְנָטַר לֵהּ. וְרָזָא דְמִלָּה, וְהָאִישׁ מִשְׁתָּאֵה לָהּ. וְלֵית אִישׁ, אֶלָּא קוּדְשָׁא בְּרִיךְ הוּא.

הה"ד יְיָ' אִישׁ מִלְחָמָה. וַיְהִי הוּא טֶרֶם כִּלָּה לְדַבֵּר וְהִנֵּה רִבְקָה יוֹצֵאת,
כְּגוֹן וְיָצָא כַבָּרָק חִצּוֹ.

242. And for this reason, she says: "O that I were in the wilderness, in a
lodging place of wayfaring men" (Yirmeyah 9:1), for then she would have
been independent, without those who turn her sin downwards, and without
her groom. And whenever a man prays, the Holy One, blessed be He,
precedes him and protects her. And the secret of the matter is to be found in
the verse: "And the man (Heb. *ish*) wondering at her" (Beresheet 24:21), for
whenever the word *Ish* (Eng. 'man') is used the reference is to the Holy
One, blessed be He, as it is written: "Hashem is a man (Heb. *ish*) of war"
(Shemot 15:3). "And it came to pass, before he had done speaking, that,
behold, Rivkah (Resh Bet Kof Hei) came out" (Beresheet 24:15), just as
"and his arrow (Heb. *habarak*, Hei Bet Resh Kof) shall go forth like the
lightning" (Zecharyah 9:14).

243. וְאִי תֵּימְרוּן, דְּהָא אוּקְמוּהָ רַבָּנָן, לַעֲשָׂרָה קַדְמָא שְׁכִינְתָּא וְאַתְיָא,
לְאֶחָד עַד דְּיָתִיב. לַעֲשָׂרָה דְּהִיא י' קַדְמָה ה'. לְאֶחָד דְּאִיהוּ ו', עַד
דְּיָתִיב, לָא אַתְיָא לְגַבֵּיהּ ה' תִּנְיָינָא. וְרָזָא דְּמִלָּה, דְּבְאֲתָר דְּלֵית תַּמָּן
י"ה, לָא אַתְיָא תַּמָּן ה'. וּמַאן דְּבָעֵי לְיַחֲדָא אַתְוָון, צָרִיךְ בִּתְחִנָּה
וּבְתַחֲנוּנֵי. וּבְג"ד, וָאֶתְחַנַּן אֶל יְיָ', בַּאֲדֹנָ"י לִשְׁכִינְתָּא בְּתַחֲנוּנִים.
וּלְקוּדְשָׁא בְּרִיךְ הוּא בְּרַחֲמֵי, עַד הָכָא.

243. You might argue that the sages taught that in a gathering of ten the
Shechinah is preceding to come among them, but does not come for a single
one until he sits down, AND WHAT DID I SAY? THAT WHENEVER A MAN
PRAYS, THE HOLY ONE, BLESSED BE HE, PRECEDES AND RECEIVES
HIM, NAMELY, EVEN A SINGLE PERSON. HE ANSWERS THAT THE
EXPLANATION IS AS FOLLOWS: In the case of ten, there is Yud (= 10) before
Hei; THAT IS TO SAY, IF THERE IS YUD HEI, THE MOCHIN OF
CHOCHMAH AND BINAH, FOR THE YUD INCLUDES THE HEI ALSO, THEN
THE SHECHINAH, WHICH IS THE SECRET OF HEI, COMES. In the case of
one, who is Vav: IF THE VAV IS ALONE WITHOUT YUD HEI, until he sits
down AND RECEIVES THE MOCHIN OF YUD HEI the second Hei OF YUD
HEI VAV HEI does not come to him. And the secret of the matter is that the

Hei THAT IS MALCHUT does not come to a place where Yud Hei are not. Whoever wishes to unite the letters YUD HEI AND VAV HEI must pray with supplications and entreaties, this being the reason for the verse: "And I besought Hashem at that time, SAYING "ADONAI ELOHIM, YOU HAVE BEGUN..." (Devarim 3:23-24), for Adonai, which is the Shechinah, is sought with entreaties, and mercy is sought from the Holy One, blessed be He. And up to here IS THE EXPLANATION FOR ARVIT.

44. "The one lamb you shall offer in the morning"

A Synopsis

The sages taught that one should not pry into the secrets of God or mysteries of the world, and so the secrets of the Torah must be kept covered up and hidden from the wicked and the ignorant. We are reminded of the role and importance of Scripture, Mishnah, Talmud and Kabbalah.

The Relevance of this Passage

The potent mystical wisdom of the Zohar is shielded from the eyes of the wicked who only seek to use these spiritual forces for negative purposes. Thus, any traces of wickedness are purged from our hearts so that we may always merit closeness to this deep well of wisdom. The mystical Light that is cast from these verses overwhelms and cleanses the negative energy created by those who propagate evil, immorality, and sexual perversion in the world.

In verse 246, the Zohar states:

"Happy are the organs that are sanctified at the time of intercourse, for they are called 'the wood of the burnt offering'"

These words project Light that heals our sexual reproductive organs, imbuing them with divine blessing. Ailments associated with Sexual Dysfunction afflicting both males and females such as Impotence and Inhibited Desire Disorder are remedied here. Our consciousness is raised, deepening our understanding of the great spiritual potential that sexual relations offer us.

The Zohar's reference to the importance and role of Scripture, Mishnah, Talmud, and Kabbalah concerns the building of a Vessel (Female Waters) that can receive and hold the Light of the Creator. Thus, this passage constructs a Vessel so that Divine Energy fills us and all Creation with boundless Light.

244. אֶת הַכֶּבֶשׂ הָאֶחָד תַּעֲשֶׂה בַבֹּקֶר וְאֵת הַכֶּבֶשׂ הַשֵּׁנִי תַּעֲשֶׂה בֵּין הָעַרְבָּיִם. דְּאִיהוּ רָזָא דְּכִבְשֵׁי דְּרַחֲמָנָא, דְּאוֹקְמוּהָ עֲלַיְיהוּ רַבָּנָן, גַּבֵּי כִּבְשֵׁי דְּרַחֲמָנָא לָמָּה לָךְ. אֶלָּא מִלִּין דְּיהוֹן תְּחוֹת כְּבְשׁוֹנֵי דְּעָלְמָא, יְהוֹן מְכוּסִין תְּחוֹת לְבוּשָׁךְ. מַה לְבוּשׁ אִיהוּ מְכַסֶּה עַל גּוּפָא, אוֹף הָכִי צָרִיךְ לְכַסָּאָה רָזִין דְּאוֹרַיְיתָא. כ"ש רָזִין דְּקָרְבְּנִין, דְּאִינּוּן כְּגַוְונָא דְּקָרִיבוּ דְּאִתְּתָא לְגַבֵּי בַּעְלָהּ.

244. "The one lamb (Heb. *keves*) you shall offer in the morning, and the other lamb you shall offer towards evening" (Shemot 29:39 and Bemidbar 28:4). And about the hidden matters (Heb. *kivshi*) of the Merciful One, the sages have taught: 'Why do you probe into the secrets of the Merciful One?', THE MEANING OF WHICH IS: Matters that are of the mysteries of the world, let them be concealed under your dress. Just as clothes cover the body, so also must the secrets of the Torah be kept covered up, and this applies even more to the secret of the sacrifices, which are like a wife drawing near to her husband, WHICH IS WHY A SACRIFICE IS CALLED 'KORBAN', FROM THE SAME ROOT AS THE WORD *KIRVAH*, MEANING NEARNESS.

245. וּמַה קְרִיבוּ דְּתַרְוַויְיהוּ צָרִיךְ בְּאִתְכַּסְיָא. אוֹף הָכִי צָרִיךְ קָרְבָּן לְכַסָּאָה לוֹן, מִבְּנֵי עַרְיָין רַשִׁיעַיָּא חֲצוּפִין, דְּלֵית לוֹן בֹּשֶׁת פָּנִים וְלָא עֲנָוָה. וְכַמָּה מִינֵי מַמְזְרִין אִינוּן, בְּנֵי עֲרָיוֹת, בְּנֵי נִדָּה, דְּנָד ה' מִנָּה, וְאִשְׁתְּכַח בְּאַתְרָהּ. שִׁפְחָה בַּת אֵל נֵכָר זוֹנָה. וְהַאי אִיהוּ רָזָא, תַּחַת שָׁלֹשׁ רָגְזָה אֶרֶץ וְגוֹ', תַּחַת עֶבֶד כִּי יִמְלוֹךְ וְנָבָל כִּי יִשְׂבַּע לָחֶם וְשִׁפְחָה כִּי תִירַשׁ גְּבִירְתָּהּ. דְּנָד ה' מֵאַתְרָאָה, דְּאִיהִי מַטְרוֹנִיתָא, יצה"ט. וְעָאלָא בְּאַתְרָהָא שִׁפְחָה יצה"ר.

245. And just as the proximity of the two of them, OF HUSBAND AND WIFE, has to be in concealment, so also must the sacrifice be concealed from the wicked, the impudent, the immoral and practicioners of incest, who have no shame and no modesty. And there are bastards of a number of sorts, children of incest, of those who have intercourse during menstruation (Heb. *nidah*). *NIDAH* MEANS THAT Hei, WHICH IS THE SHECHINAH WHO IS CALLED 'HEI', has moved (Heb. *nad*) away from her, and in her place is a bondwoman, daughter of a strange El, a prostitute. And this is a secret of: "For three things the earth is disquieted…for a slave when he becomes king; and a fool when he is filled with food…and a handmaid that is heir to her mistress" (Mishlei 30:21-23). For the Hei has moved away from its place, which is the Queen and is the Good Inclination, and in her stead has come in a handmaid, the Evil Inclination.

246. וְרָזָא דְּמִלָּה, כְּנֶגַע נִרְאָה לִי בַּבָּיִת, הַיְינוּ דָּם טָמֵא דְּנִדָּה. וּמַה הָתָם וְהִסְגִּירוֹ הַכֹּהֵן שִׁבְעַת יָמִים. אוֹף הָכִי שִׁבְעַת יָמִים תִּהְיֶה בְנִדָּתָהּ.

זַכָּאִין אִינּוּן אֵבָרִים דְּמִתְקַדְּשֵׁי בְּשַׁעַת תַּשְׁמִישׁ, דְּאִינּוּן עֲצֵי הָעוֹלָה, דַּאֲחִידָן בְּהוֹן אֶשִׁין קַדִּישִׁין, שֵׁם יְדוָד דְּאָחִיד בְּאֶשִׁין דִּלְהוֹן. ובג"ד בָּאוּרִים כַּבְּדוּ יְיָ' ע"כ כִּבְשֵׁי דְּרַחֲמָנָא, הַיְינוּ אֶת הַכֶּבֶשׂ הָאֶחָד תַּעֲשֶׂה בַבֹּקֶר וְאֵת הַכֶּבֶשׂ הַשֵּׁנִי תַּעֲשֶׂה בֵּין הָעַרְבָּיִם.

246. And the secret of the matter is to be found in the verse: "It seems to me there is as it were a plague in the house" (Vayikra 14:35), namely, the impure blood of menstruation. Just as in the one case, OF THE PLAGUE, "then the priest shall shut him up for seven days" (Vayikra 13:21), so also in the other: "she shall be seven days in her menstrual impurity" (Vayikra 15:19). Happy are the organs that are sanctified at the time of intercourse, for they are called 'the wood of the burnt offering', for they are engulfed by holy fires from the Name Yud Hei Vav Hei, WHICH IS ZEIR ANPIN, who takes hold of their fire. And for this reason IT IS WRITTEN: "Wherefore glorify Hashem in the regions of light" (Yeshayah 24:15). Thus the mysteries (Aramaic *kevesh*) of the Merciful One are: "The one lamb (Heb. *keves*) you shall offer in the morning, and the other lamb you shall offer towards evening."

247. שְׁלִימוּ דִּקְרָא, וַעֲשִׂירִית הָאֵיפָה סֹלֶת. זַכָּאָה אִיהוּ מַאן דְּאַנְגִּיד מִמּוֹחֵיהּ, טִפָּה סֹלֶת נְקִיָּה בְּלָא פְּסוֹלֶת. וְאִיהִי רְמִיזָא בְּאָת י' מִן אֲדֹנָ"י, כְּלִילָא בַּעֲשַׂר סְפִירָאן. דְּאִיהִי בְּלוּלָה בְּשֶׁמֶן כָּתִית רְבִיעִית הַהִין. וְאִיהִי בְּלוּלָה, בַּמִּקְרָא, בַּמִּשְׁנָה, בַּתַּלְמוּד, בְּקַבָּלָה.

247. And the end of the verse continues: "and a tenth part of an efah of fine flour" (Bemidbar 28:5). That is, happy is he who draws down from his brain a drop of clean refined flour without impurity and waste, AT THE TIME OF THE MATING, and this is hinted at in the letter Yud of Adonai, AND THAT IS WHY IT SAYS 'A TENTH PART' that includes the ten Sfirot. And she is to be "mingled with a fourth part of a hin of beaten oil" (Ibid.). That is, it is mingled from FOUR, NAMELY, Scripture, Mishnah, Talmud, and Kabbalah, ON WHICH THE RIGHTEOUS BEAT THEMSELVES AND SO RAISE UP THE FEMALE WATERS FOR ITS UNION.

45. The Chariot of Ezekiel

A Synopsis

The Faithful Shepherd tells us about Ezekiel's ten visions of Metatron, and we hear a good deal about the meaning of the color blue and why it is so important in the Tzitzit and the Talit. Through the sacred numerical meaning of many words and letters we are led through an explanation of the throne and the sapphire stone and the six steps and the four beasts and the four faces. We are told that Metatron includes all the stages downwards from above and upwards from below.

The Relevance of this Passage

The Zohar's description of Ezekiel's vision lifts our soul into the warm, protective embrace of the Shechinah (the Divine Presence), revealing the full splendor of Light that shines from the Ten Sfirot.

The Angelic name of *Metatron,* we are told, conceals the Hebrew word for *life* (CHET YOD **חי**, pronounced "Chai" in English), whose numerical value is eighteen.

The number 18 is achieved through the two Hebrew letters TET **ט** ("t" in English) that appear in the name Metatron. The Hebrew letter TET has the numerical value of nine. Thus, the two TETs = eighteen (nine + nine =eighteen).

Moreover, *Metatron,* as we have learned in earlier passages, embodies the concept of the restoration of youth and immortality. Thus, the power of life, of immortality, and the reversal of the aging process permeates the cells and soul of our body. This indestructible life-force flows to us from the Sfirah (dimension) of *Yesod.* As it fills our material realm, the Angel of Death and the forces of chaos are vanquished from existence.

In paragraph 250, it is said that a mighty, wise, and rich man is one who has the might to overcome his ego, who is spiritually wise, and who is rich with the tools that are needed to triumph over his negative side. Accordingly, Kabbalistic might, wisdom, and wealth are bestowed upon us in great measure, ensuring answers to all our prayers for peace, prosperity, and eternal happiness.

The Zohar goes on to explain in paragraph 252 that *Malchut* – our world – is signified by the color blue, as is Metatron, and it corresponds to the ultimate objective – the perfection of all Creation. This heavenly blue flame now washes over all existence as the final perfection is consummated by the very eyes that pour over these supernal verses.

We also learn that this cosmic blue color correlates to "the blue flame in a burning candle, which consumes the fatty parts of the burnt offerings." Hence, the fires of the ancient sacrifices are lit and set aflame in this passage as well. The healing Light associated with heart disease shines forth. Deadly fats that obstruct the arteries are burned away. Our blood is purified. Anger and other negative emotions are extracted from our hearts and liver. As with all passages of the Zohar, we can also meditate to share this healing blue flame with all those who suffer cardiovascular and liver ailments. Our action of sharing burns away all the negative and evil forces from the world, clearing the way for the ultimate healing of humanity.

Moreover, Yisrael corresponds to the human heart, while the other nations of the world correspond to the human anatomy. Thus, the spiritual arteries – the relationships between Yisrael and all nations – are enriched as negative blockages and points of conflict are eradicated, creating the opening for world peace and global harmony.

Paragraph 253 associates the color blue with the sapphire stone. Whoever "inherits this stone," the Zohar states, is protected from the fires of Hell. This protection is now bestowed upon us. The fires of Hell are eternally extinguished by the power of the blue Light and our remorseful reading of these verses.

Meditating upon paragraphs 254 and 255 shields us from negative beings who dwell in other worlds and from the flames ablaze in Hell. The 248 parts of our body and soul receive the Light of Healing that shines from the prayer known as the *Sh'ma Yisrael*. Moreover, a great secret concerning the *Tetragrammaton* (*Yud Hei Vav Hei*) and *Adonai* is revealed. It is stated that:

> THE YUD HEI VAV HEI IS THE SECRET OF WHITE, WHILE ADONAI IS THE SECRET OF BLUE, THUS COMBINING Mercy and Judgment.

When one reads the *Tetragrammaton*, one actually utters the word *Adonai*. This indicates a union between the Upper World of Mercy (*Yud Hei Vav Hei*) and the Lower World of Judgment (*Adonai*) יאהדונהי.

In accordance, we now mitigate the force of Judgment in the world through the sweet scent of Mercy, thereby eliminating harsh decrees.

In paragraph 256, the power of the *72 Names* is ignited along with the power of life and immortality, signified by the number 18 (which is the value of the Hebrew word *Chai* חי which means *life*).

The 72 Names now release 72 different spiritual influences into the

world, among them:

• The power of mind over matter יבמ.
• The annihilation of death נית.
• The creation of order out of chaos האא.
• Unconditional love for our fellow man ייז.

• The strength of consciousness and certainty so that we do not doubt or become skeptical of all these benefits. ערי.

Paragraph 257 again speaks of the angel known as *Metatron* and the Sfirah of *Yesod*. Through these words, the aging process is arrested, as the concept and truth of immortality and eternal youth is emblazoned into our consciousness.

The complete revelation of Light that accompanies the observance of the 613 observances and the spiritual perfection they help us attain shines brightly here.

In the remaining segments of this passage, many deep mysteries are expounded upon. The number 13 is mentioned. The numerical value for the Hebrew word for *one* (אחד echad) is thirteen. The numerical value for the Hebrew word for *love* (אהבה ahava) is also thirteen. And thirteen is the numerical value for the Hebrew word for *to care* (דאגה deaga).

Thus, we learn from the Zohar that if one really cares for another person, then he will unconditionally love that person and then they are one!

This wonderful but simple spiritual insight engenders love and unity among all human beings.

The number 32 spoken of in the Zohar signifies the 22 Hebrew letters and the ten Sfirot. And 45 refers to Adam, our root and source. Thus, the full spiritual power of the letters and the entire spectrum of Light that shines through the Sfirot lights up our soul and all mankind.

All of these magnificent, awe-inspiring benefits are common features of the age of Messiah, which now dawns before our eyes (appropriately through the power of our eyes) as we allow them to pore over the holy words inscribed on these pages.

248. יְחֶזְקֵאל כַּד חָמָא שְׁכִינְתָּא מִגּוֹ קְלִיפִין, חֲזָא עִמָּה עֲשַׂר סְפִירָאן. בְּלָא פְרוּדָא כְּלָל. וְאַלֵּין אִינּוּן מוֹחָא, מִלְגוֹ, כֻּלְהוּ חָזָא לוֹן מִגּוֹ נְהַר כְּבָר דִּלְתַתָּא, אִיהִי רֶכֶב אֱלֹהִים רִבּוֹתַיִם, כָּל רִבּוֹא עֲשַׂר אַלְפִין,

רבוֹתַיִם כ׳ אֶלֶף, אָפִיק תְּרֵי שְׁאֵינָן, אִשְׁתָּאֲרוּ תְּמְנֵי סָר, בְּחוּשְׁבַּן ח״י
עָלְמִין. דְּכָלִיל עֶשֶׂר סְפִירָאן, דְּאִתְלַבֵּשׁ בְּט״ט מִן מְטַטְרוֹן. ט״ט מִן
טֹטָפֹת, וְאִתְּמַר בֵּיהּ וְהָיוּ לְטֹטָפֹת בֵּין עֵינֶיךָ. מַאן עַיְינִין. אִלֵּין לְעֵילָא,
דְּאִתְּמַר בְּהוּ נִפְתְּחוּ הַשָּׁמַיִם וָאֶרְאֶה מַרְאוֹת אֱלֹהִים. מַאן מַרְאוֹת.
אִלֵּין אִינּוּן עֶשְׂרָה מַרְאוֹת דִּמְטַטְרוֹן, דְּחָזָא כִּשְׁרָגָא בְּגוֹ עֲשִׁישִׁתָּא.
תֵּשַׁע בְּאִתְגַּלְיָיא, וְחַד סָתִים.

248. When Ezekiel saw the Shechinah among the Klipot, THAT IS TO SAY, AMONG THE GARMENTS, he saw with Her ten Sfirot, without any separation whatsoever, and these are the brain that is among all of them. He saw them within the earthly river K'var (Caf Bet Resh), NAMELY, THE EARTHLY CHARIOT (RESH CAF BET), NAMELY, THE LETTERS OF K'VAR REARRANGED) OF METATRON. That is, "The Chariots of Elohim are twice ten thousand, thousands UPON THOUSANDS (HEB. SHIN'AN)" (Tehilim 68:18). "twice ten thousand" are twenty thousand. From this you should deduct two that are missing, AS SHIN'AN IS SPELLED THE SAME AS 'SHE'EINAN' (MISSING). "(SHIN'AN) THOUSANDS" ARE THE MISSING TWO THOUSANDS. Eighteen thousand remain, which is as the number of the eighteen (Chet Yud) worlds. THIS IS YESOD, WHICH IS CALLED 'CHAI' (ENG. 'LIVING' - CHET YUD,), which includes the ten Sfirot, attired in the Tet Tet (nine + nine = eighteen) of Metatron (Mem Tet Tet Resh Vav Nun). And this Tet Tet is taken from the word *totafot* (Eng. 'frontlets'), about which it is said: "and they shall be as frontlets between your eyes" (Devarim 6:8). Who are the eyes? They are those above, about which it is said: "the heavens were opened, and I saw visions of Elohim" (Yechezkel 1:1). These are the ten visions of Metatron, whom Ezekiel saw as a candle within a lantern, nine OF THE VISIONS being clear, with one being vague.

249. מַרְאָה חֲדָא דְּאִיהוּ חֵזוּ קַדְמָאָה מֵאִלֵּוּ עֲשָׂרָה, דָּא אִיהוּ דְּאִתְּמַר
בֵּיהּ, וּמִמַּעַל לָרָקִיעַ אֲשֶׁר עַל רֹאשָׁם כְּמַרְאֵה אֶבֶן סַפִּיר דְּמוּת כִּסֵּא.
וְאע״ג דְּאִתְפָּרֵשׁ לְעֵילָא, צָרִיךְ לְחַדְתָּא עָלֵיהּ מִלִּין דְּחִדּוּשִׁין.

249. One vision that he saw at the beginning of those ten VISIONS was the one about which it is said: "And above the firmament that was over their heads was the likeness of a throne, in appearance like a sapphire stone" (Yechezkel 1:26). Although this VERSE has already been explained before,

new things have to be said about it.

250. אָמַר קוּדְשָׁא בְּרִיךְ הוּא, לְמַשִׁרְיָין דִּלְעֵילָא, מַאן דִּמְצַלֵי, בֵּין יְהֵא גִבּוֹר, בֵּין יְהֵא חָכָם, בֵּין יְהֵא עָשִׁיר. בְּזַכְוָון גִּבּוֹר. חָכָם בַּתּוֹרָה. וְעָשִׁיר בַּמִּצְוֹת. לָא יֵיעוּל בְּהֵיכָלָא דָּא צְלוֹתֵיהּ, עַד דְּתִתְחֲזוּן בֵּיהּ סִימָנִין אִלֵּין, דְּיָהַב גַּרְמֵיהּ בֵּיהּ תִּקּוּנִין דִּילִי. וּבְגִין דָּא אוֹקְמוּהָ מָארֵי מַתְנִיתִין, אִם הָרַב דּוֹמֶה לְמַלְאַךְ יְיָ' צְבָאוֹת תּוֹרָה יְבַקְשׁוּ מִפִּיהוּ. לְמַאן דְּיְהֵא רָשִׁים בְּאִלֵּין סִימָנִין בִּלְבוּשֵׁיהּ, תְּקַבְּלוּן צְלוֹתֵיהּ. סִימָנָא חֲדָא דְּיְהֵא רָשִׁים בִּצְלוֹתֵיהּ, בִּתְכֵלֶת, בְּכַנְפֵי מִצְוָה צִיצִית. דְּאִיהוּ דָּמֵי לָרָקִיעַ, דְּאִיהוּ מְטַטְרוֹן. דִּיּוּקְנָא דִּילֵיהּ, תְּכֵלֶת שֶׁבַּצִּיצִית.

250. The Holy One, blessed be He, said to the heavenly encampments: 'Anyone who prays, whether he be a mighty man, a wise man, or a rich man; if he is mighty in merits BECAUSE HE OVERCOMES HIS INCLINATION; a wise man in Torah; and a rich man who is rich in the precepts, do not allow his prayer to enter this chamber until there is seen in him these signs: that he has applied My tools to himself.' For this reason, the sages of the Mishnah taught: If the rabbi is like an angel of Hashem Tzva'ot, let people come to consult him in matters of the Torah. IN OTHER WORDS, you may accept the prayer of anyone who is impressed with these signs in his dress: One sign is that he should be marked in his prayer with the blue of the FOUR corners of his fringes, for blue is like the firmament, which is Metatron, AND IT WOULD THEN FOLLOW THAT HE WOULD BE LIKE AN ANGEL OF HASHEM TZVA'OT, whose form is the blue that is in the fringes (Tzitzit).

251. וּבְגִין דָּא, שִׁעוּר הַצִּיצִית אוֹקְמוּהָ רַבָּנָן, טַלִּית שֶׁהַקָּטָן מִתְכַּסֶּה בָּהּ רֹאשׁוֹ וְרוּבּוֹ. וְהַאי אִיהוּ דְּאִתְּמַר בֵּיהּ, וְנַעַר קָטֹן נוֹהֵג בָּם. וְהַאי אִיהוּ נוֹהֵג בְּד' חַיָּין, דְּאִינּוּן ד', וְאִיהוּ כָּלִיל שֵׁשׁ מַעֲלוֹת לַכִּסֵּא, דְּאִינּוּן ו'. וּבְגִין דְּאִיהוּ כָּלִיל עֶשֶׂר, מִתְלַבְּשִׁין בֵּיהּ עֶשֶׂר סְפִירָאן, י'. וּבֵיהּ הֲוָה אִתְחֲזֵי קוּדְשָׁא בְּרִיךְ הוּא בִּשְׁכִינְתֵּיהּ, דְּאִיהִי כְּלִילָא מֵעֲשַׂר סְפִירָאן, לִנְבִיאֵי. וּמִסִּטְרָא דִּשְׁכִינְתָּא דְּאִיהִי עֲשִׁירָאָה, תְּכֵלֶת שֶׁבַּצִּיצִית, אִיהוּ תְּכֵלֶת דְּכָל גַּוְונִין.

251. And for this reason the sages set the size for fringes and taught about a cloak (Talit) that a minor wears and which covers his head and most of his body. This is the same as was said about it: "and a little child shall lead them" (Yeshayah 11:6), WHICH ALLUDES TO METATRON, THAT IS CALLED 'A LITTLE CHILD'. He leads the four living creatures, and includes "The throne had six steps" (I Melachim 10:19), NAMELY, CHESED, GVURAH, TIFERET, NETZACH, HOD AND YESOD, which are six. And since he is composed of ten, the ten Sfirot OF ZEIR ANPIN AND MALCHUT OF ATZILUT attire themselves in him, for they, too, are ten. And through him the Holy One, blessed be He, appears in His Shechinah to the prophets, for He is composed of ten Sfirot. And from the side of the Shechinah, WHICH METATRON SERVES AS GARMENT TO, which is the tenth SFIRAH and the blue of the fringes, METATRON ALSO appears as the blue of all colors, THAT IS TO SAY: ALL THE COLORS WERE INCLUDED IN THIS BLUE.

252. דְּאִיהִי תַּכְלִית דִּי' סְפִירָאן. וּבֵיה וַתֵּכֶל כָּל עֲבוֹדַת אֹהֶל מוֹעֵד. וְאִיהִי לָשׁוֹן כַּלָה. הה״ד, וַיְהִי בְּיוֹם כַּלֹת מֹשֶׁה לְהָקִים אֶת הַמִשְׁכָּן. וְאוֹקְמוּהָ רַבָּנָן, כַּלֹת כְּתִיב, וְאִיהוּ תְּכֵלֶת דְּשַׁרְגָּא, דְּאָכִיל תִּרְבִּין וְעֶלְוָון.

252. For it, MALCHUT THAT IS CALLED 'BLUE' (HEB. *T'CHELET*), is the perfection (Heb. *tachlit*) ending of the ten Sfirot, and in it "Thus was all the work of the tabernacle of the Tent of Meeting finished (Heb. *vatechel*)" (Shemot 39:32), SINCE IT IS THE ENDING OF EVERYTHING. AND THE WORD T'CHELET is derived from 'finish (Heb. *calh*)', as it is written: "And it came to pass on the day that Moses finished (Heb. *calot*) setting up the tabernacle" (Bemidbar 7:1). And the sages interpreted 'calat' AS DERIVED FROM 'CALAH (LIT. 'BRIDE'). THIS IS WHY THE SHECHINAH IS CONSIDERED BLUE, and is the blue flame in a candle, which consumes the fatty parts of the burnt offerings.

253. וְעָלֶיהָ אָמַר יְחֶזְקֵאל דְּמוּת כְּמַרְאֵה אֶבֶן סַפִּיר דְּמוּת כִּסֵּא. סְגוּלָה דְּהַאי אֶבֶן, מַאן דְּיָרִית לָהּ, לָא שַׁלְטָא נוּרָא דְּגֵיהִנָּם עָלֵיהּ. לֵית נוּרָא בְּעָלְמָא מְקַלְקֵל לָהּ, וְלָא כָּל מִינֵי מַתְכוֹת. כָּל שֶׁכֵּן מַיָּא, דְּלָא מַזִּיקוּ לָהּ. מַאן דְּיָרִית לָהּ, אִתְקַיָּים בֵּיהּ כִּי תַעֲבוֹר בַּמַּיִם אִתְּךָ אָנִי וְגו'. וְכָל

עֲלָאִין וְתַתָּאִין דְּסִטְרָא אַחֲרָא דַּחֲלִין מִנֵּיהּ. תְּכֵלֶת דְּיַמָּא בְּגִינֵיהּ
אִתְּמַר, כִּי תַעֲבוֹר בַּמַּיִם אִתְּךָ אָנִי. דִּבְסְגוּלָה דָּא, סוּס וְרוֹכְבוֹ רָמָה
בַיָּם, דָּא מְמָנָא דְּמִצְרַיִם.

253. And about her, NAMELY ABOUT THE LIGHT of CHOCHMAH IN HER, THAT IS CALLED 'BLUE', Ezekiel said: "the likeness of a throne, in appearance like a sapphire stone" (Yechezkel 1:26); and the virtue of this stone is that, whoever receives it, the fire of Gehenom has no control over him, and there is no flame in the world that can damage it, nor any type of metal, FOR IF ONE HITS THIS SAPPHIRE STONE WITH A HAMMER, THE HAMMER WILL BREAK BUT THE STONE WILL BE UNDAMAGED, AS THE SAGES SAID. Water all the more can not harm it. THUS, for whoever inherits it the verse "When you pass through the waters, I will be with you" (Yeshayah 43:2) will be upheld, and all the upper and lower beings of the Other Side are fearful of him. It was also for the blue of the sea that it was said: "When you pass through the waters, I will be with you," for with this special attribute, THE BLUE LIGHT OF MALCHUT THAT IS CALLED 'SAPPHIRE STONE', "the horse and his rider has He thrown into the sea" (Shemot 15:1), for it is the minister appointed over Egypt WHO DROWNED IN THE SEA BY MEANS OF THIS BLUE LIGHT.

254. מִגָּווֶן דָּא, דַּחֲלִין עֲלָאִין וְתַתָּאִין. מַשְׁרְיָין דְּיַמָּא דַּחֲלִין מִנֵּיהּ. וּמַשְׁרְיָין דִּרְקִיעָא דְּאִיהוּ תְּכֵלֶת, מִנֵּיהּ דַּחֲלִין. מַשְׁרְיָין דִּתְכֵלֶת דְּנוּרָא דְּגֵיהִנָּם דַּחֲלִין מִנֵּיהּ.

254. From this BLUE color the upper and lower beings are fearful; the encampments of the sea are fearful of it, and the encampments of the firmament, which is blue, hold it in awe, as do the encampments of the blue fire of Gehenom, NAMELY THE BLUE OF THE OTHER SIDE.

255. וְהַאי תְּכֵלֶת אִיהוּ דִין. דִּינָא אֲדֹנָ"י. דִּינָא דְּמַלְכוּתָא דִּינָא וּתְרֵין גַּוְונִין רְשִׁימִין בְּטַלִּית, חַד חִוָּור, וְחַד תְּכֵלֶת. וְעַל תְּרֵין גַּוְונִין אִלֵּין אִתְּמַר, וְתַחַת רַגְלָיו כְּמַעֲשֵׂה לִבְנַת הַסַּפִּיר. לִבְנַת, לוֹבֶן דְּסַפִּיר. דְּאִיהוּ כָּלִיל בִּתְרֵין גַּוְונִין, רַחֲמֵי וְדִינָא, חִוָּור וְאוּכָם. אוּכְמוּ דִּתְכֵלֶת. וְעַל תְּרֵין גַּוְונִין, רְמִיזוּ רַבָּנָן, מֵאֵימָתַי קוֹרִין אֶת שְׁמַע בְּשַׁחֲרִית, מִשֶּׁיַּכִּיר

בֵּין תְּכֵלֶת לְלָבָן. לְמֶהֱוֵי בְּרַתָּא דְּמַלְכָּא, ק״ש, יְחוּדָא דְקוּדְשָׁא בְּרִיךְ
הוּא, כָּלִיל מִתְּרֵין גַּוְונִין אִלֵּין, דְּאִינוּן יְדֹנ״ד אֲדֹנָ״י, רַחֲמֵי וְדִינָא.
כְּגַוְונָא דְקוּדְשָׁא בְּרִיךְ הוּא כָּלִיל בּ׳ גַּוְונִין, יְהֹנ״ה אֲדֹנָ״י לְמֶהֱוֵי רַחֲמֵי
וְדִינָא, כֻּסֵּא דִין וְכֻסֵּא רַחֲמִים.

255. And this blue is Judgment, FOR THE NAME OF MALCHUT IS 'ADONAI', THE LETTERS OF WHICH CAN BE REARRANGED AS *DINA* (ENG. 'LAW'), and this is the inner meaning of the saying that the law of the kingdom is indeed the law. The Talit (prayer-shawl) has two colors: white and blue, and in respect to these two colors it is said: "and there was under his feet a kind of paved work of sapphire stone" (Shemot 24:10). *Livnat* (Eng. 'paved work') is the white (Eng. 'lavan') of the sapphire, because the sapphire is composed of two colors, which are Mercy and Judgment, namely white, WHICH IS MERCY, and black, from which comes the darkness of the blue. And the sages hinted at THESE two colors when they asked: 'From what time in the morning may the Sh'ma Yisrael be recited? As soon as one can distinguish between blue and white'. For the daughter of the King, WHICH IS MALCHUT, WHICH IS THE SECRET OF the recital of the Sh'ma, which is the unity of the Holy One, blessed be He, is composed of these two colors, WHITE AND BLUE, which are Yud Hei Vav Hei Adonai. YUD HEI VAV HEI IS THE SECRET OF WHITE, WHILE ADONAI IS THE SECRET OF BLUE, SO THERE ARE BOTH Mercy and Judgment. Similarly, the Holy One, blessed be He, WHO IS ZEIR ANPIN, is composed of two colors, WHICH IS THE SECRET OF Yud Hei Vav Hei Adonai, being Mercy and Judgment, namely the Throne of Mercy and the Throne of Judgment.

256. כְּמַרְאֵה אֶבֶן סַפִּיר דְּמוּת כֻּסֵּא. מַאי דְּמוּת כֻּסֵּא. אֶלָּא לְקַבֵּל
כֻּרְסְיָיא, דְּאִית לֵיהּ ע״ב גְּשָׁרִים. דְּיֶהֱא ב״ן רָשִׁים בְּע״ב קְשָׁרִים,
וְחוּלְיָין דְּצִיצִית, לָקֳבֵל ע״ב גְּשָׁרִים דְּכֻרְסְיָיא. דְּאִינוּן ח״י קְשָׁרִים,
וְחוּלְיָין לְכָל סְטְרָא. דְּכֻרְסְיָיא דְּאִיהוּ ה׳, לְכָל סְטְרָא בְּד׳ חֵיוָן
דְּכֻרְסְיָיא, דְּאִינוּן ד׳.

256. "the likeness of a throne, in appearance like a sapphire stone" (Yechezkel 1:26): HE ASKS, IF THE SAPPHIRE STONE IS THE BLUE OF THE FRINGES, what, then, is "the likeness of a throne"? HE ANSWERS THAT

it corresponds to the throne that has 72 bridges, NAMELY 72 LIGHTS FROM THE NAME OF 72. So should a person be noted for the 72 knots and links in his fringes, corresponding to the 72 bridges of the throne. These are the eighteen knots and links on each side OF THE FOUR CORNERS OF HIS GARMENT, THAT IS, FIVE KNOTS AND THIRTEEN LINKS, AND FOUR TIMES EIGHTEEN IS 72. For the throne which is Hei, NAMELY MALCHUT, is on each corner, in the four living creatures of the throne, and they are four, PARALLEL TO THE FOUR CORNERS OF HIS RAIMENT.

257. וְשִׁית דַּרְגִּין דְּכָרְסְיָיא, דְּאִינוּן ו', וְדָא מְטַטְרוֹן, אִיהוּ כָּלִיל ד' חֵיוָון. הה"ד וְנַעַר קָטֹן נוֹהֵג בָּם. וְאִינוּן מִיכָאֵל גַּבְרִיאֵל נוּרִיאֵל רְפָאֵל. מְטַטְרוֹן שֵׁשׁ מַעֲלוֹת לַכִּסֵּא, דְּסַלְקִין שִׁית מְאָה, צִיצִית בִּתְרֵין יוֹדִי"ן. וְאִי חָסֵר יוֹד, הָא חִירֵק בְּאַתְרֵיהּ, הָכִי סַלְקָא. בְּכָל סִטְרָא בְּד' כַּנְפֵי, צִיצִית וּתְלַת עֲשַׂר חֻלְיָין דְּצִיצִית, אִינוּן תרי"ג.

257. And the six steps of the throne, which are Vav (= 6), which is Metatron, which includes four living creatures, as it is said: "and a little child shall lead them" (Yeshayah 11:6), they being Michael, Gabriel, Nuriel and Raphael. And Metatron is "The throne had six steps" (I Melachim 10:19), WHICH ARE CHESED, GVURAH, TIFERET, NETZACH, HOD AND YESOD, EACH OF WHICH IS COMPOSED OF A HUNDRED, totaling six hundred in all. Tzitzit (Eng. 'fringes'), WHEN WRITTEN OUT FULL, with two Yud's, has the numerical value OF SIX HUNDRED. And if THE WORD TZITZIT is written in the abbreviated SPELLING, with one Yud omitted, then the Chirik IS LIKE A YUD AND makes up for its omission. And on each side of the four corners of his garment there is a fringe WITH THE NUMERICAL EQUIVALENT OF 600, which, together its the thirteen links, makes 613.

258. וְעוֹד. שֵׁשׁ מַעֲלוֹת לַכִּסֵּא, בְּרָזָא דָּא וָא"ו, סָלִיק לְחֻשְׁבַּן י"ג, דְּאִתְרְמִיז בִּתְלַת תֵּיבִין, וַיִּסַּע וַיָּבֹא וַיֵּט. דְּאִינוּן וְהוּא אֲנִי וָהוּ. חָמֵשׁ קָשְׁרִין, ה' לְכָל סִטְרָא. א' טַלִּית חַד לְכֻלְּהוּ. וּבָאֵת ה' אִשְׁתְּלִים ח"י. דְּאִינוּן ט"ט. לְמֶהֱוֵי חַיָּה לְכָל סִטְרָא. כָּלִיל ד' חַיּוֹת. וּלְכָל חַיָּה, אַרְבַּע אַנְפִּין, וְאַרְבַּע גַּדְפִּין, אִינוּן ל"ב אַנְפִּין וְגַדְפִּין. וְאִינוּן תַּלְיָין מֵחַיָּה דְּאִיהוּ אָדָם.

258. In addition, "The throne had six steps": IS VAV, AND with the inner meaning OF ITS BEING SPELED OUT IN FULL, is Vav Aleph Vav; its numerical value being 13. AND THIS VAV ALEPH VAV is hinted at in three words OF THE COMBINATION OF 72 WORDS INCLUDED IN THE THREE VERSES: "And the angel Elohim, who went before the camp of Yisrael, (Heb. *vayisa*) removed...and it came between...(Heb. *vayavo*). And Moses stretched out...(Heb. *vayet*)" (Shemot 14:19-21). And these THREE WORDS are *Vahu* – Vav Hei Vav, *Ani* – Aleph Nun Yud, *Vahu* – Vav Hei Vav, THE INITIAL LETTERS OF WHICH ARE: VAV, ALEPH, VAV. AND THERE ARE Hei (= 5) knots ON THE FRINGE, namely Hei on each side OF THE FOUR CORNERS OF THE GARMENT. AND THE FULL SPELLING OF HEI, WHICH IS Aleph, is the garment itself, WHICH IS one for all of them. And with the letter Hei THAT IS JOINED WITH THE VAV ALEPH VAV, THAT AMOUNTS TO 13, the total comes to chai (= 18), which is the Tet Tet (nine + nine = eighteen) OF METATRON. AND EIGHTEEN, CHAI, HINTS AT CHAYAH, A LIVING CREATURE, one living creature on each side OF THE FOUR CORNERS, AND WHICH IS comprised of four living creatures, FOR THE FOUR CORNERS COMPRISE EACH OTHER, each living creature having four countenances and four wings, making A TOTAL OF 32 countenances and wings, all of which are dependent on the FOURTH OF THE FOUR living creatures that is THE FACE OF a man, NAMELY A MAN WEARING FRINGES.

259. וְאִינּוּן ל"ב, כְּחוּשְׁבַּן יוֹ"ד הֵ"א הֵ"א. שְׁלִימוּ דִּלְהוֹן, וָא"ו. תְּלֵיסַר חוּלְיָין בְּכָל ד' כַּנְפֵי, וְהוּא"ו מִתְיַיחֵד עִם כָּל אַרְבַּע חַיוֹת, וְאַשְׁלִים לְעֵילָא, אַשְׁלִים לְתַתָּא. עַמוּדָא דְּאֶמְצָעִיתָא אִיהוּ מְטַטְרוֹן, לְאַשְׁלְמָא לְעֵילָא, כְּגַוְונָא דְּתִפְאֶרֶת, שְׁמֵיהּ כְּשֵׁם רַבֵּיהּ. בְּצַלְמוֹ כִּדְמוּתוֹ אִתְבְּרֵי. דְּאִיהוּ כָּלִיל כָּל דַּרְגִּין, מֵעֵילָא לְתַתָּא, וּמִתַּתָּא לְעֵילָא. וְאִיהוּ אָחִיד בְּאֶמְצָעִיתָא. הה"ד, וְהַבְּרִיחַ הַתִּיכוֹן בְּתוֹךְ הַקְּרָשִׁים מַבְרִיחַ מִן הַקָּצֶה אֶל הַקָּצֶה.

259. And these, THE FRINGES, are 32 in number, AS EXPLAINED ABOVE, as is the numerical value of Yud-Vav-Dalet, Hei-Aleph, Hei-Aleph, their complement being Vav Aleph Vav, namely thirteen links of each of the four corners. And the Vav Aleph Vav unites with all the four living creatures OF THE FOUR CORNERS, and completes THE NAME YUD-VAV-DALET, HEI-ALEPH, VAV-ALEPH-VAV, HEI-ALEPH above IN ZEIR ANPIN and MALCHUT OF ATZILUT, and completes it below IN THE LIVING

CREATURES. For the purpose of the Central Column, which is Metatron, is to complete above like Tiferet OF ATZILUT, for METATRON'S name is as that of his Master, TIFERET, in whose image and according to whose likeness he was created. For he, METATRON, includes all the grades downwards from above, SINCE TIFERET AND MALCHUT OF ATZILUT ARE ATTIRED IN HIM, and also upwards from below, NAMELY INCLUDING ALL FOUR OF THE HOLY LIVING CREATURES, MICHAEL, GABRIEL, NURIEL, RAPHAEL and is attached to the center, as it is said: "And the middle bar in the midst of the boards shall reach from end to end" (Shemot 26:28).

260. וְאִיהוּ כָּלִיל ד' אַנְפִּין, וְאַרְבַּע גַּדְפִין דְּכָל חַיָּה וְחַיָּה דִּלְעֵילָא, דְּאִינּוּן, יְאֲדֹנָהִי. אָז יָשִׁיר מֹשֶׁה. בְּכָל חַיָּה אַרְבַּע אַנְפִּין, וְאַרְבַּע גַּדְפִין, כְּגַוְונָא דָא. א"ז בְּאַרְיֵה. א"ז בְּשׁוֹר. א"ז בַּנֶּשֶׁר. א"ז בָּאָדָם. דְּאִינּוּן ל"ב אַנְפִּין וְגַדְפִין, בְּחוּשְׁבַּן א"ז ד' זִמְנִין.

260. And he, METATRON, is made up of the four countenances and the four wings of each of the living creatures above IN MALE AND FEMALE, which are Yud-Aleph-Hei-Dalet-Vav-Nun-Hei-Yud, NAMELY THE COMBINATION OF THE TWO NAMES: YUD HEI VAV HEI AND ADONAI, WHICH ARE ZEIR ANPIN AND MALCHUT. "Then (Heb. *az*) sang Moses" (Shemot 15:1), FOR ZEIR ANPIN, WHICH IS THE SECRET OF MOSES, has in each of his living creatures four countenances and four wings, WHICH HAVE THE NUMERICAL VALUE OF THE WORD *AZ* (= 8). In like manner, there is *az* in a lion, *az* in an ox, *az* in an eagle, *az* in a man, making up 32 wings and countenances, four times *az*.

261. וְאִינּוּן ד' אַנְפִּין: יְדֹנָ"ד. אַרְבַּע גַּדְפִין: אֲדֹנָי. לָקֳבֵל ד' בִּגְדֵי זָהָב, וְאַרְבַּע בִּגְדֵי לָבָן, דְּלָבִישׁ כַּהֲנָא לְכַפָּרָא עַל יִשְׂרָאֵל. לָקֳבֵל, אֲדֹנָי שְׂפָתַי תִּפְתָּח. וּצְלוֹתָא. דִּתְפִלָּה יְדֹנָ"ד, בַּחֲתִימָה ח"י בִּרְכָאן דִּצְלוֹתָא. וְתִמְנֵי סְרֵי זִמְנִין יְדֹנָ"ד, אִית בְּהוֹן ע"ב אַתְוָון, בְּחוּשְׁבַּן וַיְכֻלּוּ, דִּכְלִילָן בְּצַדִּיק ח"י עָלְמִין.

261. And these four countenances are THE FOUR LETTERS OF Yud Hei Vav Hei, and the four wings ARE THE FOUR LETTERS OF Adonai, that stand for the four garments of gold, WHICH IS THE SECRET OF ADONAI, and the four

garments of white, WHICH IS THE SECRET OF YUD HEI VAV HEI, the priest wore to make atonement for Yisrael. And they stand for "Adonai, open my lips" (Tehilim 51:17), WHICH IS SAID AT THE BEGINNING OF THE AMIDAH PRAYER. And the prayer ITSELF has in each of the eighteen blessings Yud Hei Vav Hei at the end. Thus Yud Hei Vav Hei occurs eighteen times, which makes a total of 72 letters, which is the same as the numerical value of "And (they) were finished (Heb. *vaychulu*)" (Beresheet 2:1). AND THIS IS THE SECRET OF YESOD, WHICH IS CALLED '*KOL*' (ENG. 'ALL'), FOR EIGHTEEN YUD HEI VAV HEI are included in the Righteous that lives forever, WHICH IS THE SECRET OF "*VAYCHULU*."

262. וּבְאַרְבַּע חִיוָן, יְדוָ"ד אֲדֹנָי. תְּמָנֵי לְכָל סִטְרָא, אִינּוּן ל"ב אַתְוָון, וי"ג אַתְוָון, דְּאִשְׁתְּכָחוּ מִן וָה"ו אֲנִי וָה"ו, הָא תְּלַת עֲשַׂר, דְּכְלִילָן עֵילָא וְתַתָּא. בְּהוֹן אִשְׁתְּלִים אָדָם, דְּאִיהוּ מ"ה, עַמּוּדָא דְּאֶמְצָעִיתָא.

262. And EACH ONE OF the four living creatures CONTAINS Yud Hei Vav Hei Adonai, namely a total of eight LETTERS on each direction, that is, a total of 32 letters. And there are thirteen letters IN THE INITIALS OF THE THREE WORDS, Vav-Hei-Vav, Aleph-Nun-Yud, Vav-Hei-Vav, WHICH ARE VAV-ALEPH-VAV, HAVING THE NUMERICAL VALUE OF THIRTEEN. And it is thirteen, since the upper and lower beings are included in this Vav-Aleph-Vav, AS EXPLAINED ABOVE, complete man, which is the Central Column. FOR THE 32 LETTERS OF YUD HEI VAV HEI AND ADONAI ON EACH SIDE, TOGETHER WITH THE THIRTEEN OF THE VAV ALEPH VAV, COME TO 45, THE NUMERICAL VALUE OF *ADAM* (ENG. 'MAN').

46. The four Klipot surrounding the four living creatures

A Synopsis

The Faithful Shepherd tells us about the Klipot that surround the four beasts of Metatron, saying that they are "formless" and "void" and "thin" and "the deep." He compares the milling of wheat to remove the bran with the Halachah that refines Torah matters and provides food for the soul. He talks about the four archangels who control man's four good elements: water, fire, wind and earth, and the four Klipot: sin, destruction, anger and wrath. When these Klipot move away from man the Tree of Life takes control of him. In every part of the body is found water, the firmament, the spirit and the earth, and all the parts of the body are open to welcome the spirit. Were the spirit not to blow in the heart, the fire in the heart would burn up the whole body.

The Relevance of this Passage

We are now connected to the Tree of Life reality, the realm known as *Zeir Anpin,* which banishes all the *klippot* (negative blockages) from our being. Our bodies and souls are refined and made clean through the power of the Torah's precepts. The Light of Immortality is set aflame forever nourishing and rejuvenating our hearts and brains and the entire spiritual and corporeal essence of a man.

In paragraphs 267-269 our lungs and heart are healed of illnesses. Through the merit and might of Elijah the Prophet and King David's psalms, we subjugate the negative influences ('A Storm Wind'). These 'Storm Winds' are the ultimate cause behind all sickness, anger, fury, rage and wrath, and they are purged from our hearts and minds. This ensures our connection to 'heaven', the Light of the Tree of Life, and the perfection that this realm embodies.

David's psalms, we are told:
"amount to the 72 countenances, THAT IS 72 LIGHTS".

Here the Light influences the physiology of the body and our heart rate. The 72 'Lights' correspond to the medically accepted average heart rate of 72 beats per minute which engenders cardiovascular efficiency and, in turn, good health. Sin, destruction, anger and wrath are purged from our hearts and the entire world.

72 also correlates to the 72 Nations. Our read of this section sends Light from Israel to all mankind, specifically the Arab Nations (Ishmael) and the Christians (Edom), engendering goodwill, peace and brotherly love between the children of Israel and their Arab and Christian brothers. In turn, this action strengthens our own

heart (Israel) and heals our entire body (72 Nations) for each of us is a microcosm of civilization.

Paragraph 270 purges the death force from our body and banishes the Angel of Death from the world through the merit of the angels, *Michael, Gavriel, Nuriel, and Refael.*

Paragraph 271 states:

> Immediately, when these FOUR Klipot move away from man, the Tree of Life takes control over him with 72 count enances OF THE ILLUMINATION OF MALCHUT,

Here our heart is healed and strengthened while anxiety and anger are eliminated from our being.

In paragraph 275 we find the following statement:

> WERE IT NOT FOR THE CENTRAL COLUMN WHICH IS CALLED 'WIND', UNITING THE RIGHT AND THE LEFT WITH EACH OTHER, THE JUDGMENT OF THE LEFT SIDE, WHICH IS THE SECRET OF THE FIRE THAT IS IN THE HEART, WOULD BURN UP THE WHOLE BODY.

The Central Column refers to our divine trait of free will which we utilize to resist 'The Left Side', our reactive, self-destructive emotions. Herein lies the fundamental secret to good health and longevity. These negative, rash and reflexive emotions, according to both medical-science and Kabbalah, cause numerous physiological changes that affect each and every cell of the body. These changes are measurable in the nervous system, hormonal system, heart and blood pressure.

The Light of this passage strengthens our free will and gives us absolute control over the negative Left Side and all of its self-destructive desires. We achieve balance, harmony, healing and ultimately, good health.

263. לְעֵילָא בְּאִילָנָא דְּחַיֵּי, לֵית, קְלִיפִין. כִּי אֵין לָבֹא אֶל שַׁעַר הַמֶּלֶךְ בִּלְבוּשׁ שָׂק. לְתַתָּא אִית קְלִיפִין בִּמְטַטְרוֹן, דְּאִיהוּ בְּדִיוּקְנָא דְּעַמוּדָא דְּאֶמְצָעִיתָא. דִּבְזִמְנָא דְּקוּדְשָׁא בְּרִיךְ הוּא לְבַר מִמַּלְכוּתֵיהּ, אִתְכַּסֵּי בְּגַדְפִין וְאַנְפִּין דְּעֲבֵד דִּילֵיהּ, הה"ד וַיִּרְכַּב עַל כְּרוּב וַיָּעֹף.

263. Above, at the Tree of Life, WHICH IS ZEIR ANPIN, there are no Klipot, for "none might enter within the king's gate clothed with sackcloth" (Ester 4:2). Lower down, at Metatron, there are Klipot, for he, METATRON, is in

the form of the Central Column, WHICH IS ZEIR ANPIN, for when the Holy
One, blessed be He, is deprived of His Malchut, NAMELY WHEN MALCHUT
IS IN EXILE, He covers himself with the countenances and wings of His
servant, WHO IS METATRON, as it is written: "And He rode upon a Cherub
and did fly" (II Shmuel 22:11), FOR METATRON IS CALLED BOTH
'CHERUB' AND 'CHARIOT'.

264. וְאִינּוּן קְלִיפִין דְּסַחֲרִין לְד' חֵיוָן דִּמְטַטְרוֹן, אִינּוּן: תֹּהוּ, וְהִנֵּה רוּחַ
גְּדוֹלָה וְחָזָק מְפָרֵק הָרִים וּמְשַׁבֵּר סְלָעִים לֹא בָרוּחַ יְיָ'. בְּה"ו, וְאַחַר
הָרוּחַ רַעַשׁ לֹא בָרַעַשׁ יְיָ', הָא תְּרֵין קְלִיפִין, יָרוֹק וְחִוָּור, דִּקְלִיפִין
דֶּאֱגוֹזָא, חַד תֹּהוּ, קַו יָרוֹק, תִּנְיָינָא בֹּהוּ, אַבְנִין מְפוּלָמִין, קְלִיפָא
תַּקִּיפָא, כְּאַבְנָא מְפוּלָמָא. לָקֳבֵל תְּרֵין קְלִיפִין אִלֵּין, מוֹץ וְתֶבֶן דְּחִטָּה.

264. And these Klipot that surround the four living creatures of Metatron
are: A) 'formless', ABOUT WHICH IS WRITTEN: "a great and strong wind rent
the mountains, and broke in pieces the rocks before Hashem; but Hashem
was not in the wind" (I Melachim 19:11). B) 'void', ABOUT WHICH IS
WRITTEN: "and after the wind an earthquake; but Hashem was not in the
earthquake" (Ibid.). These are two Klipot, WHICH ARE THE SECRET of the
green KLIPAH and the white KLIPAH of the shells of the nut. The former,
'formless', is the green line, while the latter, 'void', is smooth stones, and is
a Klipah as hard as a smooth stone. These two Klipot are also represented
by the chaff and the straw of wheat.

265. קְלִיפָא תְּלִיתָאָה, דְּקִיקָא. לָקֳבֵל סוּבִּין דְּחִטָּה, דְּהָכָא אִיהוּ
מִתְדַּבַּק בְּחִטָּה, וְלָא יָכִיל לְאִתְפָּרְשָׁא מִתַּמָּן, עַד דְּטַחֲנִין לֵיהּ בְּרֵיחַיָּיא,
דְּאִינּוּן לָקֳבֵל טוֹחֲנוֹת דְּפוּמָא דב"נ, דְּצָרִיךְ לְמִטְחַן בְּהוֹן מִלִּין
דְּאוֹרַיְיתָא, עַד דְּיִהוֹן כְּקֶמַח סֹלֶת נְקִיָּה, וּבְנָפָה דְּאִיהִי שָׂפָה, אִתְבְּרִיר
פְּסוֹלֶת דְּאִיהִי סוּבִּין דְּאוֹרַיְיתָא עַד דְּיִשְׁתְּכַח הֲלָכָה סֹלֶת נְקִיָּה. בְּהַהוּא
זִמְנָא, נָטִיל לָהּ לִבָּא וּמוֹחָא, וְכָל אֵבְרִין דְּגוּפָא דְּאִתְפְּשַׁט בְּהוֹן
נִשְׁמָתָא, וְאִתְפַּרְנְסַת בָּהּ נִשְׁמָתָא, כְּגַוְונָא דְּגוּפָא אִתְפַּרְנְסַת בְּמִלִּין
דְּעָלְמָא, דְּזֶה לְעוּמַת זֶה עָשָׂה אֱלֹהִים, נַהֲמָא דְּגוּפָא, וְנַהֲמָא
דְּאוֹרַיְיתָא. הֲדָא הוּא דִּכְתִיב, לְכוּ לַחֲמוּ בְלַחֲמִי.

265. The third Klipah THAT SURROUNDS THE FOUR LIVING CREATURES OF METATRON is thin and is represented by the bran of wheat, for here it sticks to the wheat and cannot be separated from there without grinding it in the mill-stones, which are represented by the grinding molar TEETH in a man's jaw, with which matters of Torah have to be ground until they are as fine flour. And in a sieve, which is the lips, the waste matter, which is the bran of the Torah, is sorted out, until the Halachah is as clean fine flour. At that time, the heart and the brain and all those parts of the body through which the soul spreads, take that HALACHAH WHICH IS AS CLEAN REFINED FLOUR, and the soul lives on it just as the body lives on things from the MATERIAL world. For "The Elohim has made the one as well as the other" (Kohelet 7:14): just as THERE IS food for the body, so IS THERE food for the soul, as it is written: "Come, eat of my bread" (Mishlei 9:5).

266. וְהַאי קְלִיפָא, אִיהוּ כִּקְלִיפָא דְמִתְדַּבְּקָא בְּמוֹחָא דְּאֱגוֹזָא, וּבְזִמְנָא דְּאֱגוֹזָא אִיהִי רְכִיכָא, אִתְפְּרַשׁ הַהִיא קְלִיפָא מִמּוֹחָא דְּאֱגוֹזָא, בְּלָא קוּשְׁיָא. וּבְזִמְנָא דְּאֱגוֹזָא אִיהִי יְבֵשָׁה, קָשֶׁה לב"נ לְאַעְבְּרָא לֵיהּ מִתַּמָּן, כִּי עֲדַיִין הַקּוּשְׁיָא בִּמְקוֹמָהּ עוֹמֶדֶת. וּבְגִין דָּא מָנֵי קוּדְשָׁא בְּרִיךְ הוּא לב"נ, לְאַהֲדְרָא בִּתְיוּבְתָּא בְּבַחֲרוּתֵיהּ, קוֹדֶם דְּיַזְקִין בֵּיהּ יֵצֶר הָרָע. הה"ד, מִפְּנֵי שֵׂיבָה תָּקוּם, קוֹדֶם שֵׂיבָה דִּילָךְ. וְהַאי קְלִיפָה אִיהִי אֵשׁ, וְאִתְּמַר בָּהּ וְאַחַר הָרַעַשׁ אֵשׁ לֹא בָאֵשׁ יְיָ'. רְבִיעָאָה, תְּהוֹם. חֲלָל דְּאֱגוֹזָא, בֵּיהּ קוֹל דְּמָמָה דַקָּה, תַּמָּן קָא אָתֵי מַלְכָּא, וּמִתּוֹכָהּ כְּעֵין הַחַשְׁמַל מִתּוֹךְ הָאֵשׁ.

266. And this Klipah is like the shell that sticks to the kernel of the nut, for when the nut is soft the shell separates from the kernel without difficulty, but when the nut is dry, it is difficult for man to remove it from there, and the difficult problem still remains. For this reason, the Holy One, blessed be He, commanded man to repent during his youth, before the Evil Inclination grows old within him, as it is written: "You shall rise up before the hoary head" (Vayikra 19:32), THAT IS TO SAY: Before your own old age RISE UP IN REPENTANCE. And this Klipah is fire, about which is written: "and after the earthquake a fire; but Hashem was not in the fire" (I Melachim 19:12). The fourth KLIPAH SURROUNDING THE FOUR LIVING CREATURES OF METATRON is the deep, NAMELY, "AND DARKNESS WAS ON THE FACE OF

THE DEEP" (BERESHEET 1:2). AND THIS IS THE SECRET OF the space within the nut, about which is written: "a still small voice" (I Melachim 19:12), for this is where the King comes, AND ABOUT IT IS WRITTEN: "and out of the midst of it, as it were the color of electrum, out of the midst of the fire" (Yechezkel 1:4).

267. וְאִינּוּן קְלִיפִין, אִינּוּן רְשִׁימִין בְּד' אֵבְרִים דְּגוּפָא. בְּרִיאָה, תַּמָּן לֵיחָא, דְּמִינָהּ אִשְׁתְּכָחוּ סִרְכוֹת דְּרֵיאָה, רַגְלֶיהָ יוֹרְדוֹת מָוֶת שְׁאוֹל צְעָדֶיהָ יִתְמוֹכוּ. וְתַמָּן רוּחַ חָזָק מְפָרֵק, דְּדָפִיק בְּכַנְפֵי רֵיאָה דב"ן, וְהַאי אִיהוּ רוּחָא דְּאַסְעֵיר גּוּפֵיהּ דב"ן, מַה דְּכָפַף לֵיהּ אֵלִיָּהוּ תְּחוֹתוֹי, וְסָלִיק לְעֵילָא בֵּיהּ. הה"ד, וַיַּעַל אֵלִיָּהוּ בַּסְּעָרָה הַשָּׁמָיְמָה. וְהַאי דָּפִיק עַל רֵיאָה, דְּשׁוֹתָה כָּל מַשְׁקִין. וּבְהוֹן, וְרוּחַ אֱלֹהִים מְרַחֶפֶת עַל פְּנֵי הַמָּיִם, הַאי אִיהוּ קְלִיפָה לְרוּחָא דְּקוּדְשָׁא. לִשְׂמָאלָא, רוּחַ סְעָרָה, עֲלַיְיהוּ אִתְּמַר, לֵב חָכָם לִימִינוֹ וְלֵב כְּסִיל לִשְׂמֹאלוֹ.

267. And these FOUR Klipot are marked on the four parts of the body: in the lung, in which is moisture from which come the adhesions of the lung THAT ATTACH THE LOBES OF THE LUNG TO EACH OTHER AND ENFEEBLE IT, ABOUT WHICH IT IS WRITTEN: "Her feet go down to death; her steps take hold of Sheol" (Mishlei 5:5). And there is also the "great and strong wind rent THE MOUNTAINS," that beats in the lobes of a man's lung. This is the wind that stirs up a man's body. THIS REFERS TO THE FIRST KLIPAH, WHICH, IN EZEKIEL, IS CALLED "A STORM WIND" (YECHEZKEL 1:4), and this is the wind that Elijah subjugated and on which he ascended on high, as it is written: "And Elijah went up by a storm of wind into heaven" (II Melachim 2:11). And this WIND bangs against the lung, that imbibes all manner of drinks, concerning which is written: "And a wind from Elohim moved over the surface of the waters" (Beresheet 1:2). This is a Klipah of the Holy Spirit. To the left there is a storm wind. About them it is written: "A wise man's heart inclines him to his right hand: but a fool's heart to his left" (Kohelet 10:2).

268. דָּוִד אַעְבָּר לֵיהּ מַלְבּוֹי, וְקָטִיל לֵיהּ. הה"ד, וְלִבִּי חָלָל בְּקִרְבִּי וּבְגִין דָּא זָכָה, לְנַשְׁבָּא רוּחַ צְפוֹנִית, בְּכִנּוֹר דִּילֵיהּ. וְאִתְּמַר בֵּיהּ, כֹּה אָמַר יְיָ' מֵאַרְבַּע רוּחוֹת בֹּאִי הָרוּחַ, וַהֲוָה מְנַגֵּן בֵּיהּ בַּכִּנּוֹר, בְּד' מִינֵי

נְגּוּנִין, בְּשִׁיר פָּשׁוּט, דְּאִיהוּ י'. וּבְשִׁיר כָּפוּל, דְּאִיהוּ י"ה. וּבְשִׁיר
מְשׁוּלָשׁ, דְּאִיהוּ יד"ו. וּבְשִׁיר מְרוּבָּע, דְּאִיהוּ יְדֹוָ"ד. הָא אִינּוּן עֶשֶׂר
אַתְוָון. דְּעָבַד דָּוִד לָקֳבְלַיְיהוּ, י' מִינֵי תְּלִים. וְסַלְּקִין לְע"ב אַנְפִּין,
כְּחוּשְׁבַּן י' אַתְוָון אִלֵּין.

268. David removed it, THE STORM WIND, from his heart and killed it, as it is written: "And my heart is wounded (Heb. *chalal*) within me" (Tehilim 109:22). THAT IS, HE REMOVED THE STORMY WIND AND REMAINED WITH AN EMPTY SPACE (HEB. *CHALAL*) IN THE HEART IN ITS STEAD. And for this reason, he was privileged that a north wind should blow, NAMELY THE ILLUMINATION OF CHOCHMAH FROM THE LEFT, on his lyre, WHICH IS MALCHUT, and about it is said: "Thus says Adonai Elohim: Come from the four winds, O breath (or: 'wind')" (Yechezkel 37:9). And it used to play through it four types of melody on the lyre: a simple song, which is THE SECRET OF Yud; a double song, which is THE SECRET OF Yud Hei; a triple song, WHICH IS THE SECRET OF Yud Hei Vav; and a quadruple song, which is THE SECRET OF THE FOUR LETTERS Yud Hei Vav Hei. These, TOGETHER, are ten letters, corresponding to which David composed ten types of psalm: 'HAPPY', MASKIL, 'PSALM', 'A WRIT'... And they amount to the 72 countenances, THAT IS 72 LIGHTS, as the numerical value of these ten letters OF THE FOURFOLD YUD HEI VAV HEI.

269. וּמָתַי סְלִיקוּ בְּע"ב מִינֵי נְגּוּנָא. כַּד אִתְעֲבַר שׁוּלְטָנוּתָא דְּעָוֹן
מַשְׁחִית אַף וְחֵימָה. דִּבְהוֹן דָּפִיק רוּחַ סְעָרָה. בְּאַרְבַּע סִטְרִין, דְּסַלְּקִין
לִי' כִּתְרִין לְע"ב אוּמִין, הה"ד, וּבַאֲבוֹד רְשָׁעִים רִנָּה.

269. And when do they amount to 72 types of melody, THIS BEING THE SECRET OF THE FIRST THREE SFIROT OF THE 72-LETTER NAME? It is when the rule of iniquity, destruction, anger, and wrath passes, for in them does the storm wind beat, on the four sides, adding up to ten crowns, AS ABOVE, WITH THE FOUR LETTERS OF YUD HEI VAV HEI, IN THE DOUBLE, TRIPLE, AND QUADRUPLE SONG. THEY ARE TEN LETTERS ADDING UP TO THE NUMERICAL VALUE OF 72, AND THEY THEN SUBJUGATE 72 nations, WHICH ARE THE SEVENTY NATIONS, PLUS EDOM AND ISHMAEL, as it is written: "but when the wicked perish, there is jubilation" (Mishlei 11:10) SINCE, WHEN THE FOUR KLIPOT OF INIQUITY,

DESTRUCTION, ANGER, AND WRATH PERISH, THE FIRST THREE SFIROT ARE REVEALED, WHICH IS THE SECRET OF JUBILATION, NAMELY 72 TYPES OF MELODY.

270. דְּמִיכָּאֵ״ל גַּבְרִיאֵ״ל נוּרִיאֵ״ל רְפָאֵ״ל, שַׁלְטִין עַל ד׳ יְסוֹדִין טָבִין דב״ן, דְּאִינּוּן מַיָּא וְאֶשָׁא וְרוּחָא וְעַפְרָא, וְכָל חַד אִית לֵיהּ ד׳ אַנְפִּין. עֲוֹן מַשְׁחִית אַף וְחֵימָה, תַּלְיָין עַל מָרָה לְבָנָה, דְּרֵיאָה דְּעָבֵיד סִרְכָא. וּבְמָרָה סוּמָקָא דְּכָבֵד, דְּאִתְאֲדָם בְּמַאֲדִים. וּבְמָרָה יְרוֹקָא דְּאֲחִידָא בְּכַבְדָּא, דְּאִיהוּ חַרְבָּא דְּמַלְאַךְ הַמָּוֶת, דְּאִתְּמַר בָּהּ וְאַחֲרִיתָהּ מָרָה כַלַעֲנָה חַדָּה כְּחֶרֶב פִּיּוֹת. וּבְמָרָה שְׁחוֹרָה, לִילִית, שַׁבְתַי, שׁוּלְטָנוּתָא בַּטְּחוֹל, דְּאִיהוּ עֲצִיבוּ, שְׁאוֹל תַּחְתִּית, עֲנִיּוּתָא וַחֲשׁוֹכָא בְּכִיָה וְהֶסְפְּדָא וְרַעֲבוֹן.

270. For Michael, Gabriel, Nuriel and Raphael, WHO ARE THE LIVING CREATURES OF THE CHARIOT, control man's four good elements, which are water, fire, wind and earth, WHICH ARE THE SECRET OF CHESED AND GVURAH, TIFERET AND MALCHUT, each one of them having four countenances: LION, OX, EAGLE, MAN. And iniquity, destruction, anger, and wrath come from white gall, which is the lung in which they make an adhesion, the red gall that is in the liver that turns red with Mars (Heb. *Ma'adim,* from 'red'); the green gall (Heb. *marah*) that is attached to the liver, which is the sword of the Angel of Death, about which it is said: "her end is bitter (Heb. *marah*) as wormwood, sharp as a two edged sword" (Mishlei 5:4); and the black gall which is Lilit, WHICH IS THE PLANET Saturn (Heb. *shabtai*), which is controlled by the spleen, which is melancholia, lower Sheol, poverty and darkness, weeping, mourning and starvation.

271. מִיָּד דְּמִתְעַבְּרִין אִלֵּין קְלִיפִין מב״ן, שַׁלְטָא עֲלֵיהּ אִילָנָא דְּחַיֵּי, בְּע״ב אַנְפִּין, דְּאִינּוּן י׳ יָ״ד יד״ו יד״ון״ד, דְּאִשְׁתְּכָחוּ עֲשָׂרָה תַּלְיָין מֵאַרְבַּע רוּחוֹת, דְּאִינּוּן יְדֹוָד, דְּאִתְּמַר בְּהוֹן, כֹּה אָמַר יְדֹוָד מֵאַרְבַּע רוּחוֹת בֹּאִי הָרוּחַ, דָּא הוּא רוּחוֹ דְּמָשִׁיחַ. דְּאִתְּמַר בֵּיהּ, וְנָחָה עָלָיו רוּחַ יְיָ׳, כַּד אִיהוּ מְנַשֵּׁב בְּאֹזֶן יְמִינָא דְּלִבָּא, דְּתַמָּן חָכְמָה מִסִּטְרָא דְּחֶסֶד, דְּבֵיהּ הָרוֹצֶה לְהַחְכִּים יַדְרִים בְּחָכְמָה. וְחֶסֶ״ד נָשַׁב בְּבִינָה, דְּבַחָכְמָה י׳.

בְּבִינָה ה'. בְּתִפְאֶרֶת ו'. בְּמַלְכוּת ה'. יְדֹוָד דָּפִיק בְּכֻלְּהוּ אַרְבַּע. דְּסַלְקִין
לַעֲשַׂר. וּלע"ב מַחֲשָׁבָה דְּלִבָּא.

271. Immediately, when these FOUR Klipot move away from man, the Tree of Life takes control over him with 72 countenances OF THE ILLUMINATION OF MALCHUT, NAMELY, THE FOURFOLD YUD HEI VAV HEI THUS: Yud, Yud Hei, Yud Hei Vav, and Yud Hei Vav Hei, THE NUMERICAL VALUE OF WHICH IS 72. Thus there are ten LETTERS, coming from the four winds, which are THE FOUR LETTERS OF THE Yud Hei Vav Hei, about which it is said: "Thus says Adonai Elohim: Come from the four winds, O breath (Heb. *ruach*)." This is the spirit of Messiah, about whom it is said: "And the spirit (Heb. *ruach*) of Hashem shall rest upon him" (Yeshayah 11:2), WHICH IS THE SPIRIT OF MALCHUT, when YUD HEI VAV HEI, WHICH IS ZEIR ANPIN, blows in the right auricle of the heart, where Chochmah from the side of Chesed is, with which one who wants to gain wisdom will should turn south with wisdom. And Chesed blows in Binah, AND THEN IN ZEIR ANPIN, AND THEN IN MALCHUT. When IT BLOWS in Chochmah, it is Yud; when in Binah, Hei; when in Tiferet, Vav; and when in Malchut it is Hei. Yud Hei Vav Hei, WHICH IS ZEIR ANPIN, knocks on all four OF THESE SFIROT AND BECOMES FOUR COMBINATIONS. WHEN BEATING IN CHOCHMAH, IT IS YUD; WHEN BEATING IN BINAH, YUD HEI; WHEN BEATING IN TIFERET, YUD HEI VAV; AND WHEN IN MALCHUT, YUD HEI VAV HEI, making a total of ten LETTERS, PARALLELING THE TEN SFIROT. AND THEIR NUMERICAL VALUE IS 72, WHICH IS CHOCHMAH, NAMELY the thought of the heart.

272. דָּא יו"ד ה"א וָא"ו ה"א, יְמִינָא אִיהוּ מַיִם. וְאִיהוּ יַד הַגְּדוֹלָה. מִשְׂמָאלָא אֵשׁ. וְאִיהִי יַד הַחֲזָקָה. בְּעַמּוּדָא דְּאֶמְצָעִיתָא, י"ד רָמָה. דְּאִיהִי רוּחָא דְּקֻדְשָׁא. וְכֹלָּא בֶּן י"ד.

272. Yud-Vav-Dalet, Hei-Aleph, Vav-Aleph-Vav, Hei-Aleph HAS THE NUMERICAL VALUE OF 45, WHICH IS ZEIR ANPIN, whose right is water, and is the great hand, NAMELY CHESED AND THE RIGHT COLUMN. Its left is fire, which is the strong hand, NAMELY GVURAH AND THE LEFT COLUMN. In the Central Column THAT IS BETWEEN THEM, it is the uplifted hand, NAMELY TIFERET, WHICH IS THE CENTRAL COLUMN, which is the

Holy Spirit. And altogether it is the Son of Yud-Hei, FOR HE HAS THE MOCHIN OF THE FIRST THREE SFIROT FROM YUD-HEI.

273. כִּי רוּחַ הַחַיָּה בָּאוֹפַנִּים אֶל אֲשֶׁר יִהְיֶה שָׁמָּה הָרוּחַ לָלֶכֶת יֵלֵכוּ. בֵּיהּ מִתְנַהֲגִים מַיָּא וְאֶשָּׁא. דְּאָחִיד בְּתַרְוַויְיהוּ, וְדָפִיק בְּעַרְקִין דְּמוֹחָא, דְּאִיהוּ מַיִם. וּבְעַרְקִין דְּלִבָּא, דְּאִיהוּ אֵשׁ. וְרוּחַ בְּכַנְפֵי רֵיאָה.

273. "Wherever the spirit was minded to go, they moved...for the spirit of the living creature was in the wheels" (Yechezkel 1:20). Water and fire are directed by THE SPIRIT, for it grips both of them and throbs on the arteries of the brain, which is water AND CHOCHMAH, and on the arteries of the heart, which is fire AND BINAH. AND THE PLACE OF the spirit (wind) is in the lobes of the lung, AS ABOVE.

274. בְּכָל אֵבֶר וְאֵבֶר דְּגוּפָא, אִשְׁתְּכַח גַּלְגְּלֵי יַמָּא דְּאוֹרַיְיתָא, וְגַלְגַּלֵּי רְקִיעָא, דְּאִינּוּן אֶשָּׁא. כֻּלְּהוּ סַלְקִין וְנַחְתִּין בֵּיהּ. וְאִיהוּ אַתְרֵיהּ בֵּין רְקִיעָא וְיַמָּא, מָאנָא דִּילֵיהּ אַרְעָא, דְּאִיהִי שְׁכִינְתָּא.

274. In every part of the body are to be found THESE FOUR, NAMELY the wheels of the sea of the Torah, WHICH IS WATER, and the wheels of the firmament, which is fire, all of them ascending and descending in it, IN THE BODILY PART, FOR WATER, WHICH IS RIGHT AND CHESED DESCENDS, WHILE THE FIRE, WHICH IS THE LEFT AND GVURAH, ASCENDS. FOR THE LEFT ILLUMINATES ONLY UPWARDS FROM BELOW, WHILE it, the spirit, WHICH IS TIFERET AND THE CENTRAL COLUMN, has its place IN THE CENTER between the firmament and the sea, WHICH ARE THE LEFT AND THE RIGHT. And its vessel OF THE SPIRIT, WHICH IS TIFERET, is the earth, WHICH IS DUST, which is the Shechinah.

275. וּכְגַוְונָא דְּעוֹפִין, פְּתִיחוּ גַּדְפַיְיהוּ, לְקַבְּלָא רוּחָא לְפַרְחָא בֵּיהּ. הָכִי כָּל אֵבָרִים דְּגוּפָא, פְּתִיחָן בְּכַמָּה מְקוֹרִין, בְּכַמָּה פִּרְקִין, בְּכַמָּה עַרְקִין, בְּכַמָּה אַדְרִין דְּלִבָּא, אַדְרִין דְּמוֹחָא, לְקַבְּלָא לֵיהּ. דְּאִי לָאו דְּנָשִׁיב בְּבָתֵּין דְּלִבָּא, הֲוָה נוּרָא דְּלִבָּא, אוֹקִיד כָּל גּוּפָא. וְכַמָּה סוּלָמִין, וְאִדְּרִין, דְּעַרְקִין דְּקָנֶה דְּלִבָּא, וְקָנֶה דְּרֵיאָה, כֻּלְּהוּ מִתַּתְקְנִין לְגַבֵּיהּ.

275. And just like the birds, who spread their wings against the wind so that they can fly with it, so also all the parts of the body are open at a number of sources, at a number of joints, a number of arteries, a number of compartments of the heart and a number of areas of the brain, in order to welcome THE SPIRIT WHICH IS THE CENTRAL COLUMN. Were it not to blow in the compartments of the heart, the fire that is in the heart, WHICH IS THE SECRET OF THE LEFT COLUMN, would burn up the whole body. THAT IS TO SAY: WERE IT NOT FOR THE CENTRAL COLUMN WHICH IS CALLED 'WIND', UNITING THE RIGHT AND THE LEFT WITH EACH OTHER, THE JUDGMENTS OF THE LEFT SIDE, WHICH ARE THE SECRET OF THE FIRE THAT IS IN THE HEART, WOULD BURN UP THE WHOLE BODY. FOR THE ILLUMINATION OF THE LEFT WITHOUT THE RIGHT IS HARSH AND BITTER JUDGMENTS. And a number of ladders, NAMELY STEPS and compartments from the arteries of the aorta and trachea, are all constructed by it, BY THE WIND, WHICH IS THE CENTRAL COLUMN.

47. Voice and Speech

A Synopsis
We learn how speech arises through the body, and the effect of speaking the Sh'ma Yisrael and the Amidah. The Faithful Shepherd talks about the speech and silence of the beasts of fire in Ezekiel's vision.

The Relevance of this Passage
We are told that the two lobes of the lungs (the two halves) parallel the two lips of the mouth and, together, they help create the miracle of human speech, which ascends upwards. Speech holds tremendous spiritual power. As such, negative speech creates destructive forces that bring chaos and illness to our lives. Here, through the wisdom of the Zohar, we cleanse our mouths and lungs from any illness caused by negative speech such as slander, curses, gossip, and evil speech about another person. All the destructive words spoken throughout history are hereby corrected and cleansed.

The spiritual forces that ignite during the utterance of the healing prayer *Sh'ma Yisrael* nourishes, purifies, and heals the 248 parts of the body and soul – personally, and in the collective body of man.

The holy words of the righteous souls throughout history, recited during the *Sh'ma* and the *Amidah* prayers, are now summoned forth, kindling a great Light in our lives as they join the Upper and Lower Worlds.

276. כַּד סָלִיק דְּבוּרָא, עַל כַּנְפֵי דְרֵיאָה, אִתְעֲבֵיד קוֹל. בְּהַהוּא זִמְנָא כִּי עוֹף הַשָּׁמַיִם יוֹלִיךְ אֶת הַקּוֹל. קוֹל יְיָ' עַל הַמָּיִם. מִסִּטְרָא דְמַיָּא, דְּאִיהוּ מוֹחָא, דְּתַמָּן סָלִיק בְּכַנְפֵי רֵיאָה. קוֹל יְיָ' חוֹצֵב לַהֲבוֹת אֵשׁ, מִסִּטְרָא דְּלִבָּא, כַּד נָפִיק מִפּוּמָא, אִתְקְרֵי דִּבּוּר.

276. When speech rises, THAT IS TO SAY, AT THE BEGINNING OF THE FORMATION OF SPEECH IN A MAN, over the lobes of the lung, it there becomes a voice. At that time, IT IS SAID: "for a bird of the sky shall carry the sound" (Kohelet 10:20), "The voice of Hashem is upon the waters" (Tehilim 29:3), BECAUSE IT ASCENDS from the side of water, WHICH IS THE RIGHT, which is the brain, where it ascends through the lobes of the

lung. "The voice of Hashem hews out flames of fire" (Ibid. 7) from the side of the heart, WHICH IS THE LEFT, WHICH IS FIRE. AND WHEN THE VOICE emerges from the mouth, WHICH IS THE SECRET OF MALCHUT, it is called 'speech'.

277. וְלָקֳבֵּל תְּרֵין כַּנְפֵי רֵיאָה, דְּפַתְחִין גַּדְפִּין לְקַבְּלָא לֵיהּ, הֲדָא הוּא דִכְתִיב, וּפְנֵיהֶם וְכַנְפֵיהֶם פְּרוּדוֹת מִלְמָעְלָה. הָכִי שִׂפְוָון נַטְלִין לֵיהּ לְדִיבּוּר, וּפַרְחִין לֵיהּ לְעֵילָא.

277. And just as there are two lobes (lit. 'wings') to the lung, NAMELY THE TWO HALVES OF THE LUNG that open up to welcome the voice as it is written: "Thus were their faces: and their wings were divided upwards" (Yechezkel 1:11), FOR THE LOBES OF THE LUNGS ARE SEPARATED FROM EACH OTHER, so also are the lips TWO IN NUMBER that take the speech and cast it upwards.

278. וּכְגַוְונָא דְּאִינּוּן חֲמִשָׁה כַּנְפֵי רֵיאָה, כֻּלְּהוּ פְּתִיחָן בְּלָא סִרְכָּא, לְקַבְּלָא הַאי קוֹל, הָכִי נָמֵי צְרִיכִין לְמֶהֱוֵי חַמְשָׁא תִּקּוּנִין דְּפוּמָא, כֻּלְּהוּ פְּתִיחָן בְּלָא סִירְכָּא, בְּחָמֵשׁ תִּקּוּנִין דְּאִינּוּן: אחהע בַּגָּרוֹן. בומף בְּשִׂפְוָון. גיכק בַּחֵיךְ. דטלנ"ת בְּלִישָׁנָא. זסשרץ בַּשִׁינַיִם.

278. And just as there are five lobes to the lung, NAMELY FIVE DIVISIONS IN THE TWO HALVES OF THE LUNG, all of them being open without an adhesion to receive this voice, so must there be five constructions in the mouth, all of them open without adhesions, and the five constructions are: the guttural LETTERS Aleph, Chet, Hei and Ayin THAT ARE FORMED in the throat; the labial LETTERS Bet, Vav, Mem and Pe THAT ARE FORMED with the lips; the LETTERS Gimel, Yud, Caf and Kof THAT ARE FORMED IN THE ROOF OF THE MOUTH; Dalet, Tet, Lamed and Nun Tav THAT ARE FORMED on the tongue; and Zayin, Samech, Shin, Resh and Tzadi by the teeth.

279. וְדִבּוּר דְּיֶהֱא בְּהוֹן, בְּלָא סִרְכָּא וְעִכּוּבָא כְּלָל. הה"ד, וַיְהִי הוּא טֶרֶם כִּלָּה לְדַבֵּר וְהִנֵּה רִבְקָה יוֹצֵאת. דָּא צְלוֹתָא, דְּאִיהוּ דִבּוּר. וּבְגִינֵיהּ אִתְּמַר, אִם שְׁגוּרָה תְּפִלָּתִי בְּפִי יוֹדֵעַ אֲנִי שֶׁמְּקוּבָּל. וְאִי אִית סִרְכָּא

וְנָפְקָא בְּעֵבוּבָא, יוֹדֵעַ אֲנִי שֶׁמְטוֹרָף. בְּגִין סִרְכָא בְּרִיאָה דְּאִיהִי טְרֵפָה.

279. And speech will be in them, IN THE FIVE EMISSIONS OF THE MOUTH, without any adhesion or hindrance, as it is written: "And it came to pass, before he had done speaking, that, behold, Rivkah came out" (Beresheet 24:15), WHERE RIVKAH is the prayer, that is speech. For this reason have we learned: If the prayer is fluent in my mouth, I know that it has been accepted. But if there is an adhesion and it comes out with a hindrance, I know that my prayer is in disorder, BECAUSE there is an adhesion in the lung, which makes it unfit.

280. וְקוֹל דָּא שְׁמַע יִשְׂרָאֵל, דְּבֵיהּ וָאֶשְׁמַע אֶת קוֹל כַּנְפֵיהֶם. וְדָא יְדֹנָ"ד דְּאִיהוּ קוֹל, כַּד נָפִיק לְקַבְּלָא שְׁכִינְתָּא בִּצְלוֹתָא בַּחֲשַׁאי, דְּאִיהוּ דִּבּוּר, דְּבֵיהּ אֲדֹנָ"י שְׂפָתַי תִּפְתָּח, כָּל אֶבְרִין פְּתִיחָן כֻּלְּהוּ גַּדְפַּיְיהוּ, בַּרְמַ"ח תֵּיבִין, דְּאִינּוּן בְּד' פָּרְשִׁיָּין דִּק"ש, דִּבְהוֹן נָחִית קָלָא.

280. And this voice refers to Sh'ma Yisrael, NAMELY THE UNITY OF THE SIX WORDS OF SH'MA YISRAEL, WHICH IS THE UNIFICATION OF ZEIR ANPIN, CALLED 'VOICE', through which, "I heard the noise of their wings" (Yechezkel 1:24). When Yud Hei Vav Hei, ZEIR ANPIN, who is voice, emerges to welcome the Shechinah with whispered prayer, which is speech, NAMELY MALCHUT THAT IS CALLED 'SPEECH', of which IT IS SAID: "Adonai, open my lips" (Tehilim 51:17), all the parts, NAMELY ALL THE 248 LIGHTS OF CHESED OF ZEIR ANPIN, WHICH ARE CALLED 'THE 248 PARTS OF THE BODY', their wings, NAMELY MALCHUT WHICH IS IN EACH PART, are all of them opened by the 248 words in the four sections of the recital of Sh'ma Yisrael, through which the voice descends.

281. וְכַד נָחִית, כַּמָּה צִפֳּרִין מְצַפְצְפִין לְגַבֵּיהּ, בְּכַמָּה מִינֵי נִגּוּן, כֻּלְּהוּ עַל אֶבְרִין דְּגוּפָא, דְּאִינּוּן עַנְפֵּי אִילָנָא. וּבְכָל גַּדְפִּין דְּכָל אֶבֶר, דְּתַמָּן דִּיּוּרָא דְּצִפּוֹרָא, דְּאִיהִי אֲדֹנָ"י, בְּכָל עַנְפָּא וְעַנְפָּא, אִשְׁתְּכַח פְּתִיחָא לְגַבֵּי דְּבַעֲלָהּ. אֲדֹנָ"י שְׂפָתַי תִּפְתָּח, אִיהוּ פְּתִיחָא לְגַבֵּיהּ, בִּצְלוֹתָא דַּעֲמִידָה. לֵית אֶבֶר מֵרַמַ"ח אֶבָרִים דִּשְׁכִינְתָּא, דְּלָאו אִיהִי פְּתִיחָא לְקַבְּלָא לֵיהּ. וּבְגִ"ד אִתְקְרִיאַת שִׂיחַת מַלְאֲכֵי הַשָּׁרֵת. אִיהוּ צַפְצוּף

עוֹפוֹת, דְּאִינּוּן נִשְׁמָתִין דְּשַׁרְיָין בְּאֵבָרִים. אִיהִי שִׂיחַת דְּקָלִים, דְּאִינּוּן עַנְפִין דְּאִילָנָא.

281. And when THE VOICE descends TO WELCOME THE SHECHINAH IN THE AMIDAH PRAYER, a number of birds chirp to it, THEY BEING THE SECRET TO THE 248 LIGHTS OF THE SHECHINAH, WHICH IS THE SECRET OF SPEECH. AND FOR THIS REASON THEY CHIRP, all of them, in a number of types of melody on the parts of the body, WHICH ARE THE 248 LIGHTS OF ZEIR ANPIN, which are the branches of the tree, and on all the wings that are in every part, NAMELY ON MALCHUT WHICH IS IN EACH PART, WHICH IS CALLED 'WING'. For there is the lodging-place of the bird that is called 'Adonai', NAMELY MALCHUT. FOR THE 248 LIGHTS OF MALCHUT DWELL ON THE ASPECT OF THE WING THAT IS IN EACH OF THE 248 LIGHTS OF ZEIR ANPIN, FOR EACH ASPECT RECEIVES FROM ITS CORRESPONDING ASPECT ABOVE. For on each of the branches OF ZEIR ANPIN, MALCHUT is open to her husband, THIS BEING THE SECRET OF "Adonai, open my lips," which is an opening TO ZEIR ANPIN in the Amidah prayer. For there is not one of the 248 parts of the Shechinah that is not open to receive ZEIR ANPIN. This is why THE SHECHINAH is called 'the talk of the ministering angels', BECAUSE IT IS THE ASPECT OF SPEECH, and it is the chirping of the birds, who are the souls resting on the limbs OF THE SHECHINAH, WHICH ARE CALLED 'BIRDS'. And it is 'the talk of palm trees', which are the branches of the tree THAT ARE THE LIMBS OF ZEIR ANPIN, WHICH ARE IN THE ASPECT OF PINIONS IN EACH BRANCH, WHERE ADONAI RESTS, WHO IS SPEECH.

282. וּבְהַהוּא זִמְנָא, דְּנָחִית יְדֹוָ"ד לְגַבֵּי אֲדֹנָ"י בְּכָל אֵבֶר, אִתְּמַר בְּהוּ, בְּעָמְדָם תְּרַפֶּינָה כַּנְפֵיהֶם. וְהַאי רָזָא דְּחַשְׁמַל. חַיּוֹת אֵשׁ, עִתִּים חָשׁוֹת, וְעִתִּים מְמַלְלוֹת. וְאָמְרוּ מָארֵי מַתְנִיתִין, בְּמַתְנִיתָא תָּנָא, כְּשֶׁהַדִּבּוּר יוֹצֵא מִפִּי הַקּוּדְשָׁא בְּרִיךְ הוּא, חָשׁוֹת, וּכְשֶׁאֵין הַדִּבּוּר יוֹצֵא מִפִּי הַקּוּדְשָׁא בְּרִיךְ הוּא, מְמַלְלוֹת. בְּהַהוּא זִמְנָא דְּמִתְיַיחֲדִין קוֹל וְדִבּוּר כַּחֲדָא, דְּאִינּוּן יְאֲהדֹוָנה"י, חָשׁוֹת. אֲבָל בְּזִמְנָא דִּפְנֵיהֶם וְכַנְפֵיהֶם פְּרוּדוֹת, יְדֹוָ"ד מִן אֲדֹנָ"י בְּפֵרוּדָא, אִיהוּ אִשְׁתְּכַח בְּאַרְבַּע אַנְפֵּי חֵיוָן, כֻּלְּהוּ פְּתִיחָן, לְקַבְּלֵיהּ מְמַלְלוֹת, לְמִשְׁאַל מְזוֹנָא, בְּגִין דִּמְזוֹן לְכֹלָּא בֵּיהּ. אֲדֹנָ"י אִשְׁתְּכַח בְּכַנְפֵי הַחַיּוֹת, כֻּלְּהוּ פְּתִיחָן לְגַבֵּי חֵיוָן.

282. And at the time, when Yud Hei Vav Hei descends to Adonai, in every body part AS EACH PART OF YUD HEI VAV HEI WHICH IS ZEIR ANPIN, POURS PLENTY OVER THE CORRESPONDING PART OF MALCHUT WHICH IS ADONAI, it is said about them: "when they stood still, they let down their wings" (Yechezkel, 1:24). "WHEN THEY STOOD" HINTS AT THE UNITY OF THE AMIDAH PRAYER, FOR THEN THE WINGS, WHICH ARE THE LIMBS OF MALCHUT, ARE AT REST. And this is the secret of 'electrum' (Heb. *chashmal*), WHICH IS THE LETTERS OF SILENT AND SPEAKING LIVING CREATURES OF FIRE. These living creatures of fire are sometimes quiet (Heb. *chashot*) and sometimes speaking (Heb. *memalelot*), and the sages of the Mishnah said: 'As we learned in the Mishnah, When speech comes forth from the mouth of the Holy One, blessed be He, they are silent and when no speech comes forth from the mouth of the Holy One, blessed be He, they speak'. THE MEANING OF THIS IS THAT at the time when speech and voice are united together THAT IS, ZEIR ANPIN AND MALCHUT, which are THE COMBINATION: Yud-Aleph-Hei-Dalet-Vav-Nun-Hei-Yud DURING THE AMIDAH PRAYER, they are silent. But when their faces, WHICH IS THE SECRET OF ZEIR ANPIN, and their wings, WHICH IS THE SECRET OF MALCHUT, are divided – when Yud Hei Vav Hei is separated from Adonai, it, THE YUD HEI VAV HEI, is to be found in the four faces of the living creatures, which are all open. And before it, THE WINGS OF THE LIVING CREATURES, THAT ARE THE ASPECT OF ADONAI AND THE ASPECT OF SPEECH, they speak, requesting nourishment FROM ZEIR ANPIN, for "in it was food for all" (Daniel 4:18). Adonai WHO IS MALCHUT is to be found in the wings of the living creatures, and all of them are open to receive from the living creatures.

283. שָׁאֲגִין בְּקוֹל דְּאִיהוּ יְדֹנָ"ד, כֻּלְּהוּ בִּימִינָא. אוֹפַנִּים מְצַפְצְפָן בְּדִבּוּר, דְּאִיהוּ אֲדֹנָ"י בִּשְׂמָאלָא. בִּשְׂרָפִים מִתְחַבְּרִים קוֹל וְדִבּוּר בְּאֶמְצָעִיתָא. יְאֲהֹדֹוָנָהִי. בְּהוֹן וְעוֹף וְעוֹפֵף. הַה"ד, וַיָּעָף אֵלַי אֶחָד מִן הַשְּׂרָפִים. וְאִתְּמַר בְּהוֹן, וְעוֹף הַשָּׁמַיִם יוֹלִיךְ אֶת הַקּוֹל וּבַעַל כְּנָפַיִם יַגֵּיד דָּבָר. וּשְׂרָפִים שֵׁשׁ כְּנָפַיִם לְאֶחָד. מִסִּטְרָא דְּאָת ו', דְּאִיהוּ עַמּוּדָא דְּאֶמְצָעִיתָא, כָּלִיל יְמִינָא וּשְׂמָאלָא. וְאִיהוּ כָּלִיל שִׁית תֵּיבִין, בִּשְׁתַּיִם יְכַסֶּה פָנָיו וּבִשְׁתַּיִם יְכַסֶּה רַגְלָיו וּבִשְׁתַּיִם יְעוֹפֵף סִימָן.

283. THE LIVING CREATURES THAT ARE IN YETZIRAH roar with a voice

that is ZEIR ANPIN, CALLED Yud Hei Vav Hei. And they are all on the right, NAMELY WITH CHASSADIM. The Ofanim (Eng. 'wheels'), WHICH ARE IN ASIYAH, chirp in speech, which is FROM MALCHUT, CALLED 'Adonai', and they are on the left. In the Serafim, WHICH ARE IN BRIYAH, voice and speech become joined, BEING ZEIR ANPIN AND MALCHUT, AND THEY ARE in the center, AND THEY ATTIRE THEMSELVES BY A UNIFICATION IN THE TWO NAMES: YUD HEI VAV HEI ADONAI, AND COMBINE ONE WITH THE OTHER: Yud-Aleph-Hei-Dalet-Vav-Nun-Hei-Yud. About them IT IS SAID: "And let fowl fly" (Beresheet 1:20), AND ALSO: that is the meaning of "Then one of the Serafim flew to me" (Yeshayah 6:6), THE REFERENCE BEING TO METATRON. And it is said about them: "for a bird of the sky shall carry the sound, and that which has wings shall tell the matter" (Kohelet 10:20), WHERE THE SOUND IS FROM THE SIDE OF THE YUD HEI VAV HEI ATTIRED WITH METATRON, AND "THAT WHICH HAS THE WINGS SHALL TELL THE MATTER" IS FROM THE SIDE OF ADONAI ATTIRED WITH METATRON. "Above Him stood the Serafim; each one had six wings" (Yeshayah 6:2) is from the side of the letter Vav (= 6), which IS ATTIRED IN THEM, AND is the Central Column, incorporating Right and Left, INCLUDING THE SIX SFIROT OF CHESED, GVURAH, TIFERET, NETZACH, HOD AND YESOD, and it includes the six words OF UNIFICATION AS EXPRESSED IN THE READING OF SH'MA. And that is derived from: "with two He covered His face, with two He covered His feet, and with two He did fly" (Ibid.).

284. תִּקּוּנָא תִּנְיָינָא, וְעַל דְּמוּת הַכִּסֵּא דְּמוּת כְּמַרְאֵה אָדָם עָלָיו מִלְמָעְלָה. רְשִׁימוּ דס״ת, וְאִיהוּ כְּתִפְאֶרֶת אָדָם לָשֶׁבֶת בָּיִת.

284. FROM "AND I LOOKED" TO "APPEARANCE OF A MAN" (YECHEZKEL 1:4-26) IS CONSIDERED TO BE ONE CORRECTION, FOR THERE ARE FOUR KLIPOT, WITHIN WHICH ARE THE FOUR LIVING CREATURES, AND THE SECRET OF METATRON IS THAT IN RELATION TO THE LIVING CREATURES HE IS THE INNER MEANING OF THE FIRMAMENT WHICH IS ABOVE THEIR HEADS AND LEADS THEM, WHILE IN RELATION TO MALCHUT HE IS THE INNER MEANING OF THRONE. AND ALL OF THIS IS THE FIRST CORRECTION. The second correction is: "and upon the likeness of the throne was a likeness as the appearance of a man above upon it" (Ibid.), WHERE BY MAN IS MEANT the imprint of the scroll of the Torah, NAMELY MALCHUT THAT IS THE IMPRINT OF ZEIR ANPIN, WHO IS

CALLED 'THE TORAH SCROLL'. And this is: "According to the beauty (Heb. *Tiferet*) of man, that it may remain in the house" (Yeshayah 44:13). IN OTHER WORDS, MALCHUT IS AS THE TIFERET OF MAN, BUT NOT REALLY TIFERET ITSELF. SO ALSO HERE WHERE IT IS SAID "AS THE APPEARANCE OF A MAN," BUT NOT MAN ITSELF, IT IS APPLIED TO MALCHUT, FOR WHOM METATRON IS A THRONE.

48. The reading of Sh'ma, Tzitzit (fringes), Tefilin and the straps

A Synopsis

The sages taught that the reading of Sh'ma twice daily is as good as meditating day and night. The Faithful Shepherd goes over the meaning of the number of knots in the Talit, the four passages and the knots in the Tefilin and the length and winding of the straps. We learn that God and His Shechinah are the voice and speech of every angel, and that they are in every voice and speech of Torah, and in every voice of prayer and every single precept, and in every place of God's rule in the upper and lower worlds.

The Relevance of this Passage

This section of Zohar is technical in nature and describes the metaphysical wiring, circuitry, and instructions underlying various prayers and rituals such as the reading of *Sh'ma,* the Talit, the undergarment known as *Tzitzit,* and the *Tefilin,* which are phylacteries that are worn on the head and wrapped around the left arm of a man during morning prayers.

The immeasurable spiritual power generated by these practices ignites in this potent passage to correct all the world and to link humanity to the Upper World forevermore. A few insights are worth mentioning. The name of *Metatron* brings revitalization and the energy of immortality to our world. The *72 Names* imbue us with the power of Mind over Matter. The Light of the *Shechinah* bolsters our immune system, protecting us and the world from all forms of diseases. The energy of the *Sh'ma* shines healing Light onto the 248 parts of the body and soul. The power of the *Tefilin* ignites, and it now arrests absolutely the selfish *Desire to Receive for the Self Alone* in the souls of all men.

285. וְאוֹקְמוּהָ רַבָּנָן, כָּל הַקּוֹרֵא ק״ש עַרְבִית וְשַׁחֲרִית, כְּאִילוּ מְקַיֵּים וְהָגִיתָ בּוֹ יוֹמָם וָלַיְלָה. דְּטַלִית לְבָנָה, אִיהוּ לִימִינָא מִסְּטְרָא דְּחֶסֶד. וְאִתְּמַר, אֵל מֶלֶךְ יוֹשֵׁב עַל כִּסֵּא רַחֲמִים וּמִתְנַהֵג בַּחֲסִידוּת. וְהוּכַן בְּחֶסֶד כִּסֵּא. חֶסֶד סָלִיק ע״ב חוּלְיָין וְקִשְׁרִין דְּטַלִית.

285. The sages taught: 'Anyone reading the reading of Sh'ma Yisrael morning and evening is as though he had observed the saying that "but you shall meditate therein day and night" (Yehoshua 1:8).' THIS IS BECAUSE

THE READING OF SH'MA YISRAEL ENCOMPASSES RIGHT AND LEFT, WHICH ARE THE SECRET OF DAY AND NIGHT. HE EXPLAINS, for a Talit (prayer-shawl) is white, THAT IS TO SAY, THE ASPECT OF THE WHITE THAT IS IN THE FRINGES OF THE TALIT AND NOT THE BLUE THAT IS IN IT, is to the right from the aspect of Chesed; and it is said about it: 'Almighty King, who sits on the throne of mercy, governs with kindness (Heb. *chasidut*)', and also: "And in mercy (Heb. *chesed*) a throne is established" (Yeshayah 16:5). The numerical value of Chesed is 72, which hints at the 72 links and knots of the Talit, NAMELY FOUR TIMES EIGHTEEN.

286. וְאִית טַלִּית מִסִּטְרָא דִּמְטַטְרוֹ"ן, דְּאִיהוּ ט"ט, כָּלִיל ח"י, בֵּין קִשְׁרִין וְחוּלְיָין לְכָל סִטְרָא. ה' קִשְׁרִין לָקֳבֵל ה' חוּמְשֵׁי תּוֹרָה. וּתְלֵיסַר חוּלְיָין, לָקֳבֵל תְּלֵיסַר מְכִילָן דְּרַחֲמֵי דְּאוֹרַיְיתָא. דְּאִתְּמַר בְּהוֹן, בִּי"ג מִדּוֹת הַתּוֹרָה נִדְרֶשֶׁת.

286. And there is a Talit from the aspect of Metatron, which is the Tet Tet OF METATRON, which includes the eighteen links and knots on each corner OF THE TALIT, NAMELY five knots paralleling the five books of the Torah, and thirteen links, NAMELY THE THIRTEEN LOOPS THAT ARE WOUND AROUND THE TZIZIT, which parallel the thirteen attributes of Mercy mentioned in the Torah, about which it is said: There are thirteen attributes by which the Torah is expounded, WHICH IS THE SECRET OF THE THIRTEEN ATTRIBUTES OF MERCY THAT ARE DRAWN DOWN FROM THE THIRTEEN CHARACTERISTICS OF THE BEARD OF ARICH ANPIN.

287. וּבְגִינָה אִתְּמַר, כְּמַרְאֵה אָדָם עָלָיו מִלְמָעְלָה. בְּדִיּוּקְנָא דְּתִפְאֶרֶת, דְּאִיהוּ ת"ת עָלָיו מִלְמָעְלָה. וְאִתְקְרֵי בִּשְׁמֵיהּ, יוֹ"ד ה"א וָא"ו ה"א. כָּל הַנִּקְרָא בִשְׁמִי וְלִכְבוֹדִי בְּרָאתִיו יְצַרְתִּיו אַף עֲשִׂיתִיו. וּלְעֵילָא כְּמַרְאֵה אָדָם, דָּא שְׁכִינְתָּא, דְּאִיהִי כְּחֵיזוּ דְּעַמּוּדָא דְּאֶמְצָעִיתָא, בְּד' אַנְפִּין, וּבְעֶשֶׂר סְפִירָאן, דְּאִינּוּן אָדָם. וְאַרְבַּע אַנְפִּין דְּאָדָם, אַרְבַּע אַתְוָון. וְאִינּוּן י"ד אַתְוָון, וּבְהוֹן וּבְיַד הַנְּבִיאִים אֲדַמֶּה.

287. About MALCHUT it is said: "as the appearance of a man above upon it" (Yechezkel 1:26), NAMELY THAT MALCHUT has the form of Tiferet, which

is Tiferet of man upon him from above, and is called by the name OF
TIFERET, WHICH IS Yud-Vav-Dalet, Hei-Aleph, Vav-Aleph-Vav, Hei-
Aleph. THIS IS THE INNER MEANING OF THE VERSE: "every one that is
called by My name: for I have created him for My glory; I have formed him;
yea, I have made him" (Yeshayah 43:7). THEREFORE, "as the appearance
of a man from above" is the Shechinah, which has the form of the Central
Column, WHICH IS TIFERET, with four countenances and ten Sfirot, that are
man. THAT IS, THE TEN LETTERS YUD-VAV-DALET, HEI-ALEPH, VAV-
ALEPH-VAV, HEI ALEPH HAVE THE NUMERICAL VALUE OF *ADAM* (LIT.
'*MAN*'). And the four faces of man are the four SIMPLE letters OF YUD HEI
VAV HEI, which TOGETHER make Yud-Dalet (= 14) letters, about which IT
IS SAID: "and used similes by the hand (Heb. *yad* - Yud-Dalet) of the
prophets" (Hoshea 12:11).

288. וְעוֹד אִתְקְרֵי חַ"י, מִסְּטְרָא דְּצַדִּיק, וּבֵיהּ קוּדְשָׁא בְּרִיךְ הוּא
וּשְׁכִינְתֵּיהּ אִתְקְרֵי אָז אָדָם, דְּאִיהוּ עַמּוּדָא דְּאֶמְצָעִיתָא, טַ"ל,
וּשְׁכִינְתֵּיהּ ה'. וּבָהּ אִיהוּ אָדָם. בְּגִין דְּטַ"ל הָכִי סָלִיק בְּחוּשְׁבַּן יוֹ"ד
הֵ"א וָא"ו. וְהַאי אִיהוּ מוֹרִיד הַטַּ"ל, לְגַבֵּי הֵ"א. קֶשֶׁר דְּטַלִּית, חַ"י
עָלְמִין, דְּקָשִׁיר קוּדְשָׁא בְּרִיךְ הוּא וּשְׁכִינְתֵּיהּ בְּכָל סִטְרִין, בְּאַרְבַּע
כַּנְפוֹת דְּטַלִּית.

288. Again, THE TZITZIT is called 'living' (Heb. *Chai* = 18), NAMELY THE
THIRTEEN LINKS AND FIVE KNOTS, from the aspect of the Righteous,
WHICH IS YESOD, in whom, NAMELY BY MEANS OF WHOSE UNIFICATION,
the Holy One, blessed be He, and His Shechinah are called by the name
'man'. THAT IS, YUD HEI VAV HEI, SPELLED OUT IN FULL WITH ALEPHS,
HAS THE SAME NUMERICAL VALUE AS MAN where He, the Central Column
THAT IS ZEIR ANPIN, is YUD-VAV-DALET, HEI-ALEPH, VAV-ALEPH-
VAV, AND HAS THE NUMERICAL VALUE OF dew (Heb. *tal* = 39), while His
Shechinah is Hei-Aleph. And with Hei, the name of man IS COMPLETED.
This is because dew is in numerical value equal to Yud Vav Dalet, Hei
Aleph, Vav-Aleph-Vav. And this, THE RIGHTEOUS CALLED 'LIVING', 'causes
the dew to fall', WHICH IS YUD-VAV-DALET, HEI -ALEPH, VAV-ALEPH
-VAV onto the Hei-Aleph, WHICH IS THE SHECHINAH, FOR YESOD is the
knot of the Talit, which is eighteen worlds ON EACH SIDE, NAMELY FIVE
KNOTS AND THIRTEEN LINKS that binds together AND UNITE the Holy One,

blessed be He, and His Shechinah on all sides, with the four corners of the Talit, WHICH ARE CHESED, GVURAH, TIFERET AND MALCHUT.

289. תְּפִלִּין מִשְׂמָאלָא, הה"ד, נִשְׁבַּע יְיָ' בִּימִינוֹ וּבִזְרוֹעַ עֻזּוֹ, זוֹ תּוֹרָה. וּבִזְרוֹעַ עֻזּוֹ, אֵלּוּ תְּפִלִּין. יְהוֹ"ה בְּד' פַּרְשִׁיָּין. אֲדֹנָ"י הֵיכָלָא לְד' אַתְוָון, בְּד' בָּתֵּי דִתְפִלִּין. קֶשֶׁר שֶׁל תְּפִלִּין דְּיַד, דָּא צַדִּיק חַ"י עָלְמִין, דְּאִיהוּ קִשּׁוּרָא דְּתַרְוַוייְהוּ. בִּזְרוֹעַ שְׂמָאלָא. קֶשֶׁר דְּרֵישָׁא, דָּא עַמּוּדָא דְּאֶמְצָעִיתָא, דְּאָחִיד בֵּיה יְדֹו"ד אֶהְיֶ"ה לְעֵילָּא, דְּאִינּוּן חָכְמָ"ה וּבִינָ"ה.

289. Tefilin are THE ASPECT of the Left COLUMN, as it is said: "Hashem has sworn by His right hand, and by the arm of His strength" (Yeshayah 62:8), where "His right hand" refers to the Torah and "the arm of His strength" refers to Tefilin. The four passages IN THE TEFILIN are THE FOUR LETTERS Yud Hei Vav Hei. Adonai is a temple for the four letters, WHICH ARE THE FOUR PASSAGES in the four receptacles of the Tefilin. The knot of the hand Tefilin is the Righteous, who lives forever, WHICH IS YESOD, and is the bond between the two of them, BETWEEN THE YUD HEI VAV HEI AND 'ADONAI', on the left arm. The knot of the head TEFILIN is the Central Column, NAMELY TIFERET, by which are united together on high Yud Hei Vav Hei and Eheyeh which are Chochmah and Binah, FOR ZEIR ANPIN ASCENDS AND UNITES CHOCHMAH AND BINAH, WHICH ARE CALLED THE YUD HEI VAV HEI AND 'EHEYEH', WHERE DA'AT IS FORMED.

290. ק"ש דְּאִיהוּ יִחוּדָא בְּאֶמְצָעִיתָא, וְאִיהוּ אָחִיד בֵּין צִיצִית וּתְפִלִּין, דְּכֻלְּהוּ פַּרְשִׁיָּין דְּצִיצִית וּתְפִלִּין, אִינּוּן כְּלִילָן בְּיִחוּדָא דְק"ש. וּמִסִּטְרָא דְעַמּוּדָא דְאֶמְצָעִיתָא, דְּאִיהוּ טַלִית וּתְפִלִּין, דְּאִתְּמַר בְּהוּ, וְהָיָה לְאוֹת עַל יָדְכָה וּלְטוֹטָפוֹת בֵּין עֵינֶיךָ. וְעָשׂוּ לָהֶם צִיצִית.

290. The reading of the Sh'ma is the unification that is at the center, NAMELY THE UNIFICATION IN CHESED, GVURAH AND TIFERET, and it is held between the Tzitzit and the Tefilin, FOR THE FRINGES, THAT ARE OF THE ASPECT OF THE WHITE THAT IS IN THEM, ARE TO ITS RIGHT, AND THE TEFILIN TO ITS LEFT. For all of the passages of the Tzitzit and Tefilin

are included in the unification of the reading of the Sh'ma. And from the side of the Central Column, namely Talit and Tefilin, it is said: "And it shall be for a sign upon your hand and for frontlets between your eyes" (Shemot 13:16), AND IT IS ALSO SAID: "that they make them fringes" (Bemidbar 15:38).

291. ש' שֶׁל תְּפִילִין, הֲלָכָה לְמֹשֶׁה מִסִּינַי. וְרָאוּ כָּל עַמֵּי הָאָרֶץ כִּי שֵׁם יְיָ' נִקְרָא עָלֶיךָ וַיִּרְאוּ מִמֶּךָ. וְאוֹקְמוּהָ מַאי שֵׁם יְדוֹ"ד. אֵלּוּ תְּפִלִּין שֶׁבָּרֹאשׁ. ש' שֶׁל תְּפִלִּין. תְּרֵין שִׁינִין שִׁית מְאָה. ש' שִׁית דַּרְגִּין. וְשֶׁבַע עַנְפִין דִּתְרֵין שִׁינִין, הָא תְּלַת עֲשַׂר, וְכֹלָּא תרי"ג. וְלֵית פְּקוּדָא דְּלָאו אִיהִי שְׁקִילָא לְכָל אוֹרַיְיתָא.

291. The letter Shin of the Tefilin is a tradition Moses received on Mount Sinai, AS IT IS WRITTEN: "And all peoples of the earth shall see that you are called by the name of Hashem; and they shall be afraid of you" (Devarim 28:10). And it has been taught: What is the Yud Hei Vav Hei? It is the head Tefilin, specifically the Shin Shin of the Tefilin, THAT ARE VISIBLE ON THEM FROM THE TWO EXTERNAL SIDES. The two Shins have the numerical value of six hundred. Shin Shin are the six (Heb. *shesh*) stages CHESED, GVURAH, TIFERET, NETZACH, HOD AND YESOD THAT ARE IN ZEIR ANPIN, WHERE THE RIGHT SHIN IS CHESED, GVURAH AND TIFERET, AND THE LEFT SHIN IS NETZACH, HOD AND YESOD. The two Shins have seven branches, AS THE RIGHT SHIN HAS THREE HEADS, AND THE LEFT FOUR HEADS. TOGETHER THERE ARE SEVEN HEADS, OR SEVEN BRANCHES. This adds up to thirteen, and together they are 613, BECAUSE SEVEN BRANCHES AND SIX GRADES AMOUNT TO THIRTEEN, AND THE NUMERICAL VALUE OF THE TWO SHINS IS SIX HUNDRED. And there is no precept that is not equivalent to the whole of the Torah, IT BEING, THEREFORE, SAID ABOUT IT: "AND ALL THE PEOPLES OF THE EARTH SHALL SEE THAT YOU ARE CALLED BY THE NAME OF HASHEM..."

292. כְּגַוְונָא דָּא, כָּל מִצְוָה אִיהִי יְהוָֹ"ה. יָ"ה עִם שְׁמָ"י שס"ה. וָ"ה עִם זִכְרִי רמ"ח. ובג"ד כָּל מִצְוָה אִיהִי שְׁקִילָא לתרי"ג. וְהָא אוּקְמוּהָ, שְׁמַע יִשְׂרָאֵל כָּלִיל תרי"ג, מִסִּטְרָא דְּצִיצִית. ותרי"ג מִסִּטְרָא דִּתְפִלִּין אִיהוּ בְּכָל אֲתָר.

292. Likewise, JUST AS 613 ARE IMPLIED IN THE TEFILIN, so each precept is the Yud Hei Vav Hei, AS FOLLOWS: Yud Hei IN IT, together with 'My name' (Heb. *shmi*) have the numerical value of the 365 NEGATIVE PRECEPTS IN THE TORAH. Vav Hei IN IT, together with 'My memorial' (Heb. *zichri*) have the numerical value of the 248, POSITIVE PRECEPTS IN THE TORAH. THE TOTAL NUMBER OF PRECEPTS IS 613. This is why each precept is equivalent to the 613. And the sages have taught that the reading of the Sh'ma Yisrael, INCORPORATING TEFILIN AND THE TZITZIT contains 613 of the Tzitzit, AS TZITZIT IN NUMERICAL VALUE IS SIX HUNDRED, WHICH TOGETHER WITH THE 13 LINKS THEREOF MAKES 613. And there is also 613 from the aspect of Tefilin, LIKE THE NUMERICAL EQUIVALENT OF THE TWO SHINS ON THEM AND SO it is throughout.

293. וְהָיוּ לְטוֹטָפוֹת, טֹטָפֹת: טט, חַ"י עָלְמִין, צַדִּיק, לְקַבְלֵיהּ מְטַטְרוֹן. פָּת, תִּפְאֶרֶת. מְטַטְרוֹן סוּס דְּתִפְאֶרֶת, דְּבֵיהּ כָּל סְפִירָאן מִתְלַבְּשִׁין. וְהָכִי אִיהוּ כְּגוּפָא לְנִשְׁמָתָא. וְכַד קוּדְשָׁא בְּרִיךְ הוּא אִסְתַּלָּק מִנֵּיהּ, אִשְׁתְּאַר אָלֶם, לֵית לֵיהּ קוֹל וְלָא דִבּוּר. אִשְׁתְּכַח, דְּקוּדְשָׁא בְּרִיךְ הוּא וּשְׁכִינְתֵּיהּ אִיהוּ קוֹל וְדִבּוּר. דְּכָל מַלְאָךְ וּמַלְאָךְ. וּבְכָל קָלָא וְדִבּוּר דְּאוֹרַיְיתָא, וּבְכָל קָלָא דִצְלוֹתָא. וּבְכָל פְּקוּדָא וּפְקוּדָא. בְּכָל אֲתָר שׁוּלְטָנוּתֵיהּ בְּעֶלָּאִין וְתַתָּאִין, אִיהוּ חַיִּים דְּכֹלָּא, אִיהוּ סָבִיל כֹּלָּא.

293. "and they shall be as frontlets (Heb. *totafot*)." Totefet CAN BE SPLIT INTO TET TET AND PE TAV. THE NUMERICAL VALUE OF Tet Tet is 'living' (Heb. *chai* = 18) worlds, the Righteous, NAMELY YESOD, parallel to which is Metatron, FOR YESOD IS ATTIRED WITH METATRON. Pe Tav are Tiferet, WHOSE LETTERS MAY BE REARRANGED AS TAV-ALEPH-RESH, PE TAV (NAMELY A DESCRIPTION OF PE TAV). And Metatron is Tiferet's horse; THAT IS TO SAY TIFERET RIDES UPON HIM, for all the Sfirot dress up WITH METATRON. AT ONE TIME IT MIGHT BE TIFERET THAT WEARS HIM, AT ANOTHER YESOD AND AT ANOTHER MALCHUT, WHILE AT OTHER TIMES ALL THREE MIGHT BE ATTIRED WITH HIM. And so he is to them is as body to soul, and when the Holy One, blessed be He, removes Himself from him, METATRON is left dumb, having neither voice nor speech. For the Holy One, blessed be He, and His Shechinah are voice and speech of every angel, and THEY ARE in every voice and speech of Torah, and in every voice of prayer, and in each single precept, and in every place of His rule, among the upper and lower beings. He is the life of everything. He carries everything.

294. וְלֵית אֲדֹנָי בְּלָא יְדֹוָד, בְּגַוְונָא דְּלֵית דִּבּוּר בְּלָא קוֹל. וְלֵית קוֹל בְּלָא דִבּוּר. וְהַאי אִיהוּ קָשׁוֹט, בְּעָלְמָא דַּאֲצִילוּת. אֲבָל בְּעָלְמָא דְּפֵרוּדָא, אִית קוֹל בְּלָא דִבּוּר. קֶשֶׁר שֶׁל תְּפִלִין שַׁדַּי, אָחִיד בֵּיה עֵילָא וְתַתָּא. וְדָא צַדִּיק חַי עָלְמִין, אָחִיד בֵּין קוֹל וְדִבּוּר.

294. Just as there is no speech without voice and no voice without speech, so is there no Adonai without the Yud Hei Vav Hei. And this is true for the world of Atzilut, WHERE THERE IS NO SEPARATION EXISTS BETWEEN ZEIR ANPIN AND MALCHUT, WHO ARE VOICE AND SPEECH. But in the world of separation, NAMELY IN THE THREE WORLDS OF BRIYAH, YETZIRAH AND ASIYAH, there is voice without speech. YET IN ATZILUT THEY ARE UNITED, and the knot of the Tefilin, which is Shadai, WHICH IS YESOD, is held by them from above and from below, and this is the Righteous, the life of the worlds, who is held between voice and speech AND UNITES THEM.

295. אַדְהָכִי, הָא רַעְיָא מְהֵימָנָא אִזְדְּמַן לְגַבֵּי סָבָא, וְאָמַר סָבָא סָבָא, תְּפִלִין וְצִיצִית וּפָרָשַׁת מְזוּזָה, אִינּוּן ג' פִּקּוּדִין, כְּלִילָן בק"ש. וק"ש פִּקּוּדָא רְבִיעָאָה. וְצִיצִית אַדְכַּר ג' זִמְנִין. וּבַתְּפִלִין אַדְכַּר בְּהוּ תְּרֵין זִמְנִין אוֹת. וּבַצִּיצִית ז' שֶׁל תִּזְכְּרוּ דְּצָרִיךְ לְהַתִּיז בָּהּ. וּבִמְזוּזָה, שַׁדַּי מִלְּבַר, יְדֹו"ד מִלְּגוֹ.

295. At this point, the Faithful Shepherd come to the old man, and said: Old old man, the Tefilin and the Tzitzit and the section on the Mezuzah are three precepts that are incorporated in the reading of Sh'ma Yisrael, and the reading of Sh'ma is the fourth precept. AND THE FOUR CORRESPOND TO CHESED, GVURAH, TIFERET AND MALCHUT, WHERE THE TZITZIT AND TEFILIN ARE CHESED AND GVURAH, THE READING OF SH'MA IS TIFERET THAT UNITES THEM, AND THE MEZUZAH IS MALCHUT. The Tzitzit is mentioned three times, PARALLELING THE THREE COLUMNS, and regarding Tefilin the word 'sign', WHICH IS YESOD, is mentioned twice, ONCE FOR THE KNOT OF THE HEAD TEFILIN AND ONCE FOR THE KNOT OF THE HAND TEFILIN. In respect to the Tzitzit, the letter Zayin of the word "*tiz'keru* (Eng. 'that you remember')" (Bemidbar 15:40), has to be well stressed, FOR THIS LETTER ZAYIN (= 7) IMPLIES MALCHUT, WHICH IS

THE SEVENTH SFIRAH, AND IS THE SECRET OF THE BLUE THAT IS IN THE TZITZIT, ON WHICH THE REMEMBERING DEPENDS. And on the Mezuzah, WHICH IS MALCHUT, the name Shadai is on the outside, while Yud Hei Vav Hei is on the inside. THIS IS BECAUSE THERE ARE TWO UNIONS, THE EXTERNAL UNION WITH YESOD, AND THE INTERNAL UNION WITH TIFERET. THE FAITHFUL SHEPHERD CLARIFIED ALL THIS TO THE OLD MAN FOR HIM TO UNDERSTAND ON HIS OWN.

296. וּפָרְשָׁיָין סְתִימִין וּפְתִיחָן אֲמַאי. וְשִׁיעוּר אָרְכָּה דְּצִיצִית וְרוֹחֲבָה, דְּתָקִינוּ אֹרֶךְ כָּל הַצִּיצִית תְּרֵין עֲשַׂר אֶצְבְּעָן בְּגוּדָל. מִצְוַת תְּכֵלֶת, שָׁלִישׁ גְּדִיל, וּשְׁנֵי שְׁלִישֵׁי עֲנָף. וּבֵין קֶשֶׁר לְקֶשֶׁר כִּמְלֹא גוּדָל. וְכָל חוּלְיָא וְחוּלְיָא תִּהְיֶה מְשׁוּלֶשֶׁת. וְהָכִי תְּפִלִּין אֲמַאי בְּמוֹחָא. וְלָקֳבֵּל לִבָּא. וְשִׁיעוּר רְצוּעָתְהוֹן אֲמַאי אִינוּן עַד לִבָּא לִשְׂמָאלָא. וְעַד טַבּוּרָא לִימִינָא. וּרְצוּעָא דְּיַד עַד דְּיִכְרוֹךְ וִישַׁלֵּשׁ תְּלַת זִמְנִין בְּאֶצְבַּע צְרָדָא.

296. THE FAITHFUL SHEPHERD ANSWERS THE VARIOUS QUESTIONS THAT FACE US. Why are there open and closed sections? WHY DOES the fringe have a fixed length and width, for the length of each fringe was determined as the size of twelve thumbs? WHY was the precept of the blue fixed at one-third twisted threads and two-thirds branched untwisted threads? WHY between each pair of knots IN THE FRINGES does there have to be A SPACE OF a full thumb's breadth? AND WHY SHOULD each link be triple, NAMELY THREE LOOPS? Also, why are Tefilin on the brain and against the heart? And why is the length of the straps to the heart on the left and to the navel on the right? And why does the strap of the hand Tefilin have to be wound three times round the middle finger?

297. אֶלָּא, וַדַּאי בֶּגֶד חָשׁוּב לָאו אִיהוּ, אֶלָּא שָׁלֹשׁ עַל שָׁלֹשׁ לְכָל סְטָרָא. אִינוּן תְּרֵיסָר, לָקֳבֵּל ד' בִּגְדֵי לָבָן, וְד' בִּגְדֵי זָהָב, וְד' בִּגְדֵי דְּכֹהֵן הֶדְיוֹט. וּמִסְטְרָא דְּבִרְכַּת כֹּהֵן הֶדְיוֹט קָא רָמִיז, אַל תְּהִי בִּרְכַּת הֶדְיוֹט קַלָּה בְּעֵינֶיךָ. שָׁלִישׁ גְּדִיל, וּשְׁנֵי שְׁלִישֵׁי עֲנָף, דְּאִיהוּ תְּכֵלֶת.

297. HE ANSWERS: But the garment is certainly not important unless IT HAS three on three for each side OF THE FOUR SIDES, making twelve. And they represent the four white garments THAT PARALLEL ZEIR ANPIN, WHICH IS

THE SECRET OF THE FOUR LETTERS OF THE YUD HEI VAV HEI, and the four gold garments THAT PARALLEL MALCHUT, WHICH IS THE SECRET OF THE FOUR LETTERS OF ADONAI, and the four garments of the ordinary priest, WHO IS THE SECRET OF METATRON. In terms of the blessing of an ordinary priest, it is implied 'Let not the blessing of an ordinary man be considered lightly in your eyes'. AND, THEREFORE, the blue is one-third twisted thread, NAMELY BRAIDED, AS THIRTEEN LINKS ARE WOUND AROUND THE FRINGES, FOR IT IS PARALLEL TO THE FOUR GARMENTS OF WHITE, WHICH IS THE SECRET OF ZEIR ANPIN, WHO IS THE ROOT. And two-thirds are branched untwisted thread, WHICH SHOULD HANG LOOSE, LIKE THE BRANCHES ON A TREE.

298. וְכָל חוּלְיָא מְשׁוּלֶשֶׁת, כָּל מְשׁוּלָשׁ מִסְטְרָא דִּקְדוּשָׁה. הֲה״ד קְדוּשָׁה לְךָ יְשַׁלֵּשׁוּ. וְיִשְׂרָאֵל שְׁלִישִׁיָּה, בְּגִין דְּוּשְׁלִישִׁים עַל כֻּלּוֹ. דְּצִיצִית מִסְטְרָא דְעַמּוּדָא דְּאֶמְצָעִיתָא, דְּאִיהוּ תְּלִיתָאָה לַאֲבָהָן, וְכָל דָּבָר מְשׁוּלָשׁ, וה״ו יל״י, כָּל תֵּיבָה מְשׁוּלֶשֶׁת מִסְטְרוֹי. חוּלְיָא כְּלִילָא מִתְּלַת כְּרִיכוֹת מְשָׁלְשִׁין, דָּא שְׁכִינְתָּא. קְדוּשָׁה לְךָ יְשַׁלֵּשׁוּ. וְאִיהִי מְשׁוּלֶשֶׁת בְּעַמּוּדָא דְּאֶמְצָעִיתָא, כָּלִיל תְּלַת עַנְפֵּי אֲבָהָן, דְּאִינּוּן שׁ׳ מִן שַׁבָּת, שְׁכִינְתָּא בַּת יְחִידָה. חֲלְיָא, תְּכֵלֶת שֶׁבַּצִּיצִית.

298. And every link MUST BE triple, MADE UP OF THREE, NAMELY OF THREE LOOPS. AND THE REASON IS THAT each tripling is from the side of holiness, WHICH IS THE SECRET OF THE THREE COLUMNS, as it is written: 'They proclaim You holy three times'. And Yisrael is made up of three parts, NAMELY PRIEST, LEVITES AND YISRAEL in order to SUBJUGATE THE CAPTAINS (HEB. *SHALISHIM* - FROM *SHALOSH* (THREE)) OF THE OTHER SIDE, AS IT IS WRITTEN: "And captains over every one of them" (Shemot 14:7). For the fringe is from the side of the Central Column, WHICH IS TIFERET, which is the third of the patriarchs, FOR THE PATRIARCHS ARE CHESED, GVURAH AND TIFERET. And everything that comes in threes HAS ITS ROOT IN THE 72 WORDS THAT STARTS WITH Vav-Hei-Vav, Yud -Lamed-Yud, IN WHICH every word consists of three LETTERS. From its side, every link is composed of three triple loops, AND THE LINK is the Shechinah, WHICH IS THE SECRET OF 'They proclaim You holy three times', and is tripled in the Central Column, FOR IT RECEIVES FROM THE CENTRAL COLUMN THE THREE COLUMNS THAT ARE IN IT.

THUS is it made up of the three branches of the patriarchs, NAMELY OF NETZACH, HOD AND YESOD, WHICH ARE THE BRANCHES OF CHESED, GVURAH AND TIFERET, WHICH ARE CALLED 'PATRIARCHS'. And they are the letter Shin from the word 'Shabbat', WHICH HAS THREE HEADS, WHICH IS THE SECRET OF NETZACH, HOD AND YESOD. THE 'BAT' FROM THE WORD SHABBAT ALLUDES TO the Shechinah, who is an only daughter (Heb. *bat*), WHICH IS THE SECRET OF the link, AND THE SECRET OF the blue in the Tzitzit.

299. זַכָּאָה גּוּפָא, דְּהָכִי אִיהוּ רָשִׁים, בִּשְׁכִינְתָּא וְקוּדְשָׁא בְּרִיךְ הוּא, עַל כַּנְפֵי דְמִצְוָה. רָשִׁים בִּרְצוּעָא דְּאִיהוּ תְּפִלָּה דְּיָד, בִּתְלַת כְּרִיכוּת בְּאֶצְבַּע צְרָדָא. דְּאִיהִי כְּגַוְונָא דְחוּלְיָא, כְּרִיכָא בִּתְלַת כְּרִיכוּת בְּאֶצְבְּעָא. רָשִׁים בְּקֶשֶׁר דִּתְפִלִּין, כָּלִיל בִּתְרֵין קִשְׁרִין, סַלְקִין חַמְשָׁה עֲשַׂר מְשׁוּלְשִׁין, תְּרֵין בְּקִשְׁרָא חַד.

299. Happy is the body that is thus marked with the Shechinah and the Holy One, blessed be He, through the wings of a precept, NAMELY WITH THE THIRTEEN LINKS IN THE PRECEPT OF THE TZITZIT, and marked with the strap of the hand Tefilin on the middle finger with three loops, which is like a link, wound around with three loops round the finger. THIS ALSO CORRESPONDS TO THE THREE COLUMNS, JUST LIKE THE LINK OF THE FRINGE, AND THERE ARE FOURTEEN LINKS. And it is marked with the knot of the Tefilin that consists of two knots, THE ONE ON THE HEAD AND THE OTHER ON THE ARM, FOR THEY ALSO ARE TRIPLE. And altogether there are fifteen triplets, FOR two knots in one knot IS ALSO CONSIDERED A TRIPLE, MAKING, THEREFORE, FIFTEEN TRIPLES.

300. שְׁלֹשָׁה עֲשַׂר חוּלְיָין, אִית בְּהוֹן תִּשְׁעָה וּשְׁלֹשִׁים כְּרִיכָן, כְּחוּשְׁבַּן טַ"ל. וּשְׁלֹשָׁה עֲשַׂר חֶלְיָין, כְּחוּשְׁבַּן אֶחָד. סַלְקִין בֶּ"ן. וְהַאי אִיהוּ בֶּן יֵ"ה. עַמּוּדָא דְּאֶמְצָעִיתָא.

300. The thirteen TRIPLE links contain 39 loops, as the numerical value of the word 'dew' (Heb. *tal* = 39), which, together with the thirteen links THEMSELVES that have the numerical value of the word 'one' (Heb. *echad* = 13), adds up to 'son' (Heb. *ben* = 52). And this hints at the son of Yud Hei, which is the Central Column, ZEIR ANPIN.

301. כָּל קֶשֶׁר בְּדִיּוּקְנָא דְּכַף יְמִינָא, כָּל חוּלְיָא בְּדִיּוּקְנָא דְּאֶצְבַּע, דְּאִית בֵּיהּ תְּלַת פִּרְקִין, לָקֳבֵל תְּלַת פְּרִיכוֹת. וְהָכִי בְּכָל אֶצְבַּע תְּלַת פִּרְקִין, לְבַר מִגּוּדָל. דְּאִיהוּ שִׁעוּר בֵּין קֶשֶׁר לְקֶשֶׁר דְּצִיצִית, כִּמְלֹא גוּדָל. אִיהִי מִדָּה דְּחוֹטָמָא. וּמִדָּה דְּעַיִן יְמִינָא וּשְׂמָאלָא. וְאִיהוּ מִדָּה בֵּין עַיִן לְעַיִן. וּמִדָּה דְּאֹזֶן יְמִינָא וּשְׂמָאלָא. וּמִדָּה דְּכָל שָׂפָה וְשָׂפָה. וּמִדָּה דְּלִישָׁנָא. מִדָּה אַחַת לְכָל הַיְרִיעוֹת.

301. Each knot is in the form of a right palm. Each link is in the form of a finger with three joints, paralleling the three loops, and so it is that all the fingers have three joints except the thumb THAT HAS JUST TWO. And it is the thumb that gives the distance between each pair of knots in the fringe, FOR THERE HAS TO BE A SPACE BETWEEN THEM OF A full thumb-breadth, and this is the same measurement as the nose, the width of the right and left eye, the distance between the eyes, the measurement of the right and left ear, and of each lip, and of the tongue. "and the curtains shall be all of one measure" (Shemot 26:2).

302. אַמָּה שִׁעוּר דְּגוּפָא, לְאַרְבַּע סִטְרִין וְעֵילָא וְתַתָּא. דְּאִינּוּן שִׁית אַמּוֹת. וּבְכָל אַמָּה וְאַמָּה שְׁלֹשָׁה פִּרְקִין, ח"י פִּרְקִין בְּשִׁית אַמִּין. וְאִינּוּן רָזָא דח"י נְעֲנוּעִין דְּלוּלָב. לְשִׁית סִטְרִין. תְּלַת נַעֲנוּעִין לְכָל סִטְרָא. וַעֲלַיְיהוּ אִתְּמַר, זֹאת קוֹמָתֵךְ דָּמְתָה לְתָמָר. וְדָא שִׁעוּר קוֹמָה, מִקְוֵה יִשְׂרָאֵל בִּשְׁכִינְתָּא, אִיהוּ ח"י אַרְבַּע זִמְנִין, דְּאִינּוּן אַרְבַּע סַלְקִין שִׁבְעִים וּשְׁנַיִם.

302. Cubit (lit. 'arm') is the measure of the body in four directions and up and down, making six cubits. And each arm has three joints, NAMELY THE ASPECT OF THREE COLUMNS, making eighteen joints in the six cubits, being the secret of the eighteen wavings with WHICH WE WAVE the Lulav in six directions, three in each direction. And about them it is said: "This your stature is like a palm-tree" (Shir Hashirim 7:8). FOR A PALM-TREE GROWS IN SEVENTY YEARS, WHICH IS THE SECRET OF THE SEVEN LOWER SFIROT THAT ARE IN THE BODY, WHERE CHOCHMAH, WHICH IS THE SECRET OF THE STATURE, IS REVEALED, AND NOT IN THE HEAD, AS EXPLAINED ABOVE. AND THEREFORE THE STATURE, WHICH IS THE

SECRET OF THE FIRST THREE SFIROT, IS LIKENED TO A PALM-TREE. And this is the height of the stature, THAT IT IS ONLY IN THE BODY, that the gathering (Heb. *mikveh*) of Yisrael WHICH IS ZEIR ANPIN BESTOWS upon the Shechinah, FOR THE LETTERS OF THE WORD *MIKVEH*, REARRANGED, SPELL 'STATURE' *(HEB. KOMAH)*. THAT IS TO SAY, ZEIR ANPIN EMANATES THIS STATURE OF BODY TO MALCHUT. AND WE WAVE THE LULAV FOUR TIMES WHEN WE RECITE HALEL. This makes four times eighteen, which four times make 72, FOR THE NAME OF 72 IS THE ROOT OF THE THREE COLUMNS, AND IS THE SECRET OF THE THREE VERSES: "AND THE ANGEL OF ELOHIM, WHO WENT BEFORE THE CAMP OF YISRAEL, REMOVED...AND IT CAME... AND MOSES STRETCHED OUT" (SHEMOT 14:19-21).

303. וְרָזָא דְּחֵיוָן, קוֹמָה דִּלְהוֹן וְגַבֵּיהֶם וְגוֹבַה לָהֶם וְיִרְאָה לָהֶם וְגַבוֹתָם וְגוֹ', וְגַבֵּיהֶם, אַרְבַּע חֵיוָן דִּמְרְכַּבְתָּא תַּתָּאָה. וְגוֹבַה לָהֶם, ד' חֵיוָן דִּמְרְכַּבְתָּא מְצִיעָתָא. וְגַבוֹתָם, אַרְבַּע חֵיוָן דִּמְרְכַּבְתָּא תְּלִיתָאָה. וְכֻלְּהוּ י"ב. וְאִינּוּן מְלֵאוֹת עֵינַיִם, סָבִיב לְאַרְבַּעְתָּן, יְדֹוָד יְדֹוָד יְדֹוָד.

303. And the secret of the living creatures, their stature IS THE SECRET OF THE VERSE: "As for their backs, they were so high that they were dreadful, and their backs..." (Yechezkel 1:18). "Their backs" refers to the four living creatures of the lower Chariot, WHICH ARE FROM MALCHUT. "they were so high" refers to the four living creatures of the central Chariot, WHICH IS THE SECRET OF ZEIR ANPIN. "and their backs" refers to the four living creatures of the third Chariot, THAT ARE FROM BINAH, all of them together being twelve. And THE FOUR LIVING CREATURES OF THE THIRD CHARIOT are "full of eyes round about them four," NAMELY ROUND ABOUT THE FOUR LIVING CREATURES OF THE THIRD UPPER CHARIOT, which is the secret of Yud Hei Vav Hei, Yud Hei Vav Hei, Yud Hei Vav Hei, THAT IS TO SAY, THE SECRET OF THE THREE YUD HEI VAV HEI IN 'HASHEM REIGNS, HASHEM REIGNED, HASHEM WILL REIGN FOR EVER AND EVER'; AND THEY HAVE A TOTAL OF TWELVE LETTERS BETWEEN THEM. 'HASHEM REIGNS', REFERS TO THE CENTRAL CHARIOT; 'HASHEM REIGNED', TO THE THIRD UPPER CHARIOT; AND 'HASHEM WILL REIGN' TO THE LOWER CHARIOT.

49. Bowing and standing upright

A Synopsis
The Faithful Shepherd outlines the four occasions when one has to bow and the four occasions when he has to stand upright during prayer.

The Relevance of this Passage
This comprehensive and instructional portion expounds upon the mysteries of the Amidah prayer and the significance of bowing and standing upright during the appropriate points of the connection. In the act of revealing these hidden mysteries, the Light generated by the Amidah prayer is aroused by the Zohar in the present moment. This Light helps mankind spiritually evolve and develop, which is our ultimate purpose in life.

The act of bowing, on one level of understanding, concerns the concept of humility. Those who pray with deep humility and a feeling of spiritual poverty are assured of having their prayers answered. Accordingly, humility is born in our hearts. Our prayers for peace, prosperity and lasting fulfillment are answered.

The energy force known as miracle vibrates throughout existence by the power of the 72 Names. And the entire realm of Malchut לstands uprightה. Namely, we evolve and ascend into the realm of Zeir Anpin, the Upper World where perfection, bliss and blessedness reign supreme.

This passage, like all sections of Zohar, is layered with meaning. Some interesting insights stand out concerning the spiritual evolution of humanity and the corresponding physical reflection in the world.

On one level of understanding, the Zohar discusses the basic spiritual and physical structure of man. Rabbi Shimon writes:

> "initially, Malchut was a state of prostration, which is the secret of the bowing, and has to be raised up through the Name of the Yud Hei Vav Hei, and has to be set upright through the Divine Name, through eighteen Worlds."

Malchut, according to the Zohar, corresponds to the 'First Man'. The Zohar is indicating that prior to the First Man, pre-man, initially walked in a state of prostration, bent over like an ape. Only through the infusion of divine energy, the genetic-like letters of the Creator's Name, did man stand upright and walk on two feet. The Name that altered our nature is the Tetragrammaton, the

Yod, Hei, Vav, Hei. The numerical value of this Name is 26. There are 26 bones in each foot. And the adult vertebral (spinal) column consists of 26 bones.

In paragraph 309, the Zohar speaks of the thumb and its correlation and relevance to the realm of Keter, which corresponds to the brain and human intelligence. According to the Zohar, the thumb is the vessel that holds the Light of Wisdom (Chassadim). Namely, through the thumb, intelligence is made possible. This is the secret to the spiritual evolution of man.

Interestingly, science offers similar insights into the physical evolution of man. Only apes and primates have hands capable of grasping objects. The grasp is made possible by the opposable thumb, which moves opposite to the rest of the fingers.

Science tells us that the key characteristics that played a role in human evolution is bipedalism (standing upright while walking on two legs), and the opposable thumb. A skillful hand with a thumb-grasp made intelligence advantageous for now it could create tools. Moreover, science tells us that the brain and the hand changed at the same time in our evolutionary history.

This is merely, the physical effect of the spiritual evolution that gave rise to man in this physical world.

The Central Column is spoken of in paragraph 310 and its correlation to the thumb. Central Column is our divine trait of free will. Free Will allows us to choose to not react to primal urges and selfish desires¶the distinguishing feature of man over the animal kingdom.

Finally, we learn that the word Amen, unites the Upper and Lower worlds. The one who recites Amen, is therefore considered 'greater than the one who says the blessing'. Our read of this paragraph utters the Amen throughout the world. It echoes into the distant past and into the future, thus uniting our world with the Upper World. This unification allows the Light to immediately complete our spiritual evolution in a merciful and pleasant manner.

304. וּמָארֵי דְקוֹמָה רְשִׁימִין בְּהוֹן בִּצְלוֹתָא, בְּאָן אֲתָר. אֶלָּא כָּל הַכּוֹרֵעַ כּוֹרֵעַ בְּבָרוּךְ. וְכָל הַזּוֹקֵף זוֹקֵף בַּשֵּׁם. זְקִיפוֹת אַרְבָּעָה. וּכְרִיעוֹת ד'. הָא הָכָא קָא רָמִיז בְּאִלֵּין זְקִיפוֹת וּכְרִיעוֹת, מוֹלִיךְ וּמֵבִיא לְמִי שֶׁד' רוּחוֹת הָעוֹלָם שֶׁלּוֹ, מַעֲלֶה וּמוֹרִיד לְמִי שֶׁהַשָּׁמַיִם וְהָאָרֶץ שֶׁלּוֹ. וְאִינּוּן שִׁית סִטְרִין, שָׁמַיִם וָאָרֶץ וְד' רוּחוֹת. לְקַבֵּל תְּלַת בִּרְכָאן קַדְמָאִין, וּתְלַת

בַּתְרָאִין, בְּעוֹשֶׂה שָׁלוֹם בְּמְרוֹמָיו ד׳, כְּרִיעָה וּזְקִיפָא לִשְׂמָאלָא, וּכְרִיעָה וּזְקִיפָא לִימִינָא. וְהַאי אִיהוּ נוֹתֵן שָׁלוֹם לִשְׂמֹאלוֹ וִימִינוֹ, לִשְׂמֹאל רַבּוֹ, וְלִימִין רַבּוֹ.

304. And those who have stature are marked with these THREE CHARIOTS during prayer. Where would that be? HE ANSWERS, When one bows, one should bow at 'Blessed' (the first word of each blessing), and when returning to the upright position, one should do so at the mention of the Name. THERE ARE four occasions when one has to bow and four when one has to stand upright. ONE HAS TO BOW AND THEN STAND UPRIGHT AT THE BEGINNING AND END OF THE FIRST BLESSING (OF THE AMIDAH), AND ALSO AT THE BEGINNING AND END OF *MODIM'* (LIT. 'WE GIVE THANKS'). By so bowing and standing upright, one suggests going to and bringing to Him, to whom the four directions belong, and ascending and descending for Him to whom the heaven and the earth belong, THE SAME AS WITH THE LULAV. These are the six directions: towards heaven and towards the earth and to the four directions of the world, which parallel the first three blessings, WHICH ARE CHESED, GVURAH, AND TIFERET, and the last three blessings, WHICH ARE NETZACH, HOD AND YESOD, MAKING A TOTAL OF EIGHT BOWS AND AGAIN STANDINGS UPRIGHT. And there are four in 'May He who makes peace in His high places make peace for us and for all Yisrael', namely: bowing and again standing upright to the left and bowing and again standing upright to the right, and this is LIKE ONE WHO STANDS OPPOSITE HIS MASTER. HIS RIGHT WILL AT BE HIS MASTER'S LEFT, AND HIS LEFT WILL BE HIS MASTER'S RIGHT. He THUS offers peace to his left and his right, WHERE HIS RIGHT IS OPPOSITE his Master's left AND HIS LEFT IS OPPOSITE his Master's right.

305. הָא אִינּוּן תְּרֵיסַר, בֵּין כְּרִיעוֹת וּזְקִיפוֹת. וּבְהוֹן ע״ב עַיְינִין. ו׳ כְּרִיעוֹת בְּהוֹן ח״י נְעָנוּעִין, ג׳ בְּכָל פַּעַם, רֹאשׁ וְגוּף וְזָנָב, דְּצָרִיךְ לְמִכְרַע. בְּח״י חוּלְיָין סַלְקִין ע״ב. בְּאִלֵּין ע״ב עַיְינִין דְּקוּדְשָׁא בְּרִיךְ הוּא, נַהֲרִין ע״ב גַּדְפִין דִּשְׁכִינְתָּא, וְקַמַת עָלַיְיהוּ, וְאִתְקְרִיאַת עֲמִידָה. דִּבְקַדְמֵיתָא נְפִילָה אִיהִי, וְצָרִיךְ לְאַקָמָא לָהּ בְּשֵׁם יְדֹוָד, בְּח״י עָלְמִין, וּבְאַרְבַּע זְקִיפוֹת בְּשִׁית בִּרְכָאן, דְּאִיהוּ תִּפְאֶרֶת, כָּלִיל תְּלַת בִּרְכָאן קַדְמָאִין, וּתְלַת בִּרְכָאן בַּתְרָאִין.

305. This makes a total of twelve bows and standings upright, NAMELY FOUR BOWS AND STANDINGS UPRIGHT AT THE BEGINNING AND END OF '*AVOT*'; FOUR BOWS AND STANDINGS UPRIGHT AT THE BEGINNING AND END OF '*MODIM*'; FOUR BOWS AND STANDINGS UPRIGHT TO THE RIGHT AND LEFT DURING "MAY HE WHO MAKES PEACE." And they contain 72 eyes, FOR THEY ARE THE SIX DIRECTIONS, NAMELY TO HIM TO WHOM THE FOUR DIRECTIONS BELONG, TOGETHER WITH THE HEAVENS AND THE EARTH, AS ABOVE, AND SIX TIMES TWELVE IS 72. AND BECAUSE THEY DRAW DOWN CHOCHMAH BY MEANS OF STANDINGS UPRIGHT, THEY ARE, THEREFORE, CALLED 'EYES'. The six bows contain eighteen movements, three in each bow, for one has to bend the head, the back, and the tail, LOOSENING the eighteen vertebrae IN THE SPINE, THUS ALLUDING TO YESOD, WHICH IS CALLED 'LIVING' (HEB. *CHAI* = 18), AND THE IMPLICATION IS THAT ONE HAS TO INCLUDE YESOD IN THESE SIX BOWS. AND THE TWELVE BOWS AND STANDING UPRIGHT amount to 72 AS ABOVE. And these 72 eyes of the Holy One, blessed be He, THAT ARE BESTOWED TO MALCHUT, illuminated the 72 wings of the Shechinah that rises up over them and is called 'standing', WHICH IS THE SECRET OF THE AMIDAH (LIT. 'STANDING') PRAYER. For, initially, MALCHUT was a state of prostration, WHICH IS THE SECRET OF BOWING, and has to be raised up through the Name of Yud Hei Vav Hei, AND HAS TO BE SET UPRIGHT THROUGH THE DIVINE NAME, through eighteen worlds THROUGH YESOD, THAT IS CALLED 'LIVING', and through the four standings upright in six blessings, which is Tiferet, that includes the first three blessings and the last three blessings.

306. וְלִמְכְרַע בְּחַ"י עָלְמִין, וְהַאי אִיהוּ ו"ו ו'. כָּל הַכּוֹרֵעַ כּוֹרֵעַ בְּבָרוּךְ, וְכָל הַזּוֹקֵף זוֹקֵף בְּשֵׁם יְהֹוָה. עַמּוּדָא דְּאֶמְצָעִיתָא וְצַדִּיק ו"ו ו'. וְאִינּוּן רְמִיזִין בְּוַיִּסַּע וַיָּבֹא וַיֵּט ו"ו עִלָּאָה. אָחִיד בִּזְקִיפָה וּכְרִיעָה, וְכֻלְּהוּ סַלְּקִין ח"י בִּרְכָאן דִּצְלוֹתָא.

306. And one has to bow at the 18 worlds, NAMELY AT THE ATTRIBUTE OF YESOD WHICH IS CALLED 'LIVING' (HEB. *CHAI* = 18). And this is Vav Vav and Vav, for when one bows, one should bow at 'Blessed', WHICH IS YESOD THAT IS CALLED 'BLESSED', and when returning to the upright position, one should do so at the mention of the name Yud Hei Vav Hei, which is the Central Column, THAT IS TIFERET, WHICH IS CALLED YUD

HEI VAV HEI, and the Righteous THAT IS CALLED 'BLESSED'. And they are Vav Vav and Vav, FOR TIFERET IS THE SECRET OF THE LETTER VAV FULLY SPELLED WITH VAV VAV, WHILE YESOD IS THE SECRET OF THE LETTER VAV WRITTEN AS A SINGLE VAV. And these THREE VAVS are alluded to in THE INITIAL LETTERS OF THE THREE VERSES: "And the angel of Elohim, who went before the camp of Yisrael, removed (Heb. *vayisa*)... and it came (Heb. *vayavo*)... And Moses stretched out (Heb. *vayet*)" (Shemot 14:19-21). AND THEY ARE THE SECRET OF THE THREE COLUMNS OF THE NAME OF 72. The upper Vav Vav, WHICH IS TIFERET, is connected with standing upright and with bowing down, AND HAS THEREFORE TWO VAV'S. BUT YESOD, WHICH IS CONNECTED WITH BOWING ONLY, HAS JUST ONE VAV. And all of them, ALL THE THREE VAVS, add up to EIGHTEEN, CORRESPONDING TO THE eighteen blessings of the Amidah prayer.

307. ד' כְּרִיעוֹת בַּאֲדֹנָי, ד' זְקִיפוֹת בַּיְדֹוָד, עַמּוּדָא דְּאֶמְצָעִיתָא. וּשְׁכִינְתָּא חַי עָלְמִין, קָשִׁיר לוֹן, וְדָא יְאֲהדֹונָה"י, אָמֵן, בְּכָל בִּרְכָתָא מח"י בִּרְכָאן, ח"י זִמְנִין יְדֹוָד אִינּוּן ע"ב עַיְינִין, דְּנָהֲרִין בְּע"ב גַּדְפִּין, דְּאִינּוּן ח"י זִמְנִין אֲדֹנָי.

307. There are four bows at Adonai, and four standings upright at Yud Hei Vav Hei, which are the Central Column CALLED YUD HEI VAV HEI, and the Shechinah THAT IS CALLED 'ADONAI'. The living one of the worlds, WHICH IS YESOD, unites them, NAMELY YUD HEI VAV HEI AND ADONAI, ONE WITH THE OTHER, making: Yud-Aleph-Hei-Dalet-Vav-Nun-Hei-Yud, WHICH IS THE LETTERS OF YUD HEI VAV HEI AND ADONAI INTERWOVEN. THE NUMERICAL VALUE OF THESE IS Amen, 91. AT THE CONCLUSION OF each of the eighteen blessings OF THE PRAYER, WHERE IS YUD HEI VAV HEI, there are eighteen times THE FOUR LETTERS OF Yud Hei Vav Hei, AND EIGHTEEN TIMES FOUR AMOUNTS TO 72, WHICH ARE the 72 eyes that illuminate in the 72 wings, which are eighteen times THE FOUR LETTERS OF Adonai.

308. וְרָזָא דְּמִלָּה, וְגַבֵּיהֶן, וְגוֹבַהּ לָהֶם, וְגַבּוֹתָם. וְגַבֵּיהֶן: גַּדְפִּין. וְגוֹבַהּ לָהֶם: אַנְפִּין. וְגַבּוֹתָם: דְּאִינּוּן עָלַיְיהוּ. מְלֵאֹת עֵינַיִם סָבִיב לְאַרְבַּעְתָּן, כֻּלְּהוּ מְרוּבָּעוֹת. וְכֹלָּא קָשׁוֹט, ע' אַנְפִּין לְאוֹרַיְיתָא. גַּדְפִּין, אֲדֹנָי.

אַנְפִּין, יְהֹוָה, אֶהְיֶה. עַיְינִין, אֶהְיֶה. וְסַלְּקִין יַבַ״ק בְּחוּשְׁבַּן, אֲדֹנָי, בְּמַעֲשֶׂה. יְדֹוָד, בְּדִבּוּר. אֶהְיֶה, בְּמַחֲשָׁבָה.

308. And the secret of the matter is in the verse: "As for their rims, they were so high that they were dreadful, and their rims" (Yechezkel 1:18) THAT REFERS TO THE LIVING CREATURES. "as for their rims" REFERS TO the wings, WHICH IS MALCHUT; "they were so high" REFERS TO faces, WHICH IS ZEIR ANPIN; "and their rims," which are over them IN THE ASPECT OF BINAH, are "full of eyes round about them four," for all of them are surrounded on the four sides BY THE FOUR LETTERS. AND THERE WOULD SEEM TO BE A CONTRADICTION HERE, FOR HE HAS SAID THAT THE 72 EYES ARE IN ZEIR ANPIN. HE THUS ADDS: And everything is true, THAT IS TO SAY, ALL THREE ASPECTS, PINIONS, COUNTENANCES AND EYES, ARE ALL INCLUDED IN ZEIR ANPIN, WHICH IS CALLED 'TRUTH'. AND THE PROOF OF THIS IS TO BE FOUND IN THE SAYING 'There are Ayin (lit. 'eye' = seventy) faces to the Torah'. THUS THE TORAH, WHICH IS ZEIR ANPIN, HAS EYES AND FACES, BUT IN THE PARTICULAR ASPECT, the wings are considered Adonai, WHICH IS MALCHUT; the faces are Yud Hei Vav Hei, WHICH IS ZEIR ANPIN, and the eyes are Eheyeh, WHICH IS BINAH. The sum total OF THE THREE NAMES ADONAI, YUD HEI VAV HEI AND EHEYEH is Yud Bet Kof (= 112), AND THESE THREE LETTERS ARE THE INITIAL LETTERS OF THE WORDS YICHUD (ENG. 'UNIFICATION'), BERACHAH (ENG. 'BLESSING') AND KEDUSHAH (ENG. 'SANCTIFICATION'). THE NAME 'Adonai' ALLUDES TO THE ASPECT OF action, Yud Hei Vav Hei to THE ASPECT OF speech, and Eheyeh to THE ASPECT OF thought.

309. בְּכָל עַיִן וְעַיִן, שִׁיעוּר גּוּדָל. וְדָא ו' בֵּינוֹנִי. וּב' פִּרְקִין בְּגוּדָל, אִינּוּן י' י'. לָקֳבֵל חוֹטָמָא ו'. לָקֳבֵל בּ' נַקְבֵי חוֹטָמָא, י' י'. וְסַלְּקִין יוֹד הֵא. וְדָא וַיִּיצֶר. שִׁיעוּר דְּכָל מִדָּה וּמִדָּה, יוֹד הֵא, בְּכָל אֲתָר שָׁלְטָנוּתֵיהּ, בְּכָל אֵבֶר וְאֵבֶר. כָּל אֵבֶר, כְּגוֹן יִפְרוֹשׂ כְּנָפָיו יִקָּחֵהוּ יִשָּׂאֵהוּ עַל אֶבְרָתוֹ.

309. Each and every eye is the size of a thumb, and this is the middling Vav, NAMELY THE ASPECT OF THE CENTRAL COLUMN, OF ONLY TWO JOINTS, THE UPPER JOINT IN IT MISSING. For the thumb has but two joints which are the secret of Yud Yud. In respect to the nose, THE THUMB IS CALLED

'Vav', NAMELY MIDDLE VAV. And in respect to the two nostrils that are in the nose, WHICH ARE RIGHT AND LEFT AND NOT AS ONE, THEY ARE CALLED 'Yud Yud'. THE NUMERICAL VALUE OF THE VAV, TOGETHER WITH THE TWO LETTERS YUD is Yud-Vav-Dalet, Hei Aleph, NAMELY 26. And this is as in "*vayyitzer* (Eng. 'formed')" (Beresheet 2:7), WHICH IS SPELLED AT THE BEGINNING WITH VAV AND TWO YUD'S, WHICH TEACHES ABOUT THE SIZE OF THE THUMB. IT IS the size of each measure of Yud-Vav-Dalet, Hei-Aleph, WHICH IS THE FIRST THREE SFIROT, whenever THE FIRST THREE SFIROT have control in each and every part of the body. THAT IS TO SAY, IN EVERY LIMB THERE IS A HEAD AND A BODY, AND THE MEASURE OF THUMB CONTROLS THE MEASURE OF THE HEAD OF THE LIMB. Every limb HERE MEANS EVERY WHOLE LIMB, such as in "spreads abroad her wings, takes them, bears them on her pinions (also: 'limbs')" (Devarim 32:11). THERE ARE WINGS, WHICH ARE THE LOWER ASPECT OF THE LIMB, WHICH IS THE ASPECT OF A THREE-JOINTED FINGER, AND THERE IS THE LIMB, AND THERE IS THE ASPECT OF A THUMB OF TWO JOINTS, BECAUSE IT IS THE UPPER ASPECT WHICH IS THE SECRET OF YUD HEI THAT IS IN IT.

310. לֵית אֵבֶר בְּכָל מֶרְכַּבְתּוֹ, דְּלָאו אִיהוּ כָּל אֵבֶר בְּדִיּוּקְנֵיהּ. וּבְכָל אֲתָר אִשְׁתְּכַח, וּפְנֵיהֶם וְכַנְפֵיהֶם פְּרוּדוֹת מִלְמַעְלָה. לְקַבֵּל פָּרְשִׁיָּין פְּתִיחָן דִּתְפִלִּין. לְקַבֵּל תּוֹרָה. וְכַד לְתַתָּא, אִינּוּן סְתִימִין פָּרְשִׁיָּין, לְקַבֵּל יְאַדְדּוּנְדִי עָלַיְיהוּ. בְּאַנְפּוֹי וְגַדְפּוֹי.

310. And there is no limb in the whole of his Chariot that does not have the form of a COMPLETE limb, in his image NAMELY, THE ASPECT OF HEAD AND OF BODY, AS ABOVE, IN THE PRECEDING PARAGRAPH, and in every place you will find "Thus were their faces: and their wings were divided upwards" (Yechezkel 1:11), NAMELY IN THE ASPECT OF THE FIRST THREE SFIROT OF THE LIMB, WHERE A THUMB'S MEASURE IS IN CONTROL AS THE RIGHT AND THE LEFT OF THE CENTRAL COLUMN ARE SEPARATED, AS ABOVE. And this corresponds to the open sections (namely the Biblical text leaves the line open and continues on the subsequent line) in the Tefilin, WHICH PARALLELS THE ASPECT OF THE FIRST THREE SFIROT, WHICH ARE SEPARATED, before the Torah, WHICH IS ZEIR ANPIN, AS IT IS THE FIRST THREE SFIROT, NAMELY THE EYES AND THE FACES, AS ABOVE. And when they are below, IN THE ASPECT OF THE SIX ENDS, THERE IS

THEN A UNION BETWEEN RIGHT AND LEFT OF THE CENTRAL COLUMN, AS WELL AS BETWEEN ZEIR ANPIN AND MALCHUT, WHICH ARE RIGHT AND LEFT. And THEN the sections OF THE TEFILIN are closed (namely the next verse in the Biblical text continues on the same line), paralleling Yud-Aleph-Hei-Dalet-Vav-Nun-Hei-Yud that are on them, with their faces and their wings, WHICH ARE ZEIR ANPIN and MALCHUT, WHO ARE HERE UNITED IN EACH OTHER, AND THUS THE SECTIONS ARE CLOSED. AND HERE THEIR FACES AND THEIR WINGS ARE NOT SEPARATED, BECAUSE IT IS FROM BELOW, WHICH IS THE SIX EXTREMITIES.

311. וְקוּדְשָׁא בְּרִיךְ הוּא רָשִׁים בְּיִשְׂרָאֵל לְקַבְּלַיְיהוּ, בִּצְלוֹתָא לְמֶהֱוֵי חַבְרִים בַּהֲדַיְיהוּ, לְמִכְרַע בְּכָל גּוּפַיְיהוּ, בִּתְמַנְיֵ סְרֵי בִּרְכָאן דִּצְלוֹתָא, לְאַמְלְכָא עָלַיְיהוּ אָמֵן, וְאִיהוּ יְאָהֳדוֹנָהִי, בְּכָל אֵבֶר וְאֵבֶר דִּלְהוֹן, וְאָמַר קוּדְשָׁא בְּרִיךְ הוּא, מַאן דְּלָא הֲוֵי רָשִׁים קָדָמַייכוּ, לְמֶהֱוֵי כּוֹרֵעַ בְּבָרוּךְ, וְזוֹקֵף בַּיְהֹוָה, בְּקוֹמָה דְּגוּפָא, לָא יֵיעוּל צְלוֹתֵיהּ בְּהֵיכָלָא דִּילִי, דְּאִיהוּ אֲדֹנָי. לָא תְּקַבְּלוּן מִלִּין דִּילֵיהּ, עַל גַּדְפַּייכוּ וְאַנְפַּייכוּ, דְּכָל מַאן דִּמְצַלֵּי בַּאֲדֹנָי, וּמְצָרֵף לַיְדֹוִד אַנְפִּין דְּמַלְאָכִין, וּפְנֵיהֶם וְכַנְפֵיהֶם פְּרוּדוֹת לְעֵילָא, לְנַטְלָא יְאָהֳדוֹנָה"י, בְּמִלִּין דִּצְלוֹתָא דְּנָפְקִין מִפּוּמוֹי דְּבַר נָשׁ.

311. And the Holy One, blessed be He, makes marks on Yisrael in respect thereof, NAMELY IN RESPECT TO THE FACES AND WINGS OF THE LIVING CREATURES in the prayer, in order that Yisrael should be friends WITH THE LIVING CREATURES, namely by bowing with the whole body in the eighteen blessings of the prayer, so that He should, in each and every one of their limbs, make Amen king over them, which is the secret of Yud-Aleph-Hei Dalet-Vav-Nun-Hei-Yud, WHICH HAS THE SAME NUMERICAL VALUE AS AMEN. FOR, BY BOWING ONE DRAWS DOWN 'ADONAI' AND BY STANDING UPRIGHT ONE DRAWS DOWN YUD HEI VAV HEI, AND LATER, BY LIFE OF THE WORLDS, THE TWO OF THEM UNITE AND INTERWEAVE TOGETHER IN THE SECRET OF YUD-ALEPH-HEI-DALET VAV-NUN-HEI-YUD. And the Holy One, blessed be He, said TO THE ANGELS, WHO ARE THE FOUR LIVING CREATURES: 'Whoever is not marked before you as bowing at 'Blessed' and standing up erect at the Yud Hei Vav Hei to the full stature of his body, his prayer will not enter into My palace, which is Adonai, and you

should not accept his speeches on your wings and your faces.' For everyone who prays with Adonai and combines it with Yud Hei Vav Hei, which is the faces of the angels, NAMELY OF THE FOUR LIVING CREATURES, IT IS THEN SAID ABOUT THE LIVING CREATURES, "Thus were their faces: and their wings were divided upwards" (Yechezkel 1:11), IN THE ASPECT OF THEIR FIRST THREE SFIROT IN ORDER to welcome AFTERWARDS THE UNITY OF Yud-Aleph-Hei-Dalet-Vav-Nun-Hei-Yud, IN THEIR SIX EXTREMITIES, with the words of the prayer that issues forth from the mouth of man.

312. וְגָדוֹל הָעוֹנֶה אָמֵן יוֹתֵר מִן הַמְבָרֵךְ. דִּלְגַבֵּי אֲדֹנָי יְהֹוָה בִּצְלוֹתָא, וּפְנֵיהֶם וְכַנְפֵיהֶם פְּרוּדוֹת. לָקֵבֵּל יְהֹוָה בְּאַנְפִּין, אֲדֹנָי בְּגַדְפִּין, כְּרוּב אֶחָד מִקָּצָה מִזֶּה וּכְרוּב אֶחָד מִקָּצָה מִזֶּה. אֲבָל כַּד חָזַר שׁ"ץ צְלוֹתָא, וְעוֹנֶה אָמֵן, אִיהוּ בַּמַּחְבֶּרֶת הַשֵּׁנִית, מִתְחַבְּרִין תְּרֵין שְׁמָהָן בַּמַּחְבֶּרֶת הַשֵּׁנִית. בְּקַדְמֵיתָא, מַקְבִּילֹת הַלֻּלָאֹת אַחַת אֶל אֶחָת בַּקְּרָשִׁים, דְּאִינּוּן קֶשֶׁר אֶצְבְּעָאן. אֲבָל בְּאָמֵן, וְהָיָה הַמִּשְׁכָּן אֶחָד, דְּבֵיהּ חוֹבְרוֹת אִשָּׁה אֶל אֲחוֹתָהּ.

312. And the one who answers 'Amen' is greater than the one who says the blessing, for, regarding Adonai combined with Yud Hei Vav Hei said in ANY MAN'S prayer, IT IS SAID "Thus were their faces: and their wings were divided," for 'faces' parallels Yud Hei Vav Hei and 'their wings' PARALLELS Adonai. AND THIS IS THE SECRET OF "And make one cherub at the one end" (Shemot 25:19), WHICH IS YUD HEI VAV HEI, "and one cherub at the other end" (Ibid.), WHICH IS ADONAI; AND THE TWO ARE SEPARATED, FOR THE UNIFICATION OF YUD HEI VAV HEI AND ADONAI IN COMBINATION IS NOT ACHIEVED IN THE BLESSINGS OF THE PRAYERS, BUT ONLY IN THE AMIDAH PRAYER. But when the cantor of the service repeats the prayer, and one responds 'Amen', WHICH UNITES AND COMBINES YUD HEI VAV HEI WITH ADONAI, THE NUMERICAL VALUE OF 'AMEN' BEING THE SAME AS THAT OF THE TWO NAMES COMBINED, HE IS THUS GREATER THAN THE ONE WHO SAYS THE BLESSING. For he is in the second coupling, NAMELY IN THE LOWER JOINING OF THE SIX EXTREMITIES, for it is in the second coupling that the two names YUD HEI VAV HEI AND ADONAI join together. At the beginning, NAMELY AT THE FIRST JOINING, WHICH PARALLELS THE FIRST THREE SFIROT, "the loops held one curtain to another" (Shemot 36:12) on the boards, which are the

connection of the fingers AS THE WORD *KERASHIM* (ENG. 'BOARD') IS COMPOSED OF THE SAME LETTERS OF *KESHARIM* (ENG. 'CONNECTIONS'). FOR THEN, THE TABERNACLE IS NOT ONE ACCORDING TO THE SECRET OF YUD-ALEPH-HEI-DALET-VAV-NUN-HEI-YUD. But at THE REPETITION BY THE CANTOR OF THE PRAYERS, WHICH IS THE SECRET OF THE AMIDAH, HE ANSWERS Amen, WHICH IS THE UNIFICATION OF YUD-ALEPH-HEI-DALET-VAV-NUN-HEI-YUD, WHOSE TOTAL NUMERICAL VALUE IS AS THAT OF THE LETTERS OF THE WORD 'Amen', THEN: "the tabernacle may be one" (Shemot 26:6), for in it they are "coupled one to another" (Ibid. 3), ALLUDING TO YUD HEI VAV HEI ADONAI. THUS, GREATER IS THE ONE WHO RESPONDS WITH AMEN AT THE AMIDAH PRAYER, MORE SO THAN THE ONE WHO BLESSES DURING THE OTHER BLESSINGS OF THE PRAYER.

50. At times they are silent and at times they are speaking

A Synopsis

This section tells about the arrangement of speech in prayer. The title refers to the beasts of fire in Ezekiel's vision, and we hear that they are silent when God speaks, even as Yisrael should be quiet when the Torah is being read. Those who are silent during prayer and Halachah will receive the reward of understanding.

The Relevance of this Passage

Understanding and truth blossom in our hearts and minds. The negative chatter, morbid thoughts, and self-destructive impulses that torment our mind are, at last, silenced. A quiet calm fills our being. The voice of the Creator will now be heard in our daily lives, speaking to us through our soul. It will be our intuition that forever guides us, as opposed to the chaotic rational consciousness that emanates from the side of the Evil Inclination.

In paragraph 315 the Zohar states:

> "For those who engage in the study of the Torah for its own sake, the waters of the Torah come forth for them corrected..."

The water that comprises more than 65% of our body is now purified. Our cells flourish in this environment, engendering healing and well-being. This effect extends to the waters of our planet, which are corrected, healed, and purified. All water now possesses the properties of cleansing and healing!

313. תִּקּוּנָא תְּלִיתָאָה סֵדֶר דִּבּוּרָא דִּצְלוֹתָא, דְּבֵיהּ חֵיוָן אֶשָּׁא מְמַלְלָן. וְהַאי הִיא וָאֵרֶא כְּעֵין חַשְׁמַל כְּמַרְאֵה אֵשׁ בֵּית לָהּ סָבִיב. הַאי אִיהוּ רָזָא דְחַשְׁמַל. דְּאִינּוּן חֵיוָן אֶשָּׁא, עַתִּים חָשׁוֹת עַתִּים מְמַלְלוֹת. וְאִינּוּן דְּחָשׁוֹת לס״ת, בְּזִמְנָא דְּדִבּוּר נָפִיק מִפִּי הַקּוֹרֵא, אִיהוּ חָשִׁיב לְגַבַּיְיהוּ, כְּאִלּוּ מְקַבְּלִים אוֹרַיְיתָא בְּטוּרָא דְּסִינַי. וּבְזִמְנָא דְּאָמַר אִיהוּ אָנֹכִי, לָא אִשְׁתְּמַע קָלָא, וְלָא דִּבּוּרָא אַחֲרָא דְּחֵיוָן, אֶלָּא דִּילֵיהּ.

313. The third correction is the arrangement of speech in prayer, in which the living creatures of fire speak. And this is: "And I saw something like the color of electrum, like the appearance of fire round about enclosing it" (Yechezkel 1:27). This is the secret of the electrum: that those living

creatures of fire sometimes are silent and at other times speak. AND THEY ARE THE SECRET OF THE CONGREGATION LISTENING TO THE READING OF THE TORAH, for they are silent before the Torah scroll at this time when speech emerges from the mouth of the reader, for they consider it as though they were receiving the Torah on Mount Sinai. And when THE HOLY ONE, BLESSED BE HE, said: "I am..." (Shemot 20:2), nothing but His speech was heard, no other sound nor speech of the living creatures. AND THEREFORE, SINCE THE ONE WHO READS IN THE TORAH IS IN THE PLACE OF THE HOLY ONE, BLESSED BE HE, ON SINAI, IT IS NECESSARY THEN TO BE QUIET.

314. כְּגַוְונָא דָא, כַּד הִבּוּרָא דָא נָפִיק מִפּוּמֵיה דְקוּדְשָׁא בְּרִיךְ הוּא, חַיוֹת אֵשׁ חָשׁוֹת. וּבְזִמְנָא דְשָׁתִיק חַיוֹת אֵשׁ מְמַלְלוֹת. הָדָא הוּא דִכְתִּיב, וְכָל הָעָם רוֹאִים אֶת הַקּוֹלוֹת, קָלִין דְחֵיוָן, דַּהֲווֹ שָׁאֲגִין. וְאֶת הַלַּפִּידִים, דַּהֲווֹ נָפְקִין בְּדִבּוּר דְחֵיוָן, בְּכַמָּה מִינֵי נִגּוּן קָדָם מַלְכָּא. וְאִלֵּין דְאִינּוּן דְחָשׁוֹת לְסֵ"ת, אִינּוּן בְּדִיוּקְנַיְיהוּ דְחֵיוָן. וּמָנֵי לוֹן קוּדְשָׁא בְּרִיךְ הוּא, לְאַעֲלָא לוֹן, בְּחֶדֶר דְמַרְאֵה אֵשׁ בֵּית לָהּ.

314. And likewise AS WE HAVE SAID REGARDING "I AM," SO IS IT ALWAYS when speech emerges from the mouth of the Holy One, blessed be He: the living creatures of fire are quiet, FOR THAT IS THE TIME OF THE UNIFICATION OF VOICE AND SPEECH. And when He is silent, NAMELY BEFORE THERE IS YET UNIFICATION OF VOICE AND SPEECH, THEN, the living creatures of fire are speaking. This is as it is written: "And all the people perceived the thunderings" (lit. 'voices') (Shemot 20:15), namely the voice of the living creatures who were roaring. "and the lightnings," which were emitted with the speech of the living creatures, with many types of melody before the King, FOR THIS WAS BEFORE THE HOLY ONE, BLESSED BE HE, STARTED TO SPEAK. AND WHEN HE SAID: "I AM," THE LIVING CREATURES FELL QUIET AND NOTHING WAS TO BE HEARD EXCEPT HIS VOICE, AS EXPLAINED ABOVE. And those who are quiet at THE TIME OF THE READING FROM the scroll of the Torah have the same form as those living creatures WHO ARE QUIET AT THE TIME OF SPEECH OF THE HOLY ONE, BLESSED BE HE, AS EXPLAINED ABOVE. And the Holy One, blessed be He, commanded THAT THE LIVING CREATURES be brought into the room that is like the appearance of fire round about enclosing it.

315. וְעוֹד אִינּוּן דְּחָשׁוּת בִּצְלוֹתָא בח״י בִּרְכָאן, יֵיעֲלוּן בְּחֶדֶר דְּמַרְאָה דָא. וְעוֹד אִינּוּן דְּחָשׁוּת לַהֲלָכָה, דְּאִתְּמַר בָּהּ, אַגְרָא דִּשְׁמַעְתָּא סְבָרָא, יֵיעֲלוּן בְּחֶדֶר דְּאִיהוּ הֵיכַל דְּמַרְאָה דָא, דְּאוֹרַיְיתָא, עָלָהּ אִתְּמַר הֲלֹא כֹה דְּבָרִי כָּאֵשׁ נְאֻם יְיָ' וּכְפַטִּישׁ יְפוֹצֵץ סָלַע. וְדָא סֶלַע דְּאִתְּמַר בֵּיהּ וְדִבַּרְתֶּם אֶל הַסֶּלַע לְעֵינֵיהֶם וְנָתַן מֵימָיו. אִלֵּין דְּמִשְׁתַּדְּלִין בָּהּ לִשְׁמָהּ, נָפִיק לוֹן מַיָּא דְּאוֹרַיְיתָא מְתִיקָן, וְאִתְּמַר בְּהוֹן, וַתֵּשְׁתְּ הָעֵדָה וּבְעִירָם. וְאִלֵּין דְּלָא מִשְׁתַּדְּלִין בָּהּ לִשְׁמָהּ, נָפִיק לוֹן מַיִם מְרִירִין, דְּאִתְּמַר בְּהוֹן וַיְמָרֲרוּ אֶת חַיֵּיהֶם בַּעֲבוֹדָה קָשָׁה: דָא קוּשְׁיָא. בְּחֹמֶר: דָא קַל וָחֹמֶר. וּבִלְבֵנִים: בְּלִבּוּן הֲלָכָה.

315. Moreover, those who are silent during the prayer, during the eighteen blessings, FOR THAT IS WHERE THE UNIFICATION IS, will enter into the room of this appearance, NAMELY "LIKE THE APPEARANCE OF FIRE ROUND ABOUT ENCLOSING IT"; THIS WILL BE THEIR REWARD IN THE FUTURE. And also those who are silent before the Halachah, NAMELY THOSE WHO ARE SILENT IN ORDER TO HEAR AND UNDERSTAND THE PRACTICAL LAW AS EXPOUNDED BY THEIR RABBI, about which it is said: 'The reward of listening to the exposition of the Law is in the understanding thereof'. They will enter into the room, which is the palace of this vision, of the Torah, WHICH IS FIRE, about which it is said: "Is not My word like a fire? says Hashem; and like a hammer that breaks the rock in pieces?" (Yirmeyah 23:29). And the rock mentioned here is that about which it is said: "and speak to the rock before their eyes; and it shall give forth its water" (Bemidbar 20:8), WHICH IS MALCHUT. For those who engage in the study of the Torah for its own sake, the waters of the Torah come forth for them fit to drink, and it is said about them: "And the congregation drank, and their beasts also" (Ibid. 11). But those who do not engage in the Torah for its own sake shall find that the waters emerge for them bitter, and about them it is said: "And they made their lives bitter with hard (Heb. *kashah*) bondage, in mortar (Heb. *chomer*), and in brick (Heb. *levenim*)" (Shemot 1:14). Kashah is with difficult questioning or apparent contradictions (Heb. *kushya*): chomer refers to the exegetical principle of inference from minor to major (Heb. *kal vachomer*); and, levenim means the elucidation (Heb. *libun*) of the Halachah.

51. "And their feet were straight feet"

A Synopsis
The Faithful Shepherd undertakes a difficult explanation of a portion of Ezekiel's vision, from which we understand that people must run to the Torah and its precepts, and return in repentance.

The Relevance of this Passage
Repentance blooms in our hearts, opening up a door to the Upper Spheres. A ceaseless flow of Light pours out upon Creation.

We are connected to the angel Michael, who blankets the world with boundless Mercy, igniting and ensuring our Redemption through compassion, not destruction. The angel Gabriel fights on our behalf and triumphs over the left side (our Evil Inclination). Our prayers ascend to the Holy One through the power and secret of the "straight feet," and all mankind begins to walk in the way of the Light.

316. תִּקוּנָא רְבִיעָאָה וַחֲמִשָׁאָה, מִמַּרְאֵה מָתְנָיו וּלְמַעְלָה וּמִמַּרְאֵה מָתְנָיו וּלְמַטָּה. דִּבְהוֹן שׁוֹקֵי הַחַיּוֹת כְּנֶגֶד כֻּלָּן, וּבִסְפִירָן נֶצַח וְהוֹד. מְטַטְרוֹן אוֹת בִּצְבָא דִּילֵיה, וְאִיהוּ דִּיּוּקְנָא דְּצַדִּיק. דְּצַדִּיק אוֹת בִּצְבָא דִּלְעֵילָא, וּמְטַטְרוֹן אִיהוּ אוֹת בִּצְבָא דִּלְתַתָּא. מְטַטְרוֹן שַׁדַּי בֵּיה, וְהַחַיּוֹת רָצוֹא וָשׁוֹב כְּמַרְאֵה הַבָּזָק.

316. The fourth and fifth corrections are, "...from what appeared to be his loins upward, and from what appeared to be his loins downward" (Yechezkel 1:27), about which IT IS SAID that the legs of the living creatures are equivalent to all of them, and they are in the Sfirot of Netzach and Hod. FOR NETZACH AND HOD ARE CALLED 'LOINS', AND "FROM WHAT APPEARED TO BE HIS LOINS UPWARD" IS NETZACH, AND "FROM WHAT APPEARED TO BE HIS LOINS DOWNWARD" IS HOD. And Metatron is a sign in His army, for he has the form of the Righteous, WHICH IS YESOD, FOR RIGHTEOUS, WHICH IS YESOD OF ZEIR ANPIN, is a letter in His heavenly hosts, IN ATZILUT, while Metatron is a sign in the earthly hosts, IN BRIYAH. Metatron has Shadai in him, AS HE HAS THE SAME NUMERICAL VALUE AS THE SHADAI, ABOUT WHOM IT IS SAID: "And the living creatures ran and returned like the appearance of a flash of lightning" (Ibid. 14).

317. וְרַגְלֵיהֶם רֶגֶל יְשָׁרָה, דְּרַגְלִין דְּמַזִּיקִין כֻּלְּהוּ עֲקַלָּתוֹן. וְרַגְלֵיהֶן,
וְרַגְלִין דְּחֵיוָן, קַדִּישִׁין, אִתְּמַר בְּהוֹן וְרַגְלֵיהֶם רֶגֶל יְשָׁרָה, מִצַּד חַיָּה
דְּאִיהוּ יִשְׂרָאֵל, יִשְׂרָאֵל כָּלִיל תְּלַת חֵיוָן, דְּאִתְּמַר בְּהוֹן הָאָבוֹת הֵן הֵן
הַמֶּרְכָּבָה.

317. "And their feet were straight feet" (Ibid. 7). For the feet of the demons are crooked, while about their feet, namely about the feet of the holy living creatures, it is said: "And their feet were straight feet." This is from the aspect of a living creature, which is Yisrael, and Yisrael includes three living creatures, about whom it is said: 'The patriarchs are the Chariot'.

318. וְכַף רַגְלֵיהֶם כְּכַף רֶגֶל עֵגֶל, מִסִּטְרָא דְּחַיָּה דְּאִיהוּ שׁוֹר. וְנוֹצְצִים
כְּעֵין נְחֹשֶׁת קָלָל, מִסִּטְרָא דְּנָחָשׁ בָּרִיחַ דְּיַמָּא. דְּאִיהוּ סָלִיק לְגַבֵּיהּ
בְּיַבֶּשְׁתָּא. רָצוֹא, מִסִּטְרָא דְּנוּרִיאֵל, דְּסָלִיק רָצוֹא. וָשׁוֹב, מִסִּטְרָא
דְּשַׁדַּי. דְּהָכִי סָלִיק בְּחוּשְׁבַּן. וְאִיהוּ סָלִיק מְטַטְרוֹן.

318. "and the sole of their feet was like the sole of a calf's foot" (Ibid.) BECAUSE THEY ARE from the side of the living creature that is CALLED 'ox', WHICH IS THE SECRET OF THE LEFT COLUMN, AND THIS IS WHY THEY HAD A CALF'S FOOT. "and they sparkled like the color of burnished brass" (Ibid.), namely from the side of the slithering serpent that is in the sea and which ascends to the one on the dry land, NAMELY THAT ASCENDS TO FIGHT WITH THE SERPENT THAT IS ON THE DRY LAND. SERPENT (HEB. NACHASH) AND BRASS (HEB. NECHOSHET) ARE MALE AND FEMALE, WHICH ARE IN THE BRIGHTNESS, AND IT IS THEREFORE SAID: "AND THEY SPARKLED LIKE THE COLOR OF BURNISHED BRASS" NAMELY FROM THE SIDE OF THE SERPENT WHO ILLUMINATES IN THEM. "ran (Heb. ratzo)" (Ibid. 14), WHICH IS SAID ABOUT THE LIVING CREATURES, is from the side of Nuriel, which has the same numerical number as ratzo. SIMILARLY, "and returned (Heb. vashov)," WHICH IS SAID ABOUT THE LIVING CREATURES, is from the side of Shadai, which has the same numerical value as 'vashov'. And this is the numerical value of Metatron. AND THIS HAS ALREADY BEEN EXPLAINED ABOVE.

319. וְכַד הֲווֹ יִשְׂרָאֵל שַׁמְעִין קָלָא מִמִּזְרָח, הֲווֹ רָצִין תַּמָּן. וְלַמַּעֲרָב

הָכִי, וְכֵן לַדָּרוֹם וְלַצָּפוֹן. אָמַר קוּדְשָׁא בְּרִיךְ הוּא לְמַלְאֲכֵי הַשָּׁרֵת, אִלֵּין דְּרַהֲטִין לִצְלוֹתָא דְּמִצְוָה, וְרַהֲטִין לְפִרְקָא בְּשַׁבַּתָּא, וְרַהֲטִין לְמֶעְבַּד רְעוּתָא דִּילִי, וְתָיְיבִין בִּתְיוּבְתָּא. קַבִּילוּ לוֹן בְּהֵיכָלָא דְּהַאי מַרְאָה, דְּבְאִלֵּין סִימָנִין, אִינּוּן חַבְרִים בַּהֲדַיְיכוּ, אִינּוּן דְּרָצִין וְשָׁבִין בְּאוֹרַיְיתָא, בְּדִבּוּרָא דַּהֲלָכָה, אִינּוּן רְשִׁימִין בַּהֲדַיְיכוּ, וְאָעִילוּ לוֹן בְּהַאי הֵיכָלָא.

319. And whenever Yisrael heard the voice OF TORAH AND PRAYER from the east, they would run to the east, and similarly to the west, and likewise to the south and to the north. Te Holy One, blessed be He said to the ministering angels: "Those who run to the ordained prayer, and who run to hear the lesson on the Shabbat, and run to do My will and who repent, they are to be received in the temple of this appearance," NAMELY IN THE TEMPLE OF NETZACH AND HOD. For by these signs, THAT THEY RUN TO THE TORAH AND PRECEPTS AND RETURN IN REPENTANCE, NAMELY "RAN AND RETURNED," they are your friends. For they run and return in Torah, JUST AS THE LIVING CREATURES WHO "RAN AND RETURNED," in the speech of Halachah, and they are recorded with you, them you shall bring into this temple.

320. הָכִי כַּד מְצַלִּין יִשְׂרָאֵל, מִיכָאֵ"ל טָאס עָלְמָא בְּטִיסָא חֲדָא. וְגַבְרִיאֵ"ל טָאס בִּתְרֵין טָאסִין. וְכַד נָפִיק דִּבּוּרָא מִיִּשְׂרָאֵל, בַּהֲלָכָה, בִּצְלוֹתָא, וּבְכָל פִּקּוּדָא דִּשְׁכִינְתָּא תַּמָּן. אִינּוּן רָצִין לְגַבֵּהּ, וְשָׁבִין בָּהּ בִּשְׁלִיחוּת מָארֵיהוֹן. וּבְכָל אֲתַר דְּשַׁמְעִין קָלָא דְּאוֹרַיְיתָא, דְּתַמָּן קוּדְשָׁא בְּרִיךְ הוּא, אִינּוּן רָצִין לְגַבֵּי הַהוּא קָלָא, וְתָיְיבִין בָּהּ בִּשְׁלִיחוּתָא דְּמָארֵיהוֹן. דְּבְכָל קָלָא דְּשֵׁם יְדֹנָ"ד לֵית תַּמָּן, בְּדִבּוּרָא דְּלֵית תַּמָּן אֲדֹנָי, לָא רָצִין וְשָׁבִין תַּמָּן. ובג"ד, וְרַגְלֵיהֶם רֶגֶל יְשָׁרָה, כִּי יְשָׁרִים דַּרְכֵי יְדֹנָ"ד, בַּאֲתָר דִּידֹנָ"ד תַּמָּן, אִיהוּ דֶּרֶךְ יְשָׁרָה. וְאִי לֵית תַּמָּן יְדֹנָ"ד, לָאו אִיהוּ דֶּרֶךְ יְשָׁרָה.

320. And so it is that when Yisrael pray, Michael flies round the world with one flap of his wings, and Gabriel with two, and when the speech emerges from Yisrael in Halachah, prayer, or any precept where the Shechinah is,

they run to Her, TO THE SHECHINAH and return with Her, WITH THE SHECHINAH, on a mission from their Master, TO UNITE HER WITH YUD HEI VAV HEI. And in every place where the voice of Torah is heard, there the Holy One, blessed be He, is, and they run to that voice, and return with it on a mission from their Master. And whenever there is a voice without the Name Yud Hei Vav Hei being there, or speech without Adonai being there, MICHAEL AND GABRIEL do not run and return there. And this is why "their feet were straight feet," "for the ways of Hashem are straight" (Hoshea 14:10), THIS BEING THE SECRET OF THE CENTRAL COLUMN, where the way is straight. And if the Name Yud Hei Vav Hei is not there, the way is not straight.

321. וְעוֹד רַגְלֵיהֶם רֶגֶל יְשָׁרָה, אָמְרוּ מָארֵי מַתְנִיתִין, דְּמַאן דִּמְצַלֵּי, בָּעֵי לְתַקְּנָא רַגְלוֹי בִּצְלוֹתֵיה, כְּמַלְאֲכֵי הַשָּׁרֵת. כְּכַף רֶגֶל עֵגֶל, לְמֶהֱוֵי רָשִׁים בַּהֲדַיְיהוּ. וּבְגִין דָּא, אוֹקְמוּהָ רַבָּנָן, הַמִּתְפַּלֵּל צָרִיךְ לְכַוֵּון אֶת רַגְלָיו, שֶׁנֶּאֱמַר וְכַף רַגְלֵיהֶם כְּכַף רֶגֶל עֵגֶל. וְאָמַר קוּדְשָׁא בְּרִיךְ הוּא, אִלֵּין דְּאִינּוּן רְשִׁימִין בִּצְלוֹתַיְיהוּ הָכִי, לְכַוֵּון רַגְלוֹי כְּוָותַיְיכוּ, אַפְתְּחוּ לוֹן תַּרְעֵי הֵיכָלָא, לְאַעֲלָא בְּמַרְאָה דָּא.

321. Moreover, "And their feet were straight feet." The sages of the Mishnah said: 'One who prays should arrange his feet during his prayer as do the ministering angels', NAMELY HIS FEET SHOULD BE STRAIGHT "like the sole of a calf's foot," namely to be THUS marked among them. And for this reason the sages taught: 'When one prays, he should place his feet in proper position, as it says: "And their feet were straight feet".' And the Holy One, blessed be He, said TO THE MINISTERING ANGELS: 'Those who are thus noted in their prayer, that they place their feet as you do, for them open the gates of the temple to enter this vision' OF NETZACH AND HOD.

52. Sight, hearing, smell and speech

A Synopsis

We hear that Yud Hei Vav Hei rests on sight, hearing, smell and speech, and that Adonai rests on doing, touching, using and walking. The Faithful Shepherd explains what he means by this, and he tells us how Chochmah arose in a thought that is Binah; he says that thought and inspiration are both in the heart. The Shechinah is God's sight, hearing, sweet savor, speech, and performance of precepts – and in prayer it is also His bowing and standing. Moses says that in the future God will remove all of Lilit's children from the world, but not so the children of the Shechinah, who are Yisrael; the latter are virtuous, God-fearing men of truth who despise unjust gain. Moses tells what the sages meant when they said, 'No disciple whose inside does not correspond to his exterior may enter the house of study', and this explains why Yud Hei Vav Hei is called Adonai.

The Relevance of this Passage

The abundance of spiritual energy emanating from these mysterious verses is obviously far too vast and extensive to describe in a few short paragraphs. Suffice it to say that spiritual vision is granted to the reader, which includes the ability to perceive divinity in our daily life – in its turmoil and in its moments of tranquility.

Through the power of Ezekiel's vision and the hidden mysteries of the *Tetragrammaton* יהוה, our souls ascend into the supernal Temple, where we receive Light that perfects our being.

The smoke and fragrance of the ancient sacrifices billows from this passage and blends together to create Incense that banishes death from our being and from this world. The spiritual forces that arise through precepts, prayer, and Torah swirl in our midst. The *Shechinah* rests upon us and upon all civilization. This empowers our immune system and removes airborne diseases from the world.

Our souls are connected to the realm of *Binah* and our thoughts are aligned with the will of the Creator so that we are constantly inspired in our hearts to pursue this spiritual path. As our hearts are enlightened by the Sfirot of *Chochmah* and *Binah*, a great healing unfolds throughout the cardiovascular region.

Mankind is connected to the Upper Three Sfirot – *Keter, Chochmah*, and *Binah*; and through the *Shechinah* (the Divine Presence), a bounty of mercy is cast upon the world. Mercy washes away judgement and pain from our life.

Later in the passage, paragraph 327, the author of the Zohar speaks of (do not pronounce this name) *Lilit,* the wicked female angel who posseses no humility or modesty. She is the mother of all nefarious people who abhor spirituality and propagate only evil in this world. These are the Mixed Multitude, and you will know them by their actions for they speak evil about all those who share and disseminate the wisdom and Light of this sacred book. Here, *Lilit* and her offspring are banished from this world. Their reign of terror is ended. The Light of Kabbalah is now free to flourish the world over bringing peace and harmony to civilization as quickly as the light of a bulb expels darkness from a room.

Our world now mates with the Upper World, where the Light of Immortality shines upon us. Humility and modesty fill us so that we may receive countless blessings every moment of our lives.

In paragraph 331, the Zohar says:

> "This is how it is with men of unjust gain, for even if they had all the money in the world, it would never be enough for them."

Here we awaken appreciation for our lot in life. Our insatiable *Desire to Receive for the Self Alone* is subjugated so that we finally achieve lasting fulfillment and inner peace and calm.

In conclusion, paragraph 333 expounds upon the concealed mysteries of the *Tetragrammaton* (*Yod Hei Vav Hei*) whose true pronunciation has been a secret since the dawn of creation. We're told that in the *World to Come*, the proper utterance of this Holy Name will be spoken aloud, igniting mercy from all sides. When our eyes scan this passage, it's as if the proper vocalization of the *Tetragrammaton* is taking place. Consequently, boundless mercy now blankets our world. The World to Come – the Light of Binah – illumines all existence, and it becomes a reality in our present day.

322. תִּקּוּנָא שְׁתִיתָאָה, רָאִיתִי כְּמַרְאֵה אֵשׁ, הָכָא רְאִיָּיה מַמָּשׁ. אָמַר קוּדְשָׁא בְּרִיךְ הוּא, מַאן דְּיֵיעוּל בְּחֵיזוּ דָּא, וְיֵהֵא בִּצְלוֹתֵיהּ לְבֵיהּ לְעֵילָא, לְשֵׁם יְדֹנָ״ד, וְעֵינוֹי לְתַתָּא בִּשְׁמָא דַּאֲדֹנָ״י, תֵּיעֲלוּן בְּהֵיכָלָא דָּא, כְּגַוְונָא דְּמַלְאָכִין, וְגַבֵּיהֶן לְעֵילָא, וְיִרְאָה לָהֶם לְתַתָּא, לָקֳבֵל שְׁכִינְתָּא דְּאִיהִי יִרְאַת יְדֹנָ״ד.

322. The sixth correction is "I saw what appeared to be fire" (Yechezkel

1:27). THIS IS THE FIRST TIME THAT HE USES THE WORDS "I SAW," THIS
WAS NOT MENTIONED UP TO HERE FOR here the meaning is proper sight.
The Holy One, blessed be He said: Whoever enters in this vision, and
during his prayer his heart is lifted up at the Name of Yud Hei Vav Hei and
his eyes are cast down at the name Adonai, him shall you bring in to this
temple, for he is like the angels ABOUT WHOM IT IS WRITTEN: "As for their
rims" (Ibid. 18) above, in Yud Hei Vav Hei, "and they were dreadful (or:
'had dread')" (Ibid.), downwards, towards the Shechinah, who is the dread
of Yud Hei Vav Hei.

323. וּבִרְאִיָּיה וּשְׁמִיעָה וְרֵיחָא וְדִבּוּר, שַׁרְיָא יְדֹוָ"ד. בַּעֲשִׂיָּיה, בְּמִשּׁוּשׁ,
שְׁמּוּשׁ, הִלּוּךְ, שַׁרְיָא אֲדֹנָי. וְדָא רְאִיָּה, דְּאוֹר וְנֵר, דְּאִתְּמַר בָּה וְתוֹרָה
אוֹר. רֵיחָא דְּקָרְבְּנִין, דְּאִינּוּן צְלוֹתִין, דִּבּוּר בְּאוֹרַיְיתָא, דִּבּוּר בִּצְלוֹתָא.
וַעֲשִׂיָּיה דְּמִצְוָה, וְשִׁמּוּשׁ דִּילָה, וּמִשּׁוּשׁ דִּילָה, וְהִלּוּךְ דִּילָה. וּרְאִיָּיה
וּשְׁמִיעָה, דְּלֵית תַּמָּן אוֹרַיְיתָא וּמִצְוָה, קוּדְשָׁא בְּרִיךְ הוּא וּשְׁכִינְתֵּיה
לָא שַׁרְיָא תַּמָּן. דְּקוּדְשָׁא בְּרִיךְ הוּא שַׁרְיָא בִּרְאִיָּיה, וְכֵן שְׁכִינְתֵּיה,
דְּאוֹרַיְיתָא וְתוֹרָה אוֹר, שְׁכִינְתֵּיה רְאִיָּה דִּילֵיה יְדֹוָד בְּמַרְאָה אֵלָיו
אֶתְוַדַּע, שְׁכִינְתֵּיה.

323. The Yud Hei Vav Hei rests on sight, hearing, smell and speech, FOR
SIGHT AND HEARING ARE YUD HEI, AND SMELL AND SPEECH ARE VAV
HEI. Adonai rests on doing, touching, mating using, and walking. This sight
is THAT MODE OF VISION by light and by candle flame, about which it is
said: "...and Torah is light" (Mishlei 6:23). Smell is THE SMELL of the
sacrifices, which are prayers. Speech is about Torah; speech is in prayer,
and doing is for precepts. Mating using also is for performing a precept, as
does touching and walking. Where there is sight and hearing but no Torah
and no precepts, neither do the Holy One, blessed be He, nor His Shechinah,
rest there. For the Holy One, blessed be He, rests on sight, WHICH IS
CHOCHMAH, and so does His Shechinah, for the Torah is, "and Torah is
light," and His sight is the Shechinah. FOR Yud Hei Vav Hei, WHICH IS
ZEIR ANPIN, SAID: "make Myself known to him in a vision" (Bemidbar
12:6), WHICH IS the Shechinah, WHICH IS HIS VISION.

324. בְּמַחֲשָׁבָה מִלְּגוֹ בִּינָה, בֶּן יָהּ. יִשְׂרָאֵל עָלָה בְּמַחֲשָׁבָה. הִרְהוּר

חָכְמָה, לְחַכִּימָא בִּרְמִיזָא. חָכְמָה עָלָה בְּמַחֲשָׁבָה דְּאִיהוּ בִּינָה, מַחֲשָׁבָה
וְהִרְהוּר כֹּלָּא חַד. חָכְמָה לָא אִשְׁתְּמוֹדַע אֶלָּא בְּבִינָה, וּבִינָה בַּלֵּב.
וּבְגִין דָּא, מַחֲשָׁבָה בַּלֵּב, הִרְהוּר בַּלֵּב.

324. The thought that is within THE SENSES OF SIGHT, HEARING, SMELL,
AND SPEECH, IS Binah, WHOSE LETTERS CAN BE REARRANGED AS the
son (Heb. *ben*) of Yud Hei, because Yisrael, WHICH IS THE SECRET OF
ZEIR ANPIN, WHO IS CALLED 'SON', arose in a thought, WHICH IS THE
SECRET OF YUD HEI. Contemplation is Chochmah, a hint being sufficient
for the wise man, NAMELY AN INSPIRATION IS PRIOR TO CONCEPTUALIZING
THE THOUGHT. Chochmah arose in a thought, which is Binah, since thought
and inspiration are all one, for Chochmah is known only through Binah, and
Binah is in the heart. Thus thought is in the heart and inspiration is in the
heart.

325. וְכֵן אוֹרַיְיתָא ס״ת. מִצְוָה לִשְׁמוֹעַ. וְכֵן בְּחוֹטָמָא, רֵיחַ נִיחֹחַ
לַיהֹו״ה. שְׁכִינְתָּא אִיהִי קָרְבָּן דִּילֵיהּ, עוֹלָה דִּילֵיהּ, וּצְלוֹתָא אִיהִי
כְּקָרְבָּן, וּכְרֵיחַ נִיחֹחַ סְלִיקַת לְגַבֵּיהּ, וְאִתְקְרִיבַת לְגַבֵּיהּ בִּצְלוֹתָא, וְהָכִי
בְּדִבּוּר, הֲלֹא כֹה דְּבָרַי כָּאֵשׁ נְאֻם יְדֹנָ״ד. ה׳ שְׁכִינְתָּא, דִּבּוּר דִּילֵיהּ.

325. Likewise, THERE IS hearing in the Torah, for it is a precept that one
should hear THE READING OF the scroll of the Torah. And likewise, in the
nose there is a sweet savor to Hashem. The Shechinah is a sacrifice TO YUD
HEI VAV HEI, His burnt offering, and prayer is like a sacrifice, FOR BY
MEANS OF THE SACRIFICE OR THE PRAYER THE SHECHINAH ascends to
YUD HEI VAV HEI as a sweet savor unto Him, and is offered to Him in
prayer. And, likewise, about speech IS WRITTEN: "Is not my word like a
fire? says Hashem" (Yirmeyah 23:29). The FINAL Hei OF THE YUD HEI
VAV HEI, which is the Shechinah, is His speech.

326. כְּגַוְונָא דִשְׁכִינְתָּא, אִיהִי מַרְאָה דִּילֵיהּ, שְׁמִיעָה דִּילֵיהּ, רֵיחַ נִיחֹחַ
דִּילֵיהּ, דִּבּוּר דִּילֵיהּ, בְּרֵישָׁא. הָכִי אִיהוּ בְּיָדִין, עֲשִׂיַּית מִצְוָה דִּילֵיהּ,
בְּגוּפָא כְּרִיעָא דִּילֵיהּ. בִּצְלוֹתָא זְקִיפָא דִּילֵיהּ, בִּצְלוֹתָא עֲמִידָה דִּילֵיהּ,
דְּאִיהוּ דְּקַיְימָא קַמֵּיהּ בְּכָל אֲתַר, וּכְרַעַת לְגַבֵּיהּ, וְאִתְנַפְּלַת לְרַגְלוֹי

בִּנְפִילַת אַפַּיִם, לְמִשְׁאַל מִנֵּיהּ רַחֲמִים עַל בְּנָהָא, אִיהִי עֲנָוָה לְגַבֵּיהּ,
וְאִית לָהּ בֹּשֶׁת פָּנִים מִינֵּיהּ.

326. Just as the Shechinah is His sight, His hearing, His sweet savor, His speech, in the head, so, in the hands, She is His performance of precepts, in the body His bowing, in prayer His straightening upright; AND ALSO in the prayer, it is His standing. FOR RECEPTION OF THE FIRST THREE SFIROT IS CALLED BOTH 'STANDING UP' AND 'STANDING', AS ABOVE, for She stands before Him always, and bows before Him and falls on Her face at His feet to asks mercy from Him for Her children. She is humble before Him and she is modest in His presence.

327. וְלָא כְּשִׁפְחָה בִּישָׁא, לִילִית, חֲצוּפָה בְּלָא עֲנָוָה, לֵית לָהּ בֹּשֶׁת
פָּנִים, אִימָּא דְּעֵרֶב רַב, וּבְגִין דָּא אָמַר שְׁלֹמֹה, אֵשֶׁת חַיִל עֲטֶרֶת בַּעְלָהּ
וּכְרָקָב בְּעַצְמוֹתָיו מְבִישָׁה. דִּשְׁכִינְתָּא אִיהִי מַטְרוֹנִיתָא, שִׁפְחָה דִּילָהּ
לִילִית, לֵית לָהּ עֲנָוָה, וְלָא בֹּשֶׁת אַנְפִּין מִקּוּדְשָׁא בְּרִיךְ הוּא. וְהָכִי
בְּנָהָא עֵרֶב רַב, וְקוּדְשָׁא בְּרִיךְ הוּא עָתִיד לְאַעְבְּרָא לָהּ וְלִבְנָהָא
מֵעָלְמָא, דְּמַמְזֵרִים אִינּוּן מִבְּנֵי ט' מִדּוֹת, אָסנָ"ת מַשְׁגַּחַ"ת, מַמְזֵרֵי
דְרַבָּנָן.

327. And She is not as the wicked bondwoman CALLED 'Lilit', this who insolent, having no humility and no modesty, and she is the mother of a mixed multitude. For this reason, Solomon said: "A virtuous woman is a diadem to her husband" BEING THE SHECHINAH "but she that acts shamefully is as rottenness in his bones" (Mishlei 12:4). THIS IS THE HANDMAID LILIT. For the Shechinah is the Queen, whose handmaid is Lilit who has no humility nor modesty before the Holy One, blessed be He. And her children are similar, being a mixed multitude, and the Holy One, blessed be He, will in the future remove her and her children from the world, for they are bastards, born of the nine attributes, as described by the sages, NAMELY: THE CHILDREN OF A) A WIFE RAPED BY HER HUSBAND; B) A WIFE HATED; C) MENSTRUATING WOMAN (AT THE TIME OF INTERCOURSE); D) A WIFE WHOSE HUSBAND AT THE TIME OF INTERCOURSE THOUGHT SHE WAS SOMEONE ELSE OR HIS OTHER WIFE; E) A REBELLIOUS WIFE (AT THE TIME OF INTERCOURSE); F) A HUSBAND

DRUNK (AT THE TIME OF INTERCOURSE); G) HAVING INTERCOURSE WITH
A WIFE DIVORCED IN HIS HEART; H) A WIFE WHO IS INSOLENT; I)
CHILDREN BORN TO A WIFE WHO HAD RELATIONS IMMEDIATELY PRIOR
TO HER MARRIAGE. They are considered bastards by the Torah.

328. וְכֵן שְׁכִינָה אִיהִי שִׁמּוּשׁ דְּקוּדְשָׁא בְּרִיךְ הוּא, יִחוּד דִּילֵיהּ בְּצַדִּיק
חַי עָלְמִין. וְאִיהִי הֲלִיכָה דִּילֵיהּ, צֶדֶק לְפָנָיו יְהַלֵּךְ, לְמֶעְבַּד רְעוּתֵיהּ.
וַיְהִי הוּא טֶרֶם כִּלָּה לְדַבֵּר וְהִנֵּה רִבְקָה יוֹצֵאת, רְהִיטַת לְגַבֵּיהּ, לְמֶעְבַּד
רְעוּתֵיהּ. בִּרְאִיָּה, בִּשְׁמִיעָה, בְּרֵיחָא, בְּדִבּוּר, בַּעֲשִׂיָּה, בְּגוּפָא, בְּשִׁמּוּשׁ,
בַּהֲלוּךְ, בְּכָל אֵבֶר, אִיהִי מְצֻוָּה לְשַׁמְּשָׁא לֵיהּ, וּלְמֶעְבַּד רְעוּתֵיהּ.

328. And likewise, the Shechinah is the mating of the Holy One, blessed be
He, His union with the Righteous, who lives forever, WHICH IS YESOD.
AND THE SHECHINAH is His walk. "Righteousness shall go before Him"
(Tehilim 85:14) to act on His desire. AND THE SHECHINAH IS CALLED
'RIGHTEOUSNESS'. ALSO, "And it came to pass, before he had done
speaking, that, behold, Rivkah came out" (Beresheet 24:15) THAT IS THE
SHECHINAH THAT IS CALLED 'RIVKAH' came out to Him, to do His will.
AND SO in sight, hearing, smell, speech, doing, body, mating, walking and,
indeed, in every part, She is commanded to serve Him and to do His will.

329. וּבְנָהָא, הָכִי אִינוּן בְּדִיוּקְנָהָא, בְּנֵי עֲנָוָה, בְּנֵי בֹשֶׁת אַנְפִּין, כֻּלְּהוּ
כְּמִדּוֹת דִּילָהּ. וּבְגִין דָּא מָנֵי קוּדְשָׁא בְּרִיךְ הוּא לְמֹשֶׁה, וְאַתָּה תֶחֱזֶה
מִכָּל הָעָם אַנְשֵׁי חַיִל יִרְאֵי אֱלֹהִים אַנְשֵׁי אֱמֶת שׂוֹנְאֵי בָצַע. אַנְשֵׁי חַיִל,
מִסִּטְרָא דִּימִינָא דְּאַבְרָהָם, דְּתַמָּן רְאִיָּה דְּאוֹרַיְיתָא, מִימִינוֹ אֵשׁ דָּת
לָמוֹ. יִרְאֵי אֱלֹהִים, מִסִּטְרָא דְּיִצְחָק, דְּתַמָּן שְׁמִיעָה, דְּאָמַר חֲבַקּוּק
נְבִיאָה יְיָ' שָׁמַעְתִּי שִׁמְעֲךָ יָרֵאתִי. אַנְשֵׁי אֱמֶת, מִסִּטְרָא דְּיַעֲקֹב, דְּתַמָּן
רֵיחַ נִיחֹחַ לַיֲדוָֹד, בְּחוֹטָמָא. שׂוֹנְאֵי בָצַע, מִסִּטְרָא דְּדִבּוּר, סַמְכָּא
רְבִיעָאָה, דְּאָדָם הָרִאשׁוֹן, דְּאִתְחַבַּר בַּאֲבָהָן. תְּלַת חֵיוָן אִינוּן, אַרְיֵה
שׁוֹר נֶשֶׁר, בִּרְאִיָּיה שְׁמִיעָה רֵיחָא, אָדָם בְּדִבּוּר.

329. And the children OF THE SHECHINAH, NAMELY YISRAEL, are also of
Her form, for they have humility and modesty, all of them have Her
qualities. And this is why the Holy One, blessed be He, commanded Moses:

"Moreover you shall provide out of all the people able men, such as fear Elohim, men of truth, hating unjust gain" (Shemot 18:21). "Able men" are from the right side, which is Abraham, WHO IS CHESED THAT BECOMES CHOCHMAH, SINCE AT GREATNESS OF ZEIR ANPIN, CHESED, GVURAH AND TIFERET ASCEND AND BECOME CHOCHMAH, BINAH AND DA'AT, AS IS KNOWN, for the sight of the Torah is there, as it is written: "from His right hand went a fiery law for them" (Devarim 33:2). "such as fear of Elohim" are from the side of Isaac, WHO IS GVURAH THAT BECOMES BINAH, for hearing is there, as the prophet Habakkuk said: "Hashem, I have heard the report of You, and I am afraid" (Chavakuk 3:2). "Men of truth" are from the side of Jacob, WHO IS TIFERET THAT BECOMES DA'AT, for a sweet savor to Hashem, in the nose. "Hating unjust gain" is from the side of speech, WHICH IS MALCHUT, the fourth pillar, WHICH IS THE ASPECT OF Adam who has joined together with the patriarchs, AND IS CONSIDERED AS MALCHUT FOR THEM. AND MALCHUT IS CALLED 'MAN', FOR the three living creatures are lion, ox, and eagle, THAT ARE CHESED, GVURAH AND TIFERET in sight, hearing, and smell, AS ABOVE, AND THE FOURTH PILLAR FOR THEM IS THE FACE OF a man in speech, NAMELY THE FIRST MAN.

330. וְשַׂמְתָּ עֲלֵיהֶם שָׂרֵי אֲלָפִים, מִסִּטְרָא דְּאָת א'. וְשָׂרֵי מֵאוֹת, מִסִּטְרָא דְּאָת ד' ד' מֵאוֹת שָׁנָה דְּאִשְׁתַּעְבִּידוּ יִשְׂרָאֵל בְּמִצְרַיִם. שָׂרֵי חֲמִשִּׁים נ'. וְשָׂרֵי עֲשָׂרוֹת י'.

330. "and place such over them, to be rulers of thousands (Heb. *alafim*)," namely from the side of the letter Aleph OF ADONAI; "rulers of hundreds," from the side of the letter Dalet OF ADONAI WHICH IS THE secret of the Dalet (= 4) hundred years that Yisrael were enslaved in Egypt. "rulers of fifties," the Nun (= 50) of Adonai, "and rulers of tens" (Shemot 18:21), the Yud (= 10) OF ADONAI.

331. יִשְׂרָאֵל בְּאִינוּן מִדּוֹת אִשְׁתְּמוֹדְעוּן, דְּאִינוּן בְּנוֹי דְּקוּדְשָׁא בְּרִיךְ הוּא וּשְׁכִינְתֵּיהּ. לְמֶהֱוֵי בְּהוֹן אַנְשֵׁי חַיִל, כְּגוֹן אֵשֶׁת חַיִל עֲטֶרֶת בַּעְלָהּ, מָארֵי דְחֶסֶד. יִרְאֵי אֱלֹהִים. אַנְשֵׁי אֱמֶת, וְלָא אַנְשֵׁי שֶׁקֶר, דִּבְנֵי יִשְׂרָאֵל לֹא יַעֲשׂוּ עַוְלָה וְלֹא יְדַבְּרוּ כָזָב וְלֹא יִמָּצֵא בְּפִיהֶם לְשׁוֹן תַּרְמִית. וְשׂוֹנְאֵי בָצַע, כב"נ שָׂמַח בְּחֶלְקוֹ. וְלָא כְּעֵרֶב רַב בְּנוֹי דְּשִׁפְחָה בִּישָׁא,

דְּאִינּוּן כְּחִוְיָא דְּכָל אַרְעָא קַדְמֵיה. הה"ד וְנָחָשׁ עָפָר לַחְמוֹ, וְדָחִיל
לְמִשְׁבַּע מֵעַפְרָא, דְּדָחִיל דְּתֶחְסַר לֵיה. וְהָכִי מָארֵי בָּצַע. דְּלָא שְׂבֵעִין
מִכָּל מָמוֹן דְּעָלְמָא.

331. Yisrael are recognized by these qualities to be the children of the Holy
One, blessed be He, and His Shechinah; that is, that there should be among
them able (Heb. *chayil*) men, as in the verse: "A virtuous (Heb. *chayil*)
woman is a crown to her husband" (Mishlei 12:4), for they are people of
Chesed, CORRESPONDING TO CHESED OF ZEIR ANPIN. "such as fear
Elohim" CORRESPONDS TO GVURAH OF ZEIR ANPIN. "Men of truth"
CORRESPONDS TO TIFERET OF ZEIR ANPIN, and not men of falsehood, for
the Children of "Yisrael shall not do iniquity, nor speak lies; neither shall a
deceitful tongue be found in their mouth" (Tzfanyah 3:13). "Hating unjust
gain" CORRESPONDS TO MALCHUT, as a man who rejoices in his portion.
And they are not as a mixed multitude, the children of the wicked
bondwoman, LILIT, who are as a serpent before whom is the whole land, as
it is written: "and dust shall be the serpent's food" (Yeshayah 65:25). WITH
ALL THIS, he fears eating the dust until he is full, for he is afraid that there
will not be enough for him. This is how it is with men of unjust gain, for even
if they had all the money in the world, it would never be enough for them.

332. וּבְג"ד אוּקְמוּהָ מָארֵי מַתְנִיתִין, לֹא הַמִּדְרָשׁ הוּא הָעִיקָר אֶלָּא
הַמַּעֲשֶׂה. בְּגִין דְּקוּדְשָׁא בְּרִיךְ הוּא אִיהוּ סָתִים בְּסִתְרֵי הַתּוֹרָה, בְּמַאי
אִשְׁתְּמוֹדַע. בַּמִצְוֹת, דְּאִיהִי שְׁכִינְתֵּיה, דְּאִיהִי דִיּוּקְנֵיה. כְּגַוְונָא דְּאִיהוּ
עָנָו, שְׁכִינְתֵּיה עַנְוָה. אִיהוּ חָסִיד, וְאִיהוּ חֲסִידָה. אִיהוּ גִבּוֹר, וְאִיהִי
גִבֶּרֶת עַל כָּל אוּמִין דְּעָלְמָא. אִיהוּ אֱמֶת, וְאִיהִי אֱמוּנָה. אִיהוּ נָבִיא,
וְאִיהִי נְבִיאָה. אִיהוּ צַדִיק וְאִיהִי צַדֶּקֶת. אִיהוּ מֶלֶךְ, וְאִיהִי מַלְכוּת.
אִיהוּ חָכָם, וְאִיהִי חָכְמְתָא. אִיהוּ מֵבִין, וְאִיהִי תְּבוּנָה דִּילֵיה. אִיהוּ
כֶּתֶר, וְאִיהִי עֲטָרָה דִּילֵיה, עֲטֶרֶת תִּפְאֶרֶת. וּבְג"ד אוּקְמוּהָ רַבָּנָן, כָּל מִי
שֶׁאֵין תּוֹכוֹ כְּבָרוֹ אַל יִכָּנֵס לְבֵית הַמִּדְרָשׁ. כְּדִיוּקְנָא דְּקוּדְשָׁא בְּרִיךְ
הוּא, דְּאִיהוּ תּוֹכוֹ וּשְׁכִינְתָּא בָּרוֹ, אִיהוּ תּוֹכוֹ מִלְגוֹ, וְאִיהִי בָּרוֹ מִלְבַר.
וְלָא אִשְׁתְּנִיאַת אִיהִי דִלְבַר, מֵהַהוּא דִלְגוֹ, לְאִשְׁתְּמוֹדְעָא דְּהִיא
אֲצִילוּתֵיה, וְלֵית אַפְרָשׁוּתָא תַּמָּן כְּלָל, דְּמִבַּיִת וּמִבַחוּץ תְּצַפֶּנּוּ.

332. And this is why the sages of the Mishnah taught: 'Not the expounding of the Law is the chief thing, but the doing of it'. For the Holy One, blessed be He, is concealed by the secrets of the Torah. In what, then, can He be known? In the precepts, for they are the Shechinah, which is His form. Just as THE HOLY ONE, BLESSED BE HE, is humble, so is His Shechinah humble. He is pious and She is pious. He is valiant, and She is valiant over all the nations of the world. He is truth and She is faith. He is a prophet and She is a prophetess. He is righteous and She is righteous. He is King and She is kingdom. He is wise and She is wisdom. He understands and She is His understanding. He is a crown, and She is His diadem, "a crown of glory" (Yeshayah 62:3). This is why the sages taught: 'No disciple whose inside does not correspond to his exterior may enter the house of study.' That is, the disciple will be as the form of the Holy One, blessed be He, who is his inside and the Shechinah is his outside. He is the inside within and THE SHECHINAH is his exterior on the outside. And She that is on the outside has not changed from Him who is on the inside, that it should be known that She is His Atzilut, and there is no separation there whatsoever, THIS BEING THE SECRET OF THE VERSE: "...within and without shall you overlay it" (Shemot 25:11).

333. וּבְגִין דְּאִיהוּ יְדֹוָד, סָתִים מִלְּגָיו, לָא אִתְקְרֵי אֶלָּא בִּשְׁכִינְתֵּיה, אֲדֹנָי. וּבְגִין דָּא אָמְרוּ רַבָּנָן, לָא כְּשֶׁאֲנִי נִכְתָּב אֲנִי נִקְרָא, בעוה״ז, נִכְתָּב אֲנִי בַּידֹוָ״ד, וְנִקְרָא אֲנִי בַּאֲדֹנָ״י. אֲבָל בעוה״ב, נִכְתָּב בַּידֹוָ״ד, וְנִקְרָא בַּידֹוָ״ד. לְמֶהֱוֵי רַחֲמֵי מִכָּל סִטְרָא וּבְגִין דָּא מָנֵי קוּדְשָׁא בְּרִיךְ הוּא לְמַלְאֲכֵי הַשָּׁרֵת, מַאן דְּלָא יְהֵא תּוֹכוֹ כְּבָרוֹ, בְּכָל אֵבָרִין פְּנִימָאִין וְחִצוֹנִין, לָא יֵיעוֹל בְּהֵיכָלָא דָא. וּבְגִין דָּא אָמַר קְרָא, הַצּוּר תָּמִים פָּעֳלוֹ. תָּמִים תִּהְיֶה עִם יְיָ׳ אֱלֹהֶיךָ.

333. And since He, Yud Hei Vav Hei is concealed from within, He is called only by the name of His Shechinah, Adonai. And this is why the sages taught: 'I am not spelled as I am pronounced. In this world I am spelled with Yud Hei Vav Hei but pronounced as Adonai. In the World to Come I am pronounced with Yud Hei Vav Hei and pronounced as Yud Hei Vav Hei." And this is so that there will be mercy from all sides. And this is why the Holy One, blessed be He, commanded the ministering angels: 'Whosoever's inside does not correspond to his exterior, in all his parts, both internal and

external, that person may not enter this temple.' This is why the verse says: "He is the Rock, His work is perfect" (Devarim 32:4) and "You shall be perfect with Hashem your Elohim" (Devarim 18:13), NAMELY HIS INSIDE EXACTLY CORRESPONDS WITH HIS EXTERIOR.

53. Rainbow, Tefilin, Tzitzit, blue, white, and the reading of Sh'ma

A Synopsis
The metaphor of a marriage is used to explain the unification of Zeir Anpin and Malchut.

The Relevance of this Passage
The ultimate mating, the joining of our world of *Malchut* with Heaven – the realm of *Zeir Anpin* – occurs as our eyes wed with the letters that speak this wisdom. In turn, our own sexual relations with our spouse are imbued with holiness, generating for us divine pleasure and fulfillment.

Once again, the healing forces associated with the *Sh'ma Yisrael* prayer now remedy and regenerate the 248 parts of our body and soul. Moreover, sharing this Light with our fellow man while we meditate upon paragraph 336 and 337 heals the collective body and soul of man.

Paragraph 337 interweaves Judgment with Mercy so that leniency and great compassion mark our Final Redemption – both personally and globally.

334. תִּקּוּנָא שְׁבִיעָאָה, כְּמַרְאֵה הַקֶּשֶׁת אֲשֶׁר יִהְיֶה בֶעָנָן בְּיוֹם הַגֶּשֶׁם. אָמְרוּ רַבָּנָן, מִן וָאֵרֶא עַד כְּמַרְאֵה הַקֶּשֶׁת הֵן הֵן מַעֲשֵׂה הַמֶּרְכָּבָה. וְאָמְרוּ חֲכָמִים, כְּשֶׁהָיָה ר"ע דּוֹרֵשׁ בְּמַעֲשֵׂה מֶרְכָּבָה, יָרְדָה אֵשׁ מִן הַשָּׁמַיִם, וְסִבְּבָה הָאִילָנוֹת. וְהָיוּ מִתְקַבְּצִין מַלְאֲכֵי הַשָּׁרֵת כִּבְמִזְמוּטֵי חָתָן וְכַלָּה. בְּגִין דְּלֵית יְחוּדָא וְקִשּׁוּרָא וּמֶרְכָּבָה, לְשֵׁם יְדֹנָ"ד בַּאֲדֹנָ"י, אֶלָּא בְּצַדִּיק. דְּאִיהוּ קֶשֶׁת, דְּבֵיהּ מֶרְכַּבְתָּא שְׁלֵימָתָא דִּלְעֵילָּא, יְאָהֲדֹוָנָה"י.

334. The seventh correction is "As the appearance of the rainbow that is in the cloud in the day of rain" (Yechezkel 1:28). The sages said: 'The study of the Divine Chariot is from "And I looked AND, BEHOLD, A STORM WIND" (Ibid. 4) until "As the appearance of the rainbow," these are the study of the Divine Chariot.' And the sages further said: 'When Rabbi Akiva was expounding the study of the Divine Chariot, fire came down from heaven and engulfed the trees, and the ministering angels assembled as though at the enjoyment of groom with bride.' FOR THE CHARIOT IS THE SECRET OF

THE UNIFICATION OF YUD HEI VAV HEI AND ADONAI, WHICH ARE THE SECRET OF GROOM AND BRIDE. THIS IS THE REASON FOR THE STUDY OF THE DIVINE CHARIOT TO CONCLUDE WITH THE VERSE STARTING "AS THE APPEARANCE OF THE RAINBOW," for there is no unification and connection and Chariot for the name Yud Hei Vav Hei with Adonai other than by means of the Righteous, WHICH IS YESOD, that is CALLED 'rainbow'. For through him is the upper Chariot, which is Yud-Aleph-Hei Dalet-Vav-Nun-Hei-Yud, complete.

335. שְׁכִינְתָּא אִיהִי מַעֲשֵׂה בְּרֵאשִׁית, וְאוּקְמוּהָ, אֵין דּוֹרְשִׁין בְּמַעֲשֵׂה בְּרֵאשִׁית בִּשְׁנַיִם. בְּגִין דְּעַנְפִּין דְּאִילָנָא, אִינּוּן פְּרוּדוֹת מִלְמַעֲלָה בְּכַנְפֵי חֵיוָן, יְדוָֹ"ד לִימִינָא, אֲדֹנָ"י לִשְׂמָאלָא. חָתָן לִימִינָא, כַּלָּה לִשְׂמָאלָא. כַּד אַתְיָין לָהּ לַחוּפָּה, בְּכַמָּה מִינֵי נְגוּנָא, צְרִיכִין יִשְׂרָאֵל לְאַתְעָרָא לוֹן לְתַתָּא, בְּשִׁירוֹת וְתִשְׁבָּחוֹת, בְּכָל מִינֵי נְגוּנָא בִּצְלוֹתָא, הָא קָא אַתְיָין לַחוּפָּה.

335. The Shechinah is the Work of Creation, and it has been taught: 'The Work of Creation may not be expounded in the presence of two people.' Because the branches of the tree, WHICH ARE THE LIVING CREATURES, are divided above in the wings of the living creatures, with Yud Hei Vav Hei to the right and Adonai to the left, FOR ZEIR ANPIN IS THE SECRET OF THE CHASSADIM ON THE RIGHT, AND MALCHUT IS THE SECRET OF THE LEFT, WITHOUT ANY UNIFICATION BETWEEN THEM, AND IT FOLLOWS that the bridegroom is to the right while the bride is to the left. And when she is brought to the wedding canopy with a number of types of melody, Yisrael must awaken them from below TO THE UNIFICATION with songs and praises and all sorts of melody in prayer, for, behold, they are approaching the wedding canopy, NAMELY ARE COMING TO BE UNITED.

336. וּצְרִיכִין יִשְׂרָאֵל לְמֵיהַב קִדּוּשִׁין לַכַּלָּה. מֶחָתָנָא, בְּקִשׁוּרָא דִּתְפִלָּה דְּיָד, לְמֶהֱוֵי קְשִׁירָא לֵיהּ, וּלְעַטְּרָא לוֹן בִּתְפִילִין דְּרֵישָׁא, דְּאִיהוּ פְּאֵר, הה"ד, פְּאֵרְךָ חָבוּשׁ עָלֶיךָ. וּתְלַת כְּרִיכִין דִּרְצוּעָה, לָקֳבֵל ג' קְדוּשׁוֹת, דְּאִינּוּן קָדוֹשׁ קָדוֹשׁ קָדוֹשׁ, קְדוּשָׁה לְךָ יְשַׁלֵּשׁוּ. וְצָרִיךְ לְבָרְכָא לוֹן בְּשֶׁבַע בִּרְכָאן, דְּאִינּוּן שֶׁבַע בִּרְכוֹת דק"ש, בְּשַׁחַר שְׁתַּיִם

לְפָנֶיהָ וְאַחַת לְאַחֲרֶיהָ. וּבָעֶרֶב שְׁתַּיִם לְפָנֶיהָ וּשְׁתַּיִם לְאַחֲרֶיהָ.

336. And Yisrael must give THE RING OF marriage from the bridegroom to the bride, with the knot of the hand Tefilin, so that THE SHECHINAH should be bound to ZEIR ANPIN, and crown them with the head Tefilin, WHICH IS THE SECRET OF BRINGING DOWN TO THEM THE MOCHIN OF THE FIRST THREE SFIROT, which is glory (Heb. *pe'er*), as it is said: "Bind on your turban (Heb. *pe'er*)" (Yechezkel 24:17). And the three loops of the strap UPON THE MIDDLE FINGER parallel the three holies, which are 'Holy, Holy, Holy' "They proclaim You thrice holy'. And they have to be blessed with seven blessings, which are the seven blessings of the reading of the Sh'ma, namely: two before and one after in the morning service, and two before and two after in the evening service.

337. וְכַלָּה בְּחוּפָּה, דְּאִיהִי בְּדִיּוּקְנָא דְּכַנְפֵי מִצְוָה, בְּצִיצִיוֹת מוּזְהָבוֹת, וּתְכֵלֶת וְלָבָן, כִּסֵּא דֵין וְכִסֵּא רַחֲמִים, כָּלִיל דָּא בְּדָא. וְכַמָּה קְשָׁרִים וְחֻלְיָין, סַחֲרָנֵיהּ. בְּכַמָּה מַרְגְּלָאן וְאַבְנִין יַקִּירִין, מַלְיָין סְגוּלוֹת, סַחֲרִין לְגַבֵּיהּ, כְּדִיּוּקְנָא דְּזַגִּין וְרִמּוֹנִין, הַלְבוּשֵׁי מַלְכָּא וּמַטְרוֹנִיתָא, דְּאִינּוּן ד׳ בִּגְדֵי לָבָן, וְד׳ בִּגְדֵי זָהָב, מִסִּטְרָא דִּתְרֵין שְׁמָהָן, יְדֹוָ״ד אֲדֹנָ״י, כִּשְׁמוֹ כֵּן כִּסְאוֹ, כֵּן חוּפָּתוֹ, כֵּן לְבוּשׁוֹ. רָשִׁים שְׁמֵיהּ בְּכֹלָּא, כַּד בָּעֵי לְאַעֲלָא בְּהֵיכָלֵיהּ, לְמֶהֱוֵי תַּמָּן חָתָן בְּכַלָּתֵיהּ, בח״י בִּרְכָאן דִּצְלוֹתָא, דְּאִיהִי כְּמַרְאֵה הַקָּשֶׁת.

337. And the bride under the wedding canopy, NAMELY IN THE UNIFICATION OF THE READING OF SH'MA WHICH IS CALLED 'A WEDDING CANOPY', is in the form of the corners of the Tzitzit, which, in the fringes, are gilded. THAT IS TO SAY THAT THEY ARE BOUND WITH BLUE, WHICH IS THE SECRET OF THE ILLUMINATION OF CHOCHMAH, WHICH IS DRAWN DOWN FROM THE LEFT SIDE OF BINAH, WHICH IS CALLED 'GOLD'. AND THUS THE FRINGES ARE AS THOUGH GILDED WITH BLUE. And the blue and the white THAT ARE IN THE FRINGES are the Throne of Judgment and the Throne of Mercy interwoven with each other, FOR BLUE IS JUDGMENT AND WHITE IS MERCY. And there are a number of knots and links surrounding THE FRINGES with a number of pearls and precious stones, NAMELY THE LIGHTS OF CHOCHMAH AND CHASSADIM, full of special

qualities surrounding it in the form of bells and pomegranates of the apparel of the King and the Queen, which are the four white garments OF ZEIR ANPIN, and the four gold garments OF MALCHUT, which are from the side of the two names, Yud Hei Vav Hei and Adonai. As is His name, so is His throne, so is His wedding canopy, so is His apparel. His name is marked on all, WHICH IS YESOD, WHO IS CALLED 'ALL' when He wishes to enter His palace so the groom shall be there with His bride, in the eighteen blessings of the prayer, WHERE EIGHTEEN HINTS AT YESOD, which is "As the appearance of the rainbow," NAMELY YESOD, AS ABOVE.

54. Mystic speculations on the divine Chariot and prayer

A Synopsis

Moses speaks about the Amidah prayer, and says that everyone should pray quietly so that his neighbor can not hear him. He says that prayer can be learned from what is said about the sacrifices. We hear about Rabbi Akiva discussing the Work of the Chariot, and we are given another explanation of the rainbow.

The Relevance of this Passage

This complex section discourses on the mysteries of the *Amidah* prayer. In doing so, all the spiritual forces that ignite through this spiritual connection are summoned forth. The Light of Mercy, through the dimension known as *Chesed* and via Abraham, shines on us. This mitigates judgment, thereby eradicating chaos and suffering from our life.

The Central Column, the key to an infinite illumination of Light, is strengthened in our soul and in the world so that we forever resist the selfish desires of the Left Column, transforming ourselves into souls who *receive for the purpose of sharing.*

The power of the ancient sacrifices resurrects here to arouse Mercy and to appease the negative forces with the burning of impure fats. Our hearts and the nation of Yisrael are healed and strengthened. Our arteries and Yisrael's relationship with the other nations are cleared of obstructions, creating harmony and a constant flow of Light.

All of our prayers are strengthen and empowered so that they are answered speedily.

338. אֵין דּוֹרְשִׁין בַּמֶּרְכָּבָה בְּיָחִיד, בְּגִין דְּהַדּוֹרֵשׁ לְיָחִיד, עֲמֵיהּ הָא אִינּוּן שְׁנַיִם בַּדְרָשָׁא. וְלָא צָרִיךְ תַּמָּן לְמִשְׁמַע קַלָא בִּצְלוֹתֵיהּ. אֶלָּא רַק שְׂפָתֶיהָ נָעוֹת וְקוֹלָהּ לֹא יִשָּׁמֵעַ, וּבְהַאי רָזָא וְהַזָר הַקָּרֵב יוּמָת. וְהָכִי בִּצְלוֹתָא כָּל חַד מְצַלֵי בַּחֲשַׁאי, דְּלָא אִשְׁתְּמַע צְלוֹתֵיהּ לְגַבֵּי חַבְרֵיהּ. כְּגוֹן מַאן דְּדָרִישׁ לְחַבְרֵיהּ, וְיַשְׁתִּיק דִּבּוּר לְגַבֵּיהּ, לָא צָרִיךְ לְמֶעְבַּד אֶלָּא דִּבּוּר בַּחֲשַׁאי, דְּלָא יִשְׁמַע חַבְרֵיהּ. וּבְגַ"ד אוֹקְמוּהָ רַבָּנָן, כָּל הַמַּשְׁמִיעַ קוֹלוֹ בִּתְפִלָתוֹ, ה"ז מִקְטַנֵּי אֲמָנָה.

338. AND REGARDING THE AMIDAH PRAYER, IT WAS SAID: 'The study of

the Divine Chariot may not be expounded before one person', because he who expounds to a single person, is not THAT PERSON NOW with him during the exposition, and they are two. And he must not make sound there in his prayer, but "only her lips moved, but her voice was not heard" (I Shmuel 1:13). And in this lies the secret of the verse: "and the stranger that comes near shall be put to death" (Bemidbar 3:38). And so it is with prayer: everyone should pray quietly in such a way that his prayer is not heard by his neighbor, THIS BEING WHAT THEY REFERRED TO WHEN THEY SAID: 'THE STUDY OF THE DIVINE CHARIOT MAY NOT BE EXPOUNDED BEFORE ONE PERSON.' It is just as one who is expounding to his fellow and he wants to whisper the words to him, SO THAT HE SHOULD NOT HEAR; he does not have to do anything other than speak in silence, and then his fellow will not hear. All this is why the sages taught: 'One who says the prayer so that it can be heard is of small faith'.

339. וּבג״כ חֵיוָון אֶשָּׁא לְעֵילָא, מְמַלְלָן כְּעַנְפִּין דְּאִילָנָא, דַּהֲווֹ מִתְקַבְּצִין תַּמָּן, בְּמִזְמוּטֵי חָתָן וְכַלָּה. בְּאָן אֲתָר. בק״ש, דְּתַמָּן וְאֶשְׁמַע אֶת קוֹל כַּנְפֵיהֶם. דְּאִינּוּן ס״ד לְד׳ גַּדְפִּין, ד׳ זְמְנִין ס״ד, סַלְקִין רנ״ו. וְהַאי אִיהוּ, רָנּוּ לְיַעֲקֹב שִׂמְחָה. אֵימָתַי. לְבָתַר דְּנָטִיל נוּקְמָא מְשַׂנְאוֹי, וְיוֹקִיד טַעֲוָון דִּלְהוֹן, הה״ד וּבַאֲבוֹד רְשָׁעִים רְנָּה.

339. And this is why the heavenly living creatures of fire speak as the branches of the tree, WHICH ARE THE MINISTERING ANGELS who assemble there at the wedding feast. And where is this to happen? At the unification of the reading of Sh'ma, WHICH IS THE SECRET OF THE WEDDING CANOPY, for there IT IS SAID: "I heard the noise of their wings" (Yechezkel 1:24), FOR THE LOWER UNITY, YUD-ALEPH-HEI-DALET-VAV-NUN- HEI-YUD, IS NOT YET THERE AND THEY ARE THEREFORE SPEAKING. And there are 64 for each of the four wings. THAT IS TO SAY: THE FOUR LIVING CREATURES, EACH COMPOSED OF FOUR, MAKE SIXTEEN LIVING CREATURES. EACH LIVING CREATURE HAS FOUR WINGS, MAKING A TOTAL OF 64 WINGS. BUT THE WINGS ARE INTERWOVEN AND THERE ARE FOUR WINGS IN EACH WING, THUS 64 HAS TO BE multiplied by four, making 256, and this is: "Sing (Heb. ronu = 256) with gladness for Jacob" (Yirmeyah 31:6). And when will this be? After he has wreaked vengeance on those who hate him and burnt their deities, as it is written: "but when the wicked perish, there is jubilation (Heb. rinah)" (Mishlei 11:10) WHICH HAS

THE NUMERICAL VALUE OF 256, TOGETHER WITH THE ONE THAT REPRESENTS THE WHOLE.

340. וְתַלְיָין ס"ד, מִן תְּמַנְיָא א"ז. וְהָכִי ס"ד מִתְּמַנְיָא א"ז לְד' סְטְרִין, רנ"ו. וְכַד מָטֵי לַל"ב, דְּאִינּוּן א"ז א"ז א"ז, דְּאִינּוּן ח' ח' ח' ח', אִתְחַבַּר י' לְכָל סְטָר, לְמֶהֱוֵי ח"י יְהֹוָ"ה, בַּח"י בִּרְכָאן דִּצְלוֹתָא, דְּאִית בְּהוֹן ח"י זִמְנִין יְדֹוָ"ד, דְּסַלְקִין ע"ב. בְּהַהוּא זִמְנָא דְּמִתְחַבְּרָא יְהֹוָ"ה בַּאֲדֹנָ"י בְּח"י עָלְמִין וְאַהֲדֹרָנָהִי, מִיָּד חֵיוָן דְּאֵשׁ חָשׁוֹת. מַה כְּתִיב בְּהוֹן. בְּעָמְדָם תְּרַפֶּינָה כַנְפֵיהֶם, בְּעָמְדָם יִשְׂרָאֵל בִּצְלוֹתָא, תְּרַפֶּינָה כַנְפֵיהֶם, דְּלָא יִשְׁתְּמוֹדְעוּן עַד הַהִיא שַׁעֲתָא.

340. And the 64 are derived from eight TIMES *az* (Eng. 'then' = 8); FOR *AZ* INDICATES THE EIGHT LETTERS OF THE UNITY, YUD-ALEPH-HEI-DALET-VAV-NUN-HEI-YUD, and thus the 64 is DERIVED from eight TIMES *az*. AND WITH THE 64 ON each of the four corners, the total is 256. And when he reaches heart (Heb. *lev* = 32), which is four times *az*, which is four times the letter Chet, Yud is joined with them on each side, making 'Hashem lives', NAMELY THAT YESOD WHICH IS CALLED 'LIVING' JOINS WITH YUD HEI VAV HEI in the eighteen blessings of the prayer, in which Yud Hei Vav Hei appears eighteen times, for a total of 72 LETTERS. At the moment Yud Hei Vav Hei is joined with Adonai by the 18 worlds, namely Yud-Aleph-Hei Dalet-Vav-Nun-Hei-Yud IS FORMED BY YESOD, WHO IS CALLED 'LIFE OF THE WORLDS'. Immediately, the living creatures of fire fall silent, FOR AT THE TIME OF THE UNIFICATION THEY ARE QUIET. What is written about them? "When they stood, they let down their wings" (Yechezkel 1:24), THE MEANING OF WHICH IS: When Yisrael stand in prayer, THIS BEING THE TIME OF THE UNIFICATION, they let down their wings, that their presence should not be felt, until that time NAMELY THEY FALL SILENT.

341. וְהַאי אִיהוּ רַק שְׂפָתֶיהָ נָעוֹת. דְּאִינּוּן כַּנְפֵי הַחַיּוֹת, וְקוֹלָהּ לֹא יִשָּׁמֵעַ. מַה דַּהֲוֵי חַשְׁמַל, חֵיוָן אֶשָּׁא מְמַלְּלָן, אִינּוּן חָשׁוֹת. וּבג"ד תַּקִּינוּ צְלוֹתָא בַּחֲשַׁאי, וְהָכִי מַעֲשֵׂה מֶרְכָּבָה בַּחֲשַׁאי, לְמַלְּלָא תַּמָּן בַּחֲשַׁאי, בֵּינוֹ לְבֵין עַצְמוֹ. ג' צְלוֹתִין תַּקִּינוּ, וּבְכֻלְּהוּ ח"י יְהֹוָ"ה, דְּאִינּוּן ע"ב

אַתְוָון, בְּכָל צְלוֹתָא, בִּתְמָנֵי סְרֵי בִּרְכָאן, דְּאִינּוּן רי״ו, וּכְלִילָן בְּחֶסֶד, בְּע״ב, עִם ל״ב נְתִיבוֹת, וְהַיְינוּ ר״ן חֲסֵרִין ב׳. דִּכְלִילָן בְּעַמּוּדָא דְּאֶמְצָעִיתָא.

341. And this is the meaning of "Only her lips moved, but her voice was not heard," where lips refer to the wings of the living creatures. For the electrum was PREVIOUSLY living creatures of fire who were speaking, while NOW they are silent. And this is why silent prayer was ordained, and thus the study of the Divine Chariot is without sound, for he speaks there to himself in a whisper. Three prayers were ordained and in each one Yud Hei Vav Hei is ENUNCIATED eighteen TIMES, making 72 letters in each prayer, in the CONCLUDING SENTENCES OF EACH OF THE eighteen blessings, AND 3 TIMES 72 makes 216 LETTERS that are included in Chesed. AND THREE TIMES 72, together with the 32 paths OF CHOCHMAH comes to 250 minus two, NAMELY, ADDS UP TO 248, WHICH IS CHESED, that are included in the Central Column, WHICH IS CHESED.

342. דִּמְקָרְבָנָא אִשְׁתְּמַע צְלוֹתָא, צְלוֹתָא מִקָרְבָנָא. כְּגַוְונָא דְּאִתְּמַר בְּהוֹן, וָאֶשְׁמַע אֶת קוֹל כַּנְפֵיהֶם. הָכִי בִּכְרוּבִים, וַיִּשְׁמַע אֶת הַקוֹל מִדַּבֵּר אֵלָיו. כְּגַוְונָא דְּכֶבֶשׁ סַלְקִין וְנַחְתִּין בֵּיהּ קָרְבְּנִין וְעָלָוון. הָכִי בִּצְלוֹתָא, מַלְאֲכִין סַלְקִין תְּרֵי וְנַחְתֵּי תְּרֵי. וּכְגַוְונָא דְּסִינַי, דְּבֵיהּ מֹשֶׁה וְאַהֲרֹן סַלְקִין וְנַחְתִּין, סַלְקִין תְּרֵין וְנַחְתִּין ב׳. וּבְפִקּוּדָא דָא, אִתְרְמִיזוּ כָּל פִּקּוּדִין דְּאוֹרַיְיתָא.

342. From what is said about sacrifices, we can learn aboutprayer, and prayer is deduced from the sacrifices. Just as it is said ABOVE ABOUT PRAYER, "I heard the noise of their wings" (Yechezkel 1:24), so with regard to the Cherubs, WHICH ARE THE SECRET OF SACRIFICE, NAMELY OF THE UNIFICATION OF YUD HEI VAV HEI AND ADONAI THAT IS ATTAINED THROUGH THE SACRIFICE, AS IT IS SAID: "Then he heard the voice speaking to him" (Bemidbar 7:89). AND SO WE DEDUCE ABOUT PRAYER FROM THE SACRIFICES. ABOUT THE LATTER IT IS WRITTEN: "THE VOICE SPEAKING" WHICH HINTS AT BOTH VOICE AND SPEECH, WHICH ARE YUD HEI VAV HEI AND ADONAI. SIMILARLY, ABOUT PRAYER IT IS SAID ONLY: "I HEARD THE NOISE OF THEIR WINGS," WITHOUT SPEECH BEING

MENTIONED IN THIS CONTEXT. NEVERTHELESS, SPEECH IS ALSO INCLUDED THERE. Just as with the ramp OF THE ALTAR, on which sacrifices and burnt offerings ascend and descend, so in the prayer two angels ascend and two descend. And so it was at Mount Sinai, where Moses and Aaron ascended the mountain and descended, NAMELY two went up and two came down. And all the precepts of the Torah are implied in this precept OF PRAYER.

343. וְהָכִי כַּד הֲוָה פָּתַח ר"ע בְּמַעֲשֵׂה מֶרְכָּבָה, פּוּמֵיה הֲוָה סִינַי, וְקָלֵיה הֲוָה סֻלָּם, דְּבֵיה מַלְאֲכִין סַלְקִין וְנַחְתִּין. בְּכָל דִּבּוּר וְדִבּוּר דִּילֵיה, הֲוָה רָכִיב עֲלֵיה מַלְאָךְ מְטַטְרוֹ"ן. אִיהוּ רֶכֶב לִשְׁכִינָתָּא, דִּכְלִילָא בֵּיה סְפִירָן עַמּוּדָא דְּאֶמְצָעִיתָא, דְּאִיהוּ יוֹ"ד הֵ"א וָא"ו הֵ"א מִלְּגוֹ. דִּשְׁכִינָתָּא כְּלִילָא מִי' סְפִירָן, דִּלְבַר. וְקוּדְשָׁא בְּרִיךְ הוּא וּשְׁכִינְתֵּיה, רֶכֶב וּמֶרְכָּבָה. עַמּוּדָא דְּאֶמְצָעִיתָא, רֶכֶב לְעַלַּת הָעִלּוֹת. וּשְׁכִינְתֵּיה, רֶכֶב לְעַמּוּדָא דְּאֶמְצָעִיתָא. וְעַלַּת הָעִלּוֹת אִיהוּ דִּמְיַחֵד לְכֹלָּא, וּמְסַדֵּר לְכֹלָּא, וְנָהִיר בְּכֹלָּא. נְהוֹרֵיה אַעֲבַּר בְּנִשְׁמָתָא וְגוּפָא וּלְבוּשָׁא. וְלֵית בֵּיה שִׁנּוּי וְשׁוּתָּפוּ וְחוּשְׁבָּן וּתְמוּנָה וְדִמְיוֹן מִכָּל מֶרְכַּבְתָּא, וּמַרְאֶה וְדִמְיוֹן דְּאִתְחַזְיָיא בְּעֵין הַשֵּׂכֶל. דַּרְגִּין עִלָּאִין וְתַתָּאִין, אִינּוּן רֶכֶב וּמֶרְכַּבְתָּא לְגַבֵּיה, וַעֲלֵיה לֵית מַאן דְּרָכִיב.

343. Thus, when Rabbi Akiva started to discuss the study of the Divine Chariot, his mouth was Sinai and his voice was a ladder on which angels ascended and descended. With every speech of his, the angel Metatron would ride on it. He is a vehicle of the Shechinah, for included in him are the Sfirot of the Central Column, WHICH IS ZEIR ANPIN, which is Yud-Vav Dalet, Hei-Aleph, Vav-Aleph-Vav, Hei-Aleph. They are inside, while the Shechinah, which is composed of ten Sfirot, is outside OVER HIM. And the Holy One, blessed be He, and His Shechinah are *rechev* (Eng. 'vehicle', masc.) and *Merkavah* (Eng. 'Chariot', fem.). The Central Column is a vehicle to the Cause of Causes, WHICH IS THE ENDLESS LIGHT, while His Shechinah is a vehicle for the Central Column. And the Cause of Causes, WHICH IS THE ENDLESS LIGHT, is the All-uniting and the All-arranging and the All- illuminating. His light passes through the soul and body and apparel, and He is unchanging, and without partnership, or account or picture or likeness of any Chariot or vision or likeness that the MIND'S eyes

can summon up. The upper and lower steps are a vehicle and Chariot to Him, but none ride on Him.

344. קֶשֶׁת, סִימָן תְּקִיעָה שְׁבָרִים תְּרוּעָה. וְאִינּוּן סִימָן מֶרְכָּבָה דַּאֲבָהָן. תְּקִיעָה, דְּאַבְרָהָם. שְׁבָרִים, דְּיִצְחָק, תְּרוּעָה, דְּיַעֲקֹב. דְּאִתְּמַר בֵּיהּ וּתְרוּעַת מֶלֶךְ בּוֹ. וְג' גַּוְונִין אִתְחַזְיָין בֵּיהּ, חִוָּור סוּמָק וְיָרוֹק. וּמִסְּטְרָא דִּגְבוּרָה, אִתְקְרֵי קֶשֶׁת גִּבּוֹרִים חַתִּים. וּמִסְּטְרָא דִּימִינָא, כְּמַרְאֵה הַקֶּשֶׁת אֲשֶׁר יִהְיֶה בֶעָנָן בְּיוֹם הַגֶּשֶׁם. כַּד אִתְחֲזֵי בְּיוֹם הַגֶּשֶׁם, אַחְזֵי רַחֲמֵי. וְכַד אִתְחֲזֵי בְּלָא מִטְרָא, אַחְזֵי דִּינָא. מְעוּרָב בֵּין מִטְרָא וְשִׁמְשָׁא, אַחְזֵי דִּינָא וְרַחֲמֵי כָּלִיל. וְהַאי אִיהוּ ש' מִן שַׁדַּי, תְּלַת עַנְפֵּי אֲבָהָן, דְּאִינּוּן יְדֹנָ"ד אֱלֹהֵי"נוּ יְדֹנָ"ד, תְּלַת שְׁמָהָן לָקֳבֵל תְּלַת עַנְפֵּי אֲבָהָן. וּבְהוֹן י"ד אַתְוָון, בְּחוּשְׁבָּן ד"י מִן שַׁדַּי. וּלְבוּשׁ דְּשַׁדַּי, מְטַטְרוֹן, דְּהָכִי סָלִיק בְּחוּשְׁבַּן שַׁדַּי.

ע"כ רעיא מהימנא

344. The rainbow (Heb. *keshet* - Kof Shin Tav) stands for initials of T'kiah, Sh'varim, T'ruah and they are a sign for the patriarchs' Chariot. T'kiah is Abraham, Sh'varim Isaac, and T'ruah is Jacob, about whom it is said: "And the trumpet blast (Heb. *t'ruah*) of a king is among them" (Bemidbar 23:21). And in it three colors are visible: white, red, and green. From the side of Gvurah it, YESOD, is called "The bows of the mighty are broken" (I Shmuel 2:4), and from the right side, WHICH IS CHESED, IT IS CALLED "As the appearance of the rainbow that is in the cloud in the day of rain" (Yechezkel 1:28). When it appears on a rainy day, Mercy is visible, but when it appears when there is no rain, Judgment is visible. And when it is blended in between rain and sun, this shows that Mercy and Judgment are joined. And this is the letter Shin of Shadai (Shin-Dalet-Yud), THAT TEACHES ABOUT the three branches of the patriarchs, namely: Yud Hei Vav Hei, Our Elohim, Yud Hei Vav Hei, these being the three names that parallel the three branches of the patriarchs, WHICH ARE CHESED, GVURAH AND TIFERET. AND THESE THREE NAMES contain Yud Dalet (= 14) letters, which form the Dalet Yud of Shadai. AND SHADAI IS YESOD OF ZEIR ANPIN, and the apparel of Shadai IS Metatron, which has the same numerical value as Shadai.

End of Ra'aya Meheimna(the Faithful Shepherd)

55. Whoever recites the psalm "A praise of David" every day

A Synopsis
Rabbi Elazar says that one must recite the title psalm three times each day – twice for the food of mortal man, and once to give force to the world above.

The Relevance of this Passage
Here we inherit a portion of the *World to Come* through the merit gained by the *Praise of David* made three times daily. Again, we must be mindful of the fact that the *World to Come* refers to the Light of *Binah,* which shines in the here and now as we meditate and read through this passage. This Light bestows sustenance, order, and well-being upon us.

345. אר"ש, מַאן דְּפָתַח פִּתְחָא יֵימָא. א"ר אֶלְעָזָר, תָּנֵינָן, כָּל מַאן דְּאָמַר תְּהִלָּה לְדָוִד בְּכָל יוֹם תְּלַת זִמְנִין, אִיהוּ בַּר עָלְמָא דְּאָתֵי. וְהָא אִתְּמַר טַעֲמָא. אִי בְּגִין פַּרְנָסָה וּמְזוֹנָא דְּכָל עָלְמִין, תְּרֵין זִמְנִין אִינּוּן בְּכָל יוֹמָא בְּצַפְרָא וּבְפַנְיָיא, דִּכְתִּיב בְּתֵת יְיָ' לָכֶם בָּעֶרֶב בָּשָׂר וְגוֹ', אֲמַאי תְּלַת זִמְנִין בְּכָל יוֹמָא. אֶלָּא תְּרֵין לִמְזוֹנָא דִּבְנֵי אִינָשֵׁי וּדְכָל עָלְמָא. וְחַד לְמֵיהַב תּוּקְפָּא לְהַהוּא אֲתָר דִּפְתִיחוּ יְדוֹי.

345. Rabbi Shimon said: Let he who has started continue! (THIS IS THE REACTION OF RABBI SHIMON TO RABBI ELAZAR'S WORDS, SEE ABOVE 237). Rabbi Elazar said, we learned: Whoever recites the psalm "A praise of David" (Tehilim 145) three times daily is sure to inherit the World to Come. And we have already learned the reason, NAMELY THAT IT CONTAINS THE VERSE: "YOU OPEN YOUR HAND, AND SATISFY THE DESIRE OF EVERY LIVING THING" (IBID. 16), THIS BEING A PRAYER OVER FOOD. HE ASKS, IF THE REASON has to do with sustenance and food for all the worlds, THEN HE SHOULD SAY IT TWICE each day, twice being in the morning and the evening, for it is written: "When Hashem shall give you in the evening meat to eat, and in the morning your fill of bread" (Shemot 16:8). Why should he have to recite it three times daily? HE ANSWERS that he says it twice for the food of people, and for the whole world, and once is to give force to that place which hands are open.

346. וּתְרֵין מְזוֹנִין אִלֵּין מְשַׁנְיָין דָּא מִן דָּא, וְכֻלְּהוּ תְּלַת מְזוֹנֵי כְּתִיבֵי

הָכָא, וְאַתָּה נוֹתֵן לָהֶם אֶת אָכְלָם בְּעִתּוֹ, דָּא מְזוֹנָא דַּעֲתִירֵי, דְּיָהִיב מֵיכְלָא סַגִּי בְּעִתּוֹ, הָא חַד. תְּרֵין, דִּכְתִּיב וּמַשְׂבִּיעַ לְכָל חַי רָצוֹן, דָּא מְזוֹנָא דְּמִסְכְּנֵי, דְּאִינּוּן שְׂבֵעִין מֵרָצוֹן, וְלָא מִגּוֹ מֵיכְלָא סַגִּי. תְּלַת דִּכְתִּיב פּוֹתֵחַ אֶת יָדֶךָ, דָּא תּוּקְפָּא לְהַהוּא אֲתָר, וּבְפָתִיחוּ דִּידוֹי, נָפְקָא רָצוֹן וְשַׂבְעָא לְכֹלָּא.

346. These two foodstuffs OF MAN differ from each other, FOR THE ONE IS FOR THE RICH AND THE OTHER FOR THE POOR. And all three types of food are mentioned here IN THE PSALM "A PRAISE OF DAVID." "and you give them their food in due season" (Tehilim 145:15) refers to the food of the rich, for He gives "them their food in due season." This is the first of the three. The second is "and satisfy the desire of every living thing." This refers to the food of the poor, for they are satisfied not with much food but with what He satisfied them with. The third is the verse "You open your hand," this being strength to that place, for when He opens His hands, favor and abundance for all emerge.

347. תּוּ הָכִי אוֹלִיפְנָא, דְּלָא אִיהוּ אֶלָּא תְּרֵי זִמְנֵי, בְּגִין מְזוֹנָא וּפַרְנָסָה בְּכָל יוֹמָא. דְּאִלֵּין חִיּוּבָא עַל ב"נ. וְאִי אָמַר יַתִּיר, לָאו בְּגִין חוֹבָה אִיהוּ, אֶלָּא בְּגִין שְׁבָחָא גּוֹ תּוּשְׁבְּחָן דִּזְמִירוֹת דְּדָוִד מַלְכָּא. מ"ט. בְּגִין דְּפַרְנָסָה לָא חֲזֵי לְמִשְׁאַל אֶלָּא בָּתַר צְלוֹתָא וּפַרְנָסָה דְּמָארֵיהּ. מַלְכָּא יֵיכוּל בְּקַדְמֵיתָא וּלְבָתַר יֵיכְלוּן עַבְדּוֹי.

347. I have also learned that A MAN HAS TO SAY "A PRAISE OF DAVID" twice a day only for his daily food and sustenance. And these TWO TIMES are mandatory for a person. And if he says it more than twice, this is not in fulfillment of an obligation, but in praise among the songs of praise of King David. What is the reason? It is because it is not fitting that a man should ask for his sustenance until after the prayer, FOR THE PRAYER ITSELF is his Master's sustenance, and the King should eat first, and His servants should eat afterwards.

56. "I have eaten my honeycomb with my honey; I have drunk my wine with my milk"

56. "I have eaten my honeycomb with my honey; I have drunk my wine with my milk"

A Synopsis
Rabbi Elazar explains the title verse in the context of the prayers.

The Relevance of this Passage
The *Sh'ma Yisrael* prayer is of such vital importance that the Zohar finds it necessary to offer further insights into its purpose. For the reader, it offers us another opportunity to dip ourselves into the pristine waters of healing that nourish and regenerate the 248 parts of our body and soul.

We are told that the *Praise of David* takes place in the afternoon, just before Judgment arrives, because Favor and Mercy are still out in force. That is the appropriate time to ask for sustenance and blessing. Accordingly, here we receive financial sustenance and the power to create order out of chaos, two benefits associated with the *Praise of David*. These influences abolish poverty and chaos from the world.

348. הה"ד, בָּאתִי לְגַנִּי אֲחוֹתִי כַלָּה אָכַלְתִּי יַעֲרִי עִם דִּבְשִׁי שָׁתִיתִי יֵינִי עִם חֲלָבִי, לְבָתַר אִכְלוּ רֵעִים. אָכַלְתִּי יַעֲרִי, דָא צְלוֹתָא דִּמְיוּשָׁב. עִם דִּבְשִׁי דָא ק"ש. אָכַלְתִּי יַעֲרִי דָא צְלוֹתָא דִּמְיוּשָׁב, הַהוּא יַעַר לְבָנוֹן, יוֹצֵר אוֹר וְהָאוֹפַנִּים וְחַיּוֹת הַקֹּדֶשׁ, כָּל הָנֵי אִקְרוּן יַעַר אִילָנִין וּנְצִיבִין דְּבֵיהּ. עִם דִּבְשִׁי דָא ק"ש, דְּאִיהוּ מְתִיקוּ דְּכֹלָּא, בְּכַמָּה צוּפִין וּמְתִיקִין.

348. It is written: "I am come into my garden, my sister, my bride; I have gathered my myrrh with my spice; I have eaten my honeycomb with my honey; I have drunk my wine with my milk" (Shir Hashirim 5:1). The verse continues: "Eat, O dear ones." "I have eaten my honeycomb" refers to that part of the prayer service that is said seated; NAMELY FROM 'WHO FORMS LIGHT AND CREATES DARKNESS...' UNTIL THE READING OF SH'MA. "with my honey" refers to the recital of the Sh'ma. HE EXPLAINS, "I have eaten my honeycomb (Heb. *ya'ar*)" refers to that part of the prayer service that is said seated, BECAUSE the forest (Heb. *ya'ar*) of Lebanon WHICH IS THE WORLD OF BRIYAH, INCLUDES, 'Who forms light and creates darkness,'

including the wheels and the holy living creatures, all of which are called 'the forest of trees' and the saplings in it. "with my honey" refers to the recital of the Sh'ma, which is the sweetest of all, with much nectar and sweetness.

349. שָׁתִיתִי יֵינִי, דָּא צְלוֹתָא, דִּמְעוּמָד, מְשִׁיכוּ דְּיֵינָא עִלָּאָה דְּאִתְנְטַר. וְדָא בִּשְׁלַשׁ בִּרְכוֹת רִאשׁוֹנוֹת. עִם חֲלָבִי, אִלֵּין אִינּוּן שָׁלַשׁ בִּרְכוֹת אַחֲרוֹנוֹת, וְאִתְכְּלִילָן אִלֵּין בְּאִלֵּין. עַד כְּעַן מֵיכְלָא דְּמַלְכָּא. לְבָתַר דְּאָכַל מַלְכָּא, אִכְלוּ רֵעִים לְעֵילָּא, שְׁתוּ וְשִׁכְרוּ דּוֹדִים לְתַתָּא.

349. "I have drunk my wine" is that part of the prayer service that is said standing, for it is the drawing down of the upper cellared wine, WHICH IS THE ILLUMINATION OF CHOCHMAH THAT IS IN BINAH, AND IT IS THEREFORE SAID ABOUT IT "I HAVE DRUNK MY WINE." And this is in the first three OF THE EIGHTEEN blessings OF THE AMIDAH, PARALLELING CHOCHMAH, BINAH AND DA'AT. "with my milk" refers to the final three blessings OF THE AMIDAH, AND THEY PARALLEL NETZACH, HOD AND YESOD. AND THE ILLUMINATION OF CHASSADIM IS TERMED MILK. And the ones are included in each other, NAMELY THE ILLUMINATION OF CHOCHMAH AND OF CHASSADIM ARE INCLUDED IN EACH OTHER. To this point is the food of the King. And after the King has eaten, "Eat, O dear ones," NAMELY THE ANGELS, "drink deep, O living companions" below, NAMELY THE SOULS.

350. וע"ד לֵית חִיּוּבָא דִּמְזוֹנָא אֶלָּא לְבָתַר צְלוֹתָא. בִּצְלוֹתָא דְּמִנְחָה קוֹדֶם צְלוֹתָא מ"ט. בְּגִין דְּעַד לָא אִשְׁתְּכַח דִּינָא קַשְׁיָא, בְּעוֹד דְּאַנְפִּין דְּמַלְכָּא נְהִירִין, יֵימָא תְּהִלָּה לְדָוִד, בְּהַאי סְדוּרָא דִּמְזוֹנָא. דִּלְבָתַר דְּדִינָא שַׁרְיָא וְתָלֵי עַל עָלְמָא, לָאו שַׁעֲתָא אִיהוּ. אָתָא ר' פִּנְחָס וּנְשָׁקֵיהּ.

350. And thus there is no obligation TO OFFER PRAISES for food until after the prayer, NAMELY UNTIL AFTER THE KING HAS EATEN, AS ABOVE. And what is the reason FOR THE RECITAL OF "A PRAISE OF DAVID" (TEHILIM 145) IN THE AFTERNOON SERVICE BEFORE THE AMIDAH? IT IS BECAUSE THE AFTERNOON SERVICE CORRESPONDS TO ISAAC, WHICH IS

56. "I have eaten my honeycomb with my honey; I have drunk my wine with my milk"

JUDGMENT. SO before there is harsh Judgment, NAMELY BEFORE THE AMIDAH, while the King's countenance is still shining WITH CHESED (ENG. 'FAVOR'), let him say "A praise of David" in that order of foodstuffs IN THE THREE ASPECTS, for after THE PRAYER when Judgment prevails and impends over the world, it is an inappropriate time for that. Rabbi Pinchas came and kissed him.

57. Now there was a day when the sons of Elohim came to present themselves before Hashem"

A Synopsis

Rabbi Shimon talks about Rosh Hashanah, when harsh judgment is present in the world, telling us that the day spoken of in the title was Rosh Hashanah. We learn that "the sons of Elohim" are the supreme court, the seventy officials who always surround the King, and that everyone must take care to honor the Holy Name in order to avoid judgment.

The Relevance of this Passage

The power of Rosh Hashanah is available to us. Reading this portion with great remorse sweetens and annuls judgments otherwise in store for us, by awakening Mercy. And because this secret of Rosh Hashanah is revealed through the Zohar – the soul and essence of the Torah and the world – the effect is cosmic. The entire world is sweetened with mercy as judgments are repealed. The Supreme Court is permanently adjourned, and our adversaries – the prosecuting attorneys *Satan and Lilit* – are relieved of their duties.

351. אָמַר רִבִּי יְהוּדָה, לֵימָא לָן מֹר, מִלִּין מְעַלְּיָתָא דְּרֹאשׁ הַשָּׁנָה. פָּתַח רִבִּי שִׁמְעוֹן וְאָמַר וַיְהִי הַיּוֹם. בְּכָל אֲתָר דִּכְתִיב וַיְהִי, אִיהוּ צַעַר, וַיְהִי בִּימֵי צַעַר. וַדַּאי, וַיְהִי הַיּוֹם, יוֹמָא דְּאִית בֵּיהּ צַעַר, וְדָא הוּא רֹאשׁ הַשָּׁנָה, יוֹמָא דְּאִית בֵּיהּ דִּינָא קַשְׁיָא עַל עָלְמָא. וַיְהִי הַיּוֹם וַיַּעֲבֹר אֱלִישָׁע אֶל שׁוּנֵם, יוֹמָא דְּרֹאשׁ הַשָּׁנָה הֲוָה. וּבְכָל אֲתָר וַיְהִי הַיּוֹם, דָּא רֹאשׁ הַשָּׁנָה. וַיְהִי הַיּוֹם וַיָּבֹאוּ בְּנֵי הָאֱלֹהִים, יוֹם רֹאשׁ הַשָּׁנָה הֲוָה.

351. Rabbi Yehuda said TO RABBI SHIMON, Let my master say some beautiful things about Rosh Hashanah. Rabbi Shimon began by quoting: "Allow there was (Heb. *vayehi*) a day" (Iyov 1:6). Wherever it is written: *vayehi*, it is A TERM OF anguish. "Now there was a day" refers to anguish. Certainly "Now there was a day" refers to a day on which there is anguish, and this is Rosh Hashanah, a day on which there is harsh Judgment on the world. SIMILARLY: "And it happened one day, that Elisha passed to Shunem" (II Melachim 4:8) was on the day of Rosh Hashanah. And wherever it is said "And it happened one day" the day referred to is Rosh Hashanah. CONSEQUENTLY, "Now there was a day when the sons of the Elohim came" (Iyov 1:6) refers to the day of Rosh Hashanah.

352. בְּכָל זִמְנָא תְּרֵין יוֹמִין אִינּוּן, מַאי טַעֲמָא. בְּגִין, דִּלְהֱוֵי יִצְחָק כָּלִיל דִּינָא וְרַחֲמֵי, תְּרֵין יוֹמִין וְלָא חַד. דְּאִלְמָלֵא יִשְׁתְּכַח יְחִידָאי, יַחֲרִיב עָלְמָא. וְעַל דָּא כְּתִיב תְּרֵין זִמְנִין, וַיְהִי הַיּוֹם וַיְהִי הַיּוֹם.

352. Rosh Hashanah always lasts for two days. What is the reason for this? It is so that Isaac, WHO IS THE LEFT COLUMN, WHICH IS THE ASPECT OF ROSH HASHANAH, should be composed of Judgment and Mercy, WHICH ARE two days, and ISAAC WILL not BE JUST one. For WERE ISAAC TO BE just one, WITHOUT THE INCLUSION OF MERCY, he would destroy the world, and this is why it is written IN JOB twice: "Now there was a day" (Iyov 1:6; 2:1).

353. וַיָּבֹאוּ בְּנֵי הָאֱלֹהִים, אִלֵּין ב"ד רַבְרְבָא. בְּנֵי הָאֱלֹהִים וַדַּאי, בְּנוֹי דְּמַלְכָּא קְרִיבִין לְגַבֵּיהּ. וְאִינּוּן שַׁבְעִין מְמָנָן, דְּסַחֲרִין תְּדִירָא לְמַלְכָּא. וְאִינּוּן חַתְכִין דִּינָא עַל עָלְמָא. לְהִתְיַצֵּב עַל יְיָ', וְכִי עַל יְיָ' קַיְימֵי. אֶלָּא, בְּשַׁעֲתָא דְּאִלֵּין קַיְימֵי עַל דִּינָא, דִּינָא קַדְמָאָה דְּכֹלָּא בֵּיהּ, מַאן הוּא. דְּלָא יוֹקִיר לִשְׁמָא דְּקוּדְשָׁא בְּרִיךְ הוּא, וּדְלָא יוֹקִיר לְאוֹרַיְיתָא וּלְעַבְדּוֹי. אוֹף הָכִי, מַאן הוּא דְּלָא חָיִישׁ עַל יְקָרָא דִּשְׁמָא קַדִּישָׁא, דְּלָא יִתְחַלֵּל בְּאַרְעָא. מַאן הוּא דְּלָא חָיִישׁ לִיקָרֵיהּ דְּקוּדְשָׁא בְּרִיךְ הוּא, מַאן הוּא דְּלָא שַׁוֵּי יְקָר לִשְׁמָא דָּא. וַיָּבֹא גַּם הַשָּׂטָן בְּתוֹכָם, גַּם, לְרַבּוֹת הַהִיא נוּקְבָּא דִּילֵיהּ. אוֹף הָכִי לְהִתְיַצֵּב עַל יְיָ', דְּאִיהוּ חָיִישׁ נָמֵי לִיקָרָא דִּשְׁמָא דָּא.

353. "the sons of the Elohim came": These are certainly the supreme court, the sons of the Elohim, before whom the children of the King, NAMELY YISRAEL, draw near. And they are the seventy officials who always surround the King, and they decree sentences on the world. "to present themselves before (lit. 'upon') Hashem": HE ASKS, do they stand upon Hashem? HE ANSWERS, No, but when they stand to judge THE WORLD, the first to be judged is the one who does not honor the Holy Name and does not respect the Torah and His servants. So, too, whoever is not concerned about the honor of the Holy Name, WHICH IS THE SHECHINAH, that it be

not desecrated on earth, and whoever is not concerned over the honor of the Holy One, blessed be He, WHO IS ZEIR ANPIN, he does not give honor to this Name. "and the adversary came also amongst them" (Ibid.): "also" adds the female of the adversary, LILIT. And so it is here: "to present themselves before Hashem" means that the Satan, too, was concerned for the honor of this Name, THAT IS TO SAY, HE CAME TO INCITE AGAINST IT.

58. The righteous man suffers, the wicked man thrives

A Synopsis

Rav Hamnuna tells Elijah that a righteous man whose sins are few is punished in this world, but a man with many sins and a few good deeds is rewarded in this world. He goes on to say that people must confess their own sins to God and then He will hear, judge, and forgive him.

The Relevance of this Passage

When we confess our own sins, absolutely, to the Creator, as opposed to having our Accuser (Satan) present them as an indictment against us, the Zohar states:

"…The heavenly court leaves alone the person who expounds his own sins AND DOES NOT FIND HIM GUILTY."

This passage is our opportunity to confess and procure a favorable verdict concerning that sins we have committed. Acknowledging our misdeeds is the key to activating the power of this passage.

354. הָכָא אַפְלִיגוּ עַמּוּדִין קַדְמָאִין דְּעָלְמָא. חַד אָמַר, אִיּוֹב מֵחֲסִידֵי אוּמּוֹת הָעוֹלָם הֲוָה. וְחַד אָמַר, מֵחֲסִידֵי יִשְׂרָאֵל הֲוָה. וְאַלְקֵי, לְכַפְּרָא עַל עָלְמָא. דְּהָא יוֹמָא חַד אַשְׁכְּחֵיהּ רַב הַמְנוּנָא לְאֵלִיָּהוּ. א"ל, וַדַּאי תְּנֵינָן דְּאִית צַדִּיק וְרַע לוֹ, רָשָׁע וְטוֹב לוֹ. אָמַר, צַדִּיק, כָּל שֶׁמְּמוּעָטִין לוֹ חוֹבוֹתָיו נוֹתְנִין לוֹ בָּעוֹלָם הַזֶּה חוֹבוֹ, וְעַל כֵּן צַדִּיק וְרַע לוֹ. וְכָל שֶׁמְּרוּבִּין עֲווֹנוֹתָיו, וּמְמוּעָטִין זָכְיוֹתָיו, נוֹתְנִין לוֹ שְׂכָרוֹ בָּעוֹלָם הַזֶּה, רָשָׁע וְטוֹב לוֹ. א"ל, דִּינוֹי דְּמָארֵי עָלְמָא, עֲמִיקִין אֲבָל בְּשַׁעֲתָא דְּבָעֵי קוּדְשָׁא בְּרִיךְ הוּא לְכַפְּרָא חוֹבִין דְּעָלְמָא, אַלְקֵי בִּדְרוֹעָא דִּלְהוֹן, וְאָסֵי לְכוּלְהוּ מְתַל לָאַסְיָיא, דְּאַלְקֵי לִדְרוֹעָא, לְשֵׁיזָבָא לְכָל שַׁיְּיפִין. כְּמָה דִּכְתִיב, וְהוּא מְחוֹלָל מִפְּשָׁעֵינוּ וְגוֹ'.

354. Here the ancient pillars of the world were divided. One said: Job was one of the pious of the nations of the world, and another said: Job was one of the pious of Yisrael, but was smitten in order to atone for the world. One day Rav Hamnuna found Elijah and said to him: We have definitely learned that there is a righteous man who suffers and a wicked man who prospers. RAV HAMNUNA EXPLAINED AND said: A righteous man is one whose sins

are few and who pays the price for them in this world, and thus the righteous man suffers. But if his sins are many and his good deeds few, then he receives his reward in this world, AND THUS is a wicked man who prospers. He said to him: The judgments of the Master of the World are profound, but when the Holy One, blessed be He, wants to make atonement for the sins of the generation, He smites their arm and through this action the generation is healed. It can be likened to a doctor who smites, NAMELY LETS BLOOD IN the arm in order to save all the parts, as it is written: "But he was wounded because of our transgressions" (Yeshayah 53:5).

355. כְּמָה דְּאִתְּמַר, בְּהַהוּא יוֹמָא שֶׁל רֹאשׁ הַשָּׁנָה, דְּקַיְּימִין שַׁבְעִין קָתֶדְרָאִין לְמֵידָן דִּינָא לְעָלְמָא, כַּמָּה אִינּוּן מָארֵי תְּרִיסִין, קַטֵיגוֹרִין, דְּקַיְּימֵי לְעֵילָּא. אִלֵּין מַיְימִינִין לְזָכוּ וְאִלֵּין מַשְׂמָאלִין לְחוֹבָא, לְאַדְכְּרָא חוֹבִין דְּעָלְמָא, חוֹבִין דְּכָל חַד וְחַד. וְעַל דָּא אִצְטְרִיךְ לב"נ, לְפָרְשָׁא חוֹבוֹי, כָּל חַד וְחַד כְּמָה דְּאִיהוּ בְּגִין דְּמַאן דְּמְפָרֵשׁ חֶטָאוֹי, לָא אִתְמְסַר דִּינֵיהּ, אֶלָּא בִּידָא דְּמַלְכָּא קוּדְשָׁא בְּרִיךְ הוּא בִּלְחוֹדוֹי. וּמַאן דְּדָאִין לֵיהּ קוּדְשָׁא בְּרִיךְ הוּא, אִיהוּ לְטָב. וע"ד בָּעָא דָּוִד מַלְכָּא, שָׁפְטֵנִי אֱלֹקִים, אַנְתְּ, וְלָא אַחֲרָא. וְכֵן שְׁלֹמֹה אָמַר, לַעֲשׂוֹת מִשְׁפַּט עַבְדּוֹ, הוּא, וְלָא אַחֲרָא, וְכָל ב"ד בְּדֵילִין מִמֶּנּוּ.

355. As we have learned, on that day of Rosh Hashanah, seventy seats of justice arise to judge the world, many for the defense and many for the prosecution standing on high, those on the right for innocence and those on the left for guilt, to recall the sins of the world and the sins of each individual. A man has therefore to CONFESS AND specify his sins, each one just as it is, for whoever expounds his sins BEFORE THE HOLY ONE, BLESSED BE HE, judgment is passed on him by the Holy One, blessed be He, and by no other. And whoever is judged by the Holy One, blessed be He, it is for his good. This is why King David requested: "Judge me, Elohim" (Tehilim 43:1), You and none other. Similarly, Solomon said, "that He maintain the cause of His servant" (I Melachim 8:59). He and no other. And the HEAVENLY court leaves him.

356. וע"ד אִצְטְרִיךְ לוֹן לְפָרְשָׁא חוֹבִין דְּכָל שַׁיְּיפָא וְשַׁיְּיפָא, וְכָל מַה דְּעָבֵיד בִּפְרָט. הה"ד, חַטָּאתִי אוֹדִיעֲךָ וְגו'. לְבָתַר וְאַתָּה נָשָׂאתָ עֲוֹן

חָטָאתִי סֶלָה. מְנָלָן. מִמֹּשֶׁה, דִּכְתִיב אָנָּא חָטָא הָעָם הַזֶּה וְגוֹ'. בְּיִשְׂרָאֵל כְּתִיב, חָטָאנוּ כִּי עָזַבְנוּ אֶת יְיָ', דְּאִי תֵּימָא הַאי בְּיָחִיד, אֲבָל בְּצִבּוּר לָא. הָא כְּתִיב קְרָא דָא. וְאִי תֵּימָא הָא בְּצִבּוּר, אֲבָל שְׁלִיחָא דִּלְהוֹן לָא, הָא כְּתִיב וַיָּשָׁב מֹשֶׁה אֶל יְיָ' וְגוֹ'. וּכְתִיב וַיַּעֲשׂוּ לָהֶם וְגוֹ'. מ"ט. מַאן דִּמְפָרֵשׁ חוֹבֵיהּ, בֵּי דִינָא בְּדֵילִין מִינֵיהּ, בְּגִין דב"נ קָרִיב לְגַרְמֵיהּ, וְלָא אִתְדָּן עַל פּוּמֵיהּ.

356. This is why the sins of every limb have to be expounded, and everything that he did in detail, as it is written: "I acknowledge my sin to You" (Tehilim 32:5). And this same verse concludes: "and You forgave the iniquity of my sin. Se'la." How do we know this? We know it from Moses, for it is written: "This people has sinned a great sin" (Ibid. 31). And about Yisrael is written: "We have sinned because we have forsaken Hashem" (I Shmuel 12:10). Should you suggest THAT THE VERSE ABOUT MOSES refers to an individual alone, while in public one does not HAVE TO SPECIFY ONE'S SINS, then the other verse "WE HAVE SINNED BECAUSE WE HAVE FORSAKEN HASHEM" comes to teach the opposite, FOR IT IS SAID IN PUBLIC. And should you agree that it is to be in public, but that it is not the cantor WHO HAS TO DETAIL THE SINS, the opposite is suggested, as it is written: "And Moses returned to Hashem and said: This people has sinned a great sin...and have made them an Elohim of gold." What is the reason? It is because the heavenly court leaves alone the person who expounds his own sins AND DOES NOT FIND HIM GUILTY. Because a man may be considered as one of his own close relatives, AND A RELATIVE IS UNACCEPTABLE AS A WITNESS. He is, THEREFORE, not judged according to his OWN testimony.

357. וְתוּ, לָא שָׁבִיק לִמְקַטְרְגָא לְאוֹלָפָא עֲלֵיהּ חוֹבָא מוּמָא. דְּבַר נָשׁ יַקְדִּים וְיֵימָא, וְלָא יָהִיב דּוּכְתָּא לְאַחֲרָא לְמֵימַר. כְּדֵין קוּדְשָׁא בְּרִיךְ הוּא מָחִיל לֵיהּ, הה"ד, וּמוֹדֶה וְעוֹזֵב יְרוּחָם.

357. Moreover, he does not let the prosecutor teach guilt and fault about him, because the person himself comes first and tells all, leaving nothing for anyone else to mention. Then the Holy One, blessed be He, forgives him, as it is written: "But whoever confesses and forsakes them shall have mercy" (Mishlei 28:13).

59. Rosh Hashanah

A Synopsis

We learn why Rosh Hashanah lasts for two days, and that when people are coming to be judged Yisrael comes in first. It is important that we know the meaning of the blowing of the Shofar that arouses leniency and mercy.

The Relevance of this Passage

Rosh Hashanah is commonly known as the "Jewish New Year." Traditionally, it is also a time of judgment, when the Creator takes a reckoning of our deeds during the previous year.

But according to Kabbalah, both these depictions of Rosh Hashanah are inaccurate.

Kabbalah teaches that the Force we call *God* does not preside over a heavenly court, deciding who will be forgiven and who will be punished. And Rosh Hashanah actually occurs in the seventh month of the Hebrew Calendar, so it does not signify a new year.

Science offers us some insight into the true significance of Rosh Hashanah. A principle of physics states that for every action there is an equal reaction. Rosh Hashanah is also built upon this foundation – the universal law of cause and effect.

Though we may not be aware of it, when we behave in a contemptuous, uncivil, or rude manner, we arouse negative forces. When we cheat, lie, steal, insult, embarrass, or harm other people, a negative energy force is brought into existence. These negative forces are the unseen cause behind all the things that just "happen" to go wrong in our lives, be it illness, emotional pain, or financial adversity.

Rosh Hashanah is our opportunity to confront the negative energy aroused through the wrongful acts we have committed during the preceding year. At this special time, the spiritual cycle of the universe is structured so that the consequences of our careless misdeeds, intolerant behavior, and hurtful words return to us. These repercussions of our own actions stand in judgment before us. The court of Cause and Effect stands in session.

Moreover, this self-confrontation is not exclusive to the children of Yisrael. According to the Zohar, the experience of cause and effect is shared by all mankind.

Put in simple terms, Kabbalah teaches that reality is like a mirror. Look into a mirror and smile, and the image smiles back. If one curses at the mirror, the image curses back. When we perform a negative act in our world, the cosmic mirror – our universe – reflects that negative energy.

The Creator *never* stands in judgment of us, and we are never required to stand in judgment in front of the Creator.

Crime and punishment

There is only one Force, one energy source for the entire cosmos, just as there is but one electrical force flowing through your home. This Force is good, positive, and infinitely compassionate.

Consider this: Electricity enriches human life by providing power for an entire nation. But this same force can also be used destructively. Placing one's finger into a light socket will cause electrocution. But the nature of the electricity never changed, and it would be senseless to say that the electricity "punished" you.

In the same way, the Creator never punishes us. *We ourselves* have chosen to place our finger in the socket through wrongful conduct.

We always have the free choice of how we react to life's challenges. Even when we know something is wrong, we sometimes choose to do it anyway. And when we know something is right, we may forsake it for a negative option. The choice is always ours.

Crimes and misdemeanors

Negative activity and sin can materialize in ways both large and small. Consider the sins of *murder, evil speech,* and *adultery:*

Murder
- We can kill someone physically, or we may also kill someone emotionally and spiritually.

- We can assassinate a person's body, or we may also assassinate a person's character.

- We can destroy someone's relationships, or we may also ruin their livelihood.

Kabbalah teaches that the sin of "spilling blood" is not limited to physical violence. Spilling blood can refer to the shame and embarrassment we may cause to others, forcing the blood to rush to their faces out of humiliation.

Evil Speech
According to Kabbalah, any form of malicious speech – even about someone we have never met – is one of the most serious crimes a person can commit.

Speech has tremendous powers. When we speak badly of others, we not only damage their lives – we also damage ourselves and even the entire world. At Rosh Hashanah, our damaging words come back to haunt us. Evil speech, therefore, is a no-win

situation. According to the wisdom of the sages, people should be more concerned with what comes out of their mouths than what goes into their mouths.

Adultery

The concept of adultery is not limited to extramarital affairs. One can also covet another person's business, children, or material possessions. Envy and adultery occur when we fail fully to appreciate all that we have. And this lack of appreciation occurs when we gain our possessions through egocentric, destructive behavior.

Requesting a pardon

Now that we understand that there are real repercussions associated with our negative behavior, we may be tempted to ask for a pardon, or seek exoneration through ignorance of the law of cause and effect. But ignorance of the law is no excuse, and natural laws of the universe cannot be violated without consequences. You cannot plead ignorance of the force of gravity while you are plunging a thousand feet toward the ground.

However, it is *also* a spiritual law of the universe that when a person achieves a remarkable change in his or her own nature, the universe must respond and reflect that miraculous energy back to us. We can then use that energy to alter our destiny and deflect judgments.

The first thing we must do in order to bring about change is to admit that we are guilty. Accept responsibility. Become accountable for our actions (that, perhaps, is the hardest thing to do). Then, with all our heart and soul, we make every attempt to change our ways during the time frame of Rosh Hashanah.

This internal change begins with a mighty and majestic blast of a horn!

The secret of the Shofar

Most people associate the blowing of the Shofar with tradition. It's viewed as ceremonial activity. A symbolic act of commemoration.

However, symbolism and traditional rituals offer no practical benefit to our daily lives, according to the Kabbalist.

BUT BECAUSE WE HAVE REMAINED IGNORANT AS TO THE TRUE PURPOSE OF THE SHOFAR, ITS EFFECT IN OUR LIVES, THROUGHOUT HISTORY, HAS BEEN NEGLIGIBLE. TWO THOUSAND YEARS OF PAIN AND SUFFERING ARE EVIDENCE TO THAT HARSH TRUTH.

The Shofar's power can only be expressed when *knowledge* of its true purpose is instilled within our consciousness. *Knowing why* we sound the Shofar is the electrical current that turns it on.

THE SOUND EMANATING FROM THE HORN OPERATES LIKE A SPIRITUAL LASER BEAM THAT DISSOLVES ALL THE BLOCKAGES OF NEGATIVE ENERGY THAT WE'VE CREATED. THE MYSTICAL SOUND ALSO ACTS AS A CLEANSING AGENT THAT PERMEATES EVERY CRACK AND CREVICE IN OUR BEING, REMOVING NEGATIVE RESIDUES AND PURIFYING OUR SOUL. ONCE THESE BLOCKAGES ARE REMOVED, THE JUDGMENTS HAVE LOST THEIR TARGETS. THE EVIDENCE IS DESTROYED.

The "prosecuting attorney," the Accuser Satan, stands before the "court" – universal law of cause and effect – without a shred of evidence. Case dismissed!

Here we ignite the sounds and secrets of the Shofar. The negative energy created by the sins of man is dissolved away and all judgments are annulled.

358. בְּיוֹמֵי דר״ה, מְתַקְּנִין בֵּי דִינָא כּוּרְסְיָיא לְמַלְכָּא, לְמֵידָן כָּל עָלְמָא. וְיִשְׂרָאֵל עָאלִין בְּקַדְמֵיתָא בְּדִינָא קַמֵּיה, דְּלִיפוּש רַחֲמֵי. תְּנָן וּמִשְׁפַּט עַמּוֹ יִשְׂרָאֵל דְּבַר יוֹם בְּיוֹמוֹ, יוֹם בְּיוֹמוֹ מַאי הוּא. אֶלָּא הָנֵי תְּרֵי יוֹמִין דר״ה. אֲמַאי תְּרֵי יוֹמִין. בְּגִין דְּאִינּוּן תְּרֵי בֵּי דִינָא, דְּמִתְחַבְּרָן כַּחֲדָא. דִּינָא עִלָּאָה, דְּאִיהוּ קַשְׁיָא, בְּדִינָא תַּתָּאָה, דְּאִיהוּ רַפְיָא, וְתַרְוַויְיהוּ מִשְׁתַּכְחֵי.

358. On the days of Rosh Hashanah, the court prepares a throne for the King to judge the whole world. Yisrael come in first to be judged before Him, so that Mercy will multiply, NAMELY BEFORE ANGER IS AROUSED AT THE SINNERS OF THE WORLD. It is written "that He maintain...the cause of His people Yisrael, as each day may require" (I Melachim 8:59). What is the meaning of "as each day may require"? THE MEANING IS the two days of Rosh Hashanah. And why are there two days? Because they are two courts joined together. There is the upper Judgment, which is harsh, and the lower Judgment that is lenient, and both of them exist.

359. וְעַל דָּא לָא יַדְעֵי הָנֵי בַּבְלָאֵי, רָזָא דְּיִבָּבָא וִילָלוּתָא, וְלָא יַדְעֵי דְּתַרְוַויְיהוּ אִצְטְרִיכוּ, יְלָלוּתָא דְּאִיהוּ דִּינָא תַּקִּיפָא. תְּלַת תְּבִירִין דְּאִיהוּ דִּינָא רַפְיָא, גְּנוּחֵי גָּנַח רַפְיָא. אִינּוּן לָא יַדְעֵי, וְעַבְדִין תַּרְוַויְיהוּ. וַאֲנָן יַדְעִינָן, וְעַבְדֵּינָן תַּרְוַויְיהוּ. וְכֹלָּא נָפְקִין לְאֹרַח קְשׁוֹט.

359. And in this respect the Babylonians did not know the secret of the Sh'varim and T'ruah and that both of them are required. The T'ruah is strict Judgment. The three notes of the Sh'varim are lenient Judgment, AND IT IS LIKE someone who groans FROM HIS HEART, which is soft. They did not know WHICH OF THE TWO WAS REQUIRED, AND they THEREFORE had both of them. But we know BOTH, THAT BOTH OF THEM ARE REQUIRED, and do both OF THEM. And everything comes out by the way of truth.

360. פָּתַח וְאָמַר, תִּקְעוּ בַחֹדֶשׁ שׁוֹפָר בַּכֶּסֶה לְיוֹם חַגֵּנוּ. תִּקְעוּ בַחֹדֶשׁ שׁוֹפָר, מַאי בַחֹדֶשׁ. דָּא בֵּי דִּינָא רַפְיָא, דְּאִקְרֵי חֹדֶשׁ. בַּכֶּסֶה: דָּא דִּינָא קַשְׁיָא, פַּחַד יִצְחָק. דִּינָא דְּאִתְכַּסְּיָא תָּדִיר, דְּלָאו אִיהוּ דִּינָא בְּאִתְגַּלְּיָיא. כִּי חֹק, דָּא דִּינָא רַפְיָא. וּמִשְׁפָּט, דָּא דִּינָא בְּרַחֲמֵי. וְתַרְוַויְיהוּ אִינּוּן כַּחֲדָא. בג"כ תְּרֵין יוֹמִין, וְתַרְוַויְיהוּ בְּרָזָא חֲדָא.

360. He began by quoting: "Blow the horn at the new moon, in concealment for our feast day. For it is a statute for Yisrael...an ordinance of the Elohim of Jacob" (Tehilim 81:4-5). What is "Blow the horn at the new moon"? It means lenient Judgment, that is called "new moon." And what is "in conccalment"? This is harsh Judgment, which is ALSO TERMED 'the fear of Isaac'. It is a Judgment that is concealed permanently, NAMELY THE MANULA, which is not judgment openly. "For it is a statute" refers to lenient Judgment. "an ordinance" refers to Judgment CONTAINED with Mercy, and the two of them are there together, and this is why there are two days OF ROSH HASHANAH, both of which are of the same principle.

361. אַשְׁרֵי הָעָם יוֹדְעֵי תְרוּעָה וְגו', לָא כְּתִיב שׁמְעֵי, אוֹ תּוֹקְעֵי תְרוּעָה, אֶלָּא יוֹדְעֵי תְרוּעָה. בְּגִין חַכִּימִין דְּדַיְירִין בַּאֲוִירָא דְּאַרְעָא קַדִּישָׁא, אִינּוּן יוֹדְעֵי תְרוּעָה. רָזָא דִּתְרוּעָה, כְּמָה דִּכְתִּיב תְּרוֹעֵם בְּשֵׁבֶט בַּרְזֶל. מַאן עַמָּא כְּיִשְׂרָאֵל, דְּיַדְעִין רָזִין עִלָּאִין דְּמָארֵיהוֹן, לְמֵיעַל קַמֵּיהּ, וּלְאִתְקַשְּׁרָא בֵּיהּ. וְכָל אִינּוּן דְּיַדְעֵי רָזָא דִּתְרוּעָה, יִתְקָרְבוּן לְמֵיהַךְ בְּאוֹר פָּנָיו דְּקוּדְשָׁא בְּרִיךְ הוּא. וְדָא אוֹר קַדְמָאָה דִּגְנִיז קוּדְשָׁא בְּרִיךְ הוּא לְצַדִּיקַיָּיא. וע"ד אִצְטְרִיךְ לְמִנְדַּע לָהּ.

361. "Happy is the people that know the joyful note (Heb. *T'ruah*)"

(Tehilim 89:15). It does not say "that hear," nor does it say "that blow the sounds OF A TERU'AH," but "that know." This is because ONLY the sages who dwell in the atmosphere of the holy land are the ones who know T'ruah. The secret of the teru'ah is as it is written: "You shall break them (Heb. *teroem*) with a rod of iron" (Tehilim 2:9). What people is there like Yisrael, who know the heavenly secrets of their Master and enter in before Him and associate with Him. And all those who know the secret of the teru'ah will draw near and walk in the light of the countenance of the Holy One, blessed be He, because this is the first light that the Holy One, blessed be He, hid for the righteous. This is why it is necessary to know it, THE T'RUAH.

60. The appendix of the liver, gall, trachea, esophagus and the Shofar

A Synopsis
Rav Hamnuna talks about the iniquity of Lilit and Samael, saying that they are the liver and the appendix, and that from them emerge the gall that is the sword of the Angel of Death. On Rosh Hashanah the gall wanders the world collecting up sins, and all of Yisrael are in trouble; this is when they blow the Shofar.

The Relevance of this Passage
Extraordinary notions relating to heart disease, human behavior, healing, and world peace emerge from this ancient passage.

According to the Zohar, our reactive emotions, notably anger and rage, manifest in our liver and its appendage.

A remarkable insight is then presented in paragraph 364:

> "From the liver and the appendage, WHICH ARE SAMAEL AND LILIT, emerges the gall, which is the sword of the Angel of Death, from which come bitter drops to kill human beings."

In paragraph 365, the Zohar says that the gall:

> "...overcomes the arteries of the heart and all the arteries in the limbs of the body..."

Interestingly, *gall* is defined by Merriam Webster's Dictionary as both "bile" and "bitterness of spirit" or "rancor." This definition reinforces the Kabbalistic viewpoint that a vital connection exists between human behavior and physical health. Moreover, it is the liver that secretes gall (bile), and its primary component is cholesterol.

High levels of cholesterol are a major cause of atherosclerosis, the hardening and blockage of arteries, one of the most frequent causes of heart disease and death.

All the anger and negative reflexive emotions that we've expressed throughout the year are used by the negative angel *Lilit* during Rosh Hashanah as an indictment against us. The ensuing judgment manifests as illness and heart-related diseases. The Shofar is used to purify us, to remove the force of Satan from our arteries and cardiovascular system.

Metaphysically, it works like this:

The esophagus is spelled VAV SHIN TET (*Veshet*) ושט. However, the Zohar explains that when we are overly self-indulgent, allowing our ego and selfish desires to grow incessantly, the letter VAV ו also grows and extends into the letter NUN ן. The letters that spell esophagus are now rearranged to spell SATAN (SIN, TET, NUT) שטן. This effect is rooted in an event that took place in the Torah, in the Book of Numbers. The Children of Israel were given manna from Heaven, a spiritual substance that could taste like the finest meal one could imagine. However, a consciousness of certainty in the manna's power was the prerequisite. The Israelites did not possess this state of mind and could therefore, not connect to this spiritual energy. They demanded and received physical meat. The Satan infiltrated their bodies while the meat was in their teeth, indicating their total connection to physicality.

The Zohar states that when our own physical desires run rampant and we choose the physical world over the spiritual, the Satan again overcomes "all the limbs and the arteries" for all the 365 days of the solar year.

There is, however, recourse for the repentant heart – and it is found in the instrument of the Shofar, the trachea, and the event of Yom Kippur.

The trachea is a windpipe, just like the Shofar which is a musical windpipe. The Shofar correlates to the realm of *Binah*, where there is so much pleasure and fulfillment that there is no need for food and drink. Likewise, the trachea is not utilized when we eat or drink. Like the Shofar, only air enters our trachea.

On Yom Kippur, there is also no eating and drinking, signifying *Binah* and the unimaginable spiritual nourishment that it provides. Second, the numerical value of the "The Satan" השטן is 364, which is one number short of the 365 days of the year. This is the one day of the year when Satan is banished from our world – Yom Kippur!

Blowing the Shofar and observing Yom Kippur reestablishes our connection to Binah. The NUN in the word SATAN is reduced in size – just as we reduce our desire to consume food and drink on Yom Kippur – and it reverts back into a VAV to again spell *esophagus* in Hebrew. Satan and the force of death are now extracted from our arteries and limbs.

This splendid passage recalls the energy of Yom Kippur and it sounds the Shofar on our behalf to heal our hearts, liver, arteries, trachea, esophagus, and limbs. Good cholesterol levels rise while bad cholesterol levels decrease. Our blood is cleansed of toxins. The arteries are cleared of deadly deposits and plaque.

Yisrael, the cosmic counterpart of the human heart, also functions as the heart of mankind. Yisrael's relationship to the rest of the world is like the heart's arteries that carry blood and oxygen to the rest of the body. The nations of the world correspond to the body's organs and limbs. Hence, the same way that the heart now supplies purified blood to nourish the body, Yisrael furnishes Light to aid all the nations of the world as a result of our meditation. Furthermore, conflicts and barriers between Yisrael and all nations are henceforth eliminated, clearing the way for global harmony and lasting peace.

As Satan is absent from the world on Yom Kippur, the Light generated from this passage now banishes Satan from the other 364 days of the solar calendar, paving the way for the Messiah to arrive in our day.

362. כְּתִיב הַיּוֹתֶרֶת מִן הַכָּבֵד. וּכְתִיב וְאֶת הַיּוֹתֶרֶת עַל הַכָּבֵד. יוֹתֶרֶת מִן הַכָּבֵד, דָּא אֵשֶׁת זְנוּנִים, דְּאַזְלָא וְנָפְקָא מִן הַכָּבֵד, לְאַסְטָאָה בְּנֵי עָלְמָא, וּלְאַסְטְנָא עָלַיְיהוּ. וְשַׁבְקַת לִדְכוּרָא, לְמֶעְבַּד זְנוּנִים. וּבְג״ד הַיּוֹתֶרֶת מִן הַכָּבֵד, יוֹתֶרֶת עַל הַכָּבֵד. בָּתַר דְּעַבְדַת נִיאוּפָא, אִסְתַּלְּקַת עֲלֵיהּ. מֵצַח אִשָּׁה זוֹנָה. אִתְגַּבְּרַת עַל בַּעְלָהּ דְּאִיהוּ כָּבֵד, בְּכַעַס דְּמָרָה, אֵשֶׁת מְדָנִים, וְכַעַס, דְּשַׁלְּטָא אִיהִי עַל דְּכוּרָא דִּילָהּ. מֵצַח אִשָּׁה זוֹנָה שַׁלְטָא עַל הַכָּבֵד, אֵשֶׁת מְדָנִים וָכַעַס.

362. It is written: "the appendix of the liver" (Vayikra 9:10), and also: "the appendix above the liver" (Vayikra 3:4). "the appendix of the liver" MEANS a woman of harlotry, THAT IS LILIT, who comes out and emerges from the liver, THAT IS SAMAEL, to mislead people and denounce them, and she leaves the male to practice prostitution. And that is why IT IS WRITTEN: "the appendix of the liver"; "the appendix above the liver" MEANS THAT, after her fornications, she rises above him. She has "a harlot's forehead" (Yirmeyah 3:3) and subdues her husband, who is SAMAEL, WHO IS CALLED 'liver', with the anger of the gall, being a quarrelsome and anger-prone wife who rules over her male. THUS "The harlot's forehead" has control over the liver, WHICH IS SAMAEL, BECAUSE SHE IS a quarrelsome, angry woman AND IS THEREFORE CALLED "THE APPENDIX ABOVE THE LIVER."

363. יוֹתֶרֶת מִן הַכָּבֵד, מִן הַכָּבֵד נָפְקָא לְאַבְאָשָׁא לְכָל עָלְמָא,

וּלְמֶעְבַּד נִיאוּפִין עִם כֹּלָא. לְבָתַר אִיהִי סַלְקָא לְגַבֵּי דְכוּרָא, מֵצַח אִשָּׁה
זוֹנָה, בְּעַזוּתָא דְּאַנְפִּין, וּכְדֵין אִיהִי עַל הַכָּבֵד. וְעוֹד, יוֹתֶרֶת מִן הַכָּבֵד
אִתְקְרִיאַת מִסִּטְרָא אַחֲרָא, בָּתַר דְּנַפְקַת לְנָאֲפָא עִם כֹּלָא, יְהִיבַת
שִׁיּוּרִין לְבַעְלָהּ, וְהַאי אִיהִי יוֹתֶרֶת מִן הַכָּבֵד.

363. "the appendix of the liver:" BECAUSE SHE emerges from the liver,
WHO, AS EXPLAINED ABOVE, IS SAMAEL HER HUSBAND, in order to harm
the whole world and practice adultery with all. She then mounts the male,
with "a harlot's forehead," audaciously, and she is then above the liver.
Also, she is called "the appendix of the liver," from another point of view,
for after she has gone out to play prostitute with all, she gives the leftovers
to her husband, and this is the meaning of "the appendix of the liver,"
appendix IS DERIVED FROM LEFTOVERS.

364. מִגּוֹ כָּבֵד, וְיוֹתֶרֶת דִּילָהּ, נַפְקַת מָרָה, וְאִיהִי חַרְבָּא דְּמַלְאָךְ הַמָּוֶת,
דְּנַפְקוּ מִנָּהּ טִפִּין מְרִירָן לְקַטְלָא בְּנֵי נָשָׁא. הה"ד, וְאַחֲרִיתָהּ מָרָה
כַלַעֲנָה. וְאִיהִי תַלְיָא בַּכָּבֵד, כָּל מַרְעִין וּמוֹתָא בֵּיהּ תַּלְיָין. וְהַהוּא יוֹמָא
דר"ה מְשַׁטְּטָא בְּעָלְמָא, לְמִכְנַשׁ כָּל חוֹבֵי עָלְמָא וּכְדֵין כָּל אֵבָרִין
דְּאִינּוּן יִשְׂרָאֵל, אִינּוּן בְּעָאקוּ, דְּאִינּוּן אֵבְרֵי דְּמַטְרוֹנִיתָא, נֵר יְיָ' נִשְׁמַת
אָדָם, שְׁכִינְתָּא קַדִּישָׁא. וּכְדֵין כָּל יִשְׂרָאֵל בְּעָאקוּ, וְנַטְלֵי שׁוֹפָר
לְאִתְּעָרָא בֵּיהּ הַהוּא תְּקִיעָה וּשְׁבָרִים וּתְרוּעָה.

364. From the liver and the appendix, WHICH ARE SAMAEL AND LILIT,
emerges the gall, which is the sword of the Angel of Death, from which
come bitter drops to kill people. It is written: "Her end is bitter (Heb.
marah) as wormwood" (Mishlei 5:4). And THE GALL (HEB. MARAHA) is
hanging over the liver, all sickness and death coming from it, FROM THE
KLIPAH THAT IS CALLED 'GALL'. And on that day of Rosh Hashanah, she
prowls through the world, collecting up all the sins that are in the world.
And then all the parts, which are Yisrael, are in trouble, FOR YISRAEL are
the parts of the Shechinah, AS IT IS SAID: "The soul of man is the candle of
Hashem" (Mishlei 20:27), WHICH MEANS THAT THE SOUL OF MAN IS
DERIVED FROM THE CANDLE OF HASHEM, which is the holy Shechinah.
And then, ON ROSH HASHANAH, all Yisrael are in trouble, so they take a
Shofar to awaken with it those calls: T'kiah, Sh'varim, T'ruah.

A Synopsis

Moses talks about the participation of the body – the trachea, the lungs, the arteries, the breath, the esophagus and the mouth – in the blowing of the Shofar. He says that the Satan has no control on Yom Kippur, the Day of Atonement. Yisrael's strength is in the voice, not in eating and drinking like everyone else in the world, and it is necessary to awaken the voice with the ten Shofar verses.

רעיא מהימנא

365. אָמַר רַעְיָא מְהֵימָנָא, וַדַּאי בָּתַר דְּאֵבָרִים וְעַרְקִין דְּלִבָּא, דְּדַמְיָין לְיִשְׂרָאֵל, אִינוּן בְּעָאקוּ. צְרִיכִין לְאַתְעָרָא בְּקָנֶה, דְּאִיהוּ שׁוֹפָר. וְדָא קָנֶה דְּרֵיאָה. בָּתַר דְּכַנְפֵי רֵיאָה לָא יַכְלִין לְשַׁכְּכָא רוּגְזָא דְּמָרָה דְּאִתְגַּבְּרַת עַל עַרְקִין דְּלִבָּא, וְעַל כָּל עַרְקִין דְּאֵבָרִים דְּגוּפָא. הַהוּא רוּחָא דְּנָשִׁיב בְּהוֹן, סָלִיק בְּקָנֶה, דְּאִיהוּ שׁוֹפָר, עָלְמָא דְּאָתֵי. דְּהָכִי אוּקְמוּהָ, וֶשֶׁט, דּוּמֶה לְעָלְמָא דֵּין, דְּבֵיהּ אֲכִילָה וּשְׁתִיָּה. קָנֶה, דּוּמֶה לְעָלְמָא דְּאָתֵי, דְּלֵית בֵּיהּ אֲכִילָה וּשְׁתִיָּה.

Ra'aya Meheimna (the Faithful Shepherd)

365. The Faithful Shepherd said: Certain it is that since the limbs and the arteries of the heart, that are likened to Yisrael, are in trouble, they have to awaken in the trachea pipe, which is the secret of the Shofar, this being the windpipe connected to the lung. Since the lobes of the lung are unable to quiet the anger of the gall, which overcomes the arteries of the heart and all the arteries in the limbs of the body, that breath, WHICH IS THE SECRET OF CHASSADIM that blows in them, rises in the trachea, which is a Shofar, namely the World to Come. FOR A SHOFAR IS THE SECRET OF BINAH THAT IS CALLED 'THE WORLD TO COME'. And so it has been taught: The esophagus is like this world, WHICH IS THE SECRET OF MALCHUT, eating and drinking in it, NAMELY THE MOCHIN OF CHASSADIM AND CHOCHMAH THAT ARE TERMED EATING AND DRINKING. The trachea is likened to the World to Come, WHICH IS BINAH, for there is no eating and drinking pertain to it, FOR THOSE MOCHIN ARE NOT DISCLOSED THERE IN BINAH, BUT IN MALCHUT.

366. וּלְבָתַר דְּשָׁט ו' מִן וֶשֶׁט, בְּרִבּוּי אֲכִילָה דְּגֶזֶל אִתְאָרַךְ וְאִתְעֲבֵיד

שָׂטָן. וּמַאן גָּרִים דָּא. שָׁטוּ הָעָם וְלָקְטוּ שָׁטוּתָא דִּלְהוֹן, דְּאִתְעָרְבוּ
בְּעֵרֶב רַב שַׁטְיִין, דְּתֵאָוָה דִּלְהוֹן אֲכִילָה וּשְׁתִיָּה דְּגֶזֶל וְחָמָס, דְּשׁוֹד
עֲנִיִּים וְאֶנְקַת אֶבְיוֹנִים. בְּנוֹן כְּפוּפָה שַׁטְיִין, דְּאַכְלִין בְּלָא טְחִינָה. מַה
כְּתִיב בְּהוֹ, הַבָּשָׂר עוֹדֶנּוּ בֵּין שִׁנֵּיהֶם טֶרֶם יִכָּרֵת וְאַף יְיָ׳ חָרָה בָעָם.
אִתְפְּשַׁט ו׳ דְּשָׁטוּ, אִיהוּ דְּרוּחֵיה כָּפוּף, וְאִיהוּ נ׳. וְדָא גָרַם דְּאִתְפְּשַׁט
שָׂטָן בַּאֲכִילָה וּשְׁתִיָּה, וְאִתְגְּבַּר עַל כָּל אֵבָרִין וְעַרְקִין בְּשס"ה לֹא
תַעֲשֶׂה. כְּחוּשְׁבָּן הַשָּׂטָ"ן חָסֵר חַד, דָּא יוֹם הַכִּפּוּרִים, דְּלֵית בֵּיה אֲכִילָה
וּשְׁתִיָּה.

366. And after the Vav of esophagus (Heb. *veshet* - Vav Shin Tet) has wandered off (HEB. *shat* - Shin Tet), because of the great amount of eating that it robbed, it grew longer, AND THE VAV BECAME A FINAL NUN and becomes the Satan (Sin Tet Nun). Who caused that? "the people wandered about (Heb. *shatu*) and gathered..." (Bemidbar 11:8), 'SHATU', CAN BE DERIVED FROM THE WORD 'SH'TUT' (ENG. 'STUPIDITY'). FOR THAT ONE brought about their stupidity in that they intermingled with the foolish mixed multitude whose craving was for food and drink and robbery and violence, "For the violence done to the poor, for the sighing of the needy" (Tehilim 12:6). They went astray with a bent Nun, for they ate without grinding it. And what is written about them? "And while the meat was yet between their teeth, before it was chewed, the wrath of Hashem was inflamed against the people" (Bemidbar 11:33). For the Vav of *shatu* (Shin Tet Vav), wandered about, expanded AND BECAME A FINAL NUN, THUS MAKING THE SATAN. And he whose spirit is bowed down is as a BENT Nun, THAT IS TO SAY THAT THE SANCTITY HAD BECOME A BENT NUN, BUT THE OTHER SIDE A STRAIGHT FINAL NUN. And the result of this was that the Satan spread through eating and drinking and overcame all the limbs and the arteries with the 365 negative precepts, FOR ALL 365 DAYS OF THE SOLAR YEAR. And this is as the numerical value of Hasatan (the Satan), minus one, which is THE DAY OF Yom Kippur WHICH HE DOES NOT HAVE, on which there is no eating and drinking. THUS THE SATAN HAS NO CONTROL ON YOM KIPPUR, AND IS SHORT ONE DAY OF THE FULL 365.

367. וְאִיהוּ כְּגַוְונָא דְקָנֶה, וְאִיהוּ ו׳ בֶּן יָ"ה, מִן בִּינָה. וּבְגִינֵיה אוּקְמוּהָ
מָארֵי מַתְנִיתִין, הָרוֹאֶה קָנֶה בַּחֲלוֹם, זוֹכֶה לַחָכְמָה. הה"ד, קָנֵה חָכְמָה

קְנֵה בִינָה. דְּלֵית קָנֶה דְּאִיהוּ פָּחוּת מִתַּרְוַויְיהוּ, דְּאִינּוּן י' חָכְמָה, ה' בִּינָה. וּבג"ד, צָרִיךְ לְאִתְעָרָא בַּשׁוֹפָר, דְּאִיהוּ קָנֶה, עָלְמָא דְּאָתֵי, עוֹלָם אָרוֹךְ, אֶרֶךְ אַפַּיִם, דְּמִשְׁתַּכְּחֵי מִנֵּיהּ י"ג מְכִילִין דְּרַחֲמֵי, כְּחוּשְׁבַּן וָא"ו, א' אֶרֶךְ, ו' ו' אַפַּיִם.

367. AND YOM KIPPUR is like the trachea OF THE LUNG, WHICH IS BINAH AND THE WORLD TO COME, AS ABOVE. And it is Vav, the son (Heb. *ben*) of Yud Hei. And in respect thereof, the sages of the Mishnah taught: "He who sees a reed (Heb. *kaneh*) in a dream, attains wisdom, for it says "Get (Heb. *k'neh*) wisdom, get understanding" (Mishlei 4:5). For there is no *kaneh* that is less than both, namely, Yud Chochmah, Hei Binah, FOR THERE IS NO BINAH WITHOUT CHOCHMAH AND NO CHOCHMAH WITHOUT BINAH. And this is why they should awaken the Shofar, for it is a trachea, AS ABOVE, which is the World to Come, a long world, THAT RECEIVES FROM ARICH (ENG. 'LONG') ANPIN, from whom come the thirteen attributes of Mercy, which are in numerical value Vav-Aleph-Vav, of which the Aleph is THE SECRET OF *Erech* (Eng. 'long'), and the two Vavs are THE SECRET OF *Apayim* (Eng. 'suffering', lit. 'two noses').

368. וְאִימָּא עִלָּאָה אִיהִי תְּקִיעָה, מִסִּטְרָא דְּאַבְרָהָם. שְׁבָרִים, מִסִּטְרָא דְּיִצְחָק. תְּרוּעָה, מִסִּטְרָא דְּיַעֲקֹב. שְׁכִינְתָּא תַּתָּאָה, קֶשֶׁר דְּכֻלְּהוּ. דְּהַיְינוּ: ק' תְּקִיעָה. שׁ' שְׁבָרִים. ר' תְּרוּעָה. וְכֻלְּהוּ מְשַׁלְּשִׁין לְגַבֵּי שְׁכִינְתָּא, הה"ד, קָדוֹשׁ לְךָ יְשַׁלֵּשׁוּ. דְּלֵית קָלָא יָכִיל לְנָפְקָא לְבַר, אֶלָּא מִן הַפֶּה. אוֹף הָכִי, לֵית לְאַפְרְשָׁא שְׁכִינְתָּא מִן קוּדְשָׁא בְּרִיךְ הוּא. דְּקוּדְשָׁא בְּרִיךְ הוּא אִתְּמַר בֵּיהּ, קוֹל יְיָ' חוֹצֵב לַהֲבוֹת אֵשׁ. וּשְׁכִינְתָּא תְּפִלַת כָּל פֶּה. וְאִינּוּן סִימָנִין, קֶשֶׁר"ק קֶשׁ"ק קֶר"ק.

עד כאן רעיא מהימנא

368. And Supernal Ima is T'kiah from the side of Abraham, WHO IS CHESED. Sh'varim are from the side of Isaac, WHO IS GVURAH. T'ruah is from the side of Jacob, WHO IS TIFERET. The lower Shechinah, WHICH IS MALCHUT, is the link (Heb. *kesher* - Kof Shin Resh) between them all, FOR SHE RECEIVES THEM ALL. AND THE WORD *KESHER* IS FORMED FROM THE INITIAL LETTERS OF T'KIAH, SH'VARIM, T'RUAH, WHERE T'kiah is

Kof, Sh'varim is Shin, and T'ruah is Resh. And all of them are sounded thrice in the Shechinah, as it is written: 'They proclaim You thrice holy'. For the voice cannot come out OF THE BODY other than through the mouth. So here, too, the Shechinah must not be separated from the Holy One, blessed be He, for about the Holy One, blessed be He, it is said: "The voice of Hashem hews out flames of fire" (Tehilim 29:7). And the Shechinah is "the prayer of every mouth." And these are the mnemonics: Kof Shin Resh Kof, Kof Shin Kof, Kof Resh Kof. AND THE BLOWS ARE EXPLAINED ABOVE.

End of Ra'aya Meheimna (the Faithful Shepherd)

369. נַטְלִין שׁוֹפָר, לְאִתְּעָרָא בֵּיהּ, תְּרוּעָה וּתְקִיעָה, דִּינָא קַשְׁיָא בְּרַחֲמֵי, וּשְׁבָרִים דִּינָא רַפְיָא בְּרַחֲמֵי וּכְדֵין הָכִי יִתְּעֲרוּ לְעֵילָא לְאִתְעָרְבָא דָּא בְּדָא.

369. The Shofar is taken in order to awaken with it T'ruah and T'kiah, WHICH ARE harsh Judgment with Mercy, FOR THE T'RUAH IS HARSH JUDGMENT, AND T'KIAH IS MERCY. And Sh'varim T'KIAH means lenient Judgment with Mercy, SINCE SH'VARIM IS LENIENT JUDGMENT AND T'KIAH IS MERCY. And then they thus awaken on high and intermingle with each other, THAT IS, JUDGMENT WITH MERCY AND MERCY WITH JUDGMENT.

רעיא מהימנא

370. וּבְחִבּוּרָא קַדְמָאָה, אָמַר רַעְיָא מְהֵימְנָא, בְּהַאי אִתְכַּבְּסַם שָׂטָן, וְקָמִיט נוּ"ן מִן וֶשֶׁט, מַה דַּהֲוָה שָׂטָן לְפָנִים, תָּב לַאֲחוֹרָא, וְאִתְהַדָּר וֶשֶׁט, כְּדִבְקַדְמֵיתָא. בְּגִין דְּהַקּוֹל קוֹל יַעֲקֹב. יִשְׂרָאֵל לֵית חֵילֵיהוֹן בַּאֲכִילָה וּשְׁתִיָּה, כִּשְׁאַר עַמִּין, דְּיַרְתִין עָלְמָא דֵין, דְּחֵילֵיהוֹן בַּאֲכִילָה וּשְׁתִיָּה. אֶלָּא חֵילֵיהוֹן בְּקוֹל דָּא, דְּאִיהוּ עָלְמָא דְּאָתֵי, עוֹלָם אָרוֹךְ, דְּאִתְבְּרֵי בְּאָת יוֹ"ד, וּבְגִין דְּקוֹל דְּקוֹל שׁוֹפָר מִנֵּיהּ נָפִיק, אָמְרוּ רַבָּנָן אֵין פּוֹחֲתִין מֵעֲשָׂרָה שׁוֹפָרוֹת. וּבְאוֹת י' וַדַּאי, אִתְעֲבֵיד עוֹלָם אָרוֹךְ, דְּאִיהוּ ו' עָלְמָא דְּאָתֵי וּבְאָת ה', בָּרָא עָלְמָא דֵין, דְּאִיהִי ה' זְעֵירָא, דְּבָהּ אֲכִילָה וּשְׁתִיָּה דְּאוֹרַיְיתָא.

Ra'aya Meheimna (the Faithful Shepherd)

370. And in the first compilation, the Faithful Shepherd said that through this the Satan was mitigated and the final Nun of *veshet* (Eng. 'esophagus' - Vav Shin Tet), was folded AND IT RETURNED TO BE A VAV. Where THE ESOPHAGUS became the Satan, it is now put back, and becomes an esophagus again, as it was. This is because "the voice is the voice of Jacob" (Beresheet 27:22), for Yisrael have no power through eating and drinking, as do the other nations who inherit this world, whose strength lies in eating and drinking. But AS FOR YISRAEL, their strength is in the voice, which is the World to Come, a long world that was created with the letter Yud. And since the voice of the Shofar WHICH IS THE SECRET OF THE MOCHIN OF ZEIR ANPIN THAT ARE CALLED 'VOICE', WHICH RECEIVES FROM SHOFAR, WHICH IS BINAH, emerges from it, FROM THE YUD WHICH IS CHOCHMAH, the sages said: 'one may not blow less than...ten Shofar verses' NAMELY CORRESPONDING TO THE LETTER YUD (= 10). For with the letter Yud a long world is certainly made, which is Vav, the World to Come, NAMELY THAT RECEIVES MOCHIN OF THE WORLD TO COME, AS ABOVE. And with the letter Hei He created this world, which is small Hei, NAMELY MALCHUT, in which there is eating and drinking of the Torah, NAMELY THE MOCHIN OF CHOCHMAH AND CHASSADIM THAT ARE CALLED 'EATING' AND 'DRINKING'.

371. וְעוֹד רָזָא אַחֲרָא, בָּתַר דְּאִתְגְּזַר גְּזֵרָה בִּתְרֵין אַתְוָון, דְּאִינּוּן ה' ה', תְּרֵין בָּתֵּי דִּינִין, מַאן יָכִיל לְבַטְּלָא גְּזֵרָה דְּתַרְוַויְיהוּ. י"ו. דְּאָת הֵ"א אִימָּא עִלָּאָה. י' אָב. וּמַה כְּתִיב, כָּל נֶדֶר וְכָל שְׁבוּעַת אִסָּר לְעַנּוֹת נָפֶשׁ, דְּאִיהִי ה', אִישָׁהּ יְקִימֶנּוּ וְאִישָׁהּ יְפֵרֶנּוּ. וּבג"ד, צָרִיךְ לְאִתְעָרָא קָלָא דְּאִיהוּ ו', בַּעֲשָׂרָה שׁוֹפָרוֹת, דְּאִינּוּן י'. וְעִקָּרָא דְּלְהוֹן בִּנְשִׁימָה אַחַת, כָּל סִימָן וְסִימָן, בַּפֶּה, דְּאִיהִי י' מֵעֲשָׂרָה.

371. And there is yet another secret. For after the decree is enacted in the two letters Hei Hei, which are the two courts OF BINAH AND OF MALCHUT, who is able to rescind the decree of both of them, IF NOT Yud Vav OF YUD HEI VAV HEI. For the letter Hei OF YUD HEI VAV HEI is Supernal Ima, BINAH, and Yud is father, CHOCHMAH. And what is written? "Every vow and every binding oath to afflict the soul (which is Hei THAT IS CALLED

'SOUL', HEB. *NEFESH*), "her husband may let it stand or her husband may
make it void" (Bemidbar 30:14). HERE YUD IS THE HUSBAND OF THE
FIRST HEI, WHICH IS BINAH, AND VAV IS THE HUSBAND OF THE
SECOND HEI, WHICH IS MALCHUT. THUS THE YUD AND VAV CAN
RESCIND THE DECREE OF THE TWO HEIS. It is thus necessary to awaken
the voice, that is Vav, WHICH IS ZEIR ANPIN, with the ten Shofar verses,
that are Yud, IN ORDER TO ANNUL THE JUDGMENTS OF THE TWO HEIS,
WHICH ARE BINAH AND MALCHUT. And the main thing is that each of the
Shofar sequences should be sounded in one breath, in the mouth, which is
the tenth PART of ten, (THE SEQUENCES BEING T'KIAH, SH'VARIM,
T'RUAH, T'KIAH; TEKI'AH, SH'VARIM, T'KIAH; AND FOR T'KIAH, T'RUAH,
T'KIAH).

372. מִיַּד דְּשָׁמְעוּ מִלִּין ר"ש וְכָל חַבְרַיָּיא, אָמְרוּ, בְּרִיךְ אֱלָהָא דְּזָכֵינָא
לְמִשְׁמַע מִלִּין, מֵהַהוּא דְּאִתְקְרֵי רַבָּן שֶׁל נְבִיאִים, רַבָּן דַּחֲכָמִים, רַבָּן
דְּמַלְאֲכֵי הַשָּׁרֵת, דְּקוּדְשָׁא בְּרִיךְ הוּא וּשְׁכִינְתֵּיה מְדַבֵּר עַל פּוּמוֹי, וְכָתַב
עַל יְדוֹי רָזִין אִלֵּין, דְּלָא אִשְׁתְּמָעוּ כְּוָותַיְיהוּ מִמַּתָּן תּוֹרָה, וְעַד כְּעַן.

372. Immediately on hearing these matters, Rabbi Shimon and the friends
exclaimed: Blessed be Elohim that we have been privileged to hear such
matters from him, who is called 'the master of all the prophets', 'master of
all the sages', 'master of all the ministering angels', through whose mouth
the Holy One, blessed be He, and His Shechinah speak, and by whose hands
He wrote these secrets, the like of which have not been heard since the
revelation of the Torah until now.

373. א"ל, בּוּצִינָא קַדִּישָׁא, אַשְׁלִים מְלוּלֵי דְּרָזִין דְּחַבּוּרָא קַדְמָאָה,
לְפָרְשָׁא לוֹן, דְּהָא כָּל מָארֵי מְתִיבָתָּאן דִּלְעֵילָא, וּמָארֵי מְתִיבָתָּאן
דִּלְתַתָּא, כֻּלְּהוּ מְזוּמָנִין לְמִשְׁמַע מִלִּין אִלֵּין מִפּוּמָךְ, וּפֵירוּשִׁין דִּילָךְ.
דְּהָא חֶדְוָה וּפוּרְקָנָא, יִתְּעַר בְּהוֹן לְעֵילָא וְתַתָּא. אַל תִּתְנוּ דֳמִי, לֹא
אַנְתְּ, וְכָל סִיעֲתָא דִּילָךְ.

עד כאן רעיא מהימנא

373. THE FAITHFUL SHEPHERD said TO RABBI SHIMON: Holy Luminary,

complete the matters of the secrets of the first compilation, by expounding on them, for the heads of all of the celestial Yeshivot and the heads of all the Yeshivot below are waiting to hear these words from your mouth, with your clarifications. For thereby will rejoicing and redemption awaken in heaven above and on the earth below. "Give no rest" (Yeshayah 62:7), neither you nor any of your friends.

End of Ra'aya Meheimna (the Faithful Shepherd)

61. The liver and the heart

A Synopsis

Rabbi Shimon says that the heart (God) takes from the liver only that which is pure and clean, leaving all the foulness for Samael, who distributes it to the idol worshipping nations.

The Relevance of this Passage

Once again, we discover how the spiritual worlds mirror the function of the physical body, shedding further light on the ultimate origins of disease. In essence, when we listen to and respond to selfish impulses (reactive behavior), we succumb to the prodding of our evil adversaries – the angels *Satan/Samael* and *Lilit*. Each time we're responsive to their provocations – the rush to judgment, the urge to scream, the need to mistreat another person, the impulse to lie and deceive – their strength and hold over our body and our life increases.

Their stronghold, the Zohar tells us, is the liver. Physically, the liver filters our blood and then sends it, cleaned and purified, to the heart.

This medical truth is revealed by the Zohar's cryptic language:

> "...everything that the liver is holding it sacrifices to the heart,

which is the King, to nourish him... He takes everything that is clear and pure, NAMELY all the merits and the good deeds..."

That last statement alludes to the relationship among a good liver, purified blood, a healthy heart, and our positive behavior.

The bile of the liver absorbs fat as well as waste and toxic matter from the blood. This function is encoded into the following text of Zohar:

> "...all the foulness, the filth and the dirt, which are the bad deeds, He leaves for the liver, WHICH IS SAMAEL."

Our selfish impulses come from *Samael*. If we allow our selfish impulses to guide us in life, then *SAMAEL* has the power to send impurities of the blood from the liver to the heart. In other words, our reactive, stress-induced behavior creates negative energy that manifests physically in our body as heart disease. This truth is found in the following verse:

"And the iniquities of His people are in the arteries AND SINEWS that pulsate in the heart."

Research shows that heart disease kills twice as many people as cancer and is one of the leading causes of death. The Zohar passage that we are now discussing provides us with spiritual Light that removes stress and anxiety from our being. We are imbued with the strength to resist reactive emotions and desires – and with the ability to resist heart disease.

Our blood is cleansed. Fatty deposits, also called plaque, are extracted from the walls of our arteries and dissolved away. The entire cardiovascular system is cleared and regenerated. Heart-related illnesses and diseases are treated and cured as the Light extinguishes the dark influences of the negative adversaries.

In paragraph 375, the Zohar explains that skin sores, boils, and leprosy are rooted in the liver and toxins that remain in our body. In addition to heart disease, these Zohar verses also heal all skin-related diseases.

374. בִּתְרוּעָה וּתְקִיעָה וּשְׁבָרִים, אִתְבְּסַם כֹּלָּא דָּא בְּדָא. וְכָל מַה דְּהַהוּא כָּבֵד נָקִיט, אַקְרִיב לְגַבֵּי לֵב, דְּאִיהוּ מַלְכָּא, לְזַיְינָא. וְהַהוּא לֵב, לָאו אוֹרְחֵיהּ, וְלָאו תִּיאוּבְתֵּיהּ, בַּעֲכִירוּ דְּעוֹבָדִין דְּעַמֵּיהּ. אֶלָּא נָקִיט כָּל בְּרִירוּ, וְכָל צָחוּתָא, וְכָל זַכָּיָין, וְכָל עוֹבָדִין טָבִין. וְכָל הַהוּא עֲכִירוּ וְטִנּוּפִין וְלִכְלוּכָא דְּאִינּוּן עוֹבָדִין בִּישִׁין, אַנָּח לְכָבֵד. דְּאִתְּמַר בֵּיהּ, עֵשָׂו אִישׁ שָׂעִיר. וְכָל עַרְקִין דִּילֵיהּ, דְּאִינּוּן שְׁאַר עַמִּין עכו"ם. הה"ד, וְנָשָׂא הַשָּׂעִיר עָלָיו אֶת כָּל עֲוֹנוֹתָם. מַאי עֲוֹנוֹתָם. עֲווֹנוֹת תָּם. דְּאִתְּמַר בֵּיהּ, וְיַעֲקֹב אִישׁ תָּם. וְחוֹבִין דְּעַמֵּיהּ דְּאִינּוּן עַרְקִין וְדַפְקִין דְּלִבָּא.

374. With T'ruah, T'kiah and Sh'varim, everything is perfumed, one with the other, FOR ALL OF THE JUDGMENTS ARE MITIGATED, and everything that the liver is holding it sacrifices to the heart, which is the king, to nourish it. And it is neither the way of the heart, nor does it desire, the foulness of the deeds of its people, rather it takes everything that is clear and pure, NAMELY all the merits and the good deeds, while all the foulness, the filth and the dirt, which are the bad deeds it leaves for the liver, WHICH IS SAMAEL, about whom it is said: "Esau...is a hairy (Heb. *sair*) man" (Beresheet 27:11). And all its arteries, which are the other idol-worshipping

peoples, are as it is written: "And the goat (Heb. *seir*) shall bear upon him all their iniquities" (Vayikra 16:22). What is meant by "their iniquities" (Heb. *avonotam*)? *avonot tam*, namely the iniquities of a *tam*, a complete man, the reference being to the same one about whom it is said: "And Jacob was a plain (Heb. *tam*) man" (Beresheet 25:27). And the iniquities of its people are in the arteries AND SINEWS that pulsate in the heart.

375. וּבג"ד, שְׁחִין וְצָרַעַת וְסַפַּחַת, לְכָל אִינּוּן אֶבְרִין, מִכָּבֵד אִשְׁתְּכָחוּ, מֵאִילֵין לִכְלוּכִין דְּאִשְׁתָּאֲרוּ בֵּיה. מִלִבָּא אָתֵי כָּל בְּרִיאוּתָא, לְכָל אַבְרִין. דְּהָכִי הוּא, כֵּיוָן דְּלִבָּא נָטִיל כָּל זְכִיכוּ וּבְרִירָא וְצָחוּתָא. כָּבֵד נָטִיל כָּל מַה דְּאִשְׁתְּכַח וְאִשְׁתְּאַר מִן לִכְלוּכָא וְטִנּוּפָא. וְזָרִיק לְכָל שְׁאָר שַׁיְיפִין, דְּאִינּוּן שְׁאָר עַמִּין עכו"ם אַחֲרָנִין, בַּעַל כָּרְחַיְיהוּ. וּמִפְּסוֹלֶת דִּפְסוֹלֶת דְּכָבֵד, נָטַל טְחוֹל, דְּאִתְּמַר בֵּיה יְהִי מְאֹרֹת. מְאֵרַת יְיָ' בְּבֵית רָשָׁע.

375. And this is why boils and leprosy and skin sores of all the limbs are form the liver, deriving from the filth that remains there. From the heart comes health for all the limbs, for that is how it is: since the heart took all that is pure, clean, and bright, the liver takes what is left of the dirt and the filth and distributes it to all the other limbs, which are the other idol worshipping nations, against their will. And from the refuse of, the refuse of the liver, the spleen, WHICH IS LILIT, takes, about whom it is said: "Let there be lights (Heb. *me'orot*)" (Beresheet 1:14), WHERE THE WORD '*ME'OROT*' IS SPELLED WITHOUT VAV, WHICH CAN ALSO BE READ AS *M'ERAT*, 'THE CURSE OF,' BECAUSE LILIT WAS CREATED, as in the verse: "The curse (Heb. *m'erat*) of Hashem is in the house of the wicked" (Mishlei 3:33).

62. The spleen and the gall

A Synopsis

Moses talks about the spleen that is laughter and the gall that is anger, and says that anger is better than laughter; this illustrates his point that the righteous are punished now for their sins so that they will inherit the World to Come.

The Relevance of this Passage

The concept of laughter connects to the Patriarch Isaac, whose Hebrew name means *laughter.* Isaac is the Left Column which is *the Desire to Receive for the Self Alone,* or instant pleasure and immediate gratification.

Laughter denotes this concept. When we laugh, there is instantaneous pleasure, indicating a direct connection between the Right Column's domain of true pleasure and the Left Column's domain of the selfish Desire for Pleasure. Direct connections, however, create short-circuits. When the positive pole of a light bulb connects directly to the negative pole, without a filament to resist the current, the bulb bursts.

The Zohar is telling us, through the code word *laughter,* to avoid selfish behavior. Selfish behavior procures immediate pleasure but long-term pain and suffering. When we resist these desires, we feel we lack something "good" for the moment, but there is long-term and lasting fulfillment in store for us. This is one of the inner meanings behind the concept of receiving punishment for our sins in the present and gaining rewards for good deeds in the *World to Come.*

On another level of understanding, we are told that the Righteous choose to suffer ailments on the behalf of those in their generation who are steeped in sin as a result of selfish behavior.

Here, on the merit of the Righteous, past and present, we heal all forms of disease and illnesses, including those related to the spleen and gall bladder. As we think to share this Light with the world, the Righteous no longer have to endure illness on our behalf. All mankind benefits from this Light, as disease and sickness are eternally abolished.

רעיא מהימנא

376. עוֹד אָמַר בְּחִבּוּרָא קַדְמָאָה, אָמַר רַעְיָא מְהֵימָנָא, וְהָא אוֹקְמוּהָ

רַבָּנָן עֲלֵיהּ, טְחוֹל שׂוֹחֵק. וְאִיהוּ שְׂחוֹק הַכְּסִיל. וּבְג״ד, אוּקְמוּהָ רַבָּנָן דְּמַתְנִיתִין, אוֹי לוֹ לְמִי שֶׁהַשָּׁעָה מְשַׂחֶקֶת לוֹ. וְקֹהֶלֶת אָמַר טוֹב כַּעַס מִשְּׂחוֹק. טוֹב כַּעַס דִּכְבֵד, דְּאִיהִי מָרָה, רְצוּעָה דְּקוּדְשָׁא בְּרִיךְ הוּא, רְצוּעָה לְאַלְקָאָה בָּהּ צַדִּיקַיָּיא בְּעָלְמָא דֵּין בְּמַרְעִין בִּישִׁין, בְּמַכְתָּשִׁין, מִשְּׂחוֹק דְּשָׂחִיק לוֹן בַּטְחוֹל, בִּלְכְלוּכָא דְּהַאי עָלְמָא, דְּשׂוֹחֵק לוֹן שַׁעֲתָא בְּעוֹתְרָא. וְעוֹד, אֶרֶס דִּטְחוֹל אִיהוּ זָחִיל עָפָר, וְאִיהוּ תַּקִּיף יַתִּיר מֵאֶרֶס דְּמָרָה.

Ra'aya Meheimna (the Faithful Shepherd)

376. More was said in this first section. The Faithful Shepherd said, Did not the sages teach about it: The spleen laughs, and this is "the laughter of the fool" (Kohelet 7:6)? For this reason the sages of the Mishnah taught: Woe to him who is successful (lit. 'to whom time laughs'), FOR HE RECEIVES HIS REWARD DURING HIS LIFETIME. And Kohelet said: "Anger is better than laughter" (Ibid.). THE MEANING OF THIS IS: The anger of the liver, which is the gall, the whiplash of the Holy One, blessed be He, is a whip with which to beat the righteous in this world with bad illnesses and plagues. AND THIS IS BETTER than the laughter with which the spleen, WHICH IS LILIT, laughs at us, with the dirt of this world, and better than temporary laughter with wealth. FOR THEY RECEIVE IN THIS WORLD THE REWARD OF THE GOOD DEEDS THAT THEY DID, SO THAT THEY SHOULD UTTERLY PERISH FROM THE WORLD TO COME, WHILE THE RIGHTEOUS RECEIVE THE PUNISHMENT FOR THE SINS THEY HAVE COMMITTED IN THIS WORLD SO THAT THEY WILL INHERIT THE WORLD TO COME. moreover, venom of the spleen is crawling in the dust, and is stronger than the venom of the gall.

377. וּבְגִין דְּעֵרֶב רַב אִינּוּן שְׂאוֹר שֶׁבָּעִיסָה, וְאִינּוּן אוּמִין דְּעָלְמָא דְּמַיְינִין לְמוֹץ, יַתִּיר מְעַכְּבִין בְּגָלוּתָא עֵרֶב רַב לְיִשְׂרָאֵל, מֵאוּמִין עכו״ם. כְּמָה דְּאוּקְמוּהָ רַבָּנָן, מִי מְעַכֵּב. שְׂאוֹר שֶׁבָּעִיסָה מְעַכֵּב. דְּאִינּוּן דְּבֵקִין בְּיִשְׂרָאֵל, כַּשְׂאוֹר בַּעִיסָה. אֲבָל אוּמִין עכו״ם, לָאו אִינּוּן אֶלָּא כְּמוֹץ אֲשֶׁר תִּדְּפֶנּוּ רוּחַ.

377. And since the mixed multitude are the leaven in the dough, NAMELY THEY INTERMINGLED WITH YISRAEL AS LEAVEN IN THE DOUGH and the nations of the world are like chaff, the mixed multitude delay Yisrael in exile more than do the idol-worshipping nations. As the sages taught: what prevents us? The leaven in the dough. For THE MIXED MULTITUDE stick to Yisrael as does the leaven to the dough, but the nations of the world are no more than "like the chaff which the wind drives away" (Tehilim 1:4).

63. The scapegoat, the liver and the heart

A Synopsis

The Faithful Shepherd explains how the goat bears all of Yisrael's iniquities.

The Relevance of this Passage

The humility embodied by King David rises in our hearts. All of our iniquities are abolished, for this passage serves as the very scapegoat that absolves us of sin.

Through the Light of paragraph 378, *Satan/Samael* and *Lilit* are battered, broken, and banished from our existence. In turn, our hearts and arteries receive the Light of healing, and our livers successfully extract the poisons, toxins, and fats from our system. This cleansing occurs globally as well. The sins of man are cleansed by the "scapegoat." The world's heart, Yisrael, and the nations of the world are healed as peace and loving kindness permeate our planet.

378. וְעוֹד וְנָשָׂא הַשָּׂעִיר עָלָיו, כַּד רְעוּתֵיה לְמֶעְבַּד קוּרְצָיָא לְקוּדְשָׁא בְּרִיךְ הוּא עִם יִשְׂרָאֵל, דְּאִיהוּ נָשָׂא כָּל חוֹבִין דְּיָכִיל לְמִסְבַּל לוֹן, עַד דְּאִתְעֲבֵיד כָּבֵד, כְּמַשָּׂא כָּבֵד יִכְבְּדוּ מִמֶּנּוּ, חוֹבִין עַל גַּדְפוֹי. מֶה עָבֵיד, סָלִיק לְטוּרָא עִלָּאָה, כַּחֲמָרָא כַּד אִיהוּ בָּעֵי לְסַלְּקָא לְטוּר גָּבוֹהַּ, כְּמַשָּׂא כָּבֵד יִכְבַּד עָלֵיה. כַּד אִיהוּ לְעֵילָּא, וּבָעֵי לְסַלְּקָא לְפִי מְעוּט דְּאִשְׁתְּאַר לֵיה, אִתְיְקַר עָלֵיה מָטוּלָא, וְנָפִיל, וְאַפִּיל גַּרְמֵיה לְתַתָּא, וּבְכֹבֶד מַשָּׂא דְּאִתְתַּקַּף עָלֵיה, אִתְעֲבֵידוּ כָּל אַבְרִין דִּילֵיה פְּסָקוֹת, דְּלָא אִשְׁתְּאַר אֵבָר שְׁלִים. אוֹף הָכָא אִירַע לְסָמָאֵל וְנָחָשׁ, כָּבֵד וְיוֹתֶרֶת הַכָּבֵד, יֵצֶר הָרָע וּבַת זוּגֵיה זוֹנָה. מִתַּמָּן כָּל בַּת אֵל נֵכָר זוֹנָה.

ע״כ רעיא מהימנא

378. Also: "And the goat shall bear upon him all their iniquities" (Vayikra 16:22), when the Satan wants to inform against Yisrael before the Holy One, blessed be He. And he bears all the sins that he can carry, until he becomes heavy (Heb. *kaved*, which word also means 'liver') "like a heavy burden they are too heavy for" him (Tehilim 38:5), THAT HE CARRIES upon

his wings. What does he do? He, like an ass, ascends a high mountain, and when he gets near the top and wants to climb up that little bit more that is left for him, the weight of the burden overcomes him, and he falls, and tumbles down to the bottom, and with the weight of the burden pressing on him, all his bones are broken into pieces, until not a single limb in him remains whole. Thus, too, did it happen to Samael and the Serpent, which are liver and the appendix of the liver, the Evil Inclination and its partner, a harlot, whence every daughter of a strange El is CALLED 'a harlot'.

End of the Ra'aya Meheimna (the Faithful Shepherd)

A Synopsis
Rabbi Pinchas reiterates the information about the role of Samael, the liver. We also hear about the humility of David.

379. אָמַר רבִּי פִּנְחָס, אוֹרְחָא דָא הֲוָה מְתַקְּנָא לִי, לְמִשְׁמַע מִלִּין אִלֵּין מֵעַתִּיק יוֹמִין, זַכָּאָה עָלְמָא דְּאַנְתְּ שָׁארֵי בְּגַוֵיה. וַוי לְעָלְמָא, דְּיִשְׁתַּאֲרוּן יַתְמִין, וְלָא יַדְעִין מִלֵּי דְּאוֹרְיָיתָא כַּדְקָא יָאוּת. וַדַּאי הָכִי הוּא, דְּכָבֵד נָטִיל כֹּלָּא טַב וּבִיש. וְאע״ג דִּמְשַׁטְטָא וְלָקִיט כָּל חוֹבֵיהוֹן דְּיִשְׂרָאֵל, ה״נ זַכְיָין דִּלְהוֹן לָקִיט, בְּגִין לְקַיְּימָא קוּרְצֵיה. וְכֹלָּא הַאי וְהַאי מַקְרִיב לְגַבֵּי לֵב. וְאוֹרְחוֹי דְּלֵב, לָא נָטִיל אֶלָּא זְכִיכוּ וּבְרִירוּ וְצָחוּתָא דְּכֹלָּא, כְּמָה דְּאַמָרֵת. וּשְׁאָר טְנוּפָא וְלִכְלוּכָא, אַהְדָּר לְכָבֵד, וְנָטִיל כֹּלָּא בְּעַל כָּרְחֵיה, דִּכְתִיב וְנָשָׂא הַשָּׂעִיר עָלָיו וְגוֹ'. מִלָּה דָא אַהֲדַרְנָא, בְּגִין דְּיִתְבַּסַּם לְפוּמֵי כְּמִתְקָא דְּדוּבְשָׁא, זַכָּאָה חוּלָקֵי דְּזָכֵינָא לְהַאי, לְמֶחֱמֵי דָא בְּעֵינַי.

379. Rabbi Pinchas said TO RABBI SHIMON, This path was ordained for me to hear these things from Atik Yomin (the Ancient of Days). Happy is the world in which you reside. Woe to the world, who will remain orphans without knowing matters of Torah properly. For it is certainly like that: the liver, WHICH IS SAMAEL, takes everything, good and bad, and although it moves around and gathers in all the sins of Yisrael, it likewise gathers up their merits, too, to establish its slanderous informing FOR THE LIAR HAS TO SPEAK SOME TRUTH AT THE BEGINNING FOR PEOPLE TO BELIEVE HIM. And it sacrifices everything, BOTH MERITS AND DEMERITS, to the heart,

and the way of the heart is to take nothing but the purest, clearest and brightest of all, NAMELY THE MERITS, as you have said. And the remaining filth and dirt, WHICH ARE THE INIQUITIES, it returns to the liver, who has no choice but to take everything, as it is written: "And the goat shall bear upon him all their iniquities." I am going over this matter again, ALTHOUGH YOU HAVE ALREADY STATED IT, so that it will be sweet in my mouth as the sweetness of honey. Happy is my portion that I have been privileged to see this with my own eyes.

380. אוֹף הוּא פָּתַח וְאָמַר, יְיָ' לֹא גָבַה לִבִּי וְלֹא רָמוּ עֵינַי וְגוֹ', הַאי קְרָא אָמַר דָוִד, בְּשַׁעֲתָא דַהֲוָה אָזִיל עַל כֵּיף נַהֲרָא, אָמַר רבש"ע, כְּלוּם הֲוָה ב"נ בְּעָלְמָא, דְּאוֹדֵי וּמְשַׁבַּח לְמָארֵיה כְּוָותִי. אִזְדַמְנַת לֵיה צְפַרְדֵּעַ, א"ל, דָוִד, לֹא תִתְגָּאֶה, דַּאֲנָא עֲבָדִית יַתִּיר מִנָּך, דְּמָסָרִית גוּפָאי עַל מֵימְרָא דְמָארִי, דִּכְתִיב וְשָׁרַץ הַיְאוֹר צְפַרְדְּעִים, וְהָא אוּקְמוּהָ. וְתוּ דַּאֲנָא מְשַׁבַּח וּמְזַמֵּר לֵילְיָא וְיוֹמָא, בְּלָא שְׁכִיכוּ. בְּהַהִיא שַׁעֲתָא אָמַר דָוִד, יְיָ' לֹא גָבַה לִבִּי וְלֹא רָמוּ עֵינַי. יְיָ' לֹא גָבַה לִבִּי.

380. He, too, began by quoting: "Hashem, my heart is not haughty, nor my eyes lofty" (Tehilim 131:1). David spoke this verse when he was walking on the bank of the river, and said, Master of the Universe, has there ever been a man in the world who gave thanks and praised his Master as I have? A frog chanced by and said to him, David, do not be proud, for I have achieved more than you, for I have sacrificed my body at my Master's command, as it is written: "and the river shall bring forth frogs in swarms" (Shemot 7:28). And this, indeed, is how it has been interpreted. And also, I give praises and sing day and night, without interruption. Then at that moment, David said: "Hashem, my heart is not haughty, nor my eyes lofty." "Hashem, my heart is not haughty..." (THE CONTINUATION IS MISSING).

64. The rose

A Synopsis
We learn that when Yisrael open their hearts in repentance they immediately emit a sweet fragrance and God removes them from among the thorns.

The Relevance of this Passage
Our cold and hardened hearts are what prevent healing and joy from reaching us. Here we arouse remorse and penitence. The hearts of all men are opened. We are lifted away from the thorns, where we can now enjoy the sweet fragrance of the rose. That means that we are lifted away from Judgment, and can now enjoy the sweet scent of healing and bliss.

381. דָּא הוּא קָרְבְּנָא, דִּבְכָל יוֹמָא, וּבְכָל זְמַן וּזְמַן, לְגַבֵּי קוּדְשָׁא בְּרִיךְ הוּא. דְּאִתְכְּלִילַת כנ"י בֵּיהּ, בֵּין כָּל שְׁאַר אַכְלוּסִין, וְכָל אִילֵין פּוּלְחָנִין, אַפִּיקוּ לָהּ מִבֵּין גּוּבִין, וּמִבֵּין שְׁאַר עַמִּין. כָּךְ יִשְׂרָאֵל, כָּל זְמַן דְּאִינּוּן אֲטִימֵי לִבָּא, וְלָא פַּתְחִין בְּתִיוּבְתָּא, לָא סַלְּקִין רֵיחָא, וְלָא אָפִיק לוֹן מִגּוֹ גּוּבִין. אֲבָל כַּד פַּתְחִין בְּתִיוּבְתָּא, מִיַּד סַלְּקִין רֵיחָא, וְיַפִּיק לוֹן מִבֵּין גּוּבִין, וְיִתְהֲנֵי בְּהוּ כְּנֶסֶת יִשְׂרָאֵל. דִּכְתִיב, פִּתְחִי לִי אֲחוֹתִי רַעְיָתִי. דְּכָל זְמַן דְּשׁוֹשַׁנָּה אֲטִימָא, לֵית לָהּ רֵיחָא, וְלָא סְלִיקָא מִבֵּין גּוּבִין, וְדִיּוּרְהָא בֵּינַיְיהוּ, כְּמָה דְּאִתְּמַר. וְקוּדְשָׁא בְּרִיךְ הוּא לָא שָׁדַר לָן לְמֵהַךְ אוֹרְחָא דָּא, אֶלָּא לְאוֹלִיף מִלִּין אִלֵּין.

381. (THE BEGINNING OF THE ARTICLE IS MISSING.)...this is a sacrifice that is on every day and at every time to the Holy One, blessed be He, in which the Shechinah is included among all HER other crowds, WHO ARE YISRAEL. And all these services remove Her from among the thorns, namely from among the other nations. So it is with Yisrael. So long as they are hard-hearted and do not make a start at repenting, they do not emit fragrance, and there is none to remove them from among the thorns. But when they open their hearts in repentance, they immediately emit an aroma, and He removes them from among the thorns. And the Congregation of Yisrael, WHICH IS MALCHUT, obtains pleasure from them, as it is written: "Open to me, my sister, my love" (Shir Hashirim 5:2), for so long as the

rose is closed, it gives off no aroma and does not rise above the thorns but sits among them, as they have said. And the only reason that the Holy One, blessed be He, sent us along this path was so that we should learn these matters.

65. The eagle

A Synopsis
An eagle descends, takes a rose from among the rabbis, and flies away. Rabbi Pinchas talks about the inner meaning of this event. In the morning the rabbis see a comet, and Rabbi Pinchas says that when God calls the stars by name they run to praise him.

The Relevance of this Passage
The eagle descends upon Yisrael and all the world, removing the thorns of the rose and emitting the sweet scent of freedom and blessings all over the world. The eagle is Mercy, and it removes the judgments that weigh over our hearts, bringing freedom, health, and blessings to us and to the whole world.

Capitalizing upon David's might, we win the war against our Evil Inclination. All the wicked adversaries (our dark side) who test and challenge us go down in defeat. The streaking comet ignites "praises" to the Creator on our behalf. A "praise" denotes our connection to the Light, which allows divinity to flow to our realm of existence.

382. עַד דַּהֲווֹ יָתְבֵי, אָתָא נִשְׁרָא, וּמָאִיךְ, וְנָטִיל חַד שׁוֹשָׁנָה מִבֵּינַיְיהוּ, וְאַזְלַת. אָמְרוּ, מִכָּאן וּלְהָלְאָה, נְהַךְ לְאוֹרְחִין. קָמוּ וְאָזְלוּ. עַד הָכָא אוֹרְחָא דְּר' פִּנְחָס, וְר"ש אָזַל לֵיהּ, אִיהוּ וְר' אֶלְעָזָר, וּשְׁאַר חַבְרַיָּיא, וְר' פִּנְחָס וּשְׁאַר חַבְרַיָּיא.

382. While they were still sitting there, an eagle came, descended IN HIS FLIGHT and took one rose from among them and went. They said: From here on we shall go on our way. They arose and left. And so far they had ALL gone in the way of Rabbi Pinchas, for Rabbi Shimon went together with Rabbi Elazar and the other companions, while Rabbi Pinchas was with the other friends.

383. פָּתַח וְאָמַר ר' פִּנְחָס עַל זֶה, לַמְנַצֵּחַ עַל שׁוּשַׁן עֵדוּת מִכְתָּם לְדָוִד לְלַמֵּד, מַאי לְלַמֵּד. לְאוֹלְפָא לִבְנֵי עָלְמָא חָכְמְתָא. וְהָא אוֹקְמוּהָ, שׁוּשַׁן עֵדוּת, אִלֵּין סַנְהֶדְרֵי גְּדוֹלָה. דִּכְתִיב בָּהּ, סוּגָה בַּשּׁוֹשַׁנִּים. מִכְתָּם לְדָוִד סִימָנָא דְּאַחְזִיאוּ לֵיהּ לְדָוִד, כַּד שָׁדַר לְיוֹאָב לַאֲרַם נַהֲרַיִם וּלְאֲרַם

צוּבָא, לְאַגָחָא בְּהוּ. א"ר פִּנְחָס, דָּא אִיהוּ שׁוּשַׁן עֵדוּת דְּקַיְימָא הָכָא, הָא כֹּכְבַיָא בִּשְׁמַיָא, שְׁכִינְתָּא עֲלָן, וְדַרְגִּין עִלָּאִין בַּהֲדָהּ, וְסִיְיעָתָא קַדִּישָׁא לְתוּשְׁבַּחְתָּא, דָּא אִיהוּ שׁוּשַׁן בִּשְׁלִימוּ כַּדְקָא יֵאוֹת. קָמוּ וְאָזְלוּ. אִלֵּין הָכָא וְאִלֵּין הָכָא. אָזַל לֵיהּ ר' פִּנְחָס, וּבָת בִּכְפַר עֲקִימִין, ור' יִצְחָק ור' חִיָּיא בַּהֲדֵיהּ.

383. Rabbi Pinchas began by quoting about this, ABOUT THE EAGLE THAT TOOK THE ROSE: "To the chief musician upon Shushan-Edut; A *michtam* (Eng. 'writ') of David, to teach" (Tehilim 60:1). What is the meaning of "to teach"? It is to teach wisdom to people, and we have already expounded this. "Shushan-Edut" refers to the Great Sanhedrin, WHICH IS MALCHUT THAT ATTIRES BINAH, FOR THE MOCHIN of BINAH ARE CALLED 'EDUT' (ENG. 'TESTIMONY'). "A michtam of David" refers to a sign that was shown to David IN SHUSHAN-EDUT THAT HE WOULD WIN THE WAR, when he sent Joab to Aram Naharaim (Mesopotamia) and Aram Tzova to make war against them. Rabbi Pinchas said, This Shushan-Edut that is mentioned here is when the stars that are in the heavens and the Shechinah are over us, and with Her the upper levels, NAMELY THE MOCHIN OF BINAH THAT ARE CALLED 'TESTIMONY', and She is a holy help for extolling praises. This is Shushan, in perfection, as is fitting. They arose and went on their way, some in one direction, others in a different direction. Rabbi Pinchas went to the village of Akimin and stayed overnight, and Rabbi Yitzchak and Rabbi Chiya with him.

384. עַד דְּאַקְדִּימוּ לְמֵיזַל, יָתְבוּ וּמְחַכּוּ לִנְהוֹרָא דְצַפְרָא, זָקִיף עֵינוֹי ר' חִיָּיא, וְחָמָא אִלֵּין כּוֹכְבַיָא דְּשַׁרְבִּיטָא, דְּקָא מְרַהֲטָן וְאָזְלָן. אָמַר, וַדַּאי בְּכַמָּה זִמְנִין שָׁאֵלְנָא עַל אִלֵּין כּוֹכְבַיָא.

384. As they got up early to leave, and sat to wait for the morning light, Rabbi Chiya looked up and saw those comets: NAMELY STARS THAT CARRY ALONG A TAIL OF LIGHT BEHIND THEM, streaming in the sky. He said: a number of times I have asked about those stars. WHAT IS THEIR SIGNIFICANCE?

385. א"ר פִּנְחָס, אִלֵּין כּוֹכְבַיָא דְּשַׁרְבִּיטָא יְדִיעָן בְּסוּכְלְתָנוּ דְחַבְרַיָּיא, דְּהָא קוּדְשָׁא בְּרִיךְ הוּא בָּרָא כָּל אִינּוּן כּוֹכְבֵי רְקִיעָא, רַבְרְבִין וּזְעֵירִין.

וְכֻלְּהוּ אוֹדָן וּמְשַׁבְּחָן לְקוּדְשָׁא בְּרִיךְ הוּא. וְכַד מָטָא זִמְנַיְיהוּ לְשַׁבְּחָא,
קָרָא לוֹן קוּדְשָׁא בְּרִיךְ הוּא בִּשְׁמָא, דִּכְתִיב לְכוּלָם בְּשֵׁם יִקְרָא. וּכְדֵין
רַהֲטֵי, וְאוֹשִׁיטוּ שַׁרְבִיטָא דִּנְהוֹרָא, לְמֵהַךְ לְשַׁבְּחָא לְמָארֵיהוֹן, בְּהַהוּא
אֲתָר דְּאִתְפְּקָדָן. הֲדָא הוּא דִּכְתִיב, שְׂאוּ מָרוֹם עֵינֵיכֶם וּרְאוּ מִי בָרָא
אֵלֶּה. וְגוֹ'. אַדְּהָכִי אָתָא נְהוֹרָא, קָמוּ וְאַזְלוּ.

385. Rabbi Pinchas said, These comets are known by the understanding of
the friends, that the Holy One, blessed be He, created all these stars of the
firmament, both great and small, and they all give thanks and praise to the
Holy One, blessed be He. And when their time to sing praises comes, the
Holy One, blessed be He, calls them by name, as it is written: "He calls
them all by names" (Yeshayah 40:26). And then they run and hold out a
scepter of light to go and praise their Master in the same place where they
were numbered, as it is written: "Lift up your eyes on high and behold who
has created these things" (Ibid.). Meanwhile the light dawned. They arose
and went.

66. A great eagle and King Solomon

A Synopsis

An eagle circles over the heads of the rabbis. Rabbi Pinchas interprets this as a sign of mercy for those who are on their sick-beds, and says that this is the time for them to be healed. He calls to the eagle but it flies away, and Rabbi Chiya recalls how King Solomon used to ride on a great eagle every day to the place where Aza and Azael were imprisoned; from them Solomon learned wisdom.

The Relevance of this Passage

An abundance of healing energy pours down upon existence. Through the mysteries of the eagle, Abraham, and the morning light, the Gates of Mercy swing open so that we can heal and ultimately abolish all sickness and disease from the world. The sick are now able to rise from the bed as humanity rises from the clutches of the negative beings.

Upon the merit of Solomon, we are eternally protected from all the wicked entities who occupy the Other Side.

The Zohar then states in paragraph 391:

"And immediately they, UZA AND AZAEL, would say everything that Solomon wanted."

As Solomon controlled the two angels UZA AND AZAEL through the power of the Holy Name יהוה, we also assume control over our Evil Inclination and over the entire physical environment.

The wisdom of Solomon disseminates throughout the world as our eyes pour over the wisdom of this passage.

386. עַד דַּהֲווֹ אָזְלֵי, אָתָא נִשְׁרָא רַבְרְבָא, אַסְחַר עַל רֵישַׁיְיהוּ, וְקַיְּימָא עֲלַיְיהוּ. א"ר פִּנְחָס, וַדַּאי עִידָן רְעוּתָא הוּא הַשְׁתָּא, בָּה שַׁעֲתָא, אִתְפְּתָחוּ תַּרְעֵי דְרַחֲמֵי, לְכָל אִינּוּן בֵּי מַרְעֵי, וְהוּא זִמְנָא לְאַסְוָותָא לוֹן. ואע"ג דְּאִינּוּן אֲסִירִין דְּמַלְכָּא. דְּהָא נִשְׁרָא דָּא סִימָנָא דְרַחֲמֵי אִיהוּ.

386. While they were walking along, a large eagle came and circled their heads, remaining over them. Rabbi Pinchas said, This is certainly a favorable time, right now, and the Gates of Mercy are open for all those who are on a sick-bed, and this is the time to heal them. And although they

are the prisoners of the King, FOR THEY ARE CONFINED TO THEIR BEDS, this eagle is a sign of Mercy, FOR THE FACE OF THE EAGLE IS THE SECRET OF THE CENTRAL COLUMN, WHICH IS MERCY.

387. פָּתַח וְאָמַר, כְּנֶשֶׁר יָעִיר קִנּוֹ עַל גּוֹזָלָיו יְרַחֵף וְגוֹ'. לֵיכָּא בְּעָלְמָא מַאן דְּאִיהוּ בְּרַחֲמֵי עַל בְּנוֹי כְּנִשְׁרָא, וְהָא אוּקְמוּהָ דִכְתִיב, וְיֹאכְלוּהָ בְנֵי נֶשֶׁר, דְּאִיהוּ רַחֲמָנָא עַל בְּנוֹי. וּמִגּוֹ דְּהַשְׁתָּא עִידָן דְּרַחֲמֵי, אָתָא נִשְׁרָא דָא וְאַסְחַר עֲלָנָא. בְּשַׁעֲתָא דָא אִיהוּ רַחֲמֵי, לְכָל אִינוּן בֵּי מַרְעֵי. וְדָא אִיהוּ דִכְתִיב, יְיָ' בֹּקֶר תִּשְׁמַע קוֹלִי. וְדָא בֹּקֶר דְּאַבְרָהָם, וְאִתְעֲרוּתָא דִילֵיהּ.

387. He began by quoting: "As an eagle that stirs up her nest, broods over her young" (Devarim 32:11). There is none in the world that has mercy over its young as does the eagle. This we have already learned as it is written: "and the young vultures shall eat it" (Mishlei 30:17), for he is merciful to his children. And since now is the time of mercy, this eagle has come and circled around us. This is the time of mercy for all those who are ill AND LYING ON THEIR BEDS, and this is as is written: "My voice shall You hear in the morning, Hashem" (Tehilim 5:4), this being the morning of Abraham, WHICH IS THE SECRET OF CHESED, and the awakening OF CHESED.

388. אַדְּהָכִי, אַסְחַר נִשְׁרָא וְאַעֲבַר לְקַמַּיְיהוּ. א"ר פִּנְחָס, נִשְׁרָא נִשְׁרָא, מָה אַנְתְּ לְגַבָּן, אִי בִּשְׁלִיחוּתָא דְּמָרָךְ אָתִית, הָא אֲנָן הָכָא. אִי בְּגִין מִלָּה אַחֲרָא אָתִיתָא, הָא אֲנָן הָכָא זְמִינִין. אִתְרָם נִשְׁרָא לְעֵילָא, וְאִתְכַּסֵּי מִנַּיְיהוּ, וְאִינּוּן יָתְבוּ.

388. While he was speaking, the eagle flew in a circle and went ahead of them. Rabbi Pinchas said, Eagle, eagle, what are you doing here with us? If you have come on a mission from your Master, here we are. If you have come for something else, then, we are here, ready. The eagle flew upwards and disappeared from their sight, and they sat down.

389. א"ר חִיָּיא, הָא דִשְׁלֹמֹה מַלְכָּא תִּיוּבְתָּא הוּא, דְּתָנֵינָן, נִשְׁרָא רַבְרְבָא הֲוָה אָתֵי לְגַבֵּיהּ שְׁלֹמֹה מַלְכָּא בְּכָל יוֹמָא וְיוֹמָא, וַהֲוָה שְׁלֹמֹה

מַלְכָּא רָכִיב עַל גַּדְפָהָא, וְאוֹבִיל לֵיה ד׳ מְאָה פַּרְסֵי בְּשַׁעְתָּא חֲדָא. לְאָן אוֹבִיל לֵיה לְתַרְמוֹ״ד בַּמִּדְבָּר בְּהָרִים. אֲתָר כַּד אִיהוּ, לְגַבֵּי טוּרֵי דַּחֲשׁוֹכָא, דְּאִקְרֵי תַּרְמוֹד בַּמִּדְבָּר וְלָאו אִיהוּ אֲתָר דְּתַרְמוֹדָאֵי, אֶלָּא תַּרְמוֹד דְּאִיהוּ בַּמִּדְבָּר בְּהָרִים, וְתַמָּן מִתְכַּנְּשֵׁי כָּל רוּחִין וְסִטְרִין אַחֲרָנִין. וְהַהוּא נִשְׁרָא הֲוָה טָאס לְתַמָּן, בְּשַׁעְתָּא חֲדָא.

389. Rabbi Chiya said: This matter of King Solomon is wondrous, for we have learned that a large eagle used to come to King Solomon every day, and King Solomon would ride on the wings, and they would travel four hundred parasangs in one hour. Where did the eagle take him? "and Tarmod in the wilderness" (I Melachim 9:18), in the hills. There is a certain place among the mountains of darkness that is called "Tarmod in the wilderness," and this is not the place WHERE the Tarmodites LIVE, but Tarmod that is in the wilderness in the hills, where all the spirits AND FORCES of the Other Side gather. And that eagle would fly there in one hour.

390. כֵּיוָן דְּקָאֵים עַל הַהוּא דּוּכְתָּא, אַגְבַּהּ נִשְׁרָא, וּשְׁלֹמֹה כָּתַב פִּתְקָא, וְאַרְמֵי תַּמָּן, וְאִשְׁתְּזִיב מֵאִינּוּן רוּחִין. וְנִשְׁרָא הֲוָה מִסְתַּכַּל גּוֹ חֲשׁוֹכָא דְּטוּרִין, לַאֲתָר דְּתַמָּן עֻזָּא וְעֲזָאֵל, דְּאִינּוּן תַּמָּן אֲסִירִין בְּשַׁלְשְׁלָאֵי דְּפַרְזְלָא, נְעִיצָן גּוֹ תְּהוֹמֵי. וְלֵית יָכִילוּ לְב״נ בְּעָלְמָא לְמֵיעַל תַּמָּן, וַאֲפִילוּ עוֹפֵי שְׁמַיָא, בַּר בִּלְעָם.

390. Once the eagle stood over that place, TARMOD, the eagle drew itself up, and Solomon wrote a note and threw it down there, and THEREBY was saved from those spirits. And the eagle used to look into the darkness of the mountains, to the place where Uza and Azael were imprisoned by chains of iron, thrust and anchored in the depths; there is no man in the world that has the ability to enter there, not even birds of the heaven, with the exception of Bilaam.

391. וְכֵיוָן דְּנִשְׁרָא מִסְתַּכַּל גּוֹ חֲשׁוֹכָא רַבְרְבָא, מָאִיךְ לְתַתָּא, וְנָטִיל לֵיה לִשְׁלֹמֹה מַלְכָּא גַּדְפָהָא תְּחוֹת שְׂמָאלָא, וּמְכַסְּיָיא לֵיה. וְקָיְימָא עַל אִלֵּין שַׁלְשְׁלָאֵי, וְאַזְלָא וּמְקָרְבָא לְגַבַּיְיהוּ, וּשְׁלֹמֹה כְּדֵין אַפִּיק עִזְקָא,

דְּחָקִיק עֲלֵיה שְׁמָא קַדִּישָׁא, וְשַׁוֵּי בְּפוּמָא דְּנִשְׁרָא. וּמִיָּד, אִינּוּן הֲווֹ
אַמְרֵי, כָּל מַה דְּבָעֵי שְׁלֹמֹה מַלְכָּא, וּמִתַּמָּן הֲוָה יָדַע שְׁלֹמֹה חָכְמְתָא.
הה"ד, וַיִּבֶן וְגוֹ' אֶת תַּרְמוֹד בַּמִדְבָּר בָּאָרֶץ. וְכִי בִּנְיָינָא הֲוָה עָבֵיד
בָּאָרֶץ. אֶלָּא מַהוּ וַיִּבֶן. אִסְתְּכַּל בְּסָכְלְתָנוּ, וְיָדַע לְהַהוּא דּוּכְתָּא,
לְמִנְדַּע בֵּיה חָכְמְתָא.

391. And since the eagle used to look into the great darkness, he FLEW down low and took King Solomon under his left wing and covered him. And THE EAGLE stood upon those chains OF UZA AND AZAEL, and drew near to them. Solomon then took out a ring, on which he had engraved the Holy Name, and placed it in the eagle's mouth. And immediately they, UZA AND AZAEL, would say everything that King Solomon wanted, and from there Solomon acquired wisdom. This is as it is written: "And Solomon built (Heb. *vayiven*)... Tarmod in the wilderness, in the land" (Ibid.). HE ASKS, did he really put up a building in the land? No! So what is meaning of "*vayiven*"? VAYIVEN COMES FROM THE WORD HAVANAH (ENG. 'UNDERSTANDING'), for he looked with understanding and knew that place, TARMOD, from which he acquired wisdom.

67. The rose, part two

A Synopsis

The eagle returns, drops a rose to the rabbis, and again flies away. Rabbi Pinchas says that God sent them this rose through the agency of the eagle as testimony to the Work of Creation. He explains the meaning to be derived from the parts of the rose.

The Relevance of this Passage

The Zohar speaks of the thirteen pedals on the rose. There are also thirteen Attributes of Mercy which signify the concept of miracles and wonders. In addition, thirteen denotes one more than twelve, indicating our ascension over the influences of the twelve signs of the Zodiac.

Our read ignites all this power in our lives helping us receive the miracles we truly need. Sickness and judgment decreed to us by the planets and stars are mitigated. Moreover, miracles now become the norm, a natural part of our existence instead of a scarce and infrequent phenomenon.

We learn that the five strong leaves of the rose correspond to the fifty Gates of Binah. The fifty gates pertain to the path of spirituality leading directly to the reality of the Tree of Life. The Tree of Life is a realm of perfect, flawless order. It is the source of our joy, our pleasure, our fulfillment, and our well-being. All the wisdom of the world resides in this realm. When intuition leads us to good fortune, we have made contact with this dimension. When our immune system wards off disease, we are linked to the Tree of Life. When a miracle occurs, it flows from the Tree of Life reality. This is our ultimate objective, and we attain it now, through the very words that expound upon these mysteries.

The rose also connects to the *Sh'ma Yisrael* prayer. The *Sh'ma's* first five words signify the five strong pedals. The last word of the *Sh'ma* is *echad*, which means *one*. This corresponds to the *one* stem that holds the entire rose, and to the *one* Creator that holds all Creation. The Hebrew word *echad* has a numerical value of thirteen, just the same way that the *one* rose has thirteen pedals. Thus, the entire rose is encapsulated inside the *Sh'ma*.

Therefore, the *Sh'ma* also emits the power of the thirteen Attributes, which are miracles and wonders; as well as the fifty Gates of Binah, which are the Tree of Life reality. All of this splendid Light cast through the *Sh'ma* shines upon us now, healing

and regenerating the 248 parts of the body and soul and bringing forth our ultimate and final unification with the Light of the Creator.

Finally, paragraph 398 states that Yisrael is:

"Like the rose among the thorns..."

When the rose is closed, no fragrance is emitted. When it opens, the rose radiates a sweet fragrance. One is then impelled to take the rose out from among the thorns to inhale its aroma and behold its beauty.

When Yisrael, including all those who embrace the spiritual wisdom of Kabbalah, opens its heart and shares the Light, all the nations of the world will be inspired to inhale the sweet scent of spirituality and elevate Yisrael to its proper place. Yisrael and all mankind will ascend out of the thorns of judgment, and all the world will behold the beauty of the rose – that is, the Light of the Creator.

In accordance with these spiritual insights, these verses of Zohar open our hearts to emit a sweet aroma from our soul. We are forever lifted from out of the thorns (judgment).

392. עַד דַּהֲוֹו יַתְבֵי, הָא נִשְׁרָא אַתְיָא לְגַבַּיְיהוּ, וְשׁוֹשַׁנָּה חֲדָא בְּפוּמֵהּ, וְשָׁדֵי קַמַּיְיהוּ, וְאָזְלַת לָהּ, חָמוּ וְחַדוּ. א"ר פִּנְחָס, וְלָאו אֲמֵינָא לְכוּ, דְּנִשְׁרָא דָא בִּשְׁלִיחוּתָא דְּמָארֵהּ, אָזְלָא וְאַתְיָא. שׁוֹשַׁנָּה דָא, אִיהִי שׁוּשַׁן עֵדוּת דְּקָאֲמֵינָא, וְקוּדְשָׁא בְּרִיךְ הוּא שָׁדַר לֵיהּ לְגַבָּן.

392. And while they were still sitting, the eagle came back to them, with one rose in its mouth, which it dropped in front of them, and flew away. They saw this and rejoiced. Rabbi Pinchas said, Did I not tell you that this eagle is on a mission from its Master? This rose (Heb. *shoshanah*) is an allusion to Shushan-Edut, as I said, and the Holy One, blessed be He, sent it to us.

393. פָּתַח כְּמִלְּקַדְמִין וְאָמַר, לַמְנַצֵּחַ עַל שׁוּשַׁן עֵדוּת מִכְתָּם לְדָוִד לְלַמֵּד. וְכִי שׁוּשַׁן עֵדוּת מַאי סַהֲדוּתָא סָהִיד. אֶלָּא שׁוּשַׁן דָּא אִיהִי סַהֲדוּתָא לְמַעֲשֶׂה בְּרֵאשִׁית, וְאִיהִי סַהֲדוּתָא לכנ"י. וְאִיהִי סַהֲדוּתָא לְיִחוּדָא עִלָּאָה, וְדָא אִיהוּ. בְּגִין דְּשׁוֹשַׁנָּה דָא אִית בָּהּ תְּלֵיסַר עָלִין,

וְכֻלְּהוּ קַיְימִין בְּעִקְּרָא חֲדָא, וְאִית בָּה חָמֵשׁ עָלִין לְבַר תַּקִּיפִין, דְּחַפְיִין
לְדָא שׁוֹשַׁנָּה וְאַגִּינוּ עָלָהּ.

393. He began again and said: "To the chief musician upon Shushan-Edut; A michtam (lit. 'writ') of David, to teach" (Tehilim 60:1). HE ASKS, does this mean that Shushan is testimony (Heb. *edut*)? What is the testimony to which it testifies? AND HE ANSWERS, that this Shushan is witness to the Work of Creation, and is witness to the Congregation of Yisrael, and is witness to the heavenly unity. And this is so because in a rose (Heb. *shoshanah*) there are thirteen petals, all of them on one root, and there are five strong petals on the outside, that cover this rose and protect it.

394. וְכֹלָּא בְּרָזָא דְּחָכְמְתָא הוּא, תְּלֵיסַר עָלִין, אִלֵּין תְּלֵיסַר מְכִילָן
דְּרַחֲמֵי, דְּיָרְתָא כְּנֶסֶת יִשְׂרָאֵל מִלְּעֵילָא, וְכֻלְּהוּ אֲחִידָן בְּעִקְּרָא חֲדָא,
וְאִיהוּ בְּרִית חֲדָא וְדוּגְמָא דִּבְרִית יְסוֹדָא דְכֹלָּא. חָמֵשׁ תַּקִּיפִין דְּסַחֲרָן
עָלֵיהּ, אִלֵּין חַמְשִׁין תַּרְעִין, חֲמֵשׁ מְאָה שְׁנִין דְּאִילָנָא דְחַיֵּי, אַזְלָא בְּהוּ.

394. And it is all based on the secret of wisdom, for the thirteen leaves ALLUDE TO the thirteen attributes of Mercy that the Congregation of Yisrael, WHICH IS MALCHUT, inherits from above, FROM THE THIRTEEN ATTRIBUTES OF ARICH ANPIN. And all of them are attached to one root, which is one covenant, NAMELY YESOD OF ZEIR ANPIN, BY WHOSE MEANS MALCHUT RECEIVES THE THIRTEEN ATTRIBUTES OF MERCY OF ARICH ANPIN. AND THUS THE ROOT OF THE THIRTEEN LEAVES OF THE ROSE THAT ARE BENEATH THEM IS a pattern of the covenant, which is the foundation (Yesod) of everything. The five strong LEAVES that surround it are the fifty gates, NAMELY CHESED, GVURAH, TIFERET, NETZACH AND HOD OF BINAH, EACH ONE OF WHICH IS COMPOSED OF TEN. And they are five hundred years that the Tree of Life, WHICH IS ZEIR ANPIN, goes by, FOR IT RECEIVES THEM IN THE PLACE OF BINAH, WHOSE SFIROT ARE IN THE PRINCIPLE OF HUNDREDS, AND THEY ARE FIVE HUNDRED YEARS.

395. סַהֲדוּתָא לְעוֹבָדָא דִּבְרֵאשִׁית. כָּל עוֹבָדָא דִּבְרֵאשִׁית, כֻּלְּהוּ תֵּיבִין
יְדִיעָן בְּסוּכְלְתָנוּ, וְקַיְימָא בְּחוּשְׁבְּנָא אֱלֹהִים דְּמַעֲשֵׂה בְרֵאשִׁית. אַחְזֵי
לְעֵילָא, וְאַחְזֵי לְתַתָּא. אַחְזֵי לְעֵילָא, בְּרָזָא דְּעָלְמָא דְּאָתֵי. וְאַחְזֵי

לְתַתָּא, בְּרָזָא דִּכְנֶסֶת יִשְׂרָאֵל.

395. THE ROSE IS witness to the Work of Creation, for all the Works of Creation are words known with understanding and take part in the reckoning of Elohim of the Work of Creation, WHICH IS BINAH. And it is seen above and seen below. It is seen above, namely in the secret of the World to Come, WHICH IS BINAH, and seen below in the secret of the Congregation of Yisrael, WHICH IS MALCHUT.

396. שׁוֹשַׁנָּה סַהֲדוּתָא לְעוֹבָדָא דִּבְרֵאשִׁית, דְּקַיְּימָא בְּכָל הָנֵי סִימָנִין, דִּכְתִיב בְּרֵאשִׁית בָּרָא אֱלֹהִים, דָּא שׁוֹשַׁנָּה. תְּלֵיסַר עָלִין, אִינּוּן תְּלֵיסַר תֵּיבִין עַד אֱלֹהִים תִּנְיָינָא. וְאִינּוּן: אֶת, הַשָּׁמַיִם, וְאֶת, הָאָרֶץ, וְהָאָרֶץ, הָיְתָה, תֹהוּ, וָבֹהוּ, וְחֹשֶׁךְ, עַל, פְּנֵי, תְהוֹם, וְרוּחַ. הָא תְּלֵיסַר עָלִין דְּשׁוֹשַׁנָּה. חָמֵשׁ תַּקִּיפִין דְּסַחֲרָן לְאִלֵּין, אִינּוּן: מְרַחֶפֶת, עַל, פְּנֵי, הַמַּיִם, וַיֹּאמֶר. הָא חָמֵשׁ אַחֲרָנִין. לְבָתַר יְהִי אוֹר, הָא עִיקָּרָא וְשָׁרְשָׁא דְּשׁוֹשַׁנָּה דְּכֹלָּא וַאֲחִידָן בָּהּ.

396. The rose is witness to the Work of Creation, for it has all these signs, NAMELY THE THIRTEEN ATTRIBUTES OF MERCY AND THE FIVE SFIROT OF CHESED, GVURAH, TIFERET, NETZACH AND HOD. For it is written: "In the beginning Elohim created..." (Beresheet 1:16): This is the rose, WHICH IS BINAH AND WHICH IS MALCHUT, BECAUSE IT IS SEEN ABOVE AND SEEN BELOW, AS ABOVE IN THE PRECEDING SECTION. The thirteen leaves are the thirteen words FROM "IN THE BEGINNING ELOHIM" (BERESHEET 1:1) until "...AND A WIND FROM Elohim" (Ibid. 2), namely: ...1) the 2) heaven 3) and the 4) earth. 5) And the earth 6) was 7) without form 8) and void 9) and darkness was 10) on 11) the face of 12) the deep 13). And a wind... These, then, are the thirteen leaves of the rose THAT ALLUDE TO THE THIRTEEN ATTRIBUTES. The five stronger LEAVES that surround these thirteen are: 1) moved 2) over 3) the surface of 4) the waters. 5) And (Elohim) said; FROM THE WORD ELOHIM IN THE EXPRESSION "AND A WIND FROM ELOHIM" UNTIL "ELOHIM" IN "AND ELOHIM SAID." For there are five others THAT ALLUDE TO THE FIVE SFIROT: CHESED, GVURAH, TIFERET, NETZACH AND HOD, AS EXPLAINED ABOVE. After this comes "Let there be light," this being the prime cause and the root of the rose, for all THE GRADES ARE INCLUDED IN AND attached to it.

397. סַהֲדוּתָא לְיִחוּדָא. חֲמֵשׁ עָלִין תַּקִּיפִין, שָׁרָשִׁין וְיִחוּדָא, דַּאֲחִידָן בֵּיהּ תְּלֵיסַר עָלִין אִלֵּין. שְׁמַע יִשְׂרָאֵל יְיָ' אֱלֹהֵינוּ יְיָ', הָא חֲמֵשׁ עָלִין דְּשׁוֹשַׁנָּה. אֶחָד, דָּא הִיא עִיקָּרָא וְשָׁרְשָׁא דְּכֻלְּהוּ אֲחִידָן בֵּיהּ. רָזָא דִּתְלֵיסַר בְּחוּשְׁבָּנָא, גּוּשְׁפַּנְקָא דְּמַלְכָּא.

397. THE ROSE IS witness to the unity, for the five strong leaves are the roots and the unity to which these thirteen leaves are attached. THE FIVE WORDS, "Hear, Yisrael, Hashem our Elohim; Hashem" (Devarim 6:4), PARALLEL the five leaves of the rose, while "one" is the prime cause and the root to which all of them are attached, FOR THE WORD *ECHAD* (ENG. 'ONE') IS a secret, having the numerical value of thirteen. And this is the King's signet ring.

398. ת"ח, כְּגַוְונָא דְשׁוֹשַׁנָּה בֵּין הַחוֹחִים, הָכִי אִינּוּן יִשְׂרָאֵל בֵּין עַמִּין עכו"ם. וְהָכִי כְּנֶסֶת יִשְׂרָאֵל, בֵּין שְׁאַר אֻכְלוּסִין רַבְרְבָן מְמָנָן. כָּל זְמַן דְּשׁוֹשַׁנָּה קַיָּימָא אֲטִימָא, דְּלָא פְּתִיחָא, לֵית בָּהּ רֵיחָא, וְלָא סַלְקִין לָהּ, וְלָא מַפְקִין לָהּ מִגּוֹ גּוּבִין, בְּשַׁעֲתָא דְשׁוֹשַׁנָּה פְּתִיחָא, סַלְקָא רֵיחָא, כְּדֵין אַפִּיקוּ לָהּ מִגּוֹ גּוּבִין. וְיִתְהֲנֵי בְּהוּ כ"י, שֶׁנֶּאֱמַר פִּתְחִי לִי אֲחוֹתִי רַעְיָתִי, וְקוּדְשָׁא בְּרִיךְ הוּא לָא לָא שַׁדְרָהּ לָן אֶלָּא לְמֵיהַךְ לְאוֹרְחָן.

עד כאן רעיא מהימנא

398. Come and see: "Like the rose among the thorns" (Shir Hashirim 2:2), so are Yisrael among the idol-worshipping nations and so is the Congregation of Yisrael, WHICH IS MALCHUT, among the many other ministers appointed OVER THE NATIONS. So long as the rose stands there closed, unopened, it has no fragrance and one does not lift it out and remove it from among the thorns. When the rose is open and gives off a fragrance, then one takes it out from among the thorns. And the Congregation of Yisrael will benefit from them, as it is said: "Open to me, my sister, my love" (Shir Hashirim 5:2). And the Holy One, blessed be He, only sent to us THE EAGLE, WHO BROUGHT THE ROSE SO THAT we should continue on our journey WITH THE SHECHINAH.

End of Ra'aya Meheimna (the Faithful Sheperd)

68. Internal organs

A Synopsis
Rabbi Shimon explains to his son the secret of the inner organs, telling him about the wings of the lung that are like the wings of a dove covered with silver, Chassadim.

The Relevance of this Passage
Here we are told that the illumination of the Left is the source of all illness. That means that egotistic behavior, which includes anger, rage, jealousy, hostility, and self-indulgence, is the source of all illness. This causes the heart to burn, unless a wind from the lung can blow upon it and cool the fire. The angels Raphael and Tzidkiel represent the lungs and liver, which is mercy, and it flows to us to bring health and salvation to us and the world.

Here our lungs receive the divine Light of healing. The fire in our heart is extinguished by cool wind from our lungs. Our anger is calmed by the angels Raphael and Tzidkiel. By reading this passage, we give our lungs the capacity to eliminate our anger.

As our sins multiply, the health of our internal organs slowly begins to deteriorate. The brain, representing Mercy and the Creator, now sweetens and silences all judgments that have been building up in our hearts as a result of our iniquities. We atone for our sins as our hearts and internal organs are healed of physical ailments. Brain afflictions are also treated in this profound passage. And atonement extends to the nation of Yisrael, promoting peace and good will throughout the world. These vital benefits are bestowed upon us by virtue of the Torah's Light and the spiritual energy arising from the Sh'ma prayer connection.

Next, we learn that the kidneys correspond to the Sfirah of Gvurah, which is Judgment. Accordingly, readers are able to heal and remedy kidney disorders and diseases.

Paragraphs 409 - 410 tell us that (do not pronounce this name) Lilit corresponds to the spleen and (do not pronounce this name) Samael is the liver. Lilit is the root cause of death in children, and Samael is the Angel of Death who comes for adults.

These two paragraphs in the Zohar heal children of sickness and disease. In turn, the Light that shines here brings death to Lilit and Samael, causing the demise of the Angel of Death himself!
Meditating upon this passage on Mondays and Wednesdays further enhances the positive effects achieved by this sacred book, striking

the two demons at the root and seed-level of their evil existence.

Esau, the evil son of Isaac, also corresponds to the liver. Esau represents all those people who abhor the spiritual path and Light. Like the liver, they accept both the purities and the impurities of life, not differentiating between good and evil. Jacob, Isaac's righteous son, represents our heart, which only accepts the pure blood, the same way that the righteous always choose good over evil.

The Light cast from this verse purifies Esau. The verse purifies all the nations and our internal Evil Inclination, as wickedness is banished forever from Creation. Healing and harmony takes place in our bodies and among all nations of the world.

The Light of the *Shechinah* wraps us up and completely heals us, freeing us from sickness and disease, particularly those related directly or indirectly to the immune system (paragraphs 413 - 414). The Angel of Death is tightly wrapped up in this same Light, but he is suffocated and then snuffed out of existence. Our immune system is strengthened to perfection.

All stomach ailments are treated and remedied in paragraph 415. Sharing this Light with others in need solidifies the demise of the Angel of Death.

All the body parts, internal and external, are liberated from the Other Side – the Evil Inclination. The profound truth that all illness is firmly based in negative human behavior becomes instilled in our consciousness, removing doubts and skepticism, paving the way for the ultimate healing of our bodies and souls.

The remaining paragraphs expound in cryptic language upon sublime matters concerning the relationship between the organs of the body and their correlations to supernal worlds, spiritual beings, ancient sacrifices, and the Temple.

Most relevant to the reader are the healing benefits reaped from these verses. They refer to the disorders and maladies of the heart, the circulatory system, and the respiratory system, especially the structures and organs that have to do with breathing – the nasal cavities, the throat (pharynx), the larynx, the windpipe (trachea), the airways (bronchii), and the lung tissue.

Finally, because all this spiritual wisdom has been lost, the companions of Rabbi Shimon, the author of the Zohar, state:

> "Alas, Rabbi, when you depart from the world, who will reveal to us such deep and hidden secrets that have not been heard from the days of King Solomon until now? Happy is the generation that hears such matters! Happy is the

generation amongst whom you are! Woe to the generation that will be orphaned without you!"

For the last 2000 years, all the generations were the orphans who suffered without this great Kabbalist in their midst. However, through the worldwide revelation of this wisdom in our generation, Rabbi Shimon lives among us. Thus, happy is our generation, forevermore.

399. אָמַר ר' אֶלְעָזָר לַאֲבוּהִי, הָא שְׁמַעֲנָא אִלֵּין שַׁיְיפִין אֲטִימִין, בְּרָזָא דְקָרְבְּנִין. שַׁיְיפִין אַחֲרָנִין, רָזָא דִּלְהוֹן מַאי. א"ל רִבִּי שִׁמְעוֹן לר"א, אֶלְעָזָר בְּרִי, כָּל שְׁאַר שַׁיְיפִין דִּלְגוֹ, רָזָא עִלָּאָה אִיהוּ.

399. Rabbi Elazar said to his father, We have already heard THE EXPOSITION OF the closed organs, NAMELY THE EXTERNAL LIMBS, in the secret of the sacrifice, but what is the secret of the other organs, THE INNER ONES? Rabbi Shimon said to Rabbi Elazar: Elazar, my son, all the other organs that are internal have a supreme secret.

400. ת"ח, לִבָּא הָא אִתְּמַר, אֲבָל לֵב דָּא אִיהוּ נוּרָא דְּדָלִיק, וְאִלְמָלֵא דְּזַמִּין לְגַבֵּיהּ מַלְכָּא עִלָּאָה כַּנְפֵי רֵיאָה, דְּאַתְיָין לְקַמֵּיהּ רוּחָא, מְרוּחָא דְּנָשִׁיב מִגּוֹ בּוּסְמִין עִלָּאִין, הֲוָה אוֹקִיד לְעָלְמָא בְּרִגְעָא חֲדָא.

400. Come and see, We have already learned about the heart: The heart is a burning fire, and if the Supernal King had not arranged for it the wings of the lung that bring to it a breeze from the wind that blows with the upper spices, NAMELY FROM THE FIRST THREE SFIROT OF ZEIR ANPIN, the heart would burn up the whole world in a single moment.

401. פָּתַח וְאָמַר, וַיְיָ' הִמְטִיר עַל סְדוֹם וְעַל עֲמוֹרָה גָּפְרִית וָאֵשׁ, אֲמַאי אוֹקִיד לוֹן. בְּגִין דְּכַנְפֵי רֵיאָה לָא נְשִׁיבוּ בְּהַהִיא שַׁעֲתָא. וְסִתְרָא דְּכַנְפֵי רֵיאָה, דָּא כַּנְפֵי יוֹנָה נֶחְפָּה בַכֶּסֶף וְאִינוּן רְפָאֵל, וְצַדְקִיאֵל, וְעָלַיְיהוּ אִתְּמַר, עוֹשֶׂה מַלְאָכָיו רוּחוֹת, לְנַשְׁבָא תָּדִיר קַמֵּי לִבָּא.

401. He began by quoting: "Then Hashem caused to rain upon S'dom and upon Amorah brimstone and fire" (Beresheet 19:24). Why did He burn

them? Because at that time the wings of the lung did not blow a wind ON And the secret of these wings of the lung is the secret of the verse, "the wings of a dove covered with silver" (Tehilim 68:14). FOR DOVE, WHICH IS THE SECRET OF MALCHUT, OF WHICH THE ROOT IS FROM THE LEFT OF BINAH, FROM THE ASPECT OF THE HEART, HAS TO BE COVERED WITH SILVER, WHICH IS THE SECRET OF CHASSADIM. AND WHEN IT IS COVERED WITH SILVER IT IS THE SECRET OF THE ANGELS Raphael and Tzadkiel, WHICH COME FROM IT FOR THE HEALTH AND SALVATION OF THE WORLD. And it is said about them: "who makes the winds His messengers" (Tehilim 104:4), namely permanently to blow on the heart.

A Synopsis

Moses tells Rabbi Shimon about the inner meaning of the brain, the heart, the lungs and the kidneys, further refining his interpretation of the brain, which he says is the Throne of Mercy.

רעיא מהימנא

402. וּבְחִבּוּרָא קַדְמָאָה, אָמַר רַעְיָא מְהֵימָנָא, בּוּצִינָא קַדִּישָׁא, כָּל מַה דְּאָמַרְת שַׁפִּיר, אֲבָל מוֹחָא אִיהוּ מַיִם, לֵב אִיהוּ אֵשׁ, וְתַרְוַוייהוּ אִיהוּ רַחֲמֵי וְדִינָא, דָּא כָּסֵּא רַחֲמֵי, וְדָא כָּסֵּא דִינָא. וְקוּדְשָׁא בְּרִיךְ הוּא מֶלֶךְ, עוֹמֵד מִכָּסֵּא דִין, דְּאִיהוּ לֵב. וְיוֹשֵׁב עַל כָּסֵּא רַחֲמִים, דְּאִיהוּ מוֹחָא.

Ra'aya Meheimna (the Faithful Shepherd)

402. And in the first section, the Faithful Shepherd said TO RABBI SHIMON, Holy Luminary, everything that you have said is good, but the brain is water, the heart is fire, and the two of them are Mercy and Judgment. This, THE BRAIN, is the Throne of Mercy, while the other, THE HEART, is the Throne of Judgment. And the Holy One, blessed be He, is the King who arise from the Throne of Judgment which is the heart, and sits down on the Throne of Mercy which is the brain.

403. וְכַד חוֹבִין מִתְרַבִּין עַל אֵבָרִים, וְעַל עַרְקִין דְּלִבָּא, דְּאִיהוּ כֻּרְסַיָּיא דְּדִינָא. אִתְּמַר בְּלִבָּא, וְהַמֶּלֶךְ קָם בַּחֲמָתוֹ מִמִּשְׁתֵּה הַיַּיִן, דְּאִיהוּ יֵינָא דְּאוֹרַיְיתָא. וּבְזִמְנָא דְּכַנְפֵי רֵיאָה נָשְׁבִין עַל לִבָּא, וַחֲמַת הַמֶּלֶךְ שָׁכָכָה.

דִּתְרֵין כַּנְפֵי רֵיאָה, וְהָיוּ הַכְּרוּבִים פֹּרְשֵׂי כְנָפַיִם לְמַעְלָה סוֹכְכִים בְּכַנְפֵיהֶם עַל הַכַּפֹּרֶת, דָּא כַּפּוּרְתָּא דְלִבָּא.

403. When iniquities multiply in the organs and in the arteries of the heart, which is the Throne of Judgment, it is said of the heart: "And the king arising from the banquet of wine in his wrath" (Ester 7:7), which is the wine of the Torah. But when the wings of the lung blow on the heart, it is said: "Then the king's wrath was pacified" (Ibid. 10). For the two wings of the lung are THE SECRET OF THE VERSE, "And the Cherubs shall stretch out their wings on high, over spreading the covering with their wings" (Shemot 25:20). This is the covering of the heart.

404. וּבְמַאי וַחֲמַת הַמֶּלֶךְ שָׁכָכָה. בְּגִין וַיִּשְׁמַע אֶת הַקּוֹל, דָּא קוֹל תּוֹרָה, קוֹל דק"ש. וַיְדַבֵּר אֵלָיו, בִּצְלוֹתָא דְפוּמָא, דְּאִיהוּ אֲדֹנָי שְׂפָתַי תִּפְתָּח וּפִי יַגִּיד תְּהִלָּתֶךָ.

404. And in what way was the king's wrath appeased? It was because "then he heard the voice" (Bemidbar 7:89), this being the voice of the Torah, the voice of the reading of Sh'ma, WHICH IS THE CENTRAL COLUMN, "and it spoke to him" (Ibid.), WHICH IS THE SECRET OF THE REVELATION of CHOCHMAH THAT IS IN MALCHUT, WHICH IS CALLED 'SPEECH', and this is in the prayer that is formulated in the mouth, which is "Adonai, open my lips; and my mouth shall rehearse Your praise" (Tehilim 51:17), WHICH IS MALCHUT.

405. וְהַהוּא רוּחָא דְּנָשִׁיב בְּכַנְפֵי רֵיאָה, אִיהוּ אַפִּיק קָלָא בְּקָנֶה, דְּאִיהוּ קָנֶה חָכְמָה קְנֵה בִינָה. וְאִתְּמַר בָּהּ, כֹּה אָמַר יְיָ' מֵאַרְבַּע רוּחוֹת בֹּאִי הָרוּחַ. דְּאִינּוּן אַרְבַּע אַתְוָון יְדֹנָ"ד, וְהַאי אִיהוּ רוּחַ דְּדָפִיק בְּכָל עַרְקִין דְּלִבָּא, דְּאִתְּמַר בְּהוֹן, אֶל אֲשֶׁר יִהְיֶה שָׁמָּה הָרוּחַ לָלֶכֶת יֵלֵכוּ.

405. And that wind that blows in the wings of the lung, carries the voice out through the trachea (Heb. *kaneh*), which is "Get (Heb. *k'neh*) wisdom, get understanding" (Mishlei 4:5). FOR THE VOICE, WHICH IS ZEIR ANPIN, NAMELY VAV, IS THE SON OF YUD HEI, WHICH ARE CHOCHMAH AND BINAH. And about this it is said: "Thus says Adonai Elohim; Come from the

four winds, O breath (Heb. *ruach*)" (Yechezkel 37:9). And the four are the four letters Yud Hei Vav Hei OF ZEIR ANPIN. And this is the wind that beats and palpitates in all the arteries of the heart, about which it is said: "Wherever the spirit (Heb. *ruach*) was minded to go, they went" (Yechezkel 1:12).

406. אָמַר בּוּצִינָא קַדִּישָׁא, וַדַּאי רַעְיָא מְהֵימָנָא, דַּרְגָּא דִילָךְ אִיהִי, דְּבֵיהּ וַחֲמַת הַמֶּלֶךְ שָׁכָכָה. אַשְׁרֵי הָעָם שֶׁכָּכָ"ה, בְּגִימַטְרְיָא מֹשֶׁה. אָמַר לֵיהּ, בְּרִיךְ אַנְתְּ בּוּצִינָא קַדִּישָׁא, בּוּצִינָא דְּדָלִיק קַמֵּי מַלְכָּא וּמַטְרוֹנִיתָא. נֵר יְיָ', אִיהִי נִשְׁמָה דִּילָךְ.

406. The Holy Luminary said TO THE FAITHFUL SHEPHERD: Certainly, O Faithful Shepherd, it is your level at which it is said: "Then the king's wrath was pacified (Heb. *shachachah*)," FOR THE LEVEL OF THE FAITHFUL SHEPHERD IS THE CENTRAL COLUMN, WHICH IS ZEIR ANPIN, THAT IS CALLED 'VOICE'. "Happy is the people that is in such a case (Heb. *shecachah*)" (Tehilim 144:15), *SHACHACHAH* having the numerical value of Moses. THE FAITHFUL SHEPHERD said to him, Blessed are you, Holy Luminary, FOR YOU ARE the candle that burns before the King and His Matron. "the candle of Hashem" (Mishlei 20:27) is your soul.

407. א"ל, הָא אֲמַרַת מוֹחָא וְלִבָּא וְכַנְפֵי רֵיאָה, תְּרֵי כּוּלְיָין מַאי נִיהוּ. אָמַר רַעְיָא מְהֵימָנָא, הָא אוֹקִימְנָא בְּכַנְפֵי רֵיאָה, עוֹשֶׂה מַלְאָכָיו רוּחוֹת, כּוּלְיָין מְשָׁרְתָיו אֵשׁ לוֹהֵט. וְאִינּוּן תְּרֵין כַּנְפֵי רֵיאָה, וּתְרֵין כּוּלְיָין, לָקֳבֵל ד' חֵיוָן דְּכָרְסַיָּיא. כָּרְסַיָּיא, אִיהוּ לִבָּא בְּאֶמְצָעִיתָא.

407. RABBI SHIMON said to THE FAITHFUL SHEPHERD, You have given AN EXPLANATION for the brain, the heart, and the wings of the lungs, but what about the two kidneys? The Faithful Shepherd replied, We learned about the wings of the lungs: "who makes the winds His messengers" (Tehilim 104:4), THIS BEING THE SECRET OF CHASSADIM, WHICH ARE CALLED 'WINDS'. The kidneys ARE "the flames of fire His ministers" (Ibid.), NAMELY JUDGMENTS, and the two wings of the lung with the two kidneys stand for the four living creatures of the Throne, WHERE THE WINGS OF THE LUNG ARE LION AND EAGLE, WHICH ARE CHASSADIM, AND THE TWO

KIDNEYS ARE OX AND MAN, WHICH ARE GVUROT. And the Throne is the heart that is in the middle, WHICH IS THE THRONE OF JUDGMENT.

408. וְכֵן מוֹחָא, אִית לֵיהּ אַרְבַּע חֵיוָן, דְּאִיהוּ כֻּרְסְיָיא דְּרַחֲמֵי. וּמַאי נִיהוּ. רְאִיָּיה שְׁמִיעָה רֵיחָא דִּבּוּר. רְאִיָּיה: אַרְיֵה. שְׁמִיעָה: שׁוֹר. רֵיחָא: נִשְׁרָא. וְד' אַנְפִּין וְד' כַּנְפִין לְכָל חַד. הַדִּבּוּר: אָדָם אִיהוּ. אָחִיד עֵילָּא וְתַתָּא, דְּרוֹעִין דִּבְהוֹן וְיָדֵינוּ פְּרוּשׂוֹת כְּנִשְׁרֵי שָׁמַיִם. גּוּף אַרְיֵה, וְשׁוֹקַיִם, וְכַף רַגְלֵיהֶם כְּכַף רֶגֶל עֵגֶל. וְעַל גּוּפָא אִתְּמַר, מֶרְכֶּבֶת הַמִּשְׁנֶה. מִשְׁנָה כְּתִיב, לִישָׁנָא דְּמַתְנִיתִין.

ע"כ רעיא מהימנא

408. And so, too, does the brain have four living creatures, FOR THE BRAIN is the Throne of Mercy. And who might they be? They are sight, hearing, smell and speech. Sight is lion, NAMELY CHOCHMAH. Hearing is ox, NAMELY BINAH. Smell is eagle, NAMELY ZEIR ANPIN, and each of them has four countenances and four wings. Speech is man, NAMELY MALCHUT. He is attached above, NAMELY TO THE MOUTH OF THE HEAD, and below IN THE BODY. For ABOUT the arms of the body, IT IS SAID: 'Our hands are spread forth as the eagles of the heavens'. Body is man, THAT IS TO SAY THAT HE IS IN THE ASPECT OF MALCHUT, WHICH CLINGS TO THE CENTRAL COLUMN, WHICH IS BODY. And ABOUT the legs IT IS WRITTEN: "and the sole of their feet was like the sole of a calf's foot" (Yechezkel 1:7), WHICH INCLINE TO THE FACE OF OX, WHICH IS GVURAH. And about the body, WHICH IS MAN, it is said "the second chariot" (Beresheet 41:43), NAMELY THE CHARIOT OF MALCHUT, WHICH IS CALLED 'SECOND' (HEB. MISHNEH), but this can also be read as *Mishnah*, as in. 'we taught in the Mishnah' WHICH IS MALCHUT.

End of Ra'aya Meheimna (the Faithful Sheperd)

A Synopsis
From Rabbi Shimon we learn about the spleen, called Lilit, and the liver, called Samael or the Angel of Death.

409. טְחוֹל, פָּתַח בּוּצִינָא קַדִּישָׁא וְאָמַר, וָאֶרְאֶה אֶת כָּל הָעֲשׁוּקִים

שֶׁנַּעֲשׂוּ תַּחַת הַשֶּׁמֶשׁ וְהִנֵּה דִּמְעַת הָעֲשׁוּקִים. מַאן אִינּוּן עֲשׁוּקִים. אִלֵּין
יְנוּקִין דְּאִינּוּן בְּתוּקְפָּא דְּאִמְּהוֹן. דְּסַלְּקִין מֵעָלְמָא, ע"י מַלְאַךְ הַמָּוֶת.
וְכִי מַלְאַךְ הַמָּוֶת קָטִיל לוֹן, דְּאִיהוּ עוֹשֵׁק. אֶלָּא הָדַר וְאָמַר, וּמִיַּד
עוֹשְׁקֵיהֶם כֹּחַ וְאֵין לָהֶם מְנַחֵם. מַאן הַהוּא כֹּחַ. דָּא הוּא דִּכְתִיב, יְהִי
מְאֹרֹת בִּרְקִיעַ הַשָּׁמַיִם. וְדָא הוּא מְאֹרֹת חָסֵר וָאו, וְדָא לִילִית, דְּאִיהִי
מְמָנָא דְּהַהוּא עוֹשֵׁק.

409. WHAT IS the spleen? The Holy Luminary, NAMELY RABBI SHIMON, began: "and considered all the oppressions that are done under the sun: and behold the tears of such as were oppressed" (Kohelet 4:1). Who are those who are oppressed? They are the children who are still in need of their mother when the Angel of Death takes them from the world. HE ASKS, And is it indeed the case that the Angel of Death kills them, that he oppresses THEM? AND REPLIES, Not really, for Scripture adds: "and on the side of their oppressors there was power; but they had no comforter" (Ibid.). Then who is that power THAT KILLS THEM? The answer to this is to be found in the verse: "Let there be lights (Heb. *me'orot*) in the firmament of heaven" (Beresheet 1:14). And the word "*me'orot*" is written in the abbreviated spelling without a Vav, AND CAN BE READ *ME'EROT*. The reference, therefore, is to Lilit, who is appointed over that oppressor, AS ME'EROT MEAND CURSE.

410. וְאִיהִי אִקְרֵי טְחוֹל, וְאִיהִי אַזְלַת וְחַיְיכָא בְּיַנּוּקֵי, וּבָתַר עָבְדַת בְּהוּ
רוּגְזָא וְדִמְעָה, לְמִבְכֵּי עָלַיְיהוּ. טְחוֹל לְזִינָא דִּכְבֵד אַזְלָא. דָּא אִבְרֵי
בַּשֵּׁנִי, וְדָא בָּרְבִיעִי בְּעוֹבָדָא דִּבְרֵאשִׁית. וּבְג"ד, לֵית סִימָנָא טָבָא בַּשֵּׁנִי
וּבָרְבִיעִי. כָּבֵד מוֹתָא דְּרַבְרְבֵי, טְחוֹל מוֹתָא דְּזוּטְרֵי.

410. AND LILIT is called 'spleen', and she goes to play with children, later KILLING THEM, and creates in them anger and tears and weeping over them. The spleen goes to its own kind, the liver, WHICH IS SAMAEL, WHO IS THE ANGEL OF DEATH. This, NAMELY THE LIVER, was created on the second day OF THE WORK OF CREATION, while the other, NAMELY THE SPLEEN, was created on the fourth day of the Work of Creation. And for this reason it is not a good omen TO COMMENCE SOMETHING on Mondays or on Wednesdays. Liver is death for adults; spleen is death for children.

A Synopsis

Moses repeats some of the information from earlier sections and adds the fact that anger comes from the gall and that anyone who is angry is the same as an idol-worshipper. We learn that the Shechinah wraps the body that is sick in order to heal it, but the totally wicked person is surrounded on all sides by the Angel of Death.

רעיא מהימנא

411. וּבְחִבּוּרָא קַדְמָאָה, אָמַר רַעְיָא מְהֵימָנָא, וַדַּאי הָכִי הוּא, דְּכָבֵד אִיהוּ דַּרְגָּא דְּעֵשָׂו. עֵשָׂו הוּא אֱדוֹם. הוּא כָּנִישׁ כָּל דָּמִין, בֵּין צְלוֹלִין, בֵּין עֲכוּרִין. וְלֹא אַבְחִין בֵּין טַב לְבִישׁ. לָא עָבֵיד אַפְרָשׁוּתָא בֵּינַיְיהוּ. לִבָּא אִיהוּ יִשְׂרָאֵל, דְּאַבְחִין בֵּין טַב לְבִישׁ, בֵּין דָּם טָמֵא לְדָם טָהוֹר, וְלָא נָטִיל אֶלָּא בְּרִירוּ וְנַקְיוּ דְּהַהוּא דָּמָא, כְּבוֹרֵר אוֹכֵל מִגּוֹ פְּסוֹלֶת.

Ra'aya Meheimna (the Faithful Shepherd)

411. And in the first section, said the Faithful Shepherd, that is certainly how it is, for the liver is the level of Esau, and Esau is Edom, NAMELY IS ALL BLOOD (HEB. *DAM*), and gathers in all blood whether clear or turbid, and does not differentiate between good and bad, BETWEEN IMPURE BLOOD AND PURE BLOOD, for it makes no distinction between them. But the heart, which is Yisrael, does distinguish between good and bad, between impure blood and pure blood, and takes only the clear and the clean of that blood, like one who picks food out of the waste matter.

412. וּלְבָתַר דְּנָטִיל לִבָּא, דְּאִיהוּ יַעֲקֹב, בְּרִירוּתָא דִּדְמִים, דְּאִיהוּ לְעֵילָא. וְאִשְׁתָּאַר כָּבֵד דְּאִיהוּ עֵשָׂו בִּפְסוֹלֶת. אִיהוּ כָּעִיס עֲלֵיהּ בִּמְרָה, דְּאִיהִי גֵּיהִנָּם, דְּאִתְבְּרִיאַת בְּיוֹמָא תִּנְיָינָא, מוֹתָא דִּרְבַרְבֵי, וְאִיהִי נוּקְבָּא בִּישָׁא, אֵשׁ זָרָה, עֲבוֹדָה קָשָׁה, ע"ז קָרֵינָן לָהּ.

412. And after the heart, which is Jacob, NAMELY ZEIR ANPIN, takes the clear blood which is at the top, and the liver, which is Esau, NAMELY SAMAEL, remains in the waste matter OF THE BLOOD, it is angered at it with the gall, which is Gehenom, which was created on the second day OF

THE WORK OF CREATION, THE LIVER BEING the death of all the adults, while THE GALL is the wicked female OF SAMAEL, which is called 'a strange fire', 'hard bondage', and 'idolatry'.

413. וּבְגִין דְּמִינָהּ אִתְּעַר כַּעַס לְכָבֵד, אוֹקִמוּהָ רַבָּנָן בְּמַתְנִיתִין, כָּל הַכּוֹעֵס כְּאִילוּ עוֹבֵד ע"ז. וְלֹא עוֹד, אֶלָּא דְּלֵית שְׁרֵיפָה וַחֲמִימוּת בְּכָל מַרְעִין דְּאֶבְרִין דְּגוּפָא, אֶלָּא מִמָּרָה. דְּאִיהִי אַדְלִיקַת בְּשַׁלְהוֹבִין עַל עַרְקִין דְּכָבֵד, וּבְעֵי לְאוֹקְדָא כָּל גּוּפָא. וְאִיהוּ כְּגַוְונָא דְּיַמָּא, כַּד אִיהוּ כָּעִיס, דְּגַלֵּי יַמָּא סַלְּקִין עַד רְקִיעָא, וּבָעוּ לְנַפְקָא מִגְּבוּלַיְיהוּ, לְחַרְבָא עָלְמָא. אִי לָאו שְׁכִינְתָּא, דְּאִיהִי לַחוֹלֶה כְּחוֹל דְּאַסְחַר לְיַמָּא, דְּלָא נַפְקַת מִפוּמָהָא, אוֹף הָכִי שְׁכִינְתָּא אַסְחָרַת לְגוּפָא, וְסָמִיךְ לֵיהּ, כד"א, יְיָ' יִסְעָדֶנּוּ עַל עֶרֶשׂ דְּוָי.

413. And since the anger awakens from it, FROM THE GALL, towards the liver, the sages taught in the Mishnah: Anyone who is angry is as though he worshipped idols. And furthermore, any burning up and heat that comes with any of the illnesses of the parts of the body is only from the gall, FOR, AT THE TIME OF ILLNESS it engulfs the arteries of the liver in flames and wishes to burn up the whole body. It is like a storm in the sea and its waves reach up to the skies and want to break out of their limits and destroy the world. And this would indeed happen were it not for the Shechinah, which is for a sick person like the sand to the sea, surrounding it so that it should not break out. So, too, is the Shechinah enwrapping the body and assisting it, as it is written: "Hashem strengthens him upon the bed of sickness" (Tehilim 41:4).

414. ובג"ד אוֹקִמוּהָ מָארֵי מַתְנִיתִין, הַמְּבַקֵּר אֶת הַחוֹלֶה, לָא לִיתִיב לְמֵרַאֲשׁוֹתָיו, מִשּׁוּם דִּשְׁכִינְתָּא עַל רֵישֵׁיהּ. וְלָא לְרַגְלוֹי דְּמַלְאַךְ הַמָּוֶת לְרַגְלוֹי. הַאי לָאו לְכָל ב"נ, אֶלָּא לַבֵּינוֹנִי. אֲבָל לַצַּדִּיק גָּמוּר, יְיָ' יִסְעָדֶנּוּ עַל עֶרֶשׂ דְּוָי, עַל רֵישֵׁיהּ. וּשְׁכִינְתָּא אַסְחַר גּוּפֵיהּ, עַד רַגְלוֹי. ובג"ד אִתְּמַר בְּיַעֲקֹב, וַיֶּאֱסֹף רַגְלָיו אֶל הַמִּטָּה, וְדָא שְׁכִינְתָּא דְּאִתְּמַר בָּהּ, וְהָאָרֶץ הֲדוֹם רַגְלָי. לְרָשָׁע גָּמוּר, מַלְאַךְ הַמָּוֶת אַסְחַר לֵיהּ בְּכָל סִטְרָא. וְדָא יצה"ר, דמ"ה אַסְחַר לֵיהּ בְּכָל סִטְרָא, חַרְבָּא דִּילֵיהּ, דְּפָנָיו

מוֹרִיקוֹת, בְּטִפָּה חֲדָא מֵאִינּוּן ג׳ טִפּוֹת, דְּזָרִיק בֵּיהּ. הה״ד וְאַחֲרִיתָהּ מָרָה כַלַּעֲנָה. כָּבֵד דָּא דְּכוּרָא. יוֹתֶרֶת הַכָּבֵד נוּקְבָא.

עד כאן רעיא מהימנא

414. And for this reason the sages of the Mishnah taught: One who visits a sick person should not sit at the head of the bed because the Shechinah is over his head, nor at the foot of the bed because the Angel of Death is at his feet. And this is not the case for every person, but just for ordinary people. In the case of the perfectly righteous, "Hashem strengthens him upon the bed of sickness," namely at his head, and the Shechinah enwraps his body up to his feet. And this is why it was said about Jacob: "he gathered up his feet into the bed" (Beresheet 49:33). This is the Shechinah, about which it is said: "And the earth is My footstool" (Yeshayah 66:1), AND THE SHECHINAH IS ALSO CALLED 'BED'. In the case of the thoroughly wicked person, the Angel of Death surrounds him on every side, and this is the Evil Inclination FOR THE ANGEL OF DEATH IS THE EVIL INCLINATION. For the Angel of Death surrounds him on every side and his sword IS THE GALL, and his face turns green with one drop of the three drops that THE GALL (HEB. MARAH) sprinkles on him, as it is written: "But her end is bitter (Heb. marah) as wormwood, sharp as a two-edged sword" (Mishlei 5:4). Liver is male, WHICH IS SAMAEL, and the appendix of the liver is his female.

End of Ra'aya Meheimna (the Faithful Sheperd)

A Synopsis
We learn that the stomach is one sixtieth part of death.

415 קֵיבָה, אִיהוּ דַּרְגָּא חַד מִשִּׁתִּין דְּמוֹתָא. וְדָא אִתְקְרֵי תַּרְדֵּמָה. עֲסִירְטָא, דַּרְגָּא שְׁתִיתָאָה דְּמַלְאָךְ הַמָּוֶת. וּמִגּוֹ דְּאָתֵי מֵרָחִיק, אִיהוּ מִסִּטְרָא דְּמוֹתָא. וְלָאו מוֹתָא. רֶמֶז, חַד מִשִּׁתִּין דְּמוֹתָא.

415. The stomach is one part in sixty of death and is called 'a deep sleep' SINCE 'THE STOMACH SLEEPS', and is Asirta, which is the sixth stage of the Angel of Death. And because it came from afar it is from the side of death, but is not death itself. The hint is 'one sixtieth part of death'.

A Synopsis
The Faithful Shepherd tells us about the Good and Evil Inclination in each part of the body, about the four kinds of offerings and elements and Holy Beasts.

416. אָמַר רַעְיָא מְהֵימְנָא, בָּתַר דְּגוּפָא אִיהוּ מֵאִילָנָא דְּטוֹב וָרָע, לֵית אֵבָר בְּגוּפָא, דְּלָא אִית בֵּיהּ יֵצֶר הָרָע וְיֵצֶר טוֹב, לַבֵּינוֹנִיִּים. וְלַצַּדִּיקִים גְּמוּרִים, תְּרֵין יְצִירוֹת, דְּכַר וְנוּקְבָא, תַּרְוַוייְהוּ טוֹבִים. כְּגַוְונָא דְּחָתָן וְכַלָּה. לָרְשָׁעִים גְּמוּרִים, תְּרֵין יְצִירוֹת בִּישִׁין, דְּכַר וְנוּקְבָא, בְּכָל אֵבָר וְאֵבָר, מִסִּטְרָא דְּסָמָאֵל וְנָחָשׁ.

Ra'aya Meheimna (the Faithful Shepherd)

416. The Faithful Shepherd said, Since this body is of "the tree of knowledge of good and evil" (Beresheet 2:9), there is no part of the body that does not have in it both the Evil Inclination and the Good Inclination, THIS BEING THE CASE for ordinary people. In the case of the perfectly righteous, EACH PART DOES INDEED ALSO HAVE two inclinations, which are male and female, BUT both of them are good, being like the bride and the bridegroom. The utterly wicked have in each part of their bodies two Evil Inclinations, male and female, from the side of Samael and the Serpent.

417. וּבג״ד מִסִּטְרָא דְּאִילָנָא דְּטוֹב וָרָע, קֵיבָה אִית בָּהּ תְּרֵין דַּרְגִּין. דְּהָכִי אוֹקְמוּהָ רַבָּנָן, קֵיבָה יָשֵׁן. וְאִית שֵׁינָה, אַחַת מִשְׁתִּין בְּמוֹתָא. וְשֵׁינָה, אַחַת מִשְׁתִּין בַּנְּבוּאָה. וּבג״ד אוֹקְמוּהָ רַבָּנָן מָארֵי מְתִיבְתָּא, הַחֲלוֹמוֹת שָׁוְא יְדַבֵּרוּ, וְהָכְתִיב בַּחֲלוֹם אֲדַבֶּר בּוֹ. לָא קַשְׁיָא, כָּאן עַל יְדֵי שֵׁד. כָּאן עַל יְדֵי מַלְאָךְ. חֲלוֹם ע״י מַלְאָךְ, חַד מִשְׁתִּין בַּנְּבוּאָה. חֲלוֹם עַל יְדֵי שֵׁד, אִיהוּ שָׁוְא, מִסִּטְרָא דְּמוֹתָא. וְאִיהוּ תֶּבֶן, דְּהָכִי אוֹקְמוּהָ, כְּשֵׁם שֶׁאִי אֶפְשָׁר לְבַר בְּלָא תֶּבֶן, כָּךְ אִי אֶפְשָׁר לַחֲלוֹם בְּלָא דְּבָרִים בְּטֵלִים.

417. And it follows from this that, in terms of the Tree of Knowledge of Good and Evil, IN THE CASE OF ORDINARY PEOPLE, there are in the stomach two levels: GOOD AND EVIL. And this indeed is what the sages

taught: the stomach is asleep, and there is sleep that is one sixtieth part of death. And THERE IS ALSO sleep that is one sixtieth part of prophecy. And for this reason, the heads of the Yeshivah taught: 'IT IS WRITTEN: "and the dreams tell falsehood" (Zecharyah 10:2). Yet it is also written: "and speak to him in a dream" (Bemidbar 12:6). There is no contradiction here. In the former case it is through a demon, NAMELY THE OTHER SIDE FROM THE SIDE OF EVIL IN A MAN'S SLEEP. And in the latter case it is through an angel, WHICH IS FROM THE GOOD SIDE IN A MAN'S SLEEP. A dream through an angel is one sixtieth part of prophecy. A dream through a demon, which is falsehood, is from the side of death, and is straw. Thus indeed was it taught: Just as wheat cannot be without straw, so there cannot be a dream without some nonsense.'

418. אִצְטוֹמְכָא דָא קָרְקְבָן נִקְלָף. וְאוֹקְמוּהָ רַבָּנָן, קוּרְקְבָן טוֹחֵן, דְּאִיהוּ נָטִיל כֹּלָּא, וְשׁוֹחֵק, וּמְשַׁדֵּר לְכָל אַבְרִין. אִי אַבְרִין בְּלָא חוֹבִין, כְּגַוְונָא דְּאוֹקְמוּהָ רַבָּנָן, דְּאִית מִלִּין דִּמְעַכְּבִין יַת קָרְבָּנָא, דְּלָא נָחִית לְקַבְּלָא לֵיהּ, הַהוּא דְּשָׁדַר קוּדְשָׁא בְּרִיךְ הוּא לְקַבְּלָא דּוֹרוֹנָא דִּילֵיהּ. דְּאִית דִּמְקַבֵּל לֵיהּ קוּדְשָׁא בְּרִיךְ הוּא עַל יְדֵי אַרְיֵה, דְּאִתְּמַר בֵּיהּ וּפְנֵי אַרְיֵה אֶל הַיָּמִין לְאַרְבַּעְתָּן. וְקוּדְשָׁא בְּרִיךְ הוּא רָכִיב עֲלֵיהּ, וְנָחִית בֵּיהּ, לְקַבְּלָא הַהוּא דּוֹרוֹנָא. וְאִית דּוֹרוֹנָא דִּמְקַבֵּל לֵיהּ עַל יְדֵי שׁוֹר, דְּאִתְּמַר בֵּיהּ וּפְנֵי שׁוֹר מֵהַשְּׂמֹאל לְאַרְבַּעְתָּן.

418. The stomach is the peeled gizzard, NAMELY IT IS LIKE THE PEELED GIZZARD OF A BIRD, and the sages taught: the gizzard grinds, for it takes everything and pulverizes THE FOOD, sending it to all the parts. If the parts are without iniquities, it is as the sages taught, that there are matters that delay the sacrifice, and the one who is sent by the Holy One, blessed be He, to receive His offering, THE PEELED STOMACH MUSCLE, does not descend to accept it. For there is A GIFT that the Holy One, blessed be He, receives through the lion, about which it is said: "and they four had the face of a lion, on the right side" (Yechezkel 1:10), and the Holy One, blessed be He, rides on him, and comes down with him to receive that gift. And there is a gift that He receives through the ox, about which it is said: "And they four had the face of an ox, on the left side" (Ibid.).

419. וְאִית דּוֹרוֹנָא, דִּמְקַבֵּל עַל יְדֵי דְּנֶשֶׁר, דְּאִתְּמַר בֵּיהּ וּפְנֵי נֶשֶׁר

לְאַרְבַּעְתָּן. דְּאִינּוּן שְׁתֵּי תוֹרִים, אוֹ שְׁנֵי בְּנֵי יוֹנָה. וְאִית דּוֹרוֹנָא,
דִּמְקַבֵּל לֵיהּ ע"י דְּאָדָם דִּכְתִּיב בֵּיהּ, אָדָם כִּי יַקְרִיב מִכֶּם קָרְבָּן לַיְיָ.
בְּדִיּוּקְנָא דְּהַהוּא דְּאִתְּמַר בֵּיהּ. וּדְמוּת פְּנֵיהֶם פְּנֵי אָדָם. יְדֹנ"ד נָחִית
עֲלַיְיהוּ, לְקַבְּלָא דּוֹרוֹנָא.

419. And there is a gift that He receives through the eagle, about which it is written: "the four also had the face of an eagle" (Yechezkel 1:10), and they are "two turtledoves or two young pigeons" (Vayikra 5:7). And there is a gift that He receives by man, about whom it is written: "If any man of you bring an offering to Hashem" (Vayikra 1:2), in the form of the same one about whom it is written: "As for the likeness of their faces, they had the face of a man" (Yechezkel 1:10). THE EXPLANATION HERE IS THAT THE FOUR LIVING CREATURES ARE THE SECRET OF THE FOUR LETTERS YUD HEI VAV HEI, LION AND OX BEING YUD-HEI, AND EAGLE AND MAN BEING VAV-HEI. For Yud Hei Vav Hei descends on them to receive the sacrifice, WHICH IS THE SECRET OF THE FOUR LIVING CREATURES.

420. וְאִית חֵיוָן טִבְעִיוֹת, מְמֻנָּן עַל גּוּפִין, דְּאִינּוּן מֵאַרְבַּע יְסוֹדִין,
וְאִינּוּן דַּכְיָין. וּלְקַבְלַיְיהוּ אַרְבַּע חֵיוָן דּוֹרְסִין, מִסְאֲבִין, מְמֻנָּן עַל ד'
מְרִירָן, דְּאִינּוּן: מָרָה חִוָּורָא, מָרָה סוּמָקָא, מָרָה יְרוֹקָא, מָרָה אוּכָמָא.

420. And there are natural living creatures NAMELY ANGELS appointed over bodies that are of the four elements: FIRE, WIND, WATER AND EARTH, and they are pure. Corresponding to them are four living creatures of prey, NAMELY THE ANGELS OF DESTRUCTION, who, being impure, are appointed over the four galls, namely: white gall, red gall, green gall, and black gall, WHO ARE DEMONS, FOR ALL TEMPERATURE IN EVERY ILLNESS COMES FROM THE GALL.

421. וְאִית חֵיוָן שְׁכְלִיּוֹת, דְּסַחֲרִין לְכֻרְסַיָּיא. וְאִית לְעֵילָּא מִנַּיְיהוּ,
וּגְבוֹהִים עֲלֵיהֶם, וְאִינּוּן חֵיוָן אֱלָהִיּוֹת, מִסִּטְרָא דִּקְדוּשָׁה. וְאִית חֵיוָן
דְּסִטְרָא אַחֲרָא. וְאִתְקְרִיאוּ אֱלֹהִים אֲחֵרִים. וְאֱלָהִיּוֹת דְּקוּדְשָׁא, אֱלֹהִים
חַיִּים. וְאִלֵּין אֱלָהִיּוֹת דִּקְדוּשָׁה, אִתְקְרִיאוּ אֱלֹהֵי הָאֱלָהִיּוֹת, וְעָלַת עַל
כֹּלָּא, אֵל אָדוֹן עַל כָּל הַמַּעֲשִׂים. וְכָל זִינָא אָזִיל לְזִינֵיהּ. וּבְגִין דְּאִית

אֱלֹהִים אֲחֵרִים, אָמַר עָלַיְיהוּ, זוֹבֵחַ לָאֱלֹהִים יָחֳרָם בִּלְתִּי לַיְדֹוָ״ד לְבַדּוֹ. בְּגִין דְּלָא יִתְעָרֵב אֱלֹהִים חַיִּים עִם אֱלֹהִים אֲחֵרִים.

עד כאן רעיא מהימנא

421. And there are mental living creatures, NAMELY: THE FOUR ANGELS MICHAEL, GABRIEL, URIEL AND RAPHAEL, who surround the Throne, WHICH IS MALCHUT. And above them and higher than they are the divine living creatures from the side of holiness, NAMELY CHESED, GVURAH, TIFERET AND MALCHUT OF ZEIR ANPIN. There are also the living creatures of the Other Side, and they are called other Elohim, while the divine living creatures of holiness are CALLED "living Elohim." And those divine living creatures of holiness are called "Elohim of divinity," and the Cause of all Causes, "El, Master over all works." A kind is drawn to its own kind and so, since there are other Elohim, it is said about them: "He that sacrifices to any Elohim, save to Hashem only, he shall be utterly destroyed" (Shemot 22:19). And this is so that the living Elohim should not be mingled with the other Elohim.

End of Ra'aya Meheimna

A Synopsis
The grinding of the stomach is likened to the distribution of the offering.

422. אִצְטוֹמְכָא דָּא, נָטִיל וְשָׁחִיק, וּמְשַׁדֵּר לְכָל סִטְרִין דִּלְתַתָּא, וּמִנֵּיהּ אִתְזָנוּ תַתָּאֵי. מֵאִינּוּן שָׁתִין שְׁמָרִים לְתַתָּא, כָּל אִינּוּן רוּחִין וְסִטְרִין אַחֲרָנִין דְּאִתְזָנוּ בְּלֵילְיָא, מֵאִינּוּן אֵבָרִים וּפְדָרִים. וּשְׁאַר נַטְלִין כָּל שַׁיְיפִין, וְנָטִיל כֹּלָא כָּבֵד, וְקָרִיב לַלֵּב, כְּמָה דְּאִתְּמַר. וְדָא אִיהוּ דִּכְתִיב, וּפְנֵי אַרְיֵה אֶל הַיָּמִין. וְעַל דָּא אִתְחֲזֵי עַל מַדְבְּחָא, כְּגַוְונָא דְּאַרְיֵה אָכִיל קָרְבְּנִין. מִכָּאן וּלְהָלְאָה כָּל שְׁאַר שַׁיְיפִין, בְּרָזָא דְּגוּפָא כְּגַוְונָא דִּלְעֵילָא.

422. And the stomach takes and grinds and distributes in all directions below, NAMELY TO THE PARTS OF THE BODY, and from it are nourished the lower beings. And from those dregs all those spirits and other parties who

take their nourishment at night drink below, from those parts and fats THAT
ARE BURNT ON THE ALTAR AT NIGHT. And the remainder is taken by the
other parts, the liver taking everything and sacrificing to the heart, as we
have learned, and this is what is written: "...the face of a lion, on the right
side" (Yechezkel 1:10). Thus there appears on the altar a lion-like image
that devours the sacrifices. From here on all the other parts are in the secret
of the body on the same pattern as above.

A Synopsis

Again Moses uses the organs of the body as a metaphor for
sacrifice, the distribution of nourishment, and the acquisition of
wisdom, understanding and knowledge.

רעיא מהימנא

423. אָמַר רַעְיָא מְהֵימָנָא, בּוּצִינָא קַדִּישָׁא, וַדַּאי אִצְטוֹמְכָא בְּקַדְמֵיתָא
נָטִיל כֹּלָּא, עַד שִׁית שַׁעְתִּין, וְאוֹפֶה. קַרְקְבָן, אִיהוּ אוֹפֶה. וְרֵיאָה, אִיהִי
מַשְׁקֶה. לִבָּא מַלְכָּא. וְאִינּוּן תְּרֵין, אִינּוּן וַדַּאי אוֹפֶה וּמַשְׁקֶה, לְמֵיהַב
לְמַלְכָּא, מִשַּׁפִּירוּ דְּכָל מַאֲכָלִין וּמַשְׁקִין, רֵישָׁא דְּכֻלְּהוּ, מִבְחַר לְכֻלְּהוּ.
וְהַיְינוּ דִּכְתִּיב, אָרִיתִי מוֹרִי עִם בְּשָׂמִי אָכַלְתִּי יַעְרִי עִם דִּבְשִׁי שָׁתִיתִי
יֵינִי עִם חֲלָבִי. לְבָתַר, אִכְלוּ רֵעִים, שְׁאָר אֵבָרִים, דְּאִינּוּן חֵילִין
וּמַשְׁרְיָין דְּמַלְכָּא, דְּפָלִיג לוֹן מְזוֹנָא, ע״י שַׂר הָאוֹפִים. שְׁתוּ וְשִׁכְרוּ
דּוֹדִים, ע״י שַׂר הַמַּשְׁקִים.

Ra'aya Meheimna (the Faithful Shepherd)

423. The Faithful Shepherd said TO RABBI SHIMON, Holy Luminary, it is
certain that the omasum takes everything up to the sixth hour and bakes. For
the gizzard, WHICH IS THE OMASUM, is a baker. And the lung is a butler.
The heart is the king, and these two, THE OMASUM AND THE LUNG, are
certainly the baker and the butler who give to the king of the choicest of
food and drinks, for he is the head of them all and the choicest of them all.
And this is the meaning of what is written: "I have gathered my myrrh with
my spice; I have eaten my honeycomb with my honey; I have drunk my
wine with my milk" (Shir Hashirim 5:1). And the verse continues: "Eat, O
dear ones, and drink; drink deep, loving companions" (Ibid.). THE
COMPANIONS ARE the other parts of the body, WHICH ARE the hosts and

camps of the king who distributes food to them by means of the chief baker, WHICH IS THE OMASUM, while the drink is by means of the chief butler, WHICH IS THE LUNG.

424. וְכָבֵד אִיהוּ לִימִינָא דְּב״נ. וּבְג״ד, וּפְנֵי אַרְיֵה אֶל הַיָּמִין לְאַרְבַּעְתָּן לִימִינָא דְּמַלְכָּא, דְּאִיהוּ לִבָּא. טְחוֹל, לִשְׂמָאלָא. אִלֵּין אִינוּן מִסִּטְרָא אַחֲרָא, וּפְנֵי שׁוֹר מֵהַשְׂמֹאל. מַשְׁקֵה חַמְרָא מָזוּג בְּמַיָּא לְמַלְכָּא. וְאַרְיֵה אָכִיל, דָּא כָּבֵד, כָּנִישׁ מְזוֹנָא קַמֵּי מַלְכָּא, דְּאִיהוּ לִבָּא.

424. And the liver is on the right side of man, wherefore: "And they four had the face of a lion on the right side," namely to the right of the king, which is the heart. The spleen is to the left, and they are of the Other Side. FOR THE LIVER IS SAMAEL. AND THE SPLEEN IS LILIT, AS EXPLAINED ABOVE. "And the face of an ox on the left side," refers to the pouring out of wine mixed with water before the king, FOR WINE IS OF THE LEFT SIDE. And the lion devouring THE SACRIFICES is the liver, who collects together the food, NAMELY THE PRAYER IN THE STEAD OF THE SACRIFICES, before the king, which is the heart. IT IS, THEREFORE, ON THE RIGHT, FOR EATING COMES FROM THE RIGHT AND WINE FROM THE LEFT. AND ALL THIS REFERS TO THE TIME OF EXILE.

425. וְאִית לְאַקְשׁוּיֵי עַל הַאי. אִי כָּבֵד אִיהוּ עֵשָׂו, אֵיךְ הוּא מְתַקֵּן מְזוֹנָא לְלִבָּא. אֶלָּא וַדַּאי לִבָּא אִיהוּ בְּגַוְונָא דְּיִצְחָק. כָּבֵד עֵשָׂו, דְּאִיהוּ הַצָּד צַיִד. וְיֵימָא לֵיהּ, יָקוּם אָבִי וְיֹאכַל מִצֵּיד בְּנוֹ. אִלֵּין אִינוּן צְלוֹתִין, דְּאַזְלִין וּמִתְתַּרְכִין מֵעֲנִיִּים, וְיִצְחָק בְּצַעֲרָא וּבִיגוֹנָא, דְּלָא יַכְלִין לְכַוְּונָא לִצְלוֹתָא. וּבְגִין דָּא לָא אָמַר וְיֹאכַל מִצֵּידִי, אֶלָּא וְיֹאכַל מִצֵּיד בְּנוֹ. בְּנִי בְכוֹרִי יִשְׂרָאֵל. בְּגַוְונָא דָּא, לֵית לוֹן לְיִשְׂרָאֵל מְזוֹנָא בְּגָלוּתָא, אֶלָּא ע״י אוּמִין דְּעָלְמָא.

425. But there is a difficulty here. If the liver is Esau, how does it arrange food for the heart, WHICH IS JACOB? HE ANSWERS, the heart is certainly like Isaac, NAMELY THE LEFT COLUMN, and the liver is Esau, who hunts venison, then says to him, "Let my father arise, and eat of his son's venison" (Beresheet 27:31). This refers to the prayers of the poor who are sent away

AND ARE NOT ACCEPTED ON HIGH. And Isaac suffers trouble and anguish because they do not know how to direct the prayer. This is why ESAU did not say 'eat of my venison' but "eat of his son's venison," NAMELY OF YISRAEL, AS IT IS WRITTEN: "Yisrael is My son, My firstborn" (Shemot 4:22). Likewise, Yisrael in exile have no food except through the nations of the world.

426. אֲבָל כַּד אִינוּן בְּאַרְעָא דְיִשְׂרָאֵל, מְזוֹנֵיהוֹן ע״י שְׁכִינְתָּא. וְיַהֲון תְּרֵין כַּנְפֵי רֵיאָה מַשְׁקִין אוּמָה, שַׂר הַמַּשְׁקִים. וּתְרֵין כּוּלְיָין הָאוֹפִים, דִמְבַשְׁלִין הַזֶּרַע דְּנָחִית מִן מוֹחָא, וּמְבַשְׁלִין מַיָּא דִמְקַבְּלִין מִכַּנְפֵי רֵיאָה. וּלְבָתַר דְּיֵיכוּל מַלְכָּא, דְּאִיהוּ לִבָּא, אִתְּמַר בִּתְרֵין כּוּלְיָין דִּילֵיהּ, אִכְלוּ רֵעִים. וְלִתְרֵין כַּנְפֵי רֵיאָה, שְׁתוּ וְשִׁכְרוּ דּוֹדִים.

426. But when they are in the land of Yisrael, their food is through the Shechinah, and the two wings of the lung will give drink to the nation OF YISRAEL, FOR THEY ARE the chief butler, AS ABOVE. And the two kidneys, which are the chief baker, cook the seed that descends from the brain and cook the water that they receive from the wings of the lung. And after the king, which is the heart, has eaten, it is said of its two kidneys: "Eat, O dear ones" (Shir Hashirim 5:1), and of the two wings of the lung: "and drink; drink deep, loving companions" (Ibid.).

427. דְלִבָּא אִיהוּ כָּסֵא דִין, אַרְבַּע חֵיוָן שְׁלִיחָן דִּילֵיהּ. תְּרֵין כַּנְפֵי רֵיאָה, וּתְרֵין כּוּלְיָין, דְּכַנְפֵי רֵיאָה וּפְנֵיהֶם וְכַנְפֵיהֶם פְּרוּדוֹת מִלְמָעְלָה, לְקַבְּלָא עָלַיְיהוּ מַלְכָּא, דְּאִיהוּ רוּחַ חָכְמָה וּבִינָה רוּחַ עֵצָה וּגְבוּרָה רוּחַ דַּעַת וְיִרְאַת יְיָ׳. דְּיָתִיב עַל כֻּרְסְיָיא, דְּאִיהוּ לִבָּא, דְּכָל אִינוּן דְּפִיקִין מִתְנַהֲגִין אֲבַתְרֵיהּ, כְּחַיָּילִין בָּתַר מַלְכֵיהוֹן.

427. For the heart is the Throne of Judgment, and the four living creatures that are its messengers are the two wings of the lung and the two kidneys, NAMELY, CHESED, GVURAH, NETZACH AND HOD, for the wings of the lung ARE THE SECRET OF "Thus were their faces: and their wings were divided upwards" (Yechezkel 1:11) to welcome the King, which is "the spirit of wisdom and understanding, the spirit of counsel and might, the spirit of knowledge and of the fear of Hashem" (Yeshayah 11:2), for it is He

who sits on the Throne, which is the heart, WHICH IS THE THRONE OF JUDGMENT, and all the pulse beats follow after it as soldiers after their king.

428. וְרוּחָא דְּנָשִׁיב מִכַּנְפֵי רֵיאָה, נָשִׁיב עַל תְּרֵי נוּקְבֵי חוֹטָמָא. וְאִיהוּ קָרִיר וּצְנִינָא מִשְּׂמָאלָא. וְחָם מִיְּמִינָא. וּמִסִּטְרָא דְּמוֹחָא דְּאִיהוּ כֻּרְסְיָיא דְּרַחֲמֵי, אִיהוּ רוּחַ קַר לִימִינָא, דְּחֶסֶד. וְחָם מִשְּׂמָאלָא דִּגְבוּרָה, דְּתַמָּן לִבָּא. וּמוֹחָא מָזִיג בֵּיהּ, בְּאֶמְצָעִיתָא דְּתַרְוַויְיהוּ. אוֹף הָכִי לִבָּא מָזִיג, מִקּוֹר וָחוֹם. וּמוֹחָא אוֹף הָכִי, דִּמְקַבְּלִין דֵּין מִדֵּין.

428. And the wind that blows from the wings of the lung blows through the two nostrils of the nose, and it is cold and chilled on the left and warm on the right. And from the point of view of the brain, which is the Throne of Mercy, the cold wind is to the right, which is Chesed, and the warm is to the left, which is Gvurah, for that is where the heart is. And the brain is tempered between the two of them, THE RIGHT AND THE LEFT, and so the heart is blended of cold and hot, NAMELY BY MEANS OF THE WIND OF THE WINGS OF THE LUNG THAT BLOWS ON IT, and the brain also IS BLENDED OF COLD AND HOT, FOR THE BRAIN AND THE HEART receive from each other.

429. וּשְׂמָרִים דְּכֹלָּא, נָטִיל טְחוֹל, וּמַשְׁרְיָין דִּילֵיהּ, דְּאִינּוּן עֲבָדִים וּשְׁפָחוֹת, דְּאָמַר עֲלַיְיהוּ שְׁלֹמֹה, קָנִיתִי לִי עֲבָדִים וּשְׁפָחוֹת. תְּרֵין כֻּולְיָין אִתְקְרִיאוּ אִשִּׁים, עַל שֵׁם אִשִּׁים דִּלְעֵילָּא, דְּאִתְּמַר בְּהוּ אִשֵּׁי יְיָ' וְנַחֲלָתוֹ יֹאכֵלוּן.

429. And the spleen, with its camps, which are the bondmen and bondwoman, takes the dregs of everything. And Solomon said about them: "I acquired menservants and maidservants" (Kohelet 2:7). The two kidneys are called 'fire-offerings', named after the heavenly fire-offerings, about which it is said: "the offerings of Hashem made by fire, and His dues shall they eat" (Devarim 18:1).

430. וּבַקָּנֶה שִׁית עִזְקָאן, דְּעֲלַיְיהוּ אִתְּמַר, הָבוּ לַייָ' בְּנֵי אֵלִים. דִּבְהוֹן סָלִיק קָלָא, דְּאִתְפְּלִיג לוֹ' קָלִין דִּשְׁכִינְתָּא. וּשְׁבִיעָאָה סָלִיק לְפוּמָא,

דְּאִיהוּ כֻּרְסְיָיא. וְשִׁית עִזְקָאן דְּקָנֶה, אִינּוּן כְּגַוְונָא דְּשִׁית דַּרְגִּין
דְּכֻרְסְיָיא דְּמַלְכָּא. וְקָנֶה אִיהוּ סֻלָּם, דְּבֵיהּ מַלְאֲכֵי אֱלֹהִים עוֹלִים
וְיוֹרְדִים בּוֹ, דְּאִינּוּן הֲבָלִים סַלְקִין בֵּיהּ מִלְּבָּא, וְרוּחִין דַּאֲוֵירָא נַחְתִּין
בֵּיהּ בִּלְבָּא, לְקָרְרָא חֲמִימוּתָא, דְּלָא לוֹקִיד גּוּפָא.

430. And in the trachea there are six cartilage rings, about which it is said: "Ascribe to Hashem, O you mighty" (Tehilim 29:1), for ascending through them is the voice that subdivides into the six voices of the Shechinah, while the seventh ascends to the mouth, which is the Throne. And the six cartilage rings of the trachea are like the six steps of the King's Throne, WHICH IS THE MOUTH, and the trachea is a ladder with "the angels of Elohim ascending and descending on it" (Beresheet 28:12), FOR THE ANGELS OF ELOHIM are the vapors that ascend from the heart, while the spirits of air descend into the heart to cool its heat, so that it should not burn the body up.

431. וְכַד רוּחָא נָחִית, נָחִית בְּכַמָּה רוּחִין, כְּמַלְכָּא עִם חֵילֵיהּ. וְכַנְפֵי
רֵיאָה מְקַבְּלִין לְרוּחָא, דְּאִיהוּ מַלְכָּא עָלַיְיהוּ, כְּמָה דַּאֲמֵינָא. וּפְנֵיהֶם
וְכַנְפֵיהֶם פְּרֻדוֹת, וְהָיוּ הַכְּרוּבִים פּוֹרְשֵׂי כְנָפַיִם לְמַעְלָה.

431. And when the breath descends, it does so in a number of breaths, like a king with his soldiers. And the wings of the lung welcome the breath which is as a king over them, as I have noted: "Thus were their faces; and their wings were divided upward," THIS BEING IN ORDER TO WELCOME THE KING OVER THEM, AND ALSO: "And the Cherubs shall stretch out their wings on high" (Shemot 25:20).

432. אִי זַכָּאן אַבְרִין דְּבַר נָשׁ בְּפִקּוּדִין דְּמַלְכָּא עִלָּאָה דְּאִיהוּ רוּחַ
הַקֹּדֶשׁ, נָחִית בְּסֻלָּם, דְּאִיהוּ גָרוֹן, בְּכַמָּה רוּחִין קַדִּישִׁין, דְּאִתְּמַר
עָלַיְיהוּ, עוֹשֶׂה מַלְאָכָיו רוּחוֹת וְסַלְקִין לָקֳבֵל אִלֵּין הֲבָלִים דְּלִבָּא,
דְּאִתְּמַר עָלַיְיהוּ, מְשָׁרְתָיו אֵשׁ לוֹהֵט. וַעֲלַיְיהוּ אִתְּמַר קוֹל יְדֹנָ"ד חוֹצֵב
לַהֲבוֹת אֵשׁ. בְּגִין דְּלִבָּא אֲדֹנָי, דְּמִנֵּיהּ סַלְקִין לַהֲבוֹת אֵשׁ בְּפוּמָא
דְּאִיהוּ יְדֹנָ"ד, דְּנַחְתִּין עִמֵּיהּ כַּמָּה רוּחִין דִּקְדוּשָׁה, מֵאַרְבַּע אַתְוָון
יֶהֱוֶה. דְּאִתְּמַר עָלַיְיהוּ, כֹּה אָמַר יְדֹנָ"ד מֵאַרְבַּע רוּחוֹת בֹּאִי הָרוּחַ.

432. If the parts of man are meritorious in keeping the precepts of the Supernal King, who is the Holy Spirit, He descends on the ladder, which is the throat, with a number of holy spirits, about which it is said: "who makes the winds His messengers" (Tehilim 104:4). They rise, to accept the vapors that are in the heart, about which it is said: "the flames of fire His ministers" (Ibid.). And it is also said about them: "The voice of Hashem hews out flames of fire" (Tehilim 29:7), because the heart is Adonai, from whom ascend the flames of fire into the mouth, which is Yud Hei Vav Hei. For a number of spirits of holiness descend with Him, that is from the four letters Yud Hei Vav Hei, concerning which it is said: "Thus says Adonai Elohim; Come from the four winds, O breath (or: 'spirit')" (Yechezkel 37:9).

433. קָנֶ"ה, אִיהוּ קָנֶה חָכְמָה קָנֵה בִינָה, דְּאִינּוּן לִימִינָא דְּחֶסֶד, וְלִשְׂמָאלָא דִּגְבוּרָה. תִּפְאֶרֶת, סֻלָּם, בְּאֶמְצָעִיתָא, בְּגוּפָא כָּלִיל תְּרֵין דְּרוֹעִין, וְגוּף וּבְרִית, וּתְרֵין שׁוֹקִין. לָקֳבֵל שִׁית עִזְקָאן דְּקָנֶה.

433. The trachea (Heb. *kaneh*) is "Get (Heb. *k'neh*) wisdom, get understanding (Heb. *Binah*)" (Mishlei 4:5), for they are to the right OF THE TRACHEA, which is Chesed, THIS BEING THE SECRET OF "GET WISDOM," and to the left OF THE TRACHEA, which is Gvurah, THIS BEING THE SECRET OF "GET UNDERSTANDING." Tiferet is in the middle OF THE TRACHEA, and is a ladder AND THE SECRET OF DA'AT. And the body has SIX EXTREMITIES, NAMELY: The two arms WHICH ARE CHESED AND GVURAH, the torso and the member of covenant WHICH ARE TIFERET AND YESOD, and the two legs WHICH ARE NETZACH AND HOD. AND THE SIX EXTREMITIES OF THE BODY parallel the six cartilage rings of the trachea.

434. וְכַד נָחִית יְדֹוָ"ד לְלִבָּא, לְגַבֵּי אֲדֹנָ"י, מִתְחַבְּרִין דִּינָא בְּרַחֲמֵי בְּלִבָּא. דְּאִיהוּ יְאֲהדֹוָנָהי. וְכַד סָלִיק אֲדֹנָי לְפוּמָא, דַּאֲדֹנָי שְׂפָתַי תִּפְתָּח, לְקַבְּלָא יְהֹוָה בְּפוּמָא, לְאִתְחַבְּרָא תַּמָּן תְּרֵין שְׁמָהָן בְּחִבּוּרָא חֲדָא, יְאֲדֹוָנָדי, כְּגַוְונָא דְּמִתְחַבְּרָאן בְּלִבָּא. וּבְגִין דָּא אוּקְמוּהָ מָארֵי מַתְנִיתִין, מִי שֶׁאֵין תּוֹכוֹ כְּבָרוֹ אַל יִכָּנֵס לְבֵית הַמִּדְרָשׁ, אִי לֵית לוֹן פּוּמָא וְלִבָּא שָׁוִין.

עַד כָּאן רַעְיָא מְהֵימְנָא

434. And when Yud Hei Vav Hei descends to the heart, to Adonai, Judgment joins with Mercy in the heart, making: Yud-Aleph-Hei-Dalet-Vav Nun-Hei-Yud. And when Adonai ascends to the mouth at "Adonai, open my lips" (Tehilim 51:17) to welcome Yud Hei Vav Hei in the mouth, the two names become there one union, namely: Yud-Aleph-Hei-Dalet-Vav-Nun-Hei-Yud, just as they were combined in the heart. For this reason the sages of the Mishnah taught: 'No one whose inside does not correspond to his exterior may enter the study house', namely who does not have in his mouth the same as in his heart. FOR JUST AS THERE IS A UNIFICATION OF YUD HEI VAV HEI AND ADONAI IN THE HEART, THERE WILL ALSO BE A UNIFICATION OF YUD HEI VAV HEI AND ADONAI IN THE MOUTH.

End of Ra'aya Meheimna (the Faithful Shepherd)

A Synopsis
The six rings of cartilage in the trachea and the air and voice that blow through them are likened to the functions of the Shofar.

435. קָנֶה שִׁית עַזְקָאן בְּקָנֶה, מִתְחַבְּרָאן כַּחֲדָא, וְאִינּוּן אִקְרוּן בְּנֵי אֵלִים, מַפְּקֵי רוּחָא לְנַשְׁבָא עַל עָלְמָא. וְאַתְיָין מִסִּטְרָא דִּגְבוּרָה. וְכַד אִינּוּן מִתְחַבְּרָן כַּחֲדָא, אִינּוּן כְּגַוְונָא דְּשׁוֹפָר. וְאִלֵּין אִקְרוּ שׁוֹפָר, שׁוֹפָר שֶׁל אַיִל שֶׁל יִצְחָק. אֵלִים בְּנֵי בָשָׁן, הָבוּ לַיְיָ' בְּנֵי אֵלִים. אֵלִים דְּיִצְחָק, וּמַפְּקִין רוּחָא וְקָלָא. וְהַהוּא קָלָא נָפִיק, וְאַרְעָא בְּעֲבֵי מִטְרָא, וְאִשְׁתְּמַע לִבְרַיְיתָא לְבַר. וע"ד כְּתִיב, וְרַעַם גְּבוּרֹתָיו מִי יִתְבּוֹנָן. דְּוַדַּאי מִסִּטְרָא דִּגְבוּרָה קָא אַתְיָין. וּבְגִין דָּא אֵל הַכָּבוֹד הִרְעִים יְיָ' עַל מַיִם רַבִּים. אֵל הַכָּבוֹד רוֹעֵם לָא כְּתִיב, אֶלָּא אֵל הַכָּבוֹד הִרְעִים, עַל יְדָא דִּבְנֵי אֵלִים. וְלֵית מַאן דְּיָדַע בְּשִׁבְחָא דְּהַאי קָלָא, הה"ד מִי יִתְבּוֹנָן.

435. The six cartilage rings of the trachea are joined together, and they are called "O you mighty (Heb. *elim*)" (Tehilim 29:1). And they give forth a wind to blow over the world, and they come from the side of Gvurah, and when they join together they are like a Shofar, WHICH IS THE SECRET OF BINAH, and they are called 'Shofar', which is the secret of the Shofar (lit. 'horn') of Isaac's ram (Heb. *ayil*). AND THEY ARE "the rams (Heb. *eilim*) of the breed of Bashan" (Devarim 32:14), as it is written: "Ascribe to Hashem,

O you mighty (*elim*)" (Tehilim 29:1), for they are the *elim* of Isaac that bring forth breath and voice. And that voice goes out and meets with rain clouds and is heard by people outside. It is thus written: "but the thunder of His mighty deeds who can understand?" (Iyov 26:14), for they certainly come from the side of Gvurah. And for this reason: "the El of glory makes to thunder, Hashem is upon many waters" (Tehilim 29:3). It is not written: "The El of glory thunders" but "The El of glory makes to thunder," THE MEANING OF WHICH IS THAT HE ACTIVATES OTHERS TO DO THE THUNDERING, namely through the mighty. And there is none that recognizes the praise of this voice, which is why it is written, "who can understand?"

A Synopsis
The Faithful Shepherd tells us that voice is made from water, wind and fire, and he explains how the heart gets understanding.

436. וּבְחִבּוּרָא קַדְמָאָה, פָּתַח רַעְיָא מְהֵימְנָא וְאָמַר, וַוי לוֹן לִבְנֵי נָשָׁא, דְּאִינּוּן אֲטִימִין לִבָּא, סְתִימִין עַיְינִין, דְּלָא יַדְעִין אֲבָרִים דְּגוּפַיְיהוּ עַל מַה אִינּוּן מִתְתַּקְנִין, דְּהָא קָנֶ"ה תְּלַת חֵילִין כְּלִילָן בֵּיהּ, חַד הֶבֶל, דְּאִיהוּ לַהַב אֵשׁ, דְּנָפִיק מִן לִבָּא וְאִתְפְּלַג לְז' הֲבָלִים, דְּאָמַר קֹהֶלֶת. תִּנְיָינָא, אַוִּיר דְּעָאל לְגַבֵּיהּ מִלְּבַר. תְּלִיתָאָה, מַיִם דְּכַנְפֵי רֵיאָה, דְּאִינּוּן דְּבוּקִים בְּקָנֶה. וּמִתְּלַת אִלֵּין אִתְעֲבִיד קוֹל, מַיִם וְרוּחַ וְאֵשׁ, וּמִתְפְּלַג כָּל חַד לְז', וְאִינּוּן ז' לְהָבִים, ז' אֲוִירוֹת, ז' נְחָלִים.

Ra'aya Meheimna (the Faithful Shepherd)

436. And in the first section, the Faithful Shepherd started by saying, Woe to those people whose hearts are closed and whose eyes are unseeing, who do not know the parts of their own body, according to what they are arranged. For the trachea is composed of three forces: a) Vapor; (Heb. *hevel*, Hei-Bet-Lamed) which is a flame; (Heb. *lahav*, Lamed-Hei-Bet) a flaming fire that issues from the heart and which is divided into seven vapors or vanities as mentioned by Kohelet; b) Air, which enters it from outside; c) Water of the wings of the lung, which are attached to the trachea. And from these three, that is from water, wind, and fire, is voice made, and each one is subdivided into seven, and they are seven flames, seven airs, and seven brooks.

437. וְכַד אַעְרְעוּ לְהָבִים דְּלִבָּא, בְּעָבֵי מִטְרָא, דְּאִינּוּן כַּנְפֵי רֵיאָה, אֹרַח קָנֵה דְּרֵיאָה. הַאי אִיהוּ וְרַעַם גְּבוּרוֹתָיו מִי יִתְבּוֹנָן. דְּבֵיהּ לֵב מֵבִין בְּבִינָה, דְּאִיהִי בְּלִבָּא לִשְׂמָאלָא, גְּבוּרָה. וְחֶסֶד לִימִינָא, מַיִם דְּכַנְפֵי רֵיאָה. וְתַמָּן חָכְמָה מוֹחָא, וּמִנֵּיהּ, מַעְיַן גַּנִּים בְּאֵר מַיִם חַיִּים וְנוֹזְלִים מִן לְבָנוֹן. דְּאִיהוּ לִבוּנָא דְּמוֹחָא, נוֹזְלִים עַל קָנֶה דְּרֵיאָה. בָּתַר דְּאִסְתַּלָּקוּ עֲנָנִים דְּבִינָה לְגַבֵּי מוֹחָא.

437. And when the flames of the heart meet with the rain clouds, which are the wings of the lung, by way of the trachea of the lung, the result is: "but the thunder of His mighty deeds who can understand?" For therein the heart understands with Binah, which is in the heart on the left, which is Gvurah. And Chesed is to the right, which is the water of the wings of the lung, and Chochmah, which is brain, is there. THAT IS TO SAY THAT CHESED AND GVURAH ASCEND AND BECOME CHOCHMAH AND BINAH. And from it comes "a fountain of gardens, a well of living waters, and streams from Lebanon" (Shir Hashirim 4:15), which is the whiteness (Heb. *lavnunit*) of the brain that flows through the trachea of the lung, after the clouds of Binah have ascended to the brain.

438. וְרָזָא דְּמִלָּה מִי זֹאת עוֹלָה מִן הַמִּדְבָּר כְּתִימְרוֹת עָשָׁן. וְדָא עָשָׁן הַמַּעֲרָכָה, דְּסָלִיק מִן לִבָּא לְמוֹחָא. דְּכָל רוּחִין דְּעָלְמָא, לָא זָזִין לֵיהּ מֵאַתְרֵיהּ. חָכְמָה: כח מ"ה. כֹּחַ: בְּלִבָּא. מָה: בְּמוֹחָא. קָנֶה: תִּפְאֶרֶת, כָּלִיל ו' סְפִירָאן. ו' דַּרְגִּין אִינּוּן לְכָרְסַיָּיא, דְּאִיהִי אִימָּא. לְנַחְתָּא חָכְמָה לְגַבָּהּ, מִן מוֹחָא לְלִבָּא, דְּבָהּ לֵב מֵבִין. וּבְגִין דָּא, קָנֶה חָכְמָה קָנֶה בִינָה. בֵּיהּ אַבָּא נָחִית. בֵּיהּ אַבָּא סָלִיק. וְהַאי אִיהוּ סֻלָּם דְּבֵיהּ עוֹלִים תְּרֵי, וְיוֹרְדִים תְּרֵי.

עד כאן רעיא מהימנא

438. And the secret of the matter is in the verse: "Who is this coming out of the wilderness like columns of smoke...?" (Shir Hashirim 3:6), for this is the smoke of the arrangement on the altar that rises from the heart to the brain, which cannot be moved from its place by all the winds in the world. THE LETTERS OF THE WORD Chochmah (Chet Caf Mem Hei) form the two

words *Koach* (Caf Chet) and *Mah* (MEM HEI), BECAUSE IT IS *Koach* (Eng. 'strength') in the heart and *Mah* (Eng. 'what') in the brain. The trachea is Tiferet and incorporates six Sfirot: CHESED, GVURAH, TIFERET, NETZACH, HOD AND YESOD, which are the six steps to the Throne, which is Ima, so that Chochmah will descend to it from the brain to the heart, for with it the heart understands. For this reason IT IS WRITTEN: "Get (Heb. *k'neh*) wisdom (Heb. *Chochmah*), get understanding (Heb. *Binah*)," for Aba, WHICH IS CHOCHMAH, descends in it, and Aba ascends in it. And this is a ladder on which two ascend and two descend, FOR ABA AND IMA ARE INCORPORATED IN EACH OTHER AND DESCEND FROM THE BRAIN TO THE HEART, AND ASCEND FROM THE HEART TO THE BRAIN.

End of Ra'aya Meheimna (the Faithful Shepherd)

A Synopsis
Rabbi Shimon says that the esophagus is the stage of offerings by fire.

439. וְשֵׁט דְּבָלַע מֵיכְלָא, וּמִתַּמָּן עָאל לְכֻלְּהוּ שַׁיְיפִין, דְּאִיהִי בְּדַרְגָּא דְּאֶשִּׁים. אֶשִּׁים אִינּוּן קְרֵבִין מִיַּד, וּבָלְעֵי וְנַטְלֵי כֹּלָּא מִגּוֹ אֶשָּׁא עִלָּאָה, דְּכָלִיל לָאֶשִּׁים. וְרָזָא דָּא, אִשֵּׁי יְיָ' וְנַחֲלָתוֹ יֹאכֵלוּן. אִלֵּין אַכְלִין וּבָלְעִין, וּשְׁאָר לָא אַכְלִין הָכִי.

439. The esophagus, that swallows the food, which enters from there all the body parts, is the level of offerings by fire. These offerings by fire draw near immediately, swallowing and taking everything from the upper fire that includes the offerings by fire. And this is the secret of the verse: "the offerings of Hashem made by fire, and His dues shall they eat" (Devarim 18:1). These OFFERINGS BY devour and swallow, but the others do not eat that way.

440. וְכָל בְּנֵי עָלְמָא לְבַר, לָא יַדְעִין אֵיךְ אַכְלִין, וְלָאו רָזָא דִּלְהוֹן, אֶלָּא הַדַּרְגִּין דִּלְגוֹ אִינּוּן יַדְעִין, וְנַטְלִין מִנַּיְיהוּ. וְשֵׁט לֵית לֵיה בְּדִיקָה מִבַּחוּץ, דְּלָא יַדְעֵי, אֶלָּא מִבִּפְנִים יַדְעֵי וְנַטְלֵי עַד דְּעָאל לְבֵי טוֹחֲנָא, וְאִשְׁתְּחִיק וְאִתְבַּשַּׁל. וְנָטִיל כֹּלָּא כָּבֵד כְּמָה דְּאִתְּמַר. מֵאִלֵּין אֶשִּׁים נָפְקֵי דַּרְגִּין, דְּאַקְדְּמֵי וְנַטְלֵי בְּקַדְמֵיתָא מִכָּבֵד, וּמַאן אִינּוּן, אִלֵּין

הַטּוֹחֲנוֹת, אַכְלֵי קָרְבְּנִין וְטַחֲנֵי. וע״ד מִדְאִתְחָרַב בֵּי מַקְדְשָׁא כְּתִיב, וּבָטְלוּ הַטּוֹחֲנוֹת כִּי מֵעָטוּ. אִלֵּין טַחֲנִין בְּקַדְמֵיתָא.

440. And all the people of the world on the outside know not how they eat nor do they know their secret, but the levels that are inside do know and they take from them. For the esophagus cannot be examined from the outside, for it cannot be recognized, but on the inside it can be known and taken until it enters the mill and is pulverized and cooked. And the liver takes everything, as we had learned, but from those offerings by fire issue forth levels that take before the liver. And what are they? They are the molar TEETH, which eat and grind the sacrifices. Therefore, since the destruction of the Temple, it is written: "and the grinders cease because they are few" (Kohelet 12:3). These are the first to grind.

441. כֵּיוָן דְּאִתְטַחֲנָן, אִינּוּן דְּשַׁלְטֵי עָלַיְיהוּ, בַּלְעֵי וְנַטְלֵי, וְאִקְרוּן וֶשֶׁ״ט. אֲמַאי. אֶלָּא וֶשֶׁט, דְּיוּקְנָא דְּוָא״ו, אִיהוּ וֶשֶׁט כָּפוּף. וּלְבָתַר, שָׁט לְמֵיכַל מִשְׁתִּיָא, חַמְרָא וּמַיָא. דִּכְתִיב שָׁטוּ הָעָם וְלָקְטוּ. מֵיכְלָא לְמֵיכַל, מִשְׁתִּיָא חַמְרָא וּמַיָא, נְסוּכָא דְּיַין, וְנִסּוּכָא דְּמַיִם.

441. Once it has been ground, those who exercise control over them swallow and receive it, and they are called 'the esophagus'. Why IS THE ESOPHAGUS (HEB. *VESHET,* VAV SHIN TET) SO CALLED? Because the shape of the Vav OF '*VESHET*' is like a bowed-over esophagus. Afterwards it wanders about (Heb. *shat,* Shin Tet), to drink wine and water, as it is written: "The people went about and gathered" (Bemidbar 11:8) food to eat and to drink wine and water, namely the libation of wine and the libation of water.

442. בְּהַאי וֶשֶׁט עָאל וְאִשְׁתְּאִיב בָּרֵיאָה, אִלֵּין שְׂרָפִים, בְּשַׁלְהוֹבִיתָא דִּלְהוֹן נַטְלֵי מִשְׁתִּיָא, וְאִקְרוּן רֵיאָה, בְּחַבּוּרָא חֲדָא, וְאִשְׁתְּאִיב כֹּלָּא בְּהוֹן. וְכָל אִלֵּין, נַטְלִין כָּל חַד וְחַד, כִּדְקָא חֲזֵי לֵיהּ. וּמִדְּחָרַב בֵּי מַקְדְּשָׁא, וּבָטְלוּ הַטּוֹחֲנוֹת כִּי מֵעָטוּ כֻּלְּהוּ. דְּאִזְעֵירוּ דִּיּוּקְנַיְיהוּ וּמְזוֹנַיְיהוּ, וְלֵית יוֹמָא דְּלֵית בֵּיהּ מְאֵרָה, אָרִים קָלֵיהּ ר״ש וְאָמַר, וַוי יְרוּשְׁלֵם קַרְתָּא קַדִּישָׁא, וַוי לְעַמָּא, דְּכָל טָבָאן אִלֵּין אַבְדִין, רַבְרְבָן

גִּיבָּרִין מְמָנָן אַזְעִירוּ דְּיוּקְנַיְיהוּ, עַל דָּא בָּכוּ חַבְרַיָּיא. אָמְרוּ, וַוי רִבִּי,
כַּד תִּסְתַּלַּק מִן עָלְמָא, מַאן יְגַלֵּה רָזִין סְתִימִין עֲמִיקִין כְּאִלֵּין, דְּלָא
אִשְׁתְּמָעוּ מִן יוֹמָא דִּשְׁלֹמֹה מַלְכָּא, וְעַד הַשְׁתָּא. זַכָּאָה דָּרָא דְּשַׁמְעִין
מִלִּין אִלֵּין, וְזַכָּאָה דָּרָא דְּאַנְתְּ בְּגַוַּוּיה, וַוי לְדָרָא דְּיִשְׁתַּאֲרוּן יַתְמִין
מִנָּךְ.

442. Those Serafim with their flames enter through the esophagus and are drawn into the lung, where they take a drink, and they are called 'lung', in one union WITH THE LUNG and everything is absorbed into them. And each one of them takes as befits him. And since the destruction of the Temple, "and the grinders ceased because they were few, all of them." For their form and their food have been diminished, and there is no day that passes without a curse. Rabbi Shimon lifted up his voice and said: Woe to Jerusalem the holy city. Woe to the people that has lost all this goodness, and the image of ministers, mighty men, and officials has been reduced. The friends cried about this and said, Alas, Rabbi, when you depart from the world, who will reveal to us such deep and hidden secrets that have not been heard from the days of King Solomon until now? Happy is the generation that hears such matters! Happy is the generation amongst whom you are! Woe to the generation that will be orphaned without you!

69. Seven firmaments

A Synopsis

The Faithful Shepherd lists the seven firmaments – Curtain, Firmament, Heavens, Abode, Residence, Dwelling and Skies – and tells us a little about the first three of these.

רעיא מהימנא

443. פָּתַח רַעְיָא מְהֵימָנָא וְאָמַר, וְהָא כְּתִיב, וְשִׂפְתוֹתֵינוּ שֶׁבַח כְּמֶרְחֲבֵי רָקִיעַ. וְשֶׁבַע רְקִיעִין אִינּוּן: וִילוֹן. רָקִיעַ. שְׁחָקִים. זְבוּל. מָעוֹן. מָכוֹן. עֲרָבוֹת. שְׁחָקִים. דִּבְהוֹן רֵיחַיִם דְּטוֹחֲנִים מָן לַצַּדִּיקִים לְעָתִיד לָבֹא. וְאִינּוּן אִקְרוּן שְׁחָקִים, ע"ש וְשָׁחַקְתָּ מִמֶּנָּה הָדֵק, וְאִינּוּן נֵצַח וְהוֹד, עֲלַיְיהוּ אִתְּמַר וּשְׁחָקִים יִזְּלוּ צֶדֶק, דְּאִיהִי שְׁכִינְתָּא תַּתָּאָה.

Ra'aya Meheimna (the Faithful Shepherd)

443. The Faithful Shepherd began by saying: It is written: 'Though our lips were full of praise as the expansive firmament'. And the firmaments are seven in number: Curtain, Firmament, Heavens, Abode, Residence, Dwelling, and Skies. Heavens (Heb. *Shechakim*) is so called because therein the millstones grind the mannah for the righteous, WHICH ARE YESOD AND MALCHUT THAT ARE CALLED 'RIGHTEOUS' AND 'RIGHTEOUSNESS', for the future to come, NAMELY FROM THE EMANATION OF BINAH THAT IS CALLED 'THE FUTURE TO COME'. And the basis for the name *Shchakim* is the verse: "And you shall beat (Heb. *shachakta*) some of it very small" (Shemot 30:36). And they are Netzach and Hod, about which it is said: "and let the heavens pour down righteousness" (Yeshayah 45:8), which is the lower Shechinah, NAMELY MALCHUT, WHICH IS CALLED 'RIGHTEOUSNESS', TO WHICH BOUNTY POURS DOWN FROM HEAVENS.

444. וִילוֹן, דְּבֵיהּ מַכְנִיס עַרְבִית וּמוֹצִיא שַׁחֲרִית. רָקִיעַ, אִיהוּ יְסוֹד. דְּבֵיהּ נַהֲרִין שִׁמְשָׁא וְסִהֲרָא, דְּאִיהוּ עַמּוּדָא דְּאֶמְצָעִיתָא וּשְׁכִינְתָּא תַּתָּאָה. הה"ד, וַיִּתֵּן אוֹתָם אֱלֹהִים בִּרְקִיעַ הַשָּׁמַיִם לְהָאִיר עַל הָאָרֶץ. וְצַדִּיק אוֹת, בֵּין נֵצַח וְהוֹד. וְעֵדוּת, בֵּין תִּפְאֶרֶת וּמַלְכוּת.

444. THE FIRST FIRMAMENT, WHICH IS MALCHUT, IS CALLED 'Curtain', for it pours PLENTY into it in the evening, and brings out, THAT IS, BESTOWS, in the morning, THIS BEING THE TIME FOR EMANATING. AND THE SECOND ONE TO BE CALLED 'a Firmament' is Yesod, for in it the sun and the moon give light, for they are the Central Column, NAMELY TIFERET, and the lower Shechinah, NAMELY MALCHUT. THAT IS TO SAY THAT YESOD UNITES ZEIR ANPIN AND MALCHUT WITH EACH OTHER, AND BOTH OF THEM ILLUMINATE THROUGH IT, as it is written: "And Elohim set them in the firmament of the heaven to give light upon the earth" (Beresheet 1:17). And the Righteous, WHICH IS YESOD, IS CALLED sign when uniting Netzach and Hod, and IS CALLED testimony when uniting Tiferet and Malchut.

70. Netzach and Hod

A Synopsis

We are told that Netzach and Hod are called 'Heavens' because they are two halves of one body that must not be separated. The Faithful Shepherd talks about Netzach and Hod in connection with the sin of the Tree of Knowledge of Good and Evil, and in connection with grapes and wine. He explains why Netzach and Hod grind up the manna for the Righteous, Yesod, that is between them; he also says that Netzach and Hod are cherubim.

445. נֶצַח וְהוֹד תְּרֵין פַּלְגֵי גּוּפָא אִינּוּן, כְּגַוְונָא דִּתְרֵין תְּאוֹמִים. וּבְגִין דָּא אִתְקְרִיאוּ שְׁחָקִים. תַּרְוַוייהוּ כַּחֲדָא ו"ו אִינּוּן, מִן וֶשֶׁט, מִסִּטְרָא דִּשְׂמָאלָא. וְאִינּוּן תְּרֵין טוֹחֲנוֹת, מִסִּטְרָא דִּימִינָא.

445. Netzach and Hod are the two halves of ONE body, like two twins, which is why they are called 'Heavens'. The two of them together are Vav Vav of *veshet* (Eng. 'esophagus'), from the aspect of the left, and they are the two molar teeth from the aspect of the right.

446. וַיִּקַּח מֹשֶׁה אֶת עַצְמוֹת יוֹסֵף עִמּוֹ. עַצְמוֹת צַדִּיק יְסוֹד עָלְמִין, דַּרְגָּא דְּיוֹסֵף הַצַּדִּיק. וַעֲלַיְיהוּ אִתְּמַר, אֶת קָרְבָּנִי לַחְמִי לְאִשַּׁי. וְלֵית לֶחֶם, אֶלָּא אוֹרַיְיתָא, לְכוּ לַחֲמוּ בְּלַחְמִי. וְאִינּוּן: אַשְׁכְּלוֹת דְּצַדִּיק. וְצַדִּיק, עֵץ פְּרִי. וּבְגִינֵיהּ אִתְּמַר, וַיִּשָּׂאֻהוּ בַמּוֹט בִּשְׁנָיִם. וַאֲמַאי בַמּוֹט. בְּגִין דְּלָא הֲוָה תַּמָּן צַדִּיק.

446. "And Moses took the bones of Joseph with him" (Shemot 13:19), that is the bones of "the righteous is an everlasting foundation" (Mishlei 10:25), which is the level of Joseph the Righteous. And about them, ABOUT NETZACH AND HOD, it is said: "My offering, the provision of my sacrifices (lit. 'bread') made by fire" (Bemidbar 28:2). And by bread is meant Torah, NAMELY NETZACH AND HOD WHO FIGHT (HEB. *NILCHAMIM*) EACH OTHER BY MEANS OF GRINDING. And it is said about them: "Come, eat (Heb. *lachamu*) of my bread (Heb. *lachmi*)" (Mishlei 9:5). And they, NETZACH AND HOD, are the bunches OF GRAPES THAT ARE BESTOWED by the Righteous, WHICH IS YESOD. And the Righteous, WHICH IS YESOD, is

called 'a fruit-tree', and for it is it said: "And they bore it upon a pole (Heb. *mot*) between two" (Bemidbar 13:23). And why on a pole? WHY DOES IT NOT SAY 'AND THEY BORE IT UPON WOOD (A TREE)?' It is because the Righteous, WHO IS CALLED 'TREE', was not there. FOR YESOD, WHICH IS THE CENTRAL COLUMN, DID NOT UNITE THE TWO BUNCHES OF GRAPES, WHICH ARE NETZACH AND HOD, SO THAT THEY MIGHT BE INCLUDED IN EACH OTHER, AND THEY THEREFORE BORE IT ON A POLE BETWEEN TWO, WITHOUT BECOMING A PART IN THE RIGHTEOUS.

447. וּבְגִינַיְיהוּ אִתְּמַר בֵּיהּ, לֹא יִתֵּן לְעוֹלָם מוֹט לַצַּדִּיק, דְּאִיהוּ עֵץ, דְּאִתְּמַר בֵּיהּ, הֲיֵשׁ בָּהּ עֵץ אִם אַיִן. אַעְקְרוּ עֵץ דְּאִיהוּ צַדִּיק, אִלֵּין דְּאַפִּיקוּ שׁוּם בִּישׁ עַל אַרְעָא, וְגָרְמוּ, וַיִּשָׂאוּהוּ בַמּוֹט בִּשְׁנָיִם, ו' ו'.

447. And because NETZACH AND HOD MUST NOT BE SEPARATED, it is said ABOUT THE RIGHTEOUS, WHICH IS YESOD: "he shall never suffer the righteous to be moved (Heb. *mot*)" (Tehilim 55:23). THAT IS, YESOD WILL NEVER CEASE UNITING NETZACH AND HOD, and it is a tree, about which it is said: "Whether there is a tree in it or not" (Bemidbar 13:20). But those who spread an evil report of the land uprooted this tree, the Righteous, WHICH IS YESOD, and gave rise TO "And they bore it upon a pole between two." AND THE TWO ARE NETZACH AND HOD, IN THE ASPECTS OF Vav Vav WITHOUT THE UNIFICATION OF YESOD, FOR THE RIGHTEOUS IS COLLAPSED (HEB. *MOT*) BECAUSE THEY SPREAD AN EVIL REPORT ON THE LAND.

448. עֲלַיְיהוּ אִתְּמַר, סָחֲטָה עֲנָבִים. צַדִּיק יְסוֹד, בֵּיהּ סוֹד, דְּאִיהוּ יַיִן הַמְשׁוּמָּר בַּעֲנָבָיו מִשֵּׁשֶׁת יְמֵי בְרֵאשִׁית. דְּאִינּוּן ו' דַּרְגִּין דְּאָת ו'. וְאִינּוּן שְׂרָפִים, ו' ו', שֵׁשׁ כְּנָפַיִם לְאֶחָד. מִשְׂמָאלָא. וְאִינּוּן אַפִּיקוּ מַיִם מִימִינָא. וְצָחִין בְּשַׁלְהוֹבִיתָא דִּלְהוֹן מִסִּטְרָא דִּגְבוּרָה, וְשׁוֹאֲבִין מִסִּטְרָא דְּחֶסֶד.

448. And about NETZACH AND HOD it was said, IN CONNECTION WITH THE SIN OF THE TREE OF KNOWLEDGE OF GOOD AND EVIL, THAT EVE squeezed grapes AND GAVE TO HIM. FOR NETZACH AND HOD ARE CALLED 'BUNCHES OF GRAPES', AND GRAPES ARE THE SECRET OF THE

ILLUMINATION OF CHOCHMAH THAT IS ON THE LEFT, AND IT IS FORBIDDEN TO DRAW IT, FROM ABOVE DOWNWARDS, AND ITS BEING DRAWN DOWN FROM ABOVE IS COMPARED TO THE SQUEEZING OF GRAPES, WHICH IS THE SECRET OF THE SIN OF THE TREE OF KNOWLEDGE OF GOOD AND EVIL. The Righteous, which is Yesod, contains a secret (Heb. *sod*), FOR IN 'YESOD' THERE ARE THE LETTERS OF 'SOD'. This is the wine preserved with its grapes from the Six Days of Creation, FOR YESOD GUARDS THE GRAPES WHICH ARE THE SECRET OF THE ILLUMINATION OF CHOCHMAH, SO THAT THEY WOULD NOT BE SQUEEZED, NAMELY THAT IT SHOULD NOT BE DRAWN DOWN FROM ABOVE, BUT ONLY UPWARDS FROM BELOW. AND THE SIX DAYS OF CREATION ARE the six levels OF CHESED, GVURAH, TIFERET, NETZACH, HOD AND YESOD, of the letter Vav, WHICH IS TIFERET, THE CENTRAL COLUMN, WHICH IS TO SAY THAT YESOD RECEIVES ITS POWER OF PROTECTION FROM IT. And they are CALLED 'Seraphim' when they are Vav Vav WITHOUT UNITY, as it is written: "Serafim…each one had six wings (lit. 'six wings, six wings for each')" (Yeshayah 6:2). THAT IS, VAV (= SIX) IS MENTIONED TWICE. AND THEY ARE CALLED 'SERAFIM' FROM THE ASPECT of the left THAT IS IN THEM, and they extract water from the aspect of the right THAT IS IN THEM. And they are thirsty because of the flame that is in them from the side of Gvurah, NAMELY FROM THE LEFT SIDE, and they draw WATER from the side of Chesed.

449. וְעָלַיְיהוּ אִתְּמַר, עוֹשֶׂה מַלְאָכָיו רוּחוֹת, מִסִּטְרָא דְּעַמּוּדָא דְּאֶמְצָעִיתָא, דְּנַשְׁבִין עַל לִבָּא, דְּאִיהוּ דַּרְגָּא עֲשִׂירָאָה בְּרוּחָא דְּקוּדְשָׁא, דְּאִיהוּ בֵּינַיְיהוּ. וְאִיהוּ ו', אוֹת בְּצָבָא דִּילֵיהּ, כָּלִיל ו' פִּרְקִין דִּתְרֵין שׁוֹקִין, דִּכְתִיב בְּהוּ שׁוֹקָיו עַמּוּדֵי שֵׁשׁ, וְדָא צַדִּיק אוֹת בְּרִית.

449. About NETZACH AND HOD it is said: "who makes the winds (spirits) His messengers" (Tehilim 104:4), namely from the side of the Central Column, WHICH IS ZEIR ANPIN. THAT IS TO SAY THAT THEY ARE THE WINDS THAT ARE DRAWN DOWN FROM ZEIR ANPIN TO WITHIN THE LOBES OF THE LUNG that blow on the heart, which is the tenth level of the Holy Spirit, NAMELY MALCHUT, which is between them, NAMELY BETWEEN NETZACH AND HOD. And this is YESOD, WHICH IS the letter Vav, which is a letter in His hosts that includes the six joints of the two legs, WHICH ARE NETZACH AND HOD, EACH ONE OF WHICH HAS THREE

JOINTS, BECAUSE IT IS THE CENTRAL COLUMN. For it is written about them: "His legs are as pillars of marble (Heb. *shesh*)" (Shir Hashirim 5:15). And this is the Righteous, the sign of the covenant THAT INCLUDES THE SIX (HEB. *SHESH*) OF NETZACH AND HOD.

450. ו' עִלָּאָה, תִּפְאֶרֶת. בֵּין שִׁית פִּרְקִין דִּתְרֵין דְּרוֹעִין. וּבְגִין דָּא, ו' ו', גּוּף וּבְרִית חַשְׁבֵּינָן חַד. וְאִינּוּן פּוֹרְשֵׂי כְנָפַיִם לְמַעְלָה, לְקַבֵּל ו' עִלָּאָה עֲלַיְיהוּ. וּמִסִּטְרֵיה, אִתְקְרִיאוּ נְבִיאֵי הָאֱמֶת. סוֹכְכִים בְּכַנְפֵיהֶם עַל בְּרִית, דְּאִיהוּ ו' תִּנְיָינָא, וְצַדִּיק יְסוֹד עוֹלָם. וּבְגִין דָּא, נֶצַח וְהוֹד, טוֹחֲנִים מָן לְצַדִּיקַיָּיא, דְּאִינּוּן מִסִּטְרָא דְּצַדִּיק יְסוֹד עוֹלָם, דְּאִיהוּ בֵּינַיְיהוּ. וּבְגִין דָּא אִתְקְרִיאוּ טוֹחֲנוּת.

450. The upper Vav OF THE TWO VAV'S OF THE LETTER VAV FULLY SPELLED OUT: VAV VAV, is Tiferet, BECAUSE IT IS THE CENTRAL COLUMN between the six joints of the two arms, and because of this, body and covenant, NAMELY TIFERET AND YESOD, ARE CALLED 'Vav Vav', NAMELY THE TWO VAVS OF THE LETTER VAV WRITTEN OUT IN FULL: VAV VAV, and we consider them one. And they, NETZACH AND HOD, "shall stretch out their wings on high" (Shemot 25:20) towards the heavenly Vav that is above them, NAMELY TIFERET; and from its aspect, NETZACH AND HOD are called 'the true prophets', FOR TIFERET IS CALLED 'TRUTH'. They are "overspreading...with their wings" (Ibid.) over the covenant, NAMELY YESOD, which is the second Vav, which is "the righteous is an everlasting foundation" (Mishlei 10:25). And this is why Netzach and Hod grind up the manna for the righteous who are from the side of "the righteous is an everlasting foundation," which is between them, FOR THE RIGHTEOUS, WHICH IS YESOD, IS THE CENTRAL COLUMN BETWEEN NETZACH AND HOD, AND RECEIVES FROM THE MANNA THAT THEY GRIND, and this is why NETZACH AND HOD are called 'molars'.

451. וּמִסִּטְרָא דְּוֶשֶׁט, שָׁטוּ הָעָם וְלָקְטוּ, אִינּוּן לְקוּטוֹת דְּפִסְקוֹת דְּמַתְנִיתָא. וְטָחֲנוּ בָרֵיחַיִם, מֵהָכָא, מַאן דְּאַפִּיק מִלִּין דְּאוֹרַיְיתָא, צָרִיךְ לְמִטְחַן לוֹן בְּשִׁנַּיִים, וּלְאַפָּקָא מִלִּין שְׁלֵימִין, וְאִינּוּן מִלִּין אִתְקְרִיאוּ שְׁלֵמִים. וְאוֹחֲרָנִין, דְּאִינּוּן שַׁטְיָין, דְּאַכְלִין מִלִּין בְּהַלְעָטָה, וְלָא טוֹחֲנִין

לוֹן בַּטוֹחֲנוֹת דִּלְהוֹן וּבְשִׁנֵּיהוֹן, מַה כְּתִיב בְּהוּ, הַבָּשָׂר עוֹדֶנּוּ בֵּין שִׁנֵּיהֶם וְאַף יְיָ' חָרָה בָעָם, דְּאִינוּן, מִגִּזְעָא דְּמַאן דְּאָמַר הַלְעִיטֵנִי נָא. וְנֶצַח וְהוֹד אִתְקְרִיאוּ כְּרוּבִים.

451. And from the side of esophagus (Heb. *veshet*, Vav Shin Tet), BEFORE WHICH THERE IS GRINDING WITH THE TEETH, IT IS SAID: "The people went about (Heb. *shatu,* Shin Tet Vav), and gathered (Heb. *laktu*) it" (Bemidbar 11:8), it being the collection (Heb. *lekutot*) of JUDGMENT decisions that is in the Mishnah. "and ground it in mills" (Ibid.). It follows that whoever brings out OF HIS MOUTH words of Torah, must grind them in his teeth, NAMELY CLARIFY THEM WELL, in order to express complete words, and these words are called 'complete'. But as for the other WORDS that are scorned, these words are swallowed when eaten greedily, without being ground in their molars and their teeth, NAMELY THEY DO NOT CLARIFY FULLY THE WORDS OF THE TORAH THAT THEY BRING OUT OF THEIR MOUTHS; about them it is written: "And while the meat was yet between their teeth... the wrath of Hashem was inflamed against the people" (Bemidbar 11:33). This is because THEY COME from the root of him, who said: "Give me to swallow, I pray you..." (Beresheet 25:30), NAMELY THE WICKED ESAU. And Netzach and Hod are called 'Cherubs', WHENCE THE VERSE: "AND THE CHERUBS SHALL STRETCH OUT THEIR WINGS ON HIGH," WHICH REFERS TO NETZACH AND HOD, AS EXPLAINED IN THE PRECEDING PARAGRAPH.

71. Said Shabbat: You have given me no mate

A Synopsis
Even as the ninth Sfirah, Yesod, is not paired with another Sfirah,
the Shabbat has no partner.

452. וּתְמַנְיָא אִינּוּן: חָכְמָה, בִּינָה, גְּדוּלָה, גְּבוּרָה, תִּפְאֶרֶת, מַלְכוּת, נֶצַח, הוֹד, צַדִּיק, עֲטָרָה עַל רֵישֵׁיהּ. דְּאִיהוּ לֵית לֵיהּ זוּג. וּמַאי עֲטָרָה דִּילֵיהּ. כ"ע. וּבְגִינֵיהּ אוֹקְמוּהָ מָארֵי מַתְנִיתִין, הָעוֹלָם הַבָּא אֵין בּוֹ לֹא אֲכִילָה וְלֹא שְׁתִיָּה אֶלָּא צַדִּיקִים יוֹשְׁבִים וְעַטְרוֹתֵיהֶם בְּרָאשֵׁיהֶם. וְהַיְינוּ דְּאוֹקְמוּהָ, אָמְרָה שַׁבָּת קַמֵּי קוּדְשָׁא בְּרִיךְ הוּא, לְכֻלְּהוּ יוֹמֵי נָתַתָּ בֶּן זוּג וְלִי לֹא נָתַתָּ בֶּן זוּג.

עד כאן רעיא מהימנא

452. There are eight SFIROT: Chochmah, Binah, Greatness, Gvurah, Tiferet, Malchut, Netzach and Hod. The Righteous, WHICH IS YESOD, has a diadem on his head, for he has no mate. What is the meaning of his diadem? It refers to the upper Keter (crown). And in respect thereof the sages of the Mishnah taught: In the World to Come there is no eating or drinking, but the righteous sit with their diadems upon their heads. And this is as they taught: Shabbat pleaded before the Holy One, blessed be He: 'To all the days You have given a partner, but to me You have given no partner.'

End of Ra'aya Meheimna (the Faithful Shepherd)

72. Ayin of Sh'ma, Dalet of Echad, the name of Ayin (= 70)

A Synopsis
Rabbi Shimon gives us the concealed meaning of the letters in the title, and his explanation teaches us about rejoicing and unity.

453. פָּתַח ר"ש וְאָמַר, שְׁמַע יִשְׂרָאֵל יְיָ' אֱלֹהֵינוּ יְיָ' אֶחָד. ע' רַבְרְבָא, ד' אוֹף הָכִי. וְסִימָנָא דָא עֵד. הַיְינוּ דִכְתִיב, עַד יְיָ' בָּכֶם. אִשְׁתָּאֲרוּן אַתְוָון ש"מ, מ' פְּתוּחָה. מ"ט לָא סְתִימָא, בְּגִין דְּמ' סְתִימָא, מַלְכָּא עִלָּאָה. מ' פְּתִיחָא, מַלְכָּא תַּתָּאָה. אַתְוָון אַחֲרָנִין, אִשְׁתָּאֲרוּ א"ח, כְּבוֹד אֱלֹהִים הַסְתֵּר דָּבָר כְּתִיב.

453. Rabbi Shimon began by quoting: "Hear, Yisrael, Hashem our Elohim, Hashem is one" (Devarim 6:4). IT IS WRITTEN WITH a large letter Ayin IN THE WORD SH'MA (ENG. 'HEAR'), and so is the letter Dalet IN THE WORD ECHAD (ENG. 'ONE'). And these form the word 'ed (Ayin Dalet), a witness, as is written: "Hashem is witness against you" (I Shmuel 12:5). AND FROM THE WORD SH'MA (SHIN MEM AYIN), the letters Shin Mem remain, the Mem being open. What is the reason that the Mem is not final? (namely the form of the same letter used when it is the last letter of a word.) WHAT IS THE DIFFERENCE BETWEEN A MEDIAL OPEN MEM AND A FINAL MEM? It is that the final Mem is the upper king, NAMELY BINAH, while the medial Mem alludes to the lower king, NAMELY MALCHUT. AND THE LETTERS SHIN MEM OF THE WORD SH'MA ALLUDE TO MALCHUT. And the other letters OF ECHAD (ENG. 'ONE' - ALEPH CHET DALET) that remain are Aleph Chet. "It is the glory of Elohim to conceal a thing" (Mishlei 25:2), it is written.

454. אַשְׁכַּחְנָא בְּסִפְרָא דְרַב הַמְנוּנָא סָבָא, כָּל מַאן דִּמְיַיחֵד יְחוּדָא דָא בְּכָל יוֹמָא, חֶדְוָה זְמִינָא לֵיהּ מִלְּעֵילָּא, מֵרָזָא דְּאַתְוָון אִלֵּין, ש"מ מֵהַאי סִטְרָא. א"ח, מֵהַאי סִטְרָא. וּמְצָרֵף אַתְוָון, לְמִפְרַע שָׁרֵי, וּבְמֵישַׁר סַיֵּים. וְסִימָן אֶשְׂמַח. דִּכְתִיב אָנֹכִי אֶשְׂמַח בַּיְיָ'. מַמָּשׁ. דָּא יְחוּדָא קַדִּישָׁא. וְשַׁפִּיר אִיהוּ. וְהָכִי הוּא בְּסִפְרָא דַחֲנוֹך, דְּאָמַר כִּי הַאי גַּוְונָא, דְּמַאן דִּמְיַיחֵד יְחוּדָא דָא בְּכָל יוֹמָא, חֶדְוָה זְמִינָא לֵיהּ מִלְּעֵילָּא.

454. I have found in the book of Rav Hamnuna Saba: Whoever makes this unification every day, rejoicing is prepared for him on high, in the secret of the letters Shin Mem OF THE WORD *SH'MA* (ENG. 'HEAR') at this side, THE BEGINNING OF THE VERSE, and Aleph Chet OF THE WORD *ECHAD* at that side, THE END OF THE VERSE. And he joins the letters and starts BY JOINING TOGETHER in reverse, NAMELY THE ALEPH OF THE ALEPH CHET (FROM *ECHAD*) AT THE END OF THE VERSE IS PLACED BEFORE THE SHIN OF THE SHIN MEM (FROM *SH'MA*) AT THE BEGINNING OF THE VERSE; and he ends straightforwardly, NAMELY THE MEM OF THE *SH'MA* FIRST, AND THEN THE CHET OF *ECHAD*. The four letters so arranged, Aleph Shin Mem Chet, MAKE THE WORD *ESMACH*, as in the verse: "I will rejoice (Heb. *esmach*) in Hashem" (Tehilim 104:34). And this is so literally, for it is the holy unity, ALLUDED TO IN THE LETTERS AYIN DALET (HEB. *ED*, ENG. 'WITNESS') FOR THE LETTERS OF THE TWO WORDS *SH'MA* AND *ECHAD*, WHEN REARRANGED AS ABOVE, FORM THE TWO WORDS *ESMACH* (ENG. 'I WILL REJOICE') *ED* (ENG. 'WITNESS') and this is only right. And thus is it in the Book of Enoch, who similarly said that whoever makes this unification each day, rejoicing from above is made ready for him.

455. תּוּ אִית בֵּיהּ שמ״ע, דְּאִתְכְּלִיל מִן ע׳ רַבְרְבָא. אִלֵּין שַׁבְעִין שְׁמָהָן בְּרָזָא דַּאֲבָהָן קַדִּישִׁין, וְדָא הוּא שְׁמַע: שֵׁם ע׳. יִשְׂרָאֵל, יְיָ׳, אֱלֹהֵינוּ, יְיָ׳, אִלֵּין אַרְבַּע בָּתֵּי דִתְפִלִּין, דְּאָחִיד לוֹן א״ח. הַהוּא דְּאָמַר פְּתָחִי לִי אֲחוֹתִי רַעְיָתִי. ד׳: דָּא קֶשֶׁר שֶׁל תְּפִלִּין, דְּהִיא אֲחִידַת בְּהוּ. רָזָא לְחַכִּימִין אִתְמְסַר, דְּלָא לְגַלָּאָה. שָׁתִיק ר׳ שִׁמְעוֹן. בָּכָה וְחַיֵּיךְ, אָמַר, אֵימָא, דְּהָא וַדַּאי רַעֲוָא אִשְׁתְּכַח, וְלֵית כְּדָרָא דָא עַד דְּיֵיתֵי מַלְכָּא מְשִׁיחָא, דִּיהֵא רְשׁוּ לוֹן לְגַלָּאָה.

455. Furthermore, LET US REFLECT UPON THE WORD *SH'MA*, FOR IT INCLUDES THE TWO LETTERS Shin Mem, together with the large Ayin. These are the Ayin (= seventy) names that are in the secret of the holy patriarchs, NAMELY THE 72 NAMES IN CHESED, GVURAH AND TIFERET THAT ARE CALLED 'PATRIARCHS', OF WHICH THERE ARE SEVENTY MAIN NAMES IN THE SECRET OF THE SEVENTY MEMBERS OF THE SANHEDRIN AND TWO WITNESSES. And this is the secret of *Sh'ma*: *shem* (Eng. 'name') Ayin (= seventy), WHERE *SHEM* IS MALCHUT THAT IS COMPOSED OF THE SEVENTY NAMES. "Yisrael, Hashem our Elohim, Hashem," are the four

compartments of the Tefilin, WHICH ARE THE FOUR MOCHIN: CHOCHMAH, BINAH, THE RIGHT OF DA'AT AND THE LEFT THAT IS IN DA'AT, to which Aleph Chet (Heb. *ach*, Eng. 'brother') OF THE WORD *ECHAD* is attached. This refers to the one who said: "Open to me, my sister, my love" (Shir Hashirim 5:2), NAMELY, ZEIR ANPIN. And the Dalet OF *ECHAD* is the knot of the HEAD Tefilin, WHICH IS THE SHAPE OF DALET, for MALCHUT is attached to them. And the secret was given to the sages, but not to be revealed. Rabbi Shimon fell silent. He cried, then laughed and said: I shall tell THE SECRET, for certainly the HEAVENLY Will is abiding, for there will be no generation such as this one until King Messiah comes, in which permission will be granted to reveal it.

73. The straps and the knot of the hand Tefilin

A Synopsis
Rabbi Shimon explains why the straps of the Tefilin are arranged and fastened as they are, and he emphasizes the importance of the Yud.

456. תְּרֵין רְצוּעִין נָפְקִין, מִסְטְרָא דָא וּמִסְטְרָא דָא, רָזָא דִתְרֵין יַרְכִין דִלְתַתָּא דְּהַאי א״ח, דִּנְבִיאֵי קְשׁוֹט אֲחִידָן בְּהוּ. דְּהָא מִלְּעֵילָא נָפְקִין תְּרֵין רְצוּעִין, רָזָא דִתְרֵין דְּרוֹעִין, מִימִינָא וּמִשְׂמָאלָא, וְדָלֶ״ת אִתְאַחִידַת בְּהוּ. לְבָתַר נַחְתָּא, וְאִתְפְּשָׁטוּ יַרְכִין לְתַתָּא. כֵּיוָן דְּהִיא אִתְאַחִידַת לְעֵילָא כַּדְקָא יָאוּת, נַחְתָּא לְתַתָּא, לְאִתְאַחֲדָא בְּאַכְלוּסָהָא. וְכַד אִיהִי אִתְאַחֲדַת, אֲחִידָא בְּשִׁפּוּלֵי יַרְכִין, וּרְשִׁימוּ דְּיוֹד בְּרִית קַדִּישָׁא עָלָה מִלְּעֵילָא, כְּדֵין אִיהִי אִתְאַחֲדַת בְּיִחוּדָא חַד.

456. Two straps come out of each side, NAMELY FROM THE RIGHT AND THE LEFT, this being the secret of the two thighs THAT ARE FROM THE CHEST AND downwards of Aleph Chet, WHICH IS ZEIR ANPIN, NAMELY NETZACH AND HOD OF ZEIR ANPIN, to which the true prophets are attached. For from above, ON THE HEAD, two straps come out, which are the secret of the two arms THAT CIRCLE THE HEAD from the right and from the left, WHICH ARE THE SECRET OF CHESED AND GVURAH, and to which the Dalet, WHICH IS MALCHUT, is attached, IN THE SECRET OF THE KNOT OF THE HEAD TEFILIN. Later MALCHUT descends, and THE STRAPS, WHICH ARE THE SECRET OF the thighs below, extend downwards. For, since she is attached above, WITH THE DALET OF THE KNOT OF THE HEAD TEFILIN, as is proper, she goes down TO NETZACH, HOD AND YESOD, to hold on to her hosts, WHICH MEANS POUR PLENTY TO THE DWELLERS OF THE WORLDS OF BRIYAH, YETZIRAH AND ASIYAH. And when it becomes attached THERE, TO NETZACH HOD YESOD, she is so attached at the top of the thighs, and the imprint of the Yud, which is the Holy Covenant, NAMELY YESOD, IS over her from above, and she then unites in one unity WITH ZEIR ANPIN.

457. יוֹ״ד דָּא אִיהִי רָזָא דִּבְרִית, כָּל מַאן דְּנָטַר בְּרִית דָּא, אִיהוּ אִשְׁתְּזִיב לְעֵילָא, וְאִשְׁתְּזִיב לְתַתָּא. פִּנְחָס, בְּגִין דְּאִיהוּ קַנֵּי עַל בְּרִית

דָא, אִשְׁתְּזִיב מִן דִּינָא עִלָּאָה, וּמִן דִּינָא דִּלְתַתָּא, וּבג״כ אִתְרְשָׁם יוֹ״ד
דָא בְּגַוֵּויהּ, הה״ד, פִּינְחָס בֶּן אֶלְעָזָר בֶּן אַהֲרֹן הַכֹּהֵן וְגוֹ'.

457. Yud is the secret of the covenant, NAMELY YESOD, for everyone who
keeps this covenant will be saved above and below. Because Pinchas (*Pe
Nun-Chet-Samech*) was zealous for this covenant, he was saved from the
heavenly judgment and from earthly judgment, which is why the letter Yud
was added in him, INTO HIS NAME, as it is written: "Pinchas (Pe Yud Nun
Chet Samech), the son of Elazar..." (Bemidbar 25:11).

458. יוֹ״ד דָא, אִצְטְרִיךְ דְּלָא יִתְעֲדֵי כְּלָל מִגּוֹ תְּפִלָּה דְיַד, דְּלָא יַעֲבִיד
פֵּירוּדָא. וְכָל חֶדְוָה דִילָהּ, בְּהַאי י'. אִיהוּ יוֹ״ד דָא בִּדְכוּרָא אִיהִי, וְלָא
בְּנוּקְבָּא, אִיהוּ צַדִּיק, וְאִיהִי צֶדֶק. וּבְגִין כַּךְ, אִתְקְרִיבַת בַּהֲדָהּ, וּמַאן
דְּרָחִיק לֵיהּ מֵאֲתָר דָּא, רָחִיק הוּא מֵעִדּוּנָא דְעָלְמָא דְאָתֵי.

458. This Yud must never move from the hand Tefilin, NAMELY THE KNOT
OF THE HAND TEFILIN THAT IS IN THE SHAPE OF THE LETTER YUD,
WHICH ALLUDES TO YESOD, AS ABOVE. This is so that there should be no
separation BETWEEN YESOD, WHICH IS YUD, AND THE HAND TEFILIN,
WHICH IS MALCHUT. And the whole of MALCHUT'S rejoicing is with this
Yud, WHICH IS YESOD. And this Yud is to be found in the Male but not in
the Female. He, YESOD, IS CALLED 'Righteous' (Heb. *Tzadik* - Tzadi Dalet
Yud Kof), while she, MALCHUT, is called 'righteousness' (Heb. *Tzedek* -
Tzadi Dalet Kof), WITHOUT YUD, FOR YUD IS TO BE FOUND WITH THE
MALE AND NOT IN THE FEMALE. And this is why THE YUD is close to it ON
THE HAND TEFILIN, and whoever removes the Yud, WHICH IS YESOD,
away from this place, FROM MALCHUT, WHICH IS THE HAND TEFILIN, will
himself be far from the delights of the World to Come, NAMELY HE WILL
NOT BE PRIVILEGED TO RECEIVE THE PLENTY COMING FROM THE UNION
OF YESOD AND MALCHUT THAT IS DRAWN DOWN FROM THE UPPER
EDEN, CALLED 'THE WORLD TO COME'.

459. בִּדְכוּרָא אִיהוּ צַדִּיק, וְאִיהִי צֶדֶק בְּלָא יוֹ״ד. אִיהוּ אִישׁ. וְאִיהִי
אִשָּׁה, בְּלָא יוֹ״ד. וּבג״כ חֶדְוָה דִילָהּ, לְאִתְקָרְבָא בָּהּ, וּלְאִתְעַדְּנָא
בַּהֲדָהּ. מַאן דְּרָחִיק עִדּוּנָא דָא, יְרַחֲקוּן לֵיהּ מֵעִדּוּנָא דִּלְעֵילָא. וע״ד

כְּתִיב, כִּי מְכַבְּדַי אֲכַבֵּד וְגוֹ'.

459. In the Male he is righteous while the Female it is righteousness, without Yud. Similarly he is a man (Heb. *ish*, Aleph Yud Shin, SPELLED WITH YUD, while she is a woman (Heb. *ishah*, Aleph Shin Hei) SPELLED without Yud. This is why it is her rejoicing to come close TO THE YUD and to delight with it IN UNION. Whoever brings apart this delighting is himself removed from delight on high. And thus it is written: "for them that honor Me I will honor..." (I Shmuel 2:30).

74. "And when Pinchas...saw it, he...took a spear in his hand"

A Synopsis
We hear that the Yud was added to Pinchas' name because he halted the strong Judgment of the plague.

460. ת״ח, פִּנְחָס קָאֵים קַמֵּי דִּינָא תַּקִּיפָא דְּיִצְחָק, וְסָתִים פִּרְצָה, בְּגִין כָּךְ אַשְׁלִים לְגַבֵּי פִּנְחָס רָזָא דְּיִצְחָק. קָם קַמֵּי פִּרְצָה דִּכְתִּיב וַיַּעֲמוֹד פִּנְחָס וַיְפַלֵּל. קָם בְּפִרְצָה קַמֵּי דִּינָא דְּיִצְחָק, בְּגִין לְאַגָּנָא עֲלַיְיהוּ דְּיִשְׂרָאֵל. וע״ד כָּלִיל דָּא בְּדָא בְּחוּשְׁבָּנָא.

460. Come and see: Pinchas stood before the strong Judgment of Isaac and blocked up the breach, NAMELY HALTED THE PLAGUE, WHICH CAME FROM THE HARSH JUDGMENTS OF THE LEFT THAT IS CALLED 'ISAAC'. For this reason, the letter Yud was added to complete Pinchas' name, GIVING IT the same secret AS THE NUMERICAL VALUE of the name Isaac. He stood in the breach as it is written: "Then stood up Pinchas, and executed judgment..." (Tehilim 106:30), PINCHAS HERE BEING SPELLED WITH A YUD. He stood in the breach against the Judgment of Isaac in order to defend Yisrael, which is why their names have the same number, MEANING PINCHAS HAS THE SAME NUMERICAL VALUE AS ISAAC.

461. וְאִי תֵּימָא, הָא חוּשְׁבָּנָא לָא תַּלְיָיא אֶלָּא בְּעַיְינִין דִּילָהּ, וְהָכָא חוּשְׁבָּנָא לְעֵילָּא בְּיִצְחָק. אֶלָּא וַדַּאי הָכִי הוּא, בְּגִין דְּיִצְחָק תַּלְיָיא וְאִתְמְשַׁךְ בְּהַהוּא אֲתָר דְּאִינּוּן עַיְינִין, דְּתַמָּן דַּיְינִין דִּינִין דְּכָל עָלְמָא, דְּהָא עַיְינִין דִּילָהּ, אִינּוּן שַׁבְעִין קָתֶדְרָאִין, אֲתָר דְּדִינִין דְּעָלְמָא, וְאִקְרוּן סַנְהֶדְרִין. וע״ד כֹּלָּא חַד, בְּגִין דְּיִצְחָק וְאִינּוּן כַּחֲדָא אַזְלִין, וְכֹלָּא שַׁפִּיר.

461. You might suggest that the number, WHICH IS THE SECRET OF CHOCHMAH, is dependent on none but its eyes, NAMELY ON THE ILLUMINATION OF CHOCHMAH THAT IS IN MALCHUT, FOR EYES ARE CHOCHMAH, AND CHOCHMAH IS REVEALED ONLY IN MALCHUT AND NOT IN ANY OTHER SFIRAH, while here reckoning DEPENDS above, upon Isaac, WHO IS THE LEFT COLUMN OF ZEIR ANPIN. HE REPLIES, you are

certainly right, THAT THE RECKONING, WHICH IS THE SECRET OF CHOCHMAH, DEPENDS UPON ISAAC, since Isaac depends upon and is drawn from the place that is called 'eyes', NAMELY HE IS DRAWN TO CHOCHMAH THAT IS IN MALCHUT, where the Judgments of the whole world are judged. FOR ALL THE JUDGMENTS THAT ARE IN THE WORLD HAVE THEIR ROOT IN THE JUDGMENTS OF CHOCHMAH, for its eyes are the Ayin (= seventy, Eng. 'eye') thrones OF JUDGMENT, WHICH ARE where the judgments that are in the world are, and they are called 'the seventy members of the Sanhedrin'. AND THE NUMBER SEVENTY (AYIN = EYE) IS BECAUSE THEY ARE DRAWN FROM ITS EYES. Thus everything is one, because Isaac AND THE EYES OF MALCHUT go together, FOR MALCHUT IS BUILT UP FROM ISAAC AND HER EYES ARE FROM HIM, NAMELY FROM THE LEFT COLUMN, AND SO THE TWO OF THEM ARE REALLY ONE, and everything fits.

462. פִּנְחָס דָּא יִצְחָק, וְקָם פִּנְחָס וְדָאִין דִּינָא, וּמִתְלַבַּשׁ בִּגְבוּרָה תַּקִּיפָא דְּאִיהוּ שְׂמָאלָא. וּבג״כ זָכָה לִימִינָא. הָכָא אִתְכְּלִיל שְׂמָאלָא בִּימִינָא. הֵשִׁיב אֶת חֲמָתִי, מַאי הֵשִׁיב אֶת חֲמָתִי. אֶלָּא אִלֵּין אִינּוּן ג' מְמוּנִים דְּגֵיהִנָּם: מַשְׁחִית, אַף, וְחֵימָה. בְּגִין דְּחָמָא הַהוּא חֵמָה, דַּהֲוָה פָּשִׁיט וְאִתְמַשַּׁךְ מִסִּטְרָא דְּיִצְחָק, מָה עֲבַד, אִתְלְבַּשׁ אִיהוּ בְּיִצְחָק, וְאָחִיד בְּהַהוּא חֵימָה, כְּמַאן דְּאָחִיד בְּחַבְרֵיהּ, וְאָתִיב לֵיהּ לַאֲחוֹרָא.

462. So Pinchas is Isaac, for Pinchas stood up and judged the case OF ZIMRI AND COZBI, and put on the strong Gvurah, which is left CALLED 'ISAAC'. And because OF THIS DEED, Pinchas merited the right, NAMELY HE EARNED THE PRIESTHOOD, WHICH IS CHESED, left being here included in the right. "has turned My wrath away" (Bemidbar 25:11). What is the meaning of "turned My wrath away?" AND HE ANSWERS THAT this refers to the three officials in Gehenom WHO ARE CALLED 'Destruction', 'Anger', and 'Wrath'. For Pinchas saw that wrath spreading and being drawn down from the side of Isaac. What did he do? He put on THE LEVEL OF Isaac, WHICH IS THE ROOT OF WRATH, and then he took hold of that wrath as one who takes hold of his neighbor and pushes him back.

463. וּכְדֵין דָּן דִּינָא, וְעָבֵיד דִּינָא. דָּן דִּינָא, דְּכָל בּוֹעֵל אֲרַמִּית קַנָּאִין פּוֹגְעִין בּוֹ. וְעָבֵיד דִּינָא, דִּכְתִיב וַיִּדְקוֹר אֶת שְׁנֵיהֶם. וע״ד כְּתִיב הָכָא,

הֵשִׁיב אֶת חֲמָתִי. וּכְתִיב הָתָם, הֵשִׁיב אָחוֹר יְמִינוֹ מִפְּנֵי אוֹיֵב, מַה לְהַלָן לַאֲחוֹרָא, ה"נ לַאֲחוֹרָא. וע"ד יו"ד דְּפִינְחָס הָכָא, יו"ד דְּיִצְחָק. וְכֹלָא הוּא מֵעַל בְּנֵי יִשְׂרָאֵל, דְּכַד חָמָא הַהוּא חֵמָה, חָמָא לֵיהּ דַּהֲוָה נָחִית עַל רֵישֵׁיהוֹן דְּיִשְׂרָאֵל.

463. And then he judged the case and executed judgment. He judged according to the rule that if a man has sexual intercourse with a gentile woman, the zealots may fall upon him AND IT WAS PERMITTED TO STRIKE ZIMRI. And he passed judgment, as it is written: "and thrust both of them through" (Ibid.). Wherefore it is written: "has turned My wrath away (lit. 'back')," while elsewhere it is written: "He has turned back His right hand from before the enemy" (Eichah 2:3). Just as THE TURNING MENTIONED in the latter, is back, so also in the former case, it is back. And thus the Yud THAT WAS ADDED here to Pinchas is the Yud that is in Isaac, WHICH ALLUDES TO YESOD. And it is all "above the children of Yisrael" (Bemidbar 25:11), for when he saw that wrath, he saw it as it was descending over the heads of the children of Yisrael, AND IT IS THEREFORE WRITTEN: "HAS TURNED BACK MY WRATH BACK FROM (LIT. 'ABOVE') THE CHILDREN OF YISRAEL."

75. The letters Mem, Vav and Tav are a sign for the Angel of Death

A Synopsis

Rabbi Shimon works through some numerology and rearrangement of the letters in Mavet (Eng. 'death') to show that Pinchas was dedicated to the Holy Name of God and that he turned away God's wrath by wielding the spear. We are told that none of those who died in the plague were of Yisrael with the exception of those from the tribe of Shimon; those who died were the wicked, and the wicked are already considered to be dead.

464. מַאי חָמָא. חָמָא מ', אָת דָּא דַּהֲוָה טָאס בִּרְקִיעָא, וְדָא הוּא סִימָנָא דְּמַלְאָךְ הַמָּוֶת, דְּבַעְיָא לְאִתְבְּנָאָה בְּאָת וָא"ו וְאָת ת'. מַה עֲבַד פִּנְחָס. דַּהֲוָה מִתְלַבַּשׁ בְּיִצְחָק, כְּדֵין נָטִיל הַהוּא אָת מ', וְחָטַף לֵיהּ, וְחִבֵּר לֵיהּ בַּהֲדֵיהּ. כֵּיוָן דְּחָמָא מַלְאָךְ הַמָּוֶת, דְּפִנְחָס חָטַף לֵיהּ לְהַהוּא מ' בַּהֲדֵיהּ, מִיַּד תָּב לַאֲחוֹרָא.

464. HE ASKS, IT IS WRITTEN: "AND WHEN PINCHAS…SAW…AND TOOK A SPEAR IN HIS HAND" (BEMIDBAR 25:7). What did he see? AND ANSWERS: He saw a letter Mem flying through the sky, and this LETTER is a sign of the Angel of Death, for THE mem wants to be built up with the letter Vav and the letter Tav TO FORM THE WORD *MAVET* (ENG. 'DEATH' - MEM VAV TAV). What did Pinchas do, for he was then attired with Isaac? He then took that letter Mem and snatched it away FROM THE ANGEL OF DEATH, and joined it with himself. And when the Angel of Death saw that Pinchas had taken the letter Mem to himself, he immediately turned back.

465. מ"ט. בְּגִין דְּכַד קַנֵּי בְּלִבֵּיהּ פִּינְחָס, אִתְלְבַּשׁ בְּיִצְחָק, וְאִסְתַּלָּק לְמֶהֱוֵי בְּחוּשְׁבָּנָא ר"ח, וְהָכִי סָלִיק שְׁמֵיהּ ר"ח, וְהָכִי סָלִיק יִצְחָק. כֵּיוָן דְּחָמָא לְאָת מ' טָאס בִּרְקִיעָא, חָטַף לֵיהּ, וְחִבֵּר לֵיהּ בַּהֲדֵיהּ וְאִתְעֲבֵיד מִיַּד רמ"ח, הה"ד וַיִּקַּח רֹמַח בְּיָדוֹ.

465. HE ASKS but what is the reason BEHIND ALL THIS? HE ANSWERS, when Pinchas was zealous in his heart, he attired himself with Isaac. And he rose up to 208, which is the numerical value of his name. It is also the numerical value of Isaac. And since he saw the letter Mem flying in the sky,

he snatched it and joined it to himself, and immediately became *romach* (lit. 'a spear' - Resh Mem Chet). THAT IS, THE LETTER MEM JOINED THE NUMERICAL VALUE OF HIS NAME, RESH CHET (= 208) AND FORMED THE WORD *ROMACH*, as it is written: "and took a spear in his hand."

466. בְּגִין דְּאוֹת מ' הֲוָה סִימָנָא קַדְמָאָה לְאָדָם הָרִאשׁוֹן, לְמִבְנֵי מָוֶת עַל עָלְמָא, בְּגִין דְּאָת דָּא הֲוָה טָאס עַל רֵישֵׁיה דְּאָדָם, בְּשַׁעֲתָא דִּכְתִּיב וַתִּקַּח מִפִּרְיוֹ, מ' פִּרְיוֹ. וַהֲוָה מְחַכָּא ו"ת, בְּזִמְנָא דִּכְתִּיב, וַתֹּאכַל, וַתִּתֵּן, וַתִּפָּקַחְנָה. כְּדֵין אִתְבְּנֵי מָוֶת עַל עָלְמָא.

466. Because the letter Mem was the first mark for Adam that death was ordained over the world, because this letter flew over Adam's head at the time when, as is written: "She took of (Heb. *mi*) the fruit thereof" (Beresheet 3:6). And this MEM was waiting for the letters Vav and Tav, at the time it is written: "...and did eat (Heb. *vatochal* starts Vav Tav); and she gave (Heb. *vatiten* starts Vav Tav)... And the eyes of them both were opened (Heb. *vatipakachnah*)" (Ibid. 6-7). And thus was death (Heb. *mavet*, Mem Vav Tav) established over the world.

467. פִּנְחָס הֲוָה חָמֵי לֵיה הַשְׁתָּא הַהוּא אָת מ', טָאִיס עַל רֵישֵׁיהוֹן דְּיִשְׂרָאֵל. וְהָאֵיךְ חָמָא לֵיה. חָמָא דִּיּוּקְנָא דְּמ' פְּתוּחָה, מַלְיָא דָּמָא. כֵּיוָן דְּחָמָא לֵיה, אָמַר הָא וַדַּאי סִימָנָא דְּמַלְאָךְ הַמָּוֶת, מִיַּד חָטַף לָה, אַדְכַּר עֲלָהּ שְׁמָא מְפָרָשׁ, וְנָחִית לְהַאי אָת לְגַבֵּיה. וּמַה דַּהֲוָה ר"ח, אִתְצְרִיף רמ"ח. כְּדֵין וַיִּקַּח רֹמַח בְּיָדוֹ. וְע"ד כְּתִיב מֵעַל בְּנֵי יִשְׂרָאֵל בְּקַנְאוֹ אֶת קִנְאָתִי, דְּקַנֵּי לִשְׁמָא קַדִּישָׁא, דַּהֲווֹ מְחַבְּרִין לֵיה בִּרְשׁוּ אַחֲרָא. בְּתוֹכָם, מַאי בְּתוֹכָם. בְּגִין דַּהֲוָה אָזִל וְעָאל בְּגוֹ כַּמָּה אוּכְלוּסִין, כַּמָּה רַבְרְבָן, וּמָסַר גַּרְמֵיה לְמוֹתָא בֵּינַיְיהוּ. אֲבָל בְּתוֹכָם, בְּתוֹךְ מ', בְּתוֹךְ מ' הֲוָה מ' הַהוּא קָנְאָה דְּקַנֵּי.

467. AND SIMILARLY now Pinchas saw that same letter Mem that was flying over the heads of Yisrael. And how did he see it? He saw the shape of an open Mem covered in blood. When he saw it, he said: This is certainly a sign of the Angel of Death. He immediately snatched it, mentioned over it

the Name written in full and brought that letter down to himself. And as THE NUMERICAL VALUE OF PINCHAS is the letters Resh Chet, MEM COMBINED WITH THE RESH CHET to form Resh Mem Chet (Heb. *romach*, Eng. 'a spear'). Then he: "took a spear in his hand." And this is why it is also written: "has turned My wrath away from the children of Yisrael, in that he was zealous for My sake" (Bemidbar 25:11), for he was zealous for the Holy Name, for they had joined it to another dominion. "among them" (Ibid.). What is the meaning of "among them"? The answer is that he went in among a number of hordes and a number of great ones and gave himself over to death for their sake, IN ORDER TO SAVE THEM. THEREFORE IT IS WRITTEN: "AMONG THEM." But THE SECRET OF "among them" is as follows: The letters of "among them" (Heb. *betochham*) are, *betoch* (lit. 'within') Mem, for the zealousness that he showed was within a Mem.

468. מ"ט מ'. בְּגִין דְּאִיהִי סִימָנָא דְּמוֹת, אִיהִי סִימָנָא דְּמ' מַלְקִיּוֹת. אִיהִי סִימָנָא דְּד' מִיתוֹת ב"ד. וּמִתַּמָּן סָלִיק וְנָחִית, נָחִית וְסָלִיק, סָלִיק לְמ', וְנָחִית לְד'. נָחִית לְד', אִינּוּן ד' רוּחִין, דְּמִתְפָּרְשָׁן מִגּוֹ דְּכַר וְנוּקְבָא מִמְסָאֲבוּתָא, וּבְגִינַיְיהוּ ד' מִיתוֹת ב"ד. וּמִתַּמָּן סַלְקִין לְמ'. וְהַיְינוּ מ' סִימָנָא וּמָאנִין דְּמַלְאָךְ הַמָּוֶת. וְדָא נָטִיל פִּנְחָס, וְקָם בְּתוֹךְ מ', וע"ד וְלֹא כִלִּיתִי אֶת בְּנֵי יִשְׂרָאֵל בְּקִנְאָתִי.

468. HE ASKS, What is the reason that HE WAS ZEALOUS FOR this Mem? AND HE ANSWERS, This is because this was the sign for death, a sign for forty lashings. This is the sign of the four deaths decreed by the court, and from whence it rises and descends, descends and rises. When it rises IN NUMERICAL VALUE it amount to Mem (= 40) and when it comes down it is a Dalet (= 4), the four directions that separate from Male and Female of impurity. Because of them the four deaths are decreed by court. And from there they rise to Mem. Thus, the Mem is a sign and utensil of the Angel of Death. And this is what Pinchas took and established himself within Mem. And therefore, "I consumed not the children of Yisrael in My jealousy" (Ibid.).

469. וְכִי הַאֵיךְ הֵשִׁיב פִּנְחָס חֲמָתֵיהּ דְּקוּדְשָׁא בְּרִיךְ הוּא, וְהָכְתִיב וַיִּהְיוּ הַמֵּתִים בַּמַּגֵּפָה וְגוֹ', אִי לָא מִית חַד מִנַּיְיהוּ, הֲוָה אֲמֵינָא הֵשִׁיב אֶת חֲמָתִי, אֲבָל כֵּיוָן דְּכָל הָנֵי מִיתוּ, מ"ט הֵשִׁיב אֶת חֲמָתִי וְלֹא כִלִּיתִי אֶת

-383-

בְּנֵי יִשְׂרָאֵל. אֶלָּא וַדַּאי בְּרִירָא דְמִלָּה, וַוי לֵיהּ לב"נ דְּפָגִים זַרְעֵיהּ, וַוי לֵיהּ לְמַאן דְּלָא נָטִיר זַרְעֵיהּ כַּדְקָא יָאוּת, חַס וְשָׁלוֹם דַּאֲפִילוּ חַד מִיִּשְׂרָאֵל מִית, אֶלָּא שִׁבְטָא דְּשִׁמְעוֹן, כַּד אָתֵי אִינּוּן עֵרֶב רַב, אִתְעָרְבוּ בְּנָשִׁין דְּשִׁבְטָא דְּשִׁמְעוֹן, בָּתַר דְּאִתְגַּיָּירוּ, וְאוֹלִידוּ בְּנִין, מִנְּהוֹן מִיתוּ בַּעֵגֶל, וּמִנְּהוֹן מִיתוּ בְּמוֹתָנָא, וְאַחֲרָנִין מִיתוּ הָכָא, אִינּוּן דְּאִשְׁתָּאֲרוּ. הֲדָא הוּא דִּכְתִּיב, וַיִּהְיוּ הַמֵּתִים בַּמַּגֵּפָה, אֲשֶׁר מֵתוּ לָא כְּתִיב, אֶלָּא הַמֵּתִים, מֵתִים דְּמֵעִיקָּרָא הֲווֹ.

469. HE ASKS, How can it be said that Pinchas turned away the wrath of the Holy One, blessed be He, when it is written: "And those that died by the plague were twenty and four thousand" (Bemidbar 25:9)? Had not even one of them died, I could have said "has turned away My wrath," but since so many died it does not make sense TO SAY "turned away My wrath... so that I consumed not the children of Yisrael": AND HE ANSWERS that the matter certainly needs clarification, as follows: Woe to the person who faults his own seed. Woe to the one who does not guard his seed properly, FOR ALL THESE DIED IN THE PLAGUE. But heaven forbid, not even one of Yisrael died, with the exception of the tribe of Shimon. When the mixed multitude came, they intermingled with the women of the tribe of Shimon, after they had converted, and begot children, some of whom died at the Golden Calf episode and others of whom died in the plague; while those who remained alive died here, as it is literally written: "And the dead ones by the plague were twenty and four thousand." Scripture does not say 'which had died' but rather "the dead ones," which teaches that they were already dead, FOR THE WICKED ARE CALLED 'DEAD'.

470. וּבְגִין דְּאִסְתַּמְרוּ יִשְׂרָאֵל, וְכָל אִינּוּן זַרְעָא קַדִּישָׁא, אִתְמְנוּן כֻּלְּהוּ, בְּגִין דְּלָא חָסֵר אֲפִילוּ חַד מִנַּיְיהוּ. וע"ד כְּתִיב, וְלֹא כִלִּיתִי אֶת בְּנֵי יִשְׂרָאֵל, מִכְּלָל דְּאַחֲרָנִין כָּלוּ. וְכֵן הֵשִׁיב אֶת חֲמָתִי מֵעַל בְּנֵי יִשְׂרָאֵל, מֵעַל בְּנֵי יִשְׂרָאֵל הֵשִׁיב, אֲבָל מֵעַל אַחֲרָנִין דַּהֲווֹ עֵרֶב רַב, לָא הֵשִׁיב. וע"ד רָשִׁים קְרָא וְאָמַר, מֵעַל בְּנֵי יִשְׂרָאֵל. וּבְג"ד אִתְמְנוּן בְּנֵי יִשְׂרָאֵל כְּמִלְּקַדְּמִין, וְחִבֵּר לוֹן קוּדְשָׁא בְּרִיךְ הוּא בַּהֲדֵיהּ. כְּגַוְונָא דָּא בְּעוֹבָדָא דְעֵגֶל, דִּכְתִּיב וַיִּפּוֹל מִן הָעָם וְגוֹ'. כָּל אִינּוּן מֵעֵרֶב רַב הֲווֹ. וּלְאַחֲזָאָה

-384-

דְּלָא הֲווֹ מִבְּנֵי יִשְׂרָאֵל, מַה כְּתִיב לְבָתַר, וַיַּקְהֵל מֹשֶׁה אֶת כָּל עֲדַת בְּנֵי יִשְׂרָאֵל.

470. And because Yisrael were careful, and the holy seed were all counted and not one of them was missing, therefore it is written: "I consumed not the children of Yisrael" (Ibid. 11). The inference here is that He did consume others WHO WERE NOT OF THE CHILDREN OF YISRAEL. And so, too: "turned away My wrath from over the children of Yisrael." He turned away from over the children of Yisrael, but he did not turn it away from the others, who were a mixed multitude. And therefore Scripture explicitly states: "from the children of Yisrael." This is why the children of Yisrael were counted again and the Holy One, blessed be He joined them to Himself. Something similar happened in the case of the Golden Calf, as it is written: "And there fell of the people..." (Shemot 32:28). All of these were from the mixed multitude. To prove the point that they were not of the children of Yisrael, the verse later says: "And Moses gathered all the congregation of the children of Yisrael" (Shemot 35:1), WHICH SHOWS THAT ALL OF THEM WERE IN PERFECTION.

NOTES

NOTES

NOTES

NOTES

NOTES

NOTES

NOTES

NOTES

NOTES